BOLLINGEN SERIES LXXX

The Divine Comedy

✦

Paradiso

1: Italian Text and Translation

2: Commentary

DANTE ALIGHIERI

The Divine Comedy

TRANSLATED, WITH A COMMENTARY, BY

CHARLES S. SINGLETON

Paradiso

1: Italian Text and Translation

2: Commentary

BOLLINGEN SERIES LXXX

PRINCETON UNIVERSITY PRESS

Second Printing, with corrections, 1977
First Princeton/Bollingen Paperback printing, 1982

THIS IS VOLUME III, PARTS I AND 2, OF

THE DIVINE COMEDY OF DANTE ALIGHIERI

CONSTITUTING NUMBER LXXX IN BOLLINGEN SERIES

SPONSORED BY BOLLINGEN FOUNDATION.

THIS VOLUME, PARADISO,

IS IN TWO PARTS: ITALIAN TEXT AND TRANSLATION,

AND COMMENTARY.

*The pagination of the paperback edition follows that of the
original cloth edition.*

Library of Congress Catalogue card number 68-57090
ISBN 0-691-01844-8 pbk.
ISBN 0-691-01844-8T 3-vol. pbk.
Printed in the United States of America
by Princeton University Press, Princeton, New Jersey

CONTENTS OF PART 1

Paradiso

Italian Text and Translation

PARADISO

L<small>A GLORIA</small> di colui che tutto move
  per l'universo penetra, e risplende
  in una parte più e meno altrove.   *3*
Nel ciel che più de la sua luce prende
  fu' io, e vidi cose che ridire
  né sa né può chi di là sù discende;   *6*
perché appressando sé al suo disire,
  nostro intelletto si profonda tanto,
  che dietro la memoria non può ire.   *9*
Veramente quant' io del regno santo
  ne la mia mente potei far tesoro,
  sarà ora materia del mio canto.   *12*
O buono Appollo, a l'ultimo lavoro
  fammi del tuo valor sì fatto vaso,
  come dimandi a dar l'amato alloro.   *15*
Infino a qui l'un giogo di Parnaso
  assai mi fu; ma or con amendue
  m'è uopo intrar ne l'aringo rimaso.   *18*

CANTO I

THE GLORY of the All-Mover penetrates through the universe and reglows in one part more, and in another less. I have been in the heaven that most receives of His light, and have seen things which whoso descends from up there has neither the knowledge nor the power to relate, because, as it draws near to its desire, our intellect enters so deep that memory cannot go back upon the track. Nevertheless, so much of the holy kingdom as I could treasure up in my mind shall now be the matter of my song.

O good Apollo, for this last labor make me such a vessel of your worth as you require for granting your beloved laurel. Thus far the one peak of Parnassus has sufficed me, but now I have need of both, as I enter the arena that remains.

Entra nel petto mio, e spira tue
   sì come quando Marsïa traesti
   de la vagina de le membra sue.   *21*
O divina virtù, se mi ti presti
   tanto che l'ombra del beato regno
   segnata nel mio capo io manifesti,   *24*
vedra'mi al piè del tuo diletto legno
   venire, e coronarmi de le foglie
   che la materia e tu mi farai degno.   *27*
Sì rade volte, padre, se ne coglie
   per trïunfare o cesare o poeta,
   colpa e vergogna de l'umane voglie,   *30*
che parturir letizia in su la lieta
   delfica deïtà dovria la fronda
   peneia, quando alcun di sé asseta.   *33*
Poca favilla gran fiamma seconda:
   forse di retro a me con miglior voci
   si pregherà perché Cirra risponda.   *36*
Surge ai mortali per diverse foci
   la lucerna del mondo; ma da quella
   che quattro cerchi giugne con tre croci, *39*
con miglior corso e con migliore stella
   esce congiunta, e la mondana cera
   più a suo modo tempera e suggella.   *42*
Fatto avea di là mane e di qua sera
   tal foce quasi; e tutto era là bianco
   quello emisperio, e l'altra parte nera, *45*
quando Beatrice in sul sinistro fianco
   vidi rivolta e riguardar nel sole:
   aguglia sì non li s'affisse unquanco.   *48*

Enter into my breast and breathe there as when you drew Marsyas from the sheath of his limbs. O divine Power, if you do so lend yourself to me that I may show forth the image of the blessed realm which is imprinted in my mind, you shall see me come to your beloved tree and crown me with those leaves of which the matter and you shall make me worthy. So rarely, father, are they gathered, for triumph of caesar or of poet—fault and shame of human wills—that the Peneian frond ought to beget gladness in the glad Delphic deity whenever it causes anyone to long for it. A great flame follows a little spark: perhaps, after me, prayer shall be offered with better voices, that Cyrrha may respond.

The lamp of the world rises to mortals through different passages; but through that which joins four circles with three crosses it issues with a better course and conjoined with better stars, and tempers and stamps the wax of the world more after its own fashion. Almost such an outlet had made morning there and evening here, and all the hemisphere there was white, and the other dark, when I saw Beatrice turned to her left side and looking at the sun: never did eagle so fix his gaze thereon.

E sì come secondo raggio suole
   uscir del primo e risalire in suso,
   pur come pelegrin che tornar vuole,   *51*
così de l'atto suo, per li occhi infuso
   ne l'imagine mia, il mio si fece,
   e fissi li occhi al sole oltre nostr' uso.   *54*
Molto è licito là, che qui non lece
   a le nostre virtù, mercé del loco
   fatto per proprio de l'umana spece.   *57*
Io nol soffersi molto, né sì poco,
   ch'io nol vedessi sfavillar dintorno,
   com' ferro che bogliente esce del foco;   *60*
e di sùbito parve giorno a giorno
   essere aggiunto, come quei che puote
   avesse il ciel d'un altro sole addorno.   *63*
Beatrice tutta ne l'etterne rote
   fissa con li occhi stava; e io in lei
   le luci fissi, di là sù rimote.   *66*
Nel suo aspetto tal dentro mi fei,
   qual si fé Glauco nel gustar de l'erba
   che 'l fé consorto in mar de li altri dèi.   *69*
Trasumanar significar *per verba*
   non si poria; però l'essemplo basti
   a cui esperïenza grazia serba.   *72*
S'i' era sol di me quel che creasti
   novellamente, amor che 'l ciel governi,
   tu 'l sai, che col tuo lume mi levasti.   *75*
Quando la rota che tu sempiterni
   desiderato, a sé mi fece atteso
   con l'armonia che temperi e discerni,   *78*

An . even as a second ray is wont to issue from the first, and mount upwards again, like a pilgrim who would return home: thus of her action, infused through the eyes into my imagination, mine was made, and I fixed my eyes on the sun beyond our wont. Much is granted to our faculties there that is not granted here, by virtue of the place made for humankind as its proper abode. I did not endure it long, nor so little that I did not see it sparkle round about, like iron that comes molten from the fire. And suddenly day seemed added to day, as if He who has the power had adorned heaven with another sun.

Beatrice was standing with her eyes all fixed upon the eternal wheels, and I fixed mine on her, withdrawn from there above. Gazing upon her I became within me such as Glaucus became on tasting of the grass that made him sea-fellow of the other gods. The passing beyond humanity may not be set forth in words: therefore let the example suffice any for whom grace reserves that experience.

Whether I was but that part of me which Thou didst create last, O Love that rulest the heavens, Thou knowest, who with Thy light didst lift me. When the revolution which Thou, by being desired, makest eternal turned my attention unto itself by the harmony which Thou dost temper and distinguish,

parvemi tanto allor del cielo acceso
de la fiamma del sol, che pioggia o fiume
lago non fece alcun tanto disteso.   *81*
La novità del suono e 'l grande lume
di lor cagion m'accesero un disio
mai non sentito di cotanto acume.   *84*
Ond' ella, che vedea me sì com' io,
a quïetarmi l'animo commosso,
pria ch'io a dimandar, la bocca aprio   *87*
e cominciò: "Tu stesso ti fai grosso
col falso imaginar, sì che non vedi
ciò che vedresti se l'avessi scosso.   *90*
Tu non se' in terra, sì come tu credi;
ma folgore, fuggendo il proprio sito,
non corse come tu ch'ad esso riedi."   *93*
S'io fui del primo dubbio disvestito
per le sorrise parolette brevi,
dentro ad un nuovo più fu' inretito   *96*
e dissi: "Già contento *requïevi*
di grande ammirazion; ma ora ammiro
com' io trascenda questi corpi levi."   *99*
Ond' ella, appresso d'un pïo sospiro,
li occhi drizzò ver' me con quel sembiante
che madre fa sovra figlio deliro,   *102*
e cominciò: "Le cose tutte quante
hanno ordine tra loro, e questo è forma
che l'universo a Dio fa simigliante.   *105*
Qui veggion l'alte creature l'orma
de l'etterno valore, il qual è fine
al quale è fatta la toccata norma.   *108*

so much of the heaven seemed to me then to be kindled by the sun's flame that rain or river never made a lake so wide. The novelty of the sound and the great light kindled in me a desire to know their cause, never before felt with such keenness. Whereupon she who saw me as I saw myself, to quiet my perturbed mind, opened her lips before I opened mine to ask, and began, "You make yourself dull with false imagining, so that you do not see what you would see had you cast it off. You are not on earth, as you believe; but lightning, fleeing its proper site, never darted so fast as you are returning to yours."

If by these brief words which she smiled to me I was freed from my first perplexity, within a new one I became the more enmeshed; and I said, "I was already content concerning one great wonder; but now I marvel how it can be that I should pass through these light bodies."

Whereupon, after a pitying sigh, she turned her eyes on me with the look that a mother casts on her delirious child. And she began, "All things have order among themselves, and this is the form that makes the universe like God. Herein the high creatures behold the imprint of the Eternal Worth, which is the end wherefor the aforesaid ordinance is made.

9

Ne l'ordine ch'io dico sono accline
   tutte nature, per diverse sorti,
   più al principio loro e men vicine;   *111*
onde si muovono a diversi porti
   per lo gran mar de l'essere, e ciascuna
   con istinto a lei dato che la porti.   *114*
Questi ne porta il foco inver' la luna;
   questi ne' cor mortali è permotore;
   questi la terra in sé stringe e aduna;   *117*
né pur le creature che son fore
   d'intelligenza quest' arco saetta,
   ma quelle c'hanno intelletto e amore.   *120*
La provedenza, che cotanto assetta,
   del suo lume fa 'l ciel sempre quïeto
   nel qual si volge quel c'ha maggior fretta;   *123*
e ora lì, come a sito decreto,
   cen porta la virtù di quella corda
   che ciò che scocca drizza in segno lieto.   *126*
Vero è che, come forma non s'accorda
   molte fïate a l'intenzion de l'arte,
   perch' a risponder la materia è sorda,   *129*
così da questo corso si diparte
   talor la creatura, c'ha podere
   di piegar, così pinta, in altra parte;   *132*
e sì come veder si può cadere
   foco di nube, sì l'impeto primo
   l'atterra torto da falso piacere.   *135*
Non dei più ammirar, se bene stimo,
   lo tuo salir, se non come d'un rivo
   se d'alto monte scende giuso ad imo.   *138*

In the order whereof I speak all natures are inclined by different lots, nearer and less near unto their principle; wherefore they move to different ports over the great sea of being, each with an instinct given it to bear it on: this bears fire upwards toward the moon; this is the motive force in mortal creatures; this binds together and unites the earth. And not only does this bow shoot those creatures that lack intelligence, but also those that have intellect and love. The Providence which ordains all this, with Its light makes ever quiet that heaven within which revolves the sphere that has the greatest speed; and thither now, as to a place decreed, the virtue of that bowstring bears us on, which aims at a joyful target whatsoever it shoots.

"To be sure, even as a shape often does not accord with the intention of the art, because the material is deaf to respond, so the creature sometimes departs from this course, having the power, thus impelled, to swerve toward some other part; and even as the fire from a cloud may be seen to fall downwards, so the primal impulse, diverted by false pleasure, is turned toward earth. You should not wonder more at your rising, if I deem aright, than at a stream that falls from a mountain top to the base.

Maraviglia sarebbe in te se, privo
   d'impedimento, giù ti fossi assiso,
   com' a terra quïete in foco vivo."
Quinci rivolse inver' lo cielo il viso.   *142*

It would be a marvel if you, being freed from hindrance, had settled down below, even as stillness would be in living fire on earth."

Then she turned her gaze heavenwards again.

PARADISO

O voi che siete in piccioletta barca,
   desiderosi d'ascoltar, seguiti
   dietro al mio legno che cantando varca,   *3*
tornate a riveder li vostri liti:
   non vi mettete in pelago, ché forse,
   perdendo me, rimarreste smarriti.   *6*
L'acqua ch'io prendo già mai non si corse;
   Minerva spira, e conducemi Appollo,
   e nove Muse mi dimostran l'Orse.   *9*
Voialtri pochi che drizzaste il collo
   per tempo al pan de li angeli, del quale
   vivesi qui ma non sen vien satollo,   *12*
metter potete ben per l'alto sale
   vostro navigio, servando mio solco
   dinanzi a l'acqua che ritorna equale.   *15*
Que' glorïosi che passaro al Colco
   non s'ammiraron come voi farete,
   quando Iasón vider fatto bifolco.   *18*

CANTO II

O you that are in your little bark, eager to hear, following behind my ship that singing makes her way, turn back to see again your shores. Do not commit yourselves to the open sea, for perchance, if you lost me, you would remain astray. The water which I take was never coursed before. Minerva breathes and Apollo guides me, and nine Muses point out to me the Bears.

You other few who lifted up your necks betimes for bread of angels, on which men here subsist but never become sated of it, you may indeed commit your vessel to the deep brine, holding to my furrow ahead of the water that turns smooth again. Those glorious ones who crossed the sea to Colchis, when they saw Jason turned plowman, were not as amazed as you shall be.

La concreata e perpetüa sete
   del deïforme regno cen portava
   veloci quasi come 'l ciel vedete.   *21*
Beatrice in suso, e io in lei guardava;
   e forse in tanto in quanto un quadrel posa
   e vola e da la noce si dischiava,   *24*
giunto mi vidi ove mirabil cosa
   mi torse il viso a sé; e però quella
   cui non potea mia cura essere ascosa,   *27*
volta ver' me, sì lieta come bella,
   "Drizza la mente in Dio grata," mi disse,
   "che n'ha congiunti con la prima stella."   *30*
Parev' a me che nube ne coprisse
   lucida, spessa, solida e pulita,
   quasi adamante che lo sol ferisse.   *33*
Per entro sé l'etterna margarita
   ne ricevette, com' acqua recepe
   raggio di luce permanendo unita.   *36*
S'io era corpo, e qui non si concepe
   com' una dimensione altra patio,
   ch'esser convien se corpo in corpo repe,   *39*
accender ne dovria più il disio
   di veder quella essenza in che si vede
   come nostra natura e Dio s'unio.   *42*
Lì si vedrà ciò che tenem per fede,
   non dimostrato, ma fia per sé noto
   a guisa del ver primo che l'uom crede.   *45*
Io rispuosi: "Madonna, sì devoto
   com' esser posso più, ringrazio lui
   lo qual dal mortal mondo m'ha remoto.   *48*

The inborn and perpetual thirst for the dei-form realm bore us away, swift almost as you see the heavens. Beatrice was gazing upward, and I on her; and perhaps in that time that a bolt strikes, flies, and from the catch is re-leased, I saw myself arrived where a wondrous thing drew my sight to it. She, therefore, from whom my thoughts could not be hidden, turned toward me, as glad as she was fair, and "Direct your mind to God in gratitude," she said, "who has united us with the first star."

It seemed to me that a cloud had enveloped us, shining, dense, solid and polished, like a diamond smitten by the sun. Within itself the eternal pearl received us, as water receives a ray of light, itself remaining uncleft. If I was body (and if here we conceive not how one bulk could brook another, which must be if body enters body), the more should longing enkindle us to see that Essence wherein we behold how our nature and God united them-selves. There that which we hold by faith shall be seen, not demonstrated, but known of itself, like the first truth that man believes.

I answered, "My Lady, devoutly as I most may, I do thank Him who has removed me from the mortal world.

Ma ditemi: che son li segni bui
   di questo corpo, che là giuso in terra
   fan di Cain favoleggiare altrui?"   *51*
Ella sorrise alquanto, e poi "S'elli erra
   l'oppinïon," mi disse, "d'i mortali
   dove chiave di senso non diserra,   *54*
certo non ti dovrien punger li strali
   d'ammirazione omai, poi dietro ai sensi
   vedi che la ragione ha corte l'ali.   *57*
Ma dimmi quel che tu da te ne pensi."
   E io: "Ciò che n'appar qua sù diverso
   credo che fanno i corpi rari e densi."   *60*
Ed ella: "Certo assai vedrai sommerso
   nel falso il creder tuo, se bene ascolti
   l'argomentar ch'io li farò avverso.   *63*
La spera ottava vi dimostra molti
   lumi, li quali e nel quale e nel quanto
   notar si posson di diversi volti.   *66*
Se raro e denso ciò facesser tanto,
   una sola virtù sarebbe in tutti,
   più e men distribuita e altrettanto.   *69*
Virtù diverse esser convegnon frutti
   di princìpi formali, e quei, for ch'uno,
   seguiterieno a tua ragion distrutti.   *72*
Ancor, se raro fosse di quel bruno
   cagion che tu dimandi, o d'oltre in parte
   fora di sua materia sì digiuno   *75*
esto pianeto, o, sì come comparte
   lo grasso e 'l magro un corpo, così questo
   nel suo volume cangerebbe carte.   *78*

But tell me, what are the dusky marks of this body which there below on earth cause folk to tell the tale of Cain?"

She smiled a little, and then said to me, "If the judgment of mortals errs where the key of sense does not unlock, truly the shafts of wonder should not prick you henceforth, since even when following after the senses you see that reason's wings are short. But tell me what you yourself think of it."

And I, "That which appears to us diverse here above I suppose to be produced by rare and dense matter."

And she, "Verily you shall see that your belief is plunged deep in error, if you listen well to the argument I shall make against it.

"The eighth sphere displays to you many lights which both in quality and in magnitude can be seen to be of diverse countenances. If rarity and density alone produced this thing, one single virtue, more or less or equally distributed, would be in all. Different virtues must needs be fruits of formal principles, the which, save only one, would be destroyed, according to your reckoning. Further, were rarity the cause of that darkness whereof you make question, either this planet would thus be lacking in its matter quite through and through, or else, just as fat and lean are distributed in a body, it would alternate the pages in its volume.

Se 'l primo fosse, fora manifesto
  ne l'eclissi del sol, per trasparere
  lo lume come in altro raro ingesto.   *81*
Questo non è: però è da vedere
  de l'altro; e s'elli avvien ch'io l'altro cassi,
  falsificato fia lo tuo parere.   *84*
S'elli è che questo raro non trapassi,
  esser conviene un termine da onde
  lo suo contrario più passar non lassi;   *87*
e indi l'altrui raggio si rifonde
  così come color torna per vetro
  lo qual di retro a sé piombo nasconde.   *90*
Or dirai tu ch'el si dimostra tetro
  ivi lo raggio più che in altre parti,
  per esser lì refratto più a retro.   *93*
Da questa instanza può deliberarti
  esperïenza, se già mai la provi,
  ch'esser suol fonte ai rivi di vostr' arti.   *96*
Tre specchi prenderai; e i due rimovi
  da te d'un modo, e l'altro, più rimosso,
  tr'ambo li primi li occhi tuoi ritrovi.   *99*
Rivolto ad essi, fa che dopo il dosso
  ti stea un lume che i tre specchi accenda
  e torni a te da tutti ripercosso.   *102*
Ben che nel quanto tanto non si stenda
  la vista più lontana, lì vedrai
  come convien ch'igualmente risplenda.   *105*
Or, come ai colpi de li caldi rai
  de la neve riman nudo il suggetto
  e dal colore e dal freddo primai,   *108*

If the first were the case, this would be mani-
fest in the eclipse of the sun, by the shining
through of the light, as it does when it is
poured upon any rare matter. This is not so;
therefore we must look at the other supposi-
tion, and if it chance that I quash that, your
opinion will be refuted.

"If it be that this rarity does not pass
throughout, needs must there be a limit at
which its contrary intercepts its passing far-
ther, and thence that other's ray would be
cast back, just as color returns from the glass
that hides lead behind itself. Now you will
say that the ray shows itself dimmer there
than in other parts, because it is reflected there
from farther back. From this objection experi-
ment, which is wont to be the fountain to the
streams of your arts, may deliver you, if ever
you try it. You shall take three mirrors, and set
two of them equally remote from you, and let
the other, even more remote, meet your eyes
between the first two. Turning toward them,
cause a light to be placed behind your back
which may shine in the three mirrors and
return to you reflected from all three. Al-
though the more distant image may not reach
you so great in quantity, you will there see it
must needs be of equal brightness with the
others.

"Now—as beneath the blows of the warm
rays the substrate of the snow is left stripped
both of the color and the coldness which it
had—

così rimaso te ne l'intelletto
   voglio informar di luce sì vivace,
   che ti tremolerà nel suo aspetto.   *111*
Dentro dal ciel de la divina pace
   si gira un corpo ne la cui virtute
   l'esser di tutto suo contento giace.   *114*
Lo ciel seguente, c'ha tante vedute,
   quell' esser parte per diverse essenze,
   da lui distratte e da lui contenute.   *117*
Li altri giron per varie differenze
   le distinzion che dentro da sé hanno
   dispongono a lor fini e lor semenze.   *120*
Questi organi del mondo così vanno,
   come tu vedi omai, di grado in grado,
   che di sù prendono e di sotto fanno.   *123*
Riguarda bene omai sì com' io vado
   per questo loco al vero che disiri,
   sì che poi sappi sol tener lo guado.   *126*
Lo moto e la virtù d'i santi giri,
   come dal fabbro l'arte del martello,
   da' beati motor convien che spiri;   *129*
e 'l ciel cui tanti lumi fanno bello,
   de la mente profonda che lui volve
   prende l'image e fassene suggello.   *132*
E come l'alma dentro a vostra polve
   per differenti membra e conformate
   a diverse potenze si risolve,   *135*
così l'intelligenza sua bontate
   multiplicata per le stelle spiega,
   girando sé sovra sua unitate.   *138*

you, left thus stripped in your intellect, will I inform with light so living that it shall quiver as you look on it.

"Within the heaven of the divine peace revolves a body in whose power lies the being of all that it contains. The following heaven, which has so many things to show, distributes this being through diverse essences, distinct from it and contained by it. The other circles, by various differentiatings, dispose the distinctions which they have within themselves unto their ends and their sowings. These organs of the universe proceed, as you now see, from grade to grade, for they receive from above and operate downwards. Observe well now how I advance through this pass to the truth which you seek, so that hereafter you may know how to take the ford alone. The motion and the virtue of the holy spheres, even as the hammer's art by the smith, must needs be inspired by the blessed movers; and the heaven which so many lights make beautiful takes its stamp from the profound mind that turns it, and of that stamp makes itself the seal. And as the soul within your dust is diffused through different members and conformed to different potencies, so does the Intelligence deploy its goodness, multiplied through the stars, itself circling upon its own unity.

Virtù diversa fa diversa lega
  col prezïoso corpo ch'ella avviva,
  nel qual, sì come vita in voi, si lega.   *141*
Per la natura lieta onde deriva,
  la virtù mista per lo corpo luce
  come letizia per pupilla viva.   *144*
Da essa vien ciò che da luce a luce
  par differente, non da denso e raro;
  essa è formal principio che produce,
conforme a sua bontà, lo turbo e 'l chiaro."   *148*

Divers virtues make divers alloy with the precious body it quickens, wherein, even as life in you, it is bound. Because of the glad nature whence it flows, the mingled virtue shines through the body, as gladness does through a living pupil. Thence comes what seems different between light and light, not from density and rarity. This is the formal principle which produces, conformably with its own excellence, the dark and the bright."

PARADISO

Quel sol che pria d'amor mi scaldò 'l petto,
di bella verità m'avea scoverto,
provando e riprovando, il dolce aspetto;   3
e io, per confessar corretto e certo
me stesso, tanto quanto si convenne
leva' il capo a proferer più erto;   6
ma visïone apparve che ritenne
a sé me tanto stretto, per vedersi,
che di mia confession non mi sovvenne.   9
Quali per vetri trasparenti e tersi,
o ver per acque nitide e tranquille,
non sì profonde che i fondi sien persi,   12
tornan d'i nostri visi le postille
debili sì, che perla in bianca fronte
non vien men forte a le nostre pupille;   15
tali vid' io più facce a parlar pronte;
per ch'io dentro a l'error contrario corsi
a quel ch'accese amor tra l'omo e 'l fonte.   18

CANTO III

THAT SUN which first had heated my breast with love, proving and refuting had uncovered to me the sweet aspect of fair truth, and, to confess me corrected and assured, I raised my head more erect to speak, in measure as was meet; but a sight appeared which held me so fast to itself, to look on it, that I bethought me not of my confession.

As through smooth and transparent glass, or through clear and tranquil waters, yet not so deep that the bottom be lost, the outlines of our faces return so faint that a pearl on a white brow comes not less boldly to our eyes, so did I behold many a countenance eager to speak; wherefore I fell into the contrary error to that which kindled love between the man and the fountain.

Sùbito sì com' io di lor m'accorsi,
   quelle stimando specchiati sembianti,
   per veder di cui fosser, li occhi torsi;   *21*
e nulla vidi, e ritorsili avanti
   dritti nel lume de la dolce guida,
   che, sorridendo, ardea ne li occhi santi.   *24*
"Non ti maravigliar perch' io sorrida,"
   mi disse, "appresso il tuo püeril coto,
   poi sopra 'l vero ancor lo piè non fida,   *27*
ma te rivolve, come suole, a vòto:
   vere sustanze son ciò che tu vedi,
   qui rilegate per manco di voto.   *30*
Però parla con esse e odi e credi;
   ché la verace luce che le appaga
   da sé non lascia lor torcer li piedi."   *33*
E io a l'ombra che parea più vaga
   di ragionar, drizza'mi, e cominciai,
   quasi com' uom cui troppa voglia smaga: *36*
"O ben creato spirito, che a' rai
   di vita etterna la dolcezza senti
   che, non gustata, non s'intende mai,   *39*
grazïoso mi fia se mi contenti
   del nome tuo e de la vostra sorte."
      Ond' ella, pronta e con occhi ridenti: *42*
"La nostra carità non serra porte
   a giusta voglia, se non come quella
   che vuol simile a sé tutta sua corte.   *45*
I' fui nel mondo vergine sorella;
   e se la mente tua ben sé riguarda,
   non mi ti celerà l'esser più bella,   *48*

No sooner was I aware of them than, taking them for mirrored faces, I turned round my eyes to see of whom they were, and saw nothing; and I turned them forward again, straight into the light of the sweet guide, whose holy eyes were glowing as she smiled.

"Do not wonder," she said to me, "that I smile at your childish thought, since it does not yet trust itself upon the truth, but turns you, after its wont, to vacancy. These that you see are real substances, assigned here for failure in their vows. Wherefore speak with them and hear and believe, for the true light that satisfies them does not suffer them to turn their steps aside from it."

And I directed myself to the shade who seemed most eager to speak, and I began like a man whom excessive desire confuses, "O well-created spirit, who in the rays of life eternal do taste the sweetness which, if not tasted, is never understood, it would be a kindness to me if you satisfied me with your name and with your lot."

Whereon she, eager and with smiling eyes, "Our charity does not shut the doors against right will any more than that which wills that all Its court be like Itself. In the world I was a virgin sister, and if your memory be searched well, my being more beautiful will not conceal me from you,

ma riconoscerai ch'i' son Piccarda,
   che, posta qui con questi altri beati,
   beata sono in la spera più tarda.   *51*
Li nostri affetti, che solo infiammati
   son nel piacer de lo Spirito Santo,
   letizian del suo ordine formati.   *54*
E questa sorte che par giù cotanto,
   però n'è data, perché fuor negletti
   li nostri voti, e vòti in alcun canto."   *57*
Ond' io a lei: "Ne' mirabili aspetti
   vostri risplende non so che divino
   che vi trasmuta da' primi concetti: *60*
però non fui a rimembrar festino;
   ma or m'aiuta ciò che tu mi dici,
   sì che raffigurar m'è più latino.   *63*
Ma dimmi: voi che siete qui felici,
   disiderate voi più alto loco
   per più vedere e per più farvi amici?"   *66*
Con quelle altr' ombre pria sorrise un poco;
   da indi mi rispuose tanto lieta,
   ch'arder parea d'amor nel primo foco: *69*
"Frate, la nostra volontà quïeta
   virtù di carità, che fa volerne
   sol quel ch'avemo, e d'altro non ci asseta.   *72*
Se disïassimo esser più superne,
   foran discordi li nostri disiri
   dal voler di colui che qui ne cerne;   *75*
che vedrai non capere in questi giri,
   s'essere in carità è qui *necesse*,
   e se la sua natura ben rimiri.   *78*

but you will recognize that I am Piccarda, who, placed here with these other blessèd ones, am blessèd in the slowest sphere. Our affections, which are kindled solely in the pleasure of the Holy Ghost, rejoice in being conformed to His order. And this lot, which appears so lowly, is given to us because our vows were neglected and void in some particular."

Whereon I said to her, "In your wondrous aspects a something divine shines forth that transmutes you from recollection of former times; therefore I was not quick in calling you to mind, but now that which you tell me helps me so that I more clearly recall your features. But tell me, you who are happy here, do you desire a more exalted place, to see more, and to make yourselves more dear?"

With those other shades she first smiled a little, then answered me so glad that she seemed to burn in the first fire of love, "Brother, the power of love quiets our will and makes us wish only for that which we have and gives us no other thirst. Did we desire to be more aloft, our longings would be discordant with His will who assigns us here: which you will see is not possible in these circles if to exist in charity here is of necessity, and if you well consider what is love's nature.

Anzi è formale ad esto beato *esse*
   tenersi dentro a la divina voglia,
   per ch'una fansi nostre voglie stesse;   *81*
sì che, come noi sem di soglia in soglia
   per questo regno, a tutto il regno piace
   com' a lo re che 'n suo voler ne 'nvoglia.   *84*
E 'n la sua volontade è nostra pace:
   ell' è quel mare al qual tutto si move
   ciò ch'ella crïa o che natura face."   *87*
Chiaro mi fu allor come ogne dove
   in cielo è paradiso, *etsi* la grazia
   del sommo ben d'un modo non vi piove.   *90*
Ma sì com' elli avvien, s'un cibo sazia
   e d'un altro rimane ancor la gola,
   che quel si chere e di quel si ringrazia,   *93*
così fec' io con atto e con parola,
   per apprender da lei qual fu la tela
   onde non trasse infino a co la spuola.   *96*
"Perfetta vita e alto merto inciela
   donna più sù," mi disse, "a la cui norma
   nel vostro mondo giù si veste e vela,   *99*
perché fino al morir si vegghi e dorma
   con quello sposo ch'ogne voto accetta
   che caritate a suo piacer conforma.   *102*
Dal mondo, per seguirla, giovinetta
   fuggi'mi, e nel suo abito mi chiusi
   e promisi la via de la sua setta.   *105*
Uomini poi, a mal più ch'a bene usi,
   fuor mi rapiron de la dolce chiostra:
   Iddio si sa qual poi mia vita fusi.   *108*

Nay, it is the essence of this blessed existence to keep itself within the divine will, whereby our wills themselves are made one; so that our being thus from threshold to threshold throughout this realm is a joy to all the realm as to the King, who draws our wills to what He wills; and in His will is our peace. It is that sea to which all moves, both what It creates and what nature makes."

Then was it clear to me how everywhere in Heaven is Paradise, even if the grace of the Supreme Good does not there rain down in one same measure. But as it happens when of one food we have enough and the appetite for another still remains, that this is asked for and thanks are returned for that, so I did with gesture and with speech, to learn from her what was the web through which she had not drawn the shuttle to the end.

"Perfect life and high merit enheaven a lady more aloft," she said to me, "according to whose rule, in your world below, are those who take the robe and veil themselves that they, even till death, may wake and sleep with that Spouse who accepts every vow which love conforms unto His pleasure. From the world, to follow her, I fled while yet a girl, and in her habit I clothed me and prom-ised myself to the way of her order. Then men, more used to evil than to good, snatched me from the sweet cloister: and God knows what then my life became.

33

E quest' altro splendor che ti si mostra
da la mia destra parte e che s'accende
di tutto il lume de la spera nostra,   *111*
ciò ch'io dico di me, di sé intende;
sorella fu, e così le fu tolta
di capo l'ombra de le sacre bende.   *114*
Ma poi che pur al mondo fu rivolta
contra suo grado e contra buona usanza,
non fu dal vel del cor già mai disciolta.   *117*
Quest' è la luce de la gran Costanza
che del secondo vento di Soave
generò 'l terzo e l'ultima possanza."   *120*
Così parlommi, e poi cominciò "*Ave,
Maria*" cantando, e cantando vanio
come per acqua cupa cosa grave.   *123*
La vista mia, che tanto lei seguio
quanto possibil fu, poi che la perse,
volsesi al segno di maggior disio,   *126*
e a Beatrice tutta si converse;
ma quella folgorò nel mïo sguardo
sì che da prima il viso non sofferse;
e ciò mi fece a dimandar più tardo.   *130*

"And this other splendor which shows itself to you at my right side, and which is enkindled with all the light of our sphere, understands of herself that which I say of me. She was a sister, and from her head in like manner was taken the shadow of the sacred veil. Yet, turned back as she was into the world, against her will and against right custom, from her heart's veil she was never loosed. This is the light of the great Constance, who bore to the second blast of Swabia the third and final power."

Thus did she speak to me, and then began to sing *Ave Maria*, and, singing, vanished, as through deep water some heavy thing. My sight, which followed her so far as was possible, after it lost her, turned to the mark of greater desire and wholly reverted to Beatrice; but she so flashed upon my gaze that at first my sight endured it not; and this made me the slower with my questioning.

Intra due cibi, distanti e moventi
  d'un modo, prima si morria di fame,
  che liber' omo l'un recasse ai denti;   *3*
sì si starebbe un agno intra due brame
  di fieri lupi, igualmente temendo;
  sì si starebbe un cane intra due dame: *6*
per che s'i' mi tacea, me non riprendo,
  da li miei dubbi d'un modo sospinto,
  poi ch'era necessario, né commendo.   *9*
Io mi tacea, ma 'l mio disir dipinto
  m'era nel viso, e 'l dimandar con ello,
  più caldo assai che per parlar distinto.   *12*
Fé sì Beatrice qual fé Danïello,
  Nabuccodonosor levando d'ira,
  che l'avea fatto ingiustamente fello;   *15*
e disse: "Io veggio ben come ti tira
  uno e altro disio, sì che tua cura
  sé stessa lega sì che fuor non spira.   *18*

CANTO IV

Betweeen two foods, distant and appetizing in equal measure, a free man would die of hunger before he would bring one of them to his teeth. So would a lamb stand between two cravings of fierce wolves, in equal fear of both; so would a hound stand still between two hinds. Wherefore, if I was silent, urged in equal measure by my doubts, I neither blame nor commend myself, since it was of necessity.

I was silent, but my desire was depicted on my face, and my questioning with it, in warmer colors far than by distinct speech. Beatrice did what Daniel did, when he lifted Nebuchadnezzar out of the wrath that had made him unjustly cruel, and she said, "I see well how one and another desire so draw you on that your eagerness entangles its own self and therefore breathes not forth.

Tu argomenti: 'Se 'l buon voler dura,
   la vïolenza altrui per qual ragione
   di meritar mi scema la misura?'   *21*
Ancor di dubitar ti dà cagione
   parer tornarsi l'anime a le stelle,
   secondo la sentenza di Platone.   *24*
Queste son le question che nel tuo *velle*
   pontano igualmente; e però pria
   tratterò quella che più ha di felle.   *27*
D'i Serafin colui che più s'india,
   Moïsè, Samuel, e quel Giovanni
   che prender vuoli, io dico, non Maria,   *30*
non hanno in altro cielo i loro scanni
   che questi spirti che mo t'appariro,
   né hanno a l'esser lor più o meno anni;   *33*
ma tutti fanno bello il primo giro,
   e differentemente han dolce vita
   per sentir più e men l'etterno spiro.   *36*
Qui si mostraro, non perché sortita
   sia questa spera lor, ma per far segno
   de la celestïal c'ha men salita.   *39*
Così parlar conviensi al vostro ingegno,
   però che solo da sensato apprende
   ciò che fa poscia d'intelletto degno.   *42*
Per questo la Scrittura condescende
   a vostra facultate, e piedi e mano
   attribuisce a Dio e altro intende;   *45*
e Santa Chiesa con aspetto umano
   Gabrïel e Michel vi rappresenta,
   e l'altro che Tobia rifece sano.   *48*

You reason, 'If right will endures, by what justice can another's violence lessen the measure of my desert?' Further, that the souls appear to return to the stars, in accordance with Plato's teaching, gives you occasion for doubt. These are the questions that thrust equally upon your will. And therefore I will first treat that which has the most venom.

"Of the Seraphim he who is most in God, Moses, Samuel, and whichever John you will —I say, even Mary—have not their seats in any other heaven than these spirits which have now appeared to you, nor have they more or fewer years for their existence; but all make the first circle beautiful, and have sweet life in different measure, by feeling more and less the eternal breath. These showed themselves here, not because this sphere is allotted to them, but to afford sign of the celestial grade that is least exalted. It is needful to speak thus to your faculty, since only through sense perception does it apprehend that which it afterwards makes fit for the intellect. For this reason Scripture condescends to your capacity, and attributes hands and feet to God, having other meaning; and Holy Church represents to you with human aspect Gabriel and Michael and the other who made Tobit whole again.

Quel che Timeo de l'anime argomenta
  non è simile a ciò che qui si vede,
  però che, come dice, par che senta.   *51*
Dice che l'alma a la sua stella riede,
  credendo quella quindi esser decisa
  quando natura per forma la diede;   *54*
e forse sua sentenza è d'altra guisa
  che la voce non suona, ed esser puote
  con intenzion da non esser derisa.   *57*
S'elli intende tornare a queste ruote
  l'onor de la influenza e 'l biasmo, forse
  in alcun vero suo arco percuote.   *60*
Questo principio, male inteso, torse
  già tutto il mondo quasi, sì che Giove,
  Mercurio e Marte a nominar trascorse.   *63*
L'altra dubitazion che ti commove
  ha men velen, però che sua malizia
  non ti poria menar da me altrove.   *66*
Parere ingiusta la nostra giustizia
  ne li occhi d'i mortali, è argomento
  di fede e non d'eretica nequizia.   *69*
Ma perché puote vostro accorgimento
  ben penetrare a questa veritate,
  come disiri, ti farò contento.   *72*
Se vïolenza è quando quel che pate
  nïente conferisce a quel che sforza,
  non fuor quest' alme per essa scusate: *75*
ché volontà, se non vuol, non s'ammorza,
  ma fa come natura face in foco,
  se mille volte vïolenza il torza.   *78*

What Timaeus argues about the souls is not
like this which is seen here, for seemingly he
holds what he says for the truth. He says the
soul returns to its own star, believing it to
have been severed thence when nature gave it
for a form. But perhaps his opinion is other
than his words sound, and may be of a mean-
ing not to be derided. If he means that the
honor of their influence and the blame returns
to these wheels, perhaps his bow hits some
truth. This principle, ill-understood, once mis-
led almost the entire world, so that it ran
astray in naming Jove and Mercury and Mars.

"The other perplexity that troubles you has
less of poison, for its malice could not lead
you away from me elsewhere. For our justice
to seem unjust in mortal eyes is argument of
faith, not of heretical iniquity. But since your
understanding can well penetrate to this truth,
I will make you content as you desire.

"If it be violence when he who suffers con-
tributes nothing to what forces him, these
souls would not be excused on that account.
For will, if it will not, is not quenched, but
does as nature does in fire, though violence
wrest it aside a thousand times.

Per che, s'ella si piega assai o poco,
    segue la forza; e così queste fero
    possendo rifuggir nel santo loco.   *81*
Se fosse stato lor volere intero,
    come tenne Lorenzo in su la grada,
    e fece Muzio a la sua man severo,   *84*
così l'avria ripinte per la strada
    ond' eran tratte, come fuoro sciolte;
    ma così salda voglia è troppo rada.   *87*
E per queste parole, se ricolte
    l'hai come dei, è l'argomento casso
    che t'avria fatto noia ancor più volte.   *90*
Ma or ti s'attraversa un altro passo
    dinanzi a li occhi, tal che per te stesso
    non usciresti: pria saresti lasso.   *93*
Io t'ho per certo ne la mente messo
    ch'alma beata non poria mentire,
    però ch'è sempre al primo vero appresso;   *96*
e poi potesti da Piccarda udire
    che l'affezion del vel Costanza tenne;
    sì ch'ella par qui meco contradire.   *99*
Molte fiate già, frate, addivenne
    che, per fuggir periglio, contra grato
    si fé di quel che far non si convenne;   *102*
come Almeone, che, di ciò pregato
    dal padre suo, la propria madre spense,
    per non perder pietà si fé spietato.   *105*
A questo punto voglio che tu pense
    che la forza al voler si mischia, e fanno
    sì che scusar non si posson l'offense.   *108*

For should it bend itself much or little, it follows force: and thus did these when they had power to return to the holy place. If their will had remained whole, such as held Lawrence on the grid and made Mucius severe to his own hand, it would have urged them back, so soon as they were loosed, by the road along which they had been dragged—but such sound will is all too rare. And by these words, if you have gathered them up as you should, is the argument quashed that would have troubled you yet many times.

"But now across your path another strait confronts your eyes, such that you would not get through it by yourself before you would be exhausted. I have put it in your mind for certain that a soul in bliss cannot lie, since it is always near the Primal Truth; and then you could hear from Piccarda that Constance kept her love for the veil, so that here she seems to contradict me. Many a time ere now, brother, has it happened that unwillingly, in order to escape from danger, that was done which ought not to have been done; even as Alcmeon who, urged thereto by his father, slew his own mother, and, so as not to fail in piety, became pitiless. At this point I would have you realize that force mixes with the will, and they so act that the offenses cannot be excused.

Voglia assoluta non consente al danno;
   ma consentevi in tanto in quanto teme,
   se si ritrae, cadere in più affanno.   *111*
Però, quando Piccarda quello spreme,
   de la voglia assoluta intende, e io
   de l'altra; sì che ver diciamo insieme."   *114*
Cotal fu l'ondeggiar del santo rio
   ch'uscì del fonte ond' ogne ver deriva;
   tal puose in pace uno e altro disio.   *117*
"O amanza del primo amante, o diva,"
   diss' io appresso, "il cui parlar m'inonda
   e scalda sì, che più e più m'avviva,   *120*
non è l'affezion mia tanto profonda,
   che basti a render voi grazia per grazia;
   ma quei che vede e puote a ciò risponda.   *123*
Io veggio ben che già mai non si sazia
   nostro intelletto, se 'l ver non lo illustra
   di fuor dal qual nessun vero si spazia.   *126*
Posasi in esso, come fera in lustra,
   tosto che giunto l'ha; e giugner puollo:
   se non, ciascun disio sarebbe *frustra*.   *129*
Nasce per quello, a guisa di rampollo,
   a piè del vero il dubbio; ed è natura
   ch'al sommo pinge noi di collo in collo.   *132*
Questo m'invita, questo m'assicura
   con reverenza, donna, a dimandarvi
   d'un'altra verità che m'è oscura.   *135*
Io vo' saper se l'uom può sodisfarvi
   ai voti manchi sì con altri beni,
   ch'a la vostra statera non sien parvi."   *138*

Absolute will does not consent to the wrong, but the will consents thereto in so far as it fears, by drawing back, to fall into greater trouble. Therefore, when Piccarda says this, she means it of the absolute will, and I of the other; so that we both speak truth together."

Such was the rippling of the holy stream which issued forth from the Fount from which springs every truth, and such it set at rest one and the other desire.

"O beloved of the First Lover, O divine one," said I then, "whose speech overflows me and warms me so that it quickens me more and more, not all the depth of my affection is sufficient to render to you grace for grace; but may He who sees and can answer thereto. Well do I see that never can our intellect be wholly satisfied unless that Truth shine on it, beyond which no truth has range. Therein it rests, as a wild beast in his lair, so soon as it has reached it; and reach it it can, else every desire would be in vain. Because of this, questioning springs up like a shoot, at the foot of the truth; and this is nature which urges us to the summit, from height to height. It is this, Lady, that invites and emboldens me to question you with reverence of another truth which is obscure to me. I wish to know if man can so satisfy you for broken vows, with other goods, as not to weigh too short upon your scales."

Beatrice mi guardò con li occhi pieni
di faville d'amor così divini,
che, vinta, mia virtute diè le reni,
e quasi mi perdei con li occhi chini.   *142*

Beatrice looked on me with eyes so full of the sparkling of love and so divine that my power, vanquished, took flight, and I almost lost myself with eyes downcast.

PARADISO

"S'io ti fiammeggio nel caldo d'amore
  di là dal modo che 'n terra si vede,
  sì che del viso tuo vinco il valore,   *3*
non ti maravigliar, ché ciò procede
  da perfetto veder, che, come apprende,
  così nel bene appreso move il piede.   *6*
Io veggio ben sì come già resplende
  ne l'intelletto tuo l'etterna luce,
  che, vista, sola e sempre amore accende;   *9*
e s'altra cosa vostro amor seduce,
  non è se non di quella alcun vestigio,
  mal conosciuto, che quivi traluce.   *12*
Tu vuo' saper se con altro servigio,
  per manco voto, si può render tanto
  che l'anima sicuri di letigio."   *15*
Sì cominciò Beatrice questo canto;
  e sì com' uom che suo parlar non spezza,
  continüò così 'l processo santo: *18*
"Lo maggior don che Dio per sua larghezza
  fesse creando, e a la sua bontate
  più conformato, e quel ch'e' più apprezza,   *21*

CANTO V

"I<small>F I</small> flame on you in the warmth of love beyond the measure that is seen on earth and so vanquish the power of your eyes, do not marvel, for it comes from perfect vision which, according as it apprehends, so does it move its foot to the apprehended good. Well do I note how in your intellect already is shining the eternal light which, seen, alone and always kindles love; and if aught else seduce your love, it is naught save some vestige of that light, ill-recognized, which therein shines through. You wish to know if for an unfulfilled vow so much can be paid with other service as may secure the soul from suit."

So Beatrice began this canto, and as one who does not interrupt his speech, she thus continued her holy discourse, "The greatest gift which God in His bounty bestowed in creating, and the most conformed to His own goodness and that which He most prizes,

fu de la volontà la libertate;
   di che le creature intelligenti,
   e tutte e sole, fuoro e son dotate.   24
Or ti parrà, se tu quinci argomenti,
   l'alto valor del voto, s'è sì fatto
   che Dio consenta quando tu consenti;   27
ché, nel fermar tra Dio e l'omo il patto,
   vittima fassi di questo tesoro,
   tal quale io dico; e fassi col suo atto.   30
Dunque che render puossi per ristoro?
   Se credi bene usar quel c'hai offerto,
   di maltolletto vuo' far buon lavoro.   33
Tu se' omai del maggior punto certo;
   ma perché Santa Chiesa in ciò dispensa,
   che par contra lo ver ch'i' t'ho scoverto,   36
convienti ancor sedere un poco a mensa,
   però che 'l cibo rigido c'hai preso,
   richiede ancora aiuto a tua dispensa.   39
Apri la mente a quel ch'io ti paleso
   e fermalvi entro; ché non fa scïenza,
   sanza lo ritenere, avere inteso.   42
Due cose si convegnono a l'essenza
   di questo sacrificio: l'una è quella
   di che si fa; l'altr' è la convenenza.   45
Quest' ultima già mai non si cancella
   se non servata; e intorno di lei
   sì preciso di sopra si favella: 48
però necessitato fu a li Ebrei
   pur l'offerere, ancor ch'alcuna offerta
   si permutasse, come saver dei.   51

was the freedom of the will, with which the creatures that have intelligence, they all and they alone, were and are endowed. Now, if you argue from this, the high worth of the vow will appear to you, if it be such that God consents when you consent; for in establishing the compact between God and man, this treasure becomes the sacrifice, such as I pronounce it, and that by its own act. What then can be given in compensation? If you think to make good use of that which you have offered, you seek to do good with ill-gotten gains.

"You are now assured as to the greater point; but since Holy Church gives dispensation in this matter, which seems contrary to the truth I have declared to you, it behooves you to sit a while longer at table, for the tough food which you have taken requires still some aid for your digestion. Open your mind to that which I reveal to you, and fix it therewithin; for to have heard without retaining makes not knowledge.

"Two things constitute the essence of this sacrifice: the first is that in respect to which it is made, and the other is the covenant itself. This last is never canceled save by being kept, and concerning this was my preceding speech so precise. Therefore it was imperative upon the Hebrews to offer sacrifice in any case, though the thing offered might sometimes be changed, as you should know.

L'altra, che per materia t'è aperta,
   puote ben esser tal, che non si falla
   se con altra materia si converta.   *54*
Ma non trasmuti carco a la sua spalla
   per suo arbitrio alcun, sanza la volta
   e de la chiave bianca e de la gialla;   *57*
e ogne permutanza credi stolta,
   se la cosa dimessa in la sorpresa
   come 'l quattro nel sei non è raccolta.   *60*
Però qualunque cosa tanto pesa
   per suo valor che tragga ogne bilancia,
   sodisfar non si può con altra spesa.   *63*
Non prendan li mortali il voto a ciancia;
   siate fedeli, e a ciò far non bieci,
   come Ieptè a la sua prima mancia;   *66*
cui più si convenia dicer 'Mal feci,'
   che, servando, far peggio; e così stolto
   ritrovar puoi il gran duca de' Greci,   *69*
onde pianse Efigènia il suo bel volto,
   e fé pianger di sé i folli e i savi
   ch'udir pàrlar di così fatto cólto.   *72*
Siate, Cristiani, a muovervi più gravi:
   non siate come penna ad ogne vento,
   e non crediate ch'ogne acqua vi lavi.   *75*
Avete il novo e 'l vecchio Testamento,
   e 'l pastor de la Chiesa che vi guida;
   questo vi basti a vostro salvamento.   *78*
Se mala cupidigia altro vi grida,
   uomini siate, e non pecore matte,
   sì che 'l Giudeo di voi tra voi non rida!   *81*

The other, which is known to you as the matter, may indeed be such that there is no fault if it be exchanged for other matter. But let no one shift the load upon his shoulder at his own judgment, without the turning of both the white and the yellow key; and let him hold all changing folly unless the thing laid down be not contained in that which is taken up, as four in six. Therefore, whatever thing weighs so much through its own worth as to tip every scale cannot be made good by any other outlay.

"Let mortals never take the vow in sport. Be faithful, and with that be not perverse, as was Jephthah in his first offering, who ought rather to have said 'I did amiss,' than, by keeping his vow, to do worse. And you can find the great leader of the Greeks in like manner foolish, wherefore Iphigenia wept that her face was fair, and made weep for her both the simple and the wise who heard the tale of such a rite. Be graver, you Christians, in moving. Be not like a feather to every wind, and think not that every water may cleanse you. You have the New Testament and the Old, and the Shepherd of the Church, to guide you: let this suffice for your salvation. If evil greed cry aught else to you, be you men, and not silly sheep, so that the Jew among you may not laugh at you.

Non fate com' agnel che lascia il latte
  de la sua madre, e semplice e lascivo
  seco medesmo a suo piacer combatte!"   *84*
Così Beatrice a me com' ïo scrivo;
  poi si rivolse tutta disïante
  a quella parte ove 'l mondo è più vivo.   *87*
Lo suo tacere e 'l trasmutar sembiante
  puoser silenzio al mio cupido ingegno,
  che già nuove questioni avea davante;   *90*
e sì come saetta che nel segno
  percuote pria che sia la corda queta,
  così corremmo nel secondo regno.   *93*
Quivi la donna mia vid' io sì lieta,
  come nel lume di quel ciel si mise,
  che più lucente se ne fé 'l pianeta.   *96*
E se la stella si cambiò e rise,
  qual mi fec' io che pur da mia natura
  trasmutabile son per tutte guise!   *99*
Come 'n peschiera ch'è tranquilla e pura
  traggonsi i pesci a ciò che vien di fori
  per modo che lo stimin lor pastura,   *102*
sì vid' io ben più di mille splendori
  trarsi ver' noi, e in ciascun s'udia:
  "Ecco chi crescerà li nostri amori."   *105*
E sì come ciascuno a noi venìa,
  vedeasi l'ombra piena di letizia
  nel folgór chiaro che di lei uscia.   *108*
Pensa, lettor, se quel che qui s'inizia
  non procedesse, come tu avresti
  di più savere angosciosa carizia;   *111*

Be not like the lamb that leaves its mother's milk and, silly and wanton, fights with itself at its own pleasure."

Thus Beatrice to me, even as I write; then she turned full of longing to that part where the universe is most alive. Her silence and her changed look imposed silence on my eager mind, which already had new questionings before it. And as an arrow that strikes the target before the bowcord is quiet, so we sped into the second realm. Here I beheld my lady so glad, when she passed into that heaven's light, that the planet itself became the brighter for it; and if the star changed and smiled, what did I become, who by my very nature am subject to every kind of change?

As in a fish-pool that is still and clear the fish draw to that which comes in such manner from without that they deem it something they can feed on, so did I see full more than a thousand splendors draw towards us, and in each was heard, "Lo one who shall increase our loves!" And, as each came up to us, the shade was seen full of joy, by the bright effulgence that issued from it.

Think, reader, if this beginning went no further, how you would feel an anguished craving to know more,

e per te vederai come da questi
  m'era in disio d'udir lor condizioni,
  sì come a li occhi mi fur manifesti.   *114*
"O bene nato a cui veder li troni
  del trïunfo etternal concede grazia
  prima che la milizia s'abbandoni,   *117*
del lume che per tutto il ciel si spazia
  noi semo accesi; e però, se disii
  di noi chiarirti, a tuo piacer ti sazia."   *120*
Così da un di quelli spirti pii
  detto mi fu; e da Beatrice: "Dì, dì
  sicuramente, e credi come a dii."   *123*
"Io veggio ben sì come tu t'annidi
  nel proprio lume, e che de li occhi il traggi,
  perch' e' corusca sì come tu ridi;   *126*
ma non so chi tu se', né perché aggi,
  anima degna, il grado de la spera
  che si vela a' mortai con altrui raggi."   *129*
Questo diss' io diritto a la lumera
  che pria m'avea parlato; ond' ella fessi
  lucente più assai di quel ch'ell' era.   *132*
Sì come il sol che si cela elli stessi
  per troppa luce, come 'l caldo ha róse
  le temperanze d'i vapori spessi,   *135*
per più letizia sì mi si nascose
  dentro al suo raggio la figura santa;
  e così chiusa chiusa mi rispuose
nel modo che 'l seguente canto canta.   *139*

and by yourself you will see what my desire
was, to hear of their conditions from them,
as soon as they became manifest to my eyes.

"O happy-born, to whom Grace concedes to
see the thrones of the eternal triumph before
you leave your time of warfare, we are en-
kindled by the light that ranges through all
heaven; therefore, if you desire to draw light
from us, sate yourself at your own pleasure."
Thus was it said to me by one of those devout
spirits; and by Beatrice, "Speak, speak se-
curely, and trust even as to gods."

"I see well how you do nest yourself in your
own light, and that you dart it from your eyes,
because it sparkles when you smile; but I
know not who you are, nor why, O worthy
spirit, you have your rank in the sphere that
is veiled to mortals by another's rays." This I
said, turned toward the light which first had
spoken to me; whereon it glowed far brighter
than before. Even as the sun, which, when the
heat has consumed the tempering of the dense
vapors, conceals itself by excess of light, so, by
reason of more joy, the holy figure hid itself
from me within its own radiance and, thus
close enclosed, it answered me in such fashion
as the next canto sings.

"Poscia che Costantin l'aquila volse
    contr' al corso del ciel, ch'ella seguio
    dietro a l'antico che Lavina tolse,   3
cento e cent' anni e più l'uccel di Dio
    ne lo stremo d'Europa si ritenne,
    vicino a' monti de' quai prima uscìo;   6
e sotto l'ombra de le sacre penne
    governò 'l mondo lì di mano in mano,
    e, sì cangiando, in su la mia pervenne.   9
Cesare fui e son Iustinïano,
    che, per voler del primo amor ch'i' sento,
    d'entro le leggi trassi il troppo e 'l vano.   12
E prima ch'io a l'ovra fossi attento,
    una natura in Cristo esser, non piùe,
    credea, e di tal fede era contento;   15
ma 'l benedetto Agapito, che fue
    sommo pastore, a la fede sincera
    mi dirizzò con le parole sue.   18

CANTO VI

"After Constantine turned back the Eagle counter to the course of the heavens which it had followed behind the ancient who took Lavinia to wife, a hundred and a hundred years and more the bird of God abode on Europe's limit, near to the mountains from which it first had issued; and there it governed the world beneath the shadow of its sacred wings, from hand to hand, until by succeeding change it came into mine. I was Caesar, and am Justinian, who, by will of the Primal Love which I feel, removed from among the laws what was superfluous and vain. And before I had put my mind to this work, one nature and no more I held to be in Christ, and with that faith I was content; but the blessed Agapetus, who was the supreme pastor, directed me to the true faith by his words.

Io li credetti; e ciò che 'n sua fede era,
    vegg' io or chiaro sì, come tu vedi
    ogne contradizione e falsa e vera.   *21*

Tosto che con la Chiesa mossi i piedi,
    a Dio per grazia piacque di spirarmi
    l'alto lavoro, e tutto 'n lui mi diedi;   *24*

e al mio Belisar commendai l'armi,
    cui la destra del ciel fu sì congiunta,
    che segno fu ch'i' dovessi posarmi.   *27*

Or qui a la question prima s'appunta
    la mia risposta; ma sua condizione
    mi stringe a seguitare alcuna giunta,   *30*

perché tu veggi con quanta ragione
    si move contr' al sacrosanto segno
    e chi 'l s'appropria e chi a lui s'oppone.   *33*

Vedi quanta virtù l'ha fatto degno
    di reverenza; e cominciò da l'ora
    che Pallante morì per darli regno.   *36*

Tu sai ch'el fece in Alba sua dimora
    per trecento anni e oltre, infino al fine
    che i tre a' tre pugnar per lui ancora.   *39*

E sai ch'el fé dal mal de le Sabine
    al dolor di Lucrezia in sette regi,
    vincendo intorno le genti vicine.   *42*

Sai quel ch'el fé portato da li egregi
    Romani incontro a Brenno, incontro a Pirro,
    incontro a li altri principi e collegi;   *45*

onde Torquato e Quinzio, che dal cirro
    negletto fu nomato, i Deci e ' Fabi
    ebber la fama che volontier mirro.   *48*

I believed him, and what he held by faith I now see as clearly as you see that every contradiction is both false and true. So soon as with the Church I moved my feet, it pleased God, of His grace, to inspire me with this high task, and I gave myself entirely to it, committing arms to my Belisarius, with whom Heaven's right hand was so joined that it was a sign for me to rest from them.

"Here ends, then, my answer to the first question; but its condition constrains me to add a certain sequel to it, in order that you may see with how much reason they move against the sacred standard, both those that take it for their own and those that oppose it. See what great virtue made it worthy of reverence, beginning from the hour when Pallas died to give it sway. You know that it made its stay in Alba for three hundred years and more, till at the end, when the three fought against the three for it still. And you know what it did, through seven kings, from the wrong of the Sabine women down to the woe of Lucretia, conquering the neighboring peoples round about. You know what it did when borne by the illustrious Romans against Brennus, against Pyrrhus, and against the rest, princes and governments; whence Torquatus and Quinctius, named from his neglected locks, the Decii and the Fabii, acquired the fame which I gladly embalm.

Esso atterrò l'orgoglio de li Aràbi
   che di retro ad Anibale passaro
   l'alpestre rocce, Po, di che tu labi.   *51*

Sott' esso giovanetti trïunfaro
   Scipïone e Pompeo; e a quel colle
   sotto 'l qual tu nascesti parve amaro.   *54*

Poi, presso al tempo che tutto 'l ciel volle
   redur lo mondo a suo modo sereno,
   Cesare per voler di Roma il tolle.   *57*

E quel che fé da Varo infino a Reno,
   Isàra vide ed Era e vide Senna
   e ogne valle onde Rodano è pieno.   *60*

Quel che fé poi ch'elli uscì di Ravenna
   e saltò Rubicon, fu di tal volo,
   che nol seguiteria lingua né penna.   *63*

Inver' la Spagna rivolse lo stuolo,
   poi ver' Durazzo, e Farsalia percosse
   sì ch'al Nil caldo si sentì del duolo.   *66*

Antandro e Simeonta, onde si mosse,
   rivide e là dov' Ettore si cuba;
   e mal per Tolomeo poscia si scosse.   *69*

Da indi scese folgorando a Iuba;
   onde si volse nel vostro occidente,
   ove sentia la pompeana tuba.   *72*

Di quel che fé col baiulo seguente,
   Bruto con Cassio ne l'inferno latra,
   e Modena e Perugia fu dolente.   *75*

Piangene ancor la trista Cleopatra,
   che, fuggendoli innanzi, dal colubro
   la morte prese subitana e atra.   *78*

It cast down the pride of the Arabs that followed Hannibal across the Alpine rocks whence, Po, you do fall. Under it, Scipio and Pompey triumphed, while yet in their youth, and to that hill beneath which you were born it showed itself bitter. Afterward, near the time when all Heaven willed to bring the world to its own state of peace, Caesar, by the will of Rome, laid hold of it; and what it did from the Var even to the Rhine, the Isere beheld, and the Loire and the Seine beheld, and every valley whence Rhone is filled. What it did after it came forth from Ravenna and leaped the Rubicon was of such flight as no tongue nor pen might follow. Towards Spain it wheeled the host, then towards Durazzo, and did so smite Pharsalia that grief was felt on the burning Nile. It saw again Antandros and the Simois, whence it had set forth, and there where Hector lies; and then it shook itself again—the worse for Ptolemy. From there it fell like lightning on Juba, then turned to your west, where it heard Pompey's trumpet. Of what it wrought with the succeeding marshal, Brutus and Cassius howl in Hell, and Modena and Perugia were doleful. Because of it sad Cleopatra is still weeping who, fleeing before it, took from the viper sudden and black death.

Con costui corse infino al lito rubro;
   con costui puose il mondo in tanta pace,
   che fu serrato a Giano il suo delubro.   *81*
Ma ciò che 'l segno che parlar mi face
   fatto avea prima e poi era fatturo
   per lo regno mortal ch'a lui soggiace,   *84*
diventa in apparenza poco e scuro,
   se in mano al terzo Cesare si mira
   con occhio chiaro e con affetto puro;   *87*
ché la viva giustizia che mi spira,
   li concedette, in mano a quel ch'i' dico,
   gloria di far vendetta a la sua ira.   *90*
Or qui t'ammira in ciò ch'io ti replìco:
   poscia con Tito a far vendetta corse
   de la vendetta del peccato antico.   *93*
E quando il dente longobardo morse
   la Santa Chiesa, sotto le sue ali
   Carlo Magno, vincendo, la soccorse.   *96*
Omai puoi giudicar di quei cotali
   ch'io accusai di sopra e di lor falli,
   che son cagion di tutti vostri mali.   *99*
L'uno al pubblico segno i gigli gialli
   oppone, e l'altro appropria quello a parte,
   sì ch'è forte a veder chi più si falli.   *102*
Faccian li Ghibellin, faccian lor arte
   sott' altro segno, ché mal segue quello
   sempre chi la giustizia e lui diparte;   *105*
e non l'abbatta esto Carlo novello
   coi Guelfi suoi, ma tema de li artigli
   ch'a più alto leon trasser lo vello.   *108*

With him it coursed far as the Red Sea Shore; with him it set the world in such peace that Janus's temple was locked.

"But what the standard that makes me speak had done before, and after was to do throughout the mortal realm subject unto it, becomes in appearance little and obscure if it be looked on in the hand of the third Caesar with clear eye and pure affection; because the living Justice which inspires me granted to it, in his hand of whom I speak, the glory of doing vengeance for Its own wrath. Now marvel here at what I unfold to you: afterwards it sped with Titus to do vengeance for the vengeance of the ancient sin. Then, when the Lombard tooth bit Holy Church, under its wings Charlemagne, conquering, succored her.

"Now you may judge of such as I accused but now, and of their offenses, which are the cause of all your ills. The one opposes to the public standard the yellow lilies, and the other claims it for a party, so that it is hard to see which offends the most. Let the Ghibellines, let them practise their art under another ensign, for this one he ever follows ill who cleaves justice from it. And let not this new Charles strike it down with his Guelphs, but let him fear talons which have stripped the hide from a greater lion.

Molte fïate già pianser li figli
  per la colpa del padre, e non si creda
  che Dio trasmuti l'armi per suoi gigli!   *111*

Questa picciola stella si correda
  d'i buoni spirti che son stati attivi
  perché onore e fama li succeda: *114*

e quando li disiri poggian quivi,
  sì disvïando, pur convien che i raggi
  del vero amore in sù poggin men vivi.   *117*

Ma nel commensurar d'i nostri gaggi
  col merto è parte di nostra letizia,
  perché non li vedem minor né maggi.   *120*

Quindi addolcisce la viva giustizia
  in noi l'affetto sì, che non si puote
  torcer già mai ad alcuna nequizia.   *123*

Diverse voci fanno dolci note;
  così diversi scanni in nostra vita
  rendon dolce armonia tra queste rote.   *126*

E dentro a la presente margarita
  luce la luce di Romeo, di cui
  fu l'ovra grande e bella mal gradita.   *129*

Ma i Provenzai che fecer contra lui
  non hanno riso; e però mal cammina
  qual si fa danno del ben fare altrui.   *132*

Quattro figlie ebbe, e ciascuna reina,
  Ramondo Beringhiere, e ciò li fece
  Romeo, persona umìle e peregrina.   *135*

E poi il mosser le parole biece
  a dimandar ragione a questo giusto,
  che li assegnò sette e cinque per diece,   *138*

Many a time ere now the sons have wept for the sin of the father; and let him not believe that God will change arms for his lilies.

"This little star is adorned with good spirits who have been active in order that honor and fame might come to them. And when desires, thus deviating, tend thitherward, the rays of true love must needs mount upwards less living. But in the equal measure of our rewards with our desert is part of our joy, because we see them neither less nor greater. Hereby the living Justice makes our affection so sweet within us that it can never be bent aside to any evil. Diverse voices make sweet music, so diverse ranks in our life render sweet harmony among these wheels.

"And within this present pearl shines the light of Romeo, whose noble and beautiful work was ill rewarded; but the Provençals who wrought against him have not the laugh, and indeed he takes an ill path who makes harm for himself of another's good work. Raymond Berenger had four daughters, each of them a queen, and Romeo, a man of lowly birth and a pilgrim, did this for him. And then crooked words moved him to demand a reckoning of this just man, who had rendered him seven and five for ten.

indi partissi povero e vetusto;
   e se 'l mondo sapesse il cor ch'elli ebbe
   mendicando sua vita a frusto a frusto,
assai lo loda, e più lo loderebbe."   *142*

Thereon he departed, poor and old, and if the
world but knew the heart he had while beg-
ging his bread morsel by morsel, much as it
praises him it would praise him more."

PARADISO

"*Osanna, sanctus Deus sabaòth,*
superillustrans claritate tua
felices ignes horum malacòth!"   *3*
Così, volgendosi a la nota sua,
   fu viso a me cantare essa sustanza,
   sopra la qual doppio lume s'addua;   *6*
ed essa e l'altre mossero a sua danza,
   e quasi velocissime faville
   mi si velar di sùbita distanza.   *9*
Io dubitava e dicea "Dille, dille!"
   fra me, "dille" dicea, "a la mia donna
   che mi diseta con le dolci stille."   *12*
Ma quella reverenza che s'indonna
   di tutto me, pur per *Be* e per *ice*,
   mi richinava come l'uom ch'assonna.   *15*
Poco sofferse me cotal Beatrice
   e cominciò, raggiandomi d'un riso
   tal, che nel foco faria l'uom felice: *18*

CANTO VII

"Hosanna, sanctus Deus sabaòth,
  superillustrans claritate tua
  felices ignes horum malacòth!"
—so, revolving to his melody I saw that
substance sing, on whom a double light is
twinned; and he and the others moved in
their dance, and like swiftest sparks veiled
themselves from me by sudden distance. I
was in doubt, and was saying to myself,
"Speak to her, speak to her," I was saying,
"speak to her, to my lady who slakes my thirst
with her sweet distillings!" But that reverence
which is wholly mistress of me, only by *Be*
and by *ice*, bowed me like one who drowses.
Short while did Beatrice suffer me thus, and
she began, irradiating me with a smile such
as would make a man happy in the fire,

"Secondo mio infallibile avviso,
  come giusta vendetta giustamente
  punita fosse, t'ha in pensier miso;   *21*
ma io ti solverò tosto la mente;
  e tu ascolta, ché le mie parole
  di gran sentenza ti faran presente.   *24*
Per non soffrire a la virtù che vole
  freno a suo prode, quell' uom che non nacque,
  dannando sé, dannò tutta sua prole;   *27*
onde l'umana specie inferma giacque
  giù per secoli molti in grande errore,
  fin ch'al Verbo di Dio discender piacque   *30*
u' la natura, che dal suo fattore
  s'era allungata, unì a sé in persona
  con l'atto sol del suo etterno amore.   *33*
Or drizza il viso a quel ch'or si ragiona:
  questa natura al suo fattore unita,
  qual fu creata, fu sincera e buona;   *36*
ma per sé stessa pur fu ella sbandita
  di paradiso, però che si torse
  da via di verità e da sua vita.   *39*
La pena dunque che la croce porse
  s'a la natura assunta si misura,
  nulla già mai sì giustamente morse;   *42*
e così nulla fu di tanta ingiura,
  guardando a la persona che sofferse,
  in che era contratta tal natura.   *45*
Però d'un atto uscir cose diverse:
  ch'a Dio e a' Giudei piacque una morte;
  per lei tremò la terra e 'l ciel s'aperse.   *48*

"By my judgment, which cannot err, how just vengeance could be justly avenged, has set you pondering; but I will quickly free your mind, and do you listen, for my words will make you the gift of a great doctrine.

"By not enduring for his own good a curb upon the power that wills, that man who never was born, in damning himself damned all his progeny; wherefore the human race lay sick down there for many centuries in great error, until it pleased the word of God to descend where He, by the sole act of His eternal love, united with Himself in person the nature which had estranged itself from its Maker.

"Turn your sight now to that which now I say: this nature, which was thus united to its Maker, was, when it was created, pure and good; but by its own self it had been banished from Paradise, because it turned aside from the way of the truth and its proper life. The penalty therefore which the Cross inflicted, if it be measured by the nature assumed—none ever so justly stung; also none was ever of such great wrong, if we regard the Person who suffered it, with whom that nature was bound up. Therefore from one act issued things diverse, for one same death was pleasing to God and to the Jews; thereat the earth trembled and Heaven was opened.

73

Non ti dee oramai parer più forte,
   quando si dice che giusta vendetta
   poscia vengiata fu da giusta corte.   *51*
Ma io veggi' or la tua mente ristretta
   di pensiero in pensier dentro ad un nodo,
   del qual con gran disio solver s'aspetta.   *54*
Tu dici: 'Ben discerno ciò ch'i' odo;
   ma perché Dio volesse, m'è occulto,
   a nostra redenzion pur questo modo.'   *57*
Questo decreto, frate, sta sepulto
   a li occhi di ciascuno il cui ingegno
   ne la fiamma d'amor non è adulto.   *60*
Veramente, però ch'a questo segno
   molto si mira e poco si discerne,
   dirò perché tal modo fu più degno.   *63*
La divina bontà, che da sé sperne
   ogne livore, ardendo in sé, sfavilla
   sì che dispiega le bellezze etterne.   *66*
Ciò che da lei sanza mezzo distilla
   non ha poi fine, perché non si move
   la sua imprenta quand' ella sigilla.   *69*
Ciò che da essa sanza mezzo piove
   libero è tutto, perché non soggiace
   a la virtute de le cose nove.   *72*
Più l'è conforme, e però più le piace;
   ché l'ardor santo ch'ogne cosa raggia,
   ne la più somigliante è più vivace.   *75*
Di tutte queste dote s'avvantaggia
   l'umana creatura, e s'una manca,
   di sua nobilità convien che caggia.   *78*

No longer, now, should it seem hard to you when it is said that just vengeance was afterwards avenged by a just court.

"But now I see your mind from thought to thought entangled in a knot, from which, with great desire, it awaits release. You say, 'I follow clearly what I hear, but why God willed this sole way for our redemption is hidden from me.' This decree, brother, is buried from the eyes of everyone whose understanding is not matured within love's flame. But inasmuch as at this mark there is much aiming and little discernment, I shall tell why that way was the most fitting.

"The Divine Goodness, which spurns all envy from itself, burning within itself so sparkles that It displays the eternal beauties. That which immediately derives from it thereafter has no end, because when It seals, Its imprint may never be removed. That which rains down from it immediately is wholly free, because it is not subject to the power of the new things. It is the most conformed to it and therefore pleases It the most; for the Holy Ardor, which irradiates everything, is most living in what is most like Itself.

"With all these gifts the human creature is advantaged, and if one fails, it needs must fall from its nobility.

Solo il peccato è quel che la disfranca
  e falla dissimìle al sommo bene,
  per che del lume suo poco s'imbianca;   *81*
e in sua dignità mai non rivene,
  se non rïempie, dove colpa vòta,
  contra mal dilettar con giuste pene.   *84*
Vostra natura, quando peccò *tota*
  nel seme suo, da queste dignitadi,
  come di paradiso, fu remota;   *87*
né ricovrar potiensi, se tu badi
  ben sottilmente, per alcuna via,
  sanza passar per un di questi guadi: *90*
o che Dio solo per sua cortesia
  dimesso avesse, o che l'uom per sé isso
  avesse sodisfatto a sua follia.   *93*
Ficca mo l'occhio per entro l'abisso
  de l'etterno consiglio, quanto puoi
  al mio parlar distrettamente fisso.   *96*
Non potea l'uomo ne' termini suoi
  mai sodisfar, per non potere ir giuso
  con umiltate obedïendo poi,   *99*
quanto disobediendo intese ir suso;
  e questa è la cagion per che l'uom fue
  da poter sodisfar per sé dischiuso.   *102*
Dunque a Dio convenia con le vie sue
  riparar l'omo a sua intera vita,
  dico con l'una, o ver con amendue.   *105*
Ma perché l'ovra tanto è più gradita
  da l'operante, quanto più appresenta
  de la bontà del core ond' ell' è uscita,   *108*

Sin alone is that which disfranchises it and makes it unlike the Supreme Good, so that it is little illumined by Its light; and to its dignity it never returns unless, where fault has emptied, it fill up with just penalties against evil delight. Your nature, when it sinned totally in its seed, was removed from these dignities, even as from Paradise; nor could it recover them, if you consider carefully, by any way except the passing of one of these fords: either that God alone, solely by His clemency, had pardoned; or that man should of himself have given satisfaction for his folly. Fix your eyes now within the abyss of the Eternal Counsel, as closely fastened on my words as you are able. Man, within his own limits, could never make satisfaction, for not being able to descend in humility, by subsequent obedience, so far as in his disobedience he had intended to ascend; and this is the reason why man was shut off from power to make satisfaction by himself. Therefore it was needful for God, with His own ways, to restore man to his full life—I mean with one way, or else with both. But because the deed is so much the more prized by the doer, the more it displays of the goodness of the heart whence it issued,

la divina bontà che 'l mondo imprenta,
di proceder per tutte le sue vie,
a rilevarvi suso, fu contenta.   *111*

Né tra l'ultima notte e 'l primo die
sì alto o sì magnifico processo,
o per l'una o per l'altra, fu o fie: *114*

ché più largo fu Dio a dar sé stesso
per far l'uom sufficiente a rilevarsi,
che s'elli avesse sol da sé dimesso;   *117*

e tutti li altri modi erano scarsi
a la giustizia, se 'l Figliuol di Dio
non fosse umilïato ad incarnarsi.   *120*

Or per empierti bene ogne disio,
ritorno a dichiararti in alcun loco,
perché tu veggi lì così com' io.   *123*

Tu dici: 'Io veggio l'acqua, io veggio il foco,
l'aere e la terra e tutte lor misture
venire a corruzione, e durar poco;   *126*

e queste cose pur furon creature;
per che, se ciò ch'è detto è stato vero,
esser dovrien da corruzion sicure.'   *129*

Li angeli, frate, e 'l paese sincero
nel qual tu se', dir si posson creati,
sì come sono, in loro essere intero;   *132*

ma li alimenti che tu hai nomati
e quelle cose che di lor si fanno
da creata virtù sono informati.   *135*

Creata fu la materia ch'elli hanno;
creata fu la virtù informante
in queste stelle che 'ntorno a lor vanno.   *138*

the divine Goodness which puts its imprint on the world, was pleased to proceed by all Its ways to raise you up again; nor between the last night and the first day has there been or will there be so exalted and so magnificent a procedure, either by one or by the other; for God was more bounteous in giving Himself to make man sufficient to uplift himself again, than if He solely of Himself had remitted; and all other modes were scanty in respect to justice, if the Son of God had not humbled himself to become incarnate.

"Now, to give full satisfaction to your every wish, I go back to explain to you a certain place, that you may see it as clearly as I do. You say, 'I see water, I see fire and air and earth, and all their mixtures come to corruption and endure but little, and yet these things were created things; so that, if what I have said to you be true, they ought to be secure against corruption.'

"The angels, brother, and the pure country in which you are, may be said to be created even as they are, in their entire being; but the elements which you have named, and all things that are compounded of them, are informed by created power. Created was the matter that is in them, created was the informing virtue in these stars that wheel about them.

L'anima d'ogne bruto e de le piante
   di complession potenzïata tira
   lo raggio e 'l moto de le luci sante;   *141*
ma vostra vita sanza mezzo spira
   la somma beninanza, e la innamora
   di sé sì che poi sempre la disira.   *144*
E quinci puoi argomentare ancora
   vostra resurrezion, se tu ripensi
   come l'umana carne fessi allora
che li primi parenti intrambo fensi."   *148*

The soul of every beast and of the plants is drawn from a potentiate compound by the shining and the motion of the holy lights; but your life the Supreme Beneficence breathes forth without intermediary, and so enamors it of Itself that it desires It ever after. And hence you further can infer your resurrection, if you reflect how was the making of human flesh then when the first parents were both formed."

PARADISO

Solea creder lo mondo in suo periclo
    che la bella Ciprigna il folle amore
    raggiasse, volta nel terzo epiciclo;   *3*
per che non pur a lei faceano onore
    di sacrificio e di votivo grido
    le genti antiche ne l'antico errore;   *6*
ma Dïone onoravano e Cupido,
    quella per madre sua, questo per figlio,
    e dicean ch'el sedette in grembo a Dido;   *9*
e da costei ond' io principio piglio
    pigliavano il vocabol de la stella
    che 'l sol vagheggia or da coppa or da ciglio. *12*
Io non m'accorsi del salire in ella;
    ma d'esservi entro mi fé assai fede
    la donna mia ch'i' vidi far più bella.   *15*
E come in fiamma favilla si vede,
    e come in voce voce si discerne,
    quand' una è ferma e altra va e riede,   *18*

CANTO VIII

The world was wont to believe, to its peril, that the fair Cyprian, wheeling in the third epicycle, rayed down mad love; wherefore the ancient people in their ancient error not only to her did honor with sacrifice and votive cry, but they honored Dione and Cupid, the one as her mother, the other as her son, and they told that he had sat in Dido's lap; and from her with whom I take my start they took the name of the star which the sun woos, now behind her, now before. I was not aware of rising into it, but of being within it my lady gave me full assurance when I saw her become more beautiful.

And as we see a spark within a flame, and as a voice within a voice is distinguished when one holds the note and another comes and goes,

vid' io in essa luce altre lucerne
   muoversi in giro più e men correnti,
   al modo, credo, di lor viste interne.   *21*
Di fredda nube non disceser venti,
   o visibili o no, tanto festini,
   che non paressero impediti e lenti   *24*
a chi avesse quei lumi divini
   veduti a noi venir, lasciando il giro
   pria cominciato in li alti Serafini;   *27*
e dentro a quei che più innanzi appariro
   sonava *"Osanna"* sì, che unque poi
   di rïudir non fui sanza disiro.   *30*
Indi si fece l'un più presso a noi
   e solo incominciò: "Tutti sem presti
   al tuo piacer, perché di noi ti gioi.   *33*
Noi ci volgiam coi principi celesti
   d'un giro e d'un girare e d'una sete,
   ai quali tu del mondo già dicesti: *36*
'Voi che 'ntendendo il terzo ciel movete';
   e sem sì pien d'amor, che, per piacerti,
   non fia men dolce un poco di quïete."   *39*
Poscia che li occhi miei si fuoro offerti
   a la mia donna reverenti, ed essa
   fatti li avea di sé contenti e certi,   *42*
rivolsersi a la luce che promessa
   tanto s'avea, e "Deh, chi siete?" fue
   la voce mia di grande affetto impressa.   *45*
E quanta e quale vid' io lei far piùe
   per allegrezza nova che s'accrebbe,
   quando parlai, a l'allegrezze sue!   *48*

I saw within that light other lamps moving in a circle more and less swift according to the measure, I believe, of their internal sight. From a cold cloud winds, whether visible or not, never descended so swiftly that they would not seem impeded and slow to one who had seen those divine lights come to us, leaving the circling first begun among the high Seraphim; and within those that appeared most in front *Hosanna* sounded in such wise that never since have I been without the desire to hear it again.

Then one drew nearer to us, and alone began, "We are all ready at your pleasure, that you may have joy of us. With one circle, with one circling and with one thirst we revolve with the celestial Princes to whom you in the world did once say, '*You who move the third heaven by intellection*'; and we are so full of love that, in order to please you, a little quiet will not be less sweet to us."

After my eyes had been raised with reverence to my lady, and she had satisfied them with assurance of her consent, they turned back to the light which had promised so much; and "Say who you are" was my utterance, stamped with great affection; and, how much I saw it increase in size and brightness, through the new joy which was added to its joys when I spoke!

Così fatta, mi disse: "Il mondo m'ebbe
  giù poco tempo; e se più fosse stato,
  molto sarà di mal, che non sarebbe.   *51*
La mia letizia mi ti tien celato
  che mi raggia dintorno e mi nasconde
  quasi animal di sua seta fasciato.   *54*
Assai m'amasti, e avesti ben onde;
  che s'io fossi giù stato, io ti mostrava
  di mio amor più oltre che le fronde.   *57*
Quella sinistra riva che si lava
  di Rodano poi ch'è misto con Sorga,
  per suo segnore a tempo m'aspettava,   *60*
e quel corno d'Ausonia che s'imborga
  di Bari e di Gaeta e di Catona,
  da ove Tronto e Verde in mare sgorga.   *63*
Fulgeami già in fronte la corona
  di quella terra che 'l Danubio riga
  poi che le ripe tedesche abbandona.   *66*
E la bella Trinacria, che caliga
  tra Pachino e Peloro, sopra 'l golfo
  che riceve da Euro maggior briga,   *69*
non per Tifeo ma per nascente solfo,
  attesi avrebbe li suoi regi ancora,
  nati per me di Carlo e di Ridolfo,   *72*
se mala segnoria, che sempre accora
  li popoli suggetti, non avesse
  mosso Palermo a gridar: 'Mora, mora!'   *75*
E se mio frate questo antivedesse,
  l'avara povertà di Catalogna
  già fuggeria, perché non li offendesse;   *78*

Thus changed, it said to me, "The world held me below but little time; and had it been more, much ill shall be that would not have been. My joy, which rays around me, holds me concealed from you and hides me like a creature swathed in its own silk. Much did you love me, and had good cause; for had I remained below, I would have shown you of my love more than the leaves. That left bank which is bathed by the Rhone, after it has mingled with the Sorgue, awaited me in due time for its lord; so did that corner of Ausonia, down from where Tronto and Verde discharge into the sea, which is skirted by Bari and Gaeta and Catona. Already was shining on my brow the crown of that land which the Danube waters after it has left its German banks. And the fair Trinacria (which between Pachynus and Pelorus, on the gulf most vexed by Eurus, is darkened not by Typhoeus, but by nascent sulphur) would yet have looked to have its kings born through me from Charles and Rudolph, if ill lordship, which ever embitters the subject people, had not moved Palermo to shout, 'Die! Die!' And if my brother foresaw this, he would already shun the rapacious poverty of Catalonia, lest it make trouble for him;

ché veramente proveder bisogna
   per lui, o per altrui, sì ch'a sua barca
   carcata più d'incarco non si pogna.   *81*
La sua natura, che di larga parca
   discese, avria mestier di tal milizia
   che non curasse di mettere in arca."   *84*
"Però ch'i' credo che l'alta letizia
   che 'l tuo parlar m'infonde, segnor mio,
   là 've ogne ben si termina e s'inizia,   *87*
per te si veggia come la vegg' io,
   grata m'è più; e anco quest' ho caro
   perché 'l discerni rimirando in Dio.   *90*
Fatto m'hai lieto, e così mi fa chiaro,
   poi che, parlando, a dubitar m'hai mosso
   com' esser può, di dolce seme, amaro."   *93*
Questo io a lui; ed elli a me: "S'io posso
   mostrarti un vero, a quel che tu dimandi
   terrai lo viso come tien lo dosso.   *96*
Lo ben che tutto il regno che tu scandi
   volge e contenta, fa esser virtute
   sua provedenza in questi corpi grandi.   *99*
E non pur le nature provedute
   sono in la mente ch'è da sé perfetta,
   ma esse insieme con la lor salute: *102*
per che quantunque quest' arco saetta
   disposto cade a proveduto fine,
   sì come cosa in suo segno diretta.   *105*
Se ciò non fosse, il ciel che tu cammine
   producerebbe sì li suoi effetti,
   che non sarebbero artı, ma ruine;   *108*

for truly it is needful for him or for some
other to look to it, lest upon his laden bark a
heavier load be laid. His nature—mean
descendant from a generous forebear—would
need a knighthood that gave not its care to
the filling of coffers."

"Because I believe that the deep joy which
your words infuse in me is, even as I see it,
seen by you, my lord, there where every good
has its end and its beginning, it is the more
welcome to me; and this also I hold dear, that
you discern it gazing upon God. You have
made me glad; and so now do you make clear
to me (since in speaking you have raised the
question in my mind) how from sweet seed
may come forth bitter."

Thus I to him; and he to me, "If I can make
one truth plain to you, you will hold your
face toward that which you ask, as you now
hold your back. The Good which revolves
and contents all the realm that you are climb-
ing makes its providence become a power in
these great bodies; and not only is the nature
of things provided for in the Mind which by
itself is perfect, but, along with that nature,
their well-being; so that whatever this bow
shoots falls disposed to a foreseen end, even as
a shaft directed to its mark. Were this not so,
the heavens which you are traversing would
produce their effects in such wise that they
would be not works of art but ruins—

89

e ciò esser non può, se li 'ntelletti
   che muovon queste stelle non son manchi,
   e manco il primo, che non li ha perfetti.   *111*
Vuo' tu che questo ver più ti s'imbianchi?"
   E io "Non già; ché impossibil veggio
   che la natura, in quel ch'è uopo, stanchi."   *114*
Ond' elli ancora: "Or dì: sarebbe il peggio
   per l'omo in terra, se non fosse cive?"
   "Sì," rispuos' io; "e qui ragion non cheggio."   *117*
"E puot' elli esser, se giù non si vive
   diversamente per diversi offici?
   Non, se 'l maestro vostro ben vi scrive."   *120*
Sì venne deducendo infino a quici;
   poscia conchiuse: "Dunque esser diverse
   convien di vostri effetti le radici: *123*
per ch'un nasce Solone e altro Serse,
   altro Melchisedèch e altro quello
   che, volando per l'aere, il figlio perse.   *126*
La circular natura, ch'è suggello
   a la cera mortal fa ben sua arte,
   ma non distingue l'un da l'altro ostello.   *129*
Quinci addivien ch'Esaù si diparte
   per seme da Iacòb; e vien Quirino
   da sì vil padre, che si rende a Marte.   *132*
Natura generata il suo cammino
   simil farebbe sempre a' generanti,
   se non vincesse il proveder divino.   *135*
Or quel che t'era dietro t'è davanti:
   ma perché sappi che di te mi giova,
   un corollario voglio che t'ammanti.   *138*

and that cannot be, unless the Intelligences that move these stars be defective, and defective also the Primal Intelligence in that it did not make them perfect. Do you wish this truth to be made still clearer to you?"

And I, "No, truly; for I see it to be impossible that Nature should weary in that which is needful."

Whereupon he again, "Now say, would it be worse for man on earth if he were not a citizen?"

"Yes," I replied, "and here I ask for no proof."

"And can that be, unless men below live in diverse ways for diverse duties? Not if your master writes well of this for you." Thus he came deducing far as here, then he concluded, "Therefore the roots of your works must needs be diverse, so that one is born Solon and another Xerxes, one Melchizedek and another he who flew through the air and lost his son. Circling nature, which is a seal on the mortal wax, performs its art well, but does not distinguish one house from another. Whence it happens that Esau differs in the seed from Jacob, and Quirinus comes from so base a father that he is ascribed to Mars. The begotten nature would always make its course like its begetters, did not Divine provision overrule.

Now that which was behind you is before you; but, that you may know that I delight in you, I will have a corollary cloak you round.

Sempre natura, se fortuna trova
   discorde a sé, com' ogne altra semente
   fuor di sua regïon, fa mala prova.   *141*
E se 'l mondo là giù ponesse mente
   al fondamento che natura pone,
   seguendo lui, avria buona la gente.   *144*
Ma voi torcete a la religïone
   tal che fia nato a cignersi la spada,
   e fate re di tal ch'è da sermone;
onde la traccia vostra è fuor di strada."   *148*

Ever does Nature, if she find fortune dis-
cordant with herself, like any kind of seed
out of its proper region, come to ill result.
And if the world there below would give
heed to the foundation which Nature lays,
and followed it, it would have its people good.
But you wrest to religion one born to gird on
the sword, and you make a king of one that
is fit for sermons; so that your track is off
the road."

PARADISO

Da poi che Carlo tuo, bella Clemenza,
  m'ebbe chiarito, mi narrò li 'nganni
  che ricever dovea la sua semenza;
ma disse: "Taci e lascia muover li anni";
  sì ch'io non posso dir se non che pianto
  giusto verrà di retro ai vostri danni.
E già la vita di quel lume santo
  rivolta s'era al Sol che la rïempie
  come quel ben ch'a ogne cosa è tanto.
Ahi anime ingannate e fatture empie,
  che da sì fatto ben torcete i cuori,
  drizzando in vanità le vostre tempie!
Ed ecco un altro di quelli splendori
  ver' me si fece, e 'l suo voler piacermi
  significava nel chiarir di fori.
Li occhi di Bëatrice, ch'eran fermi
  sovra me, come pria, di caro assenso
  al mio disio certificato fermi.

CANTO IX

After your Charles, fair Clemence, had enlightened me, he told me of the frauds that his seed was destined to suffer, but he added, "Keep silence, and let the years revolve"; so that I can say nothing except that well-deserved lamentation shall follow on the wrongs done you.

And now the life of that holy light had turned again to the Sun which fills it, as to that Good which is sufficient to all things. Ah, souls deceived and creatures impious, who from such Good turn away your hearts, directing your brows to vanity!

And lo! another of those splendors made toward me and by brightening outwardly was signifying its wish to please me. Beatrice's eyes, fixed on me as before, made me assured of dear assent to my desire.

"Deh, metti al mio voler tosto compenso,
   beato spirto," dissi, "e fammi prova
   ch'i' possa in te refletter quel ch'io penso!"   *21*
Onde la luce che m'era ancor nova,
   del suo profondo, ond' ella pria cantava,
   seguette come a cui di ben far giova: *24*
"In quella parte de la terra prava
   italica che siede tra Rïalto
   e le fontane di Brenta e di Piava,   *27*
si leva un colle, e non surge molt' alto,
   là onde scese già una facella
   che fece a la contrada un grande assalto.   *30*
D'una radice nacqui e io ed ella:
   Cunizza fui chiamata, e qui refulgo
   perché mi vinse il lume d'esta stella;   *33*
ma lietamente a me medesma indulgo
   la cagion di mia sorte, e non mi noia;
   che parria forse forte al vostro vulgo.   *36*
Di questa luculenta e cara gioia
   del nostro cielo che più m'è propinqua,
   grande fama rimase; e pria che moia,   *39*
questo centesimo anno ancor s'incinqua:
   vedi se far si dee l'omo eccellente,
   sì ch'altra vita la prima relinqua.   *42*
E ciò non pensa la turba presente
   che Tagliamento e Adice richiude,
   né per esser battuta ancor si pente;   *45*
ma tosto fia che Padova al palude
   cangerà l'acqua che Vincenza bagna,
   per essere al dover le genti crude;   *48*

"Pray, blessed spirit," I said, "afford speedy fulfillment to my wish, and give me proof that what I think I can reflect on you." Whereon the light which was still new to me, from out of its depth where it first was singing, continued, as one rejoicing to do a kindness: "In that region of the depraved land of Italy that lies between the Rialto and the springs of the Brenta and the Piave there rises a hill of no great height, whence once descended a firebrand that made a great assault on the country round. I and he sprang from the same root. I was called Cunizza, and I am refulgent here because the light of this star overcame me. But I gladly pardon in myself the reason of my lot, and it does not grieve me—which might perhaps seem strange to your vulgar herd. Of this resplendent and precious jewel of our heaven which is nearest to me great fame has remained, and before it dies away this centennial year shall yet be fived. See if man should make himself excel, so that the first life may leave another after it! And this the present crowd which the Tagliamento and the Adige shut in considers not; nor yet, though it be scourged, does it repent. But soon it shall come to pass that, because her people are stubborn against duty, Padua at the marsh will stain the waters that bathe Vicenza.

e dove Sile e Cagnan s'accompagna,
   tal signoreggia e va con la testa alta,
   che già per lui carpir si fa la ragna.   *51*
Piangerà Feltro ancora la difalta
   de l'empio suo pastor, che sarà sconcia
   sì, che per simil non s'entrò in Malta.   *54*
Troppo sarebbe larga la bigoncia
   che ricevesse il sangue ferrarese,
   e stanco chi 'l pesasse a oncia a oncia,   *57*
che donerà questo prete cortese
   per mostrarsi di parte; e cotai doni
   conformi fieno al viver del paese.   *60*
Sù sono specchi, voi dicete Troni,
   onde refulge a noi Dio giudicante;
   sì che questi parlar ne paion buoni."   *63*
Qui si tacette; e fecemi sembiante
   che fosse ad altro volta, per la rota
   in che si mise com' era davante.   *66*
L'altra letizia, che m'era già nota
   per cara cosa, mi si fece in vista
   qual fin balasso in che lo sol percuota. *69*
Per letiziar là sù fulgor s'acquista,
   sì come riso qui; ma giù s'abbuia
   l'ombra di fuor, come la mente è trista. *72*
"Dio vede tutto, e tuo veder s'inluia,"
   diss' io, "beato spirto, sì che nulla
   voglia di sé a te puot' esser fuia.   *75*
Dunque la voce tua, che 'l ciel trastulla
   sempre col canto di quei fuochi pii
   che di sei ali facen la coculla,   *78*

And where Sile joins Cagnano, one lords it and
goes with his head high, for catching whom
the web is already being made. Feltre shall
yet bewail the crime of its impious shepherd,
which will be so foul that for the like nobody
ever entered Malta. Great indeed would be
the vat that should receive the blood of the
Ferrarese and weary him that should weigh
it ounce by ounce, which this courteous priest
will offer to show himself a member of his
party—and such gifts will suit the country's
way of life. Aloft are mirrors—you name
them Thrones—whence God in judgment
shines upon us, so that these words approve
themselves to us." Here she was silent, and
had to me the semblance of being turned to
other heeding, by the wheel in which she set
herself as she was before.

The other joy, which was already known
to me as precious, became to my sight like
a fine ruby on which the sun is striking.
Through rejoicing, effulgence is gained there
on high, even as a smile here; but below, the
shade darkens outwardly as the mind is sad.

"God sees all, and into Him your vision
sinks, blessed spirit," I said, "so that no wish
may steal itself from you. Why then does
your voice, which ever gladdens Heaven—
together with the singing of those devout fires
that make themselves a cowl with the six
wings—

perché non satisface a' miei disii?

Già non attendere' io tua dimanda,
s'io m'intuassi, come tu t'inmii."   *81*

"La maggior valle in che l'acqua si spanda,"
incominciaro allor le sue parole,
"fuor di quel mar che la terra inghirlanda,   *84*

tra ' discordanti liti contra 'l sole
tanto sen va, che fa meridïano
là dove l'orizzonte pria far suole.   *87*

Di quella valle fu' io litorano
tra Ebro e Macra, che per cammin corto
parte lo Genovese dal Toscano.   *90*

Ad un occaso quasi e ad un orto
Buggea siede e la terra ond' io fui,
che fé del sangue suo già caldo il porto.   *93*

Folco mi disse quella gente a cui
fu noto il nome mio; e questo cielo
di me s'imprenta, com' io fe' di lui;   *96*

ché più non arse la figlia di Belo,
noiando e a Sicheo e a Creusa,
di me infin che si convenne al pelo;   *99*

né quella Rodopëa che delusa
fu da Demofoonte, né Alcide
quando Iole nel core ebbe rinchiusa.   *102*

Non però qui si pente, ma si ride,
non de la colpa, ch'a mente non torna,
ma del valor ch'ordinò e provide.   *105*

Qui si rimira ne l'arte ch'addorna
cotanto affetto, e discernesi 'l bene
per che 'l mondo di sù quel di giù torna.   *108*

not satisfy my longings? Surely I should not wait for your request, were I in you, even as you are in me."

"The greatest valley in which the water spreads from the sea that encircles the world," he then began, "extends its discordant shores so far counter to the sun that it makes meridian of the place where before it made horizon. I was a dweller on that valley's shore, between the Ebro and the Magra, which with short course divides the Genoese from the Tuscan; and with almost the same sunset and sunrise lie Bougie and the city whence I came, which with its own blood once made its harbor warm. Folco the people called me to whom my name was known, and this heaven is imprinted by me, as I was by it: for the daughter of Belus, wronging both Sichaeus and Creusa, burned not more than I, as long as it befitted my locks; nor yet the Rhodopean maid who was deluded by Demophoön, nor Alcides when he had enclosed Iole in his heart. Yet here we repent not, but we smile, not for the fault, which returns not to mind, but for the Power that ordained and foresaw. Here we contemplate the art which so much love adorns, and we discern the good by reason of which the world below again becomes the world above.

Ma perché tutte le tue voglie piene
   ten porti che son nate in questa spera,
   procedere ancor oltre mi convene.   *111*
Tu vuo' saper chi è in questa lumera
   che qui appresso me così scintilla
   come raggio di sole in acqua mera.   *114*
Or sappi che là entro si tranquilla
   Raab; e a nostr' ordine congiunta,
   di lei nel sommo grado si sigilla.   *117*
Da questo cielo, in cui l'ombra s'appunta
   che 'l vostro mondo face, pria ch'altr' alma
   del trïunfo di Cristo fu assunta.   *120*
Ben si convenne lei lasciar per palma
   in alcun cielo de l'alta vittoria
   che s'acquistò con l'una e l'altra palma,   *123*
perch' ella favorò la prima gloria
   di Iosüè in su la Terra Santa,
   che poco tocca al papa la memoria.   *126*
La tua città, che di colui è pianta
   che pria volse le spalle al suo fattore
   e di cui è la 'nvidia tanto pianta,   *129*
produce e spande il maladetto fiore
   c'ha disvïate le pecore e li agni,
   però che fatto ha lupo del pastore.   *132*
Per questo l'Evangelio e i dottor magni
   son derelitti, e solo ai Decretali
   si studia, sì che pare a' lor vivagni.   *135*
A questo intende il papa e ' cardinali;
   non vanno i lor pensieri a Nazarette,
   là dove Gabrïello aperse l'ali.   *138*

"But in order that you may bear away with you all your desires fulfilled which have been born in this sphere, I must proceed yet further. You wish to know who is within this light which so sparkles here beside me as a sunbeam on clear water. Now know that therewithin Rahab is at rest, and being joined with our order, it is sealed by her in the highest degree. By this heaven—in which the shadow that your earth casts comes to a point—she was taken up before any other soul of Christ's triumph. And it was well-befitting to leave her in some heaven as a trophy of the lofty victory which was achieved by the one and the other palm, because she favored Joshua's first glory in the Holy Land—which little touches the memory of the Pope.

"Your city—which was planted by him who first turned his back on his Maker, and whose envy has been so bewept—produces and scatters the accursed flower that has caused the sheep and the lambs to stray, because it has made a wolf of the shepherd. For this the Gospel and the great Doctors are deserted, and only the Decretals are studied, as may be seen by their margins. Thereon the Pope and Cardinals are intent. Their thoughts go not to Nazareth whither Gabriel spread his wings.

Ma Vaticano e l'altre parti elette
di Roma che son state cimitero
a la milizia che Pietro seguette,
tosto libere fien de l'avoltero." *142*

But the Vatican and the other chosen parts of Rome which have been the burial place for the soldiery that followed Peter shall soon be free from this adultery."

PARADISO

Guardando nel suo Figlio con l'Amore
    che l'uno e l'altro etternalmente spira,
    lo primo e ineffabile Valore   *3*
quanto per mente e per loco si gira
    con tant' ordine fé ch'esser non puote
    sanza gustar di lui chi ciò rimira.   *6*
Leva dunque, lettore, a l'alte rote
    meco la vista, dritto a quella parte
    dove l'un moto e l'altro si percuote;   *9*
e lì comincia a vagheggiar ne l'arte
    di quel maestro che dentro a sé l'ama,
    tanto che mai da lei l'occhio non parte.   *12*
Vedi come da indi si dirama
    l'oblico cerchio che i pianeti porta,
    per sodisfare al mondo che li chiama.   *15*
Che se la strada lor non fosse torta,
    molta virtù nel ciel sarebbe in vano,
    e quasi ogne potenza qua giù morta;   *18*

CANTO X

Looking upon His Son with the love which the One and the Other eternally breathe forth, the primal and ineffable Power made everything that revolves through the mind or through space with such order that he who contemplates it cannot but taste of Him. Lift then your sight with me, reader, to the lofty wheels, straight to that part where the one motion strikes the other; and amorously there begin to gaze upon that Master's art who within Himself so loves it that His eye never turns from it. See how from there the oblique circle which bears the planets branches off, to satisfy the world which calls on them: and were their pathway not aslant, much virtue in the heavens would be vain, and well-nigh every potency dead here below;

e se dal dritto più o men lontano
   fosse 'l partire, assai sarebbe manco
   e giù e sù de l'ordine mondano.   21
Or ti riman, lettor, sovra 'l tuo banco,
   dietro pensando a ciò che si preliba,
   s'esser vuoi lieto assai prima che stanco.   24
Messo t'ho innanzi; omai per te ti ciba;
   ché a sé torce tutta la mia cura
   quella materia ond' io son fatto scriba.   27
Lo ministro maggior de la natura,
   che del valor del ciel lo mondo imprenta
   e col suo lume il tempo ne misura,   30
con quella parte che sù si rammenta
   congiunto, si girava per le spire
   in che più tosto ognora s'appresenta;   33
e io era con lui; ma del salire
   non m'accors' io, se non com' uom s'accorge,
   anzi 'l primo pensier, del suo venire.   36
È Bëatrice quella che sì scorge
   di bene in meglio, sì subitamente
   che l'atto suo per tempo non si sporge.   39
Quant' esser convenia da sé lucente
   quel ch'era dentro al sol dov' io entra'mi,
   non per color, ma per lume parvente!   42
Perch' io lo 'ngegno e l'arte e l'uso chiami,
   sì nol direi che mai s'imaginasse;
   ma creder puossi e di veder si brami.   45
E se le fantasie nostre son basse
   a tanta altezza, non è maraviglia;
   ché sopra 'l sol non fu occhio ch'andasse.   48

and if it parted farther or less far from the straight course, much of the order of the world, both above and below, would be defective.

Now remain, reader, upon your bench, reflecting on this of which you have a foretaste, if you would be glad far sooner than weary. I have set before you; now feed yourself, because that matter of which I am made the scribe wrests to itself all my care.

The greatest minister of nature, which imprints the world with heavenly worth and with its light measures time for us, being in conjunction with the part I have noted, was wheeling through the spirals in which it presents itself earlier every day. And I was with him, but of my ascent I was no more aware than is a man, before his first thought, aware of its coming. It is Beatrice who thus conducts from good to better, so swiftly that her act does not extend through time.

How shining in itself must have been that which was within the sun where I entered it, showing not by color but by light! Though I should call on genius, art, and practice, I could not tell it so that it could ever be imagined; but one may believe it—and let him long to see it. And if our fantasies are low for such a loftiness, it is no marvel, for our eyes never knew a light brighter than the sun.

Tal era quivi la quarta famiglia
    de l'alto Padre, che sempre la sazia,
    mostrando come spira e come figlia.   *51*
E Bëatrice cominciò: "Ringrazia,
    ringrazia il Sol de li angeli, ch'a questo
    sensibil t'ha levato per sua grazia."   *54*
Cor di mortal non fu mai sì digesto
    a divozione e a rendersi a Dio
    con tutto 'l suo gradir cotanto presto,   *57*
come a quelle parole mi fec' io;
    e sì tutto 'l mio amore in lui si mise,
    che Bëatrice eclissò ne l'oblio.   *60*
Non le dispiacque, ma sì se ne rise,
    che lo splendor de li occhi suoi ridenti
    mia mente unita in più cose divise.   *63*
Io vidi più folgór vivi e vincenti
    far di noi centro e di sé far corona,
    più dolci in voce che in vista lucenti: *66*
così cinger la figlia di Latona
    vedem talvolta, quando l'aere è pregno,
    sì che ritenga il fil che fa la zona.   *69*
Ne la corte del cielo, ond' io rivegno,
    si trovan molte gioie care e belle
    tanto che non si posson trar del regno;   *72*
e 'l canto di quei lumi era di quelle;
    chi non s'impenna sì che là sù voli,
    dal muto aspetti quindi le novelle.   *75*
Poi, sì cantando, quelli ardenti soli
    si fuor girati intorno a noi tre volte,
    come stelle vicine a' fermi poli,   *78*

Such was here the fourth family of the ex-
alted Father who ever satisfies it, showing
how He breathes forth, and how He begets.
And Beatrice began, "Give thanks, give
thanks to the Sun of the Angels who of His
grace has raised you to this visible one."

Never was heart of mortal so disposed unto
devotion and so ready, with all its gratitude,
to give itself to God, as I became at those
words. And all my love was so set on Him
that it eclipsed Beatrice in oblivion; nor did
this displease her, but she so smiled thereat
that the splendor of her smiling eyes divided
upon many things my mind intent on one.

I saw many flashing lights of surpassing
brightness make of us a center and of them-
selves a crown, more sweet in voice than shin-
ing in aspect. Thus girt we sometimes see
Latona's daughter when the air is so im-
pregnate that it holds the thread which makes
her zone. In the court of Heaven, whence I
have returned, are many gems so precious and
beautiful that they may not be taken out of
the kingdom, and of these was the song of
those lights. Let him who does not wing him-
self so that he may fly up thither await tidings
thence from the dumb.

When, so singing, those blazing suns had
circled three times round about us, like stars
neighboring the fixed poles,

donne mi parver, non da ballo sciolte,
   ma che s'arrestin tacite, ascoltando
   fin che le nove note hanno ricolte.   *81*
E dentro a l'un senti' cominciar: "Quando
   lo raggio de la grazia, onde s'accende
   verace amore e che poi cresce amando,   *84*
multiplicato in te tanto resplende,
   che ti conduce su per quella scala
   u' sanza risalir nessun discende;   *87*
qual ti negasse il vin de la sua fiala
   per la tua sete, in libertà non fora
   se non com' acqua ch'al mar non si cala.   *90*
Tu vuo' saper di quai piante s'infiora
   questa ghirlanda che 'ntorno vagheggia
   la bella donna ch'al ciel t'avvalora.   *93*
Io fui de li agni de la santa greggia
   che Domenico mena per cammino
   u' ben s'impingua se non si vaneggia.   *96*
Questi che m'è a destra più vicino,
   frate e maestro fummi, ed esso Alberto
   è di Cologna, e io Thomas d'Aquino.   *99*
Se sì di tutti li altri esser vuo' certo,
   di retro al mio parlar ten vien col viso
   girando su per lo beato serto.   *102*
Quell' altro fiammeggiare esce del riso
   di Grazïan, che l'uno e l'altro foro
   aiutò sì che piace in paradiso.   *105*
L'altro ch'appresso addorna il nostro coro,
   quel Pietro fu che con la poverella
   offerse a Santa Chiesa suo tesoro.   *108*

they seemed as ladies not released from the dance, but who stop silent, listening till they have caught the new notes. And within one I heard begin, "Since the ray of grace, by which true love is kindled and which then grows by loving, shines so multiplied in you that it brings you up that stair which none descends but to mount again, he who should deny to you the wine of his flask for your thirst would no more be at liberty than water that flows not down to the sea. You wish to know what plants these are that enflower this garland, which amorously circles round the fair lady who strengthens you for heaven. I was of the lambs of the holy flock which Dominic leads on the path where there is good fattening if they do not stray. He that is next beside me on the right was my brother and my master, and he is Albert of Cologne, and I Thomas of Aquino. If thus of all the rest you would be informed, come, following my speech with your sight, going round the blessed wreath. That next flaming comes from the smile of Gratian who served the one and the other court so well that it pleases in Paradise. The other who next adorns our choir was that Peter who, like the poor widow, offered his treasure to Holy Church.

La quinta luce, ch'è tra noi più bella,
  spira di tale amor, che tutto 'l mondo
  là giù ne gola di saper novella: *111*
entro v'è l'alta mente u' sì profondo
  saver fu messo, che, se 'l vero è vero,
  a veder tanto non surse il secondo.   *114*
Appresso vedi il lume di quel cero
  che giù in carne più a dentro vide
  l'angelica natura e 'l ministero.   *117*
Ne l'altra piccioletta luce ride
  quello avvocato de' tempi cristiani
  del cui latino Augustin si provide.   *120*
Or se tu l'occhio de la mente trani
  di luce in luce dietro a le mie lode,
  già de l'ottava con sete rimani.   *123*
Per vedere ogne ben dentro vi gode
  l'anima santa che 'l mondo fallace
  fa manifesto a chi di lei ben ode.   *126*
Lo corpo ond' ella fu cacciata giace
  giuso in Cieldauro; ed essa da martiro
  e da essilio venne a questa pace.   *129*
Vedi oltre fiammeggiar l'ardente spiro
  d'Isidoro, di Beda e di Riccardo,
  che a considerar fu più che viro.   *132*
Questi onde a me ritorna il tuo riguardo,
  è 'l lume d'uno spirto che 'n pensieri
  gravi a morir li parve venir tardo: *135*
essa è la luce etterna di Sigieri,
  che, leggendo nel Vico de li Strami,
  silogizzò invidïosi veri."   *138*

The fifth light, which is the most beautiful among us, breathes with such love that all the world there below thirsts to know tidings of it. Within it is the lofty mind to which was given wisdom so deep that, if the truth be true, there never rose a second of such full vision. At its side behold the light of that candle which, below in the flesh, saw deepest into the angelic nature and its ministry. In the next little light smiles that defender of the Christian times, of whose discourse Augustine made use. If now you are bringing your mind's eye from light to light after my praises, you are already thirsting for the eighth. Therewithin, through seeing every good, the sainted soul rejoices who makes the fallacious world manifest to any who listen well to him. The body from which it was driven lies down below in Cieldauro, and he came from martyrdom and exile to this peace. See, flaming beyond, the glowing breath of Isidore, of Bede, and of Richard who in contemplation was more than man. This one from whom your look returns to me is the light of a spirit to whom, in his grave thoughts, it seemed that death came slow. It is the eternal light of Siger who, lecturing in Straw Street, demonstrated invidious truths."

Indi, come orologio che ne chiami
   ne l'ora che la sposa di Dio surge
   a mattinar lo sposo perché l'ami,   *141*
che l'una parte e l'altra tira e urge,
   tin tin sonando con sì dolce nota,
   che 'l ben disposto spirto d'amor turge;   *144*
così vid' ïo la gloriosa rota
   muoversi e render voce a voce in tempra
   e in dolcezza ch'esser non pò nota
se non colà dove gioir s'insempra.   *148*

Then, like a clock which calls us at the hour when the Bride of God rises to sing her matins to her Bridegroom, that he may love her, in which the one part draws or drives the other, sounding *ting! ting!* with notes so sweet that the well-disposed spirit swells with love, so did I see the glorious wheel move and render voice to voice with harmony and sweetness that cannot be known except there where joy is everlasting.

PARADISO

O INSENSATA CURA de' mortali,
  quanto son difettivi silogismi
  quei che ti fanno in basso batter l'ali!   *3*
Chi dietro a *iura* e chi ad amforismi
  sen giva, e chi seguendo sacerdozio,
  e chi regnar per forza o per sofismi,   *6*
e chi rubare e chi civil negozio,
  chi nel diletto de la carne involto
  s'affaticava e chi si dava a l'ozio,   *9*
quando, da tutte queste cose sciolto,
  con Bëatrice m'era suso in cielo
  cotanto glorïosamente accolto.   *12*
Poi che ciascuno fu tornato ne lo
  punto del cerchio in che avanti s'era,
  fermossi, come a candellier candelo.   *15*
E io senti' dentro a quella lumera
  che pria m'avea parlato, sorridendo
  incominciar, faccendosi più mera: *18*
"Così com' io del suo raggio resplendo,
  sì, riguardando ne la luce etterna,
  li tuoi pensieri onde cagioni apprendo.   *21*

CANTO XI

O INSENSATE care of mortals! how false are the reasonings that make you beat your wings in downward flight. One was following after the laws, another after the *Aphorisms*, one was pursuing priesthood, and one dominion by force or craft, and another plunder, and another civil business, one was moiling, caught in the pleasures of the flesh, and another was giving himself to idleness, the while, free from all these things, I was high in heaven with Beatrice, thus gloriously received.

After each had come to the point of the circle where it was before, it stayed itself, as the taper in its stand. And within that light which first had spoken to me I heard begin, while it smiled and grew brighter, "Even as I glow with its beams, so, gazing into the Eternal Light, I perceive your thoughts and the cause of them.

Tu dubbi, e hai voler che si ricerna
   in sì aperta e 'n sì distesa lingua
   lo dicer mio, ch'al tuo sentir si sterna,   *24*
ove dinanzi dissi: 'U' ben s'impingua,'
   e là u' dissi: 'Non nacque il secondo';
   e qui è uopo che ben si distingua.   *27*
La provedenza, che governa il mondo
   con quel consiglio nel quale ogne aspetto
   creato è vinto pria che vada al fondo,   *30*
però che andasse ver' lo suo diletto
   la sposa di colui ch'ad alte grida
   disposò lei col sangue benedetto,   *33*
in sé sicura e anche a lui più fida,
   due principi ordinò in suo favore,
   che quinci e quindi le fosser per guida.   *36*
L'un fu tutto serafico in ardore;
   l'altro per sapïenza in terra fue
   di cherubica luce uno splendore.   *39*
De l'un dirò, però che d'amendue
   si dice l'un pregiando, qual ch'om prende,
   perch' ad un fine fur l'opere sue.   *42*
Intra Tupino e l'acqua che discende
   del colle eletto dal beato Ubaldo,
   fertile costa d'alto monte pende,   *45*
onde Perugia sente freddo e caldo
   da Porta Sole; e di rietro le piange
   per grave giogo Nocera con Gualdo.   *48*
Di questa costa, là dov' ella frange
   più sua rattezza, nacque al mondo un sole,
   come fa questo talvolta di Gange.   *51*

You are perplexed and would fain have my words made clearer, in plain and explicit language leveled to your understanding, where I said just now 'where there is good fattening,' and again where I said, 'there never rose a second'; and here is need that one distinguish well.

"The Providence that governs the world with that counsel in which every created vision is vanquished before it reaches the bottom, in order that the Bride of Him who, with loud cries, espoused her with the blessed blood, might go to her Delight, secure within herself and also more faithful to Him, ordained on her behalf two princes, who on this side and that might be her guides. The one was all seraphic in ardor, the other, for wisdom, was on earth a splendor of cherubic light. I will speak of one, because in praising one, whichever be taken, both are spoken of, for their labors were to one same end.

"Between the Topino and the stream that drops from the hill chosen by the blessed Ubaldo, a fertile slope hangs from a lofty mountain wherefrom Perugia feels cold and heat through Porta Sole, while behind it Nocera and Gualdo grieve under a heavy yoke. From this slope, where most it breaks its steepness a sun rose on the world, even as this is wont to rise from Ganges.

Però chi d'esso loco fa parole,
   non dica Ascesi, ché direbbe corto,
   ma Orïente, se proprio dir vuole.   *54*
Non era ancor molto lontan da l'orto,
   ch'el cominciò a far sentir la terra
   de la sua gran virtute alcun conforto;   *57*
ché per tal donna, giovinetto, in guerra
   del padre corse, a cui, come a la morte,
   la porta del piacer nessun diserra;   *60*
e dinanzi a la sua spirital corte
   et coram patre le si fece unito;
   poscia di dì in dì l'amò più forte.   *63*
Questa, privata del primo marito,
   millecent' anni e più dispetta e scura
   fino a costui si stette sanza invito;   *66*
né valse udir che la trovò sicura
   con Amiclate, al suon de la sua voce,
   colui ch'a tutto 'l mondo fé paura;   *69*
né valse esser costante né feroce,
   sì che, dove Maria rimase giuso,
   ella con Cristo pianse in su la croce.   *72*
Ma perch' io non proceda troppo chiuso,
   Francesco e Povertà per questi amanti
   prendi oramai nel mio parlar diffuso.   *75*
La lor concordia e i lor lieti sembianti,
   amore e maraviglia e dolce sguardo
   facieno esser cagion di pensier santi;   *78*
tanto che 'l venerabile Bernardo
   si scalzò prima, e dietro a tanta pace
   corse e, correndo, li parve esser tardo.   *81*

Therefore let him who talks of this place not say *Ascesi*, which would be to speak short, but *Orient*, if he would name it rightly. He was not yet very far from his rising when he began to make the earth feel, from his great virtue, a certain strengthening; for, while still a youth, he rushed into strife against his father for such a lady, to whom, as to death, none willingly unlocks the door; and before his spiritual court *et coram patre* he was joined to her, and thereafter, from day to day, he loved her ever more ardently. She, bereft of her first husband, for eleven hundred years and more, despised and obscure, remained unwooed till he came; nor had it availed to hear that he who caused fear to all the world found her undisturbed with Amyclas at the sound of his voice; nor had it availed to have been constant and undaunted so that, where Mary remained below, she wept with Christ upon the Cross.

"But, lest I should proceed too darkly, take now Francis and Poverty for these lovers in all that I have said. Their harmony and joyous semblance made love and wonder and tender looks the cause of holy thoughts; so that the venerable Bernard first bared his feet, following such great peace, and running, it seemed to him that he was slow.

Oh ignota ricchezza! oh ben ferace!
  Scalzasi Egidio, scalzasi Silvestro
  dietro a lo sposo, sì la sposa piace.   *84*
Indi sen va quel padre e quel maestro
  con la sua donna e con quella famiglia
  che già legava l'umile capestro.   *87*
Né li gravò viltà di cuor le ciglia
  per esser fi' di Pietro Bernardone,
  né per parer dispetto a maraviglia;   *90*
ma regalmente sua dura intenzione
  ad Innocenzio aperse, e da lui ebbe
  primo sigillo a sua religïone.   *93*
Poi che la gente poverella crebbe
  dietro a costui, la cui mirabil vita
  meglio in gloria del ciel si canterebbe,   *96*
di seconda corona redimita
  fu per Onorio da l'Etterno Spiro
  la santa voglia d'esto archimandrita.   *99*
E poi che, per la sete del martiro,
  ne la presenza del Soldan superba
  predicò Cristo e li altri che 'l seguiro,   *102*
e per trovare a conversione acerba
  troppo la gente e per non stare indarno,
  redissi al frutto de l'italica erba,   *105*
nel crudo sasso intra Tevero e Arno
  da Cristo prese l'ultimo sigillo,
  che le sue membra due anni portarno.   *108*
Quando a colui ch'a tanto ben sortillo
  piacque di trarlo suso a la mercede
  ch'el meritò nel suo farsi pusillo,   *111*

Oh wealth unknown, oh fertile good! Egidius bares his feet, Silvester bares his feet, following the spouse, so does the bride delight them. Then that father and master goes his way, with his lady and with that family which was already girt with the lowly cord. Nor did abjectness of heart weigh down his brow that he was Pietro Bernardone's son, nor for appearing marvelously despised; but royally he opened his stern resolve to Innocent, and had from him the first seal upon his Order.

"After the poor folk had increased behind him, whose wondrous life were better sung in Heaven's glory, then was the holy will of this chief shepherd circled with a second crown by the Eternal Spirit through Honorius. And when, in thirst for martyrdom, he, in the proud presence of the Sultan, had preached Christ and them that followed him, and, finding the people too unripe for conversion and in order not to stay in vain, had returned to the harvest of the Italian fields, then on the harsh rock between Tiber and Arno he received from Christ the last seal, which his limbs bore for two years. When it pleased Him, who had allotted him to such great good, to draw him up to the reward that he had gained in making himself lowly,

a' frati suoi, sì com' a giuste rede,
   raccomandò la donna sua più cara,
   e comandò che l'amassero a fede;   *114*

e del suo grembo l'anima preclara
   mover si volle, tornando al suo regno,
   e al suo corpo non volle altra bara.   *117*

Pensa oramai qual fu colui che degno
   collega fu a mantener la barca
   di Pietro in alto mar per dritto segno;   *120*

e questo fu il nostro patrïarca;
   per che qual segue lui, com' el comanda,
   discerner puoi che buone merce carca.   *123*

Ma 'l suo peculio di nova vivanda
   è fatto ghiotto, sì ch'esser non puote
   che per diversi salti non si spanda;   *126*

e quanto le sue pecore remote
   e vagabunde più da esso vanno,
   più tornano a l'ovil di latte vòte.   *129*

Ben son di quelle che temono 'l danno
   e stringonsi al pastor; ma son sì poche,
   che le cappe fornisce poco panno.   *132*

Or, se le mie parole non son fioche,
   se la tua audïenza è stata attenta,
   se ciò ch'è detto a la mente revoche,   *135*

in parte fia la tua voglia contenta,
   perché vedrai la pianta onde si scheggia,
   e vedra' il corrègger che argomenta

'U' ben s'impingua, se non si vaneggia.' "   *139*

to his brethren as to rightful heirs he commended his most dear lady and bade them love her faithfully; and from her bosom the glorious soul chose to set forth, returning to its own realm, and for its body would have no other bier.

"Think now what he was that was a worthy colleague to keep Peter's bark on the right course in the high sea; and such was our Patriarch; wherefore you can see that whoever follows him as he commands freights good merchandise. But his flock has grown so greedy of new fare that it cannot but be scattered through wild pastures; and the farther his sheep, remote and vagabond, go from him, the more empty of milk do they return to the fold. Some of them indeed there are who fear the harm, and keep close to the shepherd, but they are so few that little cloth suffices for their cowls.

"Now if my words have not been faint, if your listening has been intent, if you recall to mind what I have said, your wish will be content in part, for you will see the plant which is whittled away, and you will see what is intended by the correction 'where there is good fattening if they do not stray.'"

PARADISO

Sì tosto come l'ultima parola
    la benedetta fiamma per dir tolse,
    a rotar cominciò la santa mola;   *3*
e nel suo giro tutta non si volse
    prima ch'un'altra di cerchio la chiuse,
    e moto a moto e canto a canto colse;   *6*
canto che tanto vince nostre muse,
    nostre serene in quelle dolci tube,
    quanto primo splendor quel ch'e' refuse.   *9*
Come si volgon per tenera nube
    due archi paralelli e concolori,
    quando Iunone a sua ancella iube,   *12*
nascendo di quel d'entro quel di fori,
    a guisa del parlar di quella vaga
    ch'amor consunse come sol vapori,   *15*
e fanno qui la gente esser presaga,
    per lo patto che Dio con Noè puose,
    del mondo che già mai più non s'allaga: *18*

CANTO XII

As soon as the blessed flame took to speaking its last word the holy millstone began to turn, and it had not yet made a full circle when a second enclosed it round and matched motion with motion and song with song: song which, in those sweet pipes, as much surpasses our Muses, our Sirens, as a first splendor that which it throws back. As two bows, parallel and like in color, bend across a thin cloud when Juno gives the order to her handmaid—the one without born of the one within, like the voice of that wandering nymph whom love consumed as the sun does vapors—and make the people here presage, by reason of the covenant that God made with Noah, that the world shall never again be flooded;

così di quelle sempiterne rose
   volgiensi circa noi le due ghirlande,
   e sì l'estrema a l'intima rispuose.   *21*
Poi che 'l tripudio e l'altra festa grande,
   sì del cantare e sì del fiammeggiarsi
   luce con luce gaudïose e blande,   *24*
insieme a punto e a voler quetarsi,
   pur come li occhi ch'al piacer che i move
   conviene insieme chiudere e levarsi;   *27*
del cor de l'una de le luci nove
   si mosse voce, che l'ago a la stella
   parer mi fece in volgermi al suo dove;   *30*
e cominciò: "L'amor che mi fa bella
   mi tragge a ragionar de l'altro duca
   per cui del mio sì ben ci si favella.   *33*
Degno è che, dov' è l'un, l'altro s'induca:
   sì che, com' elli ad una militaro,
   così la gloria loro insieme luca.   *36*
L'essercito di Cristo, che sì caro
   costò a rïarmar, dietro a la 'nsegna
   si movea tardo, sospeccioso e raro,   *39*
quando lo 'mperador che sempre regna
   provide a la milizia, ch'era in forse,
   per sola grazia, non per esser degna;   *42*
e, come è detto, a sua sposa soccorse
   con due campioni, al cui fare, al cui dire
   lo popol disvïato si raccorse.   *45*
In quella parte ove surge ad aprire
   Zefiro dolce le novelle fronde
   di che si vede Europa rivestire,   *48*

so the two garlands of those sempiternal roses circled round us, and so did the outer correspond to the inner.

When the dance and all the great festival of both song and flames, light with light, gladsome and benign, stopped together at one instant and with one consent (even as the eyes which, at the pleasure that moves them, must needs be closed and lifted in accord), from the heart of one of the new lights there came a voice which made me seem as the needle to the star in turning me to where it was; and it began, "The love that makes me beautiful draws me to speak of the other leader on whose account such fair utterance is made here concerning mine. It is fit that where one is, the other be brought in, so that, as they warred for one same end, so together may their glory shine.

"Christ's army, which cost so dear to rearm, was moving behind the standard, slow, mistrustful and scanty, when the Emperor who reigns eternally took thought for His soldiery that was in peril, of His grace only, not that it was worthy, and, as has been said, succored His bride with two champions by whose deeds, by whose words, the scattered people were rallied.

"In that region where sweet Zephyr rises to open the new leaves wherewith Europe sees herself reclad,

non molto lungi al percuoter de l'onde
   dietro a le quali, per la lunga foga,
   lo sol talvolta ad ogne uom si nasconde,   *51*
siede la fortunata Calaroga
   sotto la protezion del grande scudo
   in che soggiace il leone e soggioga: *54*
dentro vi nacque l'amoroso drudo
   de la fede cristiana, il santo atleta
   benigno a' suoi e a' nemici crudo;   *57*
e come fu creata, fu repleta
   sì la sua mente di viva vertute
   che, ne la madre, lei fece profeta.   *60*
Poi che le sponsalizie fuor compiute
   al sacro fonte intra lui e la Fede,
   u' si dotar di mutüa salute,   *63*
la donna che per lui l'assenso diede,
   vide nel sonno il mirabile frutto
   ch'uscir dovea di lui e de le rede;   *66*
e perché fosse qual era in costrutto,
   quinci si mosse spirito a nomarlo
   del possessivo di cui era tutto.   *69*
Domenico fu detto; e io ne parlo
   sì come de l'agricola che Cristo
   elesse a l'orto suo per aiutarlo.   *72*
Ben parve messo e famigliar di Cristo:
   ché 'l primo amor che 'n lui fu manifesto,
   fu al primo consiglio che diè Cristo.   *75*
Spesse fïate fu tacito e desto
   trovato in terra da la sua nutrice,
   come dicesse: 'Io son venuto a questo.'   *78*

not far from the smiting of the waves, behind which the sun, after his long course, sometimes hides himself from every man, sits fortunate Calaroga under the protection of the mighty shield whereon the lion is subject and sovereign. Therein was born the ardent lover of the Christian faith, the holy athlete, benignant to his own and harsh to his foes. And his mind, as soon as it was created, was so full of living virtue that in his mother's womb he made her a prophetess. When the espousals were completed at the sacred font between him and the faith, where they dowered each other with mutual salvation, the lady who gave the assent for him saw in a dream the marvelous fruit destined to issue from him and from his heirs, and, that he might in very construing be what he was, a spirit from up here went forth to name him by the possessive of Him whose he wholly was. Dominic he was named, and I speak of him as of the husbandman whom Christ chose to help Him in His garden. Well did he show himself a messenger and familiar of Christ; for the first love manifested in him was for the first counsel that Christ gave. Oftentimes his nurse found him silent and awake upon the ground, as though he would say, 'I am come for this.'

Oh padre suo veramente Felice!
   oh madre sua veramente Giovanna,
   se, interpretata, val come si dice!   *81*
Non per lo mondo, per cui mo s'affanna
   di retro ad Ostïense e a Taddeo,
   ma per amor de la verace manna   *84*
in picciol tempo gran dottor si feo;
   tal che si mise a circüir la vigna
   che tosto imbianca, se 'l vignaio è reo.   *87*
E a la sedia che fu già benigna
   più a' poveri giusti, non per lei,
   ma per colui che siede, che traligna,   *90*
non dispensare o due o tre per sei,
   non la fortuna di prima vacante,
   non *decimas, quae sunt pauperum Dei,*   *93*
addimandò, ma contro al mondo errante
   licenza di combatter per lo seme
   del qual ti fascian ventiquattro piante.   *96*
Poi, con dottrina e con volere insieme,
   con l'officio appostolico si mosse
   quasi torrente ch'alta vena preme;   *99*
e ne li sterpi eretici percosse
   l'impeto suo, più vivamente quivi
   dove le resistenze eran più grosse.   *102*
Di lui si fecer poi diversi rivi
   onde l'orto catolico si riga,
   sì che i suoi arbuscelli stan più vivi.   *105*
Se tal fu l'una rota de la biga
   in che la Santa Chiesa si difese
   e vinse in campo la sua civil briga,   *108*

Oh father of him, Felice indeed! Oh mother of him, Giovanna indeed, if this, being interpreted, means as is said!

"Not for the world for whose sake men now toil after him of Ostia and after Thaddeus, but for love of the true manna, in short time he became a mighty teacher, such that he set himself to go round the vineyard, which soon turns gray if the vine-dresser is negligent. And of the seat which once was more benign to the righteous poor—not in itself, but in him who sits on it and degenerates—he asked, not to dispense two or three for six, not for the fortune of the first vacancy, not for *decimas quae sunt pauperum Dei*, but for leave to fight against the erring world for that seed of which four and twenty plants surround you. Then both with doctrine and with will, together with the apostolic office, he went forth like a torrent which a lofty vein presses out, and on the heretical stocks his force struck with most vigor where the resistances were most obstinate. From him there sprang then various streamlets whereby the catholic garden is watered, so that its bushes are more living.

"If such was the one wheel of the chariot in which Holy Church defended herself and won in the field her civil strife,

ben ti dovrebbe assai esser palese
   l'eccellenza de l'altra, di cui Tomma
   dinanzi al mio venir fu sì cortese.   *111*
Ma l'orbita che fé la parte somma
   di sua circunferenza, è derelitta,
   sì ch'è la muffa dov' era la gromma.   *114*
La sua famiglia, che si mosse dritta
   coi piedi a le sue orme, è tanto volta,
   che quel dinanzi a quel di retro gitta;   *117*
e tosto si vedrà de la ricolta
   de la mala coltura, quando il loglio
   si lagnerà che l'arca li sia tolta.   *120*
Ben dico, chi cercasse a foglio a foglio
   nostro volume, ancor troveria carta
   u' leggerebbe 'I' mi son quel ch'i' soglio'; *123*
ma non fia da Casal né d'Acquasparta,
   là onde vegnon tali a la scrittura,
   ch'uno la fugge e altro la coarta.   *126*
Io son la vita di Bonaventura
   da Bagnoregio, che ne' grandi offici
   sempre pospuosi la sinistra cura.   *129*
Illuminato e Augustin son quici,
   che fuor de' primi scalzi poverelli
   che nel capestro a Dio si fero amici.   *132*
Ugo da San Vittore è qui con elli,
   e Pietro Mangiadore e Pietro Spano,
   lo qual giù luce in dodici libelli;   *135*
Natàn profeta e 'l metropolitano
   Crisostomo e Anselmo e quel Donato
   ch'a la prim' arte degnò porre mano.   *138*

surely the excellence of the other must be very plain to you, concerning whom, before I came, Thomas was so courteous. But the track made by the topmost part of its rim is derelict; so that there is mould where the crust was. His household, which set out aright with their feet upon his footprints, is so turned about that the forward foot moves to that behind; and soon shall be seen some harvest of the bad tillage, when the tare will complain that the bin is taken from it. Nevertheless, I say, he who should search our volume leaf by leaf might still find a page where he would read, 'I am as I always was'; but it will not be from Casale or from Acquasparta, whence come such to the writing that one shuns it and the other contracts it.

"I am the living soul of Bonaventura of Bagnorea, who in the great offices always put the left-hand care behind. Illuminato and Augustine are here, who were of the first unshod poor brethren that with the cord made themselves God's friends. Hugh of St. Victor is here with them, and Peter Comestor, and Peter of Spain, who down below shines in twelve books; Nathan the prophet, and the Metropolitan Chrysostom, and Anselm, and that Donatus who deigned to set his hand to the first art;

Rabano è qui, e lucemi dallato
　il calavrese abate Giovacchino
　di spirito profetico dotato.　　　　　　　　　*141*
Ad inveggiar cotanto paladino
　mi mosse l'infiammata cortesia
　di fra Tommaso e 'l discreto latino;
e mosse meco questa compagnia."　　　　　*145*

Rabanus is here, and beside me shines the Calabrian abbot Joachim, who was endowed with prophetic spirit.

"The glowing courtesy and the well-judged discourse of Brother Thomas has moved me to celebrate so great a paladin, and with me has moved this company."

PARADISO.

Imagini, chi bene intender cupe
　　quel ch'i' or vidi — e ritegna l'image,
　　mentre ch'io dico, come ferma rupe —,　　　*3*
quindici stelle che 'n diverse plage
　　lo cielo avvivan di tanto sereno
　　che soperchia de l'aere ogne compage;　　　*6*
imagini quel carro a cu' il seno
　　basta del nostro cielo e notte e giorno,
　　sì ch'al volger del temo non vien meno;　　　*9*
imagini la bocca di quel corno
　　che si comincia in punta de lo stelo
　　a cui la prima rota va dintorno,　　　*12*
aver fatto di sé due segni in cielo,
　　qual fece la figliuola di Minoi
　　allora che sentì di morte il gelo;　　　*15*
e l'un ne l'altro aver li raggi suoi,
　　e amendue girarsi per maniera
　　che l'uno andasse al primo e l'altro al poi;　　　*18*

CANTO XIII

Let him imagine, who would rightly grasp
what I now beheld (and, while I speak, let
him hold the image firm as a rock), fifteen
stars which in different regions vivify the
heaven with such great brightness that it over-
comes every thickness of the air; let him
imagine that Wain for which the bosom of
our heaven suffices night and day so that with
the turning of the pole it does not disappear;
let him imagine the mouth of that Horn
which begins at the end of the axle on which
the first wheel revolves—all to have made of
themselves two signs in the heavens like that
which the daughter of Minos made when she
felt the chill of death; and one to have its
rays within the other, and both to revolve in
such manner that one should go first and the
other after;

e avrà quasi l'ombra de la vera
  costellazione e de la doppia danza
  che circulava il punto dov' io era: 21

poi ch'è tanto di là da nostra usanza,
  quanto di là dal mover de la Chiana
  si move il ciel che tutti li altri avanza.   24

Lì si cantò non Bacco, non Peana,
  ma tre persone in divina natura,
  e in una persona essa e l'umana.   27

Compié 'l cantare e 'l volger sua misura;
  e attesersi a noi quei santi lumi,
  felicitando sé di cura in cura.   30

Ruppe il silenzio ne' concordi numi
  poscia la luce in che mirabil vita
  del poverel di Dio narrata fumi,   33

e disse: "Quando l'una paglia è trita,
  quando la sua semenza è già riposta,
  a batter l'altra dolce amor m'invita.   36

Tu credi che nel petto onde la costa
  si trasse per formar la bella guancia
  il cui palato a tutto 'l mondo costa,   39

e in quel che, forato da la lancia,
  e prima e poscia tanto sodisfece,
  che d'ogne colpa vince la bilancia,   42

quantunque a la natura umana lece
  aver di lume, tutto fosse infuso
  da quel valor che l'uno e l'altro fece;   45

e però miri a ciò ch'io dissi suso,
  quando narrai che non ebbe 'l secondo
  lo ben che ne la quinta luce è chiuso.   48

and he will have as it were a shadow of the true constellation, and of the double dance, which was circling round the point where I was; for it is as far beyond our experience as the motion of the heaven that outspeeds all the rest is beyond the motion of the Chiana. There they sang not Bacchus, and not Paean, but Three Persons in the divine nature, and it and the human nature in one Person. The singing and the circling completed each its measure, and those holy lights gave heed to us, rejoicing as they passed from care to care.

Then the light within which the wondrous life of the poor man of God had been narrated to me broke the silence among the concordant souls, and said, "Since one straw is threshed, since its grain is now garnered, sweet charity bids me beat out the other. You believe that into the breast from which the rib was drawn to form her beautiful cheek whose palate costs dear to all the world, and into that which, pierced by the lance, made such satisfaction, both after and before, that it turns the scale against all fault, whatever of light it is allowed human nature to have was all infused by that Power which made the one and the other; and therefore you wonder at what I said above, when I declared that the excellence which is enclosed in the fifth light never had a second.

Or apri li occhi a quel ch'io ti rispondo,
  e vedräi il tuo credere e 'l mio dire
  nel vero farsi come centro in tondo.   51
Ciò che non more e ciò che può morire
  non è se non splendor di quella idea
  che partorisce, amando, il nostro Sire;   54
ché quella viva luce che sì mea
  dal suo lucente, che non si disuna
  da lui né da l'amor ch'a lor s'intrea,   57
per sua bontate il suo raggiare aduna,
  quasi specchiato, in nove sussistenze,
  etternalmente rimanendosi una.   60
Quindi discende a l'ultime potenze
  giù d'atto in atto, tanto divenendo,
  che più non fa che brevi contingenze;   63
e queste contingenze essere intendo
  le cose generate, che produce
  con seme e sanza seme il ciel movendo.   66
La cera di costoro e chi la duce
  non sta d'un modo; e però sotto 'l segno
  idëale poi più e men traluce.   69
Ond' elli avvien ch'un medesimo legno,
  secondo specie, meglio e peggio frutta;
  e voi nascete con diverso ingegno.   72
Se fosse a punto la cera dedutta
  e fosse il cielo in sua virtù supprema,
  la luce del suggel parrebbe tutta;   75
ma la natura la dà sempre scema,
  similemente operando a l'artista
  ch'a l'abito de l'arte ha man che trema.   78

Now open your eyes to that which I answer you, and you will see your belief and what I say become in the truth as the center in a circle.

"That which dies not and that which can die are naught but the splendor of that Idea which in His love our Sire begets; for that living light which so streams from its Lucent Source that It is not disunited from It, nor from the Love which is intrined with them, does of Its own goodness collect Its rays, as though reflected, in nine subsistences, Itself eternally remaining One. Thence It descends to the ultimate potentialities, downward from act to act becoming such that finally it makes but brief contingencies; and these contingencies I understand to be the generated things which the moving heavens produce with seed and without it. The wax of these and that which molds it àre not always in the same condition, and therefore under the ideal stamp it then shines now more, now less; hence it comes that one same plant, in respect to species, fruits better or worse, and that you are born with diverse dispositions. If the wax were exactly worked, and the heavens were at the height of their power, the light of the whole seal would be apparent. But nature always gives it defectively, working like the artist who in the practice of his art has a hand that trembles.

Però se 'l caldo amor la chiara vista
  de la prima virtù dispone e segna,
  tutta la perfezion quivi s'acquista.   *81*
Così fu fatta già la terra degna
  di tutta l'animal perfezïone;
  così fu fatta la Vergine pregna;   *84*
sì ch'io commendo tua oppinïone,
  che l'umana natura mai non fue
  né fia qual fu in quelle due persone.   *87*
Or s'i' non procedesse avanti piùe,
  'Dunque, come costui fu sanza pare?'
  comincerebber le parole tue.   *90*
Ma perché paia ben ciò che non pare,
  pensa chi era, e la cagion che 'l mosse,
  quando fu detto 'Chiedi,' a dimandare.   *93*
Non ho parlato sì, che tu non posse
  ben veder ch'el fu re, che chiese senno
  acciò che re sufficïente fosse;   *96*
non per sapere il numero in che enno
  li motor di qua sù, o se *necesse*
  con contingente mai *necesse* fenno;   *99*
non *si est dare primum motum esse*,
  o se del mezzo cerchio far si puote
  trïangol sì ch'un retto non avesse.   *102*
Onde, se ciò ch'io dissi e questo note,
  regal prudenza è quel vedere impari
  in che lo stral di mia intenzion percuote;   *105*
e se al "surse" drizzi li occhi chiari,
  vedrai aver solamente respetto
  ai regi, che son molti, e ' buon son rari.   *108*

Yet, if the fervent Love disposes and imprints the clear Vision of the primal Power, complete perfection is there acquired. Thus was the dust once made fit for the full perfection of a living creature, thus was the Virgin made to be with child; so that I approve your opinion that human nature never was, nor shall be, what it was in those two persons.

"Now, if I went no further, 'How, then, was that other without an equal?' would your words begin. But in order that that which is not apparent may clearly appear, consider who he was and the cause which moved him to make request when it was said to him, 'Ask.' I have not so spoken that you cannot plainly see that he was a king, who asked for wisdom, in order that he might be a worthy king; not to know the number of the mover spirits here above, nor if *necesse* with a contingent ever made *necesse*; nor *si est dare primum motum esse*; nor if in a semicircle a triangle can be so constructed that it shall have no right angle. Wherefore, if you note this along with what I said, kingly prudence is that peerless vision on which the arrow of my intention strikes. And if to 'rose' you turn your discerning eyes, you will see it has respect only to kings—who are many and the good are rare.

Con questa distinzion prendi 'l mio detto;
   e così puote star con quel che credi
   del primo padre e del nostro Diletto.   *111*

E questo ti sia sempre piombo a' piedi,
   per farti mover lento com' uom lasso
   e al sì e al no che tu non vedi: *114*

ché quelli è tra li stolti bene a basso,
   che sanza distinzione afferma e nega
   ne l'un così come ne l'altro passo;   *117*

perch' elli 'ncontra che più volte piega
   l'oppinïon corrente in falsa parte,
   e poi l'affetto l'intelletto lega.   *120*

Vie più che 'ndarno da riva si parte,
   perché non torna tal qual e' si move,
   chi pesca per lo vero e non ha l'arte.   *123*

E di ciò sono al mondo aperte prove
   Parmenide, Melisso e Brisso e molti,
   li quali andaro e non sapëan dove;   *126*

sì fé Sabellio e Arrio e quelli stolti
   che furon come spade a le Scritture
   in render torti li diritti volti.   *129*

Non sien le genti, ancor, troppo sicure
   a giudicar, sì come quei che stima
   le biade in campo pria che sien mature;   *132*

ch'i' ho veduto tutto 'l verno prima
   lo prun mostrarsi rigido e feroce,
   poscia portar la rosa in su la cima;   *135*

e legno vidi già dritto e veloce
   correr lo mar per tutto suo cammino,
   perire al fine a l'intrar de la foce.   *138*

Take my words with this distinction, and they can stand thus with what you believe of the first father and of our Beloved.

"And let this ever be as lead to your feet, to make you slow, like a weary man, in moving either to the *yes* or the *no* which you see not; for he is right low down among the fools, alike in the one and in the other case, who affirms or denies without distinguishing; because it happens that oftentimes hasty opinion inclines to the wrong side, and then fondness for it binds the intellect. Far worse than in vain does he leave the shore (since he returns not as he puts forth) who fishes for the truth and has not the art. And of this Parmenides, Melissus, Bryson, are open proofs to the world, as are the many others who went on but knew not whither. Thus did Sabellius, and Arius, and those fools who were to the Scriptures like swords, in rendering straight countenances distorted.

Moreover, let folk not be too secure in judgment, like one who should count the ears in the field before they are ripe; for I have seen first, all winter through, the thorn display itself hard and stiff, and then upon its summit bear the rose. And I have seen ere now a ship fare straight and swift over the sea through all her course, and perish at the last as she entered the harbor.

Non creda donna Berta e ser Martino,
   per vedere un furare, altro offerere,
   vederli dentro al consiglio divino;
ché quel può surgere, e quel può cadere."   *142*

Let not dame Bertha and squire Martin, if they see one steal and one make offering, believe to see them within the Divine Counsel: for the one may rise and the other may fall."

PARADISO

Dal centro al cerchio, e sì dal cerchio al centro
movesi l'acqua in un ritondo vaso,
secondo ch'è percosso fuori o dentro: *3*
ne la mia mente fé sùbito caso
questo ch'io dico, sì come si tacque
la glorïosa vita di Tommaso,   *6*
per la similitudine che nacque
del suo parlare e di quel di Beatrice,
a cui sì cominciar, dopo lui, piacque: *9*
"A costui fa mestieri, e nol vi dice
né con la voce né pensando ancora,
d'un altro vero andare a la radice.   *12*
Diteli se la luce onde s'infiora
vostra sustanza, rimarrà con voi
etternalmente sì com' ell' è ora;   *15*
e se rimane, dite come, poi
che sarete visibili rifatti,
esser porà ch'al veder non vi nòi."   *18*
Come, da più letizia pinti e tratti,
a la fïata quei che vanno a rota
levan la voce e rallegrano li atti,   *21*

CANTO XIV

F<small>ROM THE</small> center to the rim, and so from the rim to the center, the water in a round vessel moves, according as it is struck from without or within. This which I say fell suddenly into my mind as the glorious life of Thomas became silent, because of the likeness which was born of his speech and that of Beatrice, who was pleased to begin thus after him, "This man has need, and does not tell you of it, either by word or as yet in thought, to go to the root of another truth. Tell him if the light wherewith your substance blooms will remain with you eternally even as it is now; and, if it does remain, tell how, after you are made visible again, it can be that it will not hurt your sight."

As when urged and drawn on by increasing delight, those who are dancing in a ring from time to time raise their voices and gladden their motions,

così, a l'orazion pronta e divota,
   li santi cerchi mostrar nova gioia
   nel torneare e ne la mira nota.   *24*
Qual si lamenta perché qui si moia
   per viver colà sù, non vide quive
   lo refrigerio de l'etterna ploia.   *27*
Quell' uno e due e tre che sempre vive
   e regna sempre in tre e 'n due e 'n uno,
   non circunscritto, e tutto circunscrive,   *30*
tre volte era cantato da ciascuno
   di quelli spiriti con tal melodia,
   ch'ad ogne merto saria giusto muno.   *33*
E io udi' ne la luce più dia
   del minor cerchio una voce modesta,
   forse qual fu da l'angelo a Maria,   *36*
risponder: "Quanto fia lunga la festa
   di paradiso, tanto il nostro amore
   si raggerà dintorno cotal vesta.   *39*
La sua chiarezza séguita l'ardore;
   l'ardor la visïone, e quella è tanta,
   quant' ha di grazia sovra suo valore.   *42*
Come la carne glorïosa e santa
   fia rivestita, la nostra persona
   più grata fia per esser tutta quanta;   *45*
per che s'accrescerà ciò che ne dona
   di gratüito lume il sommo bene,
   lume ch'a lui veder ne condiziona;   *48*
onde la visïon crescer convene,
   crescer l'ardor che di quella s'accende,
   crescer lo raggio che da esso vene.   *51*

so at that prompt and devout petition the holy circles showed new joy in their revolving and in their marvelous melody. Whoso laments because we die here to live there on high has not seen there the refreshment of the eternal rain.

That One and Two and Three which ever lives, and ever reigns in Three and Two and One, uncircumscribed, and circumscribing all things, was thrice sung by each of those spirits with such a melody as would be adequate reward for every merit. And I heard in the divinest light of the lesser circle a modest voice, perhaps such as was that of the Angel to Mary, make answer, "As long as the feast of Paradise shall be, so long shall our love radiate around us such a garment. Its brightness follows our ardor, the ardor our vision, and that is in the measure which each has of grace beyond his merit. When the flesh, glorious and sanctified, shall be clothed on us again, our persons will be more acceptable for being all complete; wherefore whatever of gratuitous light the Supreme Good gives us will be increased, light which fits us to see Him; so that our vision needs must increase, our ardor increase which by that is kindled, our radiance increase which comes from this.

Ma sì come carbon che fiamma rende,
  e per vivo candor quella soverchia,
  sì che la sua parvenza si difende;   54
così questo folgór che già ne cerchia
  fia vinto in apparenza da la carne
  che tutto dì la terra ricoperchia;   57
né potrà tanta luce affaticarne:
  ché li organi del corpo saran forti
  a tutto ciò che potrà dilettarne."   60
Tanto mi parver sùbiti e accorti
  e l'uno e l'altro coro a dicer "Amme!"
  che ben mostrar disio d'i corpi morti: 63
forse non pur per lor, ma per le mamme,
  per li padri e per li altri che fuor cari
  anzi che fosser sempiterne fiamme.   66
Ed ecco intorno, di chiarezza pari,
  nascere un lustro sopra quel che v'era,
  per guisa d'orizzonte che rischiari.   69
E sì come al salir di prima sera
  comincian per lo ciel nove parvenze,
  sì che la vista pare e non par vera,   72
parvemi lì novelle sussistenze
  cominciare a vedere, e fare un giro
  di fuor da l'altre due circunferenze.   75
Oh vero sfavillar del Santo Spiro!
  come si fece sùbito e candente
  a li occhi miei che, vinti, nol soffriro!   78
Ma Bëatrice sì bella e ridente
  mi si mostrò, che tra quelle vedute
  si vuol lasciar che non seguir la mente.   81

But even as a coal which gives forth flame, and with its white glow outshines it, so that its visibility is maintained, so shall this effulgence which already surrounds us be surpassed in brightness by the flesh which the earth still covers; nor will such light have power to fatigue us, for the organs of the body will be strong for everything that can delight us."

So sudden and eager both the one and the other chorus seemed to me in saying "Amen," that truly they showed desire for their dead bodies—perhaps not only for themselves, but also for their mothers, for their fathers, and for the others who were dear before they became eternal flames.

And lo! round about and of equal brightness rose a lustre beyond that which was there, like a brightening horizon. And as, at rise of early evening, new lights begin to show in heaven, so that the sight does, and yet does not, seem real, it seemed to me that there I began to perceive new subsistences making a ring beyond the other two circumferences. Oh true sparkling of the Holy Spirit! how suddenly glowing it became to my eyes, which, vanquished, endured it not. But Beatrice showed herself to me so beautiful and smiling that it must be left among those sights which followed not my memory.

Quindi ripreser li occhi miei virtute
  a rilevarsi; e vidimi translato
  sol con mia donna in più alta salute.   *84*

Ben m'accors' io ch'io era più levato,
  per l'affocato riso de la stella,
  che mi parea più roggio che l'usato.   *87*

Con tutto 'l core e con quella favella
  ch'è una in tutti, a Dio feci olocausto,
  qual conveniesi a la grazia novella.   *90*

E non er' anco del mio petto essausto
  l'ardor del sacrificio, ch'io conobbi
  esso litare stato accetto e fausto;   *93*

ché con tanto lucore e tanto robbi
  m'apparvero splendor dentro a due raggi,
  ch'io dissi: "O Elïòs che sì li addobbi!"   *96*

Come distinta da minori e maggi
  lumi biancheggia tra ' poli del mondo
  Galassia sì, che fa dubbiar ben saggi;   *99*

sì costellati facean nel profondo
  Marte quei raggi il venerabil segno
  che fan giunture di quadranti in tondo.   *102*

Qui vince la memoria mia lo 'ngegno;
  ché quella croce lampeggiava Cristo,
  sì ch'io non so trovare essempro degno;   *105*

ma chi prende sua croce e segue Cristo,
  ancor mi scuserà di quel ch'io lasso,
  vedendo in quell' albor balenar Cristo.   *108*

Di corno in corno e tra la cima e 'l basso
  si movien lumi, scintillando forte
  nel congiugnersi insieme e nel trapasso: *111*

Therefrom my eyes regained power to raise
themselves again, and I saw myself, alone
with my lady, translated to a more exalted
blessedness. That I was more uplifted I per-
ceived clearly by the fiery smile of the star
which seemed to me ruddier than its wont.
With all my heart, and with that speech
which is one in all men, I made a holocaust
to God such as befitted the new grace; and
the burning of the sacrifice was not yet com-
pleted in my breast when I knew the of-
fering to be accepted and propitious, for
with such a glow and such a ruddiness splen-
dors appeared to me within two rays that I
said, "O Helios, who dost so adorn them!"

As, pricked out with greater and lesser
lights, between the poles of the Universe, the
Milky Way so gleams as to cause even the
wise to question, so did those beams, thus
constellated, make in the depth of Mars the
venerable sign which joinings of quadrants
make in a circle. Here my memory outstrips
my wit, for that Cross so flashed forth Christ
that I can find for it no fit comparison; but
he that takes up his cross and follows Christ
shall yet forgive me for what I leave untold
when he sees Christ flash in that dawn.

From horn to horn and between the top and
the base, lights were moving that sparkled
brightly as they met and passed;

così si veggion qui diritte e torte,
   veloci e tarde, rinovando vista,
   le minuzie d'i corpi, lunghe e corte,   *114*
moversi per lo raggio onde si lista
   talvolta l'ombra che, per sua difesa,
   la gente con ingegno e arte acquista.   *117*
E come giga e arpa, in tempra tesa
   di molte corde, fa dolce tintinno
   a tal da cui la nota non è intesa,   *120*
così da' lumi che lì m'apparinno
   s'accogliea per la croce una melode
   che mi rapiva, sanza intender l'inno.   *123*
Ben m'accors' io ch'elli era d'alte lode,
   però ch'a me venìa "Resurgi" e "Vinci"
   come a colui che non intende e ode.   *126*
Ïo m'innamorava tanto quinci,
   che 'nfino a lì non fu alcuna cosa
   che mi legasse con sì dolci vinci.   *129*
Forse la mia parola par troppo osa,
   posponendo il piacer de li occhi belli,
   ne' quai mirando mio disio ha posa;   *132*
ma chi s'avvede che i vivi suggelli
   d'ogne bellezza più fanno più suso,
   e ch'io non m'era lì rivolto a quelli,   *135*
escusar puommi di quel ch'io m'accuso
   per escusarmi, e vedermi dir vero:
   ché 'l piacer santo non è qui dischiuso,
perché si fa, montando, più sincero.   *139*

so we see here, straight and athwart, swift and
slow, changing appearance, the motes of bod-
ies, long and short, moving through the ray
that sometimes streaks the shade which men
with skill and art contrive for their defense.
And as viol and harp, strung with many cords
in harmony, chime sweetly for one who does
not catch the tune, so from the lights that
appeared to me there a melody gathered
through the cross which held me rapt, though
I followed not the hymn. Well I discerned it
to be of lofty praise, for there came to me:
"Rise" and "Conquer," as to one who under-
stands not, but hears; by which I was so
moved to love that till then nothing had
bound me with such sweet bonds. Perhaps my
word appears too daring, as though slighting
the pleasure of the beautiful eyes, gazing into
which my longing has repose. But he who
considers that the living seals of every beauty
have more effect the higher they are, and that
I there had not yet turned to them, may
excuse me for that whereof I accuse myself in
order to excuse myself, and may see that I
speak truth; for the holy pleasure is not ex-
cluded here, because it becomes the purer as
one mounts.

PARADISO

Bᴇɴɪɢɴᴀ ᴠᴏʟᴏɴᴛᴀᴅᴇ in che si liqua
    sempre l'amor che drittamente spira,
    come cupidità fa ne la iniqua,   *3*
silenzio puose a quella dolce lira,
    e fece quïetar le sante corde
    che la destra del cielo allenta e tira.   *6*
Come saranno a' giusti preghi sorde
    quelle sustanze che, per darmi voglia
    ch'io le pregassi, a tacer fur concorde?   *9*
Bene è che sanza termine si doglia
    chi, per amor di cosa che non duri
    etternalmente, quello amor si spoglia.   *12*
Quale per li seren tranquilli e puri
    discorre ad ora ad or sùbito foco,
    movendo li occhi che stavan sicuri,   *15*
e pare stella che tramuti loco,
    se non che da la parte ond' e' s'accende
    nulla sen perde, ed esso dura poco: *18*

CANTO XV

Gracious will, wherein right-breathing love always resolves itself, as cupidity does into grudging will, imposed silence on that sweet lyre and quieted the holy strings which the right hand of Heaven slackens and draws tight. How shall those beings be deaf to righteous prayers, who, in order to prompt me to beg of them, became silent with one consent? Right it is that he should grieve without end who, for the love of what does not endure forever, robs himself of that love.

As, through the still and cloudless evening sky a sudden fire shoots from time to time, moving the eyes that were at rest, and seeming a star that changes place, save that from where it kindles no star is lost, and it lasts but short while;

tale dal corno che 'n destro si stende
   a piè di quella croce corse un astro
   de la costellazion che lì resplende;   *21*
né si partì la gemma dal suo nastro,
   ma per la lista radïal trascorse,
   che parve foco dietro ad alabastro.   *24*
Sì pïa l'ombra d'Anchise si porse,
   se fede merta nostra maggior musa,
   quando in Eliso del figlio s'accorse.   *27*
"O sanguis meus, o superinfusa
   gratïa Deï, sicut tibi cui
   bis unquam celi ianüa reclusa?"   *30*
Così quel lume: ond' io m'attesi a lui;
   poscia rivolsi a la mia donna il viso,
   e quinci e quindi stupefatto fui;   *33*
ché dentro a li occhi suoi ardeva un riso
   tal, ch'io pensai co' miei toccar lo fondo
   de la mia gloria e del mio paradiso.   *36*
Indi, a udire e a veder giocondo,
   giunse lo spirto al suo principio cose,
   ch'io non lo 'ntesi, sì parlò profondo;   *39*
né per elezïon mi si nascose,
   ma per necessità, ché 'l suo concetto
   al segno d'i mortal si soprapuose.   *42*
E quando l'arco de l'ardente affetto
   fu sì sfogato, che 'l parlar discese
   inver' lo segno del nostro intelletto,   *45*
la prima cosa che per me s'intese,
   "Benedetto sia tu," fu, "trino e uno,
   che nel mio seme se' tanto cortese!"   *48*

so, from the horn that extends on the right, there darted a star of the resplendent constellation that is there, down to the foot of that cross; nor did the gem depart from its ribbon, but coursed along the radial strip, and seemed like fire behind alabaster. With like affection did the shade of Anchises stretch forward (if our greatest Muse merits belief), when in Elysium he perceived his son.

"*O sanguis meus, O superinfusa gratia Dei, sicut tibi cui bis unquam celi ianua reclusa?*" Thus that light; wherefore I gave my heed to it, then I turned back my sight to my lady, and on this side and that I was amazed, for in her eyes was blazing such a smile that I thought with mine I had touched the limit both of my beatitude and of my paradise.

Then, a joy to hearing and to sight, the spirit added to his first words things I did not comprehend, so deep was his speech; nor did he conceal himself from me by choice, but of necessity, for his conception was set above the mark of mortals. And when the bow of his ardent affection was so relaxed that his speech descended toward the mark of our intellect, the first thing I understood was, "Blessed be Thou, Three and One, who show such favor to my seed."

E seguì: "Grato e lontano digiuno,
  tratto leggendo del magno volume
  du' non si muta mai bianco né bruno,   *51*
solvuto hai, figlio, dentro a questo lume
  in ch'io ti parlo, mercé di colei
  ch'a l'alto volo ti vestì le piume.   *54*
Tu credi che a me tuo pensier mei
  da quel ch'è primo, così come raia
  da l'un, se si conosce, il cinque e 'l sei;   *57*
e però ch'io mi sia e perch' io paia
  più gaudïoso a te, non mi domandi,
  che alcun altro in questa turba gaia.   *60*
Tu credi 'l vero; ché i minori e ' grandi
  di questa vita miran ne lo speglio
  in che, prima che pensi, il pensier pandi;   *63*
ma perché 'l sacro amore in che io veglio
  con perpetüa vista e che m'asseta
  di dolce disïar, s'adempia meglio,   *66*
la voce tua sicura, balda e lieta
  suoni la volontà, suoni 'l disio,
  a che la mia risposta è già decreta!"   *69*
Io mi volsi a Beatrice, e quella udio
  pria ch'io parlassi, e arrisemi un cenno
  che fece crescer l'ali al voler mio.   *72*
Poi cominciai così: "L'affetto e 'l senno,
  come la prima equalità v'apparse,
  d'un peso per ciascun di voi si fenno,   *75*
però che 'l sol che v'allumò e arse,
  col caldo e con la luce è sì iguali,
  che tutte simiglianze sono scarse.   *78*

And he continued, "Happy and long-felt hunger, derived from reading in the great volume where white or dark is never changed, you have relieved, my son, within this light in which I speak to you, thanks to her who clothed you with plumes for the lofty flight. You believe that your thought flows to me from Him who is First, even as from the unit, if that be known, ray out the five and the six; and therefore who I am, and why I seem to you more joyous than another in this festive throng, you do not ask me. You believe the truth, for the lesser and the great of this life gaze into that mirror in which, before you think, you display your thought. But in order that holy love, in which I watch with perpetual vision, and which makes me thirst with sweet longing, may be the better fulfilled, let your voice, confident and bold and glad, sound forth the will, sound forth the desire, whereto my answer is already decreed."

I turned to Beatrice, and she heard before I spoke, and smiled to me a sign that made the wings of my desire increase. And I began thus, "Love and intelligence, as soon as the first Equality became visible to you, became of one weight for each of you, because the Sun which illumined you and warmed you is of such equality in its heat and light that all comparisons fall short.

Ma voglia e argomento ne' mortali,
   per la cagion ch'a voi è manifesta,
   diversamente son pennuti in ali;   *81*
ond' io, che son mortal, mi sento in questa
   disagguaglianza, e però non ringrazio
   se non col core a la paterna festa.   *84*
Ben supplico io a te, vivo topazio
   che questa gioia prezïosa ingemmi,
   perché mi facci del tuo nome sazio."   *87*
"O fronda mia in che io compiacemmi
   pur aspettando, io fui la tua radice":
   cotal principio, rispondendo, femmi.   *90*
Poscia mi disse: "Quel da cui si dice
   tua cognazione e che cent' anni e piùe
   girato ha 'l monte in la prima cornice,   *93*
mio figlio fu e tuo bisavol fue:
   ben si convien che la lunga fatica
   tu li raccorci con l'opere tue.   *96*
Fiorenza dentro da la cerchia antica,
   ond' ella toglie ancora e terza e nona,
   si stava in pace, sobria e pudica.   *99*
Non avea catenella, non corona,
   non gonne contigiate, non cintura
   che fosse a veder più che la persona.   *102*
Non faceva, nascèndo, ancor paura
   la figlia al padre, ché 'l tempo e la dote
   non fuggien quinci e quindi la misura. *105*
Non avea case di famiglia vòte;
   non v'era giunto ancor Sardanapalo
   a mostrar ciò che 'n camera si puote.   *108*

But will and faculty in mortals, for the reason that is plain to you, are not equally feathered in their wings, so that I, who am mortal, feel myself in this inequality, and therefore can only give thanks with the heart for your paternal welcome. But I beseech you, living topaz who are a gem in this precious jewel, that you satisfy me with your name."

"O my branch, in whom I took delight only expecting you, I was your root." Thus he began his answer to me, then said, "He from whom your family has its name and who a hundred years and more has circled the mountain on the first ledge, was my son and was your grandfather's father. Truly it is fitting that you should shorten his long toil with your good offices.

"Florence, within her ancient circle from which she still takes tierce and nones, abode in peace, sober and chaste. There was no necklace, no coronal, no embroidered gowns, no girdle that was more to be looked at than the person. Not yet did the daughter at her birth cause fear to the father, for the time and the dowry did not outrun due measure on this side and that. Houses empty of family there were none, nor had Sardanapalus arrived yet to show what could be done in the chamber.

Non era vinto ancora Montemalo
   dal vostro Uccellatoio, che, com' è vinto
   nel montar sù, così sarà nel calo.   *111*
Bellincion Berti vid' io andar cinto
   di cuoio e d'osso, e venir da lo specchio
   la donna sua sanza 'l viso dipinto;   *114*
e vidi quel d'i Nerli e quel del Vecchio
   esser contenti a la pelle scoperta,
   e le sue donne al fuso e al pennecchio.   *117*
Oh fortunate! ciascuna era certa
   de la sua sepultura, e ancor nulla
   era per Francia nel letto diserta.   *120*
L'una vegghiava a studio de la culla,
   e, consolando, usava l'idïoma
   che prima i padri e le madri trastulla;   *123*
l'altra, traendo a la rocca la chioma,
   favoleggiava con la sua famiglia
   d'i Troiani, di Fiesole e di Roma.   *126*
Saria tenuta allor tal maraviglia
   una Cianghella, un Lapo Salterello,
   qual or saria Cincinnato e Corniglia.   *129*
A così riposato, a così bello
   viver di cittadini, a così fida
   cittadinanza, a così dolce ostello,   *132*
Maria mi diè, chiamàta in alte grida;
   e ne l'antico vostro Batisteo
   insieme fui cristiano e Cacciaguida.   *135*
Moronto fu mio frate ed Eliseo;
   mia donna venne a me di val di Pado,
   e quindi il sopranome tuo si feo.   *138*

Not yet was Montemalo surpassed by your Uccellatoio, which, as it has been passed in the uprising, so shall it be in the fall. Bellincion Berti have I seen go girt with leather and bone, and his wife come from her mirror with unpainted face. I have seen de' Nerli and del Vecchio content in unlined skin, and their wives at the spindle and the distaff. O happy they! each one of them sure of her burial place, and none as yet deserted in her bed because of France. The one kept watch in minding the cradle, and, soothing, spoke that speech which first delights fathers and mothers. Another, as she drew the threads from the distaff, would tell her household about the Trojans, and Fiesole, and Rome. Then a Cianghella or a Lapo Salterello would have been as great a marvel as Cincinnatus and Cornelia would be now.

"To so reposeful, to so fair a life of citizens, to such a trusty community, to so sweet an abode, Mary, called on with loud cries, gave me, and in your ancient Baptistery I became at once a Christian and Cacciaguida. Moronto was my brother, and Eliseo. My wife came to me from the valley of the Po, and thence was derived your surname.

Poi seguitai lo 'mperador Currado;
  ed el mi cinse de la sua milizia,
  tanto per bene ovrar li venni in grado.   141
Dietro li andai incontro a la nequizia
  di quella legge il cui popolo usurpa,
  per colpa d'i pastor, vostra giustizia.   144
Quivi fu' io da quella gente turpa
  disviluppato dal mondo fallace,
  lo cui amor molt'anime deturpa;
e venni dal martiro a questa pace."   148

Afterward I followed the Emperor Conrad, who girt me with his knighthood, so much did I win his favor by good work. I went, in his train, against the iniquity of that law whose people, through fault of the Pastors, usurp your right. There by that foul folk was I released from the deceitful world, the love of which debases many souls, and I came from martyrdom to this peace."

PARADISO

Opoca nostra nobiltà di sangue,
   se glorïar di te la gente fai
   qua giù dove l'affetto nostro langue,   *3*
mirabil cosa non mi sarà mai:
   ché là dove appetito non si torce,
   dico nel cielo, io me ne gloriai.   *6*
Ben se' tu manto che tosto raccorce:
   sì che, se non s'appon di dì in die,
   lo tempo va dintorno con le force.   *9*
Dal "voi" che prima a Roma s'offerie,
   in che la sua famiglia men persevra,
   ricominciaron le parole mie;   *12*
onde Beatrice, ch'era un poco scevra,
   ridendo, parve quella che tossio
   al primo fallo scritto di Ginevra.   *15*
Io cominciai: "Voi siete il padre mio;
   voi mi date a parlar tutta baldezza;
   voi mi levate sì, ch'i' son più ch'io.   *18*

CANTO XVI

O OUR petty nobility of blood! if you make
folk glory in you here below where our affec-
tions languish, it will nevermore be a marvel
to me, since there where appetite is not
warped, I mean in Heaven, I myself gloried
in you. Truly you are a mantle that soon
shrinks, so that if naught be added from day
to day, time goes round about you with its
shears.

With that *You* which was first used in
Rome and in which her family least perse-
veres, my words began again; at which Bea-
trice, who was a little withdrawn, smiled and
seemed to me like her who coughed at the
first fault that is written of Guinevere. I be-
gan, "You are my father, you give me full
boldness to speak, you so uplift me that I am
more than I.

Per tanti rivi s'empie d'allegrezza
   la mente mia, che di sé fa letizia
   perché può sostener che non si spezza.   21
Ditemi dunque, cara mia primizia,
   quai fuor li vostri antichi e quai fuor li anni
   che si segnaro in vostra püerizia;   24
ditemi de l'ovil di San Giovanni
   quanto era allora, e chi eran le genti
   tra esso degne di più alti scanni."   27
Come s'avviva a lo spirar d'i venti
   carbone in fiamma, così vid' io quella
   luce risplendere a' miei blandimenti;   30
e come a li occhi miei si fé più bella,
   così con voce più dolce e soave,
   ma non con questa moderna favella,   33
dissemi: "Da quel dì che fu detto *'Ave'*
   al parto in che mia madre, ch'è or santa,
   s'alleviò di me ond' era grave,   36
al suo Leon cinquecento cinquanta
   e trenta fiate venne questo foco
   a rinfiammarsi sotto la sua pianta.   39
Li antichi miei e io nacqui nel loco
   dove si truova pria l'ultimo sesto
   da quei che corre il vostro annüal gioco.   42
Basti d'i miei maggiori udirne questo:
   chi ei si fosser e onde venner quivi,
   più è tacer che ragionare onesto.   45
Tutti color ch'a quel tempo eran ivi
   da poter arme tra Marte e 'l Batista,
   erano il quinto di quei ch'or son vivi.   48

By so many streams my mind is filled with gladness that it rejoices in itself that it can bear this and not burst. Tell me then, dear stock from which I spring, what was your ancestry and what were the years that were reckoned in your boyhood. Tell me of the sheepfold of St. John, how large it was then, and who were the folk within it worthy of the highest seats."

As a coal quickens into flame at the breathing of the winds, so did I see that light glow at my blandishments; and as it became more beautiful to my eyes, so with a voice more sweet and gentle, but not in this our modern speech, he said to me, "From that day on which *Ave* was uttered, to the birth in which my mother, who now is sainted, was lightened of me with whom she had been burdened, this fire had come to its Lion five hundred, fifty, and thirty times to rekindle itself beneath his paw. My ancestors and I were born at the place where the furthest ward is first reached by the runner in your annual game. Let it suffice to hear thus much of my forebears; as to who they were and whence they came hither, silence is more becoming than speech.

"All those able to bear arms who at that time were there, between Mars and the Baptist, were the fifth of the number now living;

Ma la cittadinanza, ch'è or mista
di Campi, di Certaldo e di Fegghine,
pura vediesi ne l'ultimo artista.   *51*
Oh quanto fora meglio esser vicine
quelle genti ch'io dico, e al Galluzzo
e a Trespiano aver vostro confine,   *54*
che averle dentro e sostener lo puzzo
del villan d'Aguglion, di quel da Signa,
che già per barattare ha l'occhio aguzzo!   *57*
Se la gente ch'al mondo più traligna
non fosse stata a Cesare noverca,
ma come madre a suo figlio benigna,   *60*
tal fatto è fiorentino e cambia e merca,
che si sarebbe vòlto a Simifonti,
là dove andava l'avolo a la cerca;   *63*
sariesi Montemurlo ancor de' Conti;
sarieno i Cerchi nel piovier d'Acone,
e forse in Valdigrieve i Buondelmonti.   *66*
Sempre la confusion de le persone
principio fu del mal de la cittade,
come del vostro il cibo che s'appone;   *69*
e cieco toro più avaccio cade
che cieco agnello; e molte volte taglia
più e meglio una che le cinque spade.   *72*
Se tu riguardi Luni e Orbisaglia
come sono ite, e come se ne vanno
di retro ad esse Chiusi e Sinigaglia,   *75*
udir come le schiatte si disfanno
non ti parrà nova cosa né forte,
poscia che le cittadi termine hanno.   *78*

but the citizenship, which is now mixed with Campi, with Certaldo, and with Figline, saw itself pure down to the humblest artisan. Oh, how much better it would be that those folk of whom I speak were neighbors, and to have your boundary at Galluzzo and at Trespiano, than to have them within and to endure the stench of the churl of Aguglione, and of him of Signa, who already has his eye sharp for jobbery.

"If the folk who are the most degenerate in the world had not been a stepmother to Caesar, but, like a mother, benignant to her son, there is one who has become a Florentine and is a money-changer and trader, who would have lived on at Simifonti where his own grandfather went a-begging. Montemurlo would still belong to its Counts, the Cerchi would be in the parish of Acone, and perhaps the Buondelmonti in Valdigreve. The intermingling of people was ever the beginning of harm to the city, as to you the food which is loaded on is to the body. And a blind bull falls more headlong than the blind lamb, and oftentimes one sword cuts better and more than five.

"If you regard Luni and Urbisaglia, how they have perished, and how are following after them Chiusi and Senigallia, it will not appear to you a strange thing or a hard, to hear how families are undone, since cities have their term.

Le vostre cose tutte hanno lor morte,
 sì come voi; ma celasi in alcuna
 che dura molto, e le vite son corte.   *81*
E come 'l volger del ciel de la luna
 cuopre e discuopre i liti sanza posa,
 così fa di Fiorenza la Fortuna: *84*
per che non dee parer mirabil cosa
 ciò ch'io dirò de li alti Fiorentini
 onde è la fama nel tempo nascosa.   *87*
Io vidi li Ughi e vidi i Catellini,
 Filippi, Greci, Ormanni e Alberichi,
 già nel calare, illustri cittadini;   *90*
e vidi così grandi come antichi,
 con quel de la Sannella, quel de l'Arca,
 e Soldanieri e Ardinghi e Bostichi.   *93*
Sovra la porta ch'al presente è carca
 di nova fellonia di tanto peso
 che tosto fia iattura de la barca,   *96*
erano i Ravignani, ond' è disceso
 il conte Guido e qualunque del nome
 de l'alto Bellincione ha poscia preso.   *99*
Quel de la Pressa sapeva già come
 regger si vuole, e avea Galigaio
 dorata in casa sua già l'elsa e 'l pome.   *102*
Grand' era già la colonna del Vaio,
 Sacchetti, Giuochi, Fifanti e Barucci
 e Galli e quei ch'arrossan per lo staio.   *105*
Lo ceppo di che nacquero i Calfucci
 era già grande, e già eran tratti
 a le curule Sizii e Arrigucci.   *108*

Your affairs all have their death, even as have you; but it is concealed in some things that last long, whereas lives are short. And as the revolution of the heaven of the moon covers and uncovers the shores without pause, so Fortune does with Florence; wherefore it should appear no wondrous thing which I shall tell of the great Florentines whose fame is hidden by time. I saw the Ughi and I saw the Catellini, Filippi, Greci, Ormanni, and Alberichi, illustrious citizens, already in decline; and I saw, great as they were ancient, dell'Arca with della Sannella, and Soldanieri and Ardinghi and Bostichi. Over the gate which at present is laden with new felony of such great weight that there will soon be jettison from the bark, were the Ravignani of whose line the Count Guido is descended and whosoever has since taken the name of the high Bellincione. Della Pressa knew already how to rule, and Galligaio had already in his house the hilt and the pommel gilded. Great already were the Vair column, the Sacchetti, Giuochi, Fifanti, Barucci, and Galli, and those that blush for the bushel. The stock from which the Calfucci sprang was already great, and already the Sizii and Arrigucci had been raised to the highest seats.

Oh quali io vidi quei che son disfatti
   per lor superbia! e le palle de l'oro
   fiorian Fiorenza in tutt' i suoi gran fatti.   *111*
Così facieno i padri di coloro
   che, sempre che la vostra chiesa vaca,
   si fanno grassi stando a consistoro.   *114*
L'oltracotata schiatta che s'indraca
   dietro a chi fugge, e a chi mostra 'l dente
   o ver la borsa, com' agnel si placa,   *117*
già venìa sù, ma di picciola gente;
   sì che non piacque ad Ubertin Donato
   che poï il suocero il fé lor parente.   *120*
Già era 'l Caponsacco nel mercato
   disceso giù da Fiesole, e già era
   buon cittadino Giuda e Infangato.   *123*
Io dirò cosa incredibile e vera:
   nel picciol cerchio s'entrava per porta
   che si nomava da quei de la Pera.   *126*
Ciascun che de la bella insegna porta
   del gran barone il cui nome e 'l cui pregio
   la festa di Tommaso riconforta,   *129*
da esso ebbe milizia e privilegio;
   avvegna che con popol si rauni
   oggi colui che la fascia col fregio.   *132*
Già eran Gualterotti e Importuni;
   e ancor saria Borgo più quïeto,
   se di novi vicin fosser digiuni.   *135*
La casa di che nacque il vostro fleto,
   per lo giusto disdegno che v'ha morti
   e puose fine al vòstro viver lieto,   *138*

Oh, how great have I seen those now undone
by their pride! and the balls of gold adorned
Florence in all her great doings. So did the
fathers of those who, whenever your church
is vacant, fatten themselves by staying in con-
sistory. The insolent breed that plays the
dragon behind him that flees, and to whoever
shows his teeth—or else his purse—becomes
mild as a lamb, was already on the rise, but of
humble stock, so that it did not please Ubertin
Donato that his father-in-law afterward
should make him their kinsman. Already had
Caponsacco descended into the market-place
down from Fiesole, and already was Giuda a
good citizen, and Infangato. One thing I will
tell, incredible and true: the little circuit was
entered by a gate named after the Della Pera.
Everyone who bears the fair ensign of the
great Baron whose name and whose worth
the feast of Thomas keeps fresh, from him
had knighthood and privilege, although he
who fringes it round is siding now with the
people. Already there were Gualterotti and
Importuni; and the Borgo would still be
quiet if they had gone fasting of new neigh-
bors. The house of which was born your
weeping, by reason of its just resentment
which has slain you and put an end to your
glad living,

era onorata, essa e suoi consorti:
  o Buondelmonte, quanto mal fuggisti
  le nozze süe per li altrui conforti!   *141*
Molti sarebber lieti, che son tristi,
  se Dio t'avesse conceduto ad Ema
  la prima volta ch'a città venisti.   *144*
Ma conveniesi, a quella pietra scema
  che guarda 'l ponte, che Fiorenza fesse
  vittima ne la sua pace postrema.   *147*
Con queste genti, e con altre con esse,
  vid' io Fiorenza in sì fatto riposo,
  che non avea cagione onde piangesse.   *150*
Con queste genti vid' io glorïoso
  e giusto il popol suo, tanto che 'l giglio
  non era ad asta mai posto a ritroso,
né per divisïon fatto vermiglio."   *154*

was honored, both itself and its consorts. O Buondelmonte, how ill for you that you did fly from its nuptials at the promptings of another. Many would be happy who now are sad if God had committed you to the Ema the first time you came to the city! but it was fitting that Florence, in her last peace, should offer a victim to that mutilated stone which guards the bridge.

"With these families, and with others with them, I saw Florence in such repose that she had no cause for wailing. With these families I saw her people so glorious and so just, that the lily was never set reversed upon the staff, nor made vermilion by division."

PARADISO

Qual venne a Climenè, per accertarsi
    di ciò ch'avëa incontro a sé udito,
    quei ch'ancor fa li padri ai figli scarsi;   *3*
tal era io, e tal era sentito
    e da Beatrice e da la santa lampa
    che pria per me avea mutato sito.   *6*
Per che mia donna "Manda fuor la vampa
    del tuo disio," mi disse, "sì ch'ella esca
    segnata bene de la interna stampa: *9*
non perché nostra conoscenza cresca
    per tuo parlare, ma perché t'ausi
    a dir la sete, sì che l'uom ti mesca."   *12*
"O cara piota mia che sì t'insusi,
    che, come veggion le terrene menti
    non capere in trïangol due ottusi,   *15*
così vedi le cose contingenti
    anzi che sieno in sé, mirando il punto
    a cui tutti li tempi son presenti;   *18*

CANTO XVII

As he who still makes fathers chary toward their sons came to Clymene to be reassured about that which he had heard against himself, such was I, and such was I perceived to be both by Beatrice and by the holy lamp which already, for my sake, had changed its place. Wherefore my lady said to me, "Put forth the flame of your desire, so that it may issue imprinted well by the internal stamp; not in order that our knowledge may increase through your speech, but that you may learn to tell your thirst, so that one may pour out drink for you."

"O dear root of me, who are so uplifted that, even as earthly minds see that two obtuse angles can not be contained in a triangle, so you, gazing upon the Point to which all times are present, do see contingent things before they exist in themselves;

mentre ch'io era a Virgilio congiunto
   su per lo monte che l'anime cura
   e discendendo nel mondo defunto,   *21*
dette mi fuor di mia vita futura
   parole gravi, avvegna ch'io mi senta
   ben tetragono ai colpi di ventura;   *24*
per che la voglia mia saria contenta
   d'intender qual fortuna mi s'appressa:
   ché saetta prevista vien più lenta."   *27*
Così diss' io a quella luce stessa
   che pria m'avea parlato; e come volle
   Beatrice, fu la mia voglia confessa.   *30*
Né per ambage, in che la gente folle
   già s'inviscava pria che fosse anciso
   l'Agnel di Dio che le peccata tolle,   *33*
ma per chiare parole e con preciso
   latin rispuose quello amor paterno,
   chiuso e parvente del suo proprio riso: *36*
"La contingenza, che fuor del quaderno
   de la vostra matera non si stende,
   tutta è dipinta nel cospetto etterno;   *39*
necessità però quindi non prende
   se non come dal viso in che si specchia
   nave che per torrente giù discende.   *42*
Da indi, sì come viene ad orecchia
   dolce armonia da organo, mi viene
   a vista il tempo che ti s'apparecchia.   *45*
Qual si partio Ipolito d'Atene
   per la spietata e perfida noverca,
   tal di Fiorenza partir ti convene.   *48*

while I was in Virgil's company, up the moun-
tain that heals the souls, and while descend-
ing through the dead world, heavy words
were said to me about my future life, though
I feel myself truly foursquare against the
blows of chance; so that my will would be
well content to hear what fortune is drawing
near me, because an arrow foreseen comes
slower." Thus said I to that same light which
had spoken to me before, and, as Beatrice
willed, my wish was confessed.

In no dark sayings, such as those in which
the foolish folk of old once ensnared them-
selves, before the Lamb of God who takes
away sins was slain, but in clear words and
with precise discourse that paternal love re-
plied, hidden and revealed by his own smile,
"Contingency, which does not extend beyond
the volume of your material world, is all de-
picted in the Eternal Vision. Yet thence it
takes not necessity, any more than from the
eyes in which it is mirrored does a ship which
is going down the stream. Therefrom, even
as sweet harmony comes from an organ to the
ear, comes to my sight the time that is in
store for you. As Hippolytus departed from
Athens, by reason of his pitiless and perfidi-
ous stepmother, so from Florence must you
depart.

Questo si vuole e questo già si cerca,
   e tosto verrà fatto a chi ciò pensa
   là dove Cristo tutto dì si merca.   *51*

La colpa seguirà la parte offensa
   in grido, come suol; ma la vendetta
   fia testimonio al ver che la dispensa.   *54*

Tu lascerai ogne cosa diletta
   più caramente; e questo è quello strale
   che l'arco de lo essilio pria saetta.   *57*

Tu proverai sì come sa di sale
   lo pane altrui, e come è duro calle
   lo scendere e 'l salir per l'altrui scale.   *60*

E quel che più ti graverà le spalle,
   sarà la compagnia malvagia e scempia
   con la qual tu cadrai in questa valle;   *63*

che tutta ingrata, tutta matta ed empia
   si farà contr' a te; ma, poco appresso,
   ella, non tu, n'avrà rossa la tempia.   *66*

Di sua bestialitate il suo processo
   farà la prova; sì ch'a te fia bello
   averti fatta parte per te stesso.   *69*

Lo primo tuo refugio e 'l primo ostello
   sarà la cortesia del gran Lombardo
   che 'n su la scala porta il santo uccello;   *72*

ch'in te avrà sì benigno riguardo,
   che del fare e del chieder, tra voi due,
   fia primo quel che tra li altri è più tardo.   *75*

Con lui vedrai colui che 'mpresso fue,
   nascendo, sì da questa stella forte,
   che notabili fier l'opere sue.   *78*

So is it willed, so already plotted, and so shall
be accomplished soon by him who ponders
upon it in the place where every day Christ
is bought and sold. The blame, as always, will
follow the injured party, in outcry; but venge-
ance shall bear witness to the truth which
dispenses it. You shall leave everything be-
loved most dearly; and this is the arrow
which the bow of exile shoots first. You shall
come to know how salt is the taste of an-
other's bread, and how hard the path to de-
scend and mount by another man's stairs.
And that which shall most weigh your
shoulders down will be the evil and senseless
company with which you shall fall into this
vale; which shall then become all ungrateful,
all mad and malevolent against you, but, soon
after, their brows, not yours, shall redden for it.
Of their brutish folly their own conduct shall
afford the proof, so that it will be for your fair
fame to have made you a party by yourself.

"Your first refuge and first inn shall be
the courtesy of the great Lombard who bears
the holy bird upon the ladder, and he will
have for you such benign regard that, in do-
ing and in asking, between you two, that will
be first which between others is the slowest.
With him you shall see one who, at his birth,
was so stamped by this strong star, that nota-
ble shall be his deeds.

Non se ne son le genti ancora accorte
   per la novella età, ché pur nove anni
   son queste rote intorno di lui torte;   *81*
ma pria che 'l Guasco l'alto Arrigo inganni,
   parran faville de la sua virtute
   in non curar d'argento né d'affanni.   *84*
Le sue magnificenze conosciute
   saranno ancora, sì che ' suoi nemici
   non ne potran tener le lingue mute.   *87*
A lui t'aspetta e a' suoi benefici;
   per lui fia trasmutata molta gente,
   cambiando condizion ricchi e mendici;   *90*
e portera'ne scritto ne la mente
   di lui, e nol dirai"; e disse cose
   incredibili a quei che fier presente.   *93*
Poi giunse: "Figlio, queste son le chiose
   di quel che ti fu detto; ecco le 'nsidie
   che dietro a pochi giri son nascose.   *96*
Non vo' però ch'a' tuoi vicini invidie,
   poscia che s'infutura la tua vita
   via più là che 'l punir di lor perfidie."   *99*
Poi che, tacendo, si mostrò spedita
   l'anima santa di metter la trama
   in quella tela ch'io le porsi ordita,   *102*
io cominciai, come colui che brama,
   dubitando, consiglio da persona
   che vede e vuol dirittamente e ama: *105*
"Ben veggio, padre mio, sì come sprona
   lo tempo verso me, per colpo darmi
   tal, ch'è più grave a chi più s'abbandona;   *108*

Not yet have folk taken due note of him,
because of his young age, for these wheels
have revolved around him only nine years;
but before the Gascon deceives the lofty
Henry, some sparks of his virtue shall appear,
in his caring naught for money or for toils.
His magnificence shall hereafter be so known,
that his very foes will not be able to keep
silent tongues about him. Look you to him
and to his benefits. By him shall many folk
be changed, the rich and the beggarly altering
their condition. And you shall bear hence
written of him in your mind, but you shall
not tell it";—and he told things past the belief
even of those who shall see them. Then he
added, "Son, these are the glosses on what
was said to you; behold the snares which are
hidden behind but a few circlings. Yet I
would not have you envious of your neigh-
bors, since your life shall be prolonged far be-
yond the punishment of their perfidies."

When by his silence the holy soul showed
he had finished setting the woof across the
warp I had held out in readiness to him, I
began, as he who, in doubt, craves counsel of
one who sees and rightly wills and loves, "I
see well, my father, how time spurs toward me
to give me such a blow as is heaviest to who-
soever is most heedless;

per che di provedenza è buon ch'io m'armi,
sì che, se loco m'è tolto più caro,
io non perdessi li altri per miei carmi.   *111*
Giù per lo mondo sanza fine amaro,
e per lo monte del cui bel cacume
li occhi de la mia donna mi levaro,   *114*
e poscia per lo ciel, di lume in lume,
ho io appreso quel che s'io ridico,
a molti fia sapor di forte agrume;   *117*
e s'io al vero son timido amico,
temo di perder viver tra coloro
che questo tempo chiameranno antico."   *120*
La luce in che rideva il mio tesoro
ch'io trovai lì, si fé prima corusca,
quale a raggio di sole specchio d'oro;   *123*
indi rispuose: "Cosciènza fusca
o de la propria o de l'altrui vergogna
pur sentirà la tua parola brusca.   *126*
Ma nondimen, rimossa ogne menzogna,
tutta tua visïon fa manifesta;
e lascia pur grattar dov' è la rogna.   *129*
Ché se la voce tua sarà molesta
nel primo gusto, vital nodrimento
lascerà poi, quando sarà digesta.   *132*
Questo tuo grido farà come vento,
che le più alte cime più percuote;
e ciò non fa d'onor poco argomento.   *135*
Però ti son mostrate in queste rote,
nel monte e ne la valle dolorosa
pur l'anime che son di fama note,   *138*

wherefore it is good that I arm myself with foresight, so that if the dearest place be taken from me, I lose not all the rest by reason of my songs. Down in the world endlessly bitter, and upon the mountain from whose fair summit my lady's eyes uplifted me, and after, through the heavens from light to light, I have learned that which, if I tell again, will have for many a savor of great bitterness; and if I am a timid friend to the truth, I fear to lose life among those who shall call this time ancient."

The light wherein was smiling the treasure I had found there first became flashing as a golden mirror in the sun, then it replied, "A conscience dark, either with its own or with another's shame, will indeed feel your speech to be harsh. But none the less, all falsehood set aside, make manifest all that you have seen; and then let them scratch where the itch is. For if at first taste your voice be grievous, yet shall it leave thereafter vital nourishment when digested. This cry of yours shall do as does the wind, which smites most upon the loftiest summits; and this shall be no little cause of honor. Therefore only the souls known of fame have been shown to you within these wheels, upon the mountain, and in the woeful valley;

che l'animo di quel ch'ode, non posa
né ferma fede per essempro ch'aia
la sua radice incognita e ascosa,
né per altro argomento che non paia." 142

for the mind of him who hears rests not nor confirms its faith by an example that has its roots unknown or hidden, nor for other proof that is not manifest."

PARADISO

Già si godeva solo del suo verbo
    quello specchio beato, e io gustava
    lo mio, temprando col dolce l'acerbo;   *3*
e quella donna ch'a Dio mi menava
    disse: "Muta pensier; pensa ch'i' sono
    presso a colui ch'ogne torto disgrava."   *6*
Io mi rivolsi a l'amoroso suono
    del mio conforto; e qual io allor vidi
    ne li occhi santi amor, qui l'abbandono: *9*
non perch' io pur del mio parlar diffidi,
    ma per la mente che non può redire
    sovra sé tanto, s'altri non la guidi.   *12*
Tanto poss' io di quel punto ridire,
    che, rimirando lei, lo mio affetto
    libero fu da ogne altro disire,   *15*
fin che 'l piacere etterno, che diretto
    raggiava in Bëatrice, dal bel viso
    mi contentava col secondo aspetto.   *18*

CANTO XVIII

ALREADY THAT blessed mirror was enjoying only its own thoughts, and I was tasting mine, tempering the bitter with the sweet, when the lady who was leading me to God said, "Change your thought: consider that I am in His presence who lightens the burden of every wrong."

I turned round at the loving sound of my Comfort, and what love I then saw in the holy eyes I leave here untold; not only because I distrust my own speech, but because of memory, which cannot return on itself so far unless Another guide it. This much of that moment can I retell, that as I gazed upon her my affection was freed from every other desire so long as the Eternal Joy that shone direct on Beatrice satisfied me from the fair eyes with its reflected aspect.

Vincendo me col lume d'un sorriso,
    ella mi disse: "Volgiti e ascolta;
    ché non pur ne' miei occhi è paradiso."   *21*
Come si vede qui alcuna volta
    l'affetto ne la vista, s'elli è tanto,
    che da lui sia tutta l'anima tolta,   *24*
così nel fiammeggiar del folgór santo,
    a ch'io mi volsi, conobbi la voglia
    in lui di ragionarmi ancora alquanto.   *27*
El cominciò: "In questa quinta soglia
    de l'albero che vive de la cima
    e frutta sempre e mai non perde foglia,   *30*
spiriti son beati, che giù, prima
    che venissero al ciel, fuor di gran voce,
    sì ch'ogne musa ne sarebbe opima.   *33*
Però mira ne' corni de la croce:
    quello ch'io nomerò, lì farà l'atto
    che fa in nube il suo foco veloce."   *36*
Io vidi per la croce un lume tratto
    dal nomar Iosuè, com' el si feo;
    né mi fu noto il dir prima che 'l fatto.   *39*
E al nome de l'alto Macabeo
    vidi moversi un altro roteando,
    e letizia era ferza del paleo.   *42*
Così per Carlo Magno e per Orlando
    due ne seguì lo mio attento sguardo,
    com' occhio segue suo falcon volando.   *45*
Poscia trasse Guiglielmo e Rinoardo
    e 'l duca Gottifredi la mia vista
    per quella croce, e Ruberto Guiscardo.   *48*

Overcoming me with the light of a smile, she said to me, "Turn and listen, for not only in my eyes is Paradise."

As sometimes here the affection is seen in the countenance if it be such that all the mind is taken up by it, so in the flaming of the holy glow to which I turned I recognized his wish to have some further speech with me; and he began, "In this fifth tier of the tree, which has life from its top and is always in fruit and never sheds its leaves, are blessed spirits which below, before they came to heaven, were of such great renown that every Muse would be rich with them. Look, therefore, upon the horns of the cross: he whom I shall name there will do as in a cloud its swift fire does."

At the naming of Joshua, even as it was done, I saw a light drawn along the cross, nor was the word noted by me before the fact; and at the name of the great Maccabeus I saw another move, wheeling, and gladness was the whip of the top. So for Charlemagne and Roland my intent gaze followed two of them, as the eye follows its falcon as he flies; next William, and Renouard and Duke Godfrey drew my sight along that cross, and Robert Guiscard too.

Indi, tra l'altre luci mota e mista,
   mostrommi l'alma che m'avea parlato
   qual era tra i cantor del cielo artista.   *51*
Io mi rivolsi dal mio destro lato
   per vedere in Beatrice il mio dovere,
   o per parlare o per atto, segnato;   *54*
e vidi le sue luci tanto mere,
   tanto gioconde, che la sua sembianza
   vinceva li altri e l'ultimo solere.   *57*
E come, per sentir più dilettanza
   bene operando, l'uom di giorno in giorno
   s'accorge che la sua virtute avanza,   *60*
sì m'accors' io che 'l mio girare intorno
   col cielo insieme avea cresciuto l'arco,
   veggendo quel miracol più addorno.   *63*
E qual è 'l trasmutare in picciol varco
   di tempo in bianca donna, quando 'l volto
   suo si discarchi di vergogna il carco,   *66*
tal fu ne li occhi miei, quando fui vòlto,
   per lo candor de la temprata stella
   sesta, che dentro a sé m'avea ricolto.   *69*
Io vidi in quella giovïal facella
   lo sfavillar de l'amor che lì era
   segnare a li occhi miei nostra favella.   *72*
E come augelli surti di rivera,
   quasi congratulando a lor pasture,
   fanno di sé or tonda or altra schiera,   *75*
sì dentro ai lumi sante creature
   volitando cantavano, e faciensi
   or *D*, or *I*, or *L* in sue figure.   *78*

Then, moving and mingling among the other lights, the soul which had spoken with me showed me how great an artist it was among the singers of that heaven.

I turned to my right side, to see in Beatrice my duty, signified either by speech or by gesture, and I saw her eyes so clear, so joyful, that her aspect surpassed all it had been at other times, even the last. And as from feeling more delight in doing well, a man from day to day becomes aware that his virtue makes advance, so did I perceive that my circling round with the heaven had increased its arc, when I saw that miracle even more adorned. And such change as comes in a moment over the face of a pale lady, when her countenance frees itself from a burden of modest shame, was presented to my eyes when I turned, because of the whiteness of the temperate sixth star which had received me within itself.

I saw in that torch of Jove the sparkling of the love that was there, trace out our speech to my eyes; and as birds, risen from the shore, as if rejoicing together at their pasture, make of themselves now a round flock, now some other shape, so within the lights holy creatures were singing as they flew, and in their figures made of themselves now *D*, now *I*, now *L*.

Prima, cantando, a sua nota moviensi;
  poi, diventando l'un di questi segni,
  un poco s'arrestavano e taciensi.   *81*
O diva Pegasëa che li 'ngegni
  fai glorïosi e rendili longevi,
  ed essi teco le cittadi e ' regni,   *84*
illustrami di te, sì ch'io rilevi
  le lor figure com' io l'ho concette:
  paia tua possa in questi versi brevi!   *87*
Mostrarsi dunque in cinque volte sette
  vocali e consonanti; e io notai
  le parti sì, come mi parver dette.   *90*
"*DILIGITE IUSTITIAM,*" primai
  fur verbo e nome di tutto 'l dipinto;
  "*QUI IUDICATIS TERRAM,*" fur sezzai.   *93*
Poscia ne l'emme del vocabol quinto
  rimasero ordinate; sì che Giove
  pareva argento lì d'oro distinto.   *96*
E vidi scendere altre luci dove
  era il colmo de l'emme, e lì quetarsi
  cantando, credo, il ben ch'a sé le move.   *99*
Poi, come nel percuoter d'i ciocchi arsi
  surgono innumerabili faville,
  onde li stolti sogliono agurarsi,   *102*
resurger parver quindi più di mille
  luci e salir, qual assai e qual poco,
  sì come 'l sol che l'accende sortille;   *105*
e quïetata ciascuna in suo loco,
  la testa e 'l collo d'un'aguglia vidi
  rappresentare a quel distinto foco.   *108*

At first, as they sang, they moved to their own notes; then, as they became one of these characters, they stopped a little and were silent.

O divine Pegasea, who give glory unto men of genius and render them long-lived, as they, through you, the cities and the kingdoms, illumine me with yourself that I may set forth their shapes, as I have them in conception; let your power appear in these brief lines.

They displayed themselves then, in five times seven vowels and consonants; and I took note of the parts as they appeared in utterance to me. *DILIGITE IUSTITIAM* were the first verb and substantive of all the design; *QUI IUDICATIS TERRAM* were the last. Then, ordered in the *M* of the fifth word they stayed, so that Jove seemed silver in that place, pricked out with gold; and I saw other lights descending where the top of the *M* was, and become quiet there, singing, I believe, the Good that draws them to Itself. Then, as on the striking of burning logs there rise innumerable sparks, wherefrom the foolish are wont to draw auguries, so thence there seemed to rise again more than a thousand lights, and mount, some much, some little, even as the Sun which kindles them allotted them; and when each had rested in its place, I saw the head and the neck of an eagle represented by that patterned fire.

Quei che dipinge lì, non ha chi 'l guidi;
   ma esso guida, e da lui si rammenta
   quella virtù ch'è forma per li nidi.   *111*
L'altra bëatitudo, che contenta
   pareva prima d'ingigliarsi a l'emme,
   con poco moto seguitò la 'mprenta.   *114*
O dolce stella, quali e quante gemme
   mi dimostraro che nostra giustizia
   effetto sia del ciel che tu ingemme!   *117*
Per ch'io prego la mente in che s'inizia
   tuo moto e tua virtute, che rimiri
   ond' esce il fummo che 'l tuo raggio vizia;   *120*
sì ch'un'altra fïata omai s'adiri
   del comperare e vender dentro al templo
   che si murò di segni e di martìri.   *123*
O milizia del ciel cu' io contemplo,
   adora per color che sono in terra
   tutti svïati dietro al malo essemplo!   *126*
Già si solea con le spade far guerra;
   ma or si fa togliendo or qui or quivi
   lo pan che 'l pïo Padre a nessun serra.   *129*
Ma tu che sol per cancellare scrivi,
   pensa che Pietro e Paulo, che moriro
   per la vigna che guasti, ancor son vivi.   *132*
Ben puoi tu dire: "I' ho fermo 'l disiro
   sì a colui che volle viver solo
   e che per salti fu tratto al martiro,
ch'io non conosco il pescator né Polo."   *136*

He who there paints has none to guide Him, but He Himself does guide, and from Him is recognized that virtue which shapes nests. The rest of the blessed spirits, which at first seemed content to form a lily on the *M*, with a slight motion completed the design.

O sweet star, how many and how bright were the gems which made it plain to me that our justice is the effect of the heaven which you engem! Wherefore I pray the Mind, in which your motion and your virtue have their beginning, that It look on the place whence issues the smoke that dims your radiance, so that once again It may be wroth at the buying and the selling in the temple which made its walls of miracles and martyrdoms. O soldiery of Heaven whom I look upon, pray for all those who have gone astray on earth, following the ill example. Of old it was the wont to make war with swords, but now it is made by taking away, now here now there, the bread which the tender Father bars from none.

But you that write only to cancel, bethink you that Peter and Paul, who died for the vineyard that you are laying waste, are still alive. Though you indeed may say, "I have my desire so set on him who willed to live alone, and who, for a dance, was dragged to martyrdom, that I know not the Fisherman nor Paul."

PARADISO

Pᴀʀᴇᴀ ᴅɪɴᴀɴᴢɪ a me con l'ali aperte
la bella image che nel dolce *frui*
liete facevan l'anime conserte;   3
parea ciascuna rubinetto in cui
raggio di sole ardesse sì acceso,
che ne' miei occhi rifrangesse lui.   6
E quel che mi convien ritrar testeso,
non portò voce mai, né scrisse incostro,
né fu per fantasia già mai compreso;   9
ch'io vidi e anche udi' parlar lo rostro,
e sonar ne la voce e "io" e "mio,"
quand' era nel concetto e "noi" e "nostro."   12
E cominciò: "Per esser giusto e pio
son io qui essaltato a quella gloria
che non si lascia vincere a disio;   15
e in terra lasciai la mia memoria
sì fatta, che le genti lì malvage
commendan lei, ma non seguon la storia."   18

CANTO XIX

With outstretched wings appeared before me the beautiful image which those inter- woven souls, joyful in their sweet fruition, were making. Each of them seemed a little ruby on which a ray of sun should glow so enkindled as to reflect it into my eyes. And that which I must now tell, never did voice report nor ink record, nor was it ever com- prised by phantasy; for I saw and also heard the beak speaking, and uttering with its voice *I* and *Mine* when in conception it was *We* and *Our*. And it began, "For being just and duteous am I here exalted to that glory which cannot be surpassed by desire; and upon earth have I left such a memory that the wicked people there commend it, but follow not its story."

Così un sol calor di molte brage
  si fa sentir, come di molti amori
  usciva solo un suon di quella image.   *21*
Ond' io appresso: "O perpetüi fiori
  de l'etterna letizia, che pur uno
  parer mi fate tutti vostri odori,   *24*
solvetemi, spirando, il gran digiuno
  che lungamente m'ha tenuto in fame,
  non trovandoli in terra cibo alcuno.   *27*
Ben so io che, se 'n cielo altro reame
  la divina giustizia fa suo specchio,
  che 'l vostro non l'apprende con velame.   *30*
Sapete come attento io m'apparecchio
  ad ascoltar; sapete qual è quello
  dubbio che m'è digiun cotanto vecchio."   *33*
Quasi falcone ch'esce del cappello,
  move la testa e con l'ali si plaude,
  voglia mostrando e faccendosi bello,   *36*
vid' io farsi quel segno, che di laude
  de la divina grazia era contesto,
  con canti quai si sa chi là sù gaude.   *39*
Poi cominciò: "Colui che volse il sesto
  a lo stremo del mondo, e dentro ad esso
  distinse tanto occulto e manifesto,   *42*
non poté suo valor sì fare impresso
  in tutto l'universo, che 'l suo verbo
  non rimanesse in infinito eccesso.   *45*
E ciò fa certo che 'l primo superbo,
  che fu la somma d'ogne creatura,
  per non aspettar lume, cadde acerbo;   *48*

Thus one sole heat makes itself felt from many embers, even as from many loves one sole sound issued from that image.

And I then, "O perpetual flowers of the eternal bliss, who make all your odors seem to me but one, breathe forth and deliver me from the great fast which has long held me hungering, not finding any food for it on earth. Well do I know that if the Divine Justice makes another realm in heaven Its mirror, yours does not apprehend It through a veil. You know how eager I prepare myself to listen; you know what is that question which is so old a fast to me."

As the falcon which, issuing from the hood, moves his head and flaps his wings, showing his will and making himself fine, such did I see that ensign which was woven of praises of the Divine Grace become, with songs such as he knows who thereabove rejoices. Then it began, "He that turned His compass round the limit of the world, and within it marked out so much both hidden and revealed, could not so imprint His power on all the universe that His word should not remain in infinite excess; and this is certified by that first proud one, who was the highest of all creatures and who, through not awaiting light, fell unripe;

e quinci appar ch'ogne minor natura
è corto recettacolo a quel bene
che non ha fine e sé con sé misura.   *51*

Dunque vostra veduta, che convene
essere alcun de' raggi de la mente
di che tutte le cose son ripiene,   *54*

non pò da sua natura esser possente
tanto, che suo principio non discerna
molto di là da quel che l'è parvente.   *57*

Però ne la giustizia sempiterna
la vista che riceve il vostro mondo,
com' occhio per lo mare, entro s'interna;   *60*

che, ben che da la proda veggia il fondo,
in pelago nol vede; e nondimeno
èli, ma cela lui l'esser profondo.   *63*

Lume non è, se non vien dal sereno
che non si turba mai; anzi è tenèbra
od ombra de la carne o suo veleno.   *66*

Assai t'è mo aperta la latebra
che t'ascondeva la giustizia viva,
di che facei question cotanto crebra;   *69*

ché tu dicevi: 'Un uom nasce a la riva
de l'Indo, e quivi non è chi ragioni
di Cristo né chi legga né chi scriva;   *72*

e tutti suoi voleri e atti buoni
sono, quanto ragione umana vede,
sanza peccato in vita o in sermoni.   *75*

Muore non battezzato e sanza fede:
ov' è questa giustizia che 'l condanna?
ov' è la colpa sua, se ei non crede?'   *78*

from which it is plain that every lesser nature is too scant a vessel for that Good which has no limit and measures Itself by Itself. Thus your vision, which must needs be one of the rays of the Mind with which all things are replete, cannot of its own nature be of such power that it should not perceive its origin to be far beyond all that is apparent to it. Therefore the sight that is granted to your world penetrates within the Eternal Justice as the eye into the sea; which, though from the shore it can see the bottom, in the open sea it sees it not, and none the less it is there, but the depth conceals it. There is no light unless it comes from that serene which is never clouded, else is it darkness, either shadow of the flesh or its poison.

"Now is laid well open to you the hiding-place which concealed from you the living Justice concerning which you have made question so incessantly. For you said, 'A man is born on the bank of the Indus, and none is there to speak, or read, or write, of Christ, and all his wishes and acts are good, so far as human reason sees, without sin in life or in speech. He dies unbaptized, and without faith. Where is this justice which condemns him? Where is his sin if he does not believe?'

Or tu chi se', che vuo' sedere a scranna,
  per giudicar di lungi mille miglia
  con la veduta corta d'una spanna?   *81*
Certo a colui che meco s'assottiglia,
  se la Scrittura sovra voi non fosse,
  da dubitar sarebbe a maraviglia.   *84*
Oh terreni animali! oh menti grosse!
  La prima volontà, ch'è da sé buona,
  da sé, ch'è sommo ben, mai non si mosse.   *87*
Cotanto è giusto quanto a lei consuona:
  nullo creato bene a sé la tira,
  ma essa, radïando, lui cagiona."   *90*
Quale sovresso il nido si rigira
  poi c'ha pasciuti la cicogna i figli,
  e come quel ch'è pasto la rimira;   *93*
cotal si fece, e sì levä i cigli,
  la benedetta imagine, che l'ali
  movea sospinte da tanti consigli.   *96*
Roteando cantava, e dicea: "Quali
  son le mie note a te, che non le 'ntendi,
  tal è il giudicio etterno a voi mortali."   *99*
Poi si quetaro quei lucenti incendi
  de lo Spirito Santo ancor nel segno
  che fé i Romani al mondo reverendi,   *102*
esso ricominciò: "A questo regno
  non salì mai chi non credette 'n Cristo,
  né pria né poi ch'el si chiavasse al legno.   *105*
Ma vedi: molti gridan 'Cristo, Cristo!'
  che saranno in giudicio assai men *prope*
  a lui, che tal che non conosce Cristo;   *108*

Now who are you who would sit upon the seat to judge at a thousand miles away with the short sight that carries but a span? Assuredly, for him who subtilizes with me, if the Scriptures were not set over you, there would be marvelous occasion for questioning. O earthly animals! O gross minds! The primal Will, which of Itself is good, has never moved from Itself, which is the supreme Good. All is just that accords with It; no created good draws It to itself, but It, raying forth, is the cause of it."

As the stork circles over her nest, when she has fed her young, and as the one which she has fed looks up to her, such became (and I so raised my brows) the blessed image which, impelled by so many counsels, moved its wings. Wheeling it sang and said, "As are my notes to you who understand them not, such is the Eternal Judgment to you mortals."

After those glowing flames of the Holy Spirit became quiet, still in the sign which made the Romans reverend to the world, it began again, "To this realm none ever rose who believed not in Christ, either before or after he was nailed to the tree. But behold, many cry Christ, Christ, who, at the Judgment, shall be far less near to Him than he who knows not Christ;

e tai Cristian dannerà l'Etïòpe,
   quando si partiranno i due collegi,
   l'uno in etterno ricco e l'altro inòpe.   *111*

Che poran dir li Perse a' vostri regi,
   come vedranno quel volume aperto
   nel qual si scrivon tutti suoi dispregi?   *114*

Lì si vedrà, tra l'opere d'Alberto,
   quella che tosto moverà la penna,
   per che 'l regno di Praga fia diserto.   *117*

Lì si vedrà il duol che sovra Senna
   induce, falseggiando la moneta,
   quel che morrà di colpo di cotenna.   *120*

Lì si vedrà la superbia ch'asseta,
   che fa lo Scotto e l'Inghilese folle,
   sì che non può soffrir dentro a sua meta.   *123*

Vedrassi la lussuria e 'l viver molle
   di quel di Spagna e di quel di Boemme,
   che mai valor non conobbe né volle.   *126*

Vedrassi al Ciotto di Ierusalemme
   segnata con un i la sua bontate,
   quando 'l contrario segnerà un emme.   *129*

Vedrassi l'avarizia e la viltate
   di quei che guarda l'isola del foco,
   ove Anchise finì la lunga etate;   *132*

e a dare ad intender quanto è poco,
   la sua scrittura fian lettere mozze,
   che noteranno molto in parvo loco.   *135*

E parranno a ciascun l'opere sozze
   del barba e del fratel, che tanto egregia
   nazione e due corone han fatte bozze.   *138*

and the Ethiop will condemn such Christians when the two companies shall be separated, the one forever rich, and the other poor. What may the Persians say to your kings, when they shall see that volume open in which are recorded all their dispraises? There shall be seen, among the deeds of Albert, that which will soon set the pen in motion, by which the Kingdom of Prague shall be made a desert. There shall be seen the woe which he who shall die by a boarskin blow is bringing upon the Seine by falsifying the coin. There shall be seen the pride that quickens thirst, which makes the Scot and the Englishman mad, so that neither can keep within his own bounds. It will show the lechery and effeminate life of him of Spain, and him of Bohemia, who never knew valor nor wished it. It will show the Cripple of Jerusalem, his goodness marked with an *I*, while an *M* will mark the opposite. It will show the avarice and cowardice of him who has in ward the Isle of Fire where Anchises ended his long life; and to give to understand how paltry he is, the writing for him shall be in contractions that will note much in little space. And plain to all shall be revealed the foul deeds of his uncle and his brother, which have dishonored so eminent a lineage and two crowns.

E quel di Portogallo e di Norvegia
lì si conosceranno, e quel di Rascia
che male ha visto il conio di Vinegia. *141*

O beata Ungheria, se non si lascia
più malmenare! e beata Navarra,
se s'armasse del monte che la fascia! *144*

E creder de' ciascun che già, per arra
di questo, Niccosïa e Famagosta
per la lor bestia si lamenti e garra,
che dal fianco de l'altre non si scosta." *148*

And he of Portugal and he of Norway shall be known there, and he of Rascia, who, to his harm, has seen the coin of Venice.

"Oh happy Hungary, if she no longer allow herself to be maltreated! and happy Navarre, if she arm herself with the mountains which bind her round! And all should believe that, for earnest of this, Nicosia and Famagosta are now lamenting and complaining because of their beast who departs not from the side of the others."

PARADISO

Quando colui che tutto 'l mondo alluma
de l'emisperio nostro sì discende,
che 'l giorno d'ogne parte si consuma,   3
lo ciel, che sol di lui prima s'accende,
subitamente si rifà parvente
per molte luci, in che una risplende;   6
e questo atto del ciel mi venne a mente,
come 'l segno del mondo e de' suoi duci
nel benedetto rostro fu tacente;   9
però che tutte quelle vive luci,
vie più lucendo, cominciaron canti
da mia memoria labili e caduci.   12
O dolce amor che di riso t'ammanti,
quanto parevi ardente in que' flailli,
ch'avieno spirto sol di pensier santi!   15
Poscia che i cari e lucidi lapilli
ond' io vidi ingemmato il sesto lume
puoser silenzio a li angelici squilli,   18

CANTO XX

WHEN HE who illumines all the world descends from our hemisphere so that day on every side is spent, the heaven, which before is kindled by him alone, suddenly shows itself again with many lights wherein one alone is shining; and this change in the sky came to my mind when the ensign of the world and of its leaders became silent in the blessed beak; because all those living lights, shining far more brightly, began songs that have lapsed and fallen from my memory.

O sweet Love, that mantlest thyself in a smile, how glowing didst thou appear in those pipes that were filled only with the breath of holy thoughts!

When the bright and precious jewels wherewith I saw the sixth luminary engemmed had imposed silence on these angelic chimes,

udir mi parve un mormorar di fiume
   che scende chiaro giù di pietra in pietra,
   mostrando l'ubertà del suo cacume.   *21*

E come suono al collo de la cetra
   prende sua forma, e sì com' al pertugio
   de la sampogna vento che penètra,   *24*

così, rimosso d'aspettare indugio,
   quel mormorar de l'aguglia salissi
   su per lo collo, come fosse bugio.   *27*

Fecesi voce quivi, e quindi uscissi
   per lo suo becco in forma di parole,
   quali aspettava il core ov' io le scrissi.   *30*

"La parte in me che vede e pate il sole
   ne l'aguglie mortali," incominciommi,
   "or fisamente riguardar si vole,   *33*

perché d'i fuochi ond' io figura fommi,
   quelli onde l'occhio in testa mi scintilla,
   e' di tutti lor gradi son li sommi.   *36*

Colui che luce in mezzo per pupilla,
   fu il cantor de lo Spirito Santo,
   che l'arca traslatò di villa in villa: *39*

ora conosce il merto del suo canto,
   in quanto effetto fu del suo consiglio,
   per lo remunerar ch'è altrettanto.   *42*

Dei cinque che mi fan cerchio per ciglio,
   colui che più al becco mi s'accosta,
   la vedovella consolò del figlio: *45*

ora conosce quanto caro costa
   non seguir Cristo, per l'esperïenza
   di questa dolce vita e de l'opposta.   *48*

I seemed to hear the murmuring of a river which falls down clear from rock to rock, showing the abundance of its high source. And as the sound takes its form at the neck of the lute, and the wind at the vent of the pipe it fills, so, without keeping me waiting longer, that murmuring of the Eagle rose up through the neck, as if it were hollow. There it became voice, and thence it issued through the beak in the form of words such as the heart whereon I wrote them was awaiting.

"That part in me which in mortal eagles sees and endures the sun you must now gaze on intently," it began to me, "because, of the fires whereof I make my shape, those with which the eye in my head is sparkling are of all their ranks the chiefs. He that shines midmost, as the pupil, was the singer of the Holy Ghost, who bore the ark about from town to town. Now he knows the merit of his song, so far as it was the effect of his own counsel, by the reward which is proportioned to it. Of the five which make an arch for my brow, he who is nearest to my beak consoled the poor widow for her son. Now he knows, by experience of this sweet life and of the opposite, how dear it costs not to follow Christ.

E quel che segue in la circunferenza
   di che ragiono, per l'arco superno,
   morte indugiò per vera penitenza: *51*
ora conosce che 'l giudicio etterno
   non si trasmuta, quando degno preco
   fa crastino là giù de l'odïerno.   *54*
L'altro che segue, con le leggi e meco,
   sotto buona intenzion che fé mal frutto,
   per cedere al pastor si fece greco: *57*
ora conosce come il mal dedutto
   dal suo bene operar non li è nocivo,
   avvegna che sia 'l mondo indi distrutto.   *60*
E quel che vedi ne l'arco declivo,
   Guiglielmo fu, cui quella terra plora
   che piagne Carlo e Federigo vivo: *63*
ora conosce come s'innamora
   lo ciel del giusto rege, e al sembiante
   del suo fulgore il fa vedere ancora.   *66*
Chi crederebbe giù nel mondo errante
   che Rifëo Troiano in questo tondo
   fosse la quinta de le luci sante?   *69*
Ora conosce assai di quel che 'l mondo
   veder non può de la divina grazia,
   ben che sua vista non discerna il fondo."   *72*
Quale allodetta che 'n aere si spazia
   prima cantando, e poi tace contenta
   de l'ultima dolcezza che la sazia,   *75*
tal mi sembiò l'imago de la 'mprenta
   de l'etterno piacere, al cui disio
   ciascuna cosa qual ell' è diventa.   *78*

And he who follows on the circumference
whereof I speak, upon the upward arc, by true
penitence delayed death. Now he knows that
the eternal judgment is not changed when
worthy prayer there below makes tomorrow's
that which was today's. The next who fol-
lows, with a good intention which bore bad
fruit, made himself Greek, together with the
laws and me, in order to give place to the
Pastor. Now he knows how the evil derived
from his good action does not harm him,
even though the world should be destroyed
thereby. And him you see in the downward
arc was William, for whom that land mourns
that weeps on account of the living Charles
and Frederick. Now he knows how Heaven
is enamored of the righteous king, as by the
effulgence of his aspect he yet makes this evi-
dent. Who would believe, down in the erring
world, that Ripheus the Trojan was the fifth
of the holy lights in this circle? Now he
knows much of the divine grace that the
world cannot see, even though his sight dis-
cerns not the bottom."

Like the lark that soars in the air, first
singing, then silent, content with the last
sweetness that satiates it, so seemed to me the
image of the imprint of the Eternal Pleasure,
by whose will everything becomes that which
it is.

E avvegna ch'io fossi al dubbiar mio
   lì quasi vetro a lo color ch'el veste,
   tempo aspettar tacendo non patio,   *81*
ma de la bocca, "Che cose son queste?"
   mi pinse con la forza del suo peso:
   per ch'io di coruscar vidi gran feste.   *84*
Poi appresso, con l'occhio più acceso,
   lo benedetto segno mi rispuose
   per non tenermi in ammirar sospeso: *87*
"Io veggio che tu credi queste cose
   perch' io le dico, ma non vedi come;
   sì che, se son credute, sono ascose.   *90*
Fai come quei che la cosa per nome
   apprende ben, ma la sua quiditate
   veder non può se altri non la prome.   *93*
Regnum celorum vïolenza pate
   da caldo amore e da viva speranza,
   che vince la divina volontate: *96*
non a guisa che l'omo a l'om sobranza,
   ma vince lei perché vuole esser vinta,
   e, vinta, vince con sua beninanza.   *99*
La prima vita del ciglio e la quinta
   ti fa maravigliar, perché ne vedi
   la regïon de li angeli dipinta.   *102*
D'i corpi suoi non uscir, come credi,
   Gentili, ma Cristiani, in ferma fede
   quel d'i passuri e quel d'i passi piedi.   *105*
Ché l'una de lo 'nferno, u' non si riede
   già mai a buon voler, tornò a l'ossa;
   e ciò di viva spene fu mercede: *108*

And albeit there I was to my questioning like glass to the color that it clothes, yet would it not endure to bide its time in silence, but by its weight and pressure forced from my lips, "How can these things be?" At which I saw a great festival of flashing lights. And then, its eye kindling yet more, the blessed sign, not to keep me in suspense and amazement, replied, "I see that you believe these things because I tell them, but you see not the *how*, so that, though believed in, they are hidden. You do as one who well apprehends a thing by name, but may not see its quiddity unless another explain it. *Regnum celorum* suffers violence from fervent love and from living hope which vanquishes the Divine will: not as man overcomes man, but vanquishes it because it wills to be vanquished, and vanquished, vanquishes with its own benignity. The first soul of the eyebrow and the fifth make you marvel, because you see the region of the Angels decked with them. They came forth from their bodies not as you think, Gentiles, but Christians, with firm faith, the one in the Feet that were to suffer, the other in the Feet that had suffered. For the one came back to his bones from Hell, where none ever returns to right will; and this was the reward of living hope,

di viva spene, che mise la possa
    ne' prieghi fatti a Dio per suscitarla,
    sì che potesse sua voglia esser mossa.   *111*

L'anima glorïosa onde si parla,
    tornata ne la carne, in che fu poco,
    credette in lui che potëa aiutarla;   *114*

e credendo s'accese in tanto foco
    di vero amor, ch'a la morte seconda
    fu degna di venire a questo gioco.   *117*

L'altra, per grazia che da sì profonda
    fontana stilla, che mai creatura
    non pinse l'occhio infino a la prima onda,   *120*

tutto suo amor là giù pose a drittura:
    per che, di grazia in grazia, Dio li aperse
    l'occhio a la nostra redenzion futura;   *123*

ond' ei credette in quella, e non sofferse
    da indi il puzzo più del paganesmo;
    e riprendiene le genti perverse.   *126*

Quelle tre donne li fur per battesmo
    che tu vedesti da la destra rota,
    dinanzi al battezzar più d'un millesmo.   *129*

O predestinazion, quanto remota
    è la radice tua da quelli aspetti
    che la prima cagion non veggion *tota*!   *132*

E voi, mortali, tenetevi stretti
    a giudicar: ché noi, che Dio vedemo,
    non conosciamo ancor tutti li eletti;   *135*

ed ènne dolce così fatto scemo,
    perché il ben nostro in questo ben s'affina,
    che quel che vole Iddio, e noi volemo."   *138*

of living hope that gave power to the prayers made to God to raise him up, that it might be possible for his will to be moved. The glorious soul I tell of, having returned to the flesh for a short time, believed in Him that was able to help him; and, believing, was kindled to such a fire of true love that on his second death he was worthy to come to this rejoicing. The other, through grace that wells from a fountain so deep that never did creature thrust eye down to its first wave, set all his love below on righteousness; wherefore, from grace to grace, God opened his eye to our future redemption, so that he believed in it, and thenceforth endured not the stench of paganism, and reproved the perverse peoples for it. Those three ladies whom you saw by the right wheel stood for baptism to him more than a thousand years before baptizing.

"O predestination, how remote is thy root from the vision of those who see not the First Cause entire! And you mortals, keep yourselves restrained in judging; for we, who see God, know not yet all the elect. And to us such defect is sweet, because our good in this good is refined, that what God wills we also will."

Così da quella imagine divina,
   per farmi chiara la mia corta vista,
   data mi fu soave medicina.   *141*
E come a buon cantor buon citarista
   fa seguitar lo guizzo de la corda,
   in che più di piacer lo canto acquista,   *144*
sì, mentre ch'e' parlò, sì mi ricorda
   ch'io vidi le due luci benedette,
   pur come batter d'occhi si concorda,
con le parole mover le fiammette.   *148*

Thus, to make my short sight clear, sweet medicine was given to me by that divine image. And as a good lutanist makes the vibration of the string accompany a good singer, by which the song gains more pleasantness, so, I remember that, while it spoke, I saw the two blessed lights, just as the winking of the eyes concords, making their flames quiver to the words.

PARADISO

Già eran li occhi miei rifissi al volto
de la mia donna, e l'animo con essi,
e da ogne altro intento s'era tolto.   *3*
E quella non ridea; ma "S'io ridessi,"
mi cominciò, "tu ti faresti quale
fu Semelè quando di cener fessi: *6*
ché la bellezza mia, che per le scale
de l'etterno palazzo più s'accende,
com' hai veduto, quanto più si sale,   *9*
se non si temperasse, tanto splende,
che 'l tuo mortal podere, al suo fulgore,
sarebbe fronda che trono scoscende.   *12*
Noi sem levati al settimo splendore,
che sotto 'l petto del Leone ardente
raggia mo misto giù del suo valore.   *15*
Ficca di retro a li occhi tuoi la mente,
e fa di quelli specchi a la figura
che 'n questo specchio ti sarà parvente."   *18*

CANTO XXI

ALREADY MY eyes were fixed again on the face of my lady, and with them my mind, and from every other intent it was withdrawn; and she did not smile, but, "Were I to smile," she began to me, "you would become such as was Semele when she turned to ashes; for my beauty which, along the steps of the eternal palace, is kindled the more, as you have seen, the higher the ascent, were it not tempered, is so resplendent that your mortal powers at its flash would be like the bough shattered by a thunderbolt. We have risen to the seventh splendor which beneath the breast of the burning Lion rays down now mingled with its power. Fix your mind after your eyes, and make of them mirrors to the figure which in this mirror shall be shown to you."

Qual savesse qual era la pastura
   del viso mio ne l'aspetto beato
   quand' io mi trasmutai ad altra cura,   *21*
conoscerebbe quanto m'era a grato
   ubidire a la mia celeste scorta,
   contrapesando l'un con l'altro lato.   *24*
Dentro al cristallo che 'l vocabol porta,
   cerchiando il mondo, del suo caro duce
   sotto cui giacque ogne malizia morta,   *27*
di color d'oro in che raggio traluce
   vid' io uno scaleo eretto in suso
   tanto, che nol seguiva la mia luce.   *30*
Vidi anche per li gradi scender giuso
   tanti splendor, ch'io pensai ch'ogne lume
   che par nel ciel, quindi fosse diffuso.   *33*
E come, per lo natural costume,
   le pole insieme, al cominciar del giorno,
   si movono a scaldar le fredde piume;   *36*
poi altre vanno via sanza ritorno,
   altre rivolgon sé onde son mosse,
   e altre roteando fan soggiorno;   *39*
tal modo parve me che quivi fosse
   in quello sfavillar che 'nsieme venne,
   sì come in certo grado si percosse.   *42*
E quel che presso più ci si ritenne,
   si fé sì chiaro, ch'io dicea pensando:
   "Io veggio ben l'amor che tu m'accenne.   *45*
Ma quella ond' io aspetto il come e 'l quando
   del dire e del tacer, si sta; ond' io,
   contra 'l disio, fo ben ch'io non dimando."   *48*

He who should know what was the pasture of my sight in her blessed aspect, when I transferred me to another care, would recognize how much it rejoiced me to be obedient to my heavenly guide, weighing the one with the other side.

Within the crystal which bears the name, circling round the world, of its beloved leader beneath whom every wickedness lay dead, I saw, of the color of gold on which a sunbeam is shining, a ladder rising up so high that my sight might not follow it. I saw, moreover, so many splendors descending along the steps, that I thought every light which appears in heaven had been poured down from it.

And, as by their natural custom, the daws move about together, at the beginning of the day, to warm their cold feathers, then some fly away not to return, some wheel round to whence they had started, while others wheeling make a stay; such movements, it seemed to me, were in that sparkling, which came in a throng, as soon as it smote upon a certain step.

And that one which stopped nearest to us became so bright that in my thought I said, "I clearly perceive the love which you are signaling to me. But she from whom I await the how and the when of speech and of silence pauses, and therefore I, counter to desire, do well not to ask."

Per ch'ella, che vedëa il tacer mio
   nel veder di colui che tutto vede,
   mi disse: "Solvi il tuo caldo disio."   *51*
E io incominciai: "La mia mercede
   non mi fa degno de la tua risposta;
   ma per colei che 'l chieder mi concede,   *54*
vita beata che ti stai nascosta
   dentro a la tua letizia, fammi nota
   la cagion che sì presso mi t'ha posta;   *57*
e dì perché si tace in questa rota
   la dolce sinfonia di paradiso,
   che giù per l'altre suona sì divota."   *60*
"Tu hai l'udir mortal sì come il viso,"
   rispuose a me; "onde qui non si canta
   per quel che Bëatrice non ha riso.   *63*
Giù per li gradi de la scala santa
   discesi tanto sol per farti festa
   col dire e con la luce che mi ammanta;   *66*
né più amor mi fece esser più presta,
   ché più e tanto amor quinci sù ferve,
   sì come il fiammeggiar ti manifesta.   *69*
Ma l'alta carità, che ci fa serve
   pronte al consiglio che 'l mondo governa,
   sorteggia qui sì come tu osserve."   *72*
"Io veggio ben," diss' io, "sacra lucerna,
   come libero amore in questa corte
   basta a seguir la provedenza etterna;   *75*
ma questo è quel ch'a cerner mi par forte,
   perché predestinata fosti sola
   a questo officio tra le tue consorte."   *78*

Whereupon she, who saw my silence in His sight who sees all, said to me, "Loose your warm desire." And I began, "My own merit does not make me worthy of your answer, but for her sake who gives me leave to ask, O blessed life that are hidden within your own joy, make known to me the cause that has placed you so near me; and tell why in this wheel the sweet symphony of Paradise is silent, which below through the others so devoutly sounds."

"You have the hearing as the sight of mortals," it replied to me, "wherefore here is no song, for that same reason for which Beatrice has not smiled. Down by the steps of the sacred ladder I descended so far only to give you glad welcome with my speech and with the light that mantles me; nor was it greater love that made me swifter; for love as much and more is burning up there, even as the flaming manifests to you; but the high charity which makes us prompt servants of the counsel which governs the world allots here as you perceive."

"I see well," said I, "O holy lamp, how free love suffices in this Court for following the eternal Providence; but this is what seems to me hard to discern, why you alone among your consorts were predestined to this office."

Né venni prima a l'ultima parola,
   che del suo mezzo fece il lume centro,
   girando sé come veloce mola;   *81*
poi rispuose l'amor che v'era dentro:
   "Luce divina sopra me s'appunta,
   penetrando per questa in ch'io m'inventro,   *84*
la cui virtù, col mio veder congiunta,
   mi leva sopra me tanto, ch'i' veggio
   la somma essenza de la quale è munta.   *87*
Quinci vien l'allegrezza ond' io fiammeggio;
   per ch'a la vista mia, quant' ella è chiara,
   la chiarità de la fiamma pareggio.   *90*
Ma quell' alma nel ciel che più si schiara,
   quel serafin che 'n Dio più l'occhio ha fisso,
   a la dimanda tua non satisfara,   *93*
però che sì s'innoltra ne lo abisso
   de l'etterno statuto quel che chiedi,
   che da ogne creata vista è scisso.   *96*
E al mondo mortal, quando tu riedi,
   questo rapporta, sì che non presumma
   a tanto segno più mover li piedi.   *99*
La mente, che qui luce, in terra fumma;
   onde riguarda come può là giùe
   quel che non pote perché 'l ciel l'assumma."   *102*
Sì mi prescrisser le parole sue,
   ch'io lasciai la quistione e mi ritrassi
   a dimandarla umilmente chi fue.   *105*
"Tra ' due liti d'Italia surgon sassi,
   e non molto distanti a la tua patria,
   tanto che ' troni assai suonan più bassi,   *108*

Nor had I come to the last word when the light made a center of its middle, and spun round like a rapid millstone. Then answered the love that was therein, "A divine light is directed on me, penetrating through this wherein I embosom myself, the virtue of which, conjoined with my vision, lifts me above myself so far that I see the Supreme Essence from which it is drawn. From this comes the joy with which I am aflame, for to my sight, in the measure of its clearness, I match the clearness of my flame. But that soul in heaven which is most enlightened, that Seraph who has his eye most fixed on God, could not satisfy your question; for that which you ask lies so deep within the abyss of the eternal statute that it is cut off from every created vision. And when you return to the mortal world, carry this back, so that it may no longer presume to move its feet toward so great a goal. The mind, which shines here, on earth is smoky, and therefore think how it can do below that which it cannot do, though heaven raise it to itself."

His words so restrained me that I left the question and drew me back to ask it humbly who it was. "Between the two shores of Italy, and not very far from your native land, rise crags so high that the thunders sound far lower down;

e fanno un gibbo che si chiama Catria,
   di sotto al quale è consecrato un ermo,
   che suole esser disposto a sola latria." *111*
Così ricominciommi il terzo sermo;
   e poi, continüando, disse: "Quivi
   al servigio di Dio mi fe' sì fermo, *114*
che pur con cibi di liquor d'ulivi
   lievemente passava caldi e geli,
   contento ne' pensier contemplativi. *117*
Render solea quel chiostro a questi cieli
   fertilemente; e ora è fatto vano,
   sì che tosto convien che si riveli. *120*
In quel loco fu' io Pietro Damiano,
   e Pietro Peccator fu' ne la casa
   di Nostra Donna in sul lito adriano. *123*
Poca vita mortal m'era rimasa,
   quando fui chiesto e tratto a quel cappello,
   che pur di male in peggio si travasa. *126*
Venne Cefàs e venne il gran vasello
   de lo Spirito Santo, magri e scalzi,
   prendendo il cibo da qualunque ostello. *129*
Or voglion quinci e quindi chi rincalzi
   li moderni pastori e chi li meni,
   tanto son gravi, e chi di rietro li alzi. *132*
Cuopron d'i manti loro i palafreni,
   sì che due bestie van sott' una pelle:
   oh pazïenza che tanto sostieni!" *135*
A questa voce vid' io più fiammelle
   di grado in grado scendere e girarsi,
   e ogne giro le facea più belle. *138*

and they make a hump whose name is Catria, beneath which a hermitage is consecrated, which once was wholly given to worship." Thus it began again to me with its third speech; then continued, "There in the service of God I became so steadfast that with food seasoned only with olive-juice I passed easily through heats and frosts, content in contemplative thoughts. That cloister used to yield abundant harvest to these heavens, and now it is become so barren that soon it needs must be revealed. In that place was I Peter Damian, and in the House of Our Lady on the Adriatic shore I was Peter the Sinner. Little of mortal life was left to me when I was sought for and dragged to that hat which ever passes down from bad to worse. Cephas came, and the great vessel of the Holy Spirit came, lean and barefoot, taking their food at whatsoever inn. Now the modern pastors require one to prop them up on this side and one on that, and one to lead them, so heavy are they, and one to hold up their trains behind. They cover their palfreys with their mantles, so that two beasts go under one hide. O patience, that do endure so much!"

At these words I saw more flamelets from step to step descending, and whirling; and every whirl made them more beautiful.

Dintorno a questa vennero e fermarsi,
e fero un grido di sì alto suono,
che non potrebbe qui assomigliarsi;
né io lo 'ntesi, sì mi vinse il tuono.　　*142*

Round about this one they came, and stopped, and uttered a cry of such deep sound that nothing here could be likened to it; nor did I understand it, so did the thunder overcome me.

PARADISO

Oppresso di stupore, a la mia guida
  mi volsi, come parvol che ricorre
  sempre colà dove più si confida;   *3*
e quella, come madre che soccorre
  sùbito al figlio palido e anelo
  con la sua voce, che 'l suol ben disporre,   *6*
mi disse: "Non sai tu che tu se' in cielo?
  e non sai tu che 'l cielo è tutto santo,
  e ciò che ci si fa vien da buon zelo?   *9*
Come t'avrebbe trasmutato il canto,
  e io ridendo, mo pensar lo puoi,
  poscia che 'l grido t'ha mosso cotanto;   *12*
nel qual, se 'nteso avessi i prieghi suoi,
  già ti sarebbe nota la vendetta
  che tu vedrai innanzi che tu muoi.   *15*
La spada di qua sù non taglia in fretta
  né tardo, ma' ch'al parer di colui
  che disïando o temendo l'aspetta.   *18*

CANTO XXII

Overwhelmed with amazement, I turned
to my guide, like a little child who always
runs back to where it has most confidence;
and she, like a mother who quickly comforts
her pale and gasping son with her voice
which is wont to reassure him, said to me,
"Do you not know that you are in heaven, do
you not know that heaven is all holy, and
that whatever is done here comes of righteous
zeal? How the song, and I by smiling, would
have transmuted you, you can now conceive,
since this cry has so much moved you; where-
in, had you understood their prayers, already
would be known to you the vengeance which
you shall see before you die. The sword of
here on high cuts not in haste nor tardily,
save to his deeming who in longing or in fear
awaits it.

Ma rivolgiti omai inverso altrui;
  ch'assai illustri spiriti vedrai,
  se com' io dico l'aspetto redui."   21
Come a lei piacque, li occhi ritornai,
  e vidi cento sperule che 'nsieme
  più s'abbellivan con mutüi rai.   24
Io stava come quei che 'n sé repreme
  la punta del disio, e non s'attenta
  di domandar, sì del troppo si teme;   27
e la maggiore e la più luculenta
  di quelle margherite innanzi fessi,
  per far di sé la mia voglia contenta.   30
Poi dentro a lei udi': "Se tu vedessi
  com' io la carità che tra noi arde,
  li tuoi concetti sarebbero espressi.   33
Ma perché tu, aspettando, non tarde
  a l'alto fine, io ti farò risposta
  pur al pensier, da che sì ti riguarde.   36
Quel monte a cui Cassino è ne la costa
  fu frequentato già in su la cima
  da la gente ingannata e mal disposta;   39
e quel son io che sù vi portai prima
  lo nome di colui che 'n terra addusse
  la verità che tanto ci soblima;   42
e tanta grazia sopra me relusse,
  ch'io ritrassi le ville circunstanti
  da l'empio cólto che 'l mondo sedusse.   45
Questi altri fuochi tutti contemplanti
  uomini fuoro, accesi di quel caldo
  che fa nascere i fiori e ' frutti santi.   48

But turn now to the others, for you shall see many illustrious spirits, if you direct your sight as I say."

As was her pleasure, I turned my eyes, and I saw a hundred little spheres which together were making themselves beautiful with their mutual rays. I was standing as one who within himself represses the prick of his desire, who does not make bold to ask, he so fears to exceed. And the greatest and most shining of those pearls came forward to satisfy my desire concerning itself. Then within it I heard, "If you could see, as I do, the charity which burns among us, you would have uttered your thoughts; but lest you, by waiting, be delayed in your lofty aim, I will make answer to the thought itself about which you are so circumspect.

"That mountain on whose slope Cassino lies was of old frequented on its summit by the folk deceived and perverse, and I am he who first bore up there His name who brought to earth that truth which so uplifts us; and such grace shone upon me that I drew away the surrounding towns from the impious worship that seduced the world. These other fires were all contemplative men, kindled by that warmth which gives birth to holy flowers and fruits.

Qui è Maccario, qui è Romoaldo,
    qui son li frati miei che dentro ai chiostri
    fermar li piedi e tennero il cor saldo."   *51*
E io a lui: "L'affetto che dimostri
    meco parlando, e la buona sembianza
    ch'io veggio e noto in tutti li ardor vostri,   *54*
così m'ha dilatata mia fidanza,
    come 'l sol fa la rosa quando aperta
    tanto divien quant' ell' ha di possanza.   *57*
Però ti priego, e tu, padre, m'accerta
    s'io posso prender tanta grazia, ch'io
    ti veggia con imagine scoverta."   *60*
Ond' elli: "Frate, il tuo alto disio
    s'adempierà in su l'ultima spera,
    ove s'adempion tutti li altri e 'l mio.   *63*
Ivi è perfetta, matura e intera
    ciascuna disïanza; in quella sola
    è ogne parte là ove sempr' era,   *66*
perché non è in loco e non s'impola;
    e nostra scala infino ad essa varca,
    onde così dal viso ti s'invola.   *69*
Infin là sù la vide il patriarca
    Iacobbe porger la superna parte,
    quando li apparve d'angeli sì carca.   *72*
Ma, per salirla, mo nessun diparte
    da terra i piedi, e la regola mia
    rimasa è per danno de le carte.   *75*
Le mura che solieno esser badia
    fatte sono spelonche, e le cocolle
    sacca son piene di farina ria.   *78*

Here is Macarius, here is Romualdus, here are my brethren who stayed their feet within the cloisters and kept a steadfast heart."

And I to him, "The affection you show in speaking with me, and the good semblance which I see and note in all your ardors, have expanded my confidence as the sun does the rose when it opens to its fullest bloom. Therefore I pray you—and do you, father, assure me if I am capable of receiving so great a grace, that I may behold you in your uncovered shape."

Whereon he, "Brother, your high desire shall be fulfilled up in the last sphere, where are fulfilled all others and my own. There every desire is perfect, mature, and whole. In that alone is every part there where it always was, for it is not in space, nor has it poles; and our ladder reaches up to it, wherefore it steals itself from your sight. All the way thither the patriarch Jacob saw it stretch its upper part, when it appeared to him so laden with Angels. But no one now lifts his foot from earth to ascend it, and my Rule remains for waste of paper. The walls, which used to be an abbey, have become dens, and the cowls are sacks full of foul meal.

Ma grave usura tanto non si tolle
   contra 'l piacer di Dio, quanto quel frutto
   che fa il cor de' monaci sì folle;   81
ché quantunque la Chiesa guarda, tutto
   è de la gente che per Dio dimanda;
   non di parenti né d'altro più brutto.   84
La carne d'i mortali è tanto blanda,
   che giù non basta buon cominciamento
   dal nascer de la quercia al far la ghianda.   87
Pier cominciò sanz' oro e sanz' argento,
   e io con orazione e con digiuno,
   e Francesco umilmente il suo convento;   90
e se guardi 'l principio di ciascuno,
   poscia riguardi là dov' è trascorso,
   tu vederai del bianco fatto bruno.   93
Veramente Iordan vòlto retrorso
   più fu, e 'l mar fuggir, quando Dio volse,
   mirabile a veder che qui 'l soccorso."   96
Così mi disse, e indi si raccolse
   al suo collegio, e 'l collegio si strinse;
   poi, come turbo, in sù tutto s'avvolse.   99
La dolce donna dietro a lor mi pinse
   con un sol cenno su per quella scala,
   sì sua virtù la mia natura vinse;   102
né mai qua giù dove si monta e cala
   naturalmente, fu sì ratto moto
   ch'agguagliar si potesse a la mia ala.   105
S'io torni mai, lettore, a quel divoto
   trïunfo per lo quale io piango spesso
   le mie peccata e 'l petto mi percuoto,   108

But heavy usury is not exacted so counter to God's pleasure as that fruit which makes the heart of monks so mad; for whatsoever the Church has in keeping is all for the folk that ask it in God's name, not for kindred, or for other filthier thing. The flesh of mortals is so soft that on earth a good beginning does not last from the springing of the oak to the bearing of the acorn. Peter began his fellowship without gold or silver, and I mine with prayer and with fasting, and Francis his with humility; and if you look at the beginning of each, and then look again whither it has strayed, you will see. the white changed to dark. Nevertheless, Jordan driven back, and the sea fleeing when God willed, were sights more wondrous than the succor here."

Thus he spoke to me, then drew back to his company, and the company closed together; then like a whirlwind all were gathered upward. My sweet lady, with only a sign, thrust me up after them by that ladder, so did her power overcome my nature; nor ever here below, where we mount and descend by nature's law, was motion so swift as might match my flight. So may I return, reader, to that devout triumph for the sake of which I often bewail my sins and beat my breast,

tu non avresti in tanto tratto e messo
   nel foco il dito, in quant' io vidi 'l segno
   che segue il Tauro e fui dentro da esso.   *111*

O glorïose stelle, o lume pregno
   di gran virtù, dal quale io riconosco
   tutto, qual che si sia, il mio ingegno,   *114*

con voi nasceva e s'ascondeva vosco
   quelli ch'è padre d'ogne mortal vita,
   quand' io senti' di prima l'aere tosco;   *117*

e poi, quando mi fu grazia largita
   d'entrar ne l'alta rota che vi gira,
   la vostra regïon mi fu sortita.   *120*

A voi divotamente ora sospira
   l'anima mia, per acquistar virtute
   al passo forte che a sé la tira.   *123*

"Tu se' sì presso a l'ultima salute,"
   cominciò Bëatrice, "che tu dei
   aver le luci tue chiare e acute;   *126*

e però, prima che tu più t'inlei,
   rimira in giù, e vedi quanto mondo
   sotto li piedi già esser ti fei;   *129*

sì che 'l tuo cor, quantunque può, giocondo
   s'appresenti a la turba trïunfante
   che lieta vien per questo etera tondo."   *132*

Col viso ritornai per tutte quante
   le sette spere, e vidi questo globo
   tal, ch'io sorrisi del suo vil sembiante;   *135*

e quel consiglio per migliore approbo
   che l'ha per meno; e chi ad altro pensa
   chiamar si puote veramente probo.   *138*

you would not have drawn out and put your finger into the fire so quickly as I saw the sign which follows the Bull, and was within it.

O glorious stars, O light impregnated with mighty power, from which I derive all my genius, whatsoever it may be, with you was rising and with you was hiding himself he who is father of every mortal life when I first felt the air of Tuscany; and then, when the grace was bestowed on me to enter the lofty wheel that bears you round, your region was assigned to me! To you my soul now devoutly sighs, that it may acquire virtue for the hard pass which draws it to itself.

"You are so near to the final blessedness," Beatrice began, "that you must have your eyes clear and keen. And therefore, before you enter farther into it, look back downward and behold how great a world I have already set beneath your feet, in order that your heart may present itself, joyous to its utmost, to the triumphant throng which comes glad through this round ether."

With my sight I returned through all and each of the seven spheres, and saw this globe such that I smiled at its paltry semblance; and that counsel I approve as best which holds it for least, and he whose thought is turned elsewhere may be called truly upright.

Vidi la figlia di Latona incensa
    sanza quell' ombra che mi fu cagione
    per che già la credetti rara e densa.   *141*

L'aspetto del tuo nato, Iperïone,
    quivi sostenni, e vidi com' si move
    circa e vicino a lui Maia e Dïone.   *144*

Quindi m'apparve il temperar di Giove
    tra 'l padre e 'l figlio; e quindi mi fu chiaro
    il varïar che fanno di lor dove;   *147*

e tutti e sette mi si dimostraro
    quanto son grandi e quanto son veloci
    e come sono in distante riparo.   *150*

L'aiuola che ci fa tanto feroci,
    volgendom' io con li etterni Gemelli,
    tutta m'apparve da' colli a le foci;

poscia rivolsi li occhi a li occhi belli.   *154*

I saw the daughter of Latona glowing without that shade for which I once believed her rare and dense. The aspect of your son, Hyperion, I there endured, and saw how Maia and Dione move around and near him. Then appeared to me the tempering of Jove between his father and his son, and then was clear to me the varying they make in their position. And all the seven were displayed to me, how great they are and swift, and how distant each from other in location. The little threshing-floor which makes us so fierce was all revealed to me from hills to river-mouths, as I circled with the eternal Twins. Then to the beauteous eyes I turned my eyes again.

PARADISO

Come l'augello, intra l'amate fronde,
   posato al nido de' suoi dolci nati
   la notte che le cose ci nasconde,   *3*
che, per veder li aspetti disïati
   e per trovar lo cibo onde li pasca,
   in che gravi labor li sono aggrati,   *6*
previene il tempo in su aperta frasca,
   e con ardente affetto il sole aspetta,
   fiso guardando pur che l'alba nasca;   *9*
così la donna mïa stava eretta
   e attenta, rivolta inver' la plaga
   sotto la quale il sol mostra men fretta: *12*
sì che, veggendola io sospesa e vaga,
   fecimi qual è quei che disïando
   altro vorria, e sperando s'appaga.   *15*
Ma poco fu tra uno e altro quando,
   del mio attender, dico, e del vedere
   lo ciel venir più e più rischiarando;   *18*
e Bëatrice disse: "Ecco le schiere
   del trïunfo di Cristo e tutto 'l frutto
   ricolto del girar di queste spere!"   *21*

CANTO XXIII

As the bird, among the beloved leaves, hav-
ing sat on the nest of her sweet brood through
the night which hides things from us, who, in
order to look upon their longed-for aspect and
to find the food wherewith to feed them,
wherein her heavy toils are pleasing to her,
foreruns the time, upon the open bough, and
with glowing love awaits the sun, fixedly gaz-
ing for the dawn to break; so was my lady
standing, erect and eager, turned toward the
region beneath which the sun shows less
haste. I, therefore, seeing her in suspense and
longing, became as he who in desire would
fain have something else, and in hope is satis-
fied. But short was the time between the one
and the other *when*, of my waiting, I mean,
and of my seeing the heavens become more
and more resplendent. And Beatrice said, "Be-
hold the hosts of Christ's triumph and all the
fruit garnered from the circling of these
spheres!"

Pariemi che 'l suo viso ardesse tutto,
  e li occhi avea di letizia sì pieni,
  che passarmen convien sanza costrutto.   *24*
Quale ne' plenilunïi sereni
  Trivïa ride tra le ninfe etterne
  che dipingon lo ciel per tutti i seni,   *27*
vid' i' sopra migliaia di lucerne
  un sol che tutte quante l'accendea,
  come fa 'l nostro le viste superne;   *30*
e per la viva luce trasparea
  la lucente sustanza tanto chiara
  nel viso mio, che non la sostenea.   *33*
Oh Bëatrice, dolce guida e cara!
  Ella mi disse: "Quel che ti sobranza
  è virtù da cui nulla si ripara.   *36*
Quivi è la sapïenza e la possanza
  ch'aprì le strade tra 'l cielo e la terra,
  onde fu già sì lunga disïanza."   *39*
Come foco di nube si diserra
  per dilatarsi sì che non vi cape,
  e fuor di sua natura in giù s'atterra,   *42*
la mente mia così, tra quelle dape
  fatta più grande, di sé stessa uscìo,
  e che si fesse rimembrar non sape.   *45*
"Apri li occhi e riguarda qual son io;
  tu hai vedute cose, che possente
  se' fatto a sostener lo riso mio."   *48*
Io era come quei che si risente
  di visïone oblita e che s'ingegna
  indarno di ridurlasi a la mente,   *51*

It seemed to me her face was all aflame, and her eyes were so full of joy that I must needs pass it by undescribed.

As in the clear skies at the full moon Trivia smiles among the eternal nymphs that deck heaven through all its depths, I saw, above thousands of lamps, a Sun which kindled each one of them as does our own the things we see above; and through its living light the lucent Substance outglowed so bright upon my vision that it endured it not.

O Beatrice, sweet guide and dear! She said to me, "That which overcomes you is power against which naught defends itself. Therein are the wisdom and the power that opened the roads between Heaven and earth, for which of old there was such long desire."

Even as fire breaks from a cloud, because it dilates so that it has not room there, and contrary to its own nature, falls down to earth, so my mind, becoming greater amid those feasts, issued from itself, and of what it became has no remembrance.

"Open your eyes and look on what I am; you have seen things such that you are become able to sustain my smile." I was as one that wakes from a forgotten dream, and who strives in vain to bring it back to mind,

quand' io udi' questa proferta, degna
   di tanto grato, che mai non si stingue
   del libro che 'l preterito rassegna.   *54*
Se mo sonasser tutte quelle lingue
   che Polimnïa con le suore fero
   del latte lor dolcissimo più pingue,   *57*
per aiutarmi, al millesmo del vero
   non si verria, cantando il santo riso
   e quanto il santo aspetto facea mero;   *60*
e così, figurando il paradiso,
   convien saltar lo sacrato poema,
   come chi trova suo cammin riciso.   *63*
Ma chi pensasse il ponderoso tema
   e l'omero mortal che se ne carca,
   nol biasmerebbe se sott' esso trema: *66*
non è pareggio da picciola barca
   quel che fendendo va l'ardita prora,
   né da nocchier ch'a sé medesmo parca.   *69*
"Perché la faccia mia sì t'innamora,
   che tu non ti rivolgi al bel giardino
   che sotto i raggi di Cristo s'infiora?   *72*
Quivi è la rosa in che 'l verbo divino
   carne si fece; quivi son li gigli
   al cui odor si prese il buon cammino."   *75*
Così Beatrice; e io, che a' suoi consigli
   tutto era pronto, ancora mi rendei
   a la battaglia de' debili cigli.   *78*
Come a raggio di sol, che puro mei
   per fratta nube, già prato di fiori
   vider, coverti d'ombra, li occhi miei;   *81*

when I heard this proffer, worthy of such gratitude that it can never be effaced from the book which records the past.

Though all those tongues which Poly-hymnia and her sisters made most rich with their sweetest milk should sound now to aid me, it would not come to a thousandth part of the truth, in singing the holy smile, and how it lit up the holy aspect; and so, depict-ing Paradise, the sacred poem must needs make a leap, even as one who finds his way cut off. But whoso thinks of the ponderous theme and of the mortal shoulder which is laden therewith, will not blame it if it trem-ble beneath the load. It is no voyage for a little bark, this which my daring prow cleaves as it goes, nor for a pilot who would spare himself.

"Why does my face so enamor you that you turn not to the fair garden which blossoms beneath the rays of Christ? Here is the Rose wherein the Divine Word became flesh; here are the lilies by whose odor the good way was taken."

Thus Beatrice; and I who to her counsels was all eager, again gave myself up to the battle of the feeble brows.

As under the sun's ray, which streams pure through a broken cloud, ere now my eyes, sheltered by shade, have seen a meadow of flowers,

vid' io così più turbe di splendori,
   folgorate di sù da raggi ardenti,
   sanza veder principio di folgóri.   *84*
O benigna vertù che sì li 'mprenti,
   sù t'essaltasti per largirmi loco
   a li occhi lì che non t'eran possenti.   *87*
Il nome del bel fior ch'io sempre invoco
   e mane e sera, tutto mi ristrinse
   l'animo ad avvisar lo maggior foço;   *90*
e come ambo le luci mi dipinse
   il quale e il quanto de la viva stella
   che là sù vince come qua giù vinse,   *93*
per entro il cielo scese una facella,
   formata in cerchio a guisa di corona,
   e cinsela e girossi intorno ad ella.   *96*
Qualunque melodia più dolce suona
   qua giù e più a sé l'anima tira,
   parrebbe nube che squarciata tona,   *99*
comparata al sonar di quella lira
   onde si coronava il bel zaffiro
   del quale il ciel più chiaro s'inzaffira.   *102*
"Io sono amore angelico, che giro
   l'alta letizia che spira del ventre
   che fu albergo del nostro disiro;   *105*
e girerommi, donna del ciel, mentre
   che seguirai tuo figlio, e farai dia
   più la spera supprema perché li entre."   *108*
Così la circulata melodia
   si sigillava, e tutti li altri lumi
   facean sonare il nome di Maria.   *111*

so saw I many hosts of splendors glowed on from above by ardent rays, though I saw not whence came the glowings. O benign Power, which doth so imprint them, Thou didst ascend so as to yield place there for the eyes that were powerless before Thee!

The name of the fair flower which I ever invoke, both morning and evening, absorbed all my mind as I gazed on the greatest flame. And when on both of my eyes had been depicted the quality and the greatness of the living star which conquers up there even as down here it conquered, there descended through the heaven a torch which formed a circle in the likeness of a crown that girt her and wheeled about her. Whatever melody sounds sweetest here below and most draws to itself the soul, would seem a cloud which, being rent, thunders, compared with the sound of that lyre wherewith was crowned the beauteous sapphire by which the brightest heaven is ensapphired.

"I am angelic love, who circle the supreme joy that breathes from out the womb which was the hostelry of our Desire; and I shall circle, Lady of Heaven, until thou shalt follow thy Son, and make the supreme sphere more divine by entering it." Thus the circling melody sealed itself, and all the other lights made Mary's name resound.

Lo real manto di tutti i volumi
    del mondo, che più ferve e più s'avviva
    ne l'alito di Dio e nei costumi,   *114*
avea sopra di noi l'interna riva
    tanto distante, che la sua parvenza,
    là dov' io era, ancor non appariva: *117*
però non ebber li occhi miei potenza
    di seguitar la coronata fiamma
    che si levò appresso sua semenza.   *120*
E come fantolin che 'nver' la mamma
    tende le braccia, poi che 'l latte prese,
    per l'animo che 'nfin di fuor s'infiamma;   *123*
ciascun di quei candori in sù si stese
    con la sua cima, sì che l'alto affetto
    ch'elli avieno a Maria mi fu palese.   *126*
Indi rimaser lì nel mio cospetto,
    "Regina celi" cantando sì dolce,
    che mai da me non si partì 'l diletto.   . *129*
Oh quanta è l'ubertà che si soffolce
    in quelle arche ricchissime che fuoro
    a seminar qua giù buone bobolce!   *132*
Quivi si vive e gode del tesoro
    che s'acquistò piangendo ne lo essilio
    di Babillòn, ove si lasciò l'oro.   *135*
Quivi trïunfa, sotto l'alto Filio
    di Dio e di Maria, di sua vittoria,
    e con l'antico e col novo concilio,
colui che tien le chiavi di tal gloria.   *139*

The royal mantle of all the world's revolving spheres, which most burns and is most quickened in the breath of God and in His workings, had, above us, its inner shore so distant that sight of it, there where I was, was not yet possible to me. Therefore my eyes had not power to follow the crowned flame which mounted upward after her offspring. And as an infant which, when it has taken the milk, stretches its arms toward its mother, its affection glowing forth, each of these splendors stretched upward with its peak, so that the deep love they had for Mary was made plain to me. Then they remained there in my sight, singing *Regina celi* so sweetly that never has the delight departed from me. Oh, how great is the abundance which is heaped up in those rich coffers, who were good sowers here below! Here they live and rejoice in the treasure which was gained with tears in the exile of Babylon, where gold was scorned. Here, under the exalted Son of God and Mary, together with both the ancient and the new council, he triumphs in his victory who holds the keys of such glory.

PARADISO

"O SODALIZIO ELETTO a la gran cena
  del benedetto Agnello, il qual vi ciba
  sì, che la vostra voglia è sempre piena,   *3*
se per grazia di Dio questi preliba
  di quel che cade de la vostra mensa,
  prima che morte tempo li prescriba,   *6*
ponete mente a l'affezione immensa
  e roratelo alquanto: voi bevete
  sempre del fonte onde vien quel ch'ei pensa."   *9*
Così Beatrice; e quelle anime liete
  si fero spere sopra fissi poli,
  fiammando, volte, a guisa di comete.   *12*
E come cerchi in tempra d'orïuoli
  si giran sì, che 'l primo a chi pon mente
  quïeto pare, e l'ultimo che voli;   *15*
così quelle carole, differente-
  mente danzando, de la sua ricchezza
  mi faciéno stimar, veloci e lente.   *18*

CANTO XXIV

"O FELLOWSHIP elect to the great supper
of the blessed Lamb, who feeds you so that
your desire is ever satisfied, since by the grace
of God this man foretastes of that which falls
from your table before death appoint his
time to him, give heed to his immense long-
ing and bedew him somewhat: you drink
ever of the fountain whence flows that which
he thinks." Thus Beatrice; and those glad
souls made themselves spheres upon fixed
poles, flaming like comets, as they whirled.
And as wheels within the fittings of clocks
revolve, so that to one who gives heed the first
seems quiet and the last to fly, so did those
carols, dancing severally fast and slow, make
me judge of their riches.

Di quella ch'io notai di più carezza
   vid' ïo uscire un foco sì felice,
   che nullo vi lasciò di più chiarezza;   *21*
e tre fïate intorno di Beatrice
   si volse con un canto tanto divo,
   che la mia fantasia nol mi ridice.   *24*
Però salta la penna e non lo scrivo:
   chè l'imagine nostra a cotai pieghe,
   non che 'l parlare, è troppo color vivo.   *27*
"O santa suora mia che sì ne prieghe
   divota, per lo tuo ardente affetto
   da quella bella spera mi disleghe."   *30*
Poscia fermato, il foco benedetto
   a la mia donna dirizzò lo spiro,
   che favellò così com' i' ho detto.   *33*
Ed ella: "O luce etterna del gran viro
   a cui Nostro Segnor lasciò le chiavi,
   ch'ei portò giù, di questo gaudio miro,   *36*
tenta costui di punti lievi e gravi,
   come ti piace, intorno de la fede,
   per la qual tu su per lo mare andavi.   *39*
S'elli ama bene e bene spera e crede,
   non t'è occulto, perché 'l viso hai quivi
   dov' ogne cosa dipinta si vede;   *42*
ma perché questo regno ha fatto civi
   per la verace fede, a glorïarla,
   di lei parlare è ben ch'a lui arrivi."   *45*
Sì come il baccialier s'arma e non parla
   fin che 'l maestro la question propone,
   per approvarla, non per terminarla,   *48*

From the one I noted as the richest I saw issue a fire so joyful that it left there none of greater brightness; and it revolved three times round Beatrice with a song so divine that my phantasy does not repeat it to me; wherefore my pen leaps and I do not write it, for our imagination, not to say our speech, is of too vivid color for such folds.

"O holy sister mine, who do so devoutly pray to us, by your ardent affection you loose me from that fair sphere"; after it had stopped, the blessed fire breathed forth these words to my lady as I have told them.

And she, "O eternal light of the great man with whom our Lord left the keys, which He bore below, of this marvelous joy, test this man on points light and grave, as pleases you, concerning the Faith by which you did walk upon the sea. Whether he loves rightly and rightly hopes and believes is not hidden from you, for you have your vision where everything is seen depicted. But since this kingdom has made its citizens by the true faith, it rightly falls to him to speak of it, that he may glorify it."

Even as the bachelor arms himself—and does not speak until the master propounds the question—in order to adduce the proof, not to decide it,

così m'armava io d'ogne ragione
  mentre ch'ella dicea, per esser presto
  a tal querente e a tal professione.   *51*
"Dì, buon Cristiano, fatti manifesto:
  fede che è?" Ond' io levai la fronte
  in quella luce onde spirava questo;   *54*
poi mi volsi a Beatrice, ed essa pronte
  sembianze femmi perch' ïo spandessi
  l'acqua di fuor del mio interno fonte.   *57*
"La Grazia che mi dà ch'io mi confessi,"
  comincia' io, "da l'alto primipilo,
  faccia li miei concetti bene espressi."   *60*
E seguitai: "Come 'l verace stilo
  ne scrisse, padre, del tuo caro frate
  che mise teco Roma nel buon filo,   *63*
fede è sustanza di cose sperate
  e argomento de le non parventi;
  e questa pare a me sua quiditate."   *66*
Allora udi': "Dirittamente senti,
  se bene intendi perché la ripuose
  tra le sustanze, e poi tra li argomenti."   *69*
E io appresso: "Le profonde cose
  che mi largiscon qui la lor parvenza,
  a li occhi di là giù son sì ascose,   *72*
che l'esser loro v'è in sola credenza,
  sopra la qual si fonda l'alta spene;
  e però di sustanza prende intenza.   *75*
E da questa credenza ci convene
  silogizzar, sanz' avere altra vista:
  però intenza d'argomento tene."   *78*

so, while she was speaking, I was arming my-
self with every reason, to be ready for such a
questioner and for such a profession.

"Speak, good Christian, and declare your-
self: Faith, what is it?" Whereon I raised my
brow to that light whence this was breathed
forth, then I turned to Beatrice, who prompt-
ly signaled to me that I should pour the water
forth from my inward fountain.

"May the grace that grants me to confess to
the Chief Centurion," I began, "cause my
conceptions to be well expressed." And I went
on, "As the veracious pen of your dear brother
wrote of it, who with you, father, put Rome
on the good path, Faith is the substance of
things hoped for and the evidence of things
not seen; and this I take to be its quiddity."

Then I heard, "Rightly do you deem, if you
understand well why he placed it among the
substances and then among the evidences."

And I thereon, "The deep things which
grant to me here the sight of themselves are
so hidden to eyes below that there their exist-
ence is in belief alone, upon which the lofty
hope is founded; and therefore it takes the
designation of substance. And from this belief
needs must we reason, without seeing more:
therefore it receives the designation of evi-
dence."

Allora udi': "Se quantunque s'acquista
  giù per dottrina, fosse così 'nteso,
  non li avria loco ingegno di sofista."   *81*
Così spirò di quello amore acceso;
  indi soggiunse: "Assai bene è trascorsa
  d'esta moneta già la lega e 'l peso;   *84*
ma dimmi se tu l'hai ne la tua borsa."
  Ond' io: "Sì ho, sì lucida e sì tonda,
  che nel suo conio nulla mi s'inforsa."   *87*
Appresso uscì de la luce profonda
  che lì splendeva: "Questa cara gioia
  sopra la quale ogne virtù si fonda,   *90*
onde ti venne?" E io: "La larga ploia
  de lo Spirito Santo, ch'è diffusa
  in su le vecchie e 'n su le nuove cuoia,   *93*
è silogismo che la m'ha conchiusa
  acutamente sì, che 'nverso d'ella
  ogne dimostrazion mi pare ottusa."   *96*
Io udi' poi: "L'antica e la novella
  proposizion che così ti conchiude,
  perché l'hai tu per divina favella?"   *99*
E io: "La prova che 'l ver mi dischiude,
  son l'opere seguite, a che natura
  non scalda ferro mai né batte incude."   *102*
Risposto fummi: "Dì, chi t'assicura
  che quell' opere fosser? Quel medesmo
  che vuol provarsi, non altri, il ti giura."   *105*
"Se 'l mondo si rivolse al cristianesmo,"
  diss' io, "sanza miracoli, quest' uno
  è tal, che li altri non sono il centesmo: *108*

Then I heard, "If all that is acquired below for doctrine were thus understood, the wit of sophist would have no place there." These words were breathed forth from that enkindled love; and it continued, "Now the alloy and the weight of this coin have been well enough examined; but tell me if you have it in your purse?" And I, "Yes, I have it so shining and so round that in its stamp nothing is doubtful to me."

Then issued from the deep light that was shining there, "This precious jewel whereon every virtue is founded, whence did it come to you?"

And I, "The plenteous rain of the Holy Spirit which is poured over the old and over the new parchments is a syllogism that has proved it to me so acutely that, in comparison with this, every demonstration seems obtuse to me."

Then I heard, "That old and that new proposition which are so conclusive to you, why do you hold them for divine discourse?"

And I, "The proof which discloses the truth to me are the works that followed, for which nature never heats iron nor beats anvil."

"Tell me," came the reply, "who assures you that these works ever were? The very thing itself which requires to be proved, and naught else, affirms them to you."

"If the world turned to Christianity without miracles," I said, "that one is such that the rest are not the hundredth part;

ché tu intrasti povero e digiuno
in campo, a seminar la buona pianta
che fu già vite e ora è fatta pruno."   *111*
Finito questo, l'alta corte santa
risonò per le spere un "Dio laudamo"
ne la melode che là sù si canta.   *114*
E quel baron che sì di ramo in ramo,
essaminando, già tratto m'avea,
che a l'ultime fronde appressavamo,   *117*
ricominciò: "La Grazia, che donnea
con la tua mente, la bocca t'aperse
infino a qui come aprir si dovea,   *120*
sì ch'io approvo ciò che fuori emerse;
ma or convien espremer quel che credi,
e onde a la credenza tua s'offerse."   *123*
"O santo padre, e spirito che vedi
ciò che credesti sì, che tu vincesti
ver' lo sepulcro più giovani piedi,"   *126*
comincia' io, "tu vuo' ch'io manifesti
la forma qui del pronto creder mio,
e anche la cagion di lui chiedesti.   *129*
E io rispondo: Io credo in uno Dio
solo ed etterno, che tutto 'l ciel move,
non moto, con amore e con disio;   *132*
e a tal creder non ho io pur prove
fisice e metafisice, ma dalmi
anche la verità che quinci piove   *135*
per Moïsè, per profeti e per salmi,
per l'Evangelio e per voi che scriveste
poi che l'ardente Spirto vi fé almi;   *138*

for you entered the field poor and hungry, to sow the good plant which was once a vine and is now become a thorn."

This ended, the high and holy court resounded a *"Te Deum laudamus"* through the spheres, in the melody which up there is sung.

And that Baron who, thus from branch to branch examining, had now drawn me on so that we were approaching the last leaves, began again, "The Grace that holds amorous discourse with your mind, till now has opened your lips aright, so that I approve what has come from them; but now you must declare what you believe and whence it was offered to your belief."

"O holy father, spirit who see that which you did so believe that you, toward the sepulchre, did outdo younger feet," I began, "you would have me declare here the form of my ready belief, and also you have asked the cause of it. And I reply: I believe in one God, sole and eternal, who, unmoved, moves all the heavens with love and with desire; and for this belief I have not only proofs physical and metaphysical, but it is given to me also in the truth that rains down hence through Moses and the Prophets and the Psalms, through the Gospel, and through you who wrote when the fiery Spirit had made you holy.

e credo in tre persone etterne, e queste
  credo una essenza sì una e sì trina,
  che soffera congiunto 'sono' ed 'este.'   *141*
De la profonda condizion divina
  ch'io tocco mo, la mente mi sigilla
  più volte l'evangelica dottrina.   *144*
Quest' è 'l principio, quest' è la favilla
  che si dilata in fiamma poi vivace,
  e come stella in cielo in me scintilla."   *147*
Come 'l segnor ch'ascolta quel che i piace,
  da indi abbraccia il servo, gratulando
  per la novella, tosto ch'el si tace;   *150*
così, benedicendomi cantando,
  tre volte cinse me, sì com' io tacqui,
  l'appostolico lume al cui comando
io avea detto: sì nel dir li piacqui!   *154*

And I believe in three Eternal Persons, and these I believe to be one essence, so one and so threefold as to comport at once with *are* and *is*. With the profound divine state whereof I now speak, the evangelic doctrine many times sets the seal upon my mind. This is the beginning, this is the spark which then dilates to a living flame and like a star in heaven shines within me."

Even as the master who listens to that which pleases him, then embraces his servant, rejoicing in his news, as soon as he is silent; so, singing benedictions on me, the apostolic light at whose bidding I had spoken encircled me three times when I was silent, I so pleased him by my speech.

PARADISO

Se mai continga che 'l poema sacro
  al quale ha posto mano e cielo e terra,
  sì che m'ha fatto per molti anni macro,   *3*
vinca la crudeltà che fuor mi serra
  del bello ovile ov' io dormi' agnello,
  nimico ai lupi che li danno guerra;   *6*
con altra voce omai, con altro vello
  ritornerò poeta, e in sul fonte
  del mio battesmo prenderò 'l cappello;   *9*
però che ne la fede, che fa conte
  l'anime a Dio, quivi intra' io, e poi
  Pietro per lei sì mi girò la fronte.   *12*
Indi si mosse un lume verso noi
  di quella spera ond' uscì la primizia
  che lasciò Cristo d'i vicari suoi;   *15*
e la mia donna, piena di letizia,
  mi disse: "Mira, mira: ecco il barone
  per cui là giù si vicita Galizia."   *18*
Sì come quando il colombo si pone
  presso al compagno, l'uno a l'altro pande,
  girando e mormorando, l'affezione;   *21*

CANTO XXV

I<small>F EVER</small> it come to pass that the sacred poem to which heaven and earth have so set hand that it has made me lean for many years should overcome the cruelty which bars me from the fair sheepfold where I slept as a lamb, an enemy to the wolves which war on it, with changed voice now and with changed fleece a poet will I return, and at the font of my baptism will I take the crown; because there I entered into the Faith that makes souls known to God; and afterward Peter, for its sake, thus encircled my brow.

Then a light moved towards us from that circle whence had issued the first-fruit which Christ left of His vicars; and my lady, full of gladness, said to me, "Look! look! Behold the Baron for whose sake, down below, folk visit Galicia."

As when the dove alights beside its mate, and the one lavishes its affection on the other, circling it and cooing,

così vid' ïo l'un da l'altro grande
  principe glorïoso essere accolto,
  laudando il cibo che là sù li prande.   24
Ma poi che 'l gratular si fu assolto,
  tacito *coram me* ciascun s'affisse,
  ignito sì che vincëa 'l mio volto.   27
Ridendo allora Bëatrice disse:
  "Inclita vita per cui la larghezza
  de la nostra basilica si scrisse,   30
fa risonar la spene in questa altezza:
  tu sai, che tante fiate la figuri,
  quante Iesù ai tre fé più carezza."   33
"Leva la testa e fa che t'assicuri:
  ché ciò che vien qua sù del mortal mondo,
  convien ch'ai nostri raggi si maturi."   36
Questo conforto del foco secondo
  mi venne; ond' io leväi li occhi a' monti
  che li 'ncurvaron pria col troppo pondo.   39
"Poi che per grazia vuol che tu t'affronti
  lo nostro Imperadore, anzi la morte,
  ne l'aula più secreta co' suoi conti,   42
sì che, veduto il ver di questa corte,
  la spene, che là giù bene innamora,
  in te e in altrui di ciò conforte,   45
dì quel ch'ell' è, dì come se ne 'nfiora
  la mente tua, e dì onde a te venne."
  Così seguì 'l secondo lume ancora.   48
E quella pïa che guidò le penne
  de le mie ali a così alto volo,
  a la risposta così mi prevenne: 51

so did I see the one great and glorious prince received by the other, praising the food which feeds them thereabove. But when the joyful greeting was completed, each stopped silent *coram me*, so aflame that it overcame my sight. Then Beatrice, smiling, said, "Illustrious life, by whom the bounty of our Court was chronicled, make hope resound in this height; you can, who did figure it all those times when Jesus showed most favor to the three."

"Lift up your head and see that you reassure yourself, for that which comes up here from the mortal world must be ripened in our beams." This assurance came to me from the second fire; whereon I lifted up my eyes unto the hills which had bent them down before with excess of weight.

"Since, of His grace, our Emperor wills that you, before your death, come face to face with His Counts in His most secret hall, so that, having seen the truth of this Court, you may strengthen in yourself and others the Hope which there below rightly enamors, say what it is, and how your mind blossoms with it, and say whence it came to you." Thus the second light continued further.

And that compassionate one, who had guided the feathers of my wings to such lofty flight, anticipated my reply thus,

"La Chiesa militante alcun figliuolo
   non ha con più speranza, com' è scritto
   nel Sol che raggia tutto nostro stuolo: *54*
però li è conceduto che d'Egitto
   vegna in Ierusalemme per vedere,
   anzi che 'l militar li sia prescritto.   *57*
Li altri due punti, che non per sapere
   son dimandati, ma perch' ei rapporti
   quanto questa virtù t'è in piacere,   *60*
a lui lasc' io, ché non li saran forti
   né di iattanza; ed elli a ciò risponda,
   e la grazia di Dio ciò li comporti."   *63*
Come discente ch'a dottor seconda
   pronto e libente in quel ch'elli è esperto,
   perché la sua bontà si disasconda,   *66*
"Spene," diss' io, "è uno attender certo
   de la gloria futura, il qual produce
   grazia divina e precedente merto.   *69*
Da molte stelle mi vien questa luce;
   ma quei la distillò nel mio cor pria
   che fu sommo cantor del sommo duce.   *72*
'Sperino in te,' ne la sua tëodia
   dice, 'color che sanno il nome tuo':
   e chi nol sa, s'elli ha la fede mia?   *75*
Tu mi stillasti, con lo stillar suo,
   ne la pistola poi; sì ch'io son pieno,
   e in altrui vostra pioggia repluo."   *78*
Mentr' io diceva, dentro al vivo seno
   di quello incendio tremolava un lampo
   sùbito e spesso a guisa di baleno.   *81*

"The Church Militant has not any child possessed of more hope, as is written in the Sun which irradiates all our host; therefore is it granted him to come from Egypt to Jerusalem, that he may see, before his term of warfare is completed. The other two points which are asked, not for sake of knowing, but that he may report how greatly this virtue is pleasing to you, I leave to him, for they will not be difficult to him, nor of vainglory; and let him answer thereto, and may the grace of God concede this to him."

As the pupil who answers the teacher, ready and eager in that wherein he is expert, so that his worth may be disclosed, "Hope," I said, "is a sure expectation of future glory, which divine grace produces, and preceding merit. From many stars this light comes to me, but he first instilled it into my heart who was the supreme singer of the Supreme Leader. 'Let them hope in Thee who know Thy name,' he says in his divine song, and who knows it not, if he have my faith. You afterwards in your Epistle did instill it into me, together with his instilling, so that I am full, and pour again your shower upon others."

While I was speaking, within the living bosom of that fire trembled a flash, sudden and frequent, like lightning;

Indi spirò: "L'amore ond' ïo avvampo
   ancor ver' la virtù che mi seguette
   infin la palma e a l'uscir del campo,   *84*
vuol ch'io respiri a te che ti dilette
   di lei; ed emmi a grato che tu diche
   quello che la speranza ti 'mpromette."   *87*
E io: "Le nove e le scritture antiche
   pongon lo segno, ed esso lo mi addita,
   de l'anime che Dio s'ha fatte amiche.   *90*
Dice Isaia che ciascuna vestita
   ne la sua terra fia di doppia vesta:
   e la sua terra è questa dolce vita;   *93*
e 'l tuo fratello assai vie più digesta,
   là dove tratta de le bianche stole,
   questa revelazion ci manifesta."   *96*
E prima, appresso al fin d'este parole,
   "Sperent in te" di sopr' a noi s'udì;
   a che rispuoser tutte le carole.   *99*
Poscia tra esse un lume si schiarì
   sì che, se 'l Cancro avesse un tal cristallo,
   l'inverno avrebbe un mese d'un sol dì.   *102*
E come surge e va ed entra in ballo
   vergine lieta, sol per fare onore
   a la novizia, non per alcun fallo,   *105*
così vid' io lo schiarato splendore
   venire a' due che si volgieno a nota
   qual conveniesi al loro ardente amore.   *108*
Misesi lì nel canto e ne la rota;
   e la mia donna in lor tenea l'aspetto,
   pur come sposa tacita e immota.   *111*

then it breathed forth, "The love whereof I am still aflame toward that virtue which followed me even to the palm and the departure from the field wills that I breathe again to you, who do delight in it; and it is my pleasure that you tell that which Hope promises to you."

And I, "The new and the old Scriptures set up the token of the souls that God has made His friends, and this points it out to me. Isaiah says that each one shall be clothed in his own land with a double garment, and his own land is this sweet life; and your brother, where he treats of the white robes, makes manifest this revelation to us far more expressly."

At first, close on the end of these words, *"Sperent in te"* was heard above us, to which all the carols made answer; then one light among them shone out so bright that if the Crab had one such crystal, winter would have a month of one unbroken day. And as a glad maiden rises and goes and enters into the dance, only to do honor to the bride, not for any failing, so did I see the brightened splendor approach the two who were wheeling to such a song as befitted their burning love. It joined there in the singing and the wheeling, and my lady kept her gaze upon them, even as a bride silent and motionless.

"Questi è colui che giacque sopra 'l petto
   del nostro pellicano, e questi fue
   di su la croce al grande officio eletto."   *114*

La donna mia così; né però piùe
   mosser la vista sua di stare attenta
   poscia che prima le parole sue.   *117*

Qual è colui ch'adocchia e s'argomenta
   di vedere eclissar lo sole un poco,
   che, per veder, non vedente diventa;   *120*

tal mi fec' ïo a quell' ultimo foco
   mentre che detto fu: "Perché t'abbagli
   per veder cosa che qui non ha loco?   *123*

In terra è terra il mio corpo, e saragli
   tanto con li altri, che 'l numero nostro
   con l'etterno proposito s'agguagli.   *126*

Con le due stole nel beato chiostro
   son le due luci sole che saliro;
   e questo apporterai nel mondo vostro."   *129*

A questa voce l'infiammato giro
   si quïetò con esso il dolce mischio
   che si facea nel suon del trino spiro,   *132*

sì come, per cessar fatica o rischio,
   li remi, pria ne l'acqua ripercossi,
   tutti si posano al sonar d'un fischio.   *135*

Ahi quanto ne la mente mi commossi,
   quando mi volsi per veder Beatrice,
   per non poter veder, benché io fossi
presso di lei, e nel mondo felice!   *139*

"This is he who lay upon the breast of our Pelican, and this is he who was chosen from upon the Cross for the great office." Thus my lady; but no more after than before her words did she move her gaze from its fixed attention.

As is he who gazes and strains to see the sun a little eclipsed, and who through seeing becomes sightless, so did I become in respect to that last fire, till it was said, "Why do you dazzle yourself in order to see that which has here no place? On earth my body is earth, and there it shall be with the rest, until our number equals the eternal purpose. With the two robes in the blessed cloister are those two lights only which ascended; and this you shall carry back into your world."

At these words the flaming circle fell silent, together with the sweet mingling made within the sound of the trinal breath, even as, to avoid fatigue or danger, oars till then struck through the water, stop all at once at the sound of a whistle.

Ah! how greatly was I stirred in my mind when I turned to see Beatrice, at not being able to see, although I was near her, and in the world of bliss.

PARADISO

Mᴇɴᴛʀ' io dubbiava per lo viso spento,
  de la fulgida fiamma che lo spense
  uscì un spiro che mi fece attento,   *3*
dicendo: "Intanto che tu ti risense
  de la vista che haï in me consunta,
  ben è che ragionando la compense.   *6*
Comincia dunque; e dì ove s'appunta
  l'anima tua, e fa ragion che sia
  la vista in te smarrita e non defunta: *9*
perché la donna che per questa dia
  regïon ti conduce, ha ne lo sguardo
  la virtù ch'ebbe la man d'Anania."   *12*
Io dissi: "Al suo piacere e tosto e tardo
  vegna remedio a li occhi, che fuor porte
  quand' ella entrò col foco ond' io sempr' ardo.   *15*
Lo ben che fa contenta questa corte,
  Alfa e O è di quanta scrittura
  mi legge Amore o lievemente o forte."   *18*

CANTO XXVI

WHILE I WAS apprehensive because of my quenched sight, there issued forth from the effulgent flame that quenched it a breath that made me attentive, and it said, "Until you have again the sense of sight which you have consumed in me, it is well that you compensate it by discourse. Begin then, and say on what aim your soul is set; and be assured that your sight in you is confounded, not destroyed; for the lady who guides you through this divine region has in her look the power which the hand of Ananias had."

And I said, "At her good pleasure, soon or late, let succor come to the eyes which were the doors when she did enter with the fire wherewith I ever burn. The good which satisfies this Court is Alpha and Omega of all the scripture which Love reads to me, either low or loud."

Quella medesma voce che paura
  tolta m'avea del sùbito abbarbaglio,
  di ragionare ancor mi mise in cura;   *21*
e disse: "Certo a più angusto vaglio
  ti conviene schiarar: dicer convienti
  chi drizzò l'arco tuo a tal berzaglio."   *24*
E io: "Per filosofici argomenti
  e per autorità che quinci scende
  cotale amor convien che in me si 'mprenti: *27*
ché 'l bene, in quanto ben, come s'intende,
  così accende amore, e tanto maggio
  quanto più di bontate in sé comprende.   *30*
Dunque a l'essenza ov' è tanto avvantaggio,
  che ciascun ben che fuor di lei si trova
  altro non è ch'un lume di suo raggio,   *33*
più che in altra convien che si mova
  la mente, amando, di ciascun che cerne
  il vero in che si fonda questa prova.   *36*
Tal vero a l'intelletto mïo sterne
  colui che mi dimostra il primo amore
  di tutte le sustanze sempiterne.   *39*
Sternel la voce del verace autore,
  che dice a Moïsè, di sé parlando:
  'Io ti farò vedere ogne valore.'   *42*
Sternilmi tu ancora, incominciando
  l'alto preconio che grida l'arcano
  di qui là giù sovra ogne altro bando."   *45*
E io udi': "Per intelletto umano
  e per autoritadi a lui concorde
  d'i tuoi amori a Dio guarda il sovrano.   *48*

The same voice that had delivered me from my fear at the sudden dazzlement gave me concern to speak again; and it said, "Assuredly you must sift with a finer sieve: you must tell who directed your bow to such a target."

And I, "By philosophic arguments, and by authority that descends from here, such love must needs imprint itself on me; for the good, inasmuch as it is good, kindles love in proportion as it is understood, and so much the more the more of good it contains in itself. Therefore, to that Essence wherein is such supremacy that whatsoever good be found outside of It is naught else save a beam of Its own radiance, more than to any other must the mind be moved, in love, of whoever discerns the truth on which this proof is founded. Such a truth he makes plain to my intelligence who demonstrates to me the first love of all the eternal substances. The voice of the veracious Author makes it plain where, speaking of Himself, He says to Moses, 'I will make you see all goodness.' You also set it forth to me in the beginning of your sublime proclamation, which more than any other heralding, declares below the mystery of this place on high."

And I heard, "On the ground of human reason and of the authorities concordant with it, the highest of all your loves looks to God;

Ma dì ancor se tu senti altre corde
   tirarti verso lui, sì che tu suone
   con quanti denti questo amor ti morde."   *51*
Non fu latente la santa intenzione
   de l'aguglia di Cristo, anzi m'accorsi
   dove volea menar mia professione.   *54*
Però ricominciai: "Tutti quei morsi
   che posson far lo cor volgere a Dio,
   a la mia caritate son concorsi: *57*
ché l'essere del mondo e l'esser mio,
   la morte ch'el sostenne perch' io viva,
   e quel che spera ogne fedel com' io,   *60*
con la predetta conoscenza viva,
   tratto m'hanno del mar de l'amor torto,
   e del diritto m'han posto a la riva.   *63*
Le fronde onde s'infronda tutto l'orto
   de l'ortolano etterno, am' io cotanto
   quanto da lui a lor di bene è porto."   *66*
Sì com' io tacqui, un dolcissimo canto
   risonò per lo cielo, e la mia donna
   dicea con li altri: "Santo, santo, santo!"   *69*
E come a lume acuto si disonna
   per lo spirto visivo che ricorre
   a lo splendor che va di gonna in gonna,   *72*
e lo svegliato ciò che vede aborre,
   sì nescïa è la sùbita vigilia
   fin che la stimativa non soccorre;   *75*
così de li occhi miei ogne quisquilia
   fugò Beatrice col raggio d'i suoi,
   che rifulgea da più di mille milia: *78*

but tell me also if you feel other cords draw you toward Him, so that you declare with how many teeth this love grips you."

The holy intention of the Eagle of Christ was not hidden, indeed it was plain to me whither he would direct my profession. Therefore I began again, "All those things whose bite can make the heart turn to God have wrought together in my love; for the being of the world and my own being, the death that He sustained that I might live, and that which every believer hopes, as do I, with the living assurance of which I spoke, have drawn me from the sea of perverse love and placed me on the shore of right love. The leaves wherewith all the garden of the Eternal Gardener is enleaved I love in measure of the good borne unto them from Him."

As soon as I was silent a most sweet song resounded through the heaven, and my lady sang with the rest, "Holy, Holy, Holy!" And as sleep is broken by a piercing light when the visual spirit runs to meet the splendor that goes from tunic to tunic, and he who awakens shrinks from what he sees, so ignorant is his sudden wakening, until his judgment comes to his aid; thus Beatrice chased away every mote from my eyes with the radiance of her own, which shone more than a thousand miles;

onde mei che dinanzi vidi poi;
　　e quasi stupefatto domandai
　　d'un quarto lume ch'io vidi tra noi.　　　　*81*
E la mia donna: "Dentro da quei rai
　　vagheggia il suo fattor l'anima prima
　　che la prima virtù creasse mai."　　　　*84*
Come la fronda che flette la cima
　　nel transito del vento, e poi si leva
　　per la propria virtù che la soblima,　　　　*87*
fec' io in tanto in quant' ella diceva,
　　stupendo, e poi mi rifece sicuro
　　un disio di parlare ond' ïo ardeva.　　　　*90*
E cominciai: "O pomo che maturo
　　solo prodotto fosti, o padre antico
　　a cui ciascuna sposa è figlia e nuro,　　　　*93*
divoto quanto posso a te supplìco
　　perché mi parli: tu vedi mia voglia,
　　e per udirti tosto non la dico."　　　　*96*
Talvolta un animal coverto broglia,
　　sì che l'affetto convien che si paia
　　per lo seguir che face a lui la 'nvoglia;　　　　*99*
e similmente l'anima primaia
　　mi facea trasparer per la coverta
　　quant' ella a compiacermi venìa gaia.　　　　*102*
Indi spirò: "Sanz' essermi proferta
　　da te, la voglia tua discerno meglio
　　che tu qualunque cosa t'è più certa;　　　　*105*
perch' io la veggio nel verace speglio
　　che fa di sé pareglio a l'altre cose,
　　e nulla face lui di sé pareglio.　　　　*108*

so that I then saw better than before; and as one amazed I asked concerning a fourth light which I saw with us. And my lady, "Within those rays the first soul which the First Power ever created gazes with love upon its Maker."

As the bough which bends its top at passing of the wind, and then uplifts itself by its own virtue which raises it, so did I, in amazement, while she was speaking, and then a desire to speak, wherewith I was burning, gave me assurance again, and I began, "O fruit that were alone produced mature, O ancient father of whom every bride is daughter and daughter-in-law, devoutly as I can, I implore you that you speak to me: you see my wish, and that I may hear you sooner I do not tell it."

Sometimes an animal that is covered so stirs that its impulse must needs be apparent, since what envelops it follows its movements: in like manner that first soul showed me, through its covering, how joyously it came to do me pleasure. Then it breathed forth, "Without its being told to me by you, I discern your wish better than you whatever is most certain to you, for I see it in the truthful Mirror which makes of Itself a reflection of all else, while of It nothing makes itself the reflection.

Tu vuogli udir quant' è che Dio mi puose
  ne l'eccelso giardino, ove costei
  a così lunga scala ti dispuose,   *111*

e quanto fu diletto a li occhi miei,
  e la propria cagion del gran disdegno,
  e l'idïoma ch'usai e che fei.   *114*

Or, figliuol mio, non il gustar del legno
  fu per sé la cagion di tanto essilio,
  ma solamente il trapassar del segno.   *117*

Quindi onde mosse tua donna Virgilio,
  quattromilia trecento e due volumi
  di sol desiderai questo concilio;   *120*

e vidi lui tornare a tutt' i lumi
  de la sua strada novecento trenta
  fïate, mentre ch'ïo in terra fu'mi.   *123*

La lingua ch'io parlai fu tutta spenta
  innanzi che a l'ovra inconsummabile
  fosse la gente di Nembròt attenta: *126*

ché nullo effetto mai razïonabile,
  per lo piacere uman che rinovella
  seguèndo il cielo, sempre fu durabile.   *129*

Opera naturale è ch'uom favella;
  ma così o così, natura lascia
  poi fare a voi secondo che v'abbella.   *132*

Pria ch'i' scendessi a l'infernale ambascia,
  I s'appellava in terra il sommo bene
  onde vien la letizia che mi fascia;   *135*

e *El* si chiamò poi: e ciò convene,
  ché l'uso d'i mortali è come fronda
  in ramo, che sen va e altra vene.   *138*

You wish to know how long it is since God placed me in the lofty garden wherein this lady prepared you for so long a stair; and how long it was a delight to my eyes; and the true cause of the great wrath; and the idiom which I used and shaped. Now know, my son, that the tasting of the tree was not in itself the cause of so long an exile, but solely the overpassing of the bound. In the place whence your lady dispatched Virgil, I longed for this assembly during four thousand three hundred and two revolutions of the sun; and while I was on earth I saw him return to all the lights of his path nine hundred and thirty times. The tongue which I spoke was all extinct before the people of Nimrod attempted their unaccomplishable work; for never was any product of reason durable forever, because of human liking, which alters, following the heavens. That man should speak is nature's doing, but whether thus or thus, nature then leaves you to follow your own pleasure. Before I descended to the anguish of Hell the Supreme Good from whom comes the joy that swathes me was named *I* on earth; and later He was called *El*: and that must needs be, for the usage of mortals is as a leaf on a branch, which goes away and another comes.

Nel monte che si leva più da l'onda,
   fu' io, con vita pura e disonesta,
   da la prim' ora a quella che seconda,
   come 'l sol muta quadra, l'ora sesta."   *142*

On the mountain which rises highest from the sea I lived pure, then guilty, from the first hour to that which follows, when the sun changes quadrant, next upon the sixth.

PARADISO

"AL Padre, al Figlio, a lo Spirito Santo,"
  cominciò, "gloria!" tutto 'l paradiso,
  sì che m'inebrïava il dolce canto.   3
Ciò ch'io vedeva mi sembiava un riso
  de l'universo; per che mia ebbrezza
  intrava per l'udire e per lo viso.   6
Oh gioia! oh ineffabile allegrezza!
  oh vita intègra d'amore e di pace!
  oh sanza brama sicura ricchezza!   9
Dinanzi a li occhi miei le quattro face
  stavano accese, e quella che pria venne
  incominciò a farsi più vivace,   12
e tal ne la sembianza sua divenne,
  qual diverrebbe Iove, s'elli e Marte
  fossero augelli e cambiassersi penne.   15
La provedenza, che quivi comparte
  vice e officio, nel beato coro
  silenzio posto avea da ogne parte,   18

CANTO XXVII

"Glory be to the Father, to the Son, and to the Holy Spirit!" all Paradise began, so that the sweet song held me rapt. What I saw seemed to me a smile of the universe, so that my rapture entered both by hearing and by sight. O joy! O ineffable gladness! O life entire of love and of peace! O wealth secure without longing!

Before my eyes the four torches stood enkindled, and that which had come first began to make itself more vivid, and in its aspect became as would Jupiter if he and Mars were birds and should exchange plumage. The Providence which there assigns turn and office had imposed silence on the blessed choir on every side,

quand' ïo udi': "Se io mi trascoloro,
   non ti maravigliar, ché, dicend' io,
   vedrai trascolorar tutti costoro.   *21*
Quelli ch'usurpa in terra il luogo mio,
   il luogo mio, il luogo mio che vaca
   ne la presenza del Figliuol di Dio,   *24*
fatt' ha del cimitero mio cloaca
   del sangue e de la puzza; onde 'l perverso
   che cadde di qua sù, là giù si placa."   *27*
Di quel color che per lo sole avverso
   nube dipigne da sera e da mane,
   vid' ïo allora tutto 'l ciel cosperso.   *30*
E come donna onesta che permane
   di sé sicura, e per l'altrui fallanza,
   pur ascoltando, timida si fane,   *33*
così Beatrice trasmutò sembianza;
   e tale eclissi credo che 'n ciel fue
   quando patì la supprema possanza.   *36*
Poi procedetter le parole sue
   con voce tanto da sé trasmutata,
   che la sembianza non si mutò piùe: *39*
"Non fu la sposa di Çristo allevata
   del sangue mio, di Lin, di quel di Cleto,
   per essere ad acquisto d'oro usata;   *42*
ma per acquisto d'esto viver lieto
   e Sisto e Pïo e Calisto e Urbano
   sparser lo sangue dopo molto fleto.   *45*
Non fu nostra intenzion ch'a destra mano
   d'i nostri successor parte sedesse,
   parte da l'altra del popol cristiano;   *48*

when I heard, "If I change color, marvel not, for, as I speak, you shall see all these change color. He who on earth usurps my place, my place, my place, which in the sight of the Son of God is vacant, has made my burial-ground a sewer of blood and of stench, so that the Perverse One who fell from here above takes comfort there below."

With that color which, by reason of the opposite sun, paints the cloud at evening and at morning, I then saw the whole heaven overspread. And as a chaste lady who is sure of herself, and at another's fault, only hearing of it, becomes timid, so did Beatrice change her semblance; and such, I believe, was the eclipse in heaven when the Supreme Power suffered.

Then his words continued, in a voice so altered from itself that his looks were not more changed, "The spouse of Christ was not nurtured on my blood and that of Linus and of Cletus, to be employed for gain of gold; but for gain of this happy life Sixtus and Pius and Calixtus and Urban shed their blood after much weeping. It was not our purpose that one part of the Christian people should sit on the right of our successors, and one part on the left;

né che le chiavi che mi fuor concesse,
   divenisser signaculo in vessillo
   che contra battezzati combattesse;   51
né ch'io fossi figura di sigillo
   a privilegi venduti e mendaci,
   ond' io sovente arrosso e disfavillo.   54
In vesta di pastor lupi rapaci
   si veggion di qua sù per tutti i paschi:
   o difesa di Dio, perché pur giaci?   57
Del sangue nostro Caorsini e Guaschi
   s'apparecchian di bere: o buon principio,
   a che vil fine convien che tu caschi!   60
Ma l'alta provedenza, che con Scipio
   difese a Roma la gloria del mondo,
   soccorrà tosto, sì com' io concipio;   63
e tu, figliuol, che per lo mortal pondo
   ancor giù tornerai, apri la bocca,
   e non asconder quel ch'io non ascondo."   66
Sì come di vapor gelati fiocca
   in giuso l'aere nostro, quando 'l corno
   de la capra del ciel col sol si tocca,   69
in sù vid' io così l'etera addorno
   farsi e fioccar di vapor trïunfanti
   che fatto avien con noi quivi soggiorno.   72
Lo viso mio seguiva i suoi sembianti,
   e seguì fin che 'l mezzo, per lo molto,
   li tolse il trapassar del più avanti.   75
Onde la donna, che mi vide assolto
   de l'attendere in sù, mi disse: "Adima
   il viso e guarda come tu se' vòlto."   78

nor that the keys which were committed to
me should become the ensign on a banner
for warfare on the baptized; nor that I should
be made a figure on a seal to sold and lying
privileges, whereat I often blush and flash.
Rapacious wolves, in shepherd's garb, are seen
from here above in all the pastures: O defense
of God, wherefore dost thou yet lie still?
Cahorsines and Gascons make ready to drink
our blood. O good beginning, to what vile
ending must you fall! But the high Provi-
dence, which with Scipio defended for Rome
the glory of the world, will succor speedily, as
I conceive. And you, my son, who, because of
your mortal weight will again return below,
open your mouth and do not hide what I
hide not."

Even as our air, when the horn of the
heavenly Goat is touched by the sun, flakes
down frozen vapors, so I saw the ether thus
adorned, flaking upwards triumphal vapors
which had made sojourn with us there. My
sight was following their semblances, and fol-
lowed, till the intermediate space became so
great that it took from it the power of passing
farther onward. Whereon my lady, who saw
me freed from gazing upwards, said to me,
"Cast your sight down and see how far you
have revolved."

Da l'ora ch'ïo avea guardato prima
   i' vidi mosso me per tutto l'arco
   che fa dal mezzo al fine il primo clima;   *81*
sì ch'io vedea di là da Gade il varco
   folle d'Ulisse, e di qua presso il lito
   nel qual si fece Europa dolce carco.   *84*
E più mi fora discoverto il sito
   di questa aiuola; ma 'l sol procedea
   sotto i mie' piedi un segno e più partito.   *87*
La mente innamorata, che donnea
   con la mia donna sempre, di ridure
   ad essa li occhi più che mai ardea;   *90*
e se natura o arte fé pasture
   da pigliare occhi, per aver la mente,
   in carne umana o ne le sue pitture,   *93*
tutte adunate, parrebber nïente
   ver' lo piacer divin che mi refulse,
   quando mi volsi al suo viso ridente.   *96*
E la virtù che lo sguardo m'indulse,
   del bel nido di Leda mi divelse
   e nel ciel velocissimo m'impulse.   *99*
Le parti sue vivissime ed eccelse
   sì uniforme son, ch'i' non so dire
   qual Bëatrice per loco mi scelse.   *102*
Ma ella, che vedëa 'l mio disire,
   incominciò, ridendo tanto lieta,
   che Dio parea nel suo volto gioire: *105*
"La natura del mondo, che quïeta
   il mezzo e tutto l'altro intorno move,
   quinci comincia come da sua meta;   *108*

From the time when I had looked before, I saw that I had moved through the whole arc which the first climate makes from its middle to its end; so that, on the one hand, beyond Cadiz, I saw the mad track of Ulysses, and on the other nearly to the shore where Europa made herself a sweet burden; and more of the space of this little threshing-floor would have been disclosed to me, but the sun was proceeding beneath my feet and was a sign and more away.

My enamored mind, which ever pays court to my lady, was more than ever burning to bring back my eyes to her; and if nature or art ever made baits to take the eye so as to possess the mind, in human flesh or in its portraiture, all these together would seem as nothing beside the divine delight that glowed upon me when I turned to her smiling face. And the power which her look granted me drew me forth from the fair nest of Leda and thrust me into the swiftest of the heavens.

Its parts, most living and exalted, are so uniform that I cannot tell which of them Beatrice chose as a place for me. But she, who saw my longing, began, smiling so glad that God seemed to rejoice in her countenance, "The nature of the universe which holds the center quiet and moves all the rest around it, begins here as from its starting-point.

e questo cielo non ha altro dove
   che la mente divina, in che s'accende
   l'amor che 'l volge e la virtù ch'ei piove.   *111*

Luce e amor d'un cerchio lui comprende,
   sì come questo li altri; e quel precinto
   colui che 'l cinge solamente intende.   *114*

Non è suo moto per altro distinto,
   ma li altri son mensurati da questo,
   sì come diece da mezzo e da quinto;   *117*

e come il tempo tegna in cotal testo
   le sue radici e ne li altri le fronde,
   omai a te può esser manifesto.   *120*

Oh cupidigia, che i mortali affonde
   sì sotto te, che nessuno ha podere
   di trarre li occhi fuor de le tue onde!   *123*

Ben fiorisce ne li uomini il volere;
   ma la pioggia continüa converte
   in bozzacchioni le sosine vere.   *126*

Fede e innocenza son reperte
   solo ne' parvoletti; poi ciascuna
   pria fugge che le guance sian coperte.   *129*

Tale, balbuzïendo ancor, digiuna,
   che poi divora, con la lingua sciolta,
   qualunque cibo per qualunque luna;   *132*

e tal, balbuzïendo, ama e ascolta
   la madre sua, che, con loquela intera,
   disïa poi di vederla sepolta.   *135*

Così si fa la pelle bianca nera
   nel primo aspetto de la bella figlia
   di quel ch'apporta mane e lascia sera.   *138*

And this heaven has no other *Where* than the divine mind, wherein is kindled the love that revolves it, and the virtue which it rains down. Light and love enclose it in a circle, as it does the others, and this engirdment He alone who girds it understands. Its motion is not determined by another's, but the others are measured by this, just as ten by its half and its fifth. And how time should have its roots in such a flower-pot, and in the others its leaves, may now be manifest to you.

"O greed, who do so plunge mortals in your depths that none has power to lift his eyes from your waves! The will blossoms well in men, but the continual rain turns the sound plums into blighted fruit. Faith and innocence are found only in little children; then each flies away before the cheeks are covered. One, so long as he lisps, keeps the fasts, who afterward, when his tongue is free, devours any food through any month; and one, while he lisps, loves his mother and listens to her, who afterward, when his speech is full, longs to see her buried. Thus the white skin turns black at the first sight of the fair daughter of him that brings morning and leaves evening.

Tu, perché non ti facci maraviglia,
   pensa che 'n terra non è chi governi;
   onde si svïa l'umana famiglia.   *141*
Ma prima che gennaio tutto si sverni
   per la centesma ch'è là giù negletta,
   raggeran sì questi cerchi superni,   *144*
che la fortuna che tanto s'aspetta,
   le poppe volgerà u' son le prore,
   sì che la classe correrà diretta;
e vero frutto verrà dopo 'l fiore."   *148*

That you marvel not at this, consider that on earth there is no one to govern, wherefore the human family goes thus astray. But before January be all unwintered, because of the hundredth part that is neglected below, these lofty circles shall so shine forth that the storm which has been so long awaited shall turn round the sterns to where the prows are, so that the fleet shall run straight; and good fruit shall follow on the flower."

PARADISO

Poscia che 'ncontro a la vita presente
 d'i miseri mortali aperse 'l vero
 quella che 'mparadisa la mia mente,   *3*
come in lo specchio fiamma di doppiero
 vede colui che se n'alluma retro,
 prima che l'abbia in vista o in pensiero,   *6*
e sé rivolge per veder se 'l vetro
 li dice il vero, e vede ch'el s'accorda
 con esso come nota con suo metro;   *9*
così la mia memoria si ricorda
 ch'io feci riguardando ne' belli occhi
 onde a pigliarmi fece Amor la corda.   *12*
E com' io mi rivolsi e furon tocchi
 li miei da ciò che pare in quel volume,
 quandunque nel suo giro ben s'adocchi,   *15*
un punto vidi che raggiava lume
 acuto sì, che 'l viso ch'elli affoca
 chiuder conviensi per lo forte acume;   *18*
e quale stella par quinci più poca,
 parrebbe luna, locata con esso
 come stella con stella si collòca.   *21*

CANTO XXVIII

AFTER SHE who imparadises my mind had declared the truth counter to the present life of wretched mortals, as one who sees in a mirror the flame of a torch which is lighted behind him before he has it in sight or in thought, and turns round to see if the glass tells him the truth, and sees that it accords with it as a song with its measure, so my memory recalls that I did, gazing into the beautiful eyes wherewith Love made the cord to capture me. And when I turned and my own were met by what appears in that revolving sphere whenever one gazes intently on its circling, I saw a point which radiated a light so keen that the eye on which it blazes needs must close because of its great keenness; and whatever star seems smallest from here would seem a moon if placed beside it like a star with neighboring star.

Forse cotanto quanto pare appresso
   alo cigner la luce che 'l dipigne
   quando 'l vapor che 'l porta più è spesso,   *24*
distante intorno al punto un cerchio d'igne
   si girava sì ratto, ch'avria vinto
   quel moto che più tosto il mondo cigne;   *27*
e questo era d'un altro circumcinto,
   e quel dal terzo, e 'l terzo poi dal quarto,
   dal quinto il quarto, e poi dal sesto il quinto.   *30*
Sopra seguiva il settimo sì sparto
   già di larghezza, che 'l messo di Iuno
   intero a contenerlo sarebbe arto.   *33*
Così l'ottavo e 'l nono; e ciascheduno
   più tardo si movea, secondo ch'era
   in numero distante più da l'uno;   *36*
e quello avea la fiamma più sincera
   cui men distava la favilla pura,
   credo, però che più di lei s'invera.   *39*
La donna mia, che mi vedëa in cura
   forte sospeso, disse: "Da quel punto
   depende il cielo e tutta la natura.   *42*
Mira quel cerchio che più li è congiunto;
   e sappi che 'l suo muovere è sì tosto
   per l'affocato amore ond' elli è punto."   *45*
E io a lei: "Se 'l mondo fosse posto
   con l'ordine ch'io veggio in quelle rote,
   sazio m'avrebbe ciò che m'è proposto;   *48*
ma nel mondo sensibile si puote
   veder le volte tanto più divine,
   quant' elle son dal centro più remote.   *51*

Perhaps as near as a halo seems to girdle the light which paints it, when the vapor that bears it is most dense, at such distance around the point a circle of fire was whirling so rapidly that it would have surpassed that motion which most swiftly girds the universe; and this was girt around by another, and that by a third, and the third by a fourth, by a fifth the fourth, then by a sixth the fifth. Thereon the seventh followed, now spread so wide that the messenger of Juno entire would be too narrow to contain it. So the eighth and the ninth; and each was moving more slowly according as it was in number more distant from the unit. And that one had the clearest flame from which the pure spark was least distant, because, I believe, it partakes more of its truth.

My lady, who saw me eager and in great suspense, said, "On that point the heavens and all nature are dependent. Look on that circle which is most conjoined to it, and know that its motion is so swift because of the burning love whereby it is spurred."

And I to her, "If the universe were disposed in the order which I see in those wheels, that which is set before me would have satisfied me. But in the world of sense the revolutions may be seen so much the more divine as they are more remote from the center.

Onde, se 'l mio disir dee aver fine
  in questo miro e angelico templo
  che solo amore e luce ha per confine,   *54*
udir convienmi ancor come l'essemplo
  e l'essemplare non vanno d'un modo,
  ché io per me indarno a ciò contemplo."   *57*
"Se li tuoi diti non sono a tal nodo
  sufficïenti, non è maraviglia:
  tanto, per non tentare, è fatto sodo!"   *60*
Così la donna mia; poi disse: "Piglia
  quel ch'io ti dicerò, se vuo' saziarti;
  e intorno da esso t'assottiglia.   *63*
Li cerchi corporai sono ampi e arti
  secondo il più e 'l men de la virtute
  che si distende per tutte lor parti.   *66*
Maggior bontà vuol far maggior salute;
  maggior salute maggior corpo cape,
  s'elli ha le parti igualmente compiute.   *69*
Dunque costui che tutto quanto rape
  l'altro universo seco, corrisponde
  al cerchio che più ama e che più sape: *72*
per che, se tu a la virtù circonde
  la tua misura, non a la parvenza
  de le sustanze che t'appaion tonde,   *75*
tu vederai mirabil consequenza
  di maggio a più e di minore a meno,
  in ciascun cielo, a süa intelligenza."   *78*
Come rimane splendido e sereno
  l'emisperio de l'aere, quando soffia
  Borea da quella guancia ond' è più leno,   *81*

Wherefore if my desire is to attain to its end in this wondrous and angelic temple which has only love and light for its confine, needs must I further hear why the model and the copy go not in one fashion, for by myself I contemplate this in vain."

"If your fingers are insufficient for such a knot, it is no wonder, so hard has it become by not being tried." So said my lady, then she continued, "Take that which I shall tell you, if you would be satisfied, and sharpen your wits about it. The material spheres are wide or narrow according to the more or less of virtue which is diffused through all their parts. Greater goodness must needs work greater weal; and the greater body, if it has its parts equally complete, contains the greater weal. Hence this sphere, which sweeps along with it all the rest of the universe, corresponds to the circle which loves most and knows most. Wherefore, if you draw your measure round the virtue, not the semblance, of the substances which appear to you in circles, you will see a wondrous correspondence of greater to more and of smaller to less, in each heaven with respect to its Intelligence."

As the hemisphere of the air remains splendid and serene when Boreas blows from his milder cheek,

per che si purga e risolve la roffia
 che pria turbava, sì che 'l ciel ne ride
 con le bellezze d'ogne sua paroffia;   *84*
così fec''ïo, poi che mi provide
 la donna mia del suo risponder chiaro,
 e come stella in cielo il ver si vide.   *87*
E poi che le parole sue restaro,
 non altrimenti ferro disfavilla
 che bolle, come i cerchi sfavillaro.   *90*
L'incendio suo seguiva ogne scintilla;
 ed eran tante, che 'l numero loro
 più che 'l doppiar de li scacchi s'inmilla.   *93*
Io sentiva osannar di coro in coro
 al punto fisso che li tiene a li *ubi*,
 e terrà sempre, ne' quai sempre fuoro.   *96*
E quella che vedëa i pensier dubi
 ne la mia mente, disse: "I cerchi primi
 t'hanno mostrato Serafi e Cherubi.   *99*
Così veloci seguono i suoi vimi,
 per somigliarsi al punto quanto ponno;
 e posson quanto a veder son soblimi.   *102*
Quelli altri amori che 'ntorno li vonno,
 si chiaman Troni del divino aspetto,
 per che 'l primo ternaro terminonno;   *105*
e dei saper che tutti hanno diletto
 quanto la sua veduta si profonda
 nel vero in che si queta ogne intelletto.   *108*
Quinci si può veder come si fonda
 l'esser beato ne l'atto che vede,
 non in quel ch'ama, che poscia seconda;   *111*

whereby the obscuring mist is cleared and dis-
solved, so that the heaven smiles to us with
the beauties of its every region, so I became
after my lady had provided me with her clear
answer, and like a star in heaven the truth
was seen.

And when she had paused in her speech,
not otherwise does molten iron throw out
sparks than the circles sparkled. Each spark
kept to its fiery ring, and they were so many
that their number stretches to more thousands
than the doubling of the chessboard. I heard
Hosannah sung from choir to choir to the
fixed point that holds them, and will forever
hold them at the *Ubi* in which they have ever
been. And she, who saw the questioning
thoughts within my mind, said, "The first
circles have shown to you the Seraphim and
the Cherubim. Thus swiftly they follow their
bonds, in order to liken themselves to the
point as most they can, and they can in pro-
portion as they are exalted in vision. Those
other loves who go round them are called
Thrones of the divine aspect, because they
terminated the first triad. And you should
know that all have delight in the measure of
the depth to which their sight penetrates the
Truth in which every intellect finds rest;
from which it may be seen that the state of
blessedness is founded on the act of vision,
not on that which loves, which follows after;

e del vedere è misura mercede,
  che grazia partorisce e buona voglia:
  così di grado in grado si procede.   *114*
L'altro ternaro, che così germoglia
  in questa primavera sempiterna
  che notturno Arïete non dispoglia,   *117*
perpetüalemente 'Osanna' sberna
  con tre melode, che suonano in tree
  ordini di letizia onde s'interna.   *120*
In essa gerarcia son l'altre dee:
  prima Dominazioni, e poi Virtudi;
  l'ordine terzo di Podestadi èe.   *123*
Poscia ne' due penultimi tripudi
  Principati e Arcangeli si girano;
  l'ultimo è tutto d'Angelici ludi.   *126*
Questi ordini di sù tutti s'ammirano,
  e di giù vincon sì, che verso Dio
  tutti tirati sono e tutti tirano.   *129*
E Dïonisio con tanto disio
  a contemplar questi ordini si mise,
  che li nomò e distinse com' io.   *132*
Ma Gregorio da lui poi si divise;
  onde, sì tosto come li occhi aperse
  in questo ciel, di sé medesmo rise.   *135*
E se tanto secreto ver proferse
  mortale in terra, non voglio ch'ammiri:
  ché chi 'l vide qua sù gliel discoperse
con altro assai del ver di questi giri."   *139*

and the merit, to which grace and good will give birth, is the measure of their vision; thus, from grade to grade the progression goes.

"The next triad that thus flowers in this eternal spring which nightly Aries does not despoil perpetually sings Hosannah with three melodies which sound in the three orders of bliss that form the triad. In this hierarchy are the next divinities, first Dominions, then Virtues; and the third are Powers. Then in the two penultimate dances, the Principalities and Archangels circle; the last is wholly of Angelic sports. These orders all gaze upward and prevail downward, so that toward God all are drawn, and all do draw. And Dionysius with such great desire set himself to contemplate these orders that he named and distinguished them, as I: but Gregory afterward differed from him, wherefore, as soon as he opened his eyes in this heaven, he smiled at himself. And if a mortal declared on earth so much of secret truth, I would not have you wonder, for he who saw it here on high disclosed it to him, with much else of the truth about these circles."

PARADISO

Quando ambedue li figli di Latona,
   coperti del Montone e de la Libra,
   fanno de l'orizzonte insieme zona,   *3*
quant' è dal punto che 'l cenìt inlibra
   infin che l'uno e l'altro da quel cinto,
   cambiando l'emisperio, si dilibra,   *6*
tanto, col volto di riso dipinto,
   si tacque Bëatrice, riguardando
   fiso nel punto che m'avëa vinto.   *9*
Poi cominciò: "Io dico, e non dimando,
   quel che tu vuoli udir, perch' io l'ho visto
   là 've s'appunta ogne *ubi* e ogne *quando*.   *12*
Non per aver a sé di bene acquisto,
   ch'esser non può, ma perché suo splendore
   potesse, risplendendo, dir '*Subsisto*,'   *15*
in sua etternità di tempo fore,
   fuor d'ogne altro comprender, come i piacque,
   s'aperse in nuovi amor l'etterno amore.   *18*

CANTO XXIX

WHEN THE two children of Latona, covered by the Ram and by the Scales, make the horizon their belt at one same moment, as long as from the instant when the zenith holds them balanced till the one and the other, changing hemispheres, are unbalanced from that belt, for so long, her face illumined with a smile, was Beatrice silent, looking fixedly at the point which had overcome me. Then she began, "I tell, not ask, what you wish to hear, for I have seen it there where every *ubi* and every *quando* is centered. Not for gain of good unto Himself, which cannot be, but that His splendor might, in resplendence, say, *'Subsisto'*—in His eternity beyond time, beyond every other bound, as it pleased Him, the Eternal Love opened into new loves.

Né prima quasi torpente si giacque;
   ché né prima né poscia procedette
   lo discorrer di Dio sovra quest' acque.   *21*
Forma e materia, congiunte e purette,
   usciro ad esser che non avia fallo,
   come d'arco tricordo tre saette.   *24*
E come in vetro, in ambra o in cristallo
   raggio resplende sì, che dal venire
   a l'esser tutto non è intervallo,   *27*
così 'l triforme effetto del suo sire
   ne l'esser suo raggiò insieme tutto
   sanza distinzïone in essordire.   *30*
Concreato fu ordine e costrutto
   a le sustanze; e quelle furon cima
   nel mondo in che puro atto fu produtto;   *33*
pura potenza tenne la parte ima;
   nel mezzo strinse potenza con atto
   tal vime, che già mai non si divima.   *36*
Ieronimo vi scrisse lungo tratto
   di secoli de li angeli creati
   anzi che l'altro mondo fosse fatto;   *39*
ma questo vero è scritto in molti lati
   da li scrittor de lo Spirito Santo,
   e tu te n'avvedrai se bene agguati;   *42*
e anche la ragione il vede alquanto,
   che non concederebbe che ' motori
   sanza sua perfezion fosser cotanto.   *45*
Or sai tu dove e quando questi amori
   furon creati e come: sì che spenti
   nel tuo disïo già son tre ardori.   *48*

Nor before, as if inert, did He lie, for neither before nor after did the moving of God upon these waters proceed. Form and matter, conjoined and simple, came into being which had no defect, as three arrows from a three-stringed bow; and as in glass, in amber, or in crystal, a ray shines so that there is no interval between its coming and its pervading all, so did the triform effect ray forth from its Lord into its being, all at once, without distinction of beginning. Therewith order was created and ordained for the substances; and those in whom pure act was produced were the summit of the universe. Pure potentiality held the lowest place; in the middle such a bond tied up potentiality with act that it is never unbound. Jerome wrote for you of the angels as being created a long stretch of ages before aught else of the universe was made; but the truth I tell is written on many a page of the scribes of the Holy Spirit, and you shall be aware of it if you look well; and also reason sees it somewhat, which would not admit that the movers could be so long without their perfection. Now you know where and when these Loves were created, and how; so that three flames of your desire are already quenched.

Né giugneriesi, numerando, al venti
   sì tosto, come de li angeli parte
   turbò il suggetto d'i vostri alimenti.   *51*
L'altra rimase, e cominciò quest' arte
   che tu discerni, con tanto diletto,
   che mai da circüir non si diparte.   *54*
Principio del cader fu il maladetto
   superbir di colui che tu vedesti
   da tutti i pesi del mondo costretto.   *57*
Quelli che vedi qui furon modesti
   a riconoscer sé da la bontate
   che li avea fatti a tanto intender presti: *60*
per che le viste lor furo essaltate
   con grazia illuminante e con lor merto,
   sì c'hanno ferma e piena volontate;   *63*
e non voglio che dubbi, ma sia certo,
   che ricever la grazia è meritorio
   secondo che l'affetto l'è aperto.   *66*
Omai dintorno a questo consistorio
   puoi contemplare assai, se le parole
   mie son ricolte, sanz' altro aiutorio.   *69*
Ma perché 'n terra per le vostre scole
   si legge che l'angelica natura
   è tal, che 'ntende e si ricorda e vole,   *72*
ancor dirò, perché tu veggi pura
   la verità che là giù si confonde,
   equivocando in sì fatta lettura.   *75*
Queste sustanze, poi che fur gioconde
   de la faccia di Dio, non volser viso
   da essa, da cui nulla si nasconde: *78*

Then, sooner than one might count to twenty, a part of the Angels disturbed the substrate of your elements. The rest remained and with such great delight began this art which you behold that they never cease from circling. The origin of the fall was the accursed pride of him whom you have seen constrained by all the weights of the universe. Those whom you see here were modest to recognize their being as from the Goodness which had made them apt for intelligence so great: wherefore their vision was exalted with illuminating grace and with their merit, so that they have their will full and established. And I would not have you doubt, but be assured that to receive grace is meritorious, in proportion as the affection is open to it.

"By now, if you have taken in my words, you may contemplate much in regard to this consistory without more help. But since it is taught in your schools on earth that the angelic nature is such that it understands and remembers and wills, I will speak further, in order that you may see in purity the truth that down there is confounded by the equivocation in such like teaching. These substances, since first they were gladdened by the face of God, have never turned their eyes from It, wherefrom nothing is concealed;

però non hanno vedere interciso
da novo obietto, e però non bisogna
rememorar per concetto diviso;   *81*
sì che là giù, non dormendo, si sogna,
credendo e non credendo dicer vero;
ma ne l'uno è più colpa e più vergogna.   *84*
Voi non andate giù per un sentiero
filosofando: tanto vi trasporta
l'amor de l'apparenza e 'l suo pensiero!   *87*
E ancor questo qua sù si comporta
con men disdegno che quando è posposta
la divina Scrittura o quando è torta.   *90*
Non vi si pensa quanto sangue costa
seminarla nel mondo e quanto piace
chi umilmente con essa s'accosta.   *93*
Per apparer ciascun s'ingegna e face
sue invenzioni; e quelle son trascorse
da' predicanti e 'l Vangelio si tace.   *96*
Un dice che la luna si ritorse
ne la passion di Cristo e s'interpuose,
per che 'l lume del sol giù non si porse;   *99*
e mente, ché la luce si nascose
da sé: però a li Spani e a l'Indi
come a' Giudei tale eclissi rispuose.   *102*
Non ha Fiorenza tanti Lapi e Bindi
quante sì fatte favole per anno
in pergamo si gridan quinci e quindi: *105*
sì che le pecorelle, che non sanno,
tornan del pasco pasciute di vento,
e non le scusa non veder lo danno.   *108*

so that their sight is never intercepted by a new object, and therefore they have no need to remember by reason of interrupted concept. Thus down there men dream while awake, believing or not believing that they speak truth—but in the one case is the greater blame and shame. You mortals do not proceed along one same path in philosophizing, so much does the love of show and the thought of it carry you away; and even this is borne with less anger up here than when the Divine Scripture is set aside or when it is perverted. They think not there how much blood it costs to sow it in the world, nor how much he pleases who humbly keeps close to it. Each one strives for display and makes his own inventions, and these are treated of by the preachers, and the Gospel is silent. One says that at Christ's passion the moon turned back and interposed itself, so that the light of the sun did not reach below—and he lies, for the light itself hid itself, so that this eclipse took place for the Spaniards and the Indians, as well as for the Jews. Florence has not so many Lapos and Bindos as fables such as these that are shouted the year long from the pulpits on every side; so that the poor sheep, who know naught, return from the pasture fed with wind—and not seeing the harm does not excuse them.

Non disse Cristo al suo primo convento:
  'Andate, e predicate al mondo ciance';
  ma diede lor verace fondamento;   *111*
e quel tanto sonò ne le sue guance,
  sì ch'a pugnar per accender la fede
  de l'Evangelio fero scudo e lance.   *114*
Ora si va con motti e con iscede
  a predicare, e pur che ben si rida,
  gonfia il cappuccio e più non si richiede.   *117*
Ma tale uccel nel becchetto s'annida,
  che se 'l vulgo il vedesse, vederebbe
  la perdonanza di ch'el si confida: *120*
per cui tanta stoltezza in terra crebbe,
  che, sanza prova d'alcun testimonio,
  ad ogne promession si correrebbe.   *123*
Di questo ingrassa il porco sant' Antonio,
  e altri assai che sono ancor più porci,
  pagando di moneta sanza conio.   *126*
Ma perché siam digressi assai, ritorci
  li occhi oramai verso la dritta strada,
  sì che la via col tempo si raccorci.   *129*
Questa natura sì oltre s'ingrada
  in numero, che mai non fu loquela
  né concetto mortal che tanto vada;   *132*
e se tu guardi quel che si revela
  per Danïel, vedrai che 'n sue migliaia
  determinato numero si cela.   *135*
La prima luce, che tutta la raia,
  per tanti modi in essa si recepe,
  quanti son li splendori a chi s'appaia.   *138*

Christ did not say to his first company, 'Go
and preach idle stories to the world,' but he
gave to them the true foundation; and that
alone sounded on their lips, so that to fight
for kindling of the faith they made shield
and lance of the Gospel. Now men go forth to
preach with jests and with buffooneries, and
so there be only a good laugh, the cowl puffs
up and nothing more is asked. But such a
bird nests in the hood's tail that if the people
saw it, they would see what pardons they are
trusting in; from which such folly has grown
on earth that without proof of any testimony
they would flock to every promise. On this
the pig of St. Anthony fattens, and others
also, who are far more pigs, paying with
money that has no stamp of coinage.

"But since we have digressed enough, turn
back your eyes now to the true path, so that
the way be shortened with the time. This na-
ture extends so exceedingly in number that
never was there speech or mortal concept
that might advance so far; and if you look at
that which is revealed by Daniel, you will
see that in his thousands no definite number
is to be found. The Primal Light that irradi-
ates them all is received by them in as many
ways as are the splendors to which It joins
Itself.

Onde, però che a l'atto che concepe
   segue l'affetto, d'amar la dolcezza
   diversamente in essa ferve e tepe.   *141*
Vedi l'eccelso omai e la larghezza
   de l'etterno valor, poscia che tanti
   speculi fatti s'ha in che si spezza,
uno manendo in sé come davanti."   *145*

Wherefore, since the affection follows upon the act of conceiving, the sweetness of love glows variously in them, more and less. Behold now the height and breadth of the Eternal Goodness, since it has made itself so many mirrors wherein it is reflected, remaining in itself One as before."

PARADISO

Forse semilia miglia di lontano
 ci ferve l'ora sesta, e questo mondo
 china già l'ombra quasi al letto piano,   *3*
quando 'l mezzo del cielo, a noi profondo,
 comincia a farsi tal, ch'alcuna stella
 perde il parere infino a questo fondo;   *6*
e come vien la chiarissima ancella
 del sol più oltre, così 'l ciel si chiude
 di vista in vista infino a la più bella.   *9*
Non altrimenti il trïunfo che lude
 sempre dintorno al punto che mi vinse,
 parendo inchiuso da quel ch'elli 'nchiude,   *12*
a poco a poco al mio veder si stinse:
 per che tornar con li occhi a Bëatrice
 nulla vedere e amor mi costrinse.   *15*
Se quanto infino a qui di lei si dice
 fosse conchiuso tutto in una loda,
 poca sarebbe a fornir questa vice.   *18*

CANTO XXX

THE SIXTH hour is glowing perhaps six thousand miles away, and this world already slopes its shadow almost to a level bed, when the midst of heaven deep above us begins to grow such that a star here and there is lost to sight at this depth; and as the brightest handmaid of the sun advances, the heaven then shuts off its lights one by one, till the fairest is gone; not otherwise the triumph that plays forever round the Point which overcame me, seeming enclosed by that which it encloses, was gradually extinguished to my sight, wherefore seeing nothing and love constrained me to return with my eyes to Beatrice. If what has been said of her so far as here were all included in a single praise, it would be too slight to serve this present turn.

La bellezza ch'io vidi si trasmoda
  non pur di là da noi, ma certo io credo
  che solo il suo fattor tutta la goda.   *21*
Da questo passo vinto mi concedo
  più che già mai da punto di suo tema
  soprato fosse comico o tragedo: *24*
ché, come sole in viso che più trema,
  così lo rimembrar del dolce riso
  la mente mia da me medesmo scema.   *27*
Dal primo giorno ch'i' vidi il suo viso
  in questa vita, infino a questa vista,
  non m'è il seguire al mio cantar preciso;   *30*
ma or convien che mio seguir desista
  più dietro a sua bellezza, poetando,
  come a l'ultimo suo ciascuno artista.   *33*
Cotal qual io la lascio a maggior bando
  che quel de la mia tuba, che deduce
  l'ardüa sua matera terminando,   *36*
con atto e voce di spedito duce
  ricominciò: "Noi siamo usciti fore
  del maggior corpo al ciel ch'è pura luce: *39*
luce intellettüal, piena d'amore;
  amor di vero ben, pien di letizia;
  letizia che trascende ogne dolzore.   *42*
Qui vederai l'una e l'altra milizia
  di paradiso, e l'una in quelli aspetti
  che tu vedrai a l'ultima giustizia."   *45*
Come sùbito lampo che discetti
  li spiriti visivi, sì che priva
  da l'atto l'occhio di più forti obietti,   *48*

The beauty I beheld transcends measure not only beyond our reach, but I truly believe that He alone who made it can enjoy it all. At this pass I concede myself defeated more than ever comic or tragic poet was defeated by a point in his theme; for, as the sun does to the sight which trembles most, even so remembrance of the sweet smile shears my memory of its very self. From the first day when in this life I saw her face, until this sight, the continuing of my song has not been cut off, but now my pursuit must desist from following her beauty further in my verses, as at his utmost reach must every artist.

Such as I leave her to a greater heralding than that of my trumpet, which draws its arduous subject to a close, with the act and voice of a leader whose task is accomplished she began again, "We have issued forth from the greatest body to the heaven which is pure light: light intellectual full of love, love of true good full of joy, joy that transcends every sweetness. Here you shall see the one and the other soldiery of Paradise, and the one in those aspects which you shall see at the last judgment."

As a sudden flash of lightning which scatters the visual spirits so that it robs the eye of the sight of the clearest objects,

così mi circunfulse luce viva,
  e lasciommi fasciato di tal velo
  del suo fulgor, che nulla m'appariva.   *51*
"Sempre l'amor che queta questo cielo
  accoglie in sé con sì fatta salute,
  per far disposto a sua fiamma il candelo."   *54*
Non fur più tosto dentro a me venute
  queste parole brievi, ch'io compresi
  me sormontar di sopr' a mia virtute;   *57*
e di novella vista mi raccesi
  tale, che nulla luce è tanto mera,
  che li occhi miei non si fosser difesi;   *60*
e vidi lume in forma di rivera
  fulvido di fulgore, intra due rive
  dipinte di mirabil primavera.   *63*
Di tal fiumana uscian faville vive,
  e d'ogne parte si mettien ne' fiori,
  quasi rubin che oro circunscrive;   *66*
poi, come inebrïate da li odori,
  riprofondavan sé nel miro gurge,
  e s'una intrava, un'altra n'uscia fori.   *69*
"L'alto disio che mo t'infiamma e urge,
  d'aver notizia di ciò che tu vei,
  tanto mi piace più quanto più turge;   *72*
ma di quest' acqua convien che tu bei
  prima che tanta sete in te si sazi":
  così mi disse il sol de li occhi miei.   *75*
Anche soggiunse: "Il fiume e li topazi
  ch'entrano ed escono e 'l rider de l'erbe
  son di lor vero umbriferi prefazi.   *78*

so round about me there shone a vivid light and left me so swathed in the veil of its effulgence that nothing was visible to me.

"Ever does the love which quiets this heaven receive into itself with such like salutation, in order to prepare the candle for its flame." No sooner had these brief words come within me than I comprehended that I was surmounting beyond my own power, and such new vision was kindled in me that there is no light so bright that my eyes could not have withstood it. And I saw a light in form of a river glowing tawny between two banks painted with marvelous spring. From out this river issued living sparks and dropped on every side into the blossoms, like rubies set in gold. Then, as if inebriated by the odors, they plunged again into the wondrous flood, and as one was entering another was issuing forth.

"The high desire which now inflames and urges you to have knowledge concerning that which you see pleases me the more the more it swells; but first you must needs drink of this water before so great a thirst in you be slaked." So spoke the sun of my eyes to me, then added, "The stream and the topazes which enter and issue, and the smiling of the grasses, are the shadowy prefaces of their truth;

Non che da sé sian queste cose acerbe;
   ma è difetto da la parte tua,
   che non hai viste ancor tanto superbe."   *81*
Non è fantin che sì sùbito rua
   col volto verso il latte, se si svegli
   molto tardato da l'usanza sua,   *84*
come fec' io, per far migliori spegli
   ancor de li occhi, chinandomi a l'onda
   che si deriva perché vi s'immegli;   *87*
e sì come di lei bevve la gronda
   de le palpebre mie, così mi parve
   di sua lunghezza divenuta tonda.   *90*
Poi, come gente stata sotto larve,
   che pare altro che prima, se si sveste
   la sembianza non süa in che disparve,   *93*
così mi si cambiaro in maggior feste
   li fiori e le faville, sì ch'io vidi
   ambo le corti del ciel manifeste.   *96*
O isplendor di Dio, per cu' io vidi
   l'alto trïunfo del regno verace,
   dammi virtù a dir com' ïo il vidi!   *99*
Lume è là sù che visibile face
   lo creatore a quella creatura
   che solo in lui vedere ha la sua pace.   *102*
E' si distende in circular figura,
   in tanto che la sua circunferenza
   sarebbe al sol troppo larga cintura.   *105*
Fassi di raggio tutta sua parvenza
   reflesso al sommo del mobile primo,
   che prende quindi vivere e potenza.   *108*

not that these things are defective in them-
selves, but on your side is the defect, in that
you do not yet have vision so exalted."

No infant, on waking far after its hour, so
suddenly rushes with face toward the milk, as
then did I, to make yet better mirrors of my
eyes, stooping to the wave which flows there
that we may be bettered in it. And even as the
eaves of my eyelids drank of it, so it seemed
to me out of its length to have become round.
Then, as folk who have been under masks
seem other than before, if they do off the
semblances not their own wherein they were
hid, so into greater festival the flowers and the
sparks did change before me that I saw both
the courts of Heaven made manifest. O splen-
dor of God whereby I saw the high triumph
of the true kingdom, give to me power to tell
how I beheld it!

A Light is thereabove which makes the
Creator visible to every creature that has his
peace only in beholding Him. It spreads so
wide a circle that the circumference would be
too large a girdle for the sun. Its whole ex-
panse is made by a ray reflected from the sum-
mit of the Primum Mobile, which therefrom
takes its life and potency;

E come clivo in acqua di suo imo
   si specchia, quasi per vedersi addorno,
   quando è nel verde e ne' fioretti opimo,   *111*
sì, soprastando al lume intorno intorno,
   vidi specchiarsi in più di mille soglie
   quanto di noi là sù fatto ha ritorno.   *114*
E se l'infimo grado in sé raccoglie
   sì grande lume, quanta è la larghezza
   di questa rosa ne l'estreme foglie!   *117*
La vista mia ne l'ampio e ne l'altezza
   non si smarriva, ma tutto prendeva
   il quanto e 'l quale di quella allegrezza.   *120*
Presso e lontano, lì, né pon né leva:
   ché dove Dio sanza mezzo governa,
   la legge natural nulla rileva.   *123*
Nel giallo de la rosa sempiterna,
   che si digrada e dilata e redole
   odor di lode al sol che sempre verna,   *126*
qual è colui che tace e dicer vole,
   mi trasse Bëatrice, e disse: "Mira
   quanto è 'l convento de le bianche stole!   *129*
Vedi nostra città quant' ella gira;
   vedi li nostri scanni sì ripieni,
   che poca gente più ci si disira.   *132*
E 'n quel gran seggio a che tu li occhi tieni
   per la corona che già v'è sù posta,
   prima che tu a queste nozze ceni,   *135*
sederà l'alma, che fia giù agosta,
   de l'alto Arrigo, ch'a drizzare Italia
   verrà in prima ch'ella sia disposta.   *138*

and as a hillside mirrors itself in water at its base, as if to look upon its own adornment when it is rich in grasses and in flowers, so above the light round and round about in more than a thousand tiers I saw all that of us have won return up there. And if the lowest rank encloses within itself so great a light, how vast is the spread of this rose in its outermost leaves! My sight lost not itself in the breadth and in the height, but took in all the extent and quality of that joy. There, near and far neither add not take away, for where God governs without intermediary, the law of nature in no way prevails.

Into the yellow of the eternal Rose, which rises in ranks and expands and breathes forth odor of praise unto the Sun which makes perpetual spring, Beatrice drew me as one who is silent and wishes to speak, and she said, "Behold how great the assembly of the white robes! See our city, how wide is its circuit! See our seats so filled that few souls are now wanted there!

"And in that great chair whereon you fix your eyes because of the crown that already is set above it, before you sup at these nuptials shall sit the soul, which on earth will be imperial, of the lofty Henry, who will come to set Italy straight before she is ready.

La cieca cupidigia che v'ammalia
  simili fatti v'ha al fantolino
  che muor per fame e caccia via la balia.   *141*
E fia prefetto nel foro divino
  allora tal, che palese e coverto
  non anderà con lui per un cammino.   *144*
Ma poco poi sarà da Dio sofferto
  nel santo officio: ch'el sarà detruso
  là dove Simon mago è per suo merto,
e farà quel d'Alagna intrar più giuso."   *148*

The blind cupidity which bewitches you has made you like the little child who dies of hunger and drives away his nurse. And such a one will then be prefect in the divine forum who openly and secretly will not go with him along one same road. But not for long shall God then suffer him in the holy office; for he shall be thrust down where Simon Magus is for his deserts, and shall make him of Alagna go deeper still."

PARADISO

IN FORMA dunque di candida rosa
  mi si mostrava la milizia santa
  che nel suo sangue Cristo fece sposa;   *3*
ma l'altra, che volando vede e canta
  la gloria di colui che la 'nnamora
  e la bontà che la fece cotanta,   *6*
sì come schiera d'ape che s'infiora
  una fïata e una si ritorna
  là dove suo laboro s'insapora,   *9*
nel gran fior discendeva che s'addorna
  di tante foglie, e quindi risaliva
  là dove 'l süo amor sempre soggiorna.   *12*
Le facce tutte avean di fiamma viva
  e l'ali d'oro, e l'altro tanto bianco,
  che nulla neve a quel termine arriva.   *15*
Quando scendean nel fior, di banco in banco
  porgevan de la pace e de l'ardore
  ch'elli acquistavan ventilando il fianco.   *18*

CANTO XXXI

I<small>N FORM</small> then of a pure white rose the saintly host was shown to me, which with His own blood Christ made His bride. But the other host—who, as it flies, sees and sings His glory who enamors it and the goodness which made it so great—like a swarm of bees which one moment enflower themselves, and the next return to where their work acquires savor—was descending into the great flower which is adorned with so many petals, and thence reascending to where its love abides forever. They had their faces all of living flame, and their wings of gold, and the rest so white that no snow reaches such a limit. When they descended into the flower, from rank to rank they proffered of the peace and the ardor which they had acquired as they fanned their sides.

Né l'interporsi tra 'l disopra e 'l fiore
   di tanta moltitudine volante
   impediva la vista e lo splendore: 21
ché la luce divina è penetrante
   per l'universo secondo ch'è degno,
   sì che nulla le puote essere ostante.   24
Questo sicuro e gaudïoso regno,
   frequente in gente antica e in novella,
   viso e amore avea tutto ad un segno.   27
Oh trina luce che 'n unica stella
   scintillando a lor vista, sì li appaga!
   guarda qua giuso a la nostra procella!   30
Se i barbari, venendo da tal plaga
   che ciascun giorno d'Elice si cuopra,
   rotante col suo figlio ond' ella è vaga,   33
veggendo Roma e l'ardüa sua opra,
   stupefaciensi, quando Laterano
   a le cose mortali andò di sopra;   36
ïo, che al divino da l'umano,
   a l'etterno dal tempo era venuto,
   e di Fiorenza in popol giusto e sano,   39
di che stupor dovea esser compiuto!
   Certo tra esso e 'l gaudio mi facea
   libito non udire e starmi muto.   42
E quasi peregrin che si ricrea
   nel tempio del suo voto riguardando,
   e spera già ridir com' ello stea,   45
su per la viva luce passeggiando,
   menava ïo li occhi per li gradi,
   mo sù, mo giù e mo recirculando.   48

Nor did the interposing of so great a flying plenitude, between what was above and the flower, impede the vision or the splendor; for the divine light so penetrates through the universe, in measure of its worthiness, that naught can be an obstacle to it. This secure and joyful kingdom, thronged with ancient and with modern folk, had look and love all directed on one mark.

O threefold Light, which, in a single star sparkling on their sight, dost so satisfy them, look down upon our tempest here below!

If the Barbarians, coming from such region as is covered every day by Helice, wheeling with her son whom she delights in, when they beheld Rome and her mighty work, when Lateran rose above all mortal things, were wonder-struck, I, who to the divine from the human, to the eternal from time had come, and from Florence to a people just and sane, with what amazement must I have been full! Truly, what with it and with the joy, I was content to hear naught and to stand mute. And as a pilgrim who is refreshed within the temple of his vow as he looks around, and already hopes to tell again how it was, so, taking my way upwards through the living light, I led my eyes along the ranks, now up, now down, and now circling about.

Vedëa visi a carità süadi,
   d'altrui lume fregiati e di suo riso,
   e atti ornati di tutte onestadi.   51
La forma general di paradiso
   già tutta mïo sguardo avea compresa,
   in nulla parte ancor fermato fiso;   54
e volgeami con voglia rïaccesa
   per domandar la mia donna di cose
   di che la mente mia era sospesa.   57
Uno intendëa, e altro mi rispuose:
   credea veder Beatrice e vidi un sene
   vestito con le genti glorïose.   60
Diffuso era per li occhi e per le gene
   di benigna letizia, in atto pio
   quale a tenero padre si convene.   63
E "Ov' è ella?" sùbito diss' io.
   Ond' elli: "A terminar lo tuo disiro
   mosse Beatrice me del loco mio;   66
e se riguardi sù nel terzo giro
   dal sommo grado, tu la rivedrai
   nel trono che suoi merti le sortiro."   69
Sanza risponder, li occhi sù levai,
   e vidi lei che si facea corona
   reflettendo da sé li etterni rai.   72
Da quella regïon che più sù tona
   occhio mortale alcun tanto non dista,
   qualunque in mare più giù s'abbandona,   75
quanto lì da Beatrice la mia vista;
   ma nulla mi facea, ché süa effige
   non discendëa a me per mezzo mista.   78

I saw faces all given to love, adorned by the light of Another, and by their own smile, and movements graced with every dignity.

My look had now taken in the general form of Paradise as a whole, and on no part as yet had my sight paused; and I turned with re-kindled will to ask my lady about things as to which my mind was in suspense. One thing I purposed, and another answered me: I thought to see Beatrice, and I saw an elder, clad like the folk in glory. His eyes and cheeks were suffused with benign gladness, his mien kindly such as befits a tender father. And, "Where is she?" I said at once; whereon he, "To terminate your desire Beatrice urged me from my place; and if you look up to the circle which is third from the highest tier, you will see her again, in the throne her merits have allotted to her."

Without answering I lifted up my eyes and saw her where she made for herself a crown as she reflected the eternal rays. From the region which thunders most high no mortal eye is so far distant, were it plunged most deep within the sea, as there from Beatrice was my sight. But to me it made no differ-ence, for her image came down to me un-blurred by aught between.

"O donna in cui la mia speranza vige,
  e che soffristi per la mia salute
  in inferno lasciar le tue vestige,   *81*
di tante cose quant' i' ho vedute,
  dal tuo podere e da la tua bontate
  riconosco la grazia e la virtute.   *84*
Tu m'hai di servo tratto a libertate
  per tutte quelle vie, per tutt' i modi
  che di ciò fare avei la potestate.   *87*
La tua magnificenza in me custodi,
  sì che l'anima mia, che fatt' hai sana,
  piacente a te dal corpo si disnodi."   *90*
Così orai; e quella, sì lontana
  come parea, sorrise e riguardommi;
  poi si tornò a l'etterna fontana.   *93*
E 'l santo sene: "Acciò che tu assommi
  perfettamente," disse, "il tuo cammino,
  a che priego e amor santo mandommi,   *96*
vola con li occhi per questo giardino;
  ché veder lui t'acconcerà lo sguardo
  più al montar per lo raggio divino.   *99*
E la regina del cielo, ond' ïo ardo
  tutto d'amor, ne farà ogne grazia,
  però ch'i' sono il suo fedel Bernardo."   *102*
Qual è colui che forse di Croazia
  viene a veder la Veronica nostra,
  che per l'antica fame non sen sazia,   *105*
ma dice nel pensier, fin che si mostra:
  "Segnor mio Iesù Cristo, Dio verace,
  or fu sì fatta la sembianza vostra?";   *108*

"O lady, in whom my hope is strong, and who for my salvation did endure to leave in Hell your footprints, of all those things which I have seen I acknowledge the grace and the virtue to be from your power and your excellence. It is you who have drawn me from bondage into liberty by all those paths, by all those means by which you had the power so to do. Preserve in me your great munificence, so that my soul, which you have made whole, may be loosed from the body, pleasing unto you." So did I pray; and she, so distant as she seemed, smiled and looked on me, then turned again to the eternal fountain.

And the holy elder said, "In order that you may consummate your journey perfectly, whereto prayer and holy love dispatched me, fly with your eyes throughout this garden; for gazing on it will better prepare your sight to mount through the divine ray. And the Queen of Heaven, for whom I am all afire with love, will grant us every grace, since I am her faithful Bernard."

As is he who comes perchance from Croatia to look on our Veronica, and whose old hunger is not sated, but says in thought so long as it is shown, "My Lord Jesus Christ, true God, was then your semblance like to this?"

tal era io mirando la vivace
  carità di colui che 'n questo mondo,
  contemplando, gustò di quella pace.   *111*
"Figliuol di grazia, quest' esser giocondo,"
  cominciò elli, "non ti sarà noto,
  tenendo li occhi pur qua giù al fondo;   *114*
ma guarda i cerchi infino al più remoto,
  tanto che veggi seder la regina
  cui questo regno è suddito e devoto."   *117*
Io levai li occhi; e come da mattina
  la parte orïental de l'orizzonte
  soverchia quella dove 'l sol declina,   *120*
così, quasi di valle andando a monte
  con li occhi, vidi parte ne lo stremo
  vincer di lume tutta l'altra fronte.   *123*
E come quivi ove s'aspetta il temo
  che mal guidò Fetonte, più s'infiamma,
  e quinci e quindi il lume si fa scemo,   *126*
così quella pacifica oriafiamma
  nel mezzo s'avvivava, e d'ogne parte
  per igual modo allentava la fiamma;   *129*
e a quel mezzo, con le penne sparte,
  vid' io più di mille angeli festanti,
  ciascun distinto di fulgore e d'arte.   *132*
Vidi a lor giochi quivi e a lor canti
  ridere una bellezza, che letizia
  era ne li occhi a tutti li altri santi;   *135*
e s'io avessi in dir tanta divizia
  quanta ad imaginar, non ardirei
  lo minimo tentar di sua delizia.   *138*

such was I, gazing on the living charity of him who, in this world, in contemplation tasted of that peace.

"Son of grace, this joyous being," he began, "will not be known to you if you hold your eyes only down here at the base; but look upon the circles, even to the most remote, until you see upon her seat the Queen to whom this realm is subject and devoted."

I lifted up my eyes; and as at morning the eastern parts of the horizon outshine that where the sun declines, so, as if going with my eyes from valley to mountain-top I saw a part on the extreme verge surpass with its light all the rest of the rim. And as the point where we await the pole that Phaethon misguided is most aglow, and on this side and on that the light diminishes, so was that pacific oriflamme quickened in the middle, on either side in equal measure tempering its flame. And at the midpoint, with outstretched wings, I saw more than a thousand Angels making festival, each one distinct in effulgence and in ministry. I saw there, smiling to their sports and to their songs, a beauty which was gladness in the eyes of all the other saints. And had I equal wealth in speech as in conception, yet would I not dare to attempt the least of her delightfulness.

Bernardo, come vide li occhi miei
nel caldo suo caler fissi e attenti,
li suoi con tanto affetto volse a lei,
che ' miei di rimirar fé più ardenti.   *142*

Bernard, when he saw my eyes fixed and intent on the object of his own burning glow, turned his own with such affection to her, that he made mine more ardent in their gazing.

Affetto al suo piacer, quel contemplante
   libero officio di dottore assunse,
   e cominciò queste parole sante: 3
"La piaga che Maria richiuse e unse,
   quella ch'è tanto bella da' suoi piedi
   è colei che l'aperse e che la punse.   6
Ne l'ordine che fanno i terzi sedi,
   siede Rachel di sotto da costei
   con Bëatrice, sì come tu vedi.   9
Sarra e Rebecca, Iudìt e colei
   che fu bisava al cantor che per doglia
   del fallo disse 'Miserere mei,'   12
puoi tu veder così di soglia in soglia
   giù digradar, com' io ch'a proprio nome
   vo per la rosa giù di foglia in foglia.   15
E dal settimo grado in giù, sì come
   infino ad esso, succedono Ebree,
   dirimendo del fior tutte le chiome;   18

CANTO XXXII

Wɪᴛʜ ʜɪs love fixed on his Delight, that contemplator freely assumed the office of a teacher, and began these holy words, "The wound which Mary closed and anointed, that one who is so beautiful at her feet is she who opened it and pierced it. Below her, in the order which the third seats make, sits Rachel with Beatrice, as you see. Sarah, Rebecca, Judith, and she who was great-grandmother of the singer who, through sorrow for his sin, cried '*Miserere mei*,' you may see, thus from rank to rank in gradation downward, as with the name of each I go downward through the rose from petal to petal. And from the seventh row downwards, even as down to it, Hebrew women follow in succession, dividing all the tresses of the flower;

perché, secondo lo sguardo che fée
  la fede in Cristo, queste sono il muro
  a che si parton le sacre scalee.   21
Da questa parte onde 'l fiore è maturo
  di tutte le sue foglie, sono assisi
  quei che credettero in Cristo venturo;   24
da l'altra parte onde sono intercisi
  di vòti i semicirculi, si stanno
  quei ch'a Cristo venuto ebber li visi.   27
E come quinci il glorïoso scanno
  de la donna del cielo e li altri scanni
  di sotto lui cotanta cerna fanno,   30
così di contra quel del gran Giovanni,
  che sempre santo 'l diserto e 'l martiro
  sofferse, e poi l'inferno da due anni;   33
e sotto lui così cerner sortiro
  Francesco, Benedetto e Augustino
  e altri fin qua giù di giro in giro.   36
Or mira l'alto proveder divino:
  ché l'uno e l'altro aspetto de la fede
  igualmente empierà questo giardino.   39
E sappi che dal grado in giù che fiede
  a mezzo il tratto le due discrezioni,
  per nullo proprio merito si siede,   42
ma per l'altrui, con certe condizioni:
  ché tutti questi son spiriti asciolti
  prima ch'avesser vere elezïoni.   45
Ben te ne puoi accorger per li volti
  e anche per le voci püerili,
  se tu li guardi bene e se li ascolti.   48

because, according to the look which their faith turned to Christ, these are the wall by which the sacred stairway is divided. On this side, wherein the flower is mature in all its petals, are seated those who believed in Christ yet to come. On the other side, where the half-circles are broken by vacant places, sit those who turned their faces toward Christ already come. And as on this side the glorious seat of the Lady of Heaven, and the other seats below it, make so great a partition, thus, opposite, does the seat of the great John who, ever holy, endured the desert and martyrdom, and then Hell for two years; and beneath him, Francis and Benedict and Augustine and others were allotted thus to divide, as far down as here, from circle to circle. Now behold the depth of the divine foresight, for one and the other aspect of the faith shall fill this garden equally. And know that, downward from the row which cleaves midway the two dividing lines, they are seated for no merit of their own, but for that of others, under certain conditions; for all these are spirits absolved before they had true power of choice. Well can you perceive it by their faces and by their childish voices, if you look well upon them and if you listen to them.

Or dubbi tu e dubitando sili;
  ma io discioglierò 'l forte legame
  in che ti stringon li pensier sottili.   *51*
Dentro a l'ampiezza di questo reame
  casüal punto non puote aver sito,
  se non come tristizia o sete o fame: *54*
ché per etterna legge è stabilito
  quantunque vedi, sì che giustamente
  ci si risponde da l'anello al dito;   *57*
e però questa festinata gente
  a vera vita non è *sine causa*
  intra sé qui più e meno eccellente.   *60*
Lo rege per cui questo regno pausa
  in tanto amore e in tanto diletto,
  che nulla volontà è di più ausa,   *63*
le menti tutte nel suo lieto aspetto
  creando, a suo piacer di grazia dota
  diversamente; e qui basti l'effetto.   *66*
E ciò espresso e chiaro vi si nota
  ne la Scrittura santa in quei gemelli
  che ne la madre ebber l'ira commota.   *69*
Però, secondo il color d'i capelli,
  di cotal grazia l'altissimo lume
  degnamente convien che s'incappelli.   *72*
Dunque, sanza mercé di lor costume,
  locati son per gradi differenti,
  sol differendo nel primiero acume.   *75*
Bastavasi ne' secoli recenti
  con l'innocenza, per aver salute,
  solamente la fede d'i parenti;   *78*

"Now you are perplexed, and in perplexity are silent; but I will loose the hard knot wherein your subtle thoughts are binding you. Within the amplitude of this realm a casual point can have no place, any more than can sorrow, or thirst, or hunger; for whatever you see is established by eternal law, so that the correspondence is exact between the ring and finger. And therefore this company, hastened to true life, is not *sine causa* more or less excellent here among themselves. The King, through whom this realm reposes in such great love and in such great delight that no will dares for more, creating all the minds in His glad sight, at His own pleasure endows with grace diversely—and here let the fact suffice. And this is clearly and expressly noted for you in Holy Scripture in those twins whose anger was stirred within their mother's womb. Therefore, according to the color of the locks, of such grace needs must the lofty light crown them according to their worth. Wherefore, without merit of their own works, they are placed in different ranks, differing only in the primal keenness of vision. In the early ages, their parents' faith alone, with their own innocence, sufficed for their salvation;

poi che le prime etadi fuor compiute,
   convenne ai maschi a l'innocenti penne
   per circuncidere acquistar virtute;   *81*
ma poi che 'l tempo de la grazia venne,
   sanza battesmo perfetto di Cristo
   tale innocenza là giù si ritenne.   *84*
Riguarda omai ne la faccia che a Cristo
   più si somiglia, ché la sua chiarezza
   sola ti può disporre a veder Cristo."   *87*
Io vidi sopra lei tanta allegrezza
   piover, portata ne le menti sante
   create a trasvolar per quella altezza,   *90*
che quantunque io avea visto davante,
   di tanta ammirazion non mi sospese,
   né mi mostrò di Dio tanto sembiante;   *93*
e quello amor che primo lì discese,
   cantando "*Ave, Maria, gratïa plena,*"
   dinanzi a lei le sue ali distese.   *96*
Rispuose a la divina cantilena
   da tutte parti la beata corte,
   sì ch'ogne vista sen fé più serena.   *99*
"O santo padre, che per me comporte
   l'esser qua giù, lasciando il dolce loco
   nel qual tu siedi per etterna sorte,   *102*
qual è quell' angel che con tanto gioco
   guarda ne li occhi la nostra regina,
   innamorato sì che par di foco?"   *105*
Così ricorsi ancora a la dottrina
   di colui ch'abbelliva di Maria,
   come del sole stella mattutina.   *108*

After those first ages were complete, it was needful for males, through circumcision, to acquire power for their innocent wings; but after the time of grace had come, without perfect baptism in Christ such innocence was held there below.

"Look now upon the face which most resembles Christ, for only its brightness can prepare you to see Christ."

I saw such gladness rain down upon her, borne in the holy minds created to fly through that height, that all I had seen before had not held me in suspense of such great marveling, nor showed me such likeness to God. And that Love which first descended there, singing "*Ave Maria, gratia plena*," now spread his wings before her. On all sides the blessed Court responded to the divine song, so that every face became the brighter therefor.

"O holy father, who for my sake endure to be here below, leaving the sweet place in which by eternal lot you have your seat, who is that angel who with such joy looks into the eyes of our Queen, so enamored that he seems afire?" Thus did I again recur to the teaching of him who drew beauty from Mary, as the morning star from the sun.

Ed elli a me: "Baldezza e leggiadria
   quant' esser puote in angelo e in alma,
   tutta è in lui; e sì volem che sia,   *111*
perch' elli è quelli che portò la palma
   giuso a Maria, quando 'l Figliuol di Dio
   carcar si volse de la nostra salma.   *114*
Ma vieni omai con li occhi sì com' io
   andrò parlando, e nota i gran patrici
   di questo imperio giustissimo e pio.   *117*
Quei due che seggon là sù più felici
   per esser propinquissimi ad Agusta,
   son d'esta rosa quasi due radici: *120*
colui che da sinistra le s'aggiusta
   è 'l padre per lo cui ardito gusto
   l'umana specie tanto amaro gusta;   *123*
dal destro vedi quel padre vetusto
   di Santa Chiesa a cui Cristo le chiavi
   raccomandò di questo fior venusto.   *126*
E quei che vide tutti i tempi gravi,
   pria che morisse, de la bella sposa
   che s'acquistò con la lancia e coi clavi,   *129*
siede lungh' esso, e lungo l'altro posa
   quel duca sotto cui visse di manna
   la gente ingrata, mobile e retrosa.   *132*
Di contr' a Pietro vedi sedere Anna,
   tanto contenta di mirar sua figlia,
   che non move occhio per cantare osanna;   *135*
e contro al maggior padre di famiglia
   siede Lucia, che mosse la tua donna
   quando chinavi, a rovinar, le ciglia.   *138*

And he to me, "Confidence and grace, as much as there can be in angel and in soul, are all in him, and we would have it so, for it is he who bore the palm down to Mary, when the Son of God willed to load Himself with the burden of our flesh.

"But come now with your eyes, as I proceed in speaking, and note the great patricians of this most just and pious empire. Those two who sit there above, most happy for being nearest to the Empress, are, as it were, two roots of this rose: he who is beside her upon the left is that Father because of whose audacious tasting the human race tastes such bitterness. On the right you see that ancient Father of Holy Church to whom Christ entrusted the keys of this beauteous flower. And he who saw, before he died, all the grievous times of the fair Bride who was won with the spear and the nails sits at his side; and beside the other rests that leader, under whom the thankless, fickle, and stubborn people lived on manna. Opposite Peter you see Anna sitting, so content to gaze upon her daughter that she moves not her eyes as she sings Hosannah. And opposite the greatest father of a family sits Lucy, who moved your lady when you were bending your brows downward to your ruin.

Ma perché 'l tempo fugge che t'assonna,
   qui farem punto, come buon sartore
   che com' elli ha del panno fa la gonna;   *141*
e drizzeremo li occhi al primo amore,
   sì che, guardando verso lui, penètri
   quant' è possibil per lo suo fulgore.   *144*
Veramente, *ne* forse tu t'arretri
   movendo l'ali tue, credendo oltrarti,
   orando grazia conven che s'impetri   *147*
grazia da quella che puote aiutarti;
   e tu mi seguirai con l'affezione,
   sì che dal dicer mio lo cor non parti."
E cominciò questa santa orazione: *151*

"But because the time flies that brings sleep upon you, we will stop here, like a good tailor that cuts the garment according to his cloth, and we will turn our eyes to the Primal Love, so that, gazing toward Him, you may penetrate, as far as that can be, into His effulgence. But lest, perchance, you fall back, moving your wings and thinking to advance, grace must be obtained by prayer, grace from her who has power to aid you; and do you follow me with your affection so that your heart depart not from my words."

And he began this holy prayer:

PARADISO

"Vergine Madre, figlia del tuo figlio,
   umile e alta più che creatura,
   termine fisso d'etterno consiglio,   *3*
tu se' colei che l'umana natura
   nobilitasti sì, che 'l suo fattore
   non disdegnò di farsi sua fattura.   *6*
Nel ventre tuo si raccese l'amore,
   per lo cui caldo ne l'etterna pace
   così è germinato questo fiore.   *9*
Qui se' a noi meridïana face
   di caritate, e giuso, intra ' mortali,
   se' di speranza fontana vivace.   *12*
Donna, se' tanto grande e tanto vali,
   che qual vuol grazia e a te non ricorre,
   sua disïanza vuol volar sanz' ali.   *15*
La tua benignità non pur soccorre
   a chi domanda, ma molte fïate
   liberamente al dimandar precorre.   *18*

CANTO XXXIII

"VIRGIN MOTHER, daughter of thy Son, humble and exalted more than any creature, fixed goal of the eternal counsel, thou art she who didst so enoble human nature that its Maker did not disdain to become its creature. In thy womb was rekindled the Love under whose warmth this flower in the eternal peace has thus unfolded. Here thou art for us the noonday torch of charity, and below among mortals thou art the living fount of hope. Lady, thou art so great and so availest, that whoso would have grace and has not recourse to thee, his desire seeks to fly without wings. Thy loving-kindness not only succors him who asks, but oftentimes freely foreruns the asking.

In te misericordia, in te pietate,
  in te magnificenza, in te s'aduna
  quantunque in creatura è di bontate.   *21*
Or questi, che da l'infima lacuna
  de l'universo infin qui ha vedute
  le vite spiritali ad una ad una,   *24*
supplica a te, per grazia, di virtute
  tanto, che possa con li occhi levarsi
  più alto verso l'ultima salute.   *27*
E io, che mai per mio veder non arsi
  più ch'i' fo per lo suo, tutti miei prieghi
  ti porgo, e priego che non sieno scarsi,   *30*
perché tu ogne nube li disleghi
  di sua mortalità co' prieghi tuoi,
  sì che 'l sommo piacer li si dispieghi.   *33*
Ancor ti priego, regina, che puoi
  ciò che tu vuoli, che conservi sani,
  dopo tanto veder, li affetti suoi.   *36*
Vinca tua guardia i movimenti umani:
  vedi Beatrice con quanti beati
  per li miei prieghi ti chiudon le mani!"   *39*
Li occhi da Dio diletti e venerati,
  fissi ne l'orator, ne dimostraro
  quanto i devoti prieghi le son grati;   *42*
indi a l'etterno lume s'addrizzaro,
  nel qual non si dee creder che s'invii
  per creatura l'occhio tanto chiaro.   *45*
E io ch'al fine di tutt' i disii
  appropinquava, sì com' io dovea,
  l'ardor del desiderio in me finii.   *48*

In thee is mercy, in thee pity, in thee munifi-
cence, in thee is found whatever of goodness
is in any creature. Now this man, who from
the lowest pit of the universe even to here
has seen one by one the spiritual lives, im-
plores thee of thy grace for power such that
he may be able with his eyes to rise still
higher toward the last salvation. And I, who
never for my own vision burned more than
I do for his, proffer to thee all my prayers,
and pray that they be not scant, that with thy
prayers thou wouldst dispel for him every
cloud of his mortality, so that the Supreme
Pleasure may be disclosed to him. Further I
pray thee, Queen, who canst do whatsoever
thou wilt, that thou preserve sound for him
his affections, after so great a vision. Let thy
protection vanquish human impulses. Be-
hold Beatrice, with how many saints, for my
prayers clasping their hands to thee."

The eyes beloved and reverenced by God,
fixed upon him who prayed, showed us how
greatly devout prayers do please her; then
they were turned to the Eternal Light,
wherein we may not believe that any crea-
ture's eye finds its way so clear.

And I, who was drawing near to the end
of all desires, raised to its utmost, even as I
ought, the ardor of my longing.

Bernardo m'accennava, e sorridea,
  perch' io guardassi suso; ma io era
  già per me stesso tal qual ei volea: *51*
ché la mia vista, venendo sincera,
  e più e più intrava per lo raggio
  de l'alta luce che da sé è vera.   *54*
Da quinci innanzi il mio veder fu maggio
  che 'l parlar mostra, ch'a tal vista cede,
  e cede la memoria a tanto oltraggio.   *57*
Qual è colüi che sognando vede,
  che dopo 'l sogno la passione impressa
  rimane, e l'altro a la mente non riede,   *60*
cotal son io, ché quasi tutta cessa
  mia visïone, e ancor mi distilla
  nel core il dolce che nacque da essa.   *63*
Così la neve al sol si disigilla;
  così al vento ne le foglie levi
  si perdea la sentenza di Sibilla.   *66*
O somma luce che tanto ti levi
  da' concetti mortali, a la mia mente
  ripresta un poco di quel che parevi,   *69*
e fa la lingua mia tanto possente,
  ch'una favilla sol de la tua gloria
  possa lasciare a la futura gente;   *72*
ché, per tornare alquanto a mia memoria
  e per sonare un poco in questi versi,
  più si conceperà di tua vittoria.   *75*
Io credo, per l'acume ch'io soffersi
  del vivo raggio, ch'i' sarei smarrito,
  se li occhi miei da lui fossero aversi.   *78*

Bernard was signing to me with a smile to look upward, but I was already of myself such as he wished; for my sight, becoming pure, was entering more and more through the beam of the lofty Light which in Itself is true.

Thenceforward my vision was greater than speech can show, which fails at such a sight, and at such excess memory fails. As is he who dreaming sees, and after the dream the passion remains imprinted and the rest returns not to the mind; such am I, for my vision almost wholly fades away, yet does the sweetness that was born of it still drop within my heart. Thus is the snow unsealed by the sun; thus in the wind, on the light leaves, the Sibyl's oracle was lost.

O Light Supreme that art so far uplifted above mortal conceiving, relend to my mind a little of what Thou didst appear, and give my tongue such power that it may leave only a single spark of Thy glory for the folk to come; for, by returning somewhat to my memory and by sounding a little in these lines, more of Thy victory shall be conceived.

I believe that, because of the keenness of the living ray which I endured, I should have been lost if my eyes had been turned from it.

E' mi ricorda ch'io fui più ardito
  per questo a sostener, tanto ch'i' giunsi
  l'aspetto mio col valore infinito.   *81*
Oh abbondante grazia ond' io presunsi
  ficcar lo viso per la luce etterna,
  tanto che la veduta vi consunsi!   *84*
Nel suo profondo vidi che s'interna,
  legato con amore in un volume,
  ciò che per l'universo si squaderna: *87*
sustanze e accidenti e lor costume
  quasi conflati insieme, per tal modo
  che ciò ch'i' dico è un semplice lume.   *90*
La forma universal di questo nodo
  credo ch'i' vidi, perché più di largo,
  dicendo questo, mi sento ch'i' godo.   *93*
Un punto solo m'è maggior letargo
  che venticinque secoli a la 'mpresa
  che fé Nettuno ammirar l'ombra d'Argo.   *96*
Così la mente mia, tutta sospesa,
  mirava fissa, immobile e attenta,
  e sempre di mirar faceasi accesa.   *99*
A quella luce cotal si diventa,
  che volgersi da lei per altro aspetto
  è impossibil che mai si consenta;   *102*
però che 'l ben, ch'è del volere obietto,
  tutto s'accoglie in lei, e fuor di quella
  è defettivo ciò ch'è lì perfetto.   *105*
Omai sarà più corta mia favella,
  pur a quel ch'io ricordo, che d'un fante
  che bagni ancor la lingua a la mammella. *108*

I remember that on this account I was the bolder to sustain it, until I united my gaze with the Infinite Goodness.

O abounding grace whereby I presumed to fix my look through the Eternal Light so far that all my sight was spent therein.

In its depth I saw ingathered, bound by love in one single volume, that which is dispersed in leaves throughout the universe: substances and accidents and their relations, as though fused together in such a way that what I tell is but a simple light. The universal form of this knot I believe that I saw, because, in telling this, I feel my joy increase.

A single moment makes for me greater oblivion than five and twenty centuries have wrought upon the enterprise that made Neptune wonder at the shadow of the Argo. Thus my mind, all rapt, was gazing, fixed, motionless and intent, ever enkindled by its gazing. In that Light one becomes such that it is impossible he should ever consent to turn himself from it for other sight; for the good, which is the object of the will, is all gathered in it, and outside of it that is defective which is perfect there.

Now will my speech fall more short, even in respect to that which I remember, than that of an infant who still bathes his tongue at the breast.

Non perché più ch'un semplice sembiante
  fosse nel vivo lume ch'io mirava,
  che tal è sempre qual s'era davante;   *111*
ma per la vista che s'avvalorava
  in me guardando, una sola parvenza,
  mutandom' io, a me si travagliava.   *114*
Ne la profonda e chiara sussistenza
  de l'alto lume parvermi tre giri
  di tre colori e d'una contenenza;   *117*
e l'un da l'altro come iri da iri
  parea reflesso, e 'l terzo parea foco
  che quinci e quindi igualmente si spiri.   *120*
Oh quanto è corto il dire e come fioco
  al mio concetto! e questo, a quel ch'i' vidi,
  è tanto, che non basta a dicer "poco."   *123*
O luce etterna che sola in te sidi,
  sola t'intendi, e da te intelletta
  e intendente te ami e arridi!   *126*
Quella circulazion che sì concetta
  pareva in te come lume reflesso,
  da li occhi miei alquanto circunspetta,   *129*
dentro da sé, del suo colore stesso,
  mi parve pinta de la nostra effige:
  per che 'l mio viso in lei tutto era messo.   *132*
Qual è 'l geomètra che tutto s'affige
  per misurar lo cerchio, e non ritrova,
  pensando, quel principio ond' elli indige,   *135*
tal era io a quella vista nova:
  veder voleva come si convenne
  l'imago al cerchio e come vi s'indova;   *138*

Not because more than one simple semblance was in the Living Light wherein I was gazing, which ever is such as it was before; but through my sight, which was growing strong in me as I looked, one sole appearance, even as I changed, was altering itself to me.

Within the profound and shining subsistence of the lofty Light appeared to me three circles of three colors and one magnitude; and one seemed reflected by the other, as rainbow by rainbow, and the third seemed fire breathed forth equally from the one and the other.

O how scant is speech, and how feeble to my conception! and this, to what I saw, is such that it is not enough to call it little.

O Light Eternal, who alone abidest in Thyself, alone knowest Thyself, and, known to Thyself and knowing, lovest and smilest on Thyself!

That circling which, thus begotten, appeared in Thee as reflected light, when my eyes had dwelt on it for a time, seemed to me depicted with our image within itself and in its own color, wherefore my sight was entirely set upon it.

As is the geometer who wholly applies himself to measure the circle, and finds not, in pondering, the principle of which he is in need, such was I at that new sight. I wished to see how the image conformed to the circle and how it has its place therein;

379

ma non eran da ciò le proprie penne:
   se non che la mia mente fu percossa
   da un fulgore in che sua voglia venne.   *141*
A l'alta fantasia qui mancò possa;
   ma già volgeva il mio disio e 'l *velle*,
   sì come rota ch'igualmente è mossa,
l'amor che move il sole e l'altre stelle.   *145*

but my own wings were not sufficient for that, save that my mind was smitten by a flash wherein its wish came to it. Here power failed the lofty phantasy; but already my desire and my will were revolved, like a wheel that is evenly moved, by the Love which moves the sun and the other stars.

INDEX

This list includes the names of persons and places mentioned in the *Paradiso*. All names are given in their conventional English form where possible, according to the translation in this volume. Even though a name may occur more than once in a single passage or canto, only its first occurrence there is listed. Italicized numbers of cantos and verses indicate indirect reference to a person or place in the verse cited.

BOLLINGEN SERIES LXXX

The Divine Comedy

✧

Paradiso

2: Commentary

DANTE ALIGHIERI

The Divine Comedy

TRANSLATED, WITH A COMMENTARY, BY

CHARLES S. SINGLETON

Paradiso

2: Commentary

CONTENTS OF PART 2

ILLUSTRATIONS

PLATE

facing page

FIGURES

on page

MAPS

facing page

ACKNOWLEDGMENTS

The sources for published material that has been quoted in the present commentary will be found in the List of Works Cited. The translations most frequently used include those of the Latin classics taken from the Loeb Classical Library, the translations of the works of Dante provided by the Temple Classics, the Confraternity-Douay translation of the Vulgate, and the translation of Aquinas' *Summa theologica* by the Fathers of the English Dominican Province in the edition of the Benziger Brothers, New York, 1947-48. Translations for which no published source was used have been provided by Charles S. Singleton.

References to the Bible are to the Vulgate; if the corresponding citation to the King James Bible differs, it is given in brackets following the Vulgate citation.

The Latin version of Aristotle that both Dante and Thomas Aquinas are assumed to have known has been quoted from the Parma edition of the *Opera omnia* of Thomas Aquinas; this "Antiqua Translatio" is the only Aristotle text quoted in the present work. Marietti editions of the Aquinas commentaries on Aristotle, which also contain the text of Aristotle in Latin, are suggested in the notes and included in the List of Works Cited for the general convenience of the reader. Bekker numbers are used in citations to the works of Aristotle to facilitate reference to any edition of Aristotle the reader may have, since Bekker numbers are not provided in the Aquinas *Opera omnia* itself; chapter numbers are those of the Loeb Classical Library.

Plate 1, a detail from *God and Scepter* (MS n. London Add. 15268) is reproduced here by permission of the British Museum. Maps 1, 2, and 4 and Figure 1 were prepared after maps and an illustration in the Temple Classics edition of *The Paradiso of Dante Alighieri*, edited by H. Oelsner and translated by P. H. Wicksteed (London, 1965). Map 3 and Figures 2 and 5 were prepared after a map and illustrations in Paget Toynbee, *A Dictionary of Proper Names and Notable Mat-*

ters in the Works of Dante, revised by Charles S. Singleton (Oxford, 1968). Figures 3 and 4 were prepared after illustrations in *La Divina Commedia*, edited by C. H. Grandgent, revised by Charles S. Singleton (Cambridge, Mass., 1972).

Commentaries on the *Divine Comedy*, both early and modern, are cited by the commentator's name alone, with no specific reference to page or verse number, because commentaries ordinarily follow the canto and verse number of the *Comedy*. The abbreviations Gr and TC are frequently used to indicate respectively the source of quotations taken from the commentaries of C. H. Grandgent and the Temple Classics. For modern authors other than commentators, the author's name and date of publication serve as citation.

Paradiso

Commentary

CANTO I

Special Note: Since Dante's *Letter to Can Grande* (*Epist.* XIII) deals in specific detail with this first canto of the *Paradiso*, dedicating the third *cantica* of the poem to that high-placed patron, the notes to *Par.* I will often refer the reader to that epistle, which should be read in its entirety at this point. The accepted text of the original Latin is to be found in *Le opere di Dante* (2d edn., 1960); the translation cited is that of the Temple Classics. For a discussion of the letter, including the question of its authenticity, and pertinent bibliography, see the *Enciclopedia dantesca*, under the entry "Epistole."

Because it is Beatrice who serves as guide through this third realm, the reader will do well to remember her several names as these have emerged in the broad patterns of meaning apparent in the last cantos of the *Purgatorio*—Revelation, Sanctifying Grace, and Wisdom. The whole event at the summit of the mountain has clearly made these three names appropriate for the "bearer of beatitude," which the name Beatrice literally means.

For a general introduction to the *Paradiso*, see Grandgent's Preliminary Note to the *cantica* (pp. 625-29 of his commentary) and the relative bibliography given by him. In general Grandgent's arguments to the cantos will be found helpful throughout.

3

1. *La Gloria*: The following verses make this "glory" primarily God's light. The reader should remember when he reaches the end of the poem that thematically the *Paradiso* describes a full circle by terminating with the light of glory, one of the three lights experienced by the pilgrim. (On the three lights, see C. S. Singleton, 1958, pp. 15-23.) However, "gloria" here should be understood primarily in the senses suggested by Dante himself in the *Letter to Can Grande* (*Epist.* XIII, 62-63):

> Similiter etiam et scientius facit auctoritas. Dicit enim Spiritus Sanctus per Hieremiam: "Celum et terram ego impleo"; et in Psalmo: "Quo ibo a spiritu tuo? et quo a facie tua fugiam? Si ascendero in celum, tu illic es; si descendero in infernum, ades. Si sumpsero pennas meas etc." Et Sapientia dicit quod "Spiritus Domini replevit orbem terrarum." Et Ecclesiasticus in quadragesimo secundo: "Gloria Domini plenum est opus eius." Quod etiam scriptura paganorum contestatur; unde Lucanus in nono: "Iuppiter est quodcunque vides, quocunque moveris."

> And authority does the same as science; for the Holy Spirit says by Jeremiah [23:24], "Do I not fill heaven and earth?" and in the psalm [138(139):7-9], "Whither shall I go from thy spirit, and whither shall I flee from thy presence? If I ascend into heaven thou art there; if I descend into hell thou art present. If I take my wings," and the rest. And *Wisdom* [1:7] says that "the spirit of the Lord filled the whole world," and *Ecclesiasticus*, in the forty-second [42:16], "His work is full of the glory of the Lord." Whereto the scripture of the pagans bears co-witness, for Lucan in the ninth [*Phars.* IX, 580], "Juppiter est quodcumque vides quocumque moveris." ("Whatsoever thou seest, wheresoever thou goest, is Jupiter.")

colui che tutto move: God as the unmoved cause of movement is a conception of Aristotelian theology (cf. "lo motor primo," *Purg.* XXV, 70). Thus the opening verse of the *Para-*

diso (like its last verse) bears the unmistakable mark of the pagan philosopher.

2-3. *per l'universo penetra . . . altrove*: See Dante's *Letter to Can Grande* (*Epist.* XIII, 64-65):

> Bene ergo dictum est cum dicit quod divinus radius sive divina gloria, "per universum penetrat et resplendet": penetrat, quantum ad essentiam; resplendet, quantum ad esse. Quod autem subicit de "magis et minus," habet veritatem in manifesto; quoniam videmus in aliquo excellentiori gradu essentiam aliquam, aliquam vero in inferiori; ut patet de celo et elementis, quorum quidem illud incorruptibile, illa vero corruptibilia sunt.

> It is therefore well said when it says that the divine ray, or divine glory *pierces and reglows* through the universe. It pierces as to essence; it reglows as to being. And what he adds as to *more and less* is manifest truth; since we see that one thing has its being in a more exalted grade, and another in a lower, as is evident with respect to the heaven and the elements, whereof that is incorruptible and these corruptible.

Much farther along in the poem, in verses that speak of the creation (specifically of the angels, but by implication of creation in general), God is said to create mirrors that reflect His light back to Him (*Par.* XXIX, 13-30).

See also *Conv.* III, xiv, 4, where Dante states: "Ancora è da sapere che lo primo agente, cioè Dio, pinge la sua virtù in cose per modo di diritto raggio, e in cose per modo di splendore reverberato; onde ne le Intelligenze raggia la divina luce sanza mezzo, ne l'altre si ripercuote da queste Intelligenze prima illuminate." ("We are further to know that the prime agent—to wit God—stamps his power upon some things after the manner of a direct ray, and upon others after the manner of a reflected splendour; for upon the intelligences the divine light rays without medium, upon other things it is reflected by those intelligences which are first enlightened.") In his *Letter to Can Grande* (*Epist.* XIII, 56-61) Dante explains:

Et sic, mediate vel inmediate, omne quod habet esse habet esse ab eo; quia ex eo quod causa secunda recipit a prima, influit super causatum ad modum recipientis et reddentis radium, propter quod causa prima est magis causa. Et hoc dicitur in libro De Causis quod "omnis causa primaria plus influit super suum causatum quam causa universalis secunda." Sed hoc quantum ad esse.

Quantum vero ad essentiam, probo sic: Omnis essentia, preter primam, est causata, aliter essent plura que essent per se necesse esse, quod est impossibile: quod causatum, vel a natura est vel ab intellectu, et quod a natura, per consequens causatum est ab intellectu, cum natura sit opus intelligentie; omne ergo quod est causatum, est causatum ab aliquo intellectu vel mediate vel inmediate. Cum ergo virtus sequatur essentiam cuius est virtus, si essentia intellectiva, est tota et unius que causat. Et sic quemadmodum prius devenire erat ad primam causam ipsius esse, sic nunc essentie et virtutis. Propter quod patet quod omnis essentia et virtus procedat a prima, et intelligentie inferiores recipiant quasi a radiante, et reddant radios superioris ad suum inferius ad modum speculorum. Quod satis aperte tangere videtur Dionysius de Celesti Hierarchia loquens. Et propter hoc dicitur in libro De Causis quod "omnis intelligentia est plena formis." Patet ergo quomodo ratio manifestat divinum lumen, id est divinam bonitatem, sapientiam et virtutem, resplendere ubique.

And thus mediately or immediately everything which is has its being from him; for it is by what the second cause received from the first cause that it has influence upon that which it causes, after the fashion of a body that receives and reflects a ray. Wherefore the first cause is cause in a higher degree; and this is what the book *De Causis* says, to wit, that "every primary cause is more influential on that which it causes, than a universal secondary cause." So much as to being.

But as to essence I prove it thus: Every essence, except the primary, is caused; otherwise there would be more than one existence of self-necessity, which is impossible. What is caused is either of nature or of intelligence; and what is of nature is consequentially caused by intellect, since nature is the work of intelligence. Everything, therefore, which is caused, is caused by some intellect, mediately or immediately. Since, then, virtue follows the essence whose virtue it is, if the essence be intellectual the whole virtue is of one [intelligence] which causes it; and thus, like as before we had to come to a first cause of being itself, so now of essence and of virtue. Wherefore it is clear that every essence and virtue proceeds from the primal one, and the lower intelligences receive it as from a radiating source, and throw the rays of their superior upon their inferior, after the fashion of mirrors. Which Dionysius, speaking of the celestial hierarchy, seems to handle clearly enough, and therefore it is said in the book *De Causis* that "every intelligence is full of forms." It is clear, then, how reason declares the divine light, that is, the divine excellence, wisdom, and virtue, to reglow everywhere.

The next canto, in discussing the reason for the dark spots in the moon, serves as a gloss to vs. 3 here. Also see *Conv.* III, vii, 2, where Dante touches on this: "Ove è da sapere che la divina bontade in tutte le cose discende, e altrimenti essere non potrebbero; ma avvegna che questa bontade si muova da simplicissimo principio, diversamente si riceve, secondo più e meno, da le cose riceventi." ("Where be it known that the divine excellence descends upon all things, and otherwise they could not exist; but although this goodness springs from the most simple principle, it is diversely received, in greater or smaller measure, by the things that receive it.")

4. *Nel ciel che più de la sua luce prende*: The tenth heaven, the Empyrean. Dante's own comment on this verse, in his *Letter to Can Grande* (*Epist.* XIII, 66-68), is:

Et postquam premisit hanc veritatem, prosequitur ab ea circumloquens Paradisum; et dicit quod fuit in celo illo quod de gloria Dei, sive de luce, recipit affluentius.

Propter quod sciendum quod illud celum est celum su-
premum, continens corpora universa et a nullo conten-
tum, intra quod omnia corpora moventur, ipso in sem-
piterna quiete permanente *** et a nulla corporali
substantia virtutem recipiens. Et dicitur empyreum,
quod est idem quod celum igne sui ardoris flagrans;
non quod in eo sit ignis vel ardor materialis, sed spiri-
tualis, quod est amor sanctus sive caritas.

And having premised this truth, he goes on from it with
a circumlocution for Paradise, and says that he "was in
that heaven which receives most abundantly of the glory
or the light of God"; wherefore you are to know that
that heaven is the supreme heaven, containing all the
bodies of the universe and contained by love, within
which all bodies move (itself abiding in eternal rest),
receiving its virtue from no corporeal substance. And
it is called the *Empyrean*, which is the same as the
heaven flaming with fire or heat, not because there is
any material fire or heat in it, but spiritual, to wit holy
love or charity.

5-9. *e vidi cose . . . ire*: Here the echo of Paul's report of his
own experience (II Cor. 12:3-4) is clearly heard. Dante him-
self, in the *Letter to Can Grande* (*Epist.* XIII, 77-79,
83-84), comments:

Et postquam dixit quod fuit in loco illo Paradisi per
suam circumlocutionem, prosequitur dicens se vidisse
aliqua que recitare non potest qui descendit. Et reddit
causam dicens "quod intellectus in tantum profundat
se" in ipsum "desiderium suum," quod est Deus, "quod
memoria sequi non potest." Ad que intelligenda scien-
dum est quod intellectus humanus in hac vita, propter
connaturalitaten et affinitatem quam habet ad substan-
tiam intellectualem separatam, quando elevatur, in tan-
tum elevatur, ut memoria post reditum deficiat propter
transcendisse humanum modum. Et hoc insinuatur
nobis per Apostolum ad Corinthios loquentem, ubi
dicit: "Scio hominem, sive in corpore sive extra corpus
nescio, Deus scit, raptum usque ad tertium celum, et

8

vidit arcana Dei, que non licet homini loqui." Ecce, postquam humanam rationem intellectus ascensione transierat, quid extra se ageretur non recordabatur. . . .

Vidit ergo, ut dicit, aliqua "que referre nescit et nequit rediens." Diligenter quippe notandum est quod dicit "nescit et nequit": nescit quia oblitus, nequit quia, si recordatur et contentum tenet, sermo tamen deficit. Multa namque per intellectum videmus quibus signa vocalia desunt: quod satis Plato insinuat in suis libris per assumptionem metaphorismorum; multa enim per lumen intellectuale vidit que sermone proprio nequivit exprimere.

And when he has said that he was in that place of Paradise, described by circumlocution, he goes on to say "that he saw certain things which he who thence descends cannot relate"; and he tells the reason, saying that "the intellect is so engulfed" in the very thing for which it longs, which is God, "that memory cannot follow." To understand which things be it known that the human intellect, when it is exalted in this life, because of its being co-natural and having affinity with a sejunct intellectual substance, it is so far exalted that after its return memory fails it, because it has transcended the measure of humanity. And this we are given to understand by the apostle, speaking *ad Corinthios* [II Cor. 12:3-4], where he says, "I know such a man (whether in the body or out of the body I know not, God knoweth), who was rapt into Paradise and heard hidden words, which it is not lawful for a man to utter." Behold, when the intellect had transcended human measure in its ascent, it remembered not the things that took place beyond its own range. . . .

He saw, then, as he says, certain things "which he who returns has not knowledge, nor power to relate"; and it must be noted carefully that he says, has "not knowledge, nor power." He has not knowledge, because he has forgotten; and he has not power, because if he remembered and retained the matter, nevertheless language fails: for we see many things by the intellect for which there are no vocal signs, of which Plato gives sufficient hint in his books by having recourse to metaphors; for he saw many things by intellectual light which he could not express in direct speech.

This theme becomes central in the final canto of the *Paradiso*.

7. *suo disire*: The object of desire, God and the vision of Him "face to face." For this use of the possessive, cf. *Purg.* XXXI, 22.

9. *memoria*: "Memoria" is the subject of the verb.

10. *Veramente*: "Veramente" here means "nevertheless," as it frequently does in the poem. Cf. the Latin *verumtamen*.

13-36. *O buono Appollo . . . risponda*: These verses contain the invocation which corresponds to those offered in *Inf.* II and in *Purg.* I. On this Dante himself comments in his *Letter to Can Grande* (*Epist.* XIII, 86-87):

> Deinde cum dicit: "O bone Apollo," etc., facit invocationem suam. Et dividitur ista pars in partes duas: in prima invocando petit; in secunda suadet Apollini petitionem factam, remunerationem quandam prenuntians; et incipit secunda pars ibi: "O divina virtus." Prima pars dividitur in partes duas: in prima petit divinum auxilium, in secunda tangit necessitatem sue petitionis, quod est iustificare ipsam, ibi: "Hucusque alterum iugum Parnassi" etc.

> Then when he says, "O good Apollo," and the rest, he makes his invocation. And that part is divided into two parts: in the first he makes petition in his invocation; in the second he suasively urges upon Apollo the petition he has made, announcing a kind of remuneration. And the second part begins here, "O divine power." The first part is divided into two parts, in the first of which he seeks the divine aid, and in the second touches upon the necessity of his petition, which is its justification. And it begins here: "up to this point one peak of Parnassus," and the rest.

13. *Appollo*: The reader will recall that the sun appears at the beginning of the poem as "the planet that leads men aright by every path" (*Inf.* I, 17-18). Apollo, of course, was the god of the Sun. See Dante, *Conv.* III, xii, 6-7.

15. *l'amato alloro*: Daphne, loved and pursued by Apollo, was changed to a laurel. See Ovid, *Metam.* I, 452-567.

16. *Parnaso*: See n. to *Purg.* XXII, 65.

19. *tue = tu*. Cf. "sùe" in *Purg.* IV, 47.

20. *Marsia*: Marsyas, a satyr of Phrygia, who, having found a flute which Minerva had thrown away in disgust because it distorted her features, discovered that it emitted of its own accord the most beautiful strains. Elated with his discovery he was rash enough to challenge Apollo to a musical contest, the conditions of which were that the victor should do what he pleased with his vanquished rival. The trial took place before the Muses as umpires, Apollo playing on the cithara, Marsyas on the flute. The decision being given in favor of the god, Apollo, to punish Marsyas for his presumption, bound him to a tree and flayed him alive. Dante here prays to Apollo to inspire him to sing as sweetly as the god played when he vanquished the satyr.

The story of Apollo and Marsyas is told by Ovid in the *Fasti* (VI, 697-708) and with more detail in the *Metamorphoses* (VI, 383-91), whence doubtless Dante took it:

> . . . satyri reminiscitur alter,
> quem Tritoniaca Latous harundine victum
> adfecit poena. "quid me mihi detrahis?" inquit;
> "a! piget, a! non est" clamabat "tibia tanti."
> clamanti cutis est summos direpta per artus,
> nec quicquam nisi vulnus erat; cruor undique manat,
> detectique patent nervi, trepidaeque sine ulla
> pelle micant venae; salientia viscera possis
> et perlucentes numerare in pectore fibras.

Another recalled the satyr whom the son of Latona had conquered in a contest on Pallas' reed, and punished. "Why do you tear me from myself?" he cried. "Oh, I repent! Oh, a flute is not worth such price!" As he screams, his skin is stripped off the surface of his body, and he is all one wound: blood flows down on every side, the sinews lie bare, his veins throb and quiver with no skin to cover them: you could count the entrails as they palpitate, and the vitals showing clearly in his breast.

See also Statius, *Theb*. IV, 186; Lucan, *Phars*. III, 205-8.

21. *la vagina*: Marsyas was flayed, thus the "vagina" ("sheath") of his limbs is his skin.

22. *divina virtù*: The invocation, with these words, now becomes more a prayer addressed to Apollo as the supreme Deity. See vs. 28, where he is called "father."

23. *ombra*: The shadowy recollection that the poet now has of the experience (see vs. 9).

25. *vedra'mi = mi vedrai*.   *diletto legno*: The laurel beloved by Apollo.

26. *le foglie*: The crown of poets was traditionally made of laurel leaves.

27. *che = di cui*.   *la materia e tu mi farai degno*: Both "materia" and "tu" are the subjects of the singular verb "farai."

29. *cesare*: Caesar, the title of the rulers of the Roman Empire, was applied by Dante to the rulers of the Holy Roman Empire and to other emperors as well. Note Dante's use of the term in reference to Frederick II (*Inf*. XIII, 65), Albert I (*Purg*. VI, 92), and Henry VII (*Epist*. V, 5). Here the reference is to emperors in general.

30. *colpa e vergogna de l'umane voglie*: "Colpa" and "vergogna" are here used in the ablative construction: "because of the sin and shame of human desires."

31-32. *che parturir letizia . . . fronda*: "Fronda" is the subject of "dovria parturir," of which "letizia" is the object. "Dovria" = *dovrebbe*.

32. *delfica deità*: Delphi was a small town on the southern slope of Mount Parnassus, famous as the site of the great temple of Apollo and the oracle who spoke in his name. The name Delphi may have derived from *adelphos* (Greek "brother"), alluding to the twin peaks of the mountain. As the name of the chief center of the worship of Apollo, the name Delphi was used to designate the god—see Ovid, *Metam*. II, 543-44: "Placuit tibi, Delphice, certe, / dum vel casta fuit vel inobservata." ("She surely found favour in thy eyes, O Delphic god, so long as she was chaste—or undetected.") The invocation to Apollo here turns, curiously, from direct to indirect address, since the "delfica deità" is Apollo himself.

33. *peneia*: Peneus, son of Oceanus and Tethys and river god of the Peneus, the chief river in Thessaly and one of the most important in Greece, was the father of Daphne, who was pursued by Apollo for her beauty.   *alcun*: The object of "asseta."

36. *Cirra*: Cirrha was a town on the Gulf of Corinth southwest of Delphi, the seat of the oracle of Apollo. It was intimately connected with Delphi and so was sometimes used as a synonym of either Apollo or Delphi. See Statius, *Theb*. III, 474-76:

> ... non Cirrha deum promiserit antro
> certius, aut frondes lucis quas fama Molossis
> Chaonias sonuisse tibi ...

Not Cirrha can more surely vouchsafe the inspiration of her grotto, nor those Chaonian leaves that are famed to rustle at thy bidding in Molossian groves.

Cirrha was also the name sometimes given to the peak of Parnassus sacred to Apollo. See Statius, *Theb*. III, 611-15:

> ... non si ipse cavo sub vertice Cirrhae,
> quisquis is est, timidis famaeque ita visus, Apollo
> mugiat insano penitus seclusus in antro,
> exspectare queam, dum pallida virgo tremendas
> nuntiet ambages. ...

Not if beneath Cirrha's caverned height he, whoe'er he is—Apollo cowards and rumour account him—were to bellow from the deep seclusion of his crazy grotto, could I wait for the pale virgin to announce the solemn riddlings!

37–44. *Surge ai mortali . . . quasi*: "In these lines Dante describes the season. On every day of the year the sun rises from a particular point in the horizon, and this point differs from day to day. The points are called *foci*, 'outlets.' The best 'outlet' is the one from which the sun emerges on March 21, the vernal equinox. This is the *foce* that 'brings together four circles with three crosses': it is the point where three great heavenly circles intersect the horizon, each of them forming a cross with it. The circles are the equator, the ecliptic, and the colure of the equinoxes; this last is a great circle that traverses the two heavenly poles and crosses the ecliptic at Aries and Libra. When the sun rises from this point, it is 'coupled with its best orbit, and with its best constellation,' namely Aries. In that sign, the sun has the most benign influence on the earth. Now on the day when Dante rose to heaven, the sun had passed 'almost' through that *foce*: it was considerably later than March 21 (it was, in fact, Wednesday, April 13, 1300); but the sun was still in Aries; 'almost this outlet,' then, 'had made morning yonder (in Eden) and evening here (in the Hemisphere of Land)' " (Gr). See Fig. 1.

It should be noted that, in place of the reading "tal foce quasi; e tutto era là bianco" accepted by Grandgent, Petrocchi and some other modern editors have adopted in vs. 44 the reading "tal foce, e quasi tutto era là bianco," arguing that "quasi" is meant to indicate that the hemisphere of water with the mountain of Purgatory at its center is only partially illuminated by the sun when it is in Aries. But this seems a less likely meaning, since Dante is speaking from a post of observation where the rising sun at least *seems* to illuminate all, whereas the fine point of having "quasi" ("almost") modify "foce," in the meaning set forth by Grandgent above, would be typical of the poet. But see Petrocchi and Chimenz for the argument in favor of the other reading.

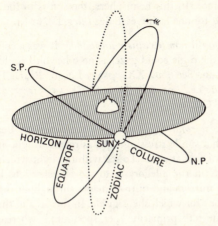

1. The circles of the equator, the zodiac, and the equinoctial
colure

39. *giugne = congiunge.*

44–45. *tutto era . . . nera*: This tells us the time of day, al-
though the signal of noon as the time of day has already been
given (*Purg.* XXXIII, 104). Now it is noon in Eden, mid-
night in Jerusalem, the hemisphere of water is all light, the
hemisphere of land all dark. It should be recalled that
the entrance into Inferno took place in the evening and that
the journey through Purgatory began at dawn. Now the up-
ward journey of Paradise will begin at high noon. The sym-
bolic value of this arrangement is rich in meaning and is, of
course, deliberately calculated. On noon, or the "sixth hour,"
as the most noble hour of the whole day, see Dante, *Conv.*
IV, xxiii, 15. The sun is in full glory then, and the *Paradiso*
has begun with an invocation addressed to Apollo, god of the
Sun.

46. *in sul sinistro fianco*: Beatrice was facing east as her
procession here at the top of the mountain finally turned and
moved in that direction (*Purg.* XXXII, 17-18), and we may
assume that she proceeded toward the east yet farther, to

reach Eunoe. In this hemisphere, the sun is to the north, or to the left for one facing east. See *Purg.* IV, 61-84.

48. *aguglia sì non li s'affisse unquanco*: It was a common belief that the eagle could gaze, as no other bird could, directly on the sun. See *Par.* XX, 31-33; Lucan, *Phars.* IX, 902-3. *li = gli*, i.e., "on it," the sun. Cf. vs. 54. *unquanco*: "Never." Cf. *Purg.* IV, 76.

49-54. *E sì come . . . uso*: The journey with Beatrice begins with a simile stressing light as reflected light and action by reflection, as it were. To see with the light which Beatrice represents in the allegory is to see by reflection, hence the stress on mirrors and mirror images throughout that part of the journey for which she is guide. In this area of the "second light" one sees primarily "per speculum," whereas beyond this second light lies the light of glory at the end, where the pilgrim will see "facie ad faciem." Cf. I Cor. 13:12: "Videmus nunc per speculum in aenigmate, tunc autem facie ad faciem." ("We see now through a mirror in an obscure manner, but then face to face.") For the three lights and such distinctions, see C. S. Singleton (1958), pp. 15-38. In the literal image of the ray of light returning upwards, it is clear that the reflector must be conceived as being horizontal, the "second" or reflected ray thus rising back up.

51. *pur come pelegrin che tornar vuole*: The burden of connotation is clear: Dante will now return "home" in returning to God, by whom his soul was created.

52-53. *così de l'atto suo . . . fece*: Dante now imitates Beatrice's own gazing at the sun.

52. *per li occhi infuso*: "Infuso" here clearly bears the suggestion of infusion, and we know that in the allegory Beatrice is (in one of her names) Sanctifying Grace, which is always infused from above, even as are the theological virtues which are seen to attend her at the end of the *Purgatorio*.

53. *ne l'imagine mia*: One may understand *imagine* to mean "imagination," but only in the sense of an "image-re-

16

ceiving" faculty of the mind. Cf. *Purg*. XVII, 13, where this same faculty is termed the "imaginativa" (and see n. to *Purg*. XVII, 13-18).

56–57. *loco fatto . . . spece*: Eden, made for man as his proper abode. Cf. Gen. 2:8, 15; *Purg*. XXVIII, 91-102.

57. *spece* = *specie*.

61–63. *e di sùbito . . . addorno*: Without knowing it, Dante has left the earth and is speeding heavenwards, rapidly rising ever closer to the sun, which explains the great increase of light. Some commentators interpret the meaning to be that he is passing through the sphere of fire which lies just below the sphere of the moon, but this seems unlikely, since the focus remains on the sun. Cf. vs. 82, " 'l grande lume."

62. *quei che puote*: God.

63. *addorno* = *adornato*.

64–66. *Beatrice . . . rimote*: Dante now turns away from the sun, which literally can be termed a mirror (cf. *Purg*. IV, 62), to Beatrice as to a mirror. See n. to vss. 49-54.

66. *le luci*: My eyes.   *rimote*: "Withdrawn" (from my upward gazing on the sun).

67. *Nel suo aspetto*: "As I thus gazed on her" is the meaning.   *fei = feci*.

67–69. *Nel suo aspetto . . . dèi*: Glaucus was a fisherman of Boeotia who, according to Ovid (*Metam*. XIII, 904-59), sat down one day on a grassy spot where no one had ever been before, to count his catch. The fish began to move about on the grass and made their way back into the sea. Thinking it must be due to some magic property in the grass, Glaucus chewed some and immediately began to yearn for the ocean. Bidding farewell to the earth, to which he would never return, he plunged into the sea and was changed into a sea god by Oceanus and Tethys. Dante compares the change wrought in himself as he gazes upon Beatrice to the transformation of Glaucus after he tasted the divine herb. On the symbolic and allegorical implications of Dante's allusion to the transformation of Glaucus, see C. S. Singleton (1958), pp. 28-29. Clearly it points to the verb "trasumanar" in the next verse as this applies to the pilgrim.

70. *Trasumanar*: "Transhumanizing," rising above the human state, as Glaucus did. Dante will now literally rise with Beatrice through the spheres and high above the mortal condition. But in terms of the kind of vision he will have while Beatrice guides him, he now passes into that mode of vision which is possible through the special grace which she represents, which is a grace *desursum descendens*, infused from on high. See the Special Note at the beginning of this canto. Actually, in its context here, the verb "trasumanar" takes on the sense of a verb of motion, "to pass beyond the human."
   per verba: Latin for "in words."

71. *poria = potrebbe*.   *però = perciò*.   *essemplo = esempio*, i.e., the example of Glaucus, in becoming a god, or godlike.

72. *a cui esperienza grazia serba*: To those who, through such a grace as is represented by Beatrice, may also rise above the human state. The verse clearly points to the allegorical journey to God in this life. Such grace may be given to everyman in the itinerary of the mind to God, here and now. "Grazia" is the subject of the verb "serba."

73. *S' = se*, "whether."   *sol di me quel che creasti*: "Only that part of me which you created," i.e., the soul. Cf. *Purg.* XXV, 70-72.

74. *novellamente*: " 'Most recently,' 'latest.'—Dante is not sure whether he took his body with him to Heaven, or left it behind. St. Paul expresses the same doubt with regard to his own experience, 2 Cor. xii, 3-4: '. . . And I knew such a man (whether in the body, or out of the body, I cannot tell; God knoweth;) How that he was caught up into paradise, and heard unspeakable words, which it is not lawful for a man to utter.' St. Augustine (*De Genesi ad Litteram*, XII, iii-vi) and St. Thomas discuss the question, but leave it undecided. The

poet considers his rapture as similar in kind to St. Paul's, and therefore repeats St. Paul's words. In the following narrative Dante seems to think of himself as still in the flesh, although he ultimately sees God. Whether St. Paul actually beheld God or not is a matter on which theologians have disagreed, St. Augustine and St. Thomas holding the affirmative opinion. Cf. Exod. xxxiii, 20: 'Thou canst not see my face: for no man shall see me, and live' " (Gr). *'l ciel*: "The heavens," the usual singular for the plural.

75. *col tuo lume mi levasti*: Since Beatrice, in the allegory, is precisely the light that uplifts the pilgrim Dante, this phrase, in direct address to the Deity, makes her a God-given light—which, of course, she is, "infused" from above.

76. *rota*: The revolution of the spheres.

77. *desiderato*: " 'By being desired.' The swift motion of the Primum Mobile, the outermost sphere of the material universe, is due to the eagerness of every one of its parts to come into contact with every part of God's own Heaven, the Empyrean; and the Primum Mobile imparts its revolution to all the heavens within it" (Gr). Cf. Dante, *Conv.* II, iii, 9:

> E questo è cagione al Primo Mobile per avere velocissimo movimento; chè per lo ferventissimo appetito ch'è 'n ciascuna parte di quello nono cielo, che è immediato a quello, d'essere congiunta con ciascuna parte di quello divinissimo ciel quieto, in quello si rivolve con tanto desiderio, che la sua velocitade è quasi incomprensibile.

> And this is the cause of the *primum mobile* having the swiftest motion, because by reason of the most fervid appetite wherewith every part of this ninth heaven, which is next below it, longeth to be conjoined with every part of this divinest, and tranquil heaven, it revolves therein with so great yearning that its swiftness is scarce to be comprehended.

That God, through being desired, moves the spheres is primarily an Aristotelian conception.

78. *con l'armonia che temperi e discerni*: The harmony of the spheres, which God is said to attune and distribute or arrange. Cf. *Purg.* XXX, 93. A text fundamental for this conception is found in Book VI of Cicero's *De re publica*. Commonly known as the *Somnium Scipionis*, it was widely read in the Middle Ages. Because of its importance, and the fact that the equivalents for Dante's two verbs *temperare* and *discernere* are found or reflected in this text, it seems appropriate to quote *De re publica* VI, xviii, 18-19 (italics added):

Quae cum intuerer stupens, ut me recepi, Quid? hic, inquam, quis est, qui conplet aures meas tantus et tam dulcis sonus?

Hic est, inquit, ille, qui intervallis disiunctus inparibus, sed tamen pro rata parte ratione *distinctis* inpulsu et motu ipsorum orbium efficitur et acuta cum gravibus *temperans* varios aequabiliter concentus efficit; nec enim silentio tanti motus incitari possunt, et natura fert, ut extrema ex altera parte graviter, ex altera autem acute sonent. quam ob causam summus ille caeli stellifer cursus, cuius conversio est concitatior, acuto ex excitato movetur sono, gravissimo autem hic lunaris atque infimus; nam terra nona inmobilis manens una sede semper haeret complexa medium mundi locum. illi autem octo cursus, in quibus eadem vis est duorum, septem efficiunt *distinctos* intervallis sonos, qui numerus rerum omnium fere nodus est; quod docti homines nervis imitati atque cantibus aperuerunt sibi reditum in hunc locum, sicut alii, qui praestantibus ingeniis in vita humana divina studia coluerunt. hoc sonitu oppletae aures hominum obsurduerunt; nec est ullus hebetior sensus in vobis, sicut, ubi Nilus ad illa, quae Catadupa nominantur, praecipitat ex altissimis montibus, ea gens, quae illum locum adcolit, propter magnitudinem sonitus sensu audiendi caret. hic vero tantus est totius mundi incitatissima conversione sonitus, ut eum aures hominum capere non possint, sicut intueri solem adversum nequitis, eiusque radiis acies vestra sensusque vincitur.

After recovering from the astonishment with which I viewed these wonders, I said: "What is this loud and agreeable sound that fills my ears?"

"That is produced," he replied, "by the onward rush and motion of the spheres themselves; the intervals between them, though unequal, being exactly arranged in a fixed proportion, by an agreeable blending of high and low tones various harmonies are produced; for such mighty motions cannot be carried on so swiftly in silence; and Nature has provided that one extreme shall produce low tones while the other gives forth high. Therefore this uppermost sphere of heaven, which bears the stars, as it revolves more rapidly, produces a high, shrill tone, whereas the lowest revolving sphere, that of the Moon, gives forth the lowest tone; for the earthly sphere, the ninth, remains ever motionless and stationary in its position in the centre of the universe. But the other eight spheres, two of which move with the same velocity, produce seven different sounds,—a number which is the key of almost everything. Learned men, by imitating this harmony on stringed instruments and in song, have gained for themselves a return to this region, as others have obtained the same reward by devoting their brilliant intellects to divine pursuits during their earthly lives. Men's ears, ever filled with this sound, have become deaf to it; for you have no duller sense than that of hearing. We find a similar phenomenon where the Nile rushes down from those lofty mountains at the place called Catadupa; the people who live near by have lost their sense of hearing on account of the loudness of the sound. But this mighty music, produced by the revolution of the whole universe at the highest speed, cannot be perceived by human ears, any more than you can look straight at the Sun, your sense of sight being overpowered by its radiance."

79–81. *parvemi tanto . . . disteso*: As Beatrice will now declare to Dante (vss. 91-93), he is already rising heavenwards faster than lightning. Some commentators take this great increase of light to mean that Dante is already traversing the sphere of fire, which was thought to be just below the sphere of the moon. However, the increase of light may simply be due to so rapid a rise toward the sun, as the phrase "fiamma del sol" seems to suggest. Cf. vss. 61-62.

85. *che vedea me sì com' io*: Beatrice knows Dante's thoughts, of course, and "reads his mind," even as Virgil was privileged to do.

87. *aprio = aprì*.

89. *falso imaginar*: Beatrice knows that Dante believes he is still on earth.

92-93. *ma folgore . . . riedi*: "When lightning descends, it leaves its proper abode, the sphere of fire. Dante's real home is the Empyrean, toward which he is returning more swiftly than lightning ever fell from the sky" (Gr). For the phenomenon of lightning in this sense, see *Par*. XXIII, 40-42. And, for the soul's return, see *Conv*. IV, xxviii, 2, where Dante says that the noble soul "ritorna a Dio, sì come a quello porto onde ella si partio quando venne ad intrare nel mare di questa vita" ("returns to God, as to that port whence she departed when she came to enter upon the sea of this life").

97. *requievi*: A Latinism, the preterite of *requiescere*, meaning "I was resting."

98. *grande ammirazion*: His wonder at the increase of light and at the harmony of the spheres.

98-99. *ma ora ammiro . . . levi*: Many commentators take "questi corpi levi" to refer to the spheres of air and fire, which lie below the sphere of the moon. But the verb "trascenda" (subjunctive of *trascendere*), and Dante's wonder, point by anticipation to the other "light bodies," the nine spheres beginning with the moon, which he knows he must pass through in his upward journey to the Empyrean. Is Dante rising in his body or not? See *Par*. II, 34-42. This is a question that is never answered within the poem. Nor did Paul answer it regarding his own rapture (II Cor. 12:2).

Though the case here is wholly different, since the pilgrim Dante is a living man, it is interesting to note that the question was commonly discussed by theologians as to how it would be possible for the elect who are to receive their glorified bodies at the Last Judgment to pass with their bodies through the spheres as they rise to the Empyrean. See Thomas Aquinas, *Summa contra Gentiles* IV, 87, the conclusion of which is as follows:

> Neque etiam huic promissioni divinae impossibilitatem affert quod corpora caelestia frangi non possunt, ut super ea gloriosa corpora subleventur, quia a virtute divina hoc fiet ut gloriosa corpora simul cum aliis corporibus esse possint; cuius rei indicium in corpore Christi praecessit, dum ad discipulos ianuis clausis intravit.

> Neither does this divine promise meet an impossibility in the assertion that celestial bodies are unbreakable so the glorious bodies may not be elevated above them. For the divine power will bring it about that the glorious bodies can be simultaneously where the other bodies are; an indication of this was given in the body of Christ when He came to the disciples, "the doors being shut" (John 20:26).

103–41. *Le cose . . . vivo*: Beatrice's answer occupies the rest of the canto and is the first striking example of the new perspective of the *Paradiso*, in which, time and again, a total view of the cosmos and its providential order is set forth. Her beginning is typical in this passage: "All things whatsoever . . ."

104–5. *hanno ordine tra loro . . . simigliante*: There is a total order and harmony in this universe created by God, and this is the form (the essential informing and governing principle) which makes God's handiwork, the universe, resemble its Maker. At the end, when the wayfaring Dante will see God "face to face," he will, in fact, see in the depth of that vision the whole universe, as it were, "bound with love into a single volume" (*Par.* XXXIII, 85-87). See Thomas Aquinas, *Summa theol.* I, q. 47, a. 3, resp.: "Ipse ordo in rebus sic a Deo creatis existens unitatem mundi manifestat. Mundus enim iste unus dicitur unitate ordinis, secundum quod quaedam ad alia ordinantur. Quaecumque autem sunt a Deo, ordinem habent ad invicem, et ad ipsum Deum." ("The very order of things created by God shows the unity of the world. For this world is called one by the unity of order, whereby some things are ordered to others. But whatever things come from God, have relation of order to each other, and to God Himself.")

106–8. *Qui veggion . . . norma*: The created universe in all its harmony and total order is there to be contemplated by those among God's creatures which have intellect, namely, angels and men, here called "high" creatures precisely because they have that "high" faculty. God made the universe for Himself and left His imprint ("orma") upon it. Things in His universe point beyond themselves, point up to Him, to the eternal worth which He is, and they are so designed by Him to do this for those creatures who have the power to contemplate the creation in this way. See Ps. 18:2[19:1]: "Caeli enarrant gloriam Dei, et opera manuum eius annuntiat firmamentum." ("The heavens declare the glory of God, and the firmament proclaims his handiwork.") The reader should consider here, in this context, that the poet has imitated God's work in his poem by the very element of the triple rhyme in which it is written: a triune Craftsman left everywhere that "orma" of a number three in His work; so does the poet in imitation thereof. See further C. S. Singleton (1949), pp. 38-41. Thus the created universe declares the glory of God, and this is ultimately its reason ("norma") for being, the "final cause" ("fine") of its total order. The following verse continues to dwell on that "ordine." See Dante, *De mon.* I, viii, 2:

De intentione Dei est ut omne causatum in tantum divinam similitudinem representet, in quantum propria natura recipere potest. Propter quod dictum est "Facia-

mus hominem ad ymaginem et similitudinem nostram";
quod licet "ad ymaginem" de rebus inferioribus ab
homine dici non possit, "ad similitudinem" tamen de
qualibet dici potest, cum totum universum nichil aliud
sit quam vestigium quoddam divine bonitatis.

It is of the intention of God that every created thing
should present the divine likeness in so far as its proper
nature is capable of receiving it. Wherefore it is said,
"Let us make man after our image and likeness." And
although "after our image" may not be said of things
lower than man, yet "after our likeness" may be said of
all things soever, since the whole universe is nought else
than a certain footprint of the divine excellence.

109–23. *Ne l'ordine . . . fretta*: Beatrice's cosmic view of this
total order among all things now touches on the motive force
within that order, which is love, natural love, an instinct in-
nate in all things. It will be recalled that the poet has built
into the exact center of his poem (his "imitation" of that
order) a discourse on love, distinguishing this natural love,
"which cannot err," from elective love. Beatrice's exposition
now is a further explanation of how this instinct, or natural
love, is indeed the primary motive force within the total order
of God's creation, as He in His providence willed it. See
Purg. XVII, 91-94, and n. to *Purg.* XVII, 91-92. There is,
of course, much Aristotelian philosophy in Beatrice's disqui-
sition, for in Dante's time Christian theology had already
taken a great deal from Aristotle.

109. *accline*: Natural love as a motive force is an instinct
which "bends," is an inclination toward something desired.
See *Purg.* XVIII, 22-27, where the term *piegare* ("to bend")
is used, and such bending is said to be love itself.

110. *tutte nature*: All created things, animate and inanimate.
Stones and flames, as well as animals, men, and angels, are
included in this conception.   *per diverse sorti*: Each class
of creatures has a different destiny, as Beatrice goes on to
state.

111–14. *più al principio . . . porti*: The ultimate principle of all things is God or the good, and in the great "chain of being" which is His creation some creatures are by their nature nearer to Him than others. There is hierarchy and degree in the total order. Angels are higher than men in that order, though both are "high," for if they are angels, they dwell forever with God, and if men, they may return to Him, returning by the motive force of natural love. See Thomas Aquinas, *Summa theol.* I, q. 59, a. 1, resp.:

> Quodcum omnia procedant ex voluntate divina, omnia suo modo per appetitum inclinantur in bonum, sed diversimode. Quaedam enim inclinantur in bonum per solam naturalem habitudinem absque cognitione, sicut plantae et corpora inanimata; et talis inclinatio ad bonum vocatur appetitus naturalis. Quaedam vero ad bonum inclinantur cum aliqua cognitione; non quidem sic quod cognoscant ipsam rationem boni, sed cognoscunt aliquod bonum particulare, sicut sensus qui cognoscit dulce et album, et aliquid huiusmodi. Inclinatio autem hanc cognitionem sequens dicitur appetitus sensitivus. Quaedam vero inclinantur ad bonum cum cognitione, qua cognoscunt ipsam boni rationem, quod est proprium intellectus; et haec perfectissime inclinantur in bonum; non quidem quasi ab alio solummodo directa in bonum, sicut ea quae cognitione carent; neque in bonum particulariter tantum sicut ea quibus est sola sensitiva cognitio; sed quasi inclinata in ipsum universale bonum; et haec inclinatio dicitur voluntas.

> Since all things flow from the Divine will, all things in their own way are inclined by appetite towards good, but in different ways. Some are inclined to good by their natural inclination, without knowledge, as plants and inanimate bodies. Such inclination towards good is called *a natural appetite*. Others, again, are inclined towards good, but with some knowledge; not that they know the aspect of goodness, but that they apprehend some particular good; as the sense, which knows the sweet, the white, and so on. The inclination which fol-

lows this apprehension is called *a sensitive appetite*.
Other things, again, have an inclination towards good,
but with a knowledge whereby they perceive the aspect
of goodness; this belongs to the intellect. This is most
perfectly inclined towards what is good; not, indeed, as
if it were merely guided by another towards good, like
things devoid of knowledge, nor towards some particu-
lar good only, as things which have only sensitive
knowledge, but as inclined towards good in general.
Such inclination is termed *will*.

See also Dante, *Conv.* III, vii, 2-5:

Ove è da sapere che la divina bontade in tutte le cose
discende, e altrimenti essere non potrebbero; ma
avvegna che questa bontade si muova da simplicissimo
principio, diversamente si riceve, secondo più e meno,
de le cose riceventi. Onde scritto è nel libro de le
Cagioni: "La prima bontade manda le sue bontadi
sopra le cose con uno discorrimento." Veramente
ciascuna cosa riceve da quello discorrimento secondo
lo modo de la sua vertù e de lo suo essere; e di ciò sensi-
bile essemplo avere potemo dal sole. Vedemo la luce del
sole, la quale è una, da uno fonte derivata, diversamente
da le corpora essere ricevuta; sì come dice Alberto, in
quello libro che fa de lo Intelletto, che certi corpi, "per
molta chiaritade di diafano avere in sè mista, tosto che 'l
sole li vede diventano tanto luminosi, che per multipli-
camento di luce in quello e ne lo loro aspetto, rendono
a li altri di sè grande splendore," sì come è l'oro e alcuna
pietra. "Certi sono che, per esser del tutto diafani, non
solamente ricevono la luce, ma quella non impediscono,
anzi rendono lei del loro colore colorata ne l'altre cose.
E certi sono tanto vincenti ne la purità del diafano, che
divegnono sì raggianti, che vincono l'armonia de
l'occhio, e non si lasciano vedere sanza fatica del viso,"
sì come sono li specchi. Certi altri sono tanto sanza dia-
fano, che quasi poco de la luce ricevono, sì come la
terra. Così la bontà di Dio è ricevuta altrimenti da le
sustanze separate, cioè da li Angeli, che sono sanza

grossezza di materia, quasi diafani per la purità de la loro forma, e altrimenti da l'anima umana.

Where be it known that the divine excellence descends upon all things, and otherwise they could not exist; but although this goodness springs from the most simple principle, it is diversely received, in greater or smaller measure, by the things that receive it. Wherefore it is written in the book *Of Causes*: "The primal excellence makes its excellences flow upon things with one flowing"; but each thing receives of this flowing according to the fashion of its power and of its being, and of this we may have an example patent to the senses from the sun. We see the light of the sun, which is one, derived from a single source, diversely received by the several bodies; as Albertus says in that book he has made *On the intellect*, that certain substances, because they have large measure of the clearness of the transparent mingled in their composition, so soon as the sun sees them become so luminous that their aspect consists in the multiplication of the light in them, and they cast a great splendour from themselves upon other substances; as are gold and certain stones. Certain there are which, because they are altogether diaphanous, not only receive the light, but without impeding it render it again, coloured with their colour, to other things. And certain there are so supreme in the purity of their transparency as to become so radiant that they vanquish the temper of the eye, and cannot be looked on without trouble of the sight; as are mirrors. Certain others are so completely without transparency that they receive but little of the light; as is earth. In like manner the excellence of God is received after one fashion by the sejunct substances, to wit the angels, which are without grossness of material, as though diaphanous, in virtue of the purity of their form; and after another fashion by the human soul.

112–14. *onde si muovono . . . porti*: Metaphorically the whole of creation is now viewed as a great sea, the sea of existence, and the creatures, impelled by natural love

("istinto," vs. 114), as so many ships or rivers destined, by
different lots, to different ports or goals.

114. *con istinto a lei dato che la porti*: This natural love is
implanted by God in everything, as its motive force.   *che
la porti*: The verb in the subjunctive expresses deliberate pur-
pose on the part of the Giver of that instinct.

115. *Questi*: This instinct, which is the subject of the verb
in this and each of the following two verses, is seen as the
motive force in three classes of creatures or natures (vs.
110): fire, animate creatures, and earth.   *ne porta*: "Ne"
is the adverb "off."   *il foco inver' la luna*: The sphere of
fire lies immediately below the sphere of the moon and is the
highest of the elemental spheres: fire, air, water, and earth,
which exist in that descending order. Thus a flame is seen to
reach upwards, as it were. Why? Because it seeks to return
to its proper sphere or locus of existence, just below the
moon. In the present context a certain passage of the *Con-
vivio* (III, iii, 2-4) can serve as a further gloss to the mean-
ing here:

> Onde è da sapere che ciascuna cosa, come detto è di
> sopra, per la ragione di sopra mostrata ha 'l suo speziale
> amore. Come le corpora simplici hanno amore naturato
> in sè a lo luogo proprio, e però la terra sempre discende
> al centro; lo fuoco ha [amore a] la circunferenza di
> sopra, lungo lo cielo de la luna, e però sempre sale a
> quello. Le corpora composte prima, sì come sono le
> minere, hanno amore a lo luogo dove la loro genera-
> zione è ordinata, e in quello crescono e acquistano
> vigore e potenza; onde vedemo la calamita sempre da
> la parte de la sua generazione ricevere vertù. Le piante,
> che sono prima animate, hanno amore a certo luogo più
> manifestamente, secondo che la complessione richiede;
> e però vedemo certe piante lungo l'acque quasi c[ontent]-
> arsi, e certe sopra li gioghi de le montagne, e certe ne
> le piagge e dappiè monti: le quali se si transmutano, o
> muoiono del tutto o vivono quasi triste, sì come cose
> disgiunte dal loro amico.

Wherefore be it known that everything, as said above, and for the reason above set forth, hath its specific love, as, for example, the simple bodies have a love which has an innate affinity to their proper place; and that is why earth ever drops to the centre; but the love of fire is for the upper circumference, under the heaven of the moon, and therefore it ever riseth thereto.

Primary compound bodies, like the minerals, have a love for the place where their generation is ordained; and therein they grow, and thence draw vigour and power. Whence we see the magnet ever receive power from the direction of its generation.

Plants, which are the primary living things, have a more manifest love for certain places, according as their composition requires; and therefore we see certain plants almost always gather along watercourses, and certain on the ridges of mountains, and certain on slopes and at the foot of hills, the which, if we transplant them, either die altogether or live as if in gloom, like things parted from the place dear to them.

116. *questi ne' cor mortali è permotore*: Mortal hearts of animals. The heart is named, of course, because this instinct is essentially an affective force, a desire. A famous passage from Augustine's *Confessions* may be appropriately remembered as another gloss on vss. 115-17, as well as on vss. 118-20. See *Conf.* XIII, 9:

In dono tuo requiescimus: ibi te fruimur. requies nostra locus noster. amor illuc attollit nos et spiritus tuus bonus exaltat humilitatem nostram de portis mortis. in bona voluntate tua pax nobis est. corpus pondere suo nititur ad locum suum. pondus non ad ima tantum est, sed ad locum suum. ignis sursum tendit, deorsum lapis. ponderibus suis aguntur, loca sua petunt. oleam infra aquam fusum super aquam attollitur, aqua supra oleum fusa infra oleum demergitur: ponderibus suis aguntur, loca sua petunt. minus ordinata inquieta sunt: ordinantur et quiescunt. pondus meum amor meus; eo feror, quocumque feror. dono tuo accendimur et sursum ferimur; inardescimus et imus. ascendimus ascensiones in corde et cantamus canticum graduum. igne tuo, igne tuo bono inardescimus et imus, quoniam sursum imus ad pacem Hierusalem, quoniam iucundatus sum in his, qui dixerunt mihi: in domum domini ibimus. ibi nos conlocabit voluntas bona, ut nihil velimus aliud quam permanere illic in aeternum.

In thy gift we rest; then we enjoy thee. Our rest is thy gift, our life's place. Love lifts us up thither, and thy good spirit advances our lowliness from the gates of death. In thy good pleasure lies our peace. Our body with its lumpishness strives towards its own place. Weight makes not downward only, but to his own place also. The fire mounts upward, a stone sinks downward. All things pressed by their own weight go towards their proper places. Oil poured in the bottom of the water, is raised above it: water poured upon oil, sinks to the bottom of the oil. They are driven by their own weights, to seek their own places. Things a little out of their places become unquiet: put them in their order again, and they are quieted. My weight is my love: by that am I carried, whithersoever I be carried. We are inflamed by thy gift, and are carried upwards: we wax hot within, and we go on. We ascend thy ways that be in our heart, and we sing a song of degrees; we glow inwardly with thy fire, with thy good fire, and we go, because we go upward to the peace of Jerusalem: for glad I was whenas they said unto me, We will go up into the house of the Lord. There will thy good pleasure settle us, that we may desire no other thing, but to dwell there for ever.

117. *la terra in sé stringe e aduna*: Augustine's words cited in the preceding note give the proper view here, for this instinct or love is a gravitational force, which causes the heavy element earth to gather itself into its proper resting-place.

118-20. *né pur . . . amore*: The tercet singles out angels and men as creatures who have intellect and love, that is, intellect and will, the two faculties of man's immortal soul. See n. on vss. 106-8.

119. *quest' arco saetta*: Beatrice's discourse is concerned with what is properly termed teleology. The term *telos*, in Greek (often in Aristotle), means the end or purpose of an action and commonly suggests the metaphor which is now implicit in Beatrice's words, namely, archery, the aiming of an arrow at some target. This figure in the present context makes God, who governs the heavens and all things, an archer who aims (through the motive force of natural love) the creature at its own proper target or resting-place. The Archer is not named as such, but His bow, His instrument in the total movement of the universe, is this love, natural love.

121. *La provedenza, che cotanto assetta*: It is God's providence that establishes and maintains this whole teleological order in the universe, which is now viewed in the order of its spheres.

122. *del suo lume fa 'l ciel sempre quieto*: The reference is to the tenth heaven, the Empyrean, which does not revolve, but is always quiet, always at rest in itself, God's light causing it to have this peace.

123. *nel qual si volge quel c'ha maggior fretta*: The heaven that turns next below the tenth heaven is the Primum Mobile, swiftest of all the spheres in its revolution. That revolution is itself caused by love or desire. See Dante, *Conv.* II, iii, 8-9.

124. *lì*: The Empyrean heaven, the final resting-place of the elect and of their natural love, in the vision of God. *decreto = decretato*. From the Latin *decretus*.

125-26. *cen porta . . . lieto*: The archery metaphor returns now with the full expression of its teleological implications. God, through natural love, aims us at Himself. It is His will that we should return to Him who creates our immortal souls directly (see *Purg.* XXV, 70-75). Natural love now becomes that force, which comes from the bowcord of the Archer, who aims us at Himself, happy target that He is.

127–35. *Vero è che . . . piacere*: But a problem arises here. How is it that some arrows fail to hit the mark? Can it be that the Almighty Archer has sometimes a faulty aim? Many souls do not return to Him, to His target which is Himself. Beatrice's discourse now contemplates this question, passing in these verses from the archery metaphor to that of art in the sense of giving shape to some object, as in the art of pottery, for example. Why is the potter's intention not always perfectly realized in the object he makes, the product of his art? The answer is that the clay does not respond perfectly to the potter's intention, it is "deaf" to it, it is not properly disposed. The failure therefore must be assigned to the matter, the clay, and not to the potter. Or, to return to the figure of the archer and the arrow that fails to hit the target, the failure must certainly be imputed to the arrow, not to the archer. But how can this be? Does the arrow in itself have the power to swerve and miss the target? The following verses return, by implication, to the archery figure and give the answer in those terms.

130. *da questo corso*: The upward course of the pilgrim now. Clearly the statement applies to the living, to their love and its direction, upwards, which is the direction of natural love.

130–32. *si diparte . . . parte*: The human creature (and Beatrice's words apply now exclusively to *living* human beings) is impelled by God-given natural love, which, according to *Purg.* XVII, 94, cannot err and always holds to the upward course in this life, always desiring God. But this same human creature is also endowed with elective love or love of choice, which *can* swerve from the course of natural love. That is, human beings have free will, which can choose to depart from the God-implanted direction of natural love—and this, of course, is sin. Again it should be recalled that the whole discourse on love and free will at the center of the poem

(*Purg.* XVI, XVII, XVIII) can serve as an excellent gloss to these verses. See also *Purg.* XXI, 64-66 (and the note to those verses), where it is made clear that elective love must be straightened or brought back to the direction of natural love. Thus the power to bend (*piegare*) or swerve is the power of free will and elective love. God launches the human soul into existence ("così pinta") or, to return to the archery figure, "shoots the arrow" at Himself, but this arrow has a quite special power given to it which no actual arrow has. This arrow may choose not to move toward the target of natural love, God, and thus fall "somewhere else."

133–35. *e sì come . . . piacere*: Like natural love, fire should always rise upward toward its "sito decreto" (vs. 124), which is above. Sometimes, however, it has a downward movement, as when lightning darts down to earth, reversing the proper or natural direction of fire. Thus the poet draws an illustration from nature to bring the reader, by such a comparison, into the focus of natural love in the human creature. This love is the "impeto primo," the innate instinct that we now understand. Lightning, of course, has no power of choice but is, in this downward motion, simply an *unnatural* movement of the element fire.

The swerving from natural love on the part of the human creature is also unnatural in being a turning-away from the upward course which that love should always follow. But unlike fire, the human creature, having elective love, turned toward earthly things through the attraction of false (i.e., sinful) pleasure—he *can* depart from the course. See *Purg.* XVII, 91-102, noting in particular vs. 97, which applies to elective love: elective love should always be in harmony with natural love, be directed on the primal good, this primal good being God. Thus the lesson in love at the center of the poem remains the best gloss available to us on Beatrice's meaning here.

135. *l'atterra*: There has been much discussion of the reading to be followed in this verse, whether it should be "s'atterra" (the reflexive verb *atterrarsi*), meaning "grounds it-

self," or "l'atterra" (the transitive verb with *lo* as the object),
meaning "grounds it." (See the relative note in Petrocchi,
whose reading is followed here.) Part of the debate has re-
sulted from some confusion concerning the meaning in this
context. With "sì l'impeto primo" Beatrice returns to natural
love in the human soul. But since this primal impulse is God-
given, how can such an instinct go wrong, when we have
been clearly told in *Purg.* XVII that it cannot? The archery
figure in the preceding verses would seem to give the proper
focus. The arrow (or natural love) is the motive force in
human hearts (vs. 116). The arrow would not move at all
if it did not have that original endowment of love as its mo-
tive force. And it cannot, by its very nature, go wrong, can-
not "ground itself." But love in the human creature, unlike
love in fire, *can* swerve to one side through the power of
elective love, which is also God-given and depends on free
will. Perhaps the best gloss on this particular point is to be
found in *Purg.* XVIII, 59-75 (and note, in *Purg.* XVIII,
46-48, 73-75, the promise made by Virgil that later Beatrice
will explain this matter).

It should be noted, however, that the reading "s'atterra"
might also make good sense in the context and with only a
slight change of focus.

136–41. *Non dei . . . vivo*: Again Beatrice turns for an ex-
ample to natural movement, now to that of gravitation, the
downward flow of water, and her focus in the argument
here is indeed close to that of Augustine in the words cited
above (n. to vs. 116). The final verse of the *Purgatorio* gives
us the pilgrim as being "puro e disposto a salire a le stelle,"
that is, without any remaining impediment in the proper up-
ward direction of his love. His love of choice is now in per-
fect harmony with his natural love, which has its natural
gravitation toward God.

The poem's basic allegory is very much to the fore here.
The upward journey of the pilgrim there reflects a *possible*
journey of "whichever" living man is uplifted in desire and
contemplation toward God: the natural gravitation of God-
given love. But love is better symbolized by fire than by

water; so Beatrice again returns to fire, to conclude her discourse. If one were to see a flame that does not reach up (toward its proper place above), this quietness would be a marvel as great as the upward flow of a river. But the flame has within it a natural love which seeks to rise. Even so the human heart.

Nor should it be forgotten that Beatrice in her triumph is dressed in the color of fire (*Purg.* XXX, 33), which is the color of love and which was the color of her dress when Dante first saw her (*Vita nuova* II, 3).

142. *Quinci rivolse inver' lo cielo il viso*: This heavenward glance of Beatrice, pointing the upward way, is a perfect conclusion to her whole argument.

CANTO II

1–18. *O voi che . . . bifolco*: This is the most remarkable address to the reader in the whole of the *Commedia*. Such addresses are encountered elsewhere, but none so long and none addressed to such a group of readers, who are here urged to turn back in their little boats. The poet *as poet* addresses these readers, and his navigational figure concerns the "voyage" of his art as it now enters upon a new sea and "crosses over" ("cantando varca") from time to eternity. It is essential to bear in mind that it is the *poet* who is speaking: if the voyage of Dante the pilgrim were meant here, the claim that no one ever sailed these waters before would be untrue, for St. Paul, uplifted to Heaven, must have passed through these spheres and completed this same journey. The claim is true only from the point of view of the poet, not from that of the wayfarer. Paul did not take us back over his experience, but Dante the poet intends to do this now, to go back over his journey, in poetry.

1–6. *O voi che . . . smarriti*: In the *Convivio* Dante recognizes that many men for various reasons are excluded from the banquet of wisdom and science. Noting that all men desire to know and that knowing is a kind of perfection, he concludes (*Conv.* I, i, 6-7):

37

Manifestamente adunque può vedere chi bene consi-
dera, che pochi rimangono quelli che a l'abito da tutti
desiderato possano pervenire, e innumerabili quasi sono
li'mpediti che di questo cibo sempre vivono affamati.
Oh beati quelli pochi che seggiono a quella mensa dove
lo pane de li angeli si manuca! e miseri quelli che con
le pecore hanno comune cibo!

Manifestly then may he perceive who rightly considers,
that few be left who may reach to that habit which is de-
sired by all; and well-nigh beyond number are they
which be hindered and which live all their lives famished
for this universal food. Oh blessed those few who sit at
the table where the bread of angels is consumed, and
wretched they who share the food of sheep!

Yet those who have followed the poet's ship so far are many,
and in their little vessels they have been able, presumably, to
navigate the waters of the *Inferno* and the *Purgatorio*. But
the *Paradiso* is as the open ocean (*pelago*), and their vessels
(that is, their minds) should not venture forth on this ocean.
One may think of this admonition in terms of the guides thus
far in the journey. The journey with Virgil is ended, and (in
spite of the fact that much philosophy was encountered
there) many readers have been able to follow through the
area or sea where Virgil is the guide. Such readers have even
navigated the last cantos of the *Purgatorio*, which include the
advent of Beatrice, the second guide, one of whose names in
the allegory is Sapientia, Wisdom which descends from on
high. But now the reader is launched with such a Lady Wis-
dom as Beatrice represents, now Dante rises with her, rises
"beyond the human" and enters upon an ocean which is too
deep even for many of those who *were* able to follow Virgil's
guidance. See C. S. Singleton (1958).

2. *desiderosi d'ascoltar*: "Tutti li uomini naturalmente de-
siderano di sapere" ("All men by nature desire to know")
is the opening statement of the *Convivio* and derives from
Aristotle.   *seguiti*: To be connected with "siete" of vs.
1, "siete seguiti." Cf. the Latin *secuti estis*.

3. *dietro al mio legno che cantando varca*: The reader will
recall that the opening of the *Purgatorio* deals in a similar
metaphor. Indeed, to look now to those verses and the navi-
gational figure they introduce, one may say that each of the
three *cantiche* can be viewed as a sea—*Inferno* a cruel one,
Purgatorio a better one, *Paradiso* an ocean—across which
the poet's genius as poet takes us. On such navigational meta-
phors, E. R. Curtius (1953, pp. 128-29) writes:

> The Roman poets are wont to compare the composition
> of a work to a nautical voyage. "To compose" is "to set
> the sails, to sail" ("vela dare": Virgil, *Georgics*, II, 41).
> At the end of the work the sails are furled ("vela
> trahere": *ibid.*, IV, 117). The epic poet voyages over
> the open sea in a great ship, the lyric poet on a river in
> a small boat. Horace makes Phoebus warn him (*Carm.*,
> IV, 15, 1):
>
> > *Phoebus volentem proelia me loqui*
> > *Victas et urbes increpuit lyra,*
> > *Ne parva Tyrrhenum per aequor*
> > *Vela darem . . .*
>
> (Phoebus, when I of battles thought to tell
> And conquered cities, struck his lyre, warning
> Lest on the open sea I set
> My little sails . . .)
>
> In poems that consist of several books each book can
> begin with "setting" the sails and end with "furling"
> them. The end of the whole work is entering port, with
> or without casting anchor (Statius, *Silvae*, IV, 89;
> *Thebais*, XII, 809; *Ilias latina*, 1063). The poet be-
> comes the sailor, his mind or his work the boat. Sailing
> the sea is dangerous, especially when undertaken by an
> "unpracticed sailor" ("rudis nauta": Fortunatus, ed.
> Leo, 114, 26) or in a "leaky boat" ("rimosa fragilis
> ingenii barca": Aldhelm [ed. Ehwald], 320, 20). Often
> the boat must be steered between cliffs ("sermonum
> cymbam inter loquelae scopulos frenare": Ennodius
> [ed. Hartel], I, 3). Alcuin fears sea-monsters (*Poetae*,

I, 198, 1321 ff.); Smaragdus the raging tides (*Poetae*, I, 609, 55 ff.). Unfavorable winds and storms often threaten.

Nautical metaphors originally belong to poetry. Pliny writes to a poet (*Ep.*, VIII, 4, 5): "Loose the hawsers, spread the sails, and let your genius voyage freely. For why should I not discourse poetically with a poet?" But Cicero had already adopted these expressions in prose. Shall he use the "oar of dialectics" or set "the sails of eloquence" at once (*Tusc.*, IV, 5, 9). Quintilian feels like a solitary sailor on the high seas (*prooemium* to Book XII). Jerome sets "the sails of interpretation" (*PL*, XXV, 903 D). His sailing breeze is the Holy Ghost (*ibid.*, 369 D). Prudentius refers to Paul's shipwreck and Peter's wanderings over the sea (ed. Bergmann, 215 f. and 245). This class of metaphor is extraordinarily widespread throughout the Middle Ages and long survives into later times.

Dante begins the second book of the *Convivio* with nautical metaphors: ". . . proemialmente ragionando . . . lo tempo chiama e domanda la mia nave uscir di porto; perchè, drizzato l' artimone de la ragione a l' òra del mio desiderio, entro in pelago."

Also note the additional examples and footnote references given by Curtius in his review of nautical metaphors, as well as his discussion of Dante in this context.

5. *in pelago*: On the deep open ocean.

6. *perdendo me*: I.e., "losing sight of me and my vessel," which now goes beyond the human ("trasumanar," *Par.* I, 70), with Beatrice guiding.

8. *Minerva*: Minerva, goddess of wisdom. Wisdom is also the name (in allegory) of Beatrice. See C. S. Singleton (1958), pp. 122-38. *spira*: In the nautical figure the meaning is "she fills my sails"; out of metaphor it is "she breathes within me." Compare this use of *spirare* in *Purg.* XXIV, 53. *conducemi Appollo*: Apollo, to whom the

opening invocation is addressed, was the god of poetry. (See n. to *Par.* I, 13.)

9. *e nove Muse*: Dante invokes the Muses at the beginning of several important passages. See, for example, *Purg.* I, 7-12, and the n. to *Purg.* I, 9-12. *l'Orse*: The "she-bears" is a term used by Dante to refer to the Big and Little Dippers (Ursa Major and Ursa Minor, the Big Bear and Little Bear) as constellations by which sailors are guided. The Little Bear contains the North Star. To indicate the pole of the northern hemisphere he speaks of the two together as "l'Orse."

10-11. *Voialtri pochi . . . angeli*: See the quotation from the *Convivio* in n. to vss. 1-6. The bread of angels is wisdom, on which the celestial Intelligences (angels) feed, as some few men may also do. The poet is singling out the privileged few, those who have devoted years to the study of philosophy and theology. The expression "bread of angels" is from the Bible. See Ps. 77[78]:25, "panem angelorum manducavit homo" ("the bread of angels was eaten by men"), and Sapien. 16:20, "pro quibus angelorum esca nutrivisti populum tuum" ("as against this, you nourished your people with food of angels").

12. *vivesi qui ma non sen vien satollo*: In *Conv.* IV, xxii, 13 Dante notes that the speculative intellect "in questa vita perfettamente lo suo uso avere non puote—lo quale averà in Dio ch'è sommo intelligibile—, se non in quanto considera lui e mira lui per li suoi effetti" ("cannot in this life have its perfect exercise, which is to see God [who is the supreme object of the intellect], save in so far as the intellect considers him and contemplates him through his effects"). See also *Purg.* XXXI, 128-29, and the corresponding note.

13. *sale*: "Salt sea." This is a Latinism (see Horace, *Epodes* XVII, 55).

14. *navigio*: The term suggests a larger ship and thus contrasts with the "little bark" of vs. 1. *solco*: Literally, "furrow"; here the wake of a ship.

15. *dinanzi a l'acqua che ritorna equale*: "Before the surface of the water becomes smooth again," without any trace ("solco") of the wake of my ship remaining visible.

16–18. *Que' gloriosi . . . bifolco*: The Argonauts, who crossed to Colchis in quest of the golden fleece, were astonished to see Jason, their leader, plowing with fire-breathing oxen and sowing dragon's teeth which grew into men. Ovid describes the scene in *Metam.* VII, 100-58.

16. *Colco*: The name of the inhabitants of Colchis (singular for plural), used to designate the country itself. Colchis was an ancient country of Asia, bounded on the west by the Euxine, on the north by the Caucasus, and on the east by Asian Iberia.

18. *Iasón*: The hero has already been encountered in Inferno. See *Inf.* XVIII, 86-96, where this famous voyage is referred to, among his other adventures, and n. to *Inf.* XVIII, 86.

19. *La concreata e perpetua sete*: This is innate natural love in man, a matter fully set forth in *Purg.* XVIII, that instinct now being called a thirst.

20. *del deiforme regno*: The Empyrean, where God is.
cen = ce ne.

21. *veloci quasi come 'l ciel vedete*: "Our 'inborn and eternal thirst' for Heaven, 'was sweeping us on almost as swift as you see the sky'—a curious comparison, since we are ordinarily not conscious of the sky's motion. If, however, we follow the position of a heavenly body from hour to hour, we discover that in a very brief period it traverses an immense distance. The sky, without seeming to move at all, is really traveling with inconceivable velocity; and so we were doing. See also *Met.*, II, 70" (Gr).

23–34. *e forse . . . dischiava*: " 'And perhaps in as much time as that in which a bolt (from a crossbow) stops and flies and quits the notch': the three incidents in the flight of the arrow are arranged in inverse order, to indicate that, to the eye, they are simultaneous. The same device is used in XXII, 109" (Gr). Other commentators, observing the curious reversal, also take the meaning to suggest simultaneity. Such a reversal, however, is by no means unique with Dante, but was known to ancient rhetoric by the Greek name of *hysteron proteron*, meaning "the last [put] first." Benvenuto refers to it as "praeposteratio." Such a figure, especially in the present context, suggests something *caused from the end*, since the eye is invited to consider the end first and then the action as seen from the end. See C. S. Singleton (1966), pp. 63-64.

26. *però = perciò*.

27. *cura*: "Interest," "concern."

30. *n'ha congiunti = ci ha congiunti.   la prima stella*: The moon.

31. *Parev' a me che nube ne coprisse*: As will now be made clear, Beatrice and Dante enter into the planet itself, and the poet is concerned to report the effects of so exceptional an experience. He is indeed causing us greater wonder than Jason's companions felt! The "matter" of the moon apparently gives the impression of a cloud to one who has actually entered into it. The reader realizes at once that the discussion of the moon which is now to follow concerns a planet conceived as being of a radically different matter than it has been thought to have since the time of Galileo. Indeed, a medieval poet and his readers (the learned few) would know from Aristotle's *De caelo*, or from medieval disquisitions on that famous text, that the moon—and everything above it— is radically different from the sublunar world.

32. *lucida*: Dante·explains in *De mon*. III, iv, 17-18 that the moon not only receives light from the sun, but also has a light of its own.

33. *adamante = diamante,* "diamond."

34. *etterna*: The heavenly spheres and all that lies above the moon are incorruptible and therefore eternal.   *margarita*: "Pearl." The comparison suggests a greater density of mat-

ter than was implied by "nube" in vs. 31, and this implica-
tion points to the problem raised by vss. 37-39.

35. *ne = ci.   recepe = riceve.* "Recepe" is from the
Latin *recipio* (infinitive, *recipere*). The body of the moon,
with the attributes suggested above, receives Dante and Bea-
trice as water does a ray of light, i.e., without any displace-
ment of the water. And this raises all the more the problem
now to be presented: if Dante is rising in his body, how can
his body pass into and through another body as a ray of light
which does not displace the substance of water?

37. *S'io era corpo*: Cf. *Par.* I, 73-75.   *qui*: Here on
earth, where all is so different. Grandgent understands "qui"
to mean "in this case"; but this, though possible, is less prob-
able than the meaning "on earth."

38. *com' una dimensione altra patio*: "How one bulk
brooked another," how one solid body could, without dis-
placement, be penetrated by another. According to Thomas
Aquinas (*Summa theol.* III, Suppl., q. 83, a. 3), it is possible
for this to be brought about by a miracle. See also Thomas
Aquinas, *Summa contra Gentiles* IV, 87.   *patio = patì.*

39. *ch'*: "Which," referring to the preceding clause.
repe: "Creeps."

40. *ne*: "Us."   *disio*: The subject of *dovria* (= *dov-
rebbe*) *accendere.*

41-45. *di veder . . . crede*: "In the 'essence' of Christ the
human and the divine natures are miraculously united. The
thought of [a human] body and the matter of the moon occu-
pying simultaneously the same space should make us eager
to rise to Heaven and behold, in the person of Christ, the
greatest miracle of the kind—a miracle which we accept on
faith, without being able to understand it. In Heaven it will
be as clear and natural as a 'primal truth,' or axiom" (Gr).

43. *Lì*: In Heaven, in the vision of God "face to face."
si vedrà ciò che tenem per fede: Precisely this desire will be
the final desire of Dante the pilgrim, and he will have it satis-

fied there, at the end. See *Par.* XXXIII, 137-45.   *tenem*
= *teniamo*.

46–48. *Madonna, sì devoto . . . remoto*: Dante is responding
to Beatrice's exhortation (vss. 29-30).

47. *lui*: God.

48. *mortal mondo*: All that lies below the sphere of the
moon; above it (and including it) all is immortal. See n. to
vs. 34.   *remoto = rimosso*.

49–51. *Ma ditemi . . . altrui*: The big question is now asked,
and Beatrice's answer will occupy the rest of this canto. For
the old belief that the spots on the moon were Cain and his
thorns, also referred to in *Inf.* XX, 126, see n. to *Inf.* XX,
126.

52–148. *Ella sorrise alquanto . . . chiaro*: Before the reader
ventures into Beatrice's long answer, he might do well to read
Grandgent's paraphrase and exposition of the whole argu-
ment, since the scholastic manner of her disquisition and her
philosophical terminology may be unfamiliar to him:

> As he pictures himself rising with Beatrice to the sphere
> of the moon, the poet takes advantage of the occasion
> to explain—through the lips of his guide—the function
> of Nature, the power to which all the activities of the
> material universe are due. By Nature Dante means the
> operation of the heavenly bodies, directed by celestial
> Intelligences, or angels, which are the ministers of God.
> The world of matter, therefore, exactly corresponds to
> the world of spirit, and is its visible image. From the
> Maker, in his Empyrean abode, descends a vital prin-
> ciple, which is received by the 9th sphere, or Primum
> Mobile, the outermost of the revolving heavens. This
> sphere, which contains no stars, is alike in all its parts;
> and for that reason it does not analyze the force be-
> stowed upon it, but imparts it, translated into material
> energy, to the heavens within its circuit. The 8th sphere
> —that of the fixed stars—by means of these bodies dif-
> ferentiates, in accordance with the needs of the world,

the single but potentially multiform power that comes from the Primum Mobile: cf. *Quaestio de Aqua et Terra* [LXX-LXXI]. This diversified power then sifts downward to the earth, passing through the other spheres, each of which combines with those energies which are akin to its own essence, and transmits them still further modified. The brightness of the heavenly bodies is due ultimately to this same power, derived from God, whose gladness is the source of all light. The various stars, according to their nature, combine to a greater or less degree with this energizing and light-giving principle; and that is why one star differs from another in glory. So it is with the moon. Some parts of this orb are less sensitive than others to the illumining energy, and hence, when seen from below, appear as spots on the lunar surface. Looked at from above, the moon has no such marks: *Par.* XXII, 139-141 (*Bull.*, VII, 235). . . .

Averroës and Albertus Magnus believed the moon spots to be the results of the presence, in some regions of the moon, of rarer matter, which was unfit to reflect the sun's light; and they attributed this opinion to Aristotle (Toynbee, 78-79). The same view is expressed by Dante in *Conv.*, II, xiii, 9. By the time he wrote the *Paradiso*, however, he had evidently become dissatisfied with such a material explanation and had worked out a more spiritual one, which applies to the stars as well as to the moon. The refutation of his former theory is conducted, in scholastic style, by Beatrice, some of whose arguments may be found in Albertus Magnus, *De Caelo et Mundo, Lib.* II, Tr. ii and iii (Toynbee, 82).

In the first place, we must assume that the obscurity of some parts of the moon is due to the same cause as the comparative dimness of some of the stars. The question then is, whether this difference in brightness is caused by a difference in density, or quantity of matter, or by a difference in quality. Now we know that each of the several heavenly bodies and groups of stars has a special influence on the earth. If the stars differed only in the density of their matter, the quality being the same, the effect of all would be the same in kind, and would differ only in degree. Different influences must be the result of different fundamental principles; and these principles, if Dante's earlier view were correct, would be reduced to one. Therefore the celestial bodies—and, by inference, the various parts of the moon—must differ in kind.

As far as the moon is concerned, there is another argument, a purely physical one. Supposing the moon contained streaks of rarer matter, these layers would either extend through the moon, from side to side, or not. If they did, we should see the sun shining through them at the time of a solar eclipse, when the moon is between the sun and the earth. If they did not, there must be dense matter behind the rare; and in that case this dense matter would reflect the light, just as if it were on the surface. But—it may be objected—the light reflected from farther back would be fainter than that reflected from the outside, and the fainter reflections would appear as spots. To be convinced that this is not true, says Beatrice, try an experiment. Aristotle has declared that experiment is the source of science (*Metaphysics*, I, i). Place three mirrors upright at a distance from you, one a little farther back than the other two. Somewhere behind you put a light in such a position that it will shine into the glasses and be reflected by them. You will see that the reflection in the three mirrors is equally bright, although its image in the more remote one is of somewhat smaller dimensions. If, as seems likely, Dante had actually performed this experiment, he must have done so under such conditions that, to the eye, his conclusion was shown to be correct.

On the philosophical and historical sources of this whole question and Beatrice's argument, the reader may profitably consult P. Toynbee (1902), pp. 78-86, cited by Grandgent above; B. Nardi (1930), pp. 3-39; E. Proto (1912); and E. G. Parodi (1922), pp. 13-41.

52–57. *Ella sorrise alquanto . . . l'ali*: Paraphrasing the meaning, Sapegno comments:

> Non dovresti ormai meravigliarti se le opinioni umane son soggette ad errare in quegli argomenti dei quali la conoscenza esatta non può esserci aperta e fornita dai sensi, poichè vedi che anche quando procede con la guida dei sensi (anche nel campo degli argomenti naturali) la nostra ragione non è in grado di spingersi molto lontano. . . . Ora qui Dante non intende rifiutare e neppure svalutare l'importanza delle cognizioni unicamente, da cui "comincia la nostra conoscenza" (*Conv.*, II, iv, 17); sì soltanto stabilire i limiti di una conoscenza razionale, che si affidi soltanto ai dati bene spesso insufficienti ed erronei dell'esperienza, anzichè prender lume da un concetto generale e, in ultima istanza, teologico.

> By now you should no longer marvel if human opinions are subject to error in those arguments in which exact knowledge cannot be clear and provided by the senses, since you see that even when it is guided by the senses (even in natural matters) our reason is not able to advance very far. . . . Now Dante at this point does not intend to refute or even invalidate the importance of cognition from which "our knowledge begins" entirely (*Conv.* II, iv, 17), but he means only to establish the limits of any rational knowledge that depends solely on the data of experience (which are quite often insufficient and erroneous) instead of gaining light from a general concept which is, finally, theological.

52. *elli = egli*. This pronoun merely anticipates the subject, "l'oppinion."

55. *dovrien = dovrebbero*.

56. *poi dietro ai sensi*: " 'Since even under the guidance of the senses.' It is no wonder that men go astray in the interpretation of spiritual things, when they cannot even explain physical phenomena" (Gr).

58. *Ma dimmi quel che tu da te ne pensi*: With this verse Dante the poet enables Dante the pilgrim to hold the opinion expressed in the *Convivio* (II, xiii, 9):

> Che se la Luna si guarda bene, due cose si veggiono in essa proprie, che non si veggiono ne l'altre stelle. L'una si è l'ombra che è in essa, la quale non è altro che raritade del suo corpo, a la quale non possono terminare li raggi del sole e ripercuotersi così come ne l'altre parti; l'altra si è la variazione de la sua luminositade, che ora luce da uno lato, e ora luce da un altro, secondo che lo sole la vede.

> For if the moon be rightly examined two special things are perceived in her which are not perceived in the other stars; the one is the shadow upon her which is nought else than the rarity of her substance, whereon the rays of the sun may not be stayed and thrown back, as from her other parts; the other is the variation of her luminosity, which now shines from the one side and now from the other, according as the sun looks upon her.

Beatrice will now refute this opinion. For the history of this particular view, see B. Nardi (1930), pp. 3-39.

63. *li = gli*, "to it," the opinion expressed by Dante.

64. *La spera ottava*: The heaven of the fixed stars, the eighth heaven counting out or upwards from that of the moon. Beatrice immediately refers the question to the lofty eighth heaven, to begin her refutation.

64-65. *molti lumi*: The stars, for in this Aristotelian-Ptolemaic cosmos *all* the stars are conceived to be "fixed" in this sphere.

65-66. *e nel quale e nel quanto . . . volti*: We see that the stars differ both in kind and in size, that is, in the quality and the quantity of their light. It is assumed that everyone—or at least the learned few—will have noticed this phenomenon.

66. *volti*: "Aspects."

67. *Se raro e denso ciò facesser tanto*: " 'If rarity and density alone produced this': i.e., this difference in apparent kind and size. There are other Tuscan examples of *tanto* = 'only' " (Gr).

67-72. *Se raro e denso . . . distrutti*: For the turn which Beatrice's refutation now takes, Sapegno's comment is most helpful:

> Ecco lo schema del suo ragionamento, che risulta difficile in quanto presuppone tutta una serie di proposizioni che dovevano apparire evidenti alla coscienza filosofica dei lettori contemporanei: l'ottavo cielo mostra ai vostri occhi molti astri che appaiono differenti nel loro aspetto per quantità e qualità di luce; queste differenze di luminosità debbono spiegarsi allo stesso modo di quelle che appaiono nel corpo lunare; ora, se esse dipendessero soltanto dalla maggiore o minore densità dei corpi, ne seguirebbe che in tutte le stelle vi sarebbe una sola virtù, cioè esse avrebbero tutte un'identica natura specifica, distinta non qualitativamente, ma solo quantitativamente (distribuita in misura maggiore, minore, od uguale, *più e men . . . e altrettanto*, in ciascuna stella). Ma questo è assurdo; le stelle fisse hanno ciascuna una diversa virtù (come è richiesto dall'ordine complesso e molteplice del mondo sublunare, sul quale quelle virtù son chiamate ad operare); e virtù diverse non possono che essere effetto di differenti principi formali; mentre, per chi accettasse la tesi di Averroè, tutti questi principi formali verrebbero ridotti ad uno solo. La teoria del raro e del denso è dunque insufficiente a spiegare, filosoficamente, una diversità che non è soltanto di ordine quantitativo, sì anche qualitativo. In altre parole: alla differenziazione delle specie nel mondo infralunare deve corrispondere nel cielo una differenza di forme; la diversa luminosità dei corpi celesti è indice di virtù attive diversamente operanti a plasmare e specificare la materia terrestre; queste virtù diverse debbono dipendere infine da principi formali distinti.

Here is the outline of her [Beatrice's] reasoning, which
is difficult [for us to follow] in that it presupposes
a whole series of propositions which must have seemed
obvious to the philosophical mentality of contemporary
readers: the eighth heaven shows you many stars that
appear different in the quantity and quality of their
light; and these differences in luminosity must be ex-
plained in the same way as those which appear in the
body of the moon; now, if these differences resulted
solely from the greater or lesser density of these bodies,
it would follow that in all the stars there would be one
single virtue, that is, the stars would all have an identical
specific nature, not distinguished qualitatively but only
quantitatively (distributed in greater, lesser, or equal
degree, "più e men . . . e altrettanto," in each star). But
this is absurd: the fixed stars have each a different vir-
tue (as is required by the complex and varied order of
the sublunar world, on which those virtues are ordained
to shed their influence); and different virtues can only
be the result of different formal principles; whereas, for
anyone who should accept the thesis of Averroës, all
these formal principles would be reduced to one only.
The theory of rarity and density is therefore insufficient
to explain, philosophically, a diversity that is not only
quantitative in kind, but also qualitative. In other
words: to the differentiation of species in the sublunar
world there must be in the heaven a corresponding dif-
ference of forms; the differing luminosity of the heav-
enly bodies indicates active virtues which operate dif-
ferently in shaping and rendering specific earthly things
[that which lies within the sublunar region of the uni-
verse]; these different virtues must result, finally, from
distinct formal principles.

The formal principle is the active principle, that is, the in-
trinsic cause which determines the specific form of a given
thing. See B. Nardi (1930), pp. 9-10; E. Proto (1912),
pp. 201-4.

67–69. *Se raro e denso . . . altrettanto*: B. Nardi (1930,
pp. 12-13) observes:

E si noti anche un'altra cosa. Rigettando la dottrina averroistica, Beatrice non intende affatto negare che alcune parti del cielo siano più dense ed altre più rare. Ma vuole che il raro e il denso . . . non sia sufficiente a spiegare la diversità sostanziale "nel quale e nel quanto" (v. 65); cossicchè, pur ammettendo il raro e il denso come condizione o disposizione materiale della diversità, questa richiede, inoltre, una diversità di principii formali intrinseci. Tale appunto è il significato di quel "tanto" del verso 67.

And let this also be noted: in rejecting the doctrine of Averroës, Beatrice does not in the least intend to deny that some parts of the heavens do indeed vary in density and rarity. But she means that this rarity and density . . . is not sufficient to explain the substantial difference "in quality and quantity" (vs. 65); so that, even admitting rarity and density as a condition or material disposition of this diversity, this latter requires, besides, a diversity of formal intrinsic principles. Such is the meaning of that "tanto" in vs. 67.

70-72. *Virtù diverse . . . distrutti*: On this point Dante's own statement in his *Questio de aqua et terra* LXX-LXXII may be cited:

Licet celum stellatum habeat unitatem in substantia, habet tamen multiplicitatem in virtute; propter quod oportuit habere diversitatem illam in partibus quam videmus, ut per organa diversa virtutes diversas influeret; et qui hec non advertit, extra limitem phylosophie se esse cognoscat. Videmus in eo differentiam in magnitudine stellarum et in luce, in figuris et ymaginibus constellationum; que quidem differentie frustra esse non possunt, ut manifestissimum esse debet omnibus in phylosophia nutritis. Unde alia est virtus huius stelle et illius, et alia huius constellationis et illius, et alia virtus stellarum que sunt citra equinoctialem, et alia earum que sunt ultra. Unde cum vultus inferiores sint similes vultibus superioribus ut Ptolomeus dicit, consequens est quod, cum iste effectus non possit reduci nisi in celum stellatum ut visum est, quod similitudo virtualis agentis consistat in illa regione celi que operit hanc terram detectam.

Although the starry heaven has unity in substance, yet it has multiplicity in virtue; and that is why it needed the diversity in its parts which we observe, in order, by diverse organs, to pour down its diverse virtues; and let him who perceives not these things know that he is outside the threshold of philosophy. We observe in this heaven difference in the magnitude and luminosity of the stars and in the figures and forms of the constellations, which differences cannot be for nought, as must be perfectly clear to all who have been nurtured in philosophy. Wherefore the virtues of this star and that differ, and likewise of this constellation and of that. And the virtue of the stars this side of the equinoctial differs from that of those beyond it. Wherefore, since the aspects of things below are like to the aspects of things above, as Ptolemy asserts, it follows that (since that effect can only be referred to the starry heaven, as we have seen) the similitude of the virtual agent abides in that region of heaven which covers this exposed land.

"These principles, 'according to thine argument, would be obliterated.' There would be one and the same nature in all the stars, and they would all have the same influence" (Gr).

72. *seguiterieno = seguiterebbero*.

73. *Ancor*: E. G. Parodi (1922, p. 20) observes that this is the *adhuc* by which the Scholastics passed to a new argument. For Beatrice's argument now, see again the final paragraph in the passage cited from Grandgent in n. to vss. 52-148.

74. *o d'oltre in parte*: "All through," from side to side. Some editors have adopted the reading "ed oltre in parte," but Petrocchi has elected "d'oltre in parte" (also adopted by others), arguing for "d'oltre" as deriving from the Provençal *d'otra*, *d'outra*. See his note, where he cites the expression *d'oltre in oltre* in the meaning *da parte a parte*.

75. *fora = sarebbe*.   *di sua materia sì digiuno*: Would thus be deficient in its matter.

76–78. *o, sì come . . . carte*: "Or else, even as in the body of an animal the fat and the lean are divided in layers which do not extend all the way through, so would there be such layers in the body of the moon, like pages in a book." Here there is a play on "volume," which means "mass," but also "volume," i.e., "book," so that the layers of the one become in metaphor the pages of the other.

79. *'l primo*: The first case (vss. 74-75). For the argument, see the quotation from Grandgent that appears in the note to vss. 52-148.

81. *ingesto*: "Introduced," i.e., as light does when introduced into any rare matter. "Ingesto" is a Latinism.

82. *però = perciò*.

85–105. *S'elli è che . . . risplenda*: For the remainder of Beatrice's refutation, see Grandgent's exposition of the argument as quoted in n. to vss. 52-148.

87. *lo suo contrario più passar non lassi*: "Its contrary [the dense] allows no further passage [of the rare]."   *lassi = lasci*.

88. *indi*: "From there," i.e., from the "termine" where the rare ends and the dense begins.   *l'altrui raggio*: The light of the sun reflected on the face of the moon.   *si rifonde*: "Is reflected."

89–90. *così come color . . . nasconde*: " 'Just as color comes back through glass' that is backed with lead, i.e., is reflected from a mirror, the glass corresponding to the rare matter, the leaden back to the dense" (Gr).

91–105. *Or dirai tu . . . risplenda*: See n. to vss. 52-148.

91. *el = egli*. The pronoun is redundant and anticipates the subject, "raggio." Cf. "elli," vs. 52.

94. *instanza*: "Objection."   *deliberarti*: "Rid you."

95. *esperienza*: The subject of "può." The term still keeps the meaning of "experiment" in Italian.

96. *ch'esser suol fonte ai rivi di vostr' arti*: The concept that experiment is the basis of human art (or of applied physical science, as we might say today) derives from Aristotle (see his *Anal. post.* II, 19, 100ᵃ), becoming, with the Scholastics, the argument *per experimentum*.

98. *d'un modo*: "To the same distance."

98–99. *più rimosso . . . ritrovi*: Let this mirror meet your eyes between the first two mirrors, but farther away.

101. *stea = stia.   accenda*: "Illuminates."

102. *ripercosso*: "Reflected."

103. *nel quanto*: "In size."   *si stenda*: "Spreads."

104. *vista*: "Image," as reflected in the mirror farthest away.

106–8. *Or, come ai colpi . . . primai*: "As, when exposed to the hot beams of the sun, the material of the snow [i.e., water] is left stripped of its previous color and cold."

107. *suggetto*: The scholastic *subiectum*, that which "lies under" a thing and is its basis, its basic matter, in this case, water.

109–11. *così rimaso te . . . aspetto*: "You, reduced to like state mentally, will I infuse with light so keen that it will quiver as it appears to you."

112. *Dentro dal ciel de la divina pace*: With this verse Beatrice makes a fresh beginning and, typically, takes the argument back to the highest heaven, *above* the eighth heaven (see vss. 64-66). This is a point of great significance, as if she were saying: only by beginning at the true beginning, with the tenth and highest heaven, the Empyrean, can the question concerning the moon spots be answered (see *Par.* I, 4).

113–14. *si gira un corpo . . . giace*: The ninth (counting out

55

from the earth) or crystalline heaven, the Primum Mobile, which in descending order lies just within the Empyrean and is the outermost material heaven. See *Conv.* II, xiv, 15-16, where Dante says:

> E così lo detto cielo ordina col suo movimento la coti-diana revoluzione di tutti li altri, per la quale ogni die tutti quelli ricevono [e mandano] qua giù la vertude di tutte le loro parti. Che se la revoluzione di questo non ordinasse ciò, poco di loro vertude qua giù verrebbe o di loro vista.

> And so doth the said heaven regulate with its movement the daily revolution of all the others, whereby every day they all receive from above [and send down] the virtue of all their parts. For if the revolution of this heaven did not thus regulate the same, little of their virtue would come down here, and little sight of them.

Thus we are told that the outermost of the material heavens, the Primum Mobile, derives a "virtue" (power) from the spiritual heaven which contains it, and it in turn transmits this power to the material universe which lies within it; and in this way we begin to follow out the passing down through the spheres of a power which, in its origin, is spiritual, is from God. The poet is presenting the view of this whole matter that was accepted in his time.

114. *contento = contenuto*.

115. *Lo ciel seguente*: The eighth heaven, the heaven of the fixed stars, with which Beatrice began her refutation (see vss. 64-66 and n. to vs. 64). With this heaven begins the process of differentiation of the power which first passed undiffer-entiated from the Empyrean to the Primum Mobile. *vedute*: Stars. See *Par.* XXIII, 30; XXX, 9.

116. *quell' esser parte per diverse essenze*: "Distributes that existence [the power transmitted by the Primum Mobile] in various types." Thus it comes to its first differentiation by passing into the stars, which are many. See Dante, *Conv.* II, xiv, 1-7.

117. *da lui distratte e da lui contenute*: "Different from it [the *essere*] but contained in it."

118. *Li altri giron*: The remaining spheres are those of the planets, which are seven. These, it is now said, continue the process of differentiation of the power (and existence), which passes to them from the stars of the eighth heaven. Cf. *Purg.* XXX, 109-11, where mention is made of this process of transmission by the "great wheels." On the derivation of this conception from Aristotelian and Neoplatonic ideas, see B. Nardi (1930), pp. 14-19. "Giron" here is the subject of "dispongono" (vs. 120), of which "distinzion" is the object.

119. *le distinzion*: The essences or virtues, deriving originally from the one virtue but now further distinguished, that is, differentiated, by these planetary spheres.

120. *a lor fini*: To the accomplishments of their effects on the sublunar world, which are according to a purpose, as we are soon to be reminded, for this transmission is not merely physical, but involves the Intelligences who move the spheres.   *lor semenze*: Their seedings, again with the suggestion of a purposive act on the part of the Intelligences that preside over this operation, which, through the spheres, "seeds," as it were, the sublunar world. Norton comments: "Each of the seven inferior heavens distributes its specific virtues in such wise as to secure their due ends, and to make them seed for the production of further effects." See Dante, *Conv.* II, vi, 9:

> Dico anche che questo spirito viene per li raggi de la stella: per che sapere si vuole che li raggi di ciascuno cielo sono la via per la quale discende la loro vertude in queste cose di qua giù. E però che li raggi non sono altro che uno lume che viene dal principio de la luce per l'aere infino a la cosa illuminata, e luce non sia se non ne la parte de la stella, però che l'altro cielo è diafano, cioè transparente, non dico che vegna questo spirito, cioè questo pensiero, dal loro cielo in tutto, ma da la loro stella.

I say then that this spirit comes upon the "rays of the star," because you are to know that the rays of each heaven are the path whereby their virtue descends upon things that are here below. And inasmuch as rays are no other than the shining which cometh from the source of the light through the air even to the thing enlightened, and the light is only in that part where the star is, because the rest of the heaven is diaphanous (that is transparent), I say not that this "spirit," to wit this thought, cometh from their heaven in its totality but from their star.

121–23. *Questi organi . . . fanno*: There is hierarchy and degree in a universe so conceived, and the transmission of the power is through degree (each higher heaven being nobler than the next lower heaven contained by it). This principle of hierarchy will be all the clearer when the transmission (downwards only) is referred to the Intelligences, or nine orders of angels, called now "beati motor" (vs. 129), that direct the nine spheres of the material cosmos.

124–26. *Riguarda bene . . . guado*: "Loco" and "guado" suggest, metaphorically, that Beatrice's disquisition is a kind of journey or fording to the final truth at which she means to arrive, and Dante must learn to follow the path of it and later be able to "ford" to it by himself.

127–29. *Lo moto . . . spiri*: The motion and the virtue (transmitted) must derive from the Intelligences, which preside over the spheres, causing them to revolve and distribute the virtue which, in the process we have followed, derives from God. Thomas Aquinas (*Summa theol.* I, q. 65, a. 4, resp.) writes:

> Sequitur ulterius quod etiam formae corporales a substantiis spiritualibus deriventur, non tanquam influentibus formas, sed tamquam moventibus ad formas. Ulterius autem reducuntur in Deum, sicut in primam causam, etiam species angelici intellectus, quae sunt quaedam seminales rationes corporalium formarum.

It follows further that even corporeal forms are derived from spiritual substances, not as emanating from them, but as the term of their movement. And, further still, the species of the angelic intellect, which are, as it were, the seminal types of corporeal forms, must be referred to God as the first cause.

The simile Dante uses here presents the action of the Intelligences as purposive, as is a smith's, which suggests that the material heaven or sphere (called an *organ*, vs. 121) is the instrument of the order of Intelligences which turn it and transmit the virtue in its downward movement. See *Conv.* IV, iv, 12, where Dante says: "La forza dunque non fu cagione movente . . . ma fu cagione instrumentale, sì come sono li colpi del martello cagione del coltello, e l'anima del fabbro è cagione efficiente e movente." ("Force then was not the moving cause . . . but was the instrumental cause, even as the blows of the hammer are the cause of the knife, whereas the mind of the smith is the efficient and moving cause.") The simile derives from Aristotle (*De anima* II, 4, 416^{a-b}) and is a commonplace in scholastic thought. The verb *spirare* suggests spiritual rather than material causality on the part of the Intelligences, which is the case.

"A difficulty seems to be caused by Dante's habit of sometimes explicitly recognising, and sometimes practically ignoring, the distinction between the heavens or heavenly bodies and their guiding and influencing Angels. There is no confusion in his own mind; but the connection between the Angels and the heavens is so close that it is often unnecessary to dwell upon the distinction, which distinction, however, is always there. It has been ignored up to this point in the present Canto. Now we find the 'differentiatings' of the Divine Power recognised as divers angelic virtues which are respectively *connected* with the divers heavenly bodies, so that the moving heaven is an 'alloy,' or union of the heavenly substance and the angelic influence. Again, the 'mingled virtue' itself that shines through the heavenly body is the personality of the Angel mingled with the creating and inspiring power of God. Cf. xxi. 82-87" (TC).

130-32. *e 'l ciel . . . suggello*: Beatrice's argument now returns to the eighth sphere, that of the fixed stars which first differentiate the virtue, as we have learned from her, but we now have the Intelligences assigned to each of the heavens brought into the picture as well. Each heaven, by way of the Intelligences which operate it, "takes from above and transmits below" (vs. 123). Often the singular *Intelligenza* is used collectively, but the plural (an entire order of angels) is understood. This is also the case with the singular "la mente profonda," meaning the minds of the presiding order of angels, which in this case is the order of the Cherubim.

131. *lui*: This eighth heaven, the heaven of the stars.

132. *prende l'image*: Receives from the mind of the presiding Intelligences their intention and transmits this downwards, by way of the differentiating stars, imprinting it as effect on the world beneath it, even as a seal stamps wax.
fassene = se ne fa, i.e., makes of it (the image) a seal, stamping the many stars of this particular heaven with the intention of the Intelligences. See Boethius, *Consol. philos.* III, ix, vss. 1-28.

133-38. *E come l'alma . . . unitate*: Sapegno comments:

In queste due terzine, e più ancora in quella che segue, Dante sembra accostarsi alla dottrina dei neoplatonici e dei filosofi arabi, che concepivano le intelligenze come anime o forme dei cieli; ma si tratta di un accostamento piuttosto apparente che sostanziale: anche per lui, come in genere per gli scolastici, il rapporto fra l'intelligenza e il corpo celeste da essa mosso è soltanto simile, e non identico, a quello fra l'anima e il corpo nell'organismo umano (cfr. *Conv.*, II, v, 18).

In these two tercets, and even more in that which follows, Dante seems close to the doctrine of the Neoplatonists and Arab philosophers, who conceived of the Intelligences as souls or forms of the heavens; but it is a closeness that is more apparent than substantial: for him, even as for the Scholastics in general, the relation between the Intelligence and the heavenly body moved by it is only similar to, not identical with, the relation between soul and body in the human organism (cf. *Conv.* II, v, 18).

See B. Nardi (1930), pp. 31-33.

133. *alma = anima.   vostra polve*: The human body ("polve" = *polvere*). The expression is from the Bible—see Gen. 3:19: "Quia pulvis es, et in pulverem reverteris." ("For dust you are and unto dust you shall return.")

135. *a diverse potenze si risolve*: "Is distributed in different faculties," i.e., is distributed in the different members of the human body that befit (are conformed to) such different faculties and are able to receive these and function accordingly.

136. *l'intelligenza*: The singular for the plural.   *sua bontate*: Its goodness, i.e., the virtue it has received from above.

137. *multiplicata per le stelle spiega*: This being the process of differentiation and distribution explained above.

138. *girando sé sovra sua unitate*: The verse turns from the outward operation of the Intelligences (in distributing and differentiating the virtue received) to the inner operation of the Intelligence, which is intellection, of which the circle is the accepted figure. See *Purg.* XXV, 75, and n. to that verse; also see *Par.* XIII, 55-60.

139-40. *Virtù diversa . . . avviva*: Each differentiated power from on high (the differentiation taking place in the eighth sphere, in the many stars it contains) "makes a different alloy" with the precious or incorruptible heavenly "body which it quickens," i.e., it does this in each of the stars first, then in the planets below, all the way down to and including the moon. This virtue is the very "life" of the star or planet, even as the spirit or soul in the human creature.

142-44. *Per la natura lieta . . . viva*: The virtue or power now passes into the figure of light (thus recalling the opening verses of the *Paradiso* where the "gloria" is in such terms).

We are thus returned to the passing-down of a light, which is also a virtue that becomes mingled with the stellar or planetary body and shines in each star variously (hence the greater or lesser light of each star) or variously in the parts of a single planet, as in the moon. Each Intelligence, like the Creator Himself (cf. *Purg.* XXV, 70), is happy in its nature, and from this happiness, now mixed (alloyed) with the star or planet, the light of a given heavenly body shines forth, as happiness in the pupil of a human eye.

To comprehend the full import of this statement, as it applies to the moon, the reader needs to be reminded that the moon spots were conceived to be visible only on the lower, earthward-turned, side of that planet. (See B. Nardi, 1930, p. 34, n. 1.) Through the simile, that downward-looking planet becomes an eye turned earthwards, in which, as in the human eye, there are darker and lighter parts. A power, which is also a light, mingled with the precious body of the planet diversely (making a different alloy here and there in the body of the planet), shines forth upon the sublunar world, working its effects there.

145–48. *Da essa vien . . . chiaro*: Beatrice concludes her argument. The light and dark parts of the moon are not due to rarity or density of its matter, but to the varying alloy of the virtue which has been transmitted downwards, originating with God.

145. *da luce a luce*: From star to star (thus the argument returns to its positive beginning in vss. 64-66).

147. *formal principio*: See n. to vss. 67-72.

148. *conforme a sua bontà*: Cf. the "bontate" of vs. 136.
turbo = torbo (from the Latin *turbidus*), "the dark." Thus the dark spots on the moon result from the lesser alloy of some of its parts, the lesser "goodness" with which here and there it is alloyed.

From a principle of material causality (rarity and density of matter) formerly held by Dante and others, Beatrice has led Dante to the principle of a spiritual causality that descends from God and variously informs His creation. "It may seem surprising to the reader on first becoming acquainted with the preceding canto, which has so little poetic charm, that Dante's first enquiry of Beatrice, after his overwhelming experience in entering the superterrestrial world, and his marvellous reception into the sphere of the Moon, should be concerning a mere physical phenomenon, and especially a matter so apparently trivial as the cause of the light and dark spots on the face of the Moon, and seemingly suggested to him only by finding himself in the body of the planet. But the surprise will vanish, and the intention of the poet will become manifest, on consideration of the full significance of the reply made by Beatrice. She begins with the lesson that in the supersensual world the evidence of the senses is not to be trusted, since even in the world of sense conclusions drawn from their evidence are often erroneous (vv. 52-105). She then proceeds to set forth the mode of operation of the Heavens, begun in the Crystalline Heaven, —the Primum Mobile,—and thence transmitted to the inferior spheres (vv. 112-123). But 'their motion and their virtue,' from which the differences in themselves and the differences in the natures and aspects of mortal things proceed, are not inherent in themselves, but are inspired by angelic Intelligences, ministers of the Divine Will to carry out the Divine plan in the order of the Universe, and to impress upon it the image of the Divine idea (vv. 127-148).

"Thus the apparently trivial question asked by Dante has led to an exposition of the Divine scheme of the Universe, requisite for the understanding of the nature of the realm into which the poet has been uplifted" (Norton).

CANTO III

1. *Quel sol*: Beatrice. *che pria d'amor mi scaldò 'l petto*: Dante's love for Beatrice began when he was nine years old. See *Vita nuova* II, 2, where Dante speaks of this.

2–3. *di bella verità . . . aspetto*: In normal prose form and order this would read "mi aveva scoperto il dolce aspetto di bella verità," i.e., the whole truth regarding the spots of the moon.

3. *riprovando*: "Refuting." The reader will recall how Beatrice began her argument by refutation (*Par*. II, 61-105).

4. *corretto e certo*: Corrected by the refutation and made certain by the truth, as expounded by Beatrice.

6. *proferer = proferire*, "to speak." *erto = eretto*.

7. *visione*: "Vision" only in the sense of "that which becomes visible." Dante uses the word in this sense elsewhere in the poem.

8. *per vedersi* = "through sight of it."

9. *non mi sovvenne*: The impersonal use in the third person of the verb *sovvenire*. Cf. *Purg*. XXVI, 147.

10. *vetri*: "Panes" of glass.

12. *persi*: This could be either the past participle of *perdere*, meaning "lost," or the adjective *perso*, meaning "dark" (cf. *Inf.* V, 89). Either meaning might serve here, but since the poet goes on to speak of reflections, the sense of the past participle seems preferable. The bottom can be seen, and the water reflects better for that reason.

13. *tornan*: "Are reflected." To Dante the faces seem to be reflected.   *postille*: Literally, "notes" such as might be found on a manuscript page surrounding the main text; here, metaphorically, "outlines," "lineaments," "contours" of the face.

14–15. *debili sì . . . pupille*: These faces are as faint to Dante's sight as is a pearl on a white forehead. The reference is to a feminine fashion of Dante's day and later, which may be seen depicted in various portraits. Hence the image arises from something familiar to the reader of the time.

17–18. *per ch'io . . . fonte*: Narcissus took his reflection in the fountain to be a real person, whereas Dante takes these real beings to be reflections, as the first part of the simile suggests and as is stated in vs. 20. See n. to *Inf.* XXX, 128.

21. *per veder di cui fosser, li occhi torsi*: Dante turns around to see the real faces which he assumes must be behind him.   *di cui = di chi.*

22. *ritorsili = li ritorsi.*

26. *appresso*: "Following."   *coto*: "Thought." It is "puerile" because completely mistaken. For another instance of "coto" in this sense, see *Inf.* XXXI, 77.

27. *poi = poiché.*   *'l vero*: These supernatural realities.   *ancor lo piè non fida*: The thought does not yet trust its foot thereon.

28. *ma te rivolve, come suole, a vòto*: The subject is "coto," which is said to turn him in error. Beatrice's chiding, begun at the summit of the mountain of Purgatory, continues in the phrase "come suole" ("as it is wont") and bears a reference

to Dante's mistaken thought concerning the moon's spots. Concerning the rhyming of "vòto" here with "voto" (pronounced *vóto*) in vs. 30, see a similar case in *Inf*. XXII, 75.
vòto = *vuoto*, "emptiness," "vanity."

29. *vere sustanze*: "Real souls," not reflected images. A "substance" is any being or thing possessing independent existence. See Dante, *Vita nuova* XXV, 1-2. The human soul is a substance, of course, by this definition.

30. *qui rilegate*: The term "relegated" is ambiguous, for it can suggest that these souls have their constant abode here in this sphere. This question is discussed in the next canto (*Par*. IV, 28-63), where we learn that the souls abide in the Empyrean and simply appear (mysteriously) in the different spheres as Dante rises from one to another. "Dante leaves us in doubt whether, in the literal sense of his narrative, the souls actually leave their seats in the Empyrean and come to meet him, or merely project their images into the several spheres. In the 8th heaven all the elect are seen by him, even those who have previously appeared below. The idea that the blessed can change their places, without losing sight of God and thus interrupting their beatitude, is in no wise contrary to Christian doctrine. St. Thomas tells us as much in his *Summa Theologiae*, Tertia, Suppl., Qu. lxix, Art. 3, and Qu. lxxxiv, Art. 1 and 2; also in *De Veritate Catholicae Fidei contra Gentiles*, IV, lxxxvi, where he discusses the active life of the spirits in Heaven. For their existence does not wholly consist of passive receptivity; they have the power of locomotion, they take interest in one another and (without diminution of their everlasting joy) in the world beneath" (Gr).

per manco di voto: The inconstant moon is the appropriate sphere in which those who were inconstant in life manifest themselves to Dante. Though we actually hear only of and from inconstant nuns, we may suppose, as Grandgent observes, "that all weak and inconstant persons who win salvation at all are to be connected with this sphere, the nuns being chosen as extreme examples."

31. *Però* = *perciò*.

32. *la verace luce*: God's light, which is the truth.

33. *da sé*: From Itself, the truth.   *torcer li piedi*: Again "feet" are used to express movements of the soul. Cf. vs. 27.

35. *drizza'mi* = *mi dirizzai*.

36. *cui* = *che* (direct object).   *smaga*: "Bewilders." Cf. *Inf.* XXV, 146; *Purg.* X, 106.

40. *grazioso* = *gradito*.

41. *del nome tuo e de la vostra sorte*: The reader will do well to note the shift here to the plural "vostra." The plural "your" includes *all* the spirits who have presented themselves in the sphere of the moon.

43. *non serra porte*: Literally, "does not close its doors," i.e., does not deny satisfaction (to any rightful desire).

44. *se non come quella*: "Any more than that" (God's love).

45. *tutta sua corte*: All the blessed in Heaven.

46. *vergine sorella*: A nun.

47. *e se la mente tua ben sé riguarda*: "If your memory examines itself well."

48. *non mi ti celerà l'esser più bella*: "L'esser più bella" is the subject of the verb.

49. *Piccarda*: Piccarda was the daughter of Simone Donati and the sister of Corso and Forese and was related by marriage to Dante through his wife, Gemma, daughter of Manetto Donati. According to the early commentators, she entered a convent but was forced thence by her brother Corso so that he might marry her to a Florentine named Rossellino della Tosa. (See n. to *Purg.* XXIV, 10.) She is spoken of in *Purg.* XXIV, 10-15, in connection with Dante's encounter with Forese, where it is said that she already enjoys her crown "on high Olympus."

50. *posta*: "Placed." The ambiguity, which was first evident in "rilegate" in vs. 30, continues here.

51. *la spera più tarda*: "The sphere of the moon, being nearest to the center, turns slowest in the diurnal revolution of the heavens. This comparative sluggishness of motion symbolizes a relatively low degree of love and of beatitude" (Gr). This means that the spirits here "placed" are lowest in the heavenly hierarchy, which explains what is said in vs. 55.

53. *piacer*: "Will." The Holy Ghost is eternal Love.

54. *letizian del suo ordine formati*: They "rejoice in whatever grade of bliss is assigned to them in that order of the universe which is the form that makes it like unto God" (Norton).

55. *par giù cotanto*: "Appears so lowly."

56. *però = per ciò.   n'è = ci è.*

57. *vòti = vuoti.*

59. *risplende non so che divino*: In the faces of these souls there now shines a wondrous supernatural light.

60. *che vi trasmuta da' primi concetti*: Which changes your appearance as it was on earth and as it is remembered ("primi concetti") by those who saw and knew you there. "Compare Dante's words to Ciacco, *Hell*, Canto vi. 43-45. In Hell anguish, in Paradise joy transfigures the spirits and makes recognition of them difficult" (Norton).

61. *festino*: From the Latin *festinus*, "quick."

63. *latino*: "Easy." This is a use of the noun as adjective or adverb which is common in early Italian. Cf. "latinamente" as used in *Conv.* II, iii, 1.

64. *voi*: The reader should note that Dante continues to speak in the plural, i.e., of all the souls "relegated" to this sphere.

66. *per più vedere e per più farvi amici*: " 'In order to see

more and make yourselves more intimate' with God. The souls that are spiritually nearest to God are endowed with the keenest intellectual vision; they therefore see God clearest and love him most" (Gr).

67. *Con quelle altr' ombre pria sorrise un poco*: Piccarda and the other souls smile at Dante's naive question.

68. *da indi*: "Then." From the Latin *deinde*.

69. *ch'arder parea d'amor nel primo foco*: Piccarda seems to glow with the love of the Holy Ghost, "first" love in this sense (see *Inf.* III, 6).

70. *Frate*: On the use of this form of address, which in the poem often introduces a statement correcting some misconceived opinion of the person spoken to, cf. *Purg.* XXVI, 115, and *passim*.

70–71. *la nostra volontà . . . carità*: "Volontà," in this construction, is the object of the verb "quieta." Cf. *Conv.* III, xv, 10, where Dante states: "E questa è la ragione per che li Santi non hanno tra loro invidia, però che ciascuno aggiugne lo fine del suo desiderio, lo quale desiderio è con la bontà de la natura misurato." ("And this is why the saints envy not one another, because each one attains the goal of his longing, which longing is commensurate with the nature of his excellence.")

71. *virtù di carità*: The "power of love" for God. *fa volerne*: "Makes us wish."

74. *foran = sarebbero*.

75. *qui ne cerne*: "Assigns us to this place" (this lowest order of beatitude).

76. *non capere*: "Have no place," "would not be fitting." *capere*: Pronounced *capére*. *in questi giri*: Piccarda now extends her statement to include all the spheres of heaven.

77. *essere in carità*: Desiring and loving in conformity with

God's will and the "first" love, the love of the Holy Ghost.

necesse: A "necessity." The Latin expression *necesse est* belongs to scholastic language and is often used to express *logical* necessity.

78. *se la sua natura ben rimiri*: "If you consider well the very nature" of love, which implies conformity of the will on the part of the lover to that of the beloved.

79. *formale*: "Essential," "inherent." *ad esto beato esse = a questo essere beato*, i.e., to this our condition of beatitude.

80–81. *tenersi dentro . . . stesse*: Piccarda continues to speak of *all* the elect and their love of God. "Tenersi dentro a la divina voglia" is another way of expressing the perfect conformity of their wills to God's, so that in Heaven the many wills are but one, in this sense.

81. *fansi = si fanno*.

82. *sem = siamo*. *soglia*: The word here means "station" or "rank." Cf. *Purg.* XXI, 69 and *passim*.

83. *a tutto il regno piace*: The subject of "piace" is the preceding clause.

84. *lo re che 'n suo voler ne 'nvoglia*: And this order pleases God who conforms our will to His. *ne = ci*.

85. *E 'n la sua volontade è nostra pace*: Cf. Eph. 2:14: "Ipse enim est pax nostra." ("For he himself is our peace.") See also the quotation from Augustine, n. to *Par.* I, 116.

86–87. *ell' è quel mare . . . face*: Just as all water comes from the sea (by evaporation) and returns to the sea by the many rivers that flow into it (cf. *Purg.* XIV, 34-36; *Par.* I, 116), so all creatures formed directly by God (angels and human souls) return to Him, and those formed by Nature seek their proper resting-place. The metaphor is explicit in Francesca's words in *Inf.* V, 98-99, where she speaks of the Po as seeking peace, while she desires peace with God, which she, being damned to Hell, shall never have.

88. *ogne dove*: Here, as *passim*, the adverb "dove" becomes a noun: every *where*, i.e., every place, station, or rank that is allotted to each soul who enjoys the beatitude of Heaven.

89. *etsi*: A Latinism, meaning "although."

90. *d'un modo*: "In the same measure," equally.

91. *elli avvien*: "It happens."

93. *chere = chiede*. *Chere*, from the Latin *quaerere*, is common in old Italian.   *e di quel*: That is, for the food already had.

95–96. *per apprender . . . spuola*: Dante would now hear more from Piccarda concerning her statement about herself in vss. 46 and 56-57. This is the cloth ("tela") which she has begun but has not finished weaving, as the metaphor of these two verses has it. Or, in Dante's desire to hear it, in the other metaphor of the two foods (one had, the other desired), this becomes the second food. Some commentators take the "tela" to refer specifically to Piccarda's broken vow itself, but this seems less acceptable as the precise meaning of the metaphor even though, out of metaphor, it amounts to the same thing.

96. *onde non trasse infino a co la spuola*: "In which she did not draw the shuttle to the end."   *co = capo*. Cf. *Inf.* XX, 76, and *passim*.

97–99. *Perfetta vita . . . vela*: The reference is to St. Clare, who, with St. Francis, founded a Franciscan conventual institution for women, the Clarisse. She was born of a noble family of Assisi in 1194, founded in 1212 under the direction of St. Francis the order of nuns which bears her name (Order of Poor Clare), and died in 1253. She was canonized, by Alexander IV, in 1255. The rule of her order was characterized by extreme austerity.

97. *inciela*: "Enheavens." Dante invents the verb.

98. *più sù*: We are never told just how high in Heaven St. Clare is, but one must think that her saintly life gives her a

very high station indeed. *a la cui norma*: "According to whose rule."

100. *perché*: "In order that." *si vegghi = si vegli* (subjunctive of *vegliare*).

101. *con quello sposo*: With Christ, in mystical union (marriage) with Him.

102. *che caritate a suo piacer conforma*: "Which love conforms to His will."

103–4. *Dal mondo . . . fuggi'mi*: To follow St. Clare, "fleeing from the world," even as St. Francis had done, in taking the vow of poverty.

104. *fuggi'mi = mi fuggii*. The reflexive pronoun is the familiar so-called pleonastic reflexive, here in its distancing function. Piccarda entered the convent of the Clarisse of Monticelli, near Florence.

105. *la via de la sua setta*: Cf. vs. 98: "norma."

106–8. *Uomini poi . . . fusi*: The men were her brother Corso Donati and his followers, who compelled her to marry. This took place around 1288. The date of her death is not known, but vs. 108 suggests that, contrary to legend, her married life outside the convent lasted for a considerable time after she was taken from it.

108. *Iddio si sa*: Here the value of the reflexive may be translated as "only" or "alone": "God only knows."
fusi = si fu. This is again the pleonastic reflexive which commonly follows the verb "to know" and in this case has its identifying value: "what my life was then," i.e., how terrible it was.

109–11. *E quest' altro splendor . . . nostra*: For the first time we are told that the spirits are resplendent in their joy and love, a feature of Paradise which will become very familiar. The reference is to the soul of the "great Constance" (as is then declared), who would seem to outshine all other spirits in this heaven of the moon, or at least to be resplendent to the maximum degree.

112. *ciò ch'io dico di me, di sé intende*: "Applies to herself what I say of me," i.e., she too was a nun who was taken from the cloister by violence and forced to marry.

114. *l'ombra de le sacre bende*: The nun's veil, called "shade" because it may be said, literally, to shade the face. As Chimenz observes, however, the "shade" is also spiritual, "shading" from the world.

115. *pur*: "Again," this being then re-echoed in the *ri-* of "rivolta."

117. *non fu dal vel del cor già mai disciolta*: "She was never stripped of the veil of the heart," i.e., she remained a nun at heart.

118-20. *Quest' è la luce . . . possanza*: This most resplendent of the souls is thus finally named "the great Constance." Constance (1154-98) was the daughter of Roger II, king of Naples and Sicily, and wife of the Emperor Henry VI, by whom she became the mother of the Emperor Frederick II. She was the last heir of the Norman dynasty. See *Purg.* III, 113.

Villani (V, 16), following the belief current among Guelphs, states that the marriage between Constance and Henry was desired by Pope Clement III and the archbishop of Palermo for the purpose of getting the kingdom out of the hands of Constance's nephew, Tancred, who showed no respect for the interests of the Church. But William the Good was still alive at the time of the marriage, and, as a matter of fact, on his death in 1189, Tancred's election was ratified by Clement, as a bar to the pretensions of Henry, though Henry's wife was the rightful heiress.

William the Good, son of William the Bad, having no issue by his wife Joan (daughter of Henry II of England), his aunt Constance became presumptive heiress to the throne, which the Emperor Frederick Barbarossa desired to acquire for his own house. To effect his object he projected an alliance between Constance and his son Henry, duke of Swabia, afterwards emperor as Henry VI. The marriage took place in 1186, when Constance was over thirty and Henry twenty-one, but their son, Frederick of Palermo, the heir to the throne, was not born until eight years later (December 1194), only four years before the death of his mother (November 1198).

It is now generally thought by historians that Constance was never a nun, as the poet would have it. Dante has simply followed a current legend. It is interesting to note (see E. Levi, 1921, p. 69) that Piccarda took the name Costanza when she entered the order.

119. *secondo vento di Soave*: "The Swabian Emperors are called 'blasts' because of the violence and the brief duration of their activity. Frederick I (Barbarossa) was the first; the 'second wind' was Constance's husband, Henry VI; the third and last was her son, Frederick II.—*Soave* (German *Schwaben*) = *Svevia*. Formerly *Soave* was the usual form" (Gr).

122. *vanio = vanì (svanì)*.

124. *seguio = seguì*.

126. *volsesi = si volse.*   *al segno di maggior disio*: Beatrice, who is a greater "target" or object of desire for Dante than is Piccarda.

CANTO IV

1-3. *Intra due cibi . . . denti*: "The familiar paradox later known as the Ass of Buridan, or the donkey and the two bales of hay, is here applied to Dante, who is eager to ask two questions and cannot decide which to put first" (Gr). See Aristotle, *De caelo* II, 13, 295^b, and Thomas Aquinas, *Summa theol.* I-II, q. 13, a. 6; cf. Ovid, *Metam.* V, 164-66.

1. *moventi*: "Attractive."

2. *d'un modo*: "Equally."

2-3. *prima si morria . . . denti*: The subject of "si morria" (= *si morirebbe*) is "liber' omo."

3. *liber' omo*: A man in full possession of his free will.

4-5. *sì si starebbe . . . lupi*: That is, immobile, like the free man, but in this case paralyzed by equal fear of the two wolves. "Intra due brame di fieri lupi" means "tra due lupi feroci e bramosi."

6. *sì si starebbe un cane intra due dame*: The third example returns to the case of equal desire, rather than fear, now on the part of a hunting dog at equal distance between two does.
    dame: The word is obsolete in the sense in which Dante

75

uses it here. Cf. the Latin *damma* and the modern Italian *daina*.

7–9. *per che . . . commendo*: Dante, equally urged by two doubts which he would have Beatrice solve, remains silent and cannot blame himself for it, since this must be the effect of such a situation, matching in its way the other three instances just cited.

10–12. *Io mi tacea . . . distinto*: Dante's desire to hear from Beatrice the answers to his questions, along with the formulation of those questions ("'l dimandar"), is evident in his face and more fervently expressed there than it would have been had he set it forth in words ("che per parlar distinto").

13–15. *Fé sì Beatrice . . . fello*: "Daniel divined the dream Nebuchadnezzar had dreamed as well as the interpretation of it (*Daniel* ii.). So Beatrice knew what problems were exercising Dante's mind as well as what were the solutions" (TC).

15. *ingiustamente fello*: Nebuchadnezzar, Chaldean king of Babylon, was about to put to death the wise men of Babylon who could not interpret a dream they had not been told.

16–18. *Io veggio . . . spira*: Dante's equally divided eagerness to have the one and the other question solved prevents his expressing either.

19–21. *Se 'l buon voler . . . misura?* The question focuses on the cases of Piccarda and Constance, whose desire to return to the convent continued in them even after they had been taken forth therefrom by violence. By what reason, then, can they be thought to deserve less, how can their "measure" of reward be less?

21. *mi scema*: The "mi" obviously generalizes the two cases, allowing them to apply to anyone.

22. *Ancor*: "Secondly."   *di dubitar ti dà cagione*: *Cagion di dubitar* is the object of "dà." The subject of the verb is the clause in the next line.

24. *secondo la sentenza di Platone*: "In the *Timaeus*, which was accessible to Dante in the Latin paraphrase of Chalcidius. Dante's direct knowledge of Plato was doubtless confined to this one dialogue. The doctrine ascribed to Plato, implicitly here and explicitly in *Conv.* [IV, xxi, 2], goes somewhat beyond the warrant of the text either in the Greek or Latin" (TC). "Plato, in his *Timaeus* (41, 42), says that the creator of the universe assigned each soul to a star, whence they were to be sown in the vessels of time. 'He who lived well during his appointed time was to return to the star which was his habitation, and there he would have a blessed and suitable existence.' Jowett's translation.—Dante's doubt has arisen from the words of Piccarda (Canto iii. 50, 51), which implied that her station was in the sphere of the Moon" (Norton). This doctrine is contrary to Christian faith. See Thomas Aquinas, *Summa theol.* III, Suppl., q. 97, a. 5. "Plato's theory appealed strongly to some of the early Christian theologians, but had to be abandoned after 540, when the Council of Constantinople decided that every soul is created by God at the birth of its body" (Gr).

25-26. *nel tuo velle pontano*: "Push upon thy will." *Velle*, as a noun, is late Latin and is common to scholastic terminology.

27. *quella che più ha di felle*: "Plato's doctrine (as understood by Dante) is poisonous because it ascribes to the admitted influences of the heavenly bodies such a prepotency as would be fatal to freewill, and therefore to morality" (TC). See *Purg.* XVI, 58-81, and XVIII, 61-75; see also Dante, *Epist.* XI, 4. "This question has the most poison, because the belief that the souls returned to the stars would be contrary to the faith that the true end of the soul is the attainment of bliss in the vision of God in the Empyrean, and would tend to divert the soul from its effort to make itself worthy of this bliss" (Norton). *felle*: The "gall" or "poison" of heresy.

28. *D'i Serafin colui che più s'india*: That Seraph of the

Seraphim, the highest order of angels, who is closest to God (enjoying His light most).

29. *Moisè, Samuel*: The statement now passes from angels to human creatures.

29–30. *e quel Giovanni che prender vuoli*: "Whichever of the Johns [the Baptist or the Evangelist] you choose."

30. *non Maria*: The statement having passed to the human order, to name Mary is to name her as the highest in that order (the "non" here having the value of "not even").

31–34. *non hanno . . . giro*: The "primo giro" is the Empyrean heaven, where God is and where the blessed and the angels see Him in direct vision, which is their beatitude. Thus Beatrice is settling one of Dante's doubts by assuring him that even the highest among angels and human creatures have the same abode as these of this lowest order. All have their seats there in the Empyrean (as the reader will see at the end of the poem), and all have eternal life there, contrary to Plato's opinion, which allowed a longer or briefer sojourn in the heavens according to the souls' respective merits.

32. *mo = ora.   appariro = apparirono.*

33. *l'esser lor*: The duration of their existence.

35–36. *e differentemente . . . spiro*: Cf. *Par.* III, 88-90. Grandgent (p. 649) comments: " 'In my Father's house are many mansions' (John xiv, 2). By 'mansions' are meant degrees of happiness: so says St. Thomas in the *Summa Theologiae*, Tertia, Suppl., Qu. xciii, Art. 2, 3; see also his Commentary on John xiv, and St. Augustine's Treatise on John, lxvii. Every soul in Heaven receives all the gladness of which it is capable, but the capacity differs. God, on creating each soul, endows it—according to his mysterious grace—with a certain degree of keenness of spiritual sight, upon which (if the soul attains Heaven) depends its vision of God, and upon the clearness of this vision depend the soul's love and joy. This is the doctrine of St. Thomas, which Dante upholds."

However, "spiro" (*spirare*) stresses love rather than vision at this point.

37. *Qui si mostraro*: The spirits have "shown themselves" to Dante, and, as the reader will see, this will be the case in each of the spheres.   *mostraro = mostrarono*.   *sortita*: "Allotted."

38. *spera = sfera*.   *lor*: "To them."   *per far segno*: "To give a sign" to Dante.

39. *de la celestial c'ha men salita*: Of their rank in the celestial sphere, the Empyrean, where they occupy the lowest seats, farthest from God. And what these spirits say of themselves applies in turn to each of the spheres that lie ahead and above. The poet's invention of this whole scheme is noteworthy, and the reader has only to consider how unsatisfactory (if not impossible) it would have been had the pilgrim risen immediately and directly to the Empyrean, in the first canto of the *Paradiso*, and remained there for thirty-two cantos! By such a device, instead, his journey can pass eventfully upwards by degrees or stages, each stage higher than the last, like so many rungs of a ladder, reaching upward all the way to God.

40–42. *Così parlar . . . degno*: The poet has Beatrice affirm that it is necessary to "speak" to human kind by way of the senses and that even the Holy Scriptures and Holy Church observe this method. The tenet thus expressed has the full support, moreover, of Aristotle's philosophy, namely, that we learn first through sense experience only.

40. *vostro*: The reader who is following the translation should note that Beatrice's affirmation shifts, with "vostro," to the plural, i.e., to a generalization regarding human kind.

41. *solo da sensato apprende*: See n. to vs. 40. On the importance of this principle to the poet as poet, see C. S. Singleton (1969), pp. 25-29. This is the essentially Aristotelian doctrine often stated as the tenet *nihil est in intellectu quin prius fuerit in sensu* ("nothing is in the intellect unless it is

first in sense experience"), a doctrine of great importance to a poet who is committed to rendering his experience in concrete imagery. The reader should connect this same tenet with the question, left open, as to whether the pilgrim makes this upward journey through the spheres in his body or not. (See *Par.* I, 73-75, and n. to *Par.* I, 74.) He would appear to be having "sensible" experience here, even as he had during his journey through Inferno and Purgatory, where he did move with his body. Thus, by indirection (but never explicitly), the poet suggests that he did indeed traverse the heavens in his body, even though this is a great mystery (cf. *Par.* II, 37-42). And Heaven, as it were, condescends to speak to him through sensible experience in each of the spheres of the upward way.

42. *fa poscia d'intelletto degno*: "According to the psychology of Aristotle and the Schoolmen, the Intellect works upon images, etc., which are retained in the mind after the sense-impressions that produced them have vanished. Thus the *imaginative* faculties receive from the faculties of *sense* the impressions which they then present to the *intellect* for it to work upon" (TC).

43-45. *Per questo . . . intende*: Thomas Aquinas, at the very beginning of his *Summa theologica*, feels the necessity of entering into such a question. See *Summa theol.* I, q. 1, a. 9, resp.:

> Respondeo dicendum quod conveniens est sacrae Scripturae divina et spiritualia sub similitudine corporalium tradere. Deus enim omnibus providet, secundum quod competit eorum naturae. Est autem naturale homini ut per sensibilia ad intelligibilia veniat; quia omnis nostra cognitio a sensu initium habet. Unde convenienter in sacra Scriptura traduntur nobis spiritualia sub metaphoris corporalium; et hoc est quod dicit Dionysius, 1 cap. Coelestis Hierarch. (circa med.): *Impossibile est nobis aliter lucere divinum radium, nisi varietate sacrorum velaminum circumvelatum.* Convenit etiam sacrae Scripturae, quae communiter omnibus proponitur, se-

cundum illud ad Rom. 1, 14: *Sapientibus et insipientibus debitor sum*, ut spiritualia sub similitudinibus corporalium proponantur, ut saltem vel sic rudes eam capiant, qui ad intelligibilia secundum se capienda non sunt idonei.

I answer that, It is befitting Holy Writ to put forward divine and spiritual truths by means of comparisons with material things. For God provides for everything according to the capacity of its nature. Now it is natural to man to attain to intellectual truths through sensible objects, because all our knowledge originates from sense. Hence in Holy Writ spiritual truths are fittingly taught under the likeness of material things. This is what Dionysius says (*Coel. Hier.* i): *We cannot be enlightened by the divine rays except they be hidden within the covering of many sacred veils.* It is also befitting Holy Writ, which is proposed to all without distinction of persons—*To the wise and to the unwise I am a debtor* (Rom. i. 14)—that spiritual truths be expounded by means of figures taken from corporeal things, in order that thereby even the simple who are unable by themselves to grasp intellectual things may be able to understand it.

Thus the poet's way of writing does not differ from God's, the Author of Holy Scripture, but can continue to seem an imitation thereof—which in so many respects it is.

44-45. *e piedi e mano attribuisce a Dio*: See Thomas Aquinas, *Summa theol.* I, q. 3, a. 1, ad 3:

Partes corporeae attribuuntur Deo in Scripturis ratione suorum actuum secundum quamdam similitudinem; sicut actus oculi est videre; unde oculus de Deo dictus significat virtutem eius ad videndum modo intelligibili, non sensibili; et simile est de aliis partibus.

Corporeal parts are attributed to God in Scripture on account of His actions, and this is owing to a certain parallel. For instance the act of the eye is to see; hence the eye attributed to God signifies His power of seeing intellectually, not sensibly; and so on with the other parts.

46–48. *e Santa Chiesa . . . sano*: Holy Church, in its many offices, follows God's way of speaking in Holy Scripture. But "vi rappresenta" in this statement seems also to apply to the paintings, icons, statues, and frescoes which are found in churches and "speak" to the people through a certain anthropomorphic imagery.

48. *e l'altro che Tobia rifece sano*: Raphael, who restored sight to old Tobit (see Tob. 11:1-15). All three angels here named are archangels.

49. *Quel che Timeo de l'anime argomenta*: Beatrice now turns to the second question, referred to in vss. 22-24. Timaeus is the chief interlocutor in the Platonic dialogue which bears that name, and it is he who expounds the opinion referred to by Beatrice. See n. to vs. 24.

51. *però che, come dice, par che senta*: "Because he seems to mean it as he expresses it," i.e., literally, not figuratively.

"The controversy still rages as to how far Plato is to be taken literally and how far Aristotle's matter-of-fact interpretation (and refutation) of his utterances is justified. Thomas Aquinas says: 'Now certain say that those poets and philosophers, and especially Plato, did not mean what the superficial sound of their words implies, but chose to hide their wisdom under certain fables and enigmatical phrases, and that Aristotle was often wont to raise objections, not to their meaning, which was sound, but to their words; lest any should be led into error by this way of speaking; and so saith Simplicius in his comment. But Alexander would have it that Plato and the other ancient philosophers meant what their words seem externally to imply; and that Aristotle strove to argue not only against their words, but against their meaning. But we need not greatly concern ourselves as to which of these is true; for the study of philosophy is not directed to ascertaining what men have believed, but how the truth of things standeth.' Simplicius (6th century) and

Alexander of Aphrodisias (2nd and 3rd centuries) are the
two greatest of the Greek commentators on Aristotle. It is
interesting to note that even Beatrice hesitates between the
two schools of interpretation" (TC).

53. *quindi*: "Therefrom," i.e., from the star which had been
its abode.   *decisa*: "Separated," "detached," from the
Latin *decidere*, "to cut off." Cf. *Purg.* XVII, 111.

54. *per forma*: The soul is the "form" of the body and, ac-
cording to the *Timaeus* (XLII), is implanted into the body.

55–57. *e forse . . . derisa*: Cf. n. to vs. 51.

55. *sentenza*: "Meaning."

56. *la voce*: His words.

57. *da non esser derisa*: "Not to be derided," i.e., worthy of
respect. See Dante, *Conv.* IV, xxi, 2-3:

> Veramente per diversi filosofi de la differenza de le
> nostre anime fue diversamente ragionato: ché Avicenna
> e Algazel volsero che esse da loro e per loro principio
> fossero nobili e vili; e Plato e altri volsero che esse pro-
> cedessero da le stelle, e fossero nobili e più e meno se-
> condo la nobilitade de la stella. Pittagora volse che tutte
> fossero d'una nobilitade, non solamente le umane, ma
> con le umane quelle de li animali bruti e de le piante,
> e le forme de le minere; e disse che tutta la differenza
> è de le corpora e de le forme. Se ciascuno fosse a difen-
> dere la sua oppinione, potrebbe essere che la veritade
> si vedrebbe essere in tutte.

> It is true that divers reasonings have been held by phi-
> losophers concerning the difference of our souls; for
> Avicenna and Algazel would have it that they in them-
> selves, and in their principle, were noble or base. Plato
> and others would have it that they proceeded from the
> stars and were noble, more or less, according to the no-
> bleness of the star. Pythagoras would have it that all
> were of like nobleness, and not only the human souls,
> but together with the human those of the brute animals

and of the plants, and the forms of the minerals; and he said that all the difference was in the bodily forms. If each were to defend his own opinion, it might be that truth would be seen to exist in all of them.

58-60. *S'elli intende . . . percuote*: "'If he means that the credit or the blame for influence (on human souls) reverts to these (heavenly) revolutions, perhaps the bow (of his speech) hits some truth.' Dante is evidently reluctant to impute fundamental error to such a philosopher as Plato" (Gr).

59. *l'onor de la influenza e 'l biasmo*: The influence of the stars was granted in the argument of Marco Lombardo (*Purg.* XVI, 73) and was generally taken for granted in medieval thought. The most striking instance, in Dante's poem, will come when Dante the pilgrim reaches the constellation of Gemini under which he was born, where (*Par.* XXII, 112-23) he acknowledges that he owes all his genius to those "glorious" stars. Indeed, the notion is fundamental to the whole structure of the *Paradiso*, for the souls seen in each of the planets were variously influenced by these heavenly bodies.

61. *Questo principio, male inteso*: This principle or doctrine of stellar influence wrongly understood. *torse*: "Led astray," "led into error."

62. *già*: In ancient times. *tutto il mondo quasi*: "Almost the whole world," the Hebrew people being the great exception.

62-63. *sì che Giove . . . trascorse*: "This passage is important as throwing light on Dante's constant assumption that the heathen deities, though in one sense 'false and lying' (*Inf.* i. 72), yet stand for some truly divine reality. We see here that idolatry springs from a misconception of the divine influences of which the heavenly bodies are the instruments. Its essential content therefore is real and divine, its form is false and impious" (TC). Cf. *Par.* VIII, 1-9; *Conv.* II, iv, 2, 6-7.

63. *trascorse*: " 'It (the world) went astray' in attributing the stellar power to heathen gods and in naming the planets after them. Cf. VIII, 1-3, 10-11.—For a rationalistic, astronomical explanation of myths, see Lucian, *On Astrology*" (Gr).

64. *L'altra dubitazion*: See vss. 19-21. Beatrice now turns to the second question.

65. *velen*: Cf. "felle," vs. 27.   *però che = perciò che*.

66. *poria = potrebbe*.   *menar da me altrove*: Beatrice here figures as Sapientia, bearer of divine truth.

67–69. *Parere ingiusta . . . nequizia*: "*Parere . . . mortali* is the subject of *è*.—*Argomento*, 'proof.'—*Nequizia*, 'iniquity.' —If man had not faith in the perfection of divine justice, he would not be troubled by apparent deviation from it" (Gr).

67. *nostra giustizia*: Beatrice speaks as one who comes from the Empyrean, hence "nostra giustizia" is to be understood as God's justice.

70. *vostro*: Beatrice continues to address all human kind.

73-74. *Se violenza . . . sforza*: Beatrice begins with a definition of the involuntary or compulsory which scholastic thought derived essentially from the third book of Aristotle's *Nicomachean Ethics*. The philosopher, in treating of the virtues, gives the following definition of the compulsory in *Eth. Nicom.* III, 1, 1109^b-1110^a (see Aquinas, *Opera omnia*, vol. XXI, p. 70, or R. M. Spiazzi, 1964, p. 111): "Videntur autem involuntaria esse, quae violenta vel propter ignorantiam facta. Violentum autem est cuius principium extra tale existens in quo nihil confert operans vel patiens. Puta si spiritus tulerit aliquo, vel homines domini existentes." ("Involuntary actions seem to be those that arise either from violence or from ignorance. The 'compulsory action' [*violentum*] is one whose principle is from outside and to which the person involved or the recipient contributes nothing, for example, if he is driven somewhere by the wind, or if he is in the power of other men.") Much that is relevant to Beatrice's argument, as it proceeds, can be found in this book of the *Nicomachean Ethics* and in the many scholastic commentaries written on it, such as that of Aquinas, which is quoted in these notes as typical.

76–78. *ché volontà . . . torza*: Here Beatrice speaks of what emerges in the argument concerning the absolute will, as opposed to the relative or qualified will, the will *secundum quid*. See Thomas Aquinas (*Summa theol.* I-II, q. 6, a. 4, resp.), who uses an example from nature to make his point, though the example is of a falling stone rather than a rising flame:

> Quod autem est coactum vel violentum, est ab exteriori principio. Unde contra rationem ipsius actus voluntatis est quod sit coactus vel violentus; sicut etiam est contra rationem naturalis inclinationis vel motus lapidis, quod feratur sursum; potest enim lapis per violentiam ferri sursum; sed quod iste motus violentus sit ex eius naturali inclinatione, esse non potest. Similiter etiam potest homo per violentiam trahi; sed quod hoc sit ex eius voluntate, repugnat rationi violentiae.

> Now what is compelled or violent is from an exterior principle. Consequently it is contrary to the nature of the will's own act, that it should be subject to compulsion and violence: just as it is also contrary to the nature of a natural inclination or movement [of a stone that is thrown upward]. For a stone may have an upward movement from violence, but that this violent movement be from its natural inclination is impossible. In like manner a man may be dragged by force: but it is contrary to the very notion of violence, that he be thus dragged of his own will.

76. *se non vuol*: Except by its own volition.   *non s'ammorza*: Cf. *Inf.* XIV, 63. This verb, commonly used of fire or a flame, already anticipates the example to be given. It is the nature of a flame to stand erect and reach upwards, and even if the wind blows it and bends it to one side a thousand

times, when the wind ceases, the flame will return to its nat-
ural upward position and movement. In the second book of
the *Nicomachean Ethics* Aristotle also uses such examples
of that which is natural. See *Eth. Nicom.* II, 1, 1103^a (in
Aquinas, *Opera omnia*, vol. XXI, p. 45, or R. M. Spiazzi,
1964, p. 69): "Puta lapis natura deorsum latus, non utique
assuescit sursum ferri: neque si decies millies assuescatur
quis eum sursum iaciens. Neque ignis deorsum, neque aliud
aliquod eorum, quae aliter innata sunt, aliter utique as-
suescet." ("Thus a stone that naturally gravitates downward
will never become accustomed to moving upward, not even
if someone should continue to throw it into the air ten thou-
sand times. Neither will fire become accustomed to tend
downward, nor will anything else that naturally tends one
way acquire the contrary custom.")

77. *face* = *fa*.

78. *torza* = *torca* (subjunctive of *torcere*).

79-80. *Per che, s'ella . . . forza*: Clearly Beatrice means that
if the flame remains bent over when the wind has ceased, then
it "follows" the violence or compulsion from without.

79. *ella*: The will.

80. *e così queste*: And thus did Piccarda and Constance,
who, when free of compulsion from without, when no longer
detained outside the convent by compulsion, could have re-
turned to the cloister. Thus their will was not "intero" (vs.
82), as implied by the following verse; or, to keep the meta-
phor of the flame, they remained "bent" by the violence, a
point that must now be dealt with (vss. 91-114).

82-84. *Se fosse stato . . . severo*: Typically Dante cites the
case of a Christian and of a pagan.

83. *Lorenzo*: St. Lawrence, a deacon of the Church of
Rome, said to have been a native of Huesca in Spain, suf-
fered martyrdom under the Emperor Valerian in 258. The
tradition is that, being commanded by the prefect of Rome
to deliver up the treasures of the Church, which had been

entrusted to his charge by Pope Sixtus II, he replied that in three days he would produce them. On the expiration of the appointed time he presented to the prefect all the sick and poor to whom he had given alms, with the words "Behold the treasures of Christ's Church." The prefect thereupon directed St. Lawrence to be tortured, in order to make him reveal where the treasures were hidden. But, torture proving ineffectual, he was stretched on an iron frame with bars, like a gridiron, beneath which a fire was kindled so that his body was gradually consumed. In the midst of his agony he is said to have remained steadfast, and to have mocked his executioners, bidding them to turn his body that it might be equally roasted on both sides.

84. *Muzio*: Gaius Mucius Scaevola, a Roman citizen who, when Lars Porsena of Clusium was besieging Rome, made his way into the enemy's camp with the intention of killing Porsena; by mistake, however, he stabbed the king's secretary instead of the king himself. Being seized, Mucius was ordered by the king to be burned alive, whereupon he thrust his right hand into a fire, which was already lighted for a sacrifice, and held it in the flames without flinching. Porsena, struck with admiration at his fortitude, ordered him to be set free; in return Mucius informed him that there were three hundred noble youths in Rome who had sworn to take the king's life, that the lot had fallen upon him to make the first attempt, and that his example would be followed by the others, each as his turn came. Porsena, impressed with this account of the determination of the Romans, made proposals of peace and withdrew from the siege. From the circumstance of the loss of his right hand, Mucius was thenceforward known as Scaevola ("left-handed"). Dante mentions Mucius in connection with this incident in *Conv.* IV, v, 13 and, with a reference to Livy (II, xii, 1-16) as his authority, in *De mon.* II, v, 14.

85–86. *così l'avria ripinte . . . sciolte*: That is, as soon as they were free to return to the convent, they would have done so.

85. *avria = avrebbe*.

86. *ond' eran tratte*: "By which they had been dragged."
   come fuoro sciolte: When the violent men who had taken them from the convent no longer held them captive or physically restrained them.

87. *ma così salda voglia è troppo rada*: I.e., the "volere intero" which Piccarda and Constance did not have and which is now called a "salda voglia."

88. *per queste parole*: By Beatrice's exposition of this whole question.

88–89. *se ricolte l'hai*: "If you have taken them in" and retained them.

89. *dei = devi.   casso*: "Quashed." Cf. *Par.* II, 83. The "argomento" which is thus quashed has reference to the apparent injustice of God's will in reducing the merit of Piccarda and Constance by placing them in the lowliest sphere. This mistaken reasoning would have continued to trouble Dante many times, had Beatrice not set him straight about it.

91–99. *Ma or . . . contradire*: But the question is not settled yet, since there is an apparent contradiction between what Piccarda said about Constance (that she had remained a nun at heart) and Beatrice's whole discourse so far. Beatrice, knowing Dante's thoughts, knows that it is necessary to settle a further point in the matter of this argument, namely the distinction between the absolute will and the relative or qualified will (*secundum quid*). Beatrice continues, of course, quite in line with the Aristotelian philosophy and with scholastic reasoning according to Aristotle.

91–93. *Ma or . . . lasso*: Beatrice, able to read Dante's thoughts, knows that another pass lies athwart his progress toward the whole truth, another problem through which he must make his way, and this he would never do without her further help (with the argument which follows).

93. *pria = prima.   saresti lasso*: These words obviously imply a struggle on Dante's part to make his way alone through this difficulty: he would be completely exhausted therein and never extricate himself if Beatrice did not help him through it.

94–96. *Io t'ho . . . appresso*: Beatrice is referring to her words in *Par.* III, 32-33.

95. *poria = potrebbe.*

96. *però ch' = perciò che.   al primo vero appresso*: Next to, i.e., in possession of, the divine truth.

97. *da Piccarda*: The reference is to Piccarda's words in *Par.* III, 117.

100–102. *Molte fiate già . . . si convenne*: Beatrice now settles this new point in terms of a "conditioned" will or in scholastic terms a *voluntas secundum quid*, as distinguished from what has been termed a "volere intero" (vs. 82) or a "salda voglia" such as St. Lawrence had (vs. 87). For the established scholastic doctrine on this point, see Thomas Aquinas, *Summa theol.* I-II, q. 6, aa. 4-6. (See n. to vss. 76-78.) Thomas' sixth article, "Whether fear causes involuntariness simply," is fundamental to this particular point, since Beatrice puts the matter in just such terms with her phrase "per fuggir periglio" (vs. 101). Thomas recalls Book III of Aristotle's *Nicomachean Ethics*, of course, where precisely such considerations come up, where the philosopher is concerned to define the difference between the voluntary and the involuntary. See *Eth. Nicom.* III, 1, 1110^a (in Aquinas, *Opera omnia*, vol. XXI, p. 70, or R. M. Spiazzi, 1964, p. 111):

> Quaecumque autem propter timorem maiorum malorum operanda sunt, vel propter bonum aliquod, puta si tyrannus praecipiat turpe aliquod operari, dominus existens parentum et filiorum, et operante quidem salventur, non operante autem moriantur, dubitationem habet utrum involuntaria sint vel voluntaria.

> Some things are done because of the fear of greater evils or because of the hope of some good. Thus a tyrant,

having in his power the parents or children of a certain man, commands him to do a disgraceful deed on condition that they will be spared if he does it but killed if he does not do it. Here a doubt arises whether his actions are voluntary or involuntary.

The instance cited here corresponds to Beatrice's "per fuggir periglio" and the case of Alcmaeon (vs. 103), which involves piety of family. Aristotle goes on in this context to observe: "Mixtae quidem igitur sunt tales operationes." ("Operations of this kind are mixed.") See vs. 107, where the verb "si mischia" expresses this notion. Thomas Aquinas recalls this (*Summa theol.* I-II, q. 6, a. 6, resp.):

Sicut Philosophus dicit in 3 Eth. (ibid.), et idem dicit Gregorius Nyssenus in lib. suo de Homine (ibid.): *huiusmodi quae per metum aguntur, mixta sunt ex voluntario et involuntario.* Id enim quod per metum agitur, in se consideratum non est voluntarium, sed fit voluntarium in casu, scilicet ad vitandum malum quod timetur.

As the Philosopher says (*Ethic.* iii) and likewise Gregory of Nyssa in his book on Man (Nemesius, *loc. cit.*), such things as are done through fear *are of a mixed character*, being partly voluntary and partly involuntary. For that which is done through fear, considered in itself, is not voluntary; but it becomes voluntary in this particular case, in order, namely, to avoid the evil feared.

The "Antiqua Translatio" (the Latin version of Aristotle known to Dante) of Aristotle's *Nicomachean Ethics* has "mixtae" here, and Thomas Aquinas keeps the term in his commentary on the *Ethics* and introduces the term "violentum secundum quid." See *Exp. Eth. Nicom.* III, lect. 1, n. 387: "Primo ostendit quid sit simpliciter violentum. Secundo quid sit violentum secundum quid, ibi, 'Quaecumque autem propter timorem.'" ("First he shows what violence is in itself. Secondly, what violence is when relative [*secundum quid*], where he says 'certain acts however done through fear.'")

100. *frate*: See n. to *Par*. III, 70. Here the term of address introduces an admonishment, as elsewhere in the poem. Cf. *Purg*. XI, 82.

101. *contra grato*: Against one's pleasure or will.

103–5. *come Almeone . . . spietato*: Alcmaeon's story is told in the note to *Purg*. XII, 50-51. The line "per non perder pietà si fé spietato" is reminiscent of Ovid (*Metam*. IX, 407-8): "Ultusque parente parentem / natus erit facto pius et sceleratus eodem." ("And his son shall avenge parent on parent, filial and accursed in the selfsame act.")

It is interesting to note that Alcmaeon is mentioned in the same book of the *Nicomachean Ethics* in which Aristotle is discussing the "mixed" type of action. See *Eth. Nicom*. III, 1, 1110$^{a\text{-}b}$ (in Aquinas, *Opera omnia*, vol. XXI, p. 72, or R. M. Spiazzi, 1964, p. 114):

> In aliquibus autem laus non sit quidem, venia autem quando propter haec operatur aliquis, quae non oportet, quae humanam naturam excedunt et nullus utique sustineret.
>
> Quaedam autem fortassis non est cogi, sed magis moriendum patientem durissima. Etenim Euripidis Alcmaeone derisoria videntur cogentia matrem occidere.
>
> Est autem difficile quandoque iudicare, quale pro quali eligendum, et quid pro quo sustinendum.
>
> Adhuc autem difficilius immorari cognitis. Ut enim in multum, quae quidem expectantur tristia, quae autem coguntur turpia. Unde laudes et vituperia sunt circa coactos vel non.

> Some actions do not deserve praise but only pardon, for example, if a person does things that are wrong because he fears evils beyond human endurance which no one would undergo in any case.
>
> Yet it is probable that there are some actions that a man cannot be forced to do and he ought to undergo death of the cruelest kind rather than do them. (The reasons that constrained Euripides' Alcmaeon to kill his mother seem to be ricidulous.)

Sometimes it is difficult to judge what is to be chosen for the price and what is to be endured for the gain.

It is still more difficult to abide by our decisions. As often happens, the expected results are painful but the compulsory acts are disgraceful. Hence we receive praise and blame according as we yield or stand firm against the constraint.

On the case of Alcmaeon, Thomas Aquinas comments (*Exp. Eth. Nicom.* III, lect. 2, n. 395): "Et ideo dicit quod Alcmae-ona, idest carmina de Alcmaeone facta ab Euripide poeta, videntur esse derisoria, in quibus narratur quod Alcmaeon coactus fuit matrem occidere ex praecepto patris sui, qui hoc sibi praeceperat in bello thebano moriens, ad quod ierat ex uxoris consilio." ("He says, therefore, that *Alcmaeona* or the poems about Alcmaeon written by Euripides seem to be sa-tirical. These poems narrate the story of Alcmaeon who was forced to kill his mother by the command of his father. The father had ordered this when dying in the Theban war to which he had gone by the advice of his wife.") The fact that Dante brings in the case of Alcmaeon in just this context shows clearly how closely he is following Book III of the *Nicomachean Ethics* as rendered in the translations thereof available to him and the commentaries thereon. But Ovid's verses are also of primary importance. See *Metam.* IX, 408, quoted above.

105. *pietà*: Filial devotion to his father, a common meaning of the Latin *pietas*.   *spietato*: "Impious," the adjectival antonym, in the Latin sense, of filial devotion, in this case, towards his mother.

106. *voglio che tu pense*: "Pense" (= *pensi*) is subjunctive: "I would have you believe."

107. *la forza al voler si mischia*: For the verb, out of Aris-totle's notion of "mixed" cases, see n. to vss. 100-102.

108. *l'offense*: "Offenses" against God, of course, and there-fore sins.

109. *Voglia assoluta*: Beatrice now introduces the technical

and specific term, the "absolute will," which is what she had termed "volere intero" in vs. 82 and "salda voglia" in vs. 87.
  danno: "Harm," "evil."

110. *consentevi = vi consente*, i.e., to the "danno." *in quanto teme*: Cf. n. to vss. 100-102.

112. *Però = perciò.*   *quello spreme = quello esprime*, i.e., what Piccarda says in *Par.* III, 117, which is then remembered in vs. 98 of the present canto.

114. *ver = il vero* (*la verità*). Thus is the apparent contradiction resolved!

115-16. *Cotal fu l'ondeggiar . . . deriva*: Through the metaphor one may glimpse, in allegory, the name of Sapientia for Beatrice here.

117. *uno e altro disio*: The two questions with which the canto began, in the figure of the ass of Buridan.

118. *amanza del primo amante*: Beloved of God as the Supreme Love. Cf. "primo Amore," *Inf.* III, 6.   *diva*: "Divine lady."

119. *m'inonda*: The verb continues the metaphor of the "santo rio," vs. 115.

120. *scalda*: Latent in the metaphor is the notion of a plant that is revived, by life-giving water and by the warmth of the sun; and in the sun, or the notion of the sun, the name of Sapientia for Beatrice is even more evident.

122. *grazia per grazia*: "Grace [thanks] for grace [favor]." Cf. Virgil, *Aen.* I, 600-601.

123. *ma quei che vede e puote*: God.

124-26. *Io veggio ben . . . spazia*: "The mind is satisfied only with that truth which contains within itself every other truth" (Gr).

126. *si spazia*: "Extends."

127. *Posasi* = *si posa, si riposa.   in esso*: In the truth.
   come fera in lustra: "As a wild beast in its lair." *Lustra*,
plural of the Latin *lustrum*, is used in older Italian as
a singular.

128. *puollo* = *lo può*.

129. *se non, ciascun disio sarebbe frustra*: The Latin *frustra*,
with the verb in the conditional, reflects a commonplace
scholastic expression, *esset frustra*, "would be in vain." And
it is a basic tenet in Aristotelian and scholastic philosophy
that "God and nature do nothing in vain." Thus, the mean-
ing here is: "If we have this natural desire implanted in us
to know the truth, it is unthinkable that it is given to us in
vain, i.e., it must be an innate desire that *can* be satisfied."
This explains the statement in the following tercet.

130–32. *Nasce per quello . . . collo*: The image is of a plant
that puts out shoot after shoot from its base. The image is
wholly natural and, by being so, is pointing to what is some-
times known in theology as man's natural desire to know
God and to love Him. Here the matter is more in terms of
God's truth, to which Beatrice (as Sapientia or Wisdom)
can lead the wayfarer, as she has just done.

130. *per   quello*: "Therefore."   *rampollo*: "Shoot,"
"sprout."

131. *ed è natura*: The whole subject of the verb "è" is the
preceding clause, "nasce . . . dubbio."

132. *ch'al sommo pinge noi di collo in collo*: As every read-
er knows by now, Dante is much given to such abrupt shifts
in metaphor. So here, immediately following on the plant
image, we are shifted to that of a journey, an upward moun-
tain climb wherein we climb from foothill to higher hill,
from peak to peak, until finally we reach the highest sum-
mit. The reader will come to see that this latter is an image
which fits the whole upward journey through the heavenly
spheres excellently well. Each new heaven or sphere, with
the doubts on Dante's part which arise there, is here

matched with the phrase "di collo in collo," and the "sommo" will be where God is finally seen "face to face." It is already evident, moreover, that the journey through Paradise is much more of an *intellectual* journey than was the journey through either Purgatory or Inferno.

133–35. *Questo m'invita . . . oscura*: Thus, following on the natural image just expressed, there springs up at once in Dante, on his upward journey, another doubt, another question that puzzles him.

136–37. *Io vo' saper . . . beni*: The question of "making amends for unfulfilled vows with other goods" is discussed by Thomas Aquinas in *Summa theol.* II-II, q. 88, aa. 10-12.

136. *sodisfarvi*: The *-vi* means "to you," that is, to the court of Heaven.

138. *la vostra statera*: "Your scales" (the possessive bearing the same reference as the *-vi* of "sodisfarvi," vs. 136).
parvi: "Deficient." The whole import of the question is made clear in the following canto.

140. *divini*: I.e., *occhi*.

141. *mia virtute*: My power of sight.   *diè = diede.*
diè le reni: "Turned its back," "fled."

142. *quasi mi perdei*: Literally, "I almost lost myself," a notion conveyed elsewhere in the poem by the verb *smarrirsi*. Cf. *Inf.* V, 72; *Par.* II, 6.

CANTO V

1–3. *S' io ti fiammeggio . . . valore*: As Dante rises from "peak to peak" (*Par.* IV, 132), that is, as he passes through question after question and their resolution by Beatrice, Beatrice's beauty increases, as the reader of the *Paradiso* comes to know full well. These opening verses present that beauty as a flaming-forth of love, not for Dante in any ordinary sense, but for truth, which Beatrice—who as Lady Wisdom has access to, being the vehicle of the divine truth ("di là dal modo che 'n terra si vede")—has been able to convey to him (see the preceding canto). In the same sense, other spirits will glow with love and with their pleasure in being able to satisfy Dante in this intellectual quest.

4–6. *ché ciò procede . . . piede*: Beatrice's words here touch on a point often repeated in the *Paradiso*. *She* has "perfect vision," but her words apply even to a mortal, who has a far more limited vision. This point concerns the priority of intellect over will: The intellect sees or apprehends first, then the will moves (in the case of a desirable good) toward the possession of what is apprehended ("nel bene appreso").

6. *move il piede*: The soul was said to have two "feet," one the intellect and the other the will. See *Inf.* I, 30, and the note to that verse.

7–9. *Io veggio . . . accende*: Clearly the verses continue the expressed doctrine as it first applies to Beatrice, but they now turn it to Dante, a mortal, first to his intellect, and then to his love, which is of the will. Already, in this lowest of the heavens, his love is kindled by the "eternal light" perceived by him, as revealed through Beatrice.

10–12. *e s'altra cosa . . . traluce*: Beatrice's discourse shifts its point of emphasis from Dante in particular to a generalization concerning all mortals on earth.

11. *vestigio*: "Unworthy things mislead the love of you mortals (*vostro amor*), not because they are evil, but because they have in them some 'trace' of the 'eternal light' " (Gr). See Dante, *De mon*. I, viii, 2: "cum totum universum nichil aliud sit quam vestigium quoddam divine bonitatis" ("since the whole universe is nought else than a certain footprint of the divine excellence"). Cf. Thomas Aquinas, *Summa theol*. I, q. 93, aa. 1-4.

12. *traluce*: God's light shines in and through created things, but our mortal apprehension can fail to see this and we can be seduced (by misapprehension) into an act of the will, into mistaken love, *malo amor*. See *Purg*. XVI, 85-93; XXX, 131-32.

13–15. *Tu vuo' saper . . . letigio*: Beatrice, reading Dante's thoughts, knows without being told by him that another question has already sprung up in his mind. It is a question that is to occupy most of this canto.

15. *che*: "Che" is the subject of "sicuri," of which "anima" is the object. *letigio*: "Contradiction" of its right to enter Heaven.

16. *Sì cominciò Beatrice questo canto*: The reader is expected to consider such a conceit on the part of the poet to mean that Beatrice *continues*, with an aspect of the argument concerning vows, her "processo santo" (vs. 18).

19–24. *Lo maggior don . . . dotate*: The argument concerns only the high creatures (see *Par*. I, 106, 120), i.e., angels and men; these and these alone receive the precious gift of free will from God. Cf. Dante, *De mon.* I, xii, 6: "Manifestum esse potest quod hec libertas sive principium hoc totius libertatis nostre, est maximum donum humane nature a Deo collatum: quia per ipsum hic felicitamur ut homines, per ipsum alibi felicitamur ut dii." ("We may further understand that this freedom [or this principle of all our freedom] is the greatest gift conferred by God on human nature; for through it we have our felicity here as men, through it we have our felicity elsewhere as deities.") See also *Purg.* XVI, 67-81, and *Purg.* XVIII, 73-75, where Virgil suggests that Beatrice will indeed deal with this matter of free will when Dante reaches her. "Fesse" (vs. 20) looks upon God's *original* endowment of the precious faculty in His first creation, of angels and then of Adam and Eve, and this past tense continues into vs. 24, "fuoro" (*furono*). But the present tense of the closing words of vs. 24 extends it to mean His continuing creation of immortal souls in human creatures. Cf. *Purg.* XXV, 70-75. For the creation of angels with free will, see Thomas Aquinas, *Summa theol.* I, q. 59, a. 3, and for free will in man, see *Summa theol.* I, q. 83.

20. *fesse = facesse.*

24. *e tutte e sole*: "All of them, and they alone."

25-27. *Or ti parrà . . . consenti*: God accepts only vows of a high moral and spiritual nature, not evil, foolish, or trivial vows. To the former He *may* consent (note the verb "consenta" in the subjunctive) even as the one who makes the vow consents, and in this lies the "high value of the vow."

29. *vittima*: The term suggests strongly something that is solemnly served up as precious and befitting.   *fassi = si fa.*

29-30. *vittima fassi . . . atto*: " 'This treasure'—free will—'precious as I describe it, becomes the offering, and it does so by its own act,' i.e., by an act of the will itself" (Gr).

31. *Dunque che render puossi per ristoro?* The implied answer to the question is, of course, nothing: for nothing can

equal in preciousness the sacrifice of the free will, God's greatest gift to man. *puossi = si può*.

32–33. *Se credi . . . lavoro*: "If thou thinkest to make amends by putting to a good use that which thou hast promised and then withdrawn, thou art like a thief who is trying to do good deeds with ill-gotten gain (*maltolletto*)" (Gr). Cf. "tollette" in *Inf*. XI, 36. Cf. vss. 13-15.

35–39. *ma perché Santa Chiesa . . . dispensa*: But Holy Church, as everyone knows, does give dispensation or release from the fulfillment of vows. Thus here lies a further problem, for Beatrice seems to contradict herself (vs. 36).

37. *convienti = ti conviene*. *un poco a mensa*: The use of the metaphor of eating and digesting for the acquisition of knowledge is a common one, basic to the title and opening chapters of Dante's own *Convivio*. Cf. *Par*. X, 22-27.

39. *dispensa*: "Digestion."

41. *fermalvi = fermalo ivi* (i.e., hold it in your mind, your memory).

43–45. *Due cose . . . convenenza*: " 'The thing of which the sacrifice is made' is the thing promised; 'the other' element in a vow 'is the act of agreement' " (Gr).

46–48. *Quest' ultima . . . favella*: The act of agreement itself (with God) *must* be carried out.

48. *si favella*: "I spoke."

49. *però = perciò*. *necessitato*: Petrocchi has preferred the past participle of *necessitare* here to the noun *necessità*, commonly given by other editors.

49–51. *però necessitato . . . dei*: The Jews, that is, were "put in the necessity of" continuing to make offerings and sacrifices to God by the Mosaic law, as explicitly prescribed in the twenty-seventh chapter of Leviticus, which is given as spoken by God directly to Moses.

50. *pur*: "Still."   *offerere = offrire*, i.e., the act itself of offering. The form *offerere* is common in early Italian.
offerta: "The thing offered." This may be exchanged. See Lev. 27.

51. *come saver dei*: I.e., you must know this, since it is so plainly stated in Leviticus and other books of the Old Testament.

52. *L'altra*: The other element, the specific subject matter of the vow (vs. 44).   *t'è aperta*: Has been described to you.

53. *puote = può*.   *non si falla*: "One does no wrong" (from *fallare*, which in a certain context, as here, can imply sin, a wrong done to God).

55. *trasmuti*: The subject of "trasmuti" is "alcun," vs. 56.
   carco: The "burden" is the substance of the vow, the "materia" of vs. 52.

56–57. *sanza la volta . . . gialla*: See *Purg.* IX, 117-26. That is, "without ecclesiastical permission."

59–60. *se la cosa . . . raccolta*: " 'If the thing put aside is not contained, as easily as four in six, in the thing assumed.' Probably no exact proportion is intended, merely a manifest superiority of the new obligation to the old" (Gr). On the whole point, see Thomas Aquinas, *Summa theol.* II-II, q. 88, especially the following, in article 10 of the question, which concerns dispensation in particular (*Summa theol.* II-II, q. 88, a. 10 resp.):

> Dispensatio voti intelligenda est ad modum dispensationis quae fit in observantia alicuius legis; quia . . . lex ponitur respiciendo ad id quod est ut in pluribus bonum. Sed quia contingit huiusmodi in aliquo casu non esse bonum, oportuit per aliquem determinari, in illo particulari casu legem non esse servandam. Et hoc proprie est dispensare in lege: nam dispensatio videtur importare quamdam commensuratam distributionem, vel ap-

plicationem communis alicuius ad ea quae sub ipso continentur; per quem modum dicitur aliquis dispensare cibum familiae.

Similiter autem ille qui vovet, quodammodo sibi statuit legem, obligans se ad aliquid quod est secundum se, et, ut in pluribus, bonum. Potest tamen contingere quod in aliquo casu sit vel simpliciter malum, vel inutile, vel maioris boni impeditivum; quod est contra rationem eius quod cadit sub voto, ut ex praedictis patet, art. 2 huius qu. Et ideo necesse est quod determinetur in tali casu votum non esse servandum.

Et si quidem absolute determinetur aliquod votum non esse servandum, dicitur esse dispensatio voti; si autem pro hoc quod servandum erat, aliquid aliud imponatur, dicitur commutatio voti. Unde minus est votum commutare quam in voto dispensare; utrumque tamen in potestate Ecclesiae consistit.

The dispensation from a vow is to be taken in the same sense as a dispensation given in the observance of a law because . . . a law is made with an eye to that which is good in the majority of instances. But since in certain cases this is not good, there is need for someone to decide that in that particular case the law is not to be observed. This is properly speaking to dispense in the law: for a dispensation would seem to denote a commensurate distribution or application of some common thing to those that are contained under it, in the same way as a person is said to dispense food to a household.

In like manner a person who takes a vow makes a law for himself as it were, and binds himself to do something which in itself and in the majority of cases is a good. But it may happen that in some particular case this is simply evil, or useless, or a hindrance to a greater good: and this is essentially contrary to that which is the matter of a vow, as is clear from what has been said above (a. 2). Therefore it is necessary, in such a case, to decide that the vow is not to be observed. And if it be decided absolutely that a particular vow is not to be observed, this is called a *dispensation* from that vow; but if some other obligation be imposed in lieu of that which was to have been observed, the vow is said to be *commuted*. Hence it is less to commute a vow than to dispense from a vow: both, however, are in the power of the Church.

61–63. *Però qualunque . . . spesa*: These verses are aimed specifically at the cases of Piccarda and Constance and religious vows, in which free will itself is served up as the offering. Free will, as Beatrice has said, is the most precious gift given us by God, and it would of course outweigh any substitute ("altra spesa"). Then, were Piccarda and Constance ever exempted by ecclesiastical authority from the fulfillment of their vows? They are here among the elect, and therefore they must have died repentant and must have been forgiven through God's mercy. Cf. *Purg.* III, 133-35, where Manfred, Constance's grandson, speaks of such mercy as possible "as long as hope prevails."

A passage in Thomas Aquinas is especially relevant here, since the case of Jephthah will now be cited in this argument (see vs. 66), being remembered in a context that, *mutatis mutandis*, applies here. See *Summa theol.* II-II, q. 88, a. 2, ad 2:

> Quod quaedam sunt quae in omnem eventum sunt bona, sicut opera virtutis; et talia bona possunt absolute cadere sub voto. Quaedam vero in omnem eventum sunt mala, sicut ea quae secundum se sunt peccata; et haec nullo modo possunt sub voto cadere. Quaedam vero sunt quidem in se considerata bona, et secundum hoc possunt cadere sub voto, possunt tamen habere malum eventum, in quo non sunt observanda. Et sic accidit in voto Iephte, qui, ut dicitur Iud. 11.[30-31]: *votum vovit Domino, dicens: Si tradideris filios Ammon in manus meas, quicumque primus egressus fuerit de foribus domus meae, mihique occurrerit revertenti in pace, eum offeram holocaustum Domino.* Hoc autem poterat malum eventum habere, si occurreret ei aliquod animal non immolandum, sicut asinus vel homo; quod etiam

accidit. Unde et Hieronymus dicit . . . : *In vovendo fuit stultus, quia discretionem non habuit, et in reddendo impius.* Praemittitur tamen ibidem, quod *factus est super eum Spiritus Domini*; quia fides et devotio ipsius, ex qua motus est ad vovendum, fuit a Spiritu sancto, propter quod ponitur in catalogo sanctorum, et propter victoriam quam obtinuit, et quia probabile est cum poenituisse de facto iniquo, quod tamen aliquod bonum figurabat.

Certain things are good, whatever be their result; such are acts of virtue, and these can be, absolutely speaking, the matter of a vow: some are evil, whatever their result may be; as those things which are sins in themselves, and these can nowise be the matter of a vow: while some, considered in themselves, are good, and as such may be the matter of a vow, yet they may have an evil result, in which case the vow must not be kept. It was thus with the vow of Jephte, who, as related in Judges xi. 30, 31, *made a vow to the Lord, saying: If Thou wilt deliver the children of Ammon into my hands, whosoever shall first come forth out of the doors of my house, and shall meet me when I return in peace, . . . the same will I offer a holocaust to the Lord.* For this could have an evil result if, as indeed happened, he were to be met by some animal which it would be unlawful to sacrifice, such as an ass or a human being. Hence Jerome says: *In vowing he was foolish, through lack of discretion, and in keeping his vow he was wicked.* Yet it is premised (*verse* 29) that *the Spirit of the Lord came upon* him, because his faith and devotion, which moved him to make that vow, were from the Holy Ghost; and for this reason he is reckoned among the saints, as also by reason of the victory which he obtained, and because it is probable that he repented of his sinful deed, which nevertheless foreshadowed something good.

64. *a ciancia*: "Lightly."

65. *bieci* = *biechi*, "squint-eyed," i.e., unreasonable. Cf.

"biece" in *Inf.* XXV, 31, and *Par.* VI, 136, and see "piage"
in *Purg.* XXV, 30.

66–68. *come Ieptè . . . peggio*: Jephthah (or Jephte), the
Gileadite, was a judge of Israel (*ca.* 1143-1137 B.C). He
sacrificed to Jehovah his only daughter in fulfillment of a vow
that if he returned victorious over the Ammonites he would
sacrifice whatever first came to meet him. The account is
given in Iudic. 11:30-31, 34:

> Votum vovit Domino, dicens: Si tradideris filios Am-
> mon in manus meas, quicumque primus fuerit egressus
> de foribus domus meae, mihique occurrerit revertenti
> cum pace a filiis Ammon, eum holocaustrum offeram
> Domino. . . .
>
> Revertente autem Iephte in Maspha domum suam,
> occurrit ei unigenita filia sua cum tympanis et choris;
> non enim habebat alios liberos.

> Jephte made a vow to the Lord. "If you deliver the Am-
> monites into my power," he said, "whoever first comes
> out of the doors of my house to meet me when I return
> in triumph from the Ammonites I shall offer up as a hol-
> ocaust to the Lord."
>
> . . . When Jephte returned to his house in Maspha, it
> was his daughter who came forth, playing the tam-
> bourines and dancing. She was an only child: he had
> neither son nor daughter besides her.

Cf. n. to vss. 61-63.

68. *servando*: "By keeping his vow."

70. *Efigènia*: According to one version of the story of the
sacrifice of Iphigenia, as a consequence of Agamemnon's
having killed a stag in the sacred grove of Diana, the goddess
in anger sent a pestilence on the Greek army and caused a
calm which prevented the Greek fleet in Aulis from sailing
against Troy. On the advice of Calchas the seer, Agamemnon
proceeded to sacrifice his daughter Iphigenia, in order to ap-
pease the wrath of the goddess (see Virgil, *Aen.* II, 116-19).
However, Iphigenia disappeared just as the fatal blow was

to fall, and in her place a beautiful deer appeared. See Ovid,
Metam. XII, 24-34:

> Permanet Aoniis Nereus violentus in undis
> bellaque non transfert, et sunt, qui parcere Troiae
> Neptunum credant, quia moenia fecerat urbi;
> at non Thestorides: nec enim nescitve tacetve
> sanguine virgineo placandam virginis iram
> esse deae. postquam pietatem publica causa
> rexque patrem vicit, castumque datura cruorem
> flentibus ante aram stetit Iphigenia ministris,
> victa dea est nubemque oculis obiecit et inter
> officium turbamque sacri vocesque precantum
> supposita fertur mutasse Mycenida cerva.

But Nereus continued to be boisterous on the Aonian
waters, and refused to transport the war. And there
were some who held that Neptune was sparing Troy be-
cause he had built its walls. But not so the son of Thes-
tor. For he was neither ignorant of the truth nor did he
withhold it, that the wrath of the virgin goddess must
be appeased with a virgin's blood. After consideration
for the public weal had overcome affection, and the fa-
ther had been vanquished by the king, and just as midst
the weeping attendants Iphigenia was standing before
the altar ready to shed her innocent blood, the goddess
was moved to pity and spread a cloud before their eyes;
and there, while the sacred rites went on, midst the con-
fusion of the sacrifice and the cries of suppliants, she is
said to have substituted a hind for the maiden of
Mycenae.

Dante adopts the version according to which Agamemnon
vowed to the goddess the fairest thing born in his realm dur-
ing the year, which turned out to be his own daughter,
Iphigenia. Benvenuto refers to a passage in the *De officiis*
(III, xxv, 95) of Cicero, which Dante evidently had in mind
when he wrote vss. 68-72:

Quid, *quod* Agamemnon cum devovisset Dianae, quod
in suo regno pulcherrimum natum esset illo anno, im-
molavit Iphigeniam, qua nihil erat eo quidem anno na-

tum pulchrius? Promissum potius non faciendum quam tam taetrum facinus admittendum fuit.

Ergo et promissa non facienda non numquam.

And once more; when Agamemnon had vowed to Diana the most beautiful creature born that year within his realm, he was brought to sacrifice Iphigenia; for in that year nothing was born more beautiful than she. He ought to have broken his vow rather than commit so horrible a crime.

Promises are, therefore, sometimes not to be kept.

Iphigenia's "bewailing her fair face (which made her an acceptable offering) is a trait transferred probably by Dante from the story of Jephthah's daughter, who, before her death, 'bewailed her virginity upon the mountains': Judges xi, 38" (Gr). Note that the name here must be pronounced *Efigènia*.

71. *i folli e i savi*: An established expression meaning everyone who heard of it, without distinction.

72. *cólto = culto*, "act of worship."

73. *a muovervi*: I.e., in the matter of making vows.

75. *e non crediate ch'ogne acqua vi lavi*: The verse has been variously interpreted. Sapegno appears to choose the more probable meaning when he paraphrases as follows: "Do not believe that any kind of water can wash you clean, as does that of baptism for original sin and holy water for venial sins; do not delude yourselves that vows are sufficient to purify you from sins committed and to assure you of salvation."

76. *Avete il novo e 'l vecchio Testamento*: See Eccles. 5:3-4[4-5]; I Tim. 6:12.

77. *e 'l pastor de la Chiesa che vi guida*: "The Pope alone has power to absolve from the greater vows" (Gr).

80. *uomini siate*: Cf. Eph. 4:14: "Ut iam non simus parvuli fluctuantes, et circumferamur omni vento doctrinae." ("And this he has done that we may be now no longer children, tossed to and fro and carried about by every wind of doctrine.")

81. *sì che 'l Giudeo di voi tra voi non rida*: See Dante, *Epist.* XI, 4: "Impietatis fautores, Iudei, Saraceni et gentes, sabbata nostra rident, et, ut fertur, conclamant: 'Ubi est Deus eorum?'" ("The champions of impiety, Jews, Saracens, and Gentiles, scoff at our sabbaths; and, as it is written, cry out 'where is their God?'")

84. *a suo piacer combatte*: Buti interprets this to mean "saltando e corneggiando" ("jumping about and tossing its horns").

87. *a quella parte ove 'l mondo è più vivo*: Beatrice looks toward the highest heaven, where God is, the Empyrean, as toward their ultimate goal. Cf. *Par.* XXIII, 113-14.

88. *e 'l trasmutar sembiante*: As they rise from sphere to sphere, Beatrice, as has been noted, becomes more and more beautiful.

91-93. *e sì come saetta . . . regno*: Again, as he does in describing movement from the top of the mountain of Purgatory to the sphere of the moon, the poet uses, as the first part of a simile, a figure which guides the eye of the reader first to the target, then back to the bowcord, which is still quivering. See *Par.* II, 23-26, and n. to *Par.* II, 23-24. Dante is certainly expressing great velocity, but his use of the figure of *hysteron proteron* here is also to be noted. There will be yet other examples in the *Paradiso*.

93. *secondo regno*: The heaven of Mercury, which symbolizes the degree of beatitude enjoyed by the souls of the ambitious.

95. *come*: "When." *nel lume di quel ciel*: Into the planet of Mercury, as the following verse makes clear.

96. *che più lucente se ne fé 'l pianeta*: The hyperbole is remarkable here: the whole planet becomes more radiant for having Beatrice in it! *fé = fece*. *'l pianeta*: Mercury.

97. *la stella*: The planet Mercury. *e rise*: The planet "smiles" for having Beatrice within itself. Cf. Dante, *Conv.*

III, viii, 11: "E che è ridere se non una corruscazione de la dilettazione de l'anima, cioè uno lume apparente di fuori secondo sta dentro?" ("And what is laughter save a coruscation of the delight of the soul, that is to say, a light appearing outwardly according as it exists within?")

But the heavens are supposed to be immutable! Men are mutable, of course, and Dante admits to being so in the extreme, so one can imagine how *he* must have changed and smiled, if the planet did!

98. *da mia natura = per la mia natura.*

101. *traggonsi = si traggono.*

102. *per modo che lo stimin lor pastura*: "In such a way that they judge it to be their food."·

103. *splendori*: These, of course, are souls, already called "splendors" in the first heaven (cf. *Par.* III, 109).

105. *Ecco chi crescerà li nostri amori*: It was explained to Dante while he was still in Purgatory that the more souls there are to be loved in Paradise, the more love there is (see *Purg.* XV, 49-78).

107. *vedeasi l'ombra piena di letizia*: The souls rejoice that they now enjoy the possibility of illuminating the living man in his doubts and questions, so that suddenly the simile is transformed from food for fish to food as increase of love.
    vedeasi = si vedeva.   *l'ombra*: In this second heaven a mere semblance of the body is still present, though very faint; in fact, joy on the part of the soul can cause it to be so resplendent that the light hides this semblance—as will soon be seen to happen (vss. 133-39). Thereafter, all souls become simply *splendori*, and any semblance of a human body that they might have is concealed by the light emanating from them.

109. *quel che qui s'inizia*: "That which begins here" is the description of this heaven.

111. *carizia = carenza*, "want," "lack," "craving."

114. *sì come*: "As soon as."   *fur = furono.*

115. *bene nato*: Cf. *Purg.* V, 60.

116. *triunfo etternal*: The condition of souls in Heaven. *grazia*: The subject of "concede."

117. *la milizia*: The warfare of life. Cf. Iob 7:1: "Militia est vita hominis super terram." ("The life of man is a warfare on earth.") The reader will encounter the two terms *trionfo* and *milizia* frequently, in one form or another, in the cantos ahead. Here "milizia" serves to distinguish the living man from the souls of the elect, he being one who is still serving in the "warfare of life."

118. *del lume che per tutto il ciel si spazia*: This is God's light (cf. the opening verses of the *Paradiso*), which is both light and love.   *si spazia*: "Extends." Cf. *Purg.* XXVI, 63; *Par.* I, 1-2.

119. *però = perciò.*

120. *di noi chiarirti*: Be enlightened about ourselves and our condition.

123. *credi come a dii*: Grandgent calls attention to Thomas Aquinas, *Summa theol.* I, q. 13, a. 9 and quotes the following passage from Boethius, *Consol. philos.* III, x, ll. 83-86, 88-89: "Nam quoniam beatitudinis adeptione fiunt homines beati, beatitudo vero est ipsa divinitas, divinitatis adeptione beatos fieri manifestum est. . . . Omnis igitur beatus deus." ("For since men are made blessed by the obtaining of blessedness, and blessedness is nothing else but divinity, it is manifest that men are made blessed by the obtaining of divinity. . . . Wherefore everyone that is blessed is a god.")

124. *t'annidi*: From *annidarsi*, "to nestle down in," a sense that will be made clearer in the final verses of the canto. Cf. vs. 138, "chiusa chiusa."

125. *de li occhi il traggi*: The light which hides the soul (in any semblance of a human body) comes from the eyes. This serves to gloss vs. 108.   *il traggi = lo trai.*

127. *aggi = abbia*.

128–29. *il grado de la spera . . . raggi*: Dante wishes to understand who the soul is and why it is assigned to the heaven of Mercury, the sphere (planet) which, more than any other, is "veiled" by the rays of the sun, for being so close to it. Speaking of Mercury in *Conv.* II, xiii, 11, Dante refers to it as "la più picciola stella del cielo" ("the smallest star of heaven") and notes that "l'altra proprietade si è che più va velata de li raggi del Sole che null'altra stella." ("The other special property is that its orbit is more veiled by the rays of the sun than that of any other star.") Thus "altrui" refers to the sun.

129. *mortai = mortali*.

131. *fessi = si fece*.

133. *stessi = stesso*. Cf. *Inf.* IX, 58.

134. *come*: "When."   *róse*: "Consumed," from *rodere*.

136–37. *per più letizia . . . santa*: The happiness of this soul is increased at being able to satisfy this living man who is visiting Heaven. Happiness manifests itself as light, and this henceforth, in the upper heavens, will render the spirits invisible, even as it does here.

138. *chiusa chiusa*: The adjective thus repeated stresses the "nestling down" of the soul in its own increased splendor, resulting from increase of happiness. Not even the eyes of this soul are visible now.

CANTO VI

1-3. *Poscia che Costantin . . . tolse*: "Constantine, transferring the seat of Empire from Rome to Byzantium, carried the Eagle from West to East, counter to the course which it took with Aeneas from Troy to Italy, where he was to become the father of the Roman people, and the founder of the Empire of whose power the bird of God was the symbol" (Norton). Byzantium was renamed Constantinople and inaugurated as the new capital in 330. (See n. to *Inf.* XIX, 116; also see *Par.* XX, 55-60.)

1. *aquila*: The object of "volse" ("turned").

3. *l'antico che Lavina tolse*: "The man of old who wedded Lavinia" was Aeneas, who brought the imperial eagle from Troy. Dante mentions Lavinia, who was the mother of Silvius and thus the co-founder of the Roman race, in *Inf.* IV, 126; *Purg.* XVII, 37; and *De mon.* II, iii, 16.

4-5. *cento e cent' anni . . . ritenne*: Constantine reigned from 306 to 337, Justinian—who is speaking—from 527 to 565. See P. Toynbee (1902), pp. 298-99:

Justinian says that when he became Emperor the Roman eagle had been at Constantinople for more than two hundred years ("cento e cent' anni e più"). Ac-

cording to the chronology accepted at the present day
this statement presents no difficulty, the period from the
foundation of Constantinople in 324 (as distinguished
from the dedication in 330) to the accession of Jus-
tinian in 527 being just over two hundred years. This,
however, was not the chronology of Dante's day. Bru-
netto Latino, for instance, in his *Trésor* (p. 82, ed. Cha-
baille) assigns the transference of the seat of empire
from Rome to Constantinople to the year 333, and the
accession of Justinian to the year 539. This gives an in-
terval of 206 years between the two dates, and I have
little doubt that the *Trésor*, with which, of course, Dante
was well acquainted, was his authority for the reckoning
of "cento e cent' anni e più."

4. *l'uccel di Dio*: The eagle, symbol of imperial power.

6. *vicino a' monti de' quai prima uscìo*: While at Constanti-
nople, the imperial eagle was relatively near the site of an-
cient Troy.

7–9. *e sotto l'ombra . . . pervenne*: In Constantinople the
Eagle, descending from emperor to emperor, governed the
world, which was under the shadow of its wings. Cf. Ps.
16[17]:8: "Sub umbra alarum tuarum protege me." ("Hide
me in the shadow of your wings.")

9. *mia*: I.e., *mano*.

10. *Cesare fui e son Iustiniano*: The same contrast between
the *fui* and the *son* is used in *Purg.* V, 88.   *Iustiniano*:
Justinian I, surnamed the Great, was emperor of Constanti-
nople from 527 to 565. He was born in Illyricum in 483,
married Theodora in 523, and died in 565. During his reign
Justinian's great general Belisarius overthrew the Vandal
kingdom in Africa and the Gothic kingdom in Italy. Jus-
tinian is best known, however, not by his conquests but by
his legislation. In *The History of the Decline and Fall of the
Roman Empire*, Edward Gibbon (1908, p. 441) says:

> The vain titles of the victories of Justinian are crumbled
> into dust; but the name of the legislator is inscribed on

a fair and everlasting monument. Under his reign, and by his care, the civil jurisprudence was digested in the immortal works of the CODE, the PANDECTS, and the INSTITUTES; the public reason of the Romans has been silently or studiously transfused into the domestic institutions of Europe; and the laws of Justinian still command the respect or obedience of independent nations.

See n. to *Purg.* VI, 88-89.

11. *per voler del primo amor ch'i' sento*: This is love of God, but with stress on the Holy Ghost. Cf. *Inf.* III, 6.

12. *d'entro le leggi trassi il troppo e 'l vano*: See n. to vs. 10 and, for Justinian's codification of the law, see n. to *Purg.* VI, 88-89.

13. *ovra = opera*, i.e., the reformation and codification of law.

14-15. *una natura . . . contento*: It was believed that Justinian was attached to the Eutychian or Monophysite heresy, which held that Christ was divine but not also human. As Butler observes, however, it appears to have been not Justinian himself, but his wife Theodora who held heterodox opinions.

16-18. *'l benedetto Agapito . . . sue*: Dante's reference here is to Agapetus I, who was pope from 535 to 536, a time when the Ostrogothic power in Italy was being destroyed by Belisarius. The story is that he was sent by Theodat, king of the Ostrogoths, to make terms with Justinian at Constantinople, and while on his mission he convinced Justinian to accept the orthodox doctrine of the two natures of Christ.

Dante's authority for his statement about the conversion of the emperor by Agapetus may have been Brunetto Latini (*Tresor* I, lxxxvii, 5), who says concerning Justinian: "Ja soit ce k'il fust au comencement en l'erreur des erites, a la fin reconut il son erreur de par le conseil Agapite, ki lors estoit apostoiles." ("Although he was in the beginning in the error of the heretics, in the end he recognized his error through the counsel of Agapetus, who was then pope.") According to the

Liber pontificalis (LIX, 2), Agapetus convinced Justinian as to the two natures of Christ: "Cui beatissimus Agapitus episcopus constantissime fidei apostolicae responsum reddidit de domino Iesu Christo Deum et hominem, hoc est duas naturas in uno Christo." ("To whom [to the Emperor Justinian] the very blessed Bishop Agapetus sent back a reply according to the very firm apostolic faith concerning our Lord Jesus Christ man and God, that is, two natures in one Christ.")

19. *li* = *gli.*

19–21. *e ciò che . . . vera*: "What he (and afterward I) accepted on faith, without being able to comprehend it, I can now see as a fact, as clearly as thou seest an axiomatic truth —for instance, that if a proposition is false, its opposite must be true (cf. *Mon.*, II, xi, 4).—Of the two natures of Christ, Dante beheld a symbolic presentment in the Griffin: *Purg.* XXXI, 121-126" (Gr). Cf. also *Par.* II, 40-45.

"It is a cardinal point of Dante's belief that in the perfect state all *effort* both of will and intellect shall cease, while their *activity* reaches its highest point. Even truths that now seem paradoxical shall be seen as axioms, and the facts that now seem perplexing or distressing shall be felt as axiomatically right and beautiful. But unfathomed depths of the Divine Nature and Will shall ever remain, adored but uncomprehended. Compare *Parad.* xix. 40-57, xxi. 82-102, etc.

"Both in this passage and in ii. 40-45 the union of the divine and human natures in Christ is the point which Dante declares will be as clear to souls in bliss as 'the initial truth which man believeth,' or is as clear to Justinian as that 'every contradiction is both false and true.' Now 'the initial truth which man believeth' is not a generic term for axiomatic truth, but a specific reference to the 'law of contradictories' on which the whole system of Aristotelian logic is built up. It asserts that the propositions *this is so* and *this is not so* cannot both be true in the same sense and at the same time. . . . And it follows immediately from this fundamental axiom, that of the two propositions 'all A's are B's' and 'some A's are not B's,' or of the two propositions 'no A's are B's' and 'some A's are B's,' one must be true and the other false. They cannot both be true or both false in the same sense at the same time. For example, if the proposition 'some A's are not B's' be true, the proposition 'all A's are B's' is false; for if not, take one of the A's that is not a B; now since all A's are B's, that particular A is a B; therefore that particular A both is and is not a B, which is impossible, *therefore*, etc. Propositions so related are called contradictories, and therefore every 'contradiction' or 'pair of contradictories' is 'both false and true' axiomatically" (TC).

25. *Belisar*: Belisarius, the famous general of the Emperor Justinian, was born on the borderland between Thrace and Illyricum *ca.* 505 and died in 565. His great achievements were the overthrow of the Vandal kingdom in Africa, the reconquest of Italy from the Goths, and the foundation of the exarchate of Ravenna upon the ruins of the Gothic dominions. When he was nearly sixty, he was accused of being privy to a conspiracy against Justinian, in consequence of which, according to the popular tradition, his property was confiscated, his eyes were put out, and he was compelled to beg in the streets of Constantinople, crying to the passers-by, "Date obolum Belisario." In truth, however, his disgrace lasted only eight months, during which he was confined to his own palace. The emperor, having satisfied himself that the charge was false, restored Belisarius to favor, and he lived in possession of his wealth and honors until his death two years later (in 565), Justinian himself dying a few months afterwards.

It is probable that Dante, who does not hint at the ingratitude of Justinian towards his great general, did not know more of the history of the latter than is contained in the medieval chronicles. Villani (II, 6) concludes his account as follows: "Belisario . . . bene avventurosamente e con vittoria in tutte parti vinse e soggiogò i ribelli dello 'mperio, e tenne in buono stato mentre vivette, infino agli anni di Cristo 565, che Giustiniano imperadore e Belisario moriro bene avventurosamente." ("Belisarius . . . with great strategy and winning victory everywhere, overcame and subjugated the rebels to the Empire and held it in good order all his lifetime until the year A.D. 565, when Justinian the emperor and Belisarius died in their daring ventures.")

26. *cui*: This is the dative.

28. *a la question prima*: See *Par.* V, 127.   *s'appunta*: "Comes to an end."

29-30. *sua condizione . . . giunta*: Justinian's reply has made it necessary for him to mention the Roman Eagle.

30. *seguitare = far seguire.*

31. *veggi = vegga* or *veda.*   *quanta*: "How little."

33. *e chi 'l s'appropria e chi a lui s'oppone*: "Chi" and "chi" (Ghibelline and Guelph) are subjects of "move."

35-36. *e cominciò . . . regno*: "It—the valor (*virtù*) of heroes—'began from that hour when Pallas'—son of the Latin king Evander—'died to give it (the *segno*) a kingdom.' Pallas, leading Latin troops to help Aeneas, was killed by Turnus (*Aen.*, X, 479-489); to avenge his death, Aeneas slew Turnus (*Aen.*, XII, 945-952), and gained possession of Latium" (Gr). Virgil represents the Trojan Aeneas, when he landed on the shores of Italy, as becoming involved in war with Turnus, king of the Latins, and as seeking and gaining the alliance of Evander, who had established a kingdom on the seven hills, afterwards to be the site of Rome.

37-39. *Tu sai . . . ancora*: The kingdom of Aeneas "was founded, however, not on the seven hills, but at Lavinium, whence it was transferred by his son Ascanius to Alba Longa where it remained for more than 300 years, till, in the reign of Tullus Hostilius (670-638 B.C.), Alba fell under Rome, on the defeat of the three Alban champions, the Curiatii, by the survivor of the three Roman champions, the Horatii" (TC).

40-41. *dal mal de le Sabine . . . Lucrezia*: "Meanwhile the Alban outcast, Romulus, had founded a camp of refuge on the Palatine (one of the seven hills), and had provided the desperadoes, who gathered there, with wives, by seizing the

Sabine women who had come to attend the public games. Under him and his six successors Rome gradually extended her power, till the outrage offered to Lucretia by Sextus, the son of the last king, so roused the indignation of the people that the monarchy was swept away (510 B.C.)" (TC).

43–53. *Sai quel ch'el . . . Scipione*: "The long period of the Republic, up to the beginning of Caesar's campaigns in Gaul (58 B.C.), is passed over rapidly by Dante, without notice of constitutional and social struggles; but the main aspects of the outward history are dealt with by rapid and effective strokes. During this period Rome established her supremacy over the other Latin tribes, repelled invasions of Italy, both by civilised and barbarous peoples, and extended her dominion by counter invasions. Lucius Quintius Cincinnatus (from cincinnus = a curl), called from the plough to the dictatorship, conquered the Aequians (458 B.C.); against Brennus (390, etc., B.C.) and his Gauls, one of the Fabii, and Titus Manlius Torquatus (as well as others, notably Camillus), distinguished themselves. The Decii,—father, son and grandson,—died self-devoted deaths in serving against the Latins (340 B.C.), the Samnites (295 B.C.) and the Greek invader Pyrrhus (280 B.C.); while the greatest of all the Fabii, Quintus Fabius Maximus (Cunctator), saved Rome from Hannibal who crossed the Alps and victoriously invaded Italy in 218 B.C., in which same year Scipio Africanus (the Elder), a boy of seventeen, won military fame by saving his father's life at the defeat of Ticinus. It was he who subsequently organised the counter invasion of Africa which compelled Hannibal to withdraw from Italy. Cf. xxvii. 61 seq." (TC).

48. *mirro*: "Embalm," "preserve."

49. *Aràbi*: "Arabs" is a term applied by an anachronism to the Carthaginians, whose territory in Dante's day was occupied by the Arabs, the reference being to their passage of the Alps under Hannibal and their subsequent defeat by Scipio Africanus.

51. *l'alpestre rocce*: Although Dante several times uses the

word "alpine" to refer to any mountainous place, here it refers to the Alps themselves.   *labi*: "You descend." From the Latin *labi*.

52–96. *Sott' esso . . . soccorse*: "By a great leap Dante now brings us to the achievement of Pompey, the great conqueror of the eastern kings and queller of the faction of Marius. He celebrated a triumph when not yet twenty-five (81 B.C.). After a passing reference to the mythical exploits of the great Romans in reducing Fiesole which overhangs Florence, and which was the refuge of Catiline (Villani, i. 31-37), we find ourselves following the career of Caesar preparatory to the founding of the Roman Empire. Lines 58-60 refer to the campaigns in Gaul (58-50 B.C.); lines 61-63 to Caesar's crossing the Rubicon (49 B.C.) between Ravenna and Rimini, thereby leaving his province, without orders from the Senate, and so formally beginning the civil war. In the same year he overcame formidable opposition in Spain, and next year unsuccessfully besieged Pompey in Dyrrachium, and then utterly defeated him at Pharsalia in Thessaly. Pompey escaped to Egypt, where he was treacherously slain by Ptolemy (lines 64-66). Caesar crossed the Hellespont and, says Lucan, visited the Troad (cf. l. 6). He took Egypt from Ptolemy and gave it to Cleopatra, subdued Juba king of Numidia who had protected his opponents after Pharsalia, and then returned to Spain (45 B.C.) where Pompey's sons had raised an army (lines 67-72). After the murder of Caesar his nephew Augustus defeated Mark Antony at Modina (43 B.C.); then, with Antony as his ally, defeated his uncle's assassins, Brutus and Cassius (cf. *Inf.* xxxiv.), at Philippi (42 B.C.), and afterwards Antony's brother Lucius at Perugia (41 B.C.). In 31 B.C. at Actium he finally defeated his rival Mark Antony, who soon afterwards committed suicide, and his example was followed by his paramour Cleopatra, who died by the tooth of a viper (lines 76-78). This made Augustus master of the whole Roman Empire to the remotest ends of Egypt, and the temple of Janus, the gates of which were always open in war-time, was, for the third time only in the history of Rome, closed in sign of universal peace. Heaven 'had brought the world to its own serene mood' (line 56), and all was ready for the birth of Christ (lines 79-81), who was crucified under Tiberius, the successor of Augustus, whereby the sin of human nature at the fall was avenged (lines 82-90). Jerusalem fell, under Titus, whereby the sin of slaying Christ was avenged on the Jews (lines 91-93).

"The epilogue of the defence of the Church by Charlemagne against the Lombard king Desiderius, whom he dethroned in A.D. 774, produces a disjointed effect upon the modern reader, but would seem natural enough to Dante and his contemporaries" (TC).

55–56. *che tutto 'l ciel . . . sereno*: See Dante, *Conv.* IV, v, 6-8:

> E però è scritto in Isaia: "Nascerà virga de la radice di Iesse, e fiore de la sua radice salirà"; e Iesse fu padre del sopra detto David. E tutto questo fu in uno temporale, che David nacque e nacque Roma, cioè che Enea venne di Troia in Italia, che fu origine de la cittad romana, sì come testimoniano le scritture. Per che assai è manifesto la divina elezione del romano imperio, per lo nascimento de la santa cittade che fu contemporaneo a la radice de la progenie di Maria. E incidentemente è da toccare che, poi che esso cielo cominciò a girare, in migliore disposizione non fu che allora quando di là su discese Colui che l'ha fatto e che 'l governa; sì come ancora per virtù di loro arti li matematici possono ritrovare. Nè 'l mondo mai non fu nè sarà sì perfettamente disposto come allora che a la voce d'un solo, principe del roman popolo e comandatore, sì come testimonia Luca evangelista. E però [che] pace universale era per tutto, che mai, più, non fu nè fia, la nave de l'umana compagnia dirittamente per dolce cammino a debito porto correa.

> Wherefore it is written in Isaiah [11:1] "a rod shall spring out of the root of Jesse and a flower shall spring up from his root." And Jesse was the father of the above-said David. And it was all at the same point of time wherein David was born and Rome was born, that

is to say Æneas came into Italy from Troy, which was
the origin of the . . . city of Rome, as testify the scrip-
tures. Whereby the divine election of the Roman em-
pire is manifest enough; to wit by the birth of the holy
city being at the same time as the root of the family of
Mary. And incidentally we may note that since the
heaven itself began to roll it ne'er was in better disposi-
tion than at the time when he who made it and who
rules it came down below; as even now by virtue of their
arts the mathematicians may retrace. Nor was the world
ever so perfectly disposed, nor shall be again, as then
when it was guided by the voice of one sole prince and
commander of the Roman peoplë, as Luke the evange-
list beareth witness. And therefore there was universal
peace which never was before nor shall be, and the ship
of the human fellowship was speeding straight to the
due port in tranquil voyage.

See also C. S. Singleton (1958), pp. 96-98.

57. *Cesare per voler di Roma il tolle*: " 'Caesar takes (*tolle*
= *toglie*) it (the *segno*) at the bidding of Rome': in accord-
ance with a popular mandate (*Phars.*, V, 389-394)" (Gr).
Caesar was regarded by Dante as the first of the Roman em-
perors—a popular misconception in the Middle Ages.

58. *Varo*: The Var is a river of southern France.

59-60. *Isara vide . . . pieno*: " 'The rivers Isère, Loire, and
Seine beheld,' and all the tributaries of the Rhone. For *Era*,
see *Giorn. dant.*, XIV, 47, and *Rendiconti del R. Istituto
Lombardo di scienze e lettere*, Serie II, Vol. XLI, p. 757. See
also H. Hauvette, *Études sur la Divine Comédie*, 226: the
Italian name for the Loire was *Era*, from Old French *Leire*
or *Lere*, understood as *L'Ere*" (Gr).

62. *e saltò Rubicon*: See *Inf.* XXVIII, 97-99.

65. *Durazzo*: Dyrrachium, the ancient Epidamnus, a seaport
in Illyria; it is the modern Durrës. *Farsalia*: Pharsalia
is the district in eastern Thessaly in which Pharsalus is situ-
ated. This was the scene of the decisive battle between Pom-

pey and Julius Caesar, which made the latter master of the Roman world in 48 B.C.

66. *sì ch'al Nil caldo si sentì del duolo*: The consequences of Caesar's victory over Pompey at Pharsalia were felt in Egypt, where Pompey was murdered.

67-68. *Antandro e Simeonta . . . rivide*: It was from the town of Antandros, near the river Simoïs, that the Eagle first set forth with Aeneas (Virgil, *Aen*. III, 5-6). When Caesar was pursuing Pompey, he stopped to visit the Troad (Lucan, *Phars*. IX, 961-99).

68. *là dov' Ettore si cuba*: Hector was buried at Troy.   *si cuba*: "Lies."

69. *e mal per Tolomeo poscia si scosse*: " 'And then shook itself, ill for Ptolemy,' who was deprived by Caesar of the kingdom of Egypt, and soon perished" (Gr).   *Tolomeo*: Ptolemy XII was king of Egypt from 51 to 47 B.C. He was the eldest son of Ptolemy Auletes, and by his father's will the sovereignty was left jointly to him and his sister Cleopatra, but the latter was expelled after sharing the throne for three years. Having collected an army, however, Cleopatra invaded Egypt and with the help of Julius Caesar, who espoused her cause, defeated her brother, who was drowned while attempting to escape. Ptolemy had been accessory to the murder of Pompey, who fled to Egypt after the battle of Pharsalia (48 B.C.). Ptolemy had his head cut off and sent to Caesar, but the latter to show his abhorrence of the deed caused the murderers to be put to death.

70. *Iuba*: Juba, king of the Numidians, was an ally of Pompey.

71. *occidente*: Spain, where the followers of Pompey were defeated in the battle of Munda.

73. *col baiulo seguente*: Augustus.   *baiulo*: A Latinism, pronounced *bàiulo* and meaning "keeper."

74. *Bruto con Cassio ne l'inferno latra*: Brutus and Cassius,

defeated by the imperial eagle, "bark" of its victory in Hell (*Inf.* XXXIV, 64-67). For the use of *latra*, cf. Dante, *Rime* CIII, 59 and *Conv.* IV, iii, 8.

75. *e Modena e Perugia fu dolente*: Mark Antony was beaten near Modena, his brother Lucius at Perugia. Dante's coupling of Modena and Perugia is a direct echo of Lucan, *Phars.* I, 41-42: "his, Caesar, Perusina fames Mutinaeque labores / accedant fatis" ("though to these be added the famine of Perusia and the horrors of Mutina").

76. *Piangene = ne piange.*   *trista*: The adjective may well be used here in the pejorative sense, with reference to Cleopatra's wantonness (*Inf.* V, 63).

77-78. *che, fuggendoli innanzi . . . atra*: After the final defeat of Mark Antony at Actium, Cleopatra, fleeing before the imperial eagle, is said to have killed herself with an asp (*colubro*).

77. *li = gli.*

79. *lito rubro*: The shore of the Red Sea. (Cf. Virgil, *Aen.* VIII, 686, "litore rubro.") With Augustus the imperial eagle reached this shore, in the conquest of Egypt.

80-81. *con costui . . . delubro*: "The temple of Janus—of which the doors were closed only in time of peace, for in time of war the god was supposed to be absent with the armies—had been locked up but twice during the whole life of the Roman Republic. But under Augustus they were closed three times; and in one of those periods when 'Heaven willed to bring the world to its own serene mood' (v. 56) it has been supposed that Christ was born; and then, 'no war, or battle's sound was heard the world around' " (Norton). See n. to vss. 55-56.

83. *era fatturo*: "Was about to do," a Latinism.

91. *t'ammira*: I.e., *meravigliati.*   *replico*: "Unfold."

92-93. *poscia con Tito . . . antico*: The Emperor Titus is referred to in *Purg.* XXI, 82-84 (see n. to those verses) by

Statius, with a reference to the point here mentioned, a point which is discussed at length in *Par.* VII, 19-51. The theory that Titus, as the destroyer of Jerusalem (in A.D. 70), was the avenger of the death of Christ was borrowed by Dante from Orosius, who, in recording the triumph of Titus after his victory, says (*Hist.* VII, iii, 8, ix, 9):

> Capta eversaque urbe Hierosolymorum, sicut prophetae praenuntiaverunt, extinctisque Iudaeis Titus, qui ad vindicandum Domini Iesu Christi sanguinem iudicio Dei fuerat ordinatus, victor triumphans cum Vespasiano patre Ianum clausit. . . . iure enim idem honos ultioni passionis Domini inpensus est, qui etiam nativitati fuerat adtributus.

> After the capture and overthrow of Jerusalem, as the prophets had foretold, and after the total destruction of the Jewish nation, Titus, who had been appointed by the decree of God to avenge the blood of the Lord Jesus Christ, celebrated with his father Vespasian his victory by a triumph and closed the Temple of Janus. . . . It was indeed right that the same honor should be paid to the avenging of the Lord's Passion as had been bestowed upon His Nativity.

94-96. *E quando il dente . . . soccorse*: "In 773 Pope Adrian I invoked the aid of Charlemagne against Desiderius, king of the Longobards or Lombards. Charlemagne—who now, in Dante's mind, represented the Empire, although he was not crowned until 800—came to the aid of the Church under the pinions of the Eagle" (Gr).

94. *dente*: The metaphor is from the Bible: cf. Pss. 3:8[7], 56:5[57:4], 123[124]:6, and Prov. 30:14.

97-99. *Omai puoi giudicar . . . mali*: Cf. vss. 31-33.

100-101. *L'uno al pubblico segno . . . oppone*: The Guelphs oppose the French arms and influence to the Empire.

101. *quello*: The "segno." *a parte*: "To a party," i.e., the Ghibelline. They appropriate the Eagle as their own sign and for their own purposes.

102. *forte*: "Hard."   *si falli*: The "si" here is the so-called pleonastic *si* used to specify identity ("which one"). For *fallare* in this sense, see *Par.* V, 53.

106. *esto Carlo novello*: "This younger Charles" is Charles II of Naples, son of Charles of Anjou. See *Purg.* XX, 79. He was not crowned until 1289 and died in 1309.

107. *Guelfi*: The Guelphs were supporters of the Church, as opposed to the Ghibellines, who were supporters of the Empire. They are mentioned by name only once in the poem. The standard of the Guelph party, in Florence, bore the arms of Clement IV, over which they later placed a small scarlet lily, as is recorded by Villani (VII, 2):

> Volle il detto papa che per suo amore la parte guelfa di Firenze portasse sempre la sua arme propria in bandiera e in suggello, la quale era, ed è, il campo bianco con una aguglia vermiglia in su uno serpente verde, la quale portarono e tennero poi, e fanno insino a' nostri presenti tempi; bene v'hanno poi aggiunto i guelfi uno giglietto vermiglio sopra il capo dell'aquila.

> The aforesaid pope decreed that in allegiance to him the Guelph party of Florence should always bear his own coat of arms on their flag and on their seal, which was and is, against a white background, a red eagle upon a green serpent, which coat of arms they did bear and did keep as they still do in our own present day; to be sure, the Guelphs later added a red lily over the head of the eagle.

li artigli: "The claws" of the imperial eagle.

109–10. *Molte fiate già . . . padre*: Charles is warned that the consequences of his folly may fall on his children.

111. *armi*: The eagle.

112. *Questa picciola stella*: Justinian now proceeds to answer Dante's second question (*Par.* V, 127-29).

114. *perché onore e fama li succeda*: "In order that honor and fame should follow them" on earth.

115–17. *e quando li disiri . . . vivi*: When desires are set on earthly honor and fame (thus deviating from true love), then it must follow that the rays of true affection mount heavenwards less intensely.

118–20. *Ma nel commensurar . . . maggi*: Part of the heavenly joy of these spirits consists in their seeing that there is an exact correspondence between their desert and their reward. One is reminded of Piccarda's words in *Par.* III, 50-57, 70-75. *Gaggi* (cf. the French *gages*) is the equivalent of the English *wages*.

120. *maggi = maggiori*. Cf. *Inf.* VI, 48; XXXI, 84.

121. *giustizia*: The subject of "addolcisce."

123. *nequizia*: "Iniquity," i.e., envy, in this case.

124–26. *Diverse voci . . . rote*: The simile (made such by "così," vs. 125) compares the harmony of many voices singing together to the harmony of the many "benches" ("scanni") or orders of blessedness witnessed by the pilgrim in these heavens. Latent here is a metaphor of cosmic harmony and order that will be variously restated in the cantos that lie ahead. There is a cosmic symphony, the cosmos is a work of art making use of darkness as well as light. In vs. 126 one hears the echo of the established notion of the harmony of the spheres. Cf. *Par.* I, 78, and see Beatrice's whole discourse in *Par.* I, 103-41, concerned as it is with cosmic order.

128–42. *Romeo . . . loderebbe*: "Raymond Berengar IV. of Provence (reigned 1209-1245), to be distinguished from his contemporary and opponent Raymond VII. of Toulouse (reigned 1222-1249), was notorious for his liberality and his patronage of poets and other men of genius. His daughter, Margaret, married Louis IX. of France (St. Louis). Eleanor married Henry III. of England. Sancha married Henry's brother, Richard of Cornwall; and Beatrice, his youngest daughter, whom he made his heiress, married Charles of Anjou after her father's death. Raymond's able and upright chamberlain, Romeo of Villeneuve (1170-1250), is also an historical character; but his name, Romeo, is the current term for one who has made a pilgrimage to Rome, or a pilgrim generally (see *Vita Nuova*, [XL, 6-7]). Hence arose the romantic legend recorded by Villani [VI, 91], and here followed by Dante. 'There came to his [Raymond Berengar's] court a certain Romeo, who was returning from S. James', and hearing the goodness of Count Raymond abode in his court, and was so wise and valorous, and came so much into favour with the Count, that he made him master and steward of all that he had. . . . Four daughters had the Count and no male child. By prudence and care the good Romeo first married the eldest for him to the good King Louis of France by giving money with her, saying to the Count, "Leave it to me, and do not grudge the cost, for if thou marriest the first well thou wilt marry all the others the better for the sake of her kinship and at less cost." And so it came to pass; for straightway the King of England, to be of kin to the King of France, took the second with little money; afterwards his carnal brother, being the king elect of the Romans, after the same manner took the third; the fourth being still to marry the good Romeo said, "For this one I desire that thou shouldst have a brave man for thy son, who may be thine heir,"—and so he did. Finding Charles, Count of Anjou, brother of King Louis of France, he said, "Give her to him for he is like to be the best man in the world," prophesying of him: and this was done. And it came to pass afterwards through envy, which destroys all good, that the barons of Provence accused the good Romeo that he had managed the Count's treasure ill, and they called upon him to give an account. The worthy Romeo said, "Count, I have served thee long while, and raised thy estate from small to great, and for this, through the false counsel of thy people, thou art little grateful. I came to thy court a poor pilgrim, and I have lived virtuously here; give me back my mule, my staff, and my scrip, as I came here, and I renounce thy service." The Count would not that he should depart; but, for nought that he could do would he remain; and, as he came so he departed, and no one knew whence he came or whither he went. But many held that he was a sainted soul' " (TC).

130. *fecer contra lui*: "Who worked against him" with their calumnies.

131. *non hanno riso*: I.e., they were punished for their evil deed by passing under the harsh rule of the Angevins, by way of Beatrice's marriage in 1246 to Charles of Anjou. Since Beatrice was her father's heiress and at the time of her marriage was countess of Provence, her union with Charles of Anjou brought Provence into the possession of the royal house of France. See *Purg.* XX, 61.   *e però mal cammina*: "And that shows that he travels an evil road." *però = perciò*.

132. *qual si fa danno*: "Whoever does himself harm."
del ben fare altrui: "By reason of another's good works." Those who maligned Romeo did themselves damage, for they sinned in envy. Cf. the definition of envy, *Purg.* XVII, 118-20.

134. *li = gli*.

136. *il*: Raymond.   *biece = bieche*, "crooked." Cf. *Par.* V, 65.

137. *ragione*: "An accounting," i.e., of his administration.

138. *che li assegnò sette e cinque per diece*: "Who had rendered him twelve for ten."   *li = gli*.   *assegnò*: The term *assegnare ragione* belongs to the mercantile language of the day (see M. Barbi, 1934, p. 251).

CANTO VII

1-3. *Osanna, sanctus Deus . . . malacòth*: " 'Hail, holy God of hosts, doubly illumining with thy brightness the happy fires of these kingdoms.' The blessed souls—'happy fires' of the heavens—are illumined first by their own intelligence and secondly by God's grace.—Of the three Hebrew words mixed with the Latin, *osanna* and *sabaòth* are used in the Bible, and *malacòth* (a mistake for *mamlacoth*) occurs in St. Jerome's preface to the Vulgate called *Prologus Galeatus*, where it is said to be equivalent to *regnorum*, 'of kingdoms' " (Gr).

5. *fu viso a me = fu visto da me*. Cf. the Latin *visum est mihi*. *essa sustanza*: Justinian.

6. *doppio lume*: Dante is probably referring here to the double light of natural intelligence and illuminating grace. There are, however, several other interpretations of the meaning, such as "the light of his beatitude doubled by that of his joy in enlightening Dante" (Norton). See *Par.* V, 131-37.
s'addua: "Is twinned." For this unusual type of verb, invented by Dante, cf. "s'incinqua" (*Par.* IX, 40) and "s'intrea" (*Par.* XIII, 57).

7. *ed essa e l'altre mossero a sua danza*: The lights now join in one dance. *sua = loro*.

129

9. *mi si velar di sùbita distanza*: The souls return to the Empyrean, their abode.   *velar = velarono*.

10–12. *Io dubitava . . . stille*: Another question has now arisen in Dante's mind, and he addresses himself in his own thoughts. "Dille" ("tell her") is used repeatedly to convey the urgency Dante feels within himself to have his thirst quenched by his lady (Beatrice), who does this, time and again, with the "sweet drops" of the truth.

14. *per Be e per ice*: "Be is the name of the letter *b*, ice is the rest of the name Bice, the shortened form of *Beatrice*. Dante is filled with reverence at the thought of the mere earthly Beatrice, and the name by which she was called: how much more reverent must he be in the presence of the heavenly Beatrice, whose full name occurs two lines below! The usual Tuscan name of *b* is *bi*; *be*, however, is Aretine" (Gr).

16. *Poco sofferse me cotal Beatrice*: "Beatrice allowed me to remain thus [with bowed head] but a little while." "Me cotal" reflects a Latin construction.

18. *faria = farebbe*.

19–21. *Secondo mio infallibile . . . miso*: No reader will forget that Beatrice can always read Dante's thoughts, which she now proceeds to do, stating that in this she is infallible. For the problem that has arisen with Dante, cf. *Par.* VI, 88-93.

21. *miso = messo*. Cf. *Inf.* XXVI, 54.

24. *sentenza*: "Doctrine."   *presente*: "Gift."

25. *Per non soffrire*: "Because he would not endure."   *la virtù che vole*: The will.

26. *freno*: The object of "soffrire."   *a suo prode*: "For his own profit."   *quell' uom che non nacque*: Adam. Dante delights in naming Adam by circumlocution. Cf. *Par.* XIII, 37-39; XXVI, 91-92.

27. *dannando sé, dannò tutta sua prole*: Thus was the burden of original sin transmitted to all mankind. This is well-

established doctrine, of course, as is that expressed in the fol-
lowing tercet.

28–33. *onde l'umana specie . . . amore*: The statement of
this standard doctrine continues. Adam's sin left all his prog-
eny "wounded" ("inferma") in intellect and in will. Fallen
man is wounded in these two faculties of his immortal soul.
See n. to *Inf.* I, 30.

29. *giù per secoli molti*: "Giù" bears the suggestion that man
was abandoned, left "below," by God, *sibi relictus* as the
theologians commonly phrase it. We learn later (*Par.* XXVI,
118-23), from Adam himself, that 5,232 years passed be-
tween the creation of Adam and the Crucifixion, which
means that man lay below in error for more than fifty cen-
turies before the Incarnation.

30. *Verbo di Dio*: Christ. Cf. Ioan. 1:1.

31. *u' = ove*, "where," i.e., to mankind.   *natura*: The
object of "unì" (vs. 32).

32. *s'era allungata*: This stresses the force of "giù" (see n.
to vs. 29).   *unì a sé in persona*: The divine Christ as-
sumed human nature, uniting it to Himself in the mystery of
the Incarnation. And this was an act of pure love. See
Thomas Aquinas, *Summa theol.* III, q. 32, a. 1, resp., where
one is reminded that "conceptionem corporis Christi tota
Trinitas est operata. Attribuitur tamen hoc Spiritui sancto."
("The whole Trinity effected the conception of Christ's
body: nevertheless, this is attributed to the Holy Ghost.")
And the Holy Ghost is eternal Love. See also *Summa theol.*
III, q. 32, a. 4, ad 1:

> Illa conceptio tria privilegia habuit: scilicet quod esset
> sine peccato originali; quod esset non puri hominis, sed
> Dei et hominis; item quod esset conceptio virginis: et
> haec tria habuit a Spiritu sancto. Et ideo dicit Damas-
> cenus quantum ad primum, quod Spiritus sanctus super-
> venit Virgini purgans ipsam, idest, praeservans, ne cum
> peccato originali conciperet.

This conception had three privileges—namely, that it was without original sin; that it was not that of a man only, but of God and man; and that it was a virginal conception. And all three were effected by the Holy Ghost. Therefore Damascene says, as to the first, that the Holy Ghost *came upon the Virgin, purifying her*— that is, preserving her from conceiving with original sin.

35–36. *questa natura . . . buona*: Human nature as it was in Adam before the Fall, "united to its Creator," was pure and good.

37–38. *ma per sé . . . paradiso*: Adam sinned by an act of his own free will, and the consequence thereof was his (and Eve's) banishment from Eden ("paradiso" here is used in the sense of the earthly Paradise).

38. *però che = perciò che*.

38–39. *si torse . . . vita*: Original sin turned human nature from the way of truth and from a perfect life in Eden.

40–42. *La pena . . . morse*: Christ assumed human nature in order to purge it, or heal it, by that assumption. See Thomas Aquinas, *Summa theol.* III, q. 31, a. 1, resp.:

> Christus humanam naturam assumpsit, ut eam a corruptione purgaret. Non autem purgatione indigebat natura humana nisi secundum quod infecta erat per originem vitiatam, qua ex Adam descendebat. Et ideo conveniens fuit ut carnem sumeret ex materia ab Adam derivata, ut ipsa natura per assumptionem curaretur.

> Christ assumed human nature in order to cleanse it of corruption. But human nature did not need to be cleansed save in as far as it was soiled in its tainted origin whereby it was descended from Adam. Therefore it was becoming that He should assume flesh of matter derived from Adam, that the nature itself might be healed by the assumption.

Christ's death on the Cross therefore *justly* atoned for original sin in Adam. Nothing was ever so just.

43–45. *e così nulla . . . natura*: Christ on earth was God, second person of the Trinity, who had assumed corrupt human nature. But He remained God, hence the Jews nailed God to the Cross. And they are responsible. See Thomas Aquinas, *Summa theol.* III, q. 46, a. 12, ad 3, where Aquinas is quoting a sermon of the Council of Ephesus:

> Sicut subditur ibidem, *non purum hominem cruci-*
> *fixerunt Iudaei, sed Deo intulerunt praesumptiones.*
> *Pone enim principem loqui per verbum, et hoc formari*
> *per litteras in charta aliqua, et dirigi civitatibus, et*
> *aliquis inobediens chartam disrumpat; ad mortis sen-*
> *tentiam deducetur, non tamquam chartam disrumpens,*
> *sed tamquam verbum imperiale disrumpens. Non ergo*
> *securus sit Iudaeus, tamquam purum hominem cruci-*
> *figens; quod enim videbat, quasi charta erat; quod au-*
> *tem in ea celabatur, imperiale Verbum erat, natum ex*
> *natura, non prolatum per linguam.*

As the passage quoted goes on to say: *The Jews did not crucify one who was simply a man; they inflicted their presumptions upon God. For suppose a prince to speak by word of mouth, and that his words are committed to writing on a parchment and sent out to the cities, and that some rebel tears up the document, he will be led forth to endure the death sentence, not for merely tearing up a document, but as destroying the imperial message. Let not the Jew, then, stand in security, as crucifying a mere man; since what he saw was as the parchment, but what was hidden under it was the imperial Word, the Son by nature, not the mere utterance of a tongue.*

Thus, says Dante, "considering the [divine] person who suffered crucifixion at their hands, never was there a greater outrage."

46–47. *Però . . . morte*: The second verse explains the first. It pleased God that Christ should die on the Cross (a point which Beatrice will now explain), and it also pleased the Jews that he should die thus. But even though the Cruci-

fixion of Christ was part of God's plan, the Jews are none-
theless accountable for their terrible deed. See Thomas
Aquinas, *Summa theol.* III, q. 47, a. 5, resp.:

Apud Iudaeos quidam erant maiores, et quidem mi-
nores. *Maiores* quidem *qui eorum principes dicebantur,*
ut dicitur in lib. QQ. veteris et novi Testam. (quaest.
66, a med., inter op. Aug.), *sicut et daemones cog-
noverunt eum esse Christum promissum in lege: omnia
enim signa videbant in eo quae dixerunt futura Prophe-
tae; mysterium autem divinitatis eius ignorabant.* Et
ideo Apostolus dicit quod *si cognovissent, nunquam
Dominum gloriae crucifixissent.* Sciendum tamen quod
eorum ignorantia non eos excusabat a crimine, quia erat
quodammodo ignorantia affectata: videbant enim evi-
dentia signa divinitatis ipsius, sed ex odio, et invidia
Christi ea pervertebant; et verbis eius, quibus se Dei
Filium fatebatur, credere noluerunt. Unde ipse de eis
dicit Ioan. 15, 22: *Si non venissem, et locutus eis non
fuissem, peccatum non haberent; nunc autem excusa-
tionem non habent de peccato suo.* Et postea subdit:
*Si opera non fecissem in eis, quae nemo alius fecit, pecca-
tum non haberent.* Et sic ex persona eorum accipi potest
quod dicitur Iob 21, 14: *Dixerunt Deo: Recede a
nobis, scientiam viarum tuarum nolumus.* Minores vero,
idest populares qui mysteria scripturae non noverant,
non plene cognoverunt ipsum esse nec Christum, nec
Filium Dei. Licet enim aliqui eorum in eum crediderint,
multitudo tamen non credidit; et si aliquando dubita-
verunt an ipse esset Christus, propter signorum multitu-
dinem et efficaciam doctrinae, ut habetur Ioan. 7, tamen
postea decepti fuerunt a suis principibus, ut eum non
crederent neque Filium Dei, neque Christum. Unde et
Petrus eis dixit: *Scio quia per ignorantiam fecistis, sicut
et principes vestri,* quia scilicet principes seducti erant.

Among the Jews some were elders, and others of lesser
degree. Now according to the author of *De Qq. Nov. et
Vet. Test., qu.* lxvi, the elders, who were called *rulers,
knew,* as did also the devils, *that He was the Christ*

promised in the Law: for they saw all the signs in Him
which the prophets said would come to pass: but they
did not know the mystery of His Godhead. Consequent-
ly the Apostle says: *If they had known it, they would*
never have crucified the Lord of glory. It must, how-
ever, be understood that their ignorance did not excuse
them from crime, because it was, as it were, affected
ignorance. For they saw manifest signs of His Godhead;
yet they perverted them out of hatred and envy of
Christ; neither would they believe His words, whereby
He avowed that He was the Son of God. Hence He
Himself says of them (Jo. xv. 22): *If I had not come,*
and spoken to them, they would not have sin; but now
they have no excuse for their sin. And afterwards He
adds (24): *If I had not done among them the works*
that no other man hath done, they would not have sin.
And so the expression employed by Job (xxi. 14) can
be accepted on their behalf: *(Who) said to God: depart*
from us, we desire not the knowledge of Thy ways.

But those of lesser degree—namely, the common folk
—who had not grasped the mysteries of the Scriptures,
did not fully comprehend that He was the Christ or the
Son of God. For although some of them believed in
Him, yet the multitude did not; and if they doubted
sometimes whether He was the Christ, on account of the
manifold signs and force of His teaching, as is stated Jo.
vii. 31, 41, nevertheless they were deceived afterwards
by their rulers, so that they did not believe Him to be
the Son of God or the Christ. Hence Peter said to them:
I know that you did it through ignorance, as did also
your rulers—namely, because they were seduced by the
rulers.

48. *tremò la terra*: Cf. *Inf.* XII, 41. The reference is to the
earthquake that shook the earth when Christ died on the
Cross (Matt. 27:51).   *e 'l ciel s'aperse*: See Thomas
Aquinas, *Summa theol.*, III, q. 49, a. 5, resp.:

Clausio ianuae est obstaculum quoddam prohibens
homines ab ingressu. Prohibebantur autem homines ab

ingressu regni caelestis propter peccatum, quia, sicut dicitur Isa. 35, 8, *Via illa sancta vocabitur, et non transibit per eam pollutus.* Est autem duplex peccatum impediens ab ingressu regni caelestis. Unum quidem commune totius humanae naturae, quod est peccatum primi parentis; et per hoc peccatum praecludebatur homini aditus regni caelestis. Unde legitur Gen. 3, 24, quod post peccatum primi parentis *collocavit Deus Cherubim et flammeum gladium atque versatilem, ad custodiendam viam ligni vitae.* Aliud autem est peccatum speciale uniuscuiusque personae, quod per proprium actum committitur uniuscuiusque hominis. Per passionem autem Christi liberati sumus, non solum a peccato communi totius humanae naturae, et quantum ad culpam, et quantum ad reatum poenae, ipso solvente pretium pro nobis, sed etiam a peccatis propriis singulorum, qui communicant eius passioni per fidem, et charitatem, et fidei sacramenta. Et ideo per passionem Christi aperta est nobis ianua regni caelestis.

The shutting of the gate is the obstacle which hinders men from entering in. But it is on account of sin that men were prevented from entering into the heavenly kingdom, since, according to Isa. xxxv. 8: *It shall be called the holy way, and the unclean shall not pass over it.* Now there is a twofold sin which prevents men from entering into the kingdom of heaven. The first is common to the whole race, for it is our first parents' sin, and by that sin heaven's entrance is closed to man. Hence we read in Gen. iii. 24 that after our first parents' sin God *placed . . . cherubim and a flaming sword, turning every way, to keep the way of the tree of life.* The other is the personal sin of each one of us, committed by our personal act.

Now by Christ's Passion we have been delivered not only from the common sin of the whole human race, both as to its guilt and as to the debt of punishment, for which He paid the penalty on our behalf; but, furthermore, from the personal sins of individuals, who share in His Passion by faith and charity and the sacraments of faith. Consequently, then, the gate of heaven's kingdom is thrown open to us through Christ's Passion.

49. *forte*: "Hard" to understand.

50–51. *quando si dice . . . corte*: See vss. 20-21 and *Par.* VI, 92-93.

51. *da giusta corte*: By Titus, i.e., by the legitimate Roman tribunal, bearing the sign of the imperial eagle.

52–57. *Ma io veggi' . . . modo*: Beatrice, reading Dante's thoughts, knows that another question, and a knotty one, has arisen in his mind: Why did God choose *this* way, as set forth above, for the redemption of mankind? For the theologian's typical answer, one may continue to turn to Thomas Aquinas, *Summa theol.* III, perhaps choosing q. 46, a. 3, where Aquinas considers whether there was a more suitable way of delivering the human race than by Christ's Passion. In his answer, Aquinas says:

Tanto aliquis modus convenientior est ad assequendum finem, quanto per ipsum plura concurrunt quae sunt expedientia fini. Per hoc autem quod homo per Christi passionem est liberatus, multa concurrerunt ad salutem hominis pertinentia praeter liberationem a peccato. Primo enim per hoc homo cognoscit quantum Deus hominem diligat, et per hoc provocatur ad eum diligendum, in quo perfectio humanae salutis consistit: unde Apostolus dicit Rom. 5, 8: *Commendat suam charitatem Deus in nobis: quoniam cum inimici essemus, Christus pro nobis mortuus est.* Secundo, quia per hoc dedit nobis exemplum obedientiae, humilitatis, constantiae, iustitiae et caeterarum virtutum in passione Christi ostensarum, quae sunt necessariae ad humanam salutem: unde dicitur 1 Pet. 2, 21: *Christus passus est pro nobis, vobis relinquens exemplum, ut sequamini vestigia eius.* Tertio, quia Christus per passionem suam non solum hominem a peccato liberavit, sed etiam gratiam iustificantem et gloriam beatitudinis ei promeruit, ut infra dicetur, quaest. 48. Quarto, quia per hoc est homini inducta major necessitas se immunem a peccato conservandi . . . secundum illud 1 Corinth. 6, 20: *Empti enim estis pretio magno: glorificate et portate Deum in corpore vestro*. Quinto, quia hoc ad majorem dignitatem hominis cessit, ut sicut homo victus fuerat et deceptus a diabolo, ita etiam homo esset qui diabolum vinceret; et sicut homo mortem meruit, ita homo moriendo mortem superaret. Unde dicitur 1 ad Corinth. 15, 57: *Deo gratias, qui dedit nobis victoriam per Dominum nostrum Iesum Christum*. Et ideo convenientius fuit quod per passionem Christi liberaremur quam per solam Dei voluntatem.

Among means to an end that one is the more suitable whereby the various concurring means employed are themselves helpful to such end. But in this that man was delivered by Christ's Passion, many other things besides deliverance from sin concurred for man's salvation. In the first place, man knows thereby how much God loves him, and is thereby stirred to love Him in return, and herein lies the perfection of human salvation; hence the Apostle says (Rom. V. 8[-9]): *God commendeth His charity towards us; for when as yet we were sinners . . . Christ died for us*. Secondly, because thereby He set us an example of obedience, humility, constancy, justice, and the other virtues displayed in the Passion, which are requisite for man's salvation. Hence it is written (1 Pet. ii. 21): *Christ also suffered for us, leaving you an example that you should follow in His steps*. Thirdly, because Christ by His Passion not only delivered man from sin, but also merited justifying grace for him and the glory of bliss, as shall be shown later (q. 48, a. 1; q. 49, aa. 1, 5). Fourthly, because by this man is all the more bound to refrain from sin, according to 1 Cor. vi. 20: *You are bought with a great price: glorify and bear God in your body*. Fifthly, because it redounded to man's greater dignity, that as man was overcome and deceived by the devil, so also it should be a man that should overthrow the devil; and as man deserved death, so a man by dying should vanquish death. Hence it is written (1 Cor. xv. 57): *Thanks be to God who hath given us the victory through our Lord Jesus Christ*. It was accordingly more fitting that we should be delivered by Christ's Passion than simply by God's good-will.

58. *frate*: The reader will note the admonitory tone of this word. Cf. *Purg.* IV, 127; XI, 82; *Par.* III, 70.

60. *adulto*: " 'Full-grown' in the flame of love. Only an infinitely loving mind can comprehend the boundless love which impelled God to sacrifice himself for man" (Gr).

61. *Veramente*: "However."   *segno*: "Target," i.e., this problem.

63. *perché tal modo fu più degno*: Thus the argument is now couched in terms of *suitability*, even as Thomas Aquinas frames it in *Summa theol.* III, q. 46, a. 3.

64–66. *La divina bontà . . . etterne*: "Divine Goodness, in its exuberant love, brings forth men and angels, just as a blazing fire sends out sparks. Thus it 'reveals its eternal beauties,' by giving them a visible, objective form in the created world. —Cf. *Cons.*, III, Metr. ix, ll. 4-6 (Boethius is addressing the Creator):

> Quem non externae pepulerunt fingere causae
> Materiae fluitantis opus, verum insita summi
> Forma boni, livore carens.

(No external causes impelled You to make this work from chaotic matter. Rather it was the form of the highest good, existing within You without envy.)" (Gr).

On the matter of the resemblance of God's creatures to Himself, E. G. Gardner (1913, pp. 106-7) notes that Dionysius and Aquinas echo Plato's *Timaeus* (XXIX).

67. *sanza mezzo*: "Immediately," "without intermediary or secondary causes."   *distilla*: "Derives."

70–72. *Ciò che da essa . . . nove*: The meaning of "libero è tutto" is explained by the clause that follows. That which is created directly by God is not subject to the power or influence of more recent things, of the heavens and their "secondary" causality—it is not subject to nature, in short. The heavens are "recent" compared to their Creator.

70. *piove*: "Piove" repeats the idea of "distilla" (vs. 67), both verbs suggesting a descent of power from above, from God.

73. *Più l'è conforme, e però più le piace*: The created thing is more like God and hence more pleasing to Him.

74-75. *ché l'ardor santo . . . vivace*: God's love shines in all things (cf. *Par.* I, 1-3), but it is most resplendent in those creatures (angels and men) which are more like Himself.

76. *dote*: Plural of *dota*, meaning "gifts," "endowments," in this case immortality and liberty, which make the human creature more like God. *s'avvantaggia*: "Has the advantage" over lesser things. And this advantage is man's "nobility," as it is termed in vs. 78.

77-78. *s'una manca . . . caggia*: The human creature needs must fall from its nobility (freedom), if it loses any one of its "advantages" or special endowments.

78. *caggia = cada.*

79. *Solo il peccato è quel che la disfranca*: Sin alone "disfranchises," i.e., takes away the God-given privilege.

80. *falla = la fa.* *dissimìle al sommo bene*: When the special "gift" (liberty) is lost, the human creature is less like God. This special gift includes reason, of course, which beasts do not have. See Thomas Aquinas, *Summa theol.* II-II, q. 64, a. 2, ad 3: "Homo peccando ab ordine rationis recedit; et ideo decidit a dignitate humana, prout scilicet homo est naturaliter liber, et propter seipsum existens; et incidit quodammodo in servitutem bestiarum." ("By sinning man departs from the order of reason, and consequently falls away from the dignity of his manhood, in so far as he is naturally free, and exists for himself, and he falls into the slavish state of the beasts.")

81. *per che*: "Wherefore."   *del lume suo poco s'im-biancia*: This obviously returns to the metaphor of light with which Beatrice's discourse on this problem began (vss. 64-66).

82-84: *e in sua dignità . . . pene*: The argument continues in terms of a "dignity" that is lost through sin, which "disfranchises." As is already clear—and will become clearer—Beatrice is speaking of the sin of Adam and Eve and its consequences for human nature. Thus, in vs. 87 "paradiso" is used to mean the earthly Paradise. The burden of expiation for sin is man's. Justice would require that he make amends, by "refilling where he had emptied," by suffering penalties equal to the sin ("mal dilettar").

85-86. *Vostra natura . . . suo*: It is important to note that the matter is kept in terms of human nature sinning when Adam, our seed, sinned. We were all in Adam (as in our seed) when Adam sinned, we all sinned when Adam sinned, that is, human nature sinned when Adam sinned. It is in this context that theology speaks of natural justice as the perfect condition lost when Adam sinned. See C. S. Singleton (1958), pp. 222-53, especially pp. 230-31.

85. *tota* = *tutta*. "Tota" is a Latinism.

86-87. *da queste dignitadi . . . remota*: The condition of original justice was lost, human nature was removed from that condition, even as it was in our first parents when they were driven from the earthly Paradise.

88-90. *né ricovrar potiensi . . . guadi*: The dignities lost by Adam's sin could not be regained except by (one or the other of) two ways (literally, "fords"). Beatrice's logic is very strict here.

91-92. *o che Dio solo . . . avesse*: One way or "ford" was this: God, through His mercy ("cortesia"), might simply have forgiven the sin of Adam.

92. *dimesso*: "Forgiven." "Dimesso" is from the Latin *di-*

mittere, used here in the sense it has in the Bible.   *per sé isso*: From the Latin *per se ipsum*, "by himself."

92-93. *o che l'uom . . . follia*: The other way would have been for man to make satisfaction for his sin.

94. *mo = ora.*

94-95. *l'abisso de l'etterno consiglio*: The infinite depths of God's eternal counsel (wisdom). Cf. *Purg.* VI, 121-22. Beatrice will now solve the dilemma, knowing God's ways, for she sees very deeply into that abyss, being herself Wisdom (in allegory).

96. *distrettamente = ben strettamente.*

97-98. *Non potea l'uomo . . . sodisfar*: The argument proceeds by looking first at the possibility of man's making amends himself for his sin, a possibility that was nil, for the reason now to be stated.

98-100. *per non potere . . . suso*: Beatrice now goes on to explain that man himself could not atone for his sin because he was unable to descend in humility to the extent that he had once aspired to rise. Adam's sin is thus put essentially in terms of his and Eve's aspiration to be as gods, according to the serpent's promise, if they should eat of the forbidden fruit. See Gen. 3:4-5: "Dixit autem serpens ad mulierem: Nequaquam morte moriemini; scit enim Deus quod in quocumque die comederitis ex eo, aperientur oculi vestri, et eritis sicut dii scientes bonum et malum." ("But the serpent said to the woman, 'No, you shall not die; for God knows that when you eat of it, your eyes will be opened and you will be like God, knowing good and evil.'") Adam's sin was one of disobedience and pride, an aspiration to rise up and be like God. Beatrice, with "ir suso" and with "disobediendo," puts the matter in these terms.

99. *con umiltate*: The needful compensatory descent is a descent to humility, which is the opposite of the prideful aspiration of our first parents.

100. *quanto disobediendo intese ir suso*: Adam and Eve

could not actually have risen up to be like God, as the serpent had promised. But their sin is measured by the degree ("quanto") of their intention or aspiration in this regard (hence, "intese"). Note that the statement is made in terms of man in general (rather than of Adam the individual), which keeps it in terms of human nature. Man could not, by his own powers, make satisfaction for original sin.

102. *dischiuso = escluso.*

103-4. *Dunque a Dio . . . vita:* "Man cannot, therefore God must" is the turn the argument now takes.

103. *con le vie sue:* God's two ways are mercy and justice. Cf. Ps. 24[25]:10: "Universae viae Domini misericordia et veritas requirentibus testamentum eius et testimonia eius." ("All the paths of the Lord are [mercy and justice] toward those who keep his covenant and his decrees.")

104. *riparar l'omo a sua intera vita:* Restore man to the rectitude he had in Eden and lost through sin.

105. *dico con l'una, o ver con amendue:* Either God could have excused man for original sin or He could have found some other way.   *con l'una:* That is, *via,* i.e., either with mercy or with justice.   *o ver con amendue:* Or with both mercy and justice.

106. *ovra = opera.*

106-7. *è più gradita da l'operante:* "Is the more pleasing to the one who performs it."

107. *appresenta:* "Demonstrates," "manifests."

111. *a rilevarvi:* Continuing in the figure of "up and down," Beatrice means mankind by the pronoun *-vi.* This will come to mean, as she continues, that in this way God made it possible for man to "raise himself" (vs. 116).

112. *ultima notte:* Judgment.   *primo die:* The Creation (cf. Matt. 24:21). The inverted order is a minor example of the figure of *hysteron proteron* (see *Par.* II, 23-24, and the

corresponding note). Here Beatrice's words survey the whole of the divine economy from the end, as it were.

113. *processo = procedimento.*

114. *o per l'una o per l'altra*: I.e., *via.*   *fie = sarà.*

115. *più largo fu Dio*: The goodness of God in choosing this way (vs. 108) continues to be the central point. Cf. vs. 91: "*cortesia.*"   *a dar sé stesso*: The Father giving the Son, second person of the Trinity, who in His sacrifice obeyed the Father.

116. *per far l'uom sufficiente a rilevarsi*: The possibility for an individual man to "raise himself" to salvation was thus established through Christ's sacrifice. This stress on the possibility of man's cooperation should be noted.

117. *che s'elli avesse sol da sé dimesso*: This was the other way or "ford" (vss. 90-93), the one which God did not choose.   *elli = egli.*

118-19. *e tutti . . . giustizia*: Justice remains the keynote, though mercy (God's other way) is not obscured by this.

120. *non fosse umiliato ad incarnarsi*: Christ's very Incarnation is viewed as a humiliation, God becoming man being the great descent that opened the way to heaven, by making it possible for man to descend low enough. But the greatest humiliation was death on the Cross. Cf. Phil. 2:8, where it is said that Christ, appearing as a man, "humiliavit semetipsum factus obediens usque ad mortem, mortem autem crucis" ("humbled himself, becoming obedient to death, even to death on a cross").

At this point, the reader should pause to consider that descent before ascent, a master pattern of Christian thought, is the basic conceptual necessity of the whole journey through Hell, up to the girding-on of the rush of humility when the wayfaring Dante reaches the shore of Mount Purgatory. On this pattern, generally overlooked in Dante studies, see C. S. Singleton (1966), pp. 75-79.

122. *in alcun loco*: This "certain place" is the distinction be-

tween direct creation by God and formation through inter-
mediary or secondary causes (vss. 67-72).

123. *veggi = vegga, veda.*

124–25. *Tu dici . . . terra*: Beatrice thus names the four ele-
ments that make up the sublunar world.

125. *e tutte lor misture*: All that which is formed by the vari-
ous combinations of these elements.

126. *venire a corruzione, e durar poco*: This *seems* to con-
tradict what Beatrice has said previously (vss. 67-72), but
she will now explain.

127. *e queste cose pur furon creature*: The tense of the verb,
in the past abolute, is significant, suggesting that God might
have created the elements and their mixtures in His original
creation. In that case they should be incorruptible (vs. 129).

129. *dovrien = dovrebbero.*

130–32. *Li angeli . . . intero*: A typical use of *frate* may be
noted here (see n. to *Par.* III, 70). Dante is now being ad-
monished to correct his thinking, for he ought to know that
God in His original creation made the angels and the heavens
or heavenly spheres, the "country" in which Dante now finds
himself (cf. *Par.* XXIX, 32-33, 35-36). And these were cre-
ated entire, i.e., in their complete being, without further
change or modification ("in loro essere intero").

133–41. *ma li alimenti . . . sante*: As stated in vss. 136-38
brute matter ("la materia ch'elli hanno") and the informing
virtue which the heavenly spheres shed on the sublunar world
were also created in God's first creation (cf. *Par.* XXIX,
22-24). But the four elements named and their "mixtures"
(vss. 124-25) are formed indirectly by operation of the in-
forming virtues of the spheres, the planets, and the stars, over
which the angelic Intelligences preside (see *Par.* II, 112-38).
These things, therefore, are not created directly by God, and
this is the main point (see vss. 67-72). "The *prima materia*
is *informed* (i.e. so combined with a 'form' or ideal and es-
sential principle as to pass from the possibility of being *any-*

thing to the actuality of being *something*) not direct by God, but by created powers, i.e. angels or heavenly influences. The transforming and vivifying power of the sun (and in lesser degree the moon) was supposed to have its analogies in equally real but less obvious influences of the other heavenly bodies, especially the planets. It is these heavenly influences collectively that draw the 'soul' or *life* of plant (nutritive and reproductive) or animal (sensitive and locomotive) from the stage of potentiality in the germinal material into that of ac-tuality in the living things itself" (TC).

139. *L'anima d'ogne bruto e de le piante*: For the concep-tion of the souls which animals and plants have (the sensitive and the vegetative respectively), see *Purg*. XXV, 52-60, and the corresponding notes.

140. *complession potenziata*: The terminology continues to be primarily Aristotelian as in so many other passages in the *Paradiso*.

142–44. *ma vostra vita . . . disira*: Compare *Purg*. XXV, especially vss. 70-75, where it is explained that God breathes the immortal soul into the fully formed fetus. Thus each hu-man soul is created directly by God. Moreover, this loving God inspires each soul with a love and desire for Himself (natural love).

145–48. *E quinci . . . fensi*: "I.e. 'from the distinctions now drawn'; for the bodies both of Adam and Eve were made immediately by God, and when the work of redemption is finally consummated (after the last judgment) man's body will be restored to the dignity which it lost only by sin. The argument is Anselm's. He meets the obvious objection that it does not cover the case of the 'resurrection unto wrath,' by urging that if the saved rejoice both in body and soul, it is but fitting that the lost should suffer in both" (TC).

145. *quinci*: "Hence."

147. *fessi = si fece*.

148. *fensi = si fecero*.

CANTO VIII

1–3. *Solea creder . . . raggiasse*: "The belief that 'mad love' was sent down from a star by a goddess was a dangerous one" (Gr).

1. *mondo*: "Mondo" is the subject of the verb.   *in suo periclo*: "To its peril." *Periclo* is a Latinism.

2. *Ciprigna*: Venus, so called from her birth in Cyprus.
il folle amore: Carnal love.

3. *raggiasse*: See *Conv.* II, vi, 9, where Dante states that "li raggi di ciascuno cielo sono la via per la quale discende la loro vertude in queste cose di qua giù." ("The rays of each heaven are the path whereby their virtue descends upon things that are here below.") Cf. *Par.* VII, 141.   *volta nel terzo epiciclo*: This identifies the goddess with the planet, as if she had her abode there and turned with it. "The spheres that bear the various stars are transparent hollow globes of light matter, turning all together from east to west, and, in addition, possessing each an independent revolution in another direction and at a different speed. Moreover, the heaven of Venus—like those of the Moon, Mercury, Mars, Jupiter, and Saturn—has, attached to itself, a little revolving sphere carrying the planet. The circuit of this smaller ball is called an *epicycle*. Mathematically, an epicycle is defined as

147

a circle whose center is on the circumference of a greater one. By means of this device (and others) the Ptolemaic astronomers explained the varying distances of each planet from the earth. Every heavenly body, except the sun and the fixed stars, has three different revolutions: the general diurnal course, the periodic orbit of the individual sphere, and the accompanying turn of the epicycle. The sun and the fixed stars have the first two. In the heaven of Venus Dante and his guide find the third of the epicycles" (Gr).

6. *l'antico errore*: Paganism. Cf. *Inf.* I, 72.

7. *Dione*: Daughter of Oceanus and Tethys, Dione was the mother of Venus, whence Venus is sometimes called Dionaea. *Cupido*: Pronounced *Cupìdo*. Cupid was the well-known son of Venus.

9. *e dicean ch'el sedette in grembo a Dido*: The allusion is to the account given by Virgil of how Cupid in the form of Ascanius sat in Dido's lap and inspired her fatal passion for Aeneas. See *Aen.* I, 657-60, 715-19:

> At Cytherea novas artes, nova pectore versat
> consilia, ut faciem mutatus et ora Cupido
> pro dulci Ascanio veniat, donisque furentem
> incendat reginam atque ossibus implicet ignem.
>
> . . . .
>
> ille ubi complexu Aeneae colloque pependit
> et magnum falsi implevit genitoris amorem,
> reginam petit. haec oculis, haec pectore toto
> haeret et interdum gremio fovet, inscia Dido,
> insidat quantus miserae deus. . . .

But the Cytherean revolves in her breast new wiles, new schemes; how Cupid, changed in face and form, may come in the stead of sweet Ascanius, and by his gifts kindle the queen to madness and send the flame into her very marrow. . . . He, when he has hung in embrace on Aeneas' neck and satisfied the deluded father's deep love, goes to the queen. She with her eyes, with all her heart clings to him and anon fondles him in her bosom, knowing not, poor Dido, how great a god settles there to her sorrow.

10. *costei*: Venus.   *principio*: "Beginning" of this canto.

11. *vocabol = vocabolo*, "name."

12. *che*: The object of "vagheggia" ("woos").   *or da coppa or da ciglio*: "*Da coppa*, 'at nape,' i.e., behind; *da ciglio*, 'at brow,' i.e., before: according as Venus is morning or evening star. For the odd expression *da coppa*, cf. *Aen.*, I, 402: (Venus) 'avertens rosea *cervice* refulsit.' (As she turned away, her roseate neck flashed bright.)" (Gr).

13. *in ella = in essa*, in the planet Venus itself.

15. *far = farsi*.

19. *essa luce*: The light of the planet.   *altre lucerne*: These lights are the souls of the blessed that have descended to greet the wayfarer on his upward flight. From now on the souls will be seen thus, as covering and hiding with their own radiance any human semblance they might have, which radiance expresses their joy.

20–21. *muoversi in giro . . . interne*: The souls turn about as in a dance, moving more or less fast, according, as Dante believes, to their "internal vision," that is, the vision of God, which they do not cease to have even though they have left the Empyrean to show themselves here.

22–23. *Di fredda nube . . . no*: "When winds become ignited, they are 'visible' in the form of lightning or meteors: cf. *Purg.* V, 37-39" (Gr). See E. Moore (1896), pp. 132-33.

26. *giro*: Round dance.

27. *in*: "Among."   *in li alti Serafini*: In the Empyrean, in company with the Seraphim, the highest of the angels.

28. *appariro = apparirono*.

29. *Osanna*: A cry of welcome. Cf. *Purg.* XXIX, 51.

32. *sem presti = siamo pronti*.

33. *gioi*: Present subjunctive of *gioiare*, "have joy."

34. *principi* = *principati*, Principalities, the angels who pre-side over the sphere of Venus. "Principi" is pronounced *prìncipi*.

35. *d'un giro e d'un girare e d'una sete*: These souls revolve in perfect harmony with the angels who turn this planet and who are addressed in the opening verse of the *canzone* now to be cited by this spirit. "Giro" has reference to the dimen-sion of their circle, "girare" to the velocity of their circling.
    un . . . un . . . una: "Selfsame."   *d'una sete*: These spir-its have the same desire (thirst) to contemplate God as do the Principalities.

36. *tu del mondo* = *tu dal mondo*, that is, "you, when in the world."

37. *Voi che 'ntendendo il terzo ciel movete*: This is the first verse of the first *canzone* of the *Convivio*, amply commented on by the poet in that work. See *Conv.* II, ii, 7, where Dante says:

> Adunque dico che la canzone proposta è contenuta da tre parti principali. La prima è lo primo verso di quella: ne la quale s'inducono a udire ciò che dire intendo certe Intelligenze, o vero per più usato modo volemo dire Angeli, le quali sono a la revoluzione del cielo di Venere, sì come movitori di quello.

> I say then that the ode before us is composed of three chief parts. The first is the first verse of it, wherein are introduced, that they may hearken to that which I in-tend to say, certain Intelligences, or, to name them after the more customary use, certain Angels, which are set over the revolution of the heaven of Venus, as its movers.

'ntendendo = *intendendo*. The angels move the sphere by intellection, and solely by intellection, as Dante states in *Conv.* II, vi, 1 in his commentary on this verse: "con lo intel-letto solo" ("with the intellect alone"). In the *Convivio*

Dante holds that the angels who turn the third heaven are the Thrones, not the Principalities (*Conv.* II, v, 13).

38. *sem = siamo*.

39. *fia = sarà.   un poco di quiete*: Even though this is the heaven of love, how far we may now feel we are from the circle of the lovers in Inferno, where "a little quiet" was allowed to Francesca and Paolo that they might speak with Dante (*Inf.* V, 96)!

40. *si fuoro offerti = si furono rivolti*.

41. *reverenti*: I.e., in asking her permission to speak with these souls.

42. *di sé contenti e certi*: Beatrice gives her full consent, so that Dante's eyes are made content and certain in their request.

43. *rivolsersi = si rivolsero*.

44. *s'avea = si era* (the use of the auxiliary *avere* with reflexive verbs is common in older Italian, as every reader of the poem knows by now).   *Deh, chi siete?* This is a much-debated reading. Some would have the question in the singular, since the answer is in the first person, and accordingly propose readings such as "Di' chi se' tu" and variants thereof. But Petrocchi's note on the manuscript evidence and on the sense of the question in the plural is persuasive. The pilgrim wants to know more about the whole group of souls. The present speaker has already served as the spokesman for the group as a whole (cf. a similar situation in *Par.* III, 40-41), and others will speak out (in the next canto), identifying themselves.

46-48. *E quanta e quale . . . sue*: The light, which is the radiance that hides the soul, increases in size ("quanta") and in intensity ("quale") in anticipation of the happiness this soul will feel in answering Dante's question.

46. *piùe = più* (the familiar epenthesis).

49. *Così fatta*: In the increase of joy.

49-50. *Il mondo m'ebbe giù poco tempo*: Charles Martel, the speaker, who will now identify himself with ample references, died at the age of twenty-four.

51. *molto sarà di mal, che non sarebbe*: "Much evil which shall be would not have befallen." For the curious construction, cf. *Par.* VI, 142.

54. *quasi animal di sua seta fasciato*: A silkworm.

55-57. *Assai m'amasti . . . fronde*: "In the spring of 1294 Charles Martel visited Florence with a brilliant retinue, and was received with unprecedented magnificence, as G. Villani relates in his *Croniche*, VIII, xiii. We may infer from the present canto that our poet then made his personal acquaintance. Indeed, we are justified in conjecturing that Charles, on this occasion, heard and applauded Dante's *canzone* (the first in the *Convivio*), *Voi che 'ntendendo il terzo ciel movete*, which was presumably the great literary novelty in Florence at the time of his visit; for he greets Dante in heaven with a reference to this poem. This episode affords, then, a clue to the date of composition of the *canzone* in question. When they met in Santa Maria Novella, Dante won the admiration of Charles by his perfect calligraphy, and was offered the post of *dictator pulcherrimus*" (Gr).

56-57. *io ti mostrava . . . fronde*: I should have shown you the fruit of my love.

58-84. *Quella sinistra riva . . . arca*: The spirit amply identifies himself as Charles Martel. The eldest son of Charles II of Naples and Mary of Hungary, he was born in 1271 and died in 1295 at the age of twenty-four. In September 1289 his father created him vicar of the realm, and in 1292 he was invested by his mother with the kingdom of Hungary. In 1287 he married Clemence of Habsburg, daughter of the Emperor Rudolf I. The date of his death, August 1295, is proved by a letter written, under the date August 30, 1295, by Boniface VIII to Mary of Hungary, appointing her regent of the kingdom of Naples and condoling with her on the death of her son. For the text of the letter, see P. Toynbee (1968), p. 145.

58-60. *Quella sinistra riva . . . m'aspettava*: "Provence, which lies on the left of the Rhone below its confluence with the Sorgue, was the dowry of Beatrice, wife of Charles of Anjou, Charles Martel's grandfather: cf. VI, 133-134; *Purg.* XX, 61-62" (Gr).

61. *quel corno*: The verb "m'aspettava" is understood as repeated.   *Ausonia*: A name for Italy used by the Latin poets.

61-62. *s'imborga di Bari . . . Catona*: "*S' imborga*, 'is skirted': *borghi* means 'outskirts,' 'suburbs'" (Gr). Dante uses the towns of Bari, Gaeta, and Catona to indicate the eastern, western, and southern confines of the kingdom of Naples, won by Charles of Anjou.

63. *da ove*: "From the point where."   *Tronto e Verde in mare sgorga*: The rivers Tronto, on the east side, and Verde (now called the Liri or Garigliano), on the west, separate the kingdom of Naples from the Papal States at the north.

64. *Fulgeami = mi fulgeva*.

65-66. *quella terra . . . abbandona*: Hungary.

67. *Trinacria*: Sicily, conquered by Charles of Anjou. *caliga*: " 'Is darkened' by clouds of smoke from Etna" (Gr).

68-69. *tra Pachino e Peloro . . . briga*: Cape Passero (Pachynus) is at the southeast point of the island of Sicily, and Cape Faro (Pelorus) is at the northeast extremity of the island. Eurus was the name given by the ancients to the east or southeast wind.

70. *non per Tifeo ma per nascente solfo*: "The darkness from Etna is not due, as Ovid sang (*Met.*, V, 346-356), to the struggles of the giant Typhoeus, buried under the whole island of Sicily, but is caused by the effect of the sun's heat

on 'sulphur in formation'" (Gr). See Ristoro d'Arezzo, *Della comp.* VII, iv, 7 (pp. 217-19).

71–75. *attesi avrebbe . . . mora*: "Sicily would now be awaiting a line of kings descended from Charles of Anjou and Rudolph of Hapsburg (respectively the grandfather and the father-in-law of Charles Martel), if the revolution of 1282, called the Sicilian Vespers, breaking out in Palermo with the cry 'Death to the French!' had not driven Charles's people from the island and given the crown to Peter III of Aragon" (Gr).

72. *per me*: Through Charles Martel.

73. *mala segnoria*: The tyrannical government of Charles I. *accora*: "Afflicts."

76–78. *E se mio frate . . . offendesse*: "Charles Martel's brother Robert succeeded his father, Charles II, in 1309; he had been chosen for the succession before 1300. Robert, who had spent some years as a hostage for his father in Spain, is represented as having adopted the traditional miserliness of Catalonia" (Gr). Or, as other commentators contend, the "avara povertà di Catalogna" may refer to the miserliness of Catalan officials appointed by Charles to high positions.

78. *fuggeria = fuggerebbe. li = gli.*

80. *per lui, o per altrui = da lui o da altrui.*

80–81. *sì ch'a sua barca . . . pogna*: That even more burdens (administrative difficulties) not be added to the ship of state that he, Robert, will inherit and pilot and that is already "laden" with troubles.

81. *pogna = ponga.*

82–84. *La sua natura . . . arca*: Robert's "stingy" nature descended from a "lavish" one. The reference may be to Charles II, or perhaps to Robert's grandfather, Charles of Anjou, since Charles II is judged to be avaricious in *Purg.* XX, 79-84 and is repeatedly condemned by Dante.

83. *milizia*: From the Latin *milites*, which, under the emperors, had the meaning of "court-officials."

84. *mettere in arca*: "To put [money] into the chest," "to fill the coffer"—either his or their own—by oppression of the people.

85. *Però = perciò*.

85-90. *Però ch'i' credo . . . Dio*: Sapegno paraphrases the meaning of these verses thus: "Since I believe that the great joy which your words give me is seen by you in God, the beginning and end of all good, with the same clarity as I see it in myself (and without my seeking to express it in a way that would be inadequate in any case), that joy is the dearer to me; moreover, this increase of joy is also dear to me since you discern it by gazing, as one of the blessed, on God."

88. *per te si veggia = da te si veda*.

91. *mi fa chiaro = fammi chiaro* (imperative), *chiariscimi*.

93. *com' esser può, di dolce seme, amaro*: "How bitter [fruit] can come from sweet seed," as in the case of Robert (see vss. 82-84).

95. *un vero = una verità*.

95-96. *a quel che tu dimandi . . . dosso*: You will have before your eyes the explanation of the point that puzzles you now and that you are turning your back on. Cf. vs. 136.

97-99. *Lo ben . . . grandi*: The whole concept expressed in these verses is a variation on a familiar theme. Cf. *Par.* II, 112-48, especially. But now the accent is on providence rather than on the process of transmission of the power by God.

97. *Lo ben*: God.   *il regno che tu scandi*: "The realm that you ascend," i.e., the heavenly spheres. "Scandi" is a Latinism, from *scandere*, "to climb," "to ascend."

98-99. *fa esser virtute . . . grandi*: "Makes Its providence to be a power ['virtute'] in these great bodies" (the planets

155

and the stars). Cf. Deut. 4:19: "ne forte elevatis oculis ad caelum, videas solem et lunam et omnia astra caeli, et errore deceptus adores ea et colas quae creavit Dominus Deus tuus in ministerium cunctis gentibus quae sub caelo sunt" ("and when you look up to the heavens and behold the sun and the moon and all the stars in the heavens and deceived by error you adore them and worship that which the Lord your God created for the lot of all nations under the heavens").

100–102. *E non pur . . . salute*: Sapegno paraphrases the meaning thus: "In the divine mind, which is perfect in itself, the various natures are *provedute*, that is, *prevedute*, determined, not only in respect to their being, but also in respect to the disposition to fulfill their place in the universal order, this disposition being their welfare (*salute*)."

103–5. *per che quantunque . . . diretta*: Again the archery figure to express the divine teleology, everywhere visible in His created universe. See *Par*. I, 125-26 and the corresponding note.

106. *il ciel*: The heavens, plural. Cf. "regno," vs. 97. *cammine = cammini*.

107. *producerebbe = produrrebbe*. *li suoi effetti*: "Its effects" (on the world below).

108. *che non sarebbero arti, ma ruine*: If God's providence were not directing the whole order and operation, the result would be not His art, but chaos, a "ruination."

109–11. *se li 'ntelletti . . . perfetti*: The whole statement in the "if" clause is unthinkable. Defect in the subordinate Intelligences would imply defect in God, which is impossible.

109. *li 'ntelletti*: The angels (Intelligences) who turn these spheres by intellection. See vs. 37.

110. *manchi*: "Deficient."

111. *il primo*: I.e., *intelletto*, God.

112. *ti s'imbianchi*: "Be made clear to you."

113. *Non già*: I.e., *no certo*, "certainly not."

114. *la natura*: In this present context, "natura" includes God (*natura naturans*) and nature in the sense of *natura naturata* or the total order of creation. See *Questio de aqua et terra* XLIV, where Dante writes:

> Propter quod sciendum est quod Natura universalis non frustratur suo fine; unde, licet natura particularis aliquando propter inobedientiam materie ab intento fine frustretur, Natura tamen universalis nullo modo potest a sua intentione deficere, cum Nature universali equaliter actus et potentia rerum, que possunt esse et non esse, subiaceant.

> And therefore be it known that universal nature is not baulked of her goal. And so, though particular nature may be baulked of her intended goal by the recalcitrance of matter, yet universal nature can in no sort fail of her intention, since both the actuality and the potentiality of things which may be or not be, are equally subject to universal nature.

The argument is a familiar one in scholastic thought deriving from Aristotle. See also *Conv.* IV, xxiv, 10 and *De mon.* I, x, 1: "cum Deus et natura in necessariis non deficiat" ("since God and nature fails not in things necessary").

115–16. *sarebbe il peggio . . . cive*: The argument now turns to the social order among men on earth and derives, of course, from Aristotle. See *Polit.* I, 1, 1253ᵃ: "Homo natura civile animal est." ("Man is by nature a social animal.")

116. *cive*: Citizen, a social being, one who is part of a social order. From the Latin *civis*.

117. *cheggio = chiedo*.

118–19. *E puot' elli . . . offici?* Can he, man, be a citizen, i.e., live a civil life, if the social order is not made up of many different natures and functions?

120. *'l maestro vostro*: Aristotle. Dante's statement in the

Convivio (IV, iv, 1-2) of Aristotle's thought in this regard may serve as gloss here:

Lo fondamento radicale de la imperiale maiestade, secondo lo vero, è la necessità de la umana civilitade, che a uno fine è ordinata, cioè a vita felice; a la quale nullo per sè è sufficiente a venire sanza l'aiutorio d'alcuno, con ciò sia cosa che l'uomo abbisogna di molte cose, a le quali uno solo satisfare non può. E però dice lo Filosofo che l'uomo naturalmente è compagnevole animale. E sì come un uomo a sua sufficienza richiede compagnia dimestica di famiglia, così una casa a sua sufficienza richiede una vicinanza: altrimenti molti difetti sosterrebbe che sarebbero impedimento di felicitade. E però che una vicinanza [a] sé non può in tutto satisfare, conviene a satisfacimento di quella essere la cittade. Ancora la cittade richiede a le sue arti e a le sue difensioni vicenda avere e fratellanza con le circavicine cittadi; e però fu fatto lo regno.

The root foundation of the imperial majesty is in truth the necessity of human civility; which is ordained for a certain end, to wit the life of felicity; to the which no man is sufficient to attain by himself without the aid of any, inasmuch as man hath need of many things which no one is able to provide alone.

Wherefore the Philosopher saith that man is by nature a social animal. And as an individual man requires the companionship of home and household for his completeness, so likewise a household requires a district for its completeness, since otherwise it would suffer many defects which would be a hindrance to felicity. And since a district cannot satisfy itself in everything, needs must there be a city for its satisfaction. And further the city requires for its arts and for its defence to have mutual relations and brotherhood with the neighbouring cities; wherefore the kingdom was instituted.

121. *quici* = *qui*.

123. *effetti*: "Works."   *radici*: The "roots" are the dispositions of men.

124–26. *per ch'un nasce . . . perse*: "One is born a legisla-
tor, or Solon; another a general, or Xerxes; another a priest,
or Melchisedech (Gen. xiv, 18); another a mechanic, or
Daedalus (who lost his son Icarus while they were flying
through the air: cf. *Inf*. XVII, 109-111)" (Gr).

127–29. *La circular natura . . . ostello*: Nature is here re-
garded as the operation of the heavens that turn about the
earth, hence "circular" or "revolving" nature. This nature
now becomes, through metaphor, a "stamp" on "the mortal
wax," i.e., men, and this is part of Nature's "art," which is
well performed. But even though Nature stamps well, she
makes no distinctions between individuals with respect to
lineage. "Ostello"—literally, "inn"—is the individual who
receives the stellar influence.

130–32. *Quinci addivien . . . Marte*: "Esau and Jacob,
though brothers, were radically different from the start: Gen.
xxv, 21-27. Quirinus, or Romulus, was the son of such a poor
father that his paternity was ascribed to the god Mars" (Gr).

133. *Natura generata*: The character of the offspring.

134. *a' generanti*: The parents.

135. *se non vincesse il proveder divino*: But God's provi-
dence intervenes, through the *virtù* that descends from Him
through the heavens, and prevents the constant and uniform
descent of the nature and character from parent to offspring.

136. *Or quel che t'era dietro t'è davanti*: Cf. vs. 96.

137. *di te mi giova*: "I delight in you."

138. *un corollario voglio che t'ammanti*: " 'I will have thee
cloak thyself in a corollary.' The corollary is added to the
demonstration, as a cloak to a suit of clothes. Cf. *Purg*.
XXVIII, 136" (Gr). See Boethius, *Consol. philos*. III, x, ll.
81-83: "Veluti geometrae solent demonstratis propositis
aliquid inferre . . . ita ego quoque tibi veluti corollarium
dabo." ("As the geometricians are wont, out of their propo-
sitions which they have demonstrated, to infer . . . so will I
give thee as it were a *corollarium*.")

139–41. *Sempre natura . . . prova*: "Natura" is now used in the sense of "natura generata" (vs. 133), the natural disposition of the individual when born.

140. *com' ogne altra semente*: The natural order of this principle is stressed by an image clearly from nature, that of the seed that falls on a soil or into a place or climate not suited to it.

142–44. *E se 'l mondo . . . gente*: If mortals would only heed the foundation that nature lays (the given character and disposition of the individual child), then in consequence people would be good, i.e., the seed (to recall the metaphor) would grow as it should.

145–46. *Ma voi torcete . . . spada*: But you mortals twist to religion, i.e., force to become a monk or a priest, one who is born to gird on the sword, to be a warrior.

146. *fia = sarà* (connoting possibility, as in modern Italian).

147. *tal ch'è da sermone*: This seems a clear reference to Robert, Charles' brother (vs. 76), who was much given to writing sermons and whom Villani (XII, 10) terms "grandissimo maestro in teologia" ("a very great master in theology").

148. *onde la traccia vostra è fuor di strada*: Hence your mortal way strays from the right path. "The condensed argument of the reply of Charles Martel to Dante's question is made the more difficult to follow, because of the various meanings in which the word *nature* is employed. First, in v. 100 *natures* signify the products of Nature in its generic sense; in v. 114 *Nature* stands for the personified order of the created world; in v. 127 'the circular nature' is equivalent to the system of the spheres; in vv. 133 and 139 *nature* is used for the individual creature, though in the latter instance it is held by many commentators to signify Nature with the same meaning which it has in v. 142, where the word is employed in its generic and personified sense" (Norton).

CANTO IX

1. *Clemenza*: The Clemence whom the poet apostrophizes here may be either the wife or the daughter of Charles Martel of Hungary, and there is considerable doubt among commentators as to which Clemence the poet is addressing. Charles' wife, Clemence of Habsburg, daughter of the Emperor Rudolf I, died in 1295, in the same epidemic that claimed her royal husband's life when he was only twenty-four years of age. Therefore, in the fictional time of the poem, Charles and Clemence had both died five years before. Would the poet address in this fashion a Clemence, spouse of Charles, who was already dead? Some commentators have held this to be unlikely, and have therefore argued that Charles' daughter is intended, Clemence of Anjou, who was born of Charles and Clemence of Habsburg at Naples in 1293, and who was married to King Louis X of France in 1315, and lived until 1328. Thus, in addressing the daughter, the poet would be addressing a living Clemence.

The arguments for and against the one identification and the other are many. Any reader interested in exploring them will find them expounded in the *Enciclopedia dantesca* under the entries "Clemenza d'Asburgo" and "Clemenza d'Angiò." All things considered, and despite some serious objections to be reckoned with, Clemence of Habsburg, spouse of Charles, would seem the more likely candidate. A strong argument in favor of this choice is the address *"tuo,"* which is more properly said to a *wife* than to a *daughter*, and *"vostri"* (vs. 6) likewise seems to point to husband and wife, rather than to father and daughter. However, no conclusive proof is available.

3. *la sua semenza*: His son, Charles Robert (Carobert), who was king of Hungary from 1308 to 1342. Born in 1288, he was the son of Charles Martel and Clemence of Habsburg. On the death of Otto of Bavaria (in 1308) he succeeded to the throne of Hungary, of which his father had been titular king (1292-95), and on the death (in 1309) of his grandfather, Charles II, he claimed the throne of Naples also; his claim, however, was disputed by his uncle Robert (eldest surviving son of Charles II), who appealed in person to Pope Clement V and, obtaining a decision in his favor, was crowned king of Naples at Avignon, June 1309 (Villani, VIII, 112), his nephew being at the same time recognized by Clement as king of Hungary. Dante is referring, in vss. 2-3, to the fact that Charles Robert was deprived of his right of succession to the throne of Naples.

4. *muover*: Other editors have "volger" instead. See Petrocchi's justification of "muover" in his vol. I, *Introduzione*, pp. 231-32.

5-6. *pianto giusto*: "A just punishment," literally "just lamentation."

6. *ai vostri danni*: Readers of the translation should note the plural "vostri" here.

7. *la vita*: The soul. Cf. *Par.* XII, 127.

8. *al Sol*: To God.

9. *tanto*: "Sufficient."

10. *fatture*: "Creatures," "men." Cf. *Purg.* XVII, 102.

11. *sì fatto ben*: God, as referred to in the verses immediately preceding.

1. Hungary and surrounding area

12. *le vostre tempie*: "Your faces," "your eyes" (literally, "brows").

14. *'l suo voler piacermi*: The object of "significava" in the following verse.

18. *fermi = mi fecero.*

19–21. *Deh, metti al mio voler . . . penso*: Dante begs the unknown soul to answer without waiting to be questioned.

22. *nova*: Unknown.

23. *cantava*: Cf. *Par*. VIII, 28-30.

24. *seguette — seguì.   a cui — colui al quale.*

25–26. *la terra prava italica*: All Italy is judged by these words.

26–27. *che siede tra Rialto . . . Piava*: The March of Treviso, in the northeast corner of Italy, lies between Venice (indicated here by the Rialto, the largest of the islands on which the city is built) and the Alps, where the rivers Brenta and Piave have their source.

27. *Brenta*: See n. to *Inf*. XV, 7.   *Piava*: The Piave, a river of northern Italy, which rises in the Carnic Alps and flowing south and southeast through Venetia falls into the Gulf of Venice some twenty miles from Venice.

28. *colle*: The hill of Romano whereon the castle of the Ezzelino family stood.

29–30. *una facella . . . assalto*: The "torch" or scourge of mankind is Ezzelino (or Azzolino) III da Romano, the most infamous and bloodthirsty of the petty tyrants of medieval Italy (cf. *Inf*. XII, 110). He was born in 1194, in the little hill town of Romano, and died in 1259. Ezzelino extended his cruel rule beyond the March of Treviso and over much of the Venetian territory, as far as Mantua and Trent.

31. *D'una radice*: Of the same parents.   *ella*: The "facella" (Ezzelino).

32. *Cunizza*: A sister of the Ghibelline Ezzelino III da Romano and youngest daughter of Ezzelino II and Adelaide di Mangona, Cunizza was born *ca.* 1198 and in 1222 was married, for political reasons, to the Guelph captain Count Riccardo di San Bonifazio of Verona. Shortly after her marriage she became enamored of the troubadour Sordello, by whom (*ca.* 1226), with the connivance of her brother, she was abducted from Verona and conveyed back to Ezzelino's court. Her intrigue with Sordello did not last long (although it appears to have been renewed later at Treviso), and she then went to the court of her brother Alberico at Treviso, where she abandoned herself to a knight named Bonio, with whom, according to the old chronicler Rolandino (*Cronica* I, 3, p. 18) she wandered about the world, leading a life of pleasure.

After the death of Bonio, who was slain while defending Treviso on behalf of Alberico against his brother Ezzelino, Cunizza was married by the latter to Aimerio, count of Breganze; after his death, he having fallen a victim to a quarrel with Ezzelino, she married a gentleman of Verona; and subsequently she married a fourth husband in the person of Salione Buzzacarini of Padua, Ezzelino's astrologer. In or about 1260, both Ezzelino and Alberico being dead, and the fortunes of her house being at a low ebb, Cunizza went to reside in Florence, where in 1265, in the house of Cavalcante de' Cavalcanti, the father of Dante's friend Guido, she executed a deed granting their freedom to her father's and brothers' slaves, with the exception of those who had been concerned in the betrayal of Alberico. In 1279, being then about eighty, she made her will, whereby she bequeathed her possessions to the sons of Count Alessandro degli Alberti of Mangona, her mother's family. She probably died not long after this date, no further mention of her having been preserved.

33. *esta stella*: Venus.

34–36. *ma lietamente . . . vulgo*: I condone the fact that I was so much under the influence of the planet Venus, indeed it pains me not at all ("e non mi noia"), which fact would be hard ("forte") for men on earth to understand.

37–39. *Di questa luculenta . . . rimase*: The reference will soon be clear, for the light to whom she refers will be the next to speak.

40. *questo centesimo anno ancor s'incinqua*: "This centennial year shall yet be fived," shall return five times, i.e., five centuries shall pass. The year is 1300.

42. *altra vita*: "Altra vita" (a life of fame on earth) is the object of "relinqua" ("shall leave"). Cf. *Par.* XVII, 98, 119-20.

43–44. *la turba presente . . . richiude*: The March of Treviso is designated by the two rivers which bound it on east and west respectively, the Tagliamento and the Adige.

46–48. *ma tosto fia . . . crude*: Padua is a city of Venezia Euganea in northeast Italy, on the Bacchiglione (which joins the Brenta a few miles south of Padua), west of Venice and southeast of Vicenza. It claims to be the oldest city in Italy and to have been founded shortly after the fall of Troy by the Trojan Antenor. On February 12, 1237 Ezzelino IV da Romano, with the help of Frederick II and the Ghibellines, obtained possession of the city, but, on the proclamation of the crusade against him by Pope Alexander IV in 1256, he was expelled by the Paduan Guelphs and the Venetians. After the death of Ezzelino in 1259, the Guelphs of Padua asserted their independence and conquered Vicenza (1265), whence, however, they were driven out, in 1314, by Can Grande della Scala, who was at that time imperial vicar in Vicenza.

47. *Vincenza*: Vicenza is a town in northern Italy, in Venetia, on the Bacchiglione, northeast of Verona and northwest of Padua. The water that bathes it is the Bacchiglione, which actually forms swamps around the city.

48. *per essere al dover le genti crude*: "Because the people are stubborn against duty" which is owed to the imperial authority.

49. *dove Sile e Cagnan s'accompagna*: The Sile and the

Cagnano (which is now known as the Botteniga) are two small rivers in upper Italy in Venetia. They unite at Treviso.

50–51. *tal signoreggia . . . ragna*: The reference is to Rizzardo da Camino, son of Gherardo da Camino (see *Purg.* XVI, 124), whom he succeeded in the lordship of Treviso in 1306, having shared the office with his father from 1300 on; he married Giovanna, daughter of Nino Visconti of Pisa, and was (according to the most trustworthy accounts) murdered in 1312 by a half-witted servitor, while playing at chess in his own palace with Alteniero degli Azzoni, who had planned the assassination in order to avenge the honor of his wife, whom Rizzardo had seduced.

52–54. *Piangerà Feltro . . . Malta*: The main facts of the incident referred to appear to be as follows. In 1314, while Alessandro Novello of Treviso was bishop of Feltre (1298-1320), certain Ferrarese Ghibellines of the house of Fontana, having failed in a conspiracy against Pino della Tosa, King Robert's vicar in Ferrara, took refuge in Feltre and placed themselves under the protection of the bishop. The latter, however, on the requisition of Pino, delivered them up (in July of that year), and they were taken back to Ferrara and publicly executed with their confederates (thirty in all). By this act of treachery the bishop incurred such great odium that he was forced to quit Feltre and retire into a monastery, where he died in 1320.

54. *Malta*: Malta is the name of several different prisons. On an island in Lake Bolsena was a dungeon of that name, for guilty prelates. See the *Enciclopedia dantesca* under the entry "Malta." See also M. Antonelli (1921).

55. *bigoncia*: "Vat."

59. *parte*: "Party" (Guelph).

61. *Troni*: The Thrones are the angels that direct the seventh sphere, the heaven of Saturn.

62. *onde refulge a noi Dio giudicante*: These angels are executors of God's judgments. Thomas Aquinas (*Summa*

theol. I, q. 108, a. 6, resp.) notes: "*Throni* dicuntur secundum Gregorium . . . *per quos Deus sua iudicia exercet.*" ("The *Thrones*, according to Gregory . . . are so called *because through them God accomplishes His judgments.*") See Gregory, *Homil.* XXXIV, 10.

63. *sì che questi parlar ne paion buoni*: "We see mirrored in the Thrones the punishment that God has in store for the sinners, and therefore we can speak with satisfaction of their misdeeds" (Gr).

65. *rota*: The round dance of bright souls.

67. *letizia*: The happy spirit mentioned in vs. 37.

69. *balasso*: A kind of ruby that took its name from the region in Asia from which it was imported, Arabic *balakṣh,* the modern Persian province of Badakhshān.   *percuota*: The subjunctive form expresses the hypothetical.

70. *Per letiziar là sù fulgor s'acquista*: Cf. *Par.* V, 126.

71. *qui*: On earth.   *giù*: In Hell. Some commentators, however, take "giù" to refer also to those on earth.

73. *s'inluia*: A word made up by Dante, from the pronoun *lui*, meaning "hims itself," i.e., identifies itself with him. Cf. vs. 81 for other similar forms.

74–75. *nulla voglia . . . fuia*: "No wish can be a thief of itself [can steal or secrete itself] from you," i.e., you can see my wish in God. For another example of *fuia* in this sense, cf. Inf. XII, 90.

77. *fuochi*: The Seraphim, ministers of divine love.

78. *sei ali*: For the six wings of the Seraphim, see Isa. 6:2, and for the six wings of the fallen seraph, Satan, see *Inf.* XXXIV, 46.   *coculla*: The gown and hood of a monk, the whole outer garment.

81. *s'io m'intuassi, come tu t'inmii*: "If I could *thou* me, as thou *meest* thee." The verbs are constructed, in the same fashion as that in vs. 73, from *tu* and *mi*.

82. *La maggior valle*: The Mediterranean, which was thought to extend from west to east 90° or a quarter of the earth's circumference.

84. *quel mar che la terra inghirlanda*: The great ocean which was thought to surround all the land.

85. *discordanti*: "Inharmonious," varied.   *contra 'l sole*: "As the opening of the sea is at the west end, it is thought of as stretching from west to east" (Gr).

86–87. *che fa meridiano . . . suole*: "The meridian of any place is a great circle passing through its zenith and nadir and the two celestial poles. The horizon of a place is a great heavenly circle midway between its zenith and its nadir, the plane of the circle being at right angles to that of the meridian. The two circles are, then, 90° apart. When the water enters the Mediterranean, at the Strait, its zenith is that of Gibraltar and its horizon traverses the zenith of Jerusalem: but when it reaches the eastern end of the sea, its meridian is that of Jerusalem and its horizon passes through the zenith of Gibraltar" (Gr).

88. *litorano*: "Shore-dweller."

89–90. *tra Ebro e Macra . . . Toscano*: Between the Spanish river Ebro and the Italian Magra or Macra. Cf. *Inf.* XXIV, 145; *Purg.* VIII, 116. The Magra, which under the Roman Empire, from the time of Augustus, formed the boundary between Liguria and Etruria, in Dante's day divided the Genoese territory from Tuscany for a relatively short distance ("per cammin corto").

92. *Buggea*: Bougie, a town in North Africa, in Algeria, on the gulf of the same name. In the Middle Ages it was a very important commercial port, its chief article of export being wax and wax candles, whence the latter came to be known as "bougies." Bougie is situated about 115 miles east of Algiers and is on almost the same meridian as Marseilles.
la terra: The city, Marseilles.

93. *che fé del sangue suo già caldo il porto*: In 49 B.C. there

was a fierce naval battle in the harbor of Marseilles between Caesar's fleet and the local supporters of Pompey. See *Purg.* XVIII, 101-2. Also see *Phars.* III, 572-73, where Lucan writes: "Cruor altus in unda / Spumat, et obducti concreto sanguine fluctus." ("Their blood foamed deep upon the wave, and a crust of gore covered the sea.")

94. *Folco*: Folquet de Marseille, famous Provençal troubadour who flourished as a poet from 1180 to 1195, was born *ca.* 1160 and died in 1231. According to the old Provençal biography, he was the son of a rich merchant of Genoa, who bequeathed him a large fortune. Devoting himself to a life of pleasure, Folquet became a frequenter of courts, his special patrons being Richard Coeur de Lion, Alfonso VIII of Castile, Raymond V, count of Toulouse, and Barral de Baux, viscount of Marseilles and lord of the city (1188-92). He attached himself and paid court to the wife of the last, composing songs in her honor, but she appears to have rejected his addresses. After her death and the deaths of the princes whose favor he had enjoyed, Folquet retired from the world and became (*ca.* 1195) a Cistercian monk; he persuaded his wife to enter a convent with their two sons. In 1201 he became an abbot in the diocese of Toulon and in 1205 was appointed bishop of Toulouse. In the latter capacity he was deeply implicated in the sanguinary persecution of the Albigensian heretics (1208-29).

96. *imprenta*: Cf. *Par.* VII, 69.   *com' io fe' di lui*: "As I did [i.e., was stamped] with it."

97. *la figlia di Belo*: Dido. See n. to *Inf.* V, 61-62.

98. *noiando e a Sicheo e a Creusa*: Dido, by her passion for Aeneas, wronged her dead husband, Sichaeus, and Aeneas' dead wife, Creusa.

99. *di me, infin che si convenne al pelo*: "Than I did, as long as it befitted my hair," i.e., until I turned gray.

100–101. *né quella Rodopea . . . Demofoonte*: The Thracian princess Phyllis, thinking herself forsaken by her lover

Demophoön, son of Theseus, hanged herself. Cf. Ovid, *Heroides* II, 147-48.

100. *Rodopea*: Pronounced *Rodopéa*. Rhodope is the name of a mountain range on the edge of Thrace near which Phyllis lived.

101–2. *né Alcide . . . rinchiusa*: Alcides was Hercules, grandson of Alcaeus and son of Jupiter and Alcmene. He lost his life as a result of his infatuation for the Thessalian princess Iole. See Ovid, *Heroides* IX. Cf. *Inf.* XII, 67-68.

103–5. *Non però . . . provide*: "The memory of sin is removed by Lethe, although the souls, seeing all things in God, have an objective knowledge of their past wickedness, and recognize the eternal fitness of the dispositions originally given them by the stars" (Gr). See Thomas Aquinas, *Summa theol.* III, Suppl., q. 87; Augustine, *De civ. Dei* XXII, xxx, 4. See also E. G. Gardner (1913), p. 73.

103. *però = perciò*.

105. *valor*: Divine power.

107. *cotanto affetto*: The subject of "addorna" of which "l'arte" is the object. *discernesi = si discerne*.
'l bene: The divine goodness.

108. *per che 'l mondo di sù quel di giù torna*: "By reason of which the world below [mankind] again becomes the world above." A difficult and much discussed line. It should be noted, in favor of this interpretation, that the verb ("torna") in rhyme must not have the same meaning in the two verses in which it appears (a rule not to be violated). The reference is to the "harvest out of time" which comes about through the turning of the spheres and their influence on human creatures, and this is a result of God's love ("affetto"); for He, loving Creator that He is, wishes every soul that He creates to return to Him. His providence works through the operation of the spheres on the world below, whence the elect return to Him.

109. *piene*: "Entirely satisfied."

112. *lumera*: "Light."

114. *mera = pure.*

115-16. *Or sappi che . . . Raab*: "The story of Rahab is re-
lated in Joshua ii. When Joshua was trying to take Jericho,
he sent to the city two spies, who lodged in the house of 'an
harlot named Rahab.' Their presence becoming known to the
enemy, their hostess saved them by sending the pursuers on
a false clue, hiding her guests on the roof of the house, and,
when the coast was clear, letting them 'down by a cord
through the window, for her house was upon the town wall.'
In return, they promised safety for her and her relatives when
Jericho should fall; as a token, she was to 'bind' a 'line of
scarlet thread in the window.' Her service resulted in the vic-
tory of the Children of Israel; and when the city was cursed,
Joshua proclaimed (vi, 17): 'Only Rahab the harlot shall
live, she and all that are with her in the house, because she
hid the messengers that we sent.' Thus, too, she won salva-
tion, and, according to Dante, was the first soul 'assumed' by
the heaven of Venus, when the Hebrew spirits were liberated
from Limbus. 'Likewise also was not Rahab the harlot justi-
fied by works,' says James ii, 25, 'when she had received the
messengers and had sent them out another way?' And in
Hebrews xi, 31, we read: 'By faith the harlot Rahab perished
not with them that believed not.' In the allegorical exposition
of the Scriptures, Joshua often figures as a symbol of Christ,
while Rahab is sometimes interpreted as the Church, which
he saved by the 'scarlet thread' of his blood" (Gr).

116-17. *e a nostr' ordine . . . si sigilla*: " 'And, she being
united to our order, it (the order) is sealed with her in the
highest degree.' Rahab is the supreme representative of our
order of beatitude" (Gr).

118-19. *Da questo cielo . . . face*: "The earth's conical
shadow reaches the sphere of Venus and touches the planet
when Venus is at its least, but not when it is at its greatest,
distance from our globe: cf. *Conv.*, II, vi, 10. The shadow,

according to Ptolemy and Alfraganus, is 871,000 miles long" (Gr). See P. Toynbee (1902), pp. 76-77; E. Moore (1903), p. 30. The shadow reaches no farther than Venus, hence it falls only over the first three heavens, wherein are seen spirits who were too much influenced by mundane inclinations.

119-20. *pria ch'altr' alma . . . assunta*: The triumph of Christ here referred to is His harrowing of Hell (cf. *Inf.* IV, 46-63), when (as we now learn) Rahab was among those who were taken to Heaven by Christ, indeed, was the first to be chosen for such a triumph.

121-22. *Ben si convenne . . . cielo*: "It was indeed fitting to leave her, in some heaven." This is to be understood symbolically, of course, for Rahab dwells in the Empyrean with all the blessed, but was "left in" (i.e., "assigned to") the heaven of Venus (cf. *Par.* IV, 28-48) and accordingly has descended with the other souls influenced by this planet to meet the pilgrim on his upward way.

122-23. *l'alta vittoria . . . palma*: Christ's great victory over Hell by the Crucifixion, when His hands (*palme*) were nailed to the Cross.

124. *favorò = favorì.*

124-25. *la prima gloria . . . Terra Santa*: Joshua was the successor of Moses and conqueror of the land of Canaan.

126. *che poco tocca al papa la memoria*: Which (the Holy Land) is well-nigh forgotten by the pope. This judgment is then repeated in vs. 137.

127-29. *La tua città . . . pianta*: Florence is a "plant" of the devil.

128-29. *che pria . . . pianta*: Satan was the first creature to turn away from God, and in his fallen and evil condition he envied Adam and Eve, causing them to sin—with such lamentable consequences for humankind.

129. *e di cui è la 'nvidia tanto pianta*: See Sapien. 2:24: "Invidia autem diaboli mors introivit in orbem terrarum."

("But by the envy of the devil, death entered the world.")
Cf. *Inf.* I, 111.

130. *il maladetto fiore*: The florin, coined by Florence, which was imprinted on one side with the lily.

131. *le pecore e li agni*: The Christian flock.

132. *però che = perciò che.   fatto ha lupo del pastore*: Avidity for riches has turned the pope and ecclesiastics generally into greedy wolves, and they thus set an example for their flock. Cf. *Inf.* VII, 46-48; *Purg.* XVI, 100-102.

133. *Per questo*: Because of this greed for riches.

133–35. *Per questo . . . studia*: The decretals are the papal decrees or epistles, usually written in reply to some question of general ecclesiastical law. They form the groundwork of a large part of the law of the Church. A compilation of them, with additions of his own, was issued by Pope Gregory IX in 1234 and, with further additions, by Pope Boniface VIII in 1298 and again, in 1314, by Pope Clement V. Previously, sometime before 1150, Gratian of Bologna had published his *Decretum*, a general collection of canons, papal epistles, and sentences of fathers, in imitation of the *Pandectae*. This work appears to have been the chief authority on the canon law in the Middle Ages. The code of the papal decretals was promulgated as the great statute law of Christendom, superior in its authority to all secular laws. The book of Gregory's decretals was issued as the authorized text to be used in all courts and schools of law.

The dative "ai Decretali" is used with "si studia," as with the Latin *studere*, i.e., "men busy themselves about." The decretals are studied for financial profit. Cf. Dante, *Epist.* XI, 16; *De mon.* III, iii, 9-11.

135. *sì che pare a' lor vivagni*: As is evident from their margins, full of notes and much worn.

136. *intende*: The verb in the singular serves a double subject.

137–38. *Nazarette . . . l'ali*: Nazareth, in the Holy Land, scene of the Annunciation, where Gabriel "opened his wings" before Mary, in an attitude of homage which many painters have represented.

139. *Vaticano*: The Vatican hill at Rome, on the right bank of the Tiber, where St. Peter's basilica (San Pietro in Vaticano) and the Vatican palace are located. The latter has been the usual residence of the popes ever since the return from Avignon in the latter part of the fourteenth century, the papal residence in Dante's time having been the Lateran palace. The Vatican hill, as having been the reputed scene of the martyrdom of Peter and of numbers of the early Christians, is held to be the most sacred quarter of all Rome. *l'altre parti elette*: The holy places of Rome, where the followers of Peter were tortured, slain, and buried.

142. *avoltero = adultèro, adulterio*. Cf. *Inf*. XIX, 1-4; *Purg*. XXXIII, 37-45.

CANTO X

1–3. *Guardando nel suo Figlio . . . Valore*: As almost always in the poem (see the inscription of the gate of Hell, *Inf.* III, 5-6 and the corresponding note), the act of creation is assigned to the triune God, the Trinity, with the familiar names: the Son is Christ, the Love is the Holy Ghost, whereas God the Father is here designated as "the first and ineffable Power." The act of creation is itself an act of love, a "spiration," also termed, in theology, a "procession." See Singleton (1954), pp. 39-41. Cf. Thomas Aquinas, *Summa theol.* I, q. 45, a. 6, resp.:

> Creare est proprie causare sive producere esse rerum. Cum autem omne agens agat sibi simile, principium actionis considerari potest ex actionis effectu; ignis enim est qui generat ignem. Et ideo creare convenit Deo secundum suum esse, quod est eius essentia, quae est communis tribus personis. Unde creare non est proprium alicui personae, sed commune toti Trinitati.
>
> Sed tamen divinae personae secundum rationem suae processionis habent causalitatem respectu creationis rerum. Ut enim supra ostensum est, qu. 14, art. 8, et qu. 19, art. 4, cum de Dei scientia et voluntate ageretur, Deus est causa rerum per suum intellectum et voluntatem, sicut artifex rerum artificiatarum. Artifex autem

per verbum in intellectu conceptum, et per amorem suae
voluntatis ad aliquid relatum, operatur. Unde et Deus
Pater operatus est creaturam per suum verbum, quod
est Filius, et per suum amorem, qui est Spiritus sanctus.
Et secundum hoc processiones personarum sunt ra-
tiones productionis creaturarum, in quantum includunt
essentialia attributa, quae sunt scientia et voluntas.

To create is, properly speaking, to cause or produce the
being of things. And as every agent produces its like, the
principle of action can be considered from the effect of
the action; for it must be fire that generates fire. And
therefore to create belongs to God according to His be-
ing, that is, His essence, which is common to the three
Persons. Hence to create is not proper to any one Per-
son, but is common to the whole Trinity.

Nevertheless the divine Persons, according to the na-
ture of their procession, have a causality respecting the
creation of things. For as was said above (q. 14, a. 8;
q. 19, a. 4), when treating of the knowledge and will of
God, God is the cause of things by His intellect and will,
just as the craftsman is cause of the things made by his
craft. Now the craftsman works through the word con-
ceived in his mind, and through the love of his will re-
garding some object. Hence also God the Father made
the creature through His Word, which is His Son; and
through His Love, which is the Holy Ghost. And so the
processions of the Persons are the type of the produc-
tions of creatures inasmuch as they include the essential
attributes, knowledge, and will.

2. *che l'uno e l'altro etternalmente spira*: "L'uno e l'altro"
is the subject and "che" is the object of "spira." According
to orthodox Roman Catholic faith, the Holy Ghost (or divine
love) emanates from both Father and Son and consists in
their eternal love for each other. Cf. Thomas Aquinas,
Summa theol. I, qq. 36 and 37. "Note the special frequency
of references to the Trinity in this and the next following
cantos. Also the emphasis laid, in line 2, on the procession
of the Holy Ghost *from the Son* as well as from the Father.

The *filioque* controversy was one of the chief sources of the alienation between the East and West, which, after widening for centuries, resulted at last in the great schism of 1054 by which the Greek and Latin Churches were severed" (TC).

4. *quanto per mente e per loco si gira*: This phrase is the object of "fé" in vs. 5 and is a statement intended to designate the *totality* of creation, whether conceived by the mind or objectively existing in space.

5. *con tant' ordine fé*: The celebration of the total order of the universe is indeed a central theme of the *Paradiso* from its first canto to its last.

6. *lui*: "Lo primo . . . Valore," vs. 3.   *chi ciò rimira*: The subject of "puote" in vs. 5.

7. *Leva dunque, lettore*: This invitation to the reader, which extends through vs. 27, is to a "feast of contemplation" of this total order. The first twenty-seven verses of this canto which bears the perfect number ten have quite correctly been viewed by commentators as marking, thematically, a fresh beginning, so that the first nine cantos, which deal with the first three of the heavenly spheres, are an initial subdivision of the *Paradiso*. This is the more fitting, moreover, in that the post of observation to which the reader is invited and from which he is to scan mentally the whole order in its operation is the heaven of the sun, indeed the very sun itself, which symbolically represents intellectual light, or wisdom.

9. *dove l'un moto e l'altro si percuote*: "The 'two motions' are the diurnal and the annual revolutions of the sun, represented by the celestial equator and the celestial ecliptic. They 'strike,' or cross, each other at Aries, in which constellation the sun is at the time of Dante's journey" (Gr).

10. *lì*: "From there."   *comincia*: Imperative.   *vagheggiar*: "Gaze rapturously."

11–12. *quel maestro . . . parte*: God the creator who lovingly sustains His creation and its admirable operation, seeing it perpetually, and first of all, within Himself.

11. *l'*: Like the "lei" in the next verse, this stands for the "arte" of vs. 10.

13–14. *Vedi come . . . porta*: At Aries the ecliptic slants across the equator.

13. *si dirama*: "Branches."

14. *oblico = obliquo.* *pianeti*: The seven planets move through the signs of the zodiac, and thus their influence is properly distributed and modified.

15. *chiama*: "Invokes," i.e., needs.

16–18. *Che se la strada . . . morta*: If the ecliptic, or zodiac, were not thus slanting, the solar and stellar influence could not operate as it does. Cf. Dante, *Conv*. III, v, 13-14, 21. There would be no seasons, and hence no generation.

16. *torta*: I.e., *obliqua*.

19–21. *e se dal dritto . . . mondano*: "If the obliquity of the ecliptic were greater or less, the succession of the seasons would not be so effective on the part of the globe where there is land" (Gr). Cf. Ristoro d'Arezzo, *Della comp*. II, 3.

20. *manco = manchevole*.

21. *giù e sù*: On either side of the equator. Cf. *Purg*. IV, 63.

22. *riman*: Imperative.

23. *si preliba*: "Is foretasted." Cf. *Par*. XXIV, 4, where the same familiar metaphor is again used in the context of an intellectual "banquet." Also see Dante, *De vulg. eloqu*. I, iv, 5.

25. *Messo t'ho innanzi*: *Mettere* sustains the metaphor of eating at table, since it was frequently used in this sense in early Italian. Cf. Boccaccio, *Decam*. I, 5 (vol. I, p. 52, l. 18).
    ti ciba: Imperative.

27. *quella materia ond' io son fatto scriba*: The "matter" is the very journey with Beatrice which is always given as a real event of which the poet is not the inventor, but (as under-

scored here) the "scribe."   *scriba = scrivano*. "Scriba"
is a Latinism.

28. *Lo ministro maggior de la natura*: The proem of twenty-
seven verses (see n. to vs. 7) being completed, the new be-
ginning is in the name of the sun, now termed "the greatest
minister," the planet in which the wayfarer finds himself
with Beatrice. Cf. Gen. 1:16: "Fecitque Deus duo luminaria
magna: luminare maius ut praeesset diei, et luminare minus
ut praeesset nocti, et stellas." ("God made the two great
lights, the greater light to rule the day and the smaller one to
rule the night, and he made the stars.")

29. *che del valor del ciel lo mondo imprenta*: The downward
transmission of this "valor" through the planets is set forth
in *Par.* II, 112-48.

30. *ne = ci*.

31. *quella parte*: Aries.   *sù*: Vss. 8-9.   *si rammenta*:
"Is mentioned."

32-33. *si girava . . . s'appresenta*: "The sun's apparent
course around the earth, from day to day, is spiral. In the
spring season it rises every day farther north and earlier than
the day before" (Gr).

32. *spire = spirali*.

35-36. *se non com' . . . venire*: "Any more than one per-
ceives the coming of a thought before it begins." "Del suo
venire" depends on "s'accorge."

36. *suo*: "Its," the thought's.

37. *scorge*: "Guides." See *Purg.* XVII, 18, and cf. the noun
scorta ("guide") *passim*.

38. *di bene in meglio*: The first three heavens were a "bene,"
but the heaven of the sun is certainly a "meglio," in every
respect. The journey now passes beyond the earth's shadow
and directly into the greatest luminary of all, the sun itself.

39. *per tempo non si sporge*: "Has no extension in time."

41–42. *era dentro al sol . . . parvente*: The souls of the wise (*sapienti*) are brighter than the sun. See Dan. 12:3: "Qui autem docti fuerint fulgebunt quasi splendor firmamenti." ("But they that are learned shall shine as the brightness of the firmament.") See also Matt. 13:43: "Tunc iusti fulgebunt sicut sol in regno Patris eorum." ("Then the just will shine forth like the sun in the kingdom of their Father.") *Docti* is, in fact, the proper name, along with that of *sapienti*, for the souls who now appear in the sun to greet Dante. They are "quel ch'era dentro al sol." "Era . . . parvente" means "was manifest."

41. *entra'mi = mi entrai*, the pronoun being the distancing reflexive frequently noticed before.

43. *Perch'*: "Though." *chiami*: "Invoke."

45. *puossi = si può*. *di veder si brami*: " 'Let men long to see it!' Let them make themselves fit for Heaven" (Gr).

46. *le fantasie nostre*: "Our powers of imagination" which, in this life, receive images through the senses; but our sense of sight knows no brighter light than that of the sun, as stated in vs. 48.

49–51. *Tal era . . . figlia*: To the "fourth family," the *sapienti* who now present themselves in the sun, it is given to contemplate the mode of God's spiration and how the Son is generated by the Father, i.e., the greatest mystery of the Christian faith, the Trinity, in its operation, as set forth in the verses that open this canto. The central presence of trinitarian imagery will be noted in the poet's account of his experience in the heaven of the sun.

53. *il Sol de li angeli*: God. See *Conv.* III, xii, 7, where Dante writes:

> Nullo sensibile in tutto lo mondo è più degno di farsi essemplo di Dio che'l sole. Lo quale di sensibile luce sé prima e poi tutte le corpora celestiali e le elementali allumina: così Dio prima sé con luce intellettuale allumina, e poi le [creature] celestiali e l'altre intelligibili.

No object of sense in all the universe is more worthy to be made the symbol of God than the sun, which enlightens, with the light of sense, itself first, and then all the celestial and elemental bodies; and in like manner God illuminates first himself with intellectual light and then the celestial and other creatures accessible to the intellect.

53–54. *ch'a questo sensibil*: That is, *sole sensibile*, i.e., this sun which we perceive with our senses.

55. *digesto*: "Disposed."

57. *gradir*: "Grateful assent."

59. *lui*: God.

60. *eclissò*: An eclipse now *within* the sun!

61. *se ne rise*: "Rejoiced at this."

63. *mia mente unita in più cose divise*: " 'Divided among many things my mind, which was concentrated on one.' The blessed souls are revealed again" (Gr).

64. *vincenti*: I.e., surpassing the light of the sun.

65. *far di noi centro e di sé far corona*: Beatrice, who in allegory is Sapientia, is now surrounded and "crowned," as it were, by this circle of the *sapienti*, and such will the configuration remain with two other crowns later joining this first one, thus celebrating, by their number, the Trinity.

67–68. *così cinger . . . talvolta*: Latona's daughter is Diana, the Moon. Sometimes, in moist weather, we see the moon "girdled" with a shining halo. Cf. *Purg.* XXIX, 78.

69. *il fil che fa la zona*: The "thread" which makes the belt (*zona*) is the light from the moon.

70. *Ne la corte del cielo*: Cf. *Inf.* II, 125.

71. *gioie*: "Jewels." "Torraca cites from Marco Polo a couple of passages describing eastern countries whose rulers will

not allow the rubies and pearls, which abound there, to be 'taken out of the kingdom'" (Gr).

74–75. *chi non s'impenna . . . novelle*: Cf. *Purg.* X, 125; XII, 95. "Wings" and "acquiring wings" for the upward flight apply in metaphor to such a flight *now* in contemplation, i.e., to an experience similar to the one the wayfarer Dante is having. There is no point in anyone's awaiting word from one who has had such an experience and returns to the world of the living since he must be "mute" about certain ineffable things seen and heard there.

76. *Poi* = *poi che*, "when."

77. *fuor* = *furono*. *tre volte*: Again the number of the Trinity.

78. *come stelle vicine a' fermi poli*: Beatrice and Dante at the center of this round dance are the "fixed poles," but the dance is primarily in honor of Beatrice, for she is Sapientia, and these are *sapienti*.

79–81. *donne mi parver . . . ricolte*: In the *Bullettino della Società Dantesca Italiana* N.S. IV (1897), p. 180 there is the following quotation from V. Borghini, who describes the customary dance done by women singing a *ballata* (dance song):

> Dimostra l'uso delle ballate, nelle quali quella che guida il canto dice la prima stanza stando ferma; la qual finita, il ballo tutto, volgendosi, la replica cantando, e finita, si ferma; e la madonna della canzone pur ferma dice la stanza nuova, la quale finisce nella rima della prima, e subito finita, il ballo si muove in cerchio, cantando pur la stanza che si chiama il ritornello.

He represents the customary manner of dancing to a *ballata*, in which the lady who leads the song recites the first stanza [the *ripresa* or *ritornello*], standing still; when she has done this, the entire group of dancers moves in a round dance, repeating the stanza, and when finished, stops; then the lady of the song [i.e., who first began the song], again standing still, sings the next

stanza, which ends rhyming with the first whereupon
the group again does a round dance, singing again the
stanza called *ritornello*.

The ladies hold one another by the hand. The phrase "non
da ballo sciolte" catches the dance at the moment when the
group, still in dance formation, awaits the end of the leader's
singing of the stanza ("le nove note") in order to resume
their round dance. A simile bringing to mind such a scene,
familiar to any contemporary reader of the poem, serves to
humanize the imagery of the *Paradiso* in a notable manner:
for clearly souls that are only bright lights do not exactly re-
semble dancing ladies.

82. *Quando*: "Since."

84. *verace amore*: Love of God.

86. *quella scala*: The ladder of contemplation, a figure which
appears elsewhere in the *Paradiso*. Cf. *Par.* XXII, 68-74.

87. *u' = ove.   u' sanza risalir nessun discende*: "Here is
a distinct promise of Dante's ultimate salvation. Cf. *Purg.* II,
91-92" (Gr).

88. *qual ti negasse il vin de la sua fiala*: "Whichever one of
us should refuse to pour of his wine to quench your thirst,"
i.e., to know who these souls are.

89. *fora = sarebbe*.

90. *se non com'*: " 'Any more than.' It would be as unnat-
ural for one of these souls to refuse to satisfy Dante, as it
would be for water not to run downhill" (Gr).

91–93. *Tu vuo' saper . . . t'avvalora*: Dante's "thirst" is now
clearly stated, and what was a "crown" of lights now becomes
a "garland" for Beatrice. "Vagheggia" belongs to amatory
parlance. These, we learn, were and are *sapienti* and appro-
priately garland Beatrice, whose name in allegory is Sapien-
tia. (See C. S. Singleton, 1958, pp. 122-38.) But her other
name is Sanctifying Grace, and as such she also "uplifts" to
Heaven, having descended from there.

94. *agni = agnelli.* *santa greggia*: The Dominican order.

95. *Domenico*: St. Dominic, whose life is recounted in *Par.* XII, 46-105. See n. to *Par.* XII, 55-56.

96. *u' ben s'impingua se non si vaneggia*: "The speaker, St. Thomas Aquinas, who belonged to the Dominican order, declares that St. Dominic led his flock over a road where the sheep 'fatten well, if they do not stray,' i.e., they have abundance of spiritual food, as long as they adhere to his rule. This expression calls for an explanation in the next canto" (Gr). Cf. Prov. 11:25: "Anima quae benedicit impinguabitur." ("He who confers benefits will be made fat.")

97-98. *Questi che m'è . . . fummi*: Thomas' "brother and master" is to his right in the circle.

98. *fummi = mi fu.*

98-99. *ed esso Alberto è di Cologna*: Albert of Cologne, now St. Albert (canonized 1932), better known as Albertus Magnus. Named Doctor Universalis on account of his vast learning, he was born of noble parents at Lauingen on the Danube in Swabia between 1193 and 1206. After studying at Padua, he joined the Dominican order in 1223 and under its rules studied theology at Bologna and elsewhere. Subsequently he was appointed to lecture at Cologne, where the order had a house, and he taught for several years there and at Regensburg, Freiburg, Strasbourg, Hildesheim, and Paris. Among his pupils was Thomas Aquinas; in 1248 Albertus returned to Cologne with Thomas Aquinas. In 1254 he was elected provincial of the Dominican order at Worms, and in 1260 he was appointed bishop of Regensburg. Sometime after 1262 he retired to Cologne, where he died, November 15, 1280.

Albertus was a most voluminous writer, his collected works (printed at Lyons in 1651) filling twenty-one folio volumes. Six are devoted to commentaries on Aristotle, five on the Scriptures, two on Dionysius the Areopagite, three on the *Sentences* of Peter Lombard, the remaining five containing his *Summa theologica, Summa de creaturis*, a treatise on the Virgin, and various opuscula, one of which is on alchemy. Albertus was the earliest among the Latins, as Avicenna had been among the Arabs, to make known the complete doctrine of Aristotle; he wrote not merely commentaries, but paraphrases and illustrative treatises on each of Aristotle's works.

99. *Thomas d'Aquino*: Thomas Aquinas, the famous scholastic theologian and philosopher, who was of noble descent and closely allied to several of the royal houses of Europe, was born in 1225 or 1226 at Roccasecca, the castle of his father, the count of Aquino, in northwest Campania. He received his early education at the Benedictine monastery of Monte Cassino, which was close to his home, and he afterwards studied for six years at the University of Naples, which he left at the age of sixteen. In 1243-44, in spite of the opposition of his family (which was only overcome by the intervention of Pope Innocent IV), he became a Dominican and shortly after was sent to study under Albertus Magnus at Cologne. In 1245 he accompanied Albertus to Paris and remained with him there for three years, during which he took a prominent part in the controversy between the university and the Begging Friars as to the liberty of teaching, being chosen to defend his order against the famous Guillaume de Saint-Amour, the champion of the university, whom he successfully confuted. In 1248 he returned with Albertus to Cologne, where he began his career as a teacher. In 1257 he became doctor of theology at the Sorbonne (at the same time as his friend Bonaventura) and began to lecture on that subject in Paris, where he speedily acquired a great reputation. In 1263 he attended a chapter of the Dominican order in London; five years later he was lecturing in Rome and Bologna; and in 1271 he was again in Paris, lecturing and at the same time busied with the affairs of the Church and acting as adviser to his kinsman, Louis VIII. In 1272 he returned to his native country, at the instance of Charles of Anjou, to assume the office of professor at the University of Naples, having previously refused the archbishopric of Naples and the abbacy of Monte Cassino. In January 1274 he was sum-

moned by Gregory X to attend the Council of Lyons, which had been called in the hope of bringing about a union of the Greek and Latin Churches. Though ill at the time, he set out on the journey, but died, after lingering for some weeks at the Cistercian monastery of Fossanova, near Terracina on the borders of Campania and Latium, March 7, 1274, a groundless suspicion being entertained that he had been poisoned at the instance of King Charles (Dante mentions Aquinas in this connection in *Purg.* XX, 69). Within fifty years of his death, Thomas Aquinas, who during his lifetime had been known as the Angelic Doctor, was canonized by Pope John XXII (in 1323, two years after Dante's death).

In allowing Aquinas to be spokesman for the first garland of lights Dante has given him the most prominent place there, even though Aquinas himself politely defers to Albertus.

101. *ten vien = vientene* (imperative).

102. *serto*: "Wreath."

104. *Grazian*: Gratian (Franciscus Gratianus), founder of the science of canon law, was born about the end of the eleventh century at Chiusi in Tuscany (or, according to some, at Carraria near Orvieto). In early life he appears to have become a Benedictine monk and to have entered the Camaldolese monastery of Classe near Ravenna, whence he afterwards removed to that of San Felice at Bologna. Here he spent many years in the preparation of his great work, the celebrated *Concordia discordantium canonum*, better known as the *Decretum Gratiani*, which was completed before 1150. In this work, which forms the first part of the *Corpus iuris canonici* and which he compiled from the Holy Scriptures, the canons of the apostles and of the councils, the decretals of the popes, and the writings of the fathers, Gratian brought into agreement the laws of the ecclesiastical and secular courts.

107. *Pietro*: Peter Lombard, otherwise known as Magister Sententiarum (from the title of his work *Sententiarum libri*

quatuor), was born near Novara, in what is now Piedmont but formerly was part of Lombardy, *ca.* 1100. He studied first at Bologna and then at Paris, where he was sent with letters from Bernard of Clairvaux. After holding a theological chair at Paris for many years, he was in 1159 appointed bishop of Paris, but died shortly after, either in 1160 or 1164. He is said to have been a pupil of Abelard at one time. He was also, together with Richard of St. Victor, a pupil of the celebrated Hugh of St. Victor. Peter Lombard's best known work, the *Libri sententiarum quatuor*, is, as its name implies, primarily a collection of the "sentences," i.e., the opinions of the Fathers. These are distributed into four books, of which the first treats of the Godhead, the second of creation and the creature, the third of the Incarnation and redemption, the fourth of the seven sacraments and eschatology. It attained immense popularity and became the favorite textbook in the theological schools and the subject of innumerable commentaries. *che con la poverella*: Here the allusion is to the opening sentence in the preface of his book, which he presents, like the widow's mite (Luc. 21:2), as a humble offering to God: "Cupientes aliquid de penuria ac tenuitate nostra cum paupercula in gazophylacium Domini mittere." ("Desiring to contribute somewhat of our poverty and our little store [of knowledge] to the treasury of the Lord, as did the poor widow [her two mites].")

109–10. *La quinta luce . . . amor*: The "fifth light," that of Solomon, is the "most beautiful" of all the circle, since it comes from the love which phrased the Song of Solomon (Canticle of Canticles), the epithalamium of Christ and Church. He revealed truth in Proverbs and Ecclesiastes.

111. *gola*: "Is greedy." *novella*: "News," concerning its fate. Some theologians maintained, as did Jerome, that Solomon was saved, while others maintained, as did Augustine, that he was damned. See III Reg. 11:4-12.

112–14. *entro v'è . . . secondo*: See III Reg. 3:12: "Dedi tibi cor sapiens et intelligens, in tantum ut nullus ante te similis tui fuerit nec post te surrecturus sit." ("[I] have given thee a wise and understanding heart; insomuch that there hath been no one like thee before thee, nor shall arise after thee.") "It is apparent that the phrase 'no second ever rose,' in l. 114, has raised in Dante's mind a question which is answered in Canto XIII" (Gr).

115–17. *il lume di quel cero . . . ministero*: "The 'candle' is Dionysius the Areopagite, St. Paul's convert in Athens (Acts xvii, 34), to whom was ascribed a Neoplatonic work of the 5th or 6th century, called *De Caelesti Hierarchia*, the great authority on the orders of the angels, their nature, their functions, and their relation to the heavens. Cf. XXVIII, 130-139; also Letter to Can Grande [*Epist*. XIII, 60]" (Gr).

118–20. *Ne l'altra piccioletta luce . . . provide*: Since this light is not actually named, the commentators have varied in their identification of it, but most would still seem to hold that it must be the spirit of Paulus Orosius, the historian. Orosius was a Spanish priest, born towards the end of the fourth century. He visited Augustine at Hippo in 413 or 414, and, after staying for a time in Africa as his disciple, he was sent by Augustine, in 415, to Jerome in Palestine. After attending a synod at Jerusalem, at which he arraigned Pelagius for heresy, he returned to North Africa, where he is believed to have died—the date of his death is unknown. His best-known work is the *Historiarum adversum paganos libri VII*, written at the suggestion of Augustine (to whom it was dedicated and to whose *De civitate Dei* it was intended to be subsidiary) to prove by the evidence of history that the condition of the world had not grown worse since the introduction of Christianity, as the pagans asserted. This work, which attained a wide popularity, was translated into Anglo-Saxon (in a free and abridged version) by Alfred the Great and into Italian (towards the beginning of the fourteenth century) by Bono Giamboni.

121. *trani*: From *tranare, trainare,* "to draw."

124. *Per vedere*: "Through seeing."

125. *l'anima santa*: The soul of Boethius (Anicius Manlius

Severinus Boethius), Roman statesman and philosopher, who was born at Rome *ca.* 480 and died at Pavia (Ticinum) in 524. Gibbon (1908, pp. 197-98) describes him as "the last of the Romans whom Cato or Tully could have acknowledged for their countryman." His father, Flavius Manlius Boethius, was consul in 487 and died soon after. As a wealthy orphan Boethius inherited the patrimony and honors of the Anician family and was educated under the care of the chief men at Rome. He also studied at Athens and translated or commented on the geometry of Euclid, the music of Pythagoras, the arithmetic of Nicomachus, the mechanics of Archimedes, the astronomy of Ptolemy, the theology of Plato, and the logic of Aristotle, with the commentary of Porphyry. To his works was due to a great extent the knowledge of Aristotle up to the thirteenth century. He was no less distinguished for his virtue than for his learning, and he was always ready to relieve the poor and oppressed. He married Rusticiana, daughter of the senator Symmachus, by whom he had two sons. From Theodoric, king of the Ostrogoths, who was then master of Italy, he received the title of patrician while still a youth, and in 510 he was made consul, an honor which twelve years later (522) was conferred upon his two sons. But his good fortune did not last; his powerful position and bold maintenance of justice aroused jealousy and hatred, and he was accused by his enemies of plotting against Theodoric. The king, believing him guilty, threw him into prison at Pavia, while the senate without a trial passed a sentence against him of confiscation and death. After he had spent some time in prison he was put to death by torture, a cord being fastened round his head and tightened until his eyes were forced from their sockets; he was then beaten with clubs until he expired. He was buried in the church of San Pietro in Ciel d'Oro, where in 722 a tomb was erected to his memory by Liutprand, king of the Lombards; this was replaced in 990 by a more magnificent one erected by the Emperor Otto III, for which Pope Sylvester II wrote an inscription. The church was reconstructed in the twelfth century, and restored in 1899; behind the altar in the crypt is a small marble sarcophagus of the sixth century in Ravennate style, in which the bones of Boethius have been preserved since 1923; below it is an inscription in Latin elegiacs. It was during his imprisonment at Pavia that Boethius wrote his most celebrated work, the *De consolatione philosophiae*. In the Middle Ages Boethius was regarded as a martyr who died in defense of the Christian faith. He is known in the Church as St. Severinus. Boethius is frequently mentioned by Dante in his prose works (for the references see P. Toynbee, 1968, p. 102). See the *Enciclopedia dantesca* under the entry "Boezio."

128. *Cieldauro*: The basilica of San Pietro in Ciel d'Oro ("with the golden ceiling") in Pavia (see n. to vs. 125).

131. *Isidoro*: Isidorus Hispalensis, St. Isidore of Seville, a learned Spaniard, was one of the most influential writers of the early Middle Ages and a father of the Western Church. He was the son of a wealthy and distinguished native of Cartagena, where he was born *ca.* 570. His elder brother Leander was archbishop of Seville, in which dignity Isidore succeeded him in 600; he died at Seville in 636. He devoted himself to the conversion of the Visigoths from Arianism and wrote many works, the most important of which were the *Etymologiarum sive Originum libri XX*, a widely used encyclopedia of the scientific knowledge of the age, the *De ecclesiasticis officiis*, and the *Libri sententiarum*. Brunetto Latini made extensive use of the *Etymologies* in certain portions of his *Tresor*. Isidore completed the Mozarabic missal and breviary, which had been begun by his brother Leander. He followed Boethius in his treatment of logic, as he himself was followed by Bede.

Beda: The Venerable Bede, Anglo-Saxon monk, the father of English history, and most eminent writer of his age, was born *ca.* 673, at Monkwearmouth, near Wearmouth (modern Sunderland) in the northeast of county Durham. At the age of seven he was received into the monastery at Wearmouth, where he was educated. In his nineteenth year he was ordained deacon, and in his thirtieth he became priest. After three years at Wearmouth he removed to the newly founded monastery at Jarrow, where he spent the rest of his life in

study and writing and where he died in 735. He was the au-
thor of a large number of works, chiefly ecclesiastical, the
most important being his ecclesiastical history of England
(*Historia ecclesiastica gentis Anglorum*) in five books, which
he brought down to 731, within four years of his death. He
was made doctor of the Church by Pope Leo XIII in 1899.

131–32. *Riccardo . . . viro*: Richard of St. Victor, said to be
a native of Scotland, was a celebrated scholastic philosopher
and theologian and chief of the mystics of the twelfth century.
He studied at the University of Paris, where he became one
of the canons-regular of the Augustinian monastery of St.
Victor, of which he was appointed sub-prior in 1159 and
prior in 1162. He was, with Peter Lombard, a pupil of the
famous Hugh of St. Victor and a friend of Bernard of Clair-
vaux, to whom several of his works are dedicated. He died
at St. Victor in 1173. His writings, which are freely quoted
by Thomas Aquinas, consist of commentaries on parts of the
Old Testament, Paul's Epistles, and the Apocalypse, as well
as of works on moral and dogmatic subjects and on mystical
contemplation, the last of which earned him the title of Mag-
nus Contemplator, which Dante's phrase "più che viro"
("more than man") seems to echo.

132. *più che viro*: Cf. "trasumanar" in *Par.* I, 70 and the
context in which it is used, and see the notes to vss. 67-69
and 70 of that canto. Richard is said to go beyond the human
measure in the same sense of contemplation and is so re-
ferred to in Dante's *Letter to Can Grande* (*Epist.* XIII, 80),
where his work on contemplation is cited.   *viro*: A
Latinism.

133. *Questi onde a me ritorna il tuo riguardo*: The twelfth
light to be named completes the circle.   *riguardo =
sguardo*.

134–35. *'n pensieri gravi*: "Immersed in deep problems."

135. *a morir li parve venir tardo*: " 'Thought that he was
moving too slowly toward death.'—He was eager to reach
Heaven, where his questions might be answered" (Gr).
li = gli.

136. *Sigieri*: Siger de Brabant was professor of the University of Paris in the thirteenth century, but little is known about him (see the bibliographies on him in P. Toynbee, 1968, p. 576, and the *Enciclopedia dantesca* under the entry "Sigieri"). It is clear that Siger took a prominent part in the violent disputes which arose between the lay members of the University of Paris and the friars of the mendicant orders concerning the teaching of Aristotle's philosophy. In 1266 he and Guillaume de Saint-Amour were publicly refuted by Thomas Aquinas, the champion of the Dominicans. He was no doubt one of those at whom, in 1270, a general condemnation of Averroism was aimed, and in 1277 the famous list of condemned propositions issued by Bishop Étienne Tempier was certainly directed at him and his colleague Boethius of Dacia. Finding himself excommunicated thereby, Siger appears to have fled to Rome to appeal to the jurisdiction of the pope, for by October 23, 1277, when he was cited to appear before the tribunal by the inquisitor Simon du Val, he had already escaped. The exact date of Siger's death is uncertain, but he is believed to have been stabbed to death by a demented servant, at Orvieto, between 1281 and 1284.

137. *leggendo nel Vico de li Strami*: Siger lectured in the Latin Quarter, in the Rue du Fouarre (Straw Street). It is now called Rue Dante.

138. *silogizzò invidiosi veri*: "Demonstrated enviable truths." For the use of "invidiosi," cf. Dante, *Epist.* V, 5.

139. *ne = ci.   chiami*: "Calls," "awakens." This is a hypothetical subjunctive.

140. *ne l'ora*: At dawn, the hour of Matins.   *la sposa di Dio*: The Church, the traditional epithet in connection with the *sposo*, who is Christ.

141. *a mattinar lo sposo perché l'ami*: Literally, given the context, "mattinar" means "to sing matins." But the phrase "perché l'ami" brings out a meaning which that verb had in amorous secular usage, namely "to court" by singing *mattinate* beneath the window of the beloved.

142. *che = in cui.*

144. *turge*: "Swells" (with the love of God).

146. *tempra*: "Modulation."

147. *pò = può.*

148. *s'insempra*: A word coined by Dante from *sempre*.

CANTO XI

1. *cura*: "Concerns."

2. *difettivi silogismi*: "False reasonings."

3. *in basso batter l'ali*: Again the familiar metaphor, implying the upward flight of contemplation and concern for heavenly things, which men forget to engage in, even though they have the "wings" to do so, here and now in this life. Cf. *Purg.* XII, 95-96.

4. *iura*: "Law," the study of law, both civil and canonical. "Iura" is a Latinism.   *amforismi = aforismi*, i.e., the study of medicine, so referred to because the *Aphorisms* of Hippocrates served as a textbook of medicine. The *Aphorisms* attributed to Hippocrates comprised one of the chief medical authorities in the Middle Ages. Galen wrote a commentary upon them which, with the *Aphorisms* themselves, was translated into Latin from an Arabic version in the eleventh century. Benvenuto defines an aphorism as a "maxima in medicina" ("maxim in medicine").

5. *sacerdozio*: "Priesthood," or the studies which lead to it.

6-7. *e chi regnar . . . rubare*: "Regnar" and "rubare" are objects of "seguendo" in vs. 5, as are the other activities named.

6. *per sofismi*: "By trickery," "by deception." Both "per forza" and "per sofismi" can bring to mind what Guido da Montefeltro said of himself in Hell ("l'opere mie / non furon leonine, ma di volpe," *Inf.* XXVII, 74-75), which reflects the same two notions of violence and fraud.

10–12. *quando, da tutte queste cose . . . accolto*: The contemplative life guided by wisdom and the lofty heights to which it can attain (even to the heaven of the sun, which symbolizes wisdom itself) has uplifted the wayfarer and placed him "far from the madding crowd's ignoble strife," and now in memory he exults over this.

11. *m'era*: The use of the so-called pleonastic reflexive here is an excellent example of its distancing function. Cf. *Inf.* VII, 94 and *passim*.

13. *ciascuno*: Each of the twelve spirits surrounding Dante and Beatrice, appearing here as lights only.   *ne lo*: For the unusual rhyme, cf. *Purg.* XVII, 55.

15. *fermossi = si fermò.   come a candellier candelo*: The image suggests a circular chandelier seen when it is motionless, with each of the candles set into its place.   *candelo = candela.*

16. *quella lumera*: The light is the soul of Thomas Aquinas.

18. *mera*: "Clear." Cf. *Par.* IX, 114. The further brightening of the light is its smile ("sorridendo").

21. *li tuoi pensieri onde cagioni apprendo*: "I apprehend whence you derive your thoughts," i.e., what occasions them in you. Thus Thomas, seeing Dante's thoughts by gazing into God's light, can formulate them.

22. *Tu dubbi = tu dubiti.   si ricerna*: Subjunctive of *ricernere*, "to re-explain," by distinguishing (cf. vs. 27). Through its derivation from the Latin *cernere*, the verb can suggest "sifting," in this case "resifting." The subject is "lo dicer mio" in vs. 24.

24. *si sterna*: A Latinism, here in the subjunctive, from

sternere, in the sense of "to spread something out flat," "to level." In the reflexive form here it means "to be leveled," i.e., "made plainer."

25. *U' = ubi (ove).* *U' ben s'impingua*: See *Par.* X, 96.

26. *Non nacque il secondo*: The verb has been changed here from the "surse" of *Par.* X, 114, to "nacque."

28-30. *La provedenza . . . fondo*: Thomas begins his clarification of the first "problem" with verses which restate the central theme of the *Paradiso.*

29. *quel consiglio*: God's counsel.

29-30. *ogne aspetto creato*: The sight of every angel and every man, his intellect or capacity to understand. Cf. *Par.* VII, 94-95; XXI, 94-96. Also see *Purg.* III, 34-37.

31. *però che = perciò che,* "in order that." *andasse*: The subject is "sposa" in vs. 32. *lo suo diletto*: Christ, the Bridegroom.

32. *la sposa*: The Church. *colui*: Christ. *alte grida*: See Matt. 27:46: "Et circa horam nonam clamavit Iesus voce magna dicens: Eli, eli, lamma sabacthani? hoc est: Deus meus, Deus meus, ut quid dereliquisti me?" ("But about the ninth hour Jesus cried out with a loud voice, saying, 'Eli, Eli, lema sabacthani,' that is, 'My God, my God, why hast thou forsaken me?' ")

33. *disposò lei col sangue benedetto*: Christ wedded the Church with his blood, on the Cross.

34. *in sé sicura e anche a lui più fida*: Both phrases depend on "andasse," vs. 31.

35. *principi*: Pronounced *prìncipi.* The two "princes," as we are to learn, are St. Francis and St. Dominic. *ordinò*: "Instituted." Cf. *Inf.* VII, 78. *in suo favore*: "In her behalf."

37. *L'un fu tutto serafico in ardore*: St. Francis, called "seraphic" because the Seraphim, the highest order of angels,

2. The location of Assisi

represent love (they are conceived to be of the color of fire which is the color of love). Cf. Thomas Aquinas, *Summa theol.* I, q. 63, a. 7, ad 1: "Seraphim autem interpretatur *ardentes*, sive *incendentes*." ("While *Seraphim* means *those who are on fire*, or *who set on fire*.")

38–39. *l'altro . . . splendore*: St. Dominic, in whom wisdom and knowledge are stressed by the epithet "di cherubica luce uno splendore." See Thomas Aquinas, *Summa theol.* I, q. 63, a. 7, ad 1: "Cherubim interpretatur *plenitudo scientiae*." ("Cherubim is interpreted *fulness of knowledge*.")

40. *un*: St. Francis.

40–41. *però che . . . prende*: We describe both by praising one, whichever one we choose.

42. *ad un fine*: "To one end."   *sue*: "Their."

43–51. *Intra Tupino . . . Gange*: These verses locate Assisi, where Francis was born. Assisi is situated between the river Topino and the Chiascio, which runs into it below. The Topino empties into the Tiber. (See Map 2, facing p. 196.)

44. *del colle eletto dal beato Ubaldo*: On the hill, in the vicinity of Gubbio, from which the Chiascio river flows, St. Ubald had his hermitage, before he became bishop of Gubbio. He died in 1160.

45. *fertile costa d'alto monte pende*: The west slope of Monte Subasio, facing Perugia, is less steep than the other side.

46–48. *onde Perugia . . . Gualdo*: "The gate called Porta Sole is on the side of Perugia nearest to Subasio. The town feels the effect of the summer sun and the winter snow on the mountain. East of the range to which Subasio belongs are the little towns of Nocera and Gualdo, which 'weep because of the heavy mountain chain' of the Apennines on their east. The Monte di Nocera may be seen, from Porta Sole, covered with snow in mid-April" (Gr).

50. *rattezza*: "Steepness" (cf. the description in *Purg.* XII, 103). Assisi lies on a spur of the mountain.   *sole*: "Even before Dante, St. Francis had been called a Sun, a traditional appellation with the Franciscans" (Gr).

51. *come fa questo talvolta di Gange*: The "questo" is the real sun, where Dante now is. The sun rises from the Ganges, due east from Jerusalem, at the vernal equinox.

52–54. *Però chi . . . vuole*: The spot from which this new sun rose should be called Orient, or Dayspring. See Luc. 1:78: "Visitavit nos oriens ex alto." ("The Dayspring from on high has visited us.") Cf. Zach. 3:8, "adducam servum meum Orientem" ("I will bring my servant the Orient") and Zach. 6:12, "ecce vir Oriens nomen eius" ("behold a man, the Orient is his name"). "The usual form of the name Assisi, in the Tuscan of Dante's day, was *Ascesi*, which may be interpreted as meaning 'I have risen.' While this is suggestive of dayspring, it is inadequate (*corto*): 'Orient' is the only fit word" (Gr). See Bonaventura (*Legenda sancti Francisci, Prologus* 1), who applies to Francis the words of Apoc. 7:2: "Vidi alterum angelum ascendentem ab ortu solis." ("I saw another angel ascending from the rising of the sun.")

55. *orto*: The term keeps the simile of a rising sun (see preceding note), but here signifies "birth."

56–57. *ch'el cominciò . . . conforto*: The terms "virtute" and "conforto" keep to the metaphor of the sun.

58–59. *ché per tal donna . . . corse*: Francis was about twenty-four when he began to woo Poverty ("tal donna"). For this "war with his father" and other details of Francis' life, see n. to vs. 74.

59–60. *a cui . . . diserra*: To which lady (Poverty, as is made clear in vs. 74) no one willingly opens—i.e., unlocks—the door, any more than anyone welcomes death. The phrase "porta del piacer" as referring to the will is made somewhat clearer through the use of this same metaphor by Virgil in his words to Dante in the discussion of love and free will at the center of the poem (*Purg.* XVIII, 61-63), where the will is said to hold the "threshold of assent."

61. *corte*: The episcopal court of Assisi.

62. *coram patre*: For the phrase "coram patre," which is from the Bible, see Matt. 10:33: "coram Patre meo" ("before my Father"). *le si fece unito*: E. G. Gardner (1913, p. 233) notes that the conception of the mystical marriage with Poverty is indicated only slightly by Tommaso da Celano and Bonaventura.

64. *Questa*: Poverty. *primo marito*: Christ.

65–66. *millecent' anni e più . . . invito*: From Christ to Francis no one had cared for Poverty.

66. *si stette*: This is again the reflexive in its distancing— here "isolating"—function.

67–69. *né valse udir . . . paura*: " 'And it availed not that men heard how he who terrified the whole world (Caesar) found her, with Amyclas (a poor fisherman), fearless at the sound of his voice.' See *Phars.*, V, 515-531. Amyclas, who had nothing to lose, was not afraid when Caesar knocked at his door; he was 'securus belli'—fearless of war. But even this example of the advantages of indigence—upon which Lucan moralizes (cf. *Conv.*, IV, xiii, 12)—did not make Poverty seem desirable" (Gr).

70. *feroce*: "Fearless."

71–72. *dove Maria . . . croce*: "When even Mary had to remain at the foot of the cross, Poverty accompanied her Spouse: Christ's raiment was taken from him" (Gr). See Mar. 15:24: "Et crucifigentes eum diviserunt vestimenta eius, mittentes sortem super eis, quis quid tolleret." ("Then they crucified him, and divided his garments, casting lots for them to see what each should take.")

72. *pianse*: Some texts have "salse" for "pianse." On this variant, see Petrocchi.

74. *Francesco*: St. Francis of Assisi (Giovanni Francesco Bernardone), son of Pietro di Bernardone, a wool-merchant of Assisi, was born in 1181 or 1182 and died in 1226. In his youth he was given up to a life of pleasure and prodigality, but was always open-handed to the poor. On one occasion at least he bore arms, for he was taken prisoner in a skirmish between Assisi and Perugia. When he was about twenty he was seized with a severe illness, which gave his thoughts a serious turn; and after a second illness at Spoleto (*ca.* 1206), while he was on his way to join a military expedition, he determined to devote himself to a religious life.

Vowing himself to poverty, which he spoke of as his bride, Francis renounced every sort of worldly goods, including even his clothes, which he stripped off in the presence of the bishop, to whom his enraged father had appealed for the protection of his property. Two or three years after this, he heard one day in church the injunction of Christ to His apostles (Matt. 10:9-10): "Nolite possidere aurum, neque argentum, neque pecuniam in zonis vestris, non peram in via, neque duas tunicas, neque calceamenta, neque virgam." ("Do not keep gold, or silver, or money in your girdles, nor wallet for your journey, nor two tunics, nor sandals, nor staff.") He cast aside shoes, staff, and girdle and girt himself with a cord, which subsequently became the distinguishing mark of his order, sometimes known as the Cordeliers. He soon began to gather followers around him, whom he sent forth to preach, and in 1209 he drew up the rules of his order, the members of which were called Friars Minor in token of humility. The order first received the verbal sanction of Innocent III.

In 1212 Francis was presented by the Benedictines of Monte Subasio with the little church of the Porziuncola (Santa Maria degli Angeli) in the vicinity of Assisi, which became the home of his order, and in the same year the first order of nuns was founded by St. Clare under his direction. In 1219 he went to Egypt with the object of converting the sultan and preached to him in his camp before Damietta, but without success. On his return he founded (in 1221) his tertiary order of penitents of both sexes; and in 1223 his order was solemnly confirmed by a bull of Honorius III. In 1224, in the solitude of Monte della Verna in the Apennines, he received in a vision the stigmata, or marks of the Crucifixion, in his hands, feet, and side. After two years of great bodily suffering he died near Assisi, October 4, 1226. His body was laid first in the cathedral of Assisi, but was claimed four years later by the brethren of his order and removed to their church outside the walls. He was canonized in 1228 by Gregory IX, who appointed October 4, the date of his death, to be observed as his festival.

Lives of St. Francis were written within a few years of his death; one of the best known is that by Bonaventura, who as an infant had been miraculously healed by him. This and the one by Tommaso da Celano were the chief sources of Dante's information as to the details of the life of the saint.

74–75. *Francesco e Povertà . . . prendi*: "Francesco e Povertà" is the object of the imperative "prendi."

75. *nel mio parlar diffuso*: "In my long figurative discourse" —for ten tercets (vss. 43-72), in fact.

76–78. *La lor concordia . . . santi*: " 'Love, wonder, and sweet gaze made their concord and their glad looks to be a source of holy thoughts' in the beholders" (Gr).

78. *facieno = facevano*.

79. *Bernardo*: Francis' first disciple was Bernardo da Quintavalle, a wealthy merchant of Assisi, where he was a person of much importance. At first, though attracted by St. Francis, he distrusted him, but having convinced himself of his sincerity, he submitted himself to his direction, sold all his possessions for the benefit of the poor, and embraced the rule of poverty. Dante's account follows that of Tommaso da Celano (see P. Toynbee, 1968, p. 93).

80. *si scalzò*: Francis and his followers went barefoot, imitating the apostles. See Luc. 22:35.

81. *li = gli*.

82. *ferace*: "Fruitful."

83. *Egidio*: Aegidius of Assisi (Blessed Giles), one of Francis' three earliest followers, was the author of a book called *Verba aurea*. He died at Perugia in 1262.   *Silvestro*: One of Francis' earliest followers, Sylvester is said to have been a priest and to have supplied Francis with stone for church-building, about the price of which he disputed on one occasion, whereupon Francis added a handful of gold to his previous payment. Sylvester soon after, struck with remorse at his own greed in contrast with the contempt for gold displayed by Francis, abandoned his former life and became one of Francis' disciples. He died *ca.* 1240.

85. *Indi*: "Then."

85–87. *Indi sen va . . . capestro*: Francis, with Poverty and with his followers, went off to Rome.

87. *capestro*: "Cord," "rope." Francis substituted a rope for the usual belt as a sign of humility.

88. *Né li gravò viltà di cuor le ciglia*: "Viltà di cuor" is the subject of "gravò." For the expression, see *Purg*. XVII, 52. *li = gli*.

89. *per esser fi' di Pietro Bernardone*: Francis' father was a wool-merchant, therefore of the middle class and not noble. Bonaventura, in his *Legenda sancti Francisci* (VI, 1), written in 1261-63, relates that when Francis heard himself lauded as a holy man, he would bid one of his friars to vilify him, and on being thus reproached with his low birth and his father's occupation, he would reply that it was fitting for the son of Pietro di Bernardone to hear such things (see P. Toynbee, 1968, p. 95).   *fi'*: The apocopated form of *figlio* was common Tuscan usage of the day.

90. *dispetto a maraviglia*: "Wondrously despicable." When Francis first visited the papal court, his appearance excited derision.

92. *Innocenzio*: Innocent III (Giovanni Lotario de' Conti) was elected pope (in succession to Celestine III) in 1198, at the age of thirty-seven, and died at Perugia, July 16, 1216.

93. *sigillo*: "Seal," approval.   *religione*: "Order." "In 1210, Innocent III verbally, and with some reluctance, sanctioned St. Francis's Rule, which seemed to him harsh and dangerous" (Gr).

94. *la gente poverella*: Francis' followers, dedicated to poverty, were at first known as the "poveri d'Assisi" (the poor ones of Assisi) and only later as the Friars Minor.

96. *meglio in gloria del ciel si canterebbe*: "Were better sung in Heaven's glory" than thus related by me.

97–99. *di seconda corona . . . archimandrita*: " 'The holy purpose of this Arch-shepherd was rounded with a second crown by the Eternal Breath (the Holy Ghost) through Honorius.'—In 1223 St. Francis obtained a definite, official sanction of his Rule from Honorius III" (Gr).

99. *archimandrita*: " 'Head of the fold,' a term of the Greek Church, is one of the words that Dante got from the *Magnae Derivationes* of Uguccione da Pisa. It is used of the Pope in Ep. XI, 13; of St. Peter in *Mon.*, III, ix, 17" (Gr).

100–102. *E poi che . . . seguiro*: In 1219 Francis and some of his disciples accompanied the crusaders to Egypt, where he preached before the sultan of Egypt, called also in Dante's time the sultan of Babylon. Francis joined the crusaders' army before Damietta and at the risk of his life made his way into the camp of the sultan, al-Malik al-Kámil, and summoned him to embrace Christianity. The sultan received him courteously and listened to him, but remained unconvinced, even when Francis offered to prove his faith by entering the fire. Finally, after pressing gifts upon him which Francis refused, the sultan dismissed him in safety to the crusaders' camp, from which he returned to Italy.

102. *li altri*: The apostles.

103. *per trovare*: "Finding."   *acerba*: "Unripe."

105. *redissi = si redì*, "he returned." The infinitive is *reddire*, from the Latin *redire*.   *al frutto de l'italica erba*: To

Italy, where better fruit (results) could be had, i.e., where conversion was easier.

106. *nel crudo sasso intra Tevero e Arno*: Francis retired to a shelter built by his followers on the wild and rugged Monte della Verna, between the upper Arno and the source of the Tiber.

107. *da Cristo prese l'ultimo sigillo*: There, in 1224, Christ or, as some painters have represented it, a seraph appeared to him and imprinted on his hands, feet, and side the stigmata, or marks of Christ's five wounds. This miracle, attested by contemporary evidence, was confirmed by three papal bulls. See n. to vs. 74.

108. *che le sue membra due anni portarno*: These marks he bore until his death in 1226. He died in Porziuncola, where the church of Santa Maria degli Angeli is now located, in the plain below Assisi.

109. *colui*: God.   *sortillo = lo sortì*, "chose him."

111. *pusillo*: A Latinism, meaning "little," lowly.

113. *donna*: Poverty.

115–17. *e del suo grembo . . . bara*: Francis, desiring to rise to Heaven "from the lap" of Poverty, commanded his followers to strip his body, after his death, and let it lie for some time on the bare ground.

118. *colui*: St. Dominic. (See vss. 40-42.) Aquinas has thus concluded his encomium of St. Francis and now turns to his own order, the Dominicans.

119–20. *barca di Pietro*: The Church.

120. *in alto mar*: Where navigation is difficult and fraught with danger.   *per dritto segno*: Directed toward the right goal, i.e., set on the right course.

121. *il nostro patriarca*: St. Dominic, whose life is recounted in *Par.* XII.

123. *merce = merci*. Continuing the navigation metaphor, this refers, figuratively, to spiritual goods, virtues and deserts. *carca = carica*.

124-25. *Ma 'l suo peculio . . . ghiotto*: The sharp criticism by this Dominican of his own order (following the eulogy of Francis' order) begins here.

124. *peculio*: "Flock," referring to the Dominicans. Cf. *Purg.* XXVII, 83.   *nova vivanda*: Worldly gain.

126. *diversi*: "Distant," "remote" (from the Latin *deverto*). *salti*: "Wild pastures" (from the Latin *saltus*).

128. *da esso*: "From him" (Dominic).

129. *di latte vòte*: I.e., without the spiritual good they should have fed on.

130. *Ben son*: The "ben" is concessive: "There are *indeed*." *di*: The partitive.

131. *stringonsi = si stringono*.

131-32. *ma son sì poche . . . panno*: I.e., it takes but little cloth to furnish them all with cowls, since they are so few. "Poco panno" is the subject.

134. *audienza*: "Listening."

135. *revoche = rivochi*, "recall."

136. *in parte*: Only the first of the two points of Dante's confusion (vss. 25-26) has been clarified.

137. *la pianta*: The Dominican order.   *onde si scheggia*: Which is torn, "chipped away," by the degenerate mass of Dominicans.

138. *corrègger*: The infinitive is used as a noun, "correction," referring to the qualifying phrase "se non si vaneggia." *che argomenta*: In more normal prose order this might be "ciò che il correggere argomenta" ("what the qualification means"), the qualification being the restrictive clause "se non si vaneggia."

CANTO XII

2. *per dir tolse = prese a dire*, but in the sense of "finished uttering," having just said "se non si vaneggia" (*Par.* XI, 139).

3. *mola*: " 'Millstone': the ring of spirits. In a mill, the two grindstones operate concurrently, and both are necessary" (Gr). It should be noted that a millstone turns horizontally, as does this ring of lights.

5. *di cerchio la chiuse*: "Encircled it."

6. *colse*: "Matched."

7–8. *nostre muse, nostre serene*: Figuratively, poetry and song as we know them here on earth. Cf. *Purg.* XIX, 19, for the form *serena* instead of *sirena* and for the word used in the sense of one who sings (although it is used there in a pejorative sense, which is absent here).

8. *tube*: "Pipes," the singing souls.

9. *quanto primo splendor quel ch'e' refuse*: As a direct ray surpasses its reflection, the one it has reflected. *e' = egli.*

refuse: *Refuse* is the preterite (here used with a present-tense meaning) of *rifondere*, "to throw back." See, for an equivalent use of this verb, *Par.* II, 88.

12. *ancella*: Iris, the rainbow. Daughter of Thaumas and Electra, Iris was the personification of the rainbow, which was regarded as the messenger of the gods and (among later writers) of Juno in particular (Virgil, *Aen*. IV, 694; V, 606; IX, 2, 5; Ovid, *Metam*. I, 271).   *iube*: "Commands." The Latin is *iubet*.

13. *nascendo di quel d'entro quel di fori*: The outer arc of a double rainbow is called the reflection, or echo, of the inner one. It was formerly thought to be an actual reflection.

14-15. *quella vaga ch'amor consunse*: The "wanderer" is the nymph Echo, who used to keep Juno engaged by incessantly talking to her, while Jupiter sported with the nymphs. Juno, on finding this out, punished Echo by changing her into an echo. In this state the nymph fell in love with Narcissus, but, her love not being returned, she pined away in grief, so that nothing remained of her but her voice. Dante got the story from Ovid (*Metam*. III, 356-401).

15. *come sol vapori*: "Sol" is here the subject of *consuma* (present tense), understood but not used.

16. *presaga*: "Confident," or "weather-wise," in this case.

17. *per*: "Because of."   *lo patto che Dio con Noè puose*: The reference is to the covenant which God made with Noah that never again should there be a flood to destroy the earth (Gen. 9:8-17).

18. *s'allaga*: "Shall be flooded."

20. *volgiensi = si volgevano*. Pronounced *volgìensi*.

22. *tripudio*: "Dance." The word is a Latinism.

23. *sì . . . sì*: "Both . . . and."

25. *a punto e a voler*: "At one instant and of one accord."

26. *piacer*: "Will."   *i = li*.

27. *conviene insieme chiudere e levarsi*: " 'Must be closed and lifted together.' The two circles operate simultaneously,

like a pair of eyes. Dante seems here to confuse the *turning* of the eyes, which must affect both at once, with shutting and opening, which may affect one without the other" (Gr).

29. *ago*: The "needle" of a compass.   *stella*: The North Star, or north.

30. *in volgermi al suo dove*: The image is exact, for Dante, being—as it were—inside the circle of so many points of a compass, acts as does the needle.   *dove*: "Place." Here, as often in the poem, the adverb is used as a noun.

31. *L'amor*: "Love of God."

32. *tragge = trae*.   *l'altro duca*: St. Dominic.

33. *per cui del mio sì ben ci si favella*: " 'For whose sake there is such fair speech here concerning mine.' St. Thomas, for love of his own leader, St. Dominic, has been praising St. Francis" (Gr).

34. *s'induca*: "Be mentioned."

35. *ad una*: Together and for the same cause.   *militaro = militarono*.

37–38. *L'essercito di Cristo . . . riarmar*: "The Christian army," made helpless by sin, had been "re-armed" by Christ's atonement.

38. *'nsegna*: The Cross.

41. *la milizia*: The "essercito," vs. 37.   *in forse*: In doubt and in danger.

43. *come è detto*: See *Par.* XI, 43-117.

46–47. *In quella parte . . . Zefiro*: Spain is the country nearest the source of Zephyr, the west wind. Cf. Ovid, *Metam.* I, 63-64: "Vesper et occiduo quae litora sole tepescunt, / proxima sunt Zephyro." ("The western shores which glow with the setting sun are the place of Zephyrus.") E. G. Gardner (1913, p. 245) notes that Petrus Ferrandi compares Dominic to Hesperus, rising from the west.

48. *rivestire = rivestirsi.*

49-52. *non molto lungi . . . Calaroga*: Compared with Italy, Caleruega, in Old Castile, is "not very far" from the Atlantic. "Spain lying due west of the Italian peninsula, the sun sets behind its Atlantic shore at the time of the vernal equinox (in the summer the direction is northwest)" (Gr). See M. Porena (1924), p. 157. Cf. *Par.* XI, 51. Note also *Aen.* XI, 913-14, where Virgil writes:

> ni roseus fessos iam gurgite Phoebus Hibero
> tinguat equos noctemque die labente reducat.

But ruddy Phoebus now laves his weary team in the Iberian flood, and, as day ebbs, brings back the night.

49. *al = dal.*

50. *foga*: " 'Flight,' its long spring course" (Gr).

51. *talvolta*: "Note that the *talvolta* occurs in l. 51 in both XI and XII: the *onde* of this canto are evidently contrasted with the *Gange* of XI" (Gr).   *ad ogne uom si nasconde*: "When the sun sinks over the Atlantic, it 'hides itself from every man,' because there is no land beyond" (Gr).

52. *Calaroga*: Caleruega, a village of Old Castile, in the province of Burgos (not to be confused with Calahorra, ancient Calagurris).

53-54. *sotto la protezion . . . soggioga*: The shield of Castile has two lions and two castles quartered, one lion above a castle and one below.

55-56. *l'amoroso drudo de la fede cristiana*: Since the life of St. Dominic begins here, the reader may understand better the details which follow if he has in mind a general brief account of the saint's life. Dominic was born between 1170 and 1175 in the village of Caleruega in Old Castile. He is supposed to have belonged to the noble family of Guzmán but there seems to be no certain evidence of this. His mother is said to have dreamed before he was born that she gave birth to a dog with a torch in its mouth, which set the world on fire. At the age of fourteen he went to the University of Palencia, where he studied theology for ten or twelve years. He was early noted for his self-denial and charity, it being told of him that during a famine he sold his clothes to feed the poor and that, in order to ransom the brother of a poor woman who appealed to him for help, he offered to sell himself as a slave to the Moors. In 1195 he became canon of the cathedral of Osma. In 1203 he accompanied the bishop on a diplomatic mission to Denmark (or more probably, to the French or Italian Marches) and thence to Rome. On his way back, two years later, he remained for some time in Languedoc, where he took an active part in the Albigensian crusade, preaching—and, according to some accounts, even fighting—against the heretics. In 1215 he accompanied Folquet de Marseille, bishop of Toulouse, to the Lateran Council. In the same year, on his return to Toulouse, he founded his order of Preaching Friars, which was formally recognized by Honorius III in 1216. By the latter he was appointed master of the sacred palace at Rome, where he henceforth resided. In 1219 the center of his order was established at Bologna, Dominican convents having by this time been founded in Italy, Spain, France, Germany, Poland, and England. He died in August 1221 at Bologna, where he was buried, his remains being preserved in the marble tomb by Nicola Pisano in the church of San Domenico. He was canonized soon after his death (in 1234) by Gregory IX, who declared that he no more doubted the sanctity of Dominic than that of Peter or Paul.

58–60. *e come fu creata . . . profeta*: "Before his birth, his mother dreamed that she brought forth a black and white dog with a burning torch in its mouth. Black and white are the Dominican colors; the torch signifies zeal; the word *Dominicani* suggests *Domini canes*, 'dogs of the Lord' " (Gr).

58. *repleta*: "Full." The word is a Latinism.

60. *lei*: "Her" (the mother).

61–63. *Poi che le sponsalizie . . . salute*: "His baptism is conceived as a wedding. He espoused Faith, as Francis (in

ll. 61-63 of XI) espoused Poverty. Dominic and Faith 'dow-
ered each other with mutual health.' Dante evidently plotted
out cantos XI and XII, to make them parallel, line by line.
Francis and Dominic are the symmetrical 'two wheels' of the
Chariot of the Church" (Gr).

63. *u' = ubi (ove)*.   *dotar = dotarono*.

64. *la donna che per lui l'assenso diede*: His godmother, who
presented him for baptism. In the traditional ceremony, the
priest asked: "Do you wish to be baptized?" His godmother,
giving the assent for the child, replied: "I do."

65–66. *vide nel sonno . . . rede*: His godmother dreamed
that he bore a star on his forehead which illumined the
world. This, by stressing light, points to the *intellectual* gifts
and pursuits of Dominic (cf. vs. 85) and his followers ("le
rede"), in contrast with the *affective* direction of Francis
and his order (cf. *Par*. XI, 112).

67. *e perché fosse qual era in costrutto*: "And that he might
be in name [verbal construct] what he was in reality." Basic
to the notion here expressed is the familiar dictum *nomina
sunt consequentia rerum* (names are the consequence of
things). Cf. Dante, *Vita nuova* XIII, 4; XXIV, 4; *Purg*.
XIII, 109-10.

68. *quinci*: From Heaven.

69. *del possessivo di cui era tutto*: *Dominicus* (the posses-
sive adjective of *Dominus*), meaning "the Lord's." Cf.
Thomas Aquinas, *Summa theol*. III, q. 16, a. 3, resp.

71–72. *l'agricola che Cristo . . . aiutarlo*: "Among the in-
terpretations of the name *Dominicus* in the *Legenda Aurea*
is 'keeper of the vineyard of the Lord' " (Gr). See Jacobus
de Varagine, *Legenda aurea* CXIII. Cf. *Par*. XXVI, 64-65.

71. *agricola = agricoltore*, "husbandman."

71–75. *Cristo . . . Cristo*: "Note that in ll. 71, 73, 75 *Cristo*
is in rhyme with itself. The same thing occurs in XIV, 104;

XIX, 104; XXXII, 83. In the *Commedia* Dante will not allow *Cristo* to rhyme with any other word" (Gr).

73. *messo*: Past participle used as a noun, meaning "messenger." *famigliar*: A follower, one of the household (cf. *Purg.* XXIX, 136).

75. *al primo consiglio che diè Cristo*: This probably refers to the first of the beatitudes (Matt. 5:3; see also Luc. 6:20), "beati pauperes spiritu" ("blessed are the poor in spirit"), taken to refer to humility (cf. *Purg.* XII, 110-11), which seems to agree best with what is said of the child in vss. 76-78. But some commentators interpret otherwise. Grandgent observes: "The 'counsels' of Christ are poverty, continence, and obedience, and the first of these is poverty: 'Sell what thou hast, and give to the poor' (Mat. xix, 21). Dante insists that St. Dominic, as well as St. Francis, was a lover of Poverty. Their love is declared in ll. 73-75 of XI and XII."

78. *Io son venuto a questo*: The words seem to echo Christ's (Mar. 1:38): "Ad hoc enim veni." ("For this is why I have come.")

79-81. *Oh padre suo . . . dice*: Again the notion supported by the dictum cited above (vss. 67-69). His father's name, "Felice," means "happy." His mother's name, "Giovanna," signifies in Hebrew "the grace of the Lord," an interpretation cited by several of Dante's authorities. See E. G. Parodi (1898).

81. *se*: This "if" does not express doubt, but affirms true doctrine. Cf. *Par.* VIII, 120.

82. *Non per lo mondo*: The phrase depends on the affirmation of vs. 85, i.e., Dominic did not become a great doctor to seek worldly gain. *mo = ora*.

82-83. *s'affanna di retro . . . Taddeo*: "Labors in pursuit of the Ostian and Taddeo," i.e., what they represent.

83. *Ostiense*: Belonging to Ostia, a village in Latium, just east of the ancient Ostia, about twenty miles southwest of

Rome and now about four from the mouth of the Tiber. Originally it was at the mouth, as the name Ostia implies. It is an episcopal see. The reference is to Enrico da Susa (Enrico Bartolomei), the author of a famous commentary on the decretals (*Summa titulorum decretalium,* or *Summa Hostiensis*) and cardinal bishop of Ostia (1261-71).

Taddeo: Probably Taddeo d'Alderotto of Bologna (or, according to some, of Pescia), celebrated physician of the latter half of the thirteenth century (*ca.* 1235-95) and reputed founder of the scientific school of medicine at the University of Bologna. He wrote commentaries on the works of Hippocrates and Galen, with philosophical illustrations. But some commentators take the reference to be to one Taddeo dei Pepoli, who was a contemporary of Dante and specialized in canon law and jurisprudence.

84. *la verace manna*: True knowledge, "the bread of angels" (cf. *Par.* II, 11).

85. *gran dottor*: Cf. *Par.* XI, 38-39. Dominic became a profound theologian, the shining light of the prophecy in vss. 64-66. He studied at the University of Palencia.   *feo = fece.*

86. *circuir*: "To go about." From the Latin *circumire.*

86–87. *la vigna . . . reo*: The vineyard grows "white" (not green, as it should be) if neglected by the vineyardist. Dominic cared for the vineyard of the Lord (the Church), dressing it and guarding it.

88–89. *E a la sedia . . . giusti*: The papal chair "which once was kinder" than it is now.

88. *a la sedia*: "Of the chair." "A la sedia" depends on "addimandò" in vs. 94.

89–90. *non per lei . . . traligna*: "The difference in its disposition is 'not because of itself' (the Papal office has not changed), but because of the degeneracy of its latterday occupants" (Gr). "A marked case of severing the ideal Papacy from the actual Popes. The Papacy *in itself* is as benign to the poor as ever; but the degenerate Pope (Boniface VIII) makes it manifest itself in other fashion" (TC).

91-93. *non dispensare . . . Dei*: "His application was not for leave to plunder on condition of paying a third or a half of the plunder to pious purposes, nor a petition for the first fat appointment that should fall vacant, or for leave to apply the tithes to his own purposes" (TC). "These phrases are the object of *addimandò* in l. 94: permission to dole out in charity only a third or a half of the money on hand, 'the income of the first vacancy,' 'the tithes which belong to God's poor' —he asked for none of these things" (Gr).

94. *mondo errante*: "The *erring world* = the heretics, notably the Albigenses, against whom Dominic's efforts were mainly directed" (TC).

95. *seme*: The faith, the seed from which sprang the bright souls which "enfold" Dante. Cf. Luc. 8:11.

98. *officio*: "Authorization." Dominic went to Rome with Folquet de Marseille (*Par.* IX, 94) and asked permission to found a new order; official sanction was given in 1216. See n. to vss. 55-56.

99. *ch'alta vena preme*: "Pushed forth by a high spring," or perhaps a deep spring. The adjective can bear either meaning in the context.

100-102. *e ne li sterpi eretici . . . grosse*: The verses continue the metaphor of the torrent. "Sterpi" suggests barren, fruitless growths (cf. *Inf.* XIII, 7 and 37), the reference being chiefly to the heretics in Provence ("quivi dove . . .") and to Dominic's role in the Albigensian crusade.

103. *Di lui si fecer poi diversi rivi*: From this "torrent" many lesser streams branched off. The reference may be simply to all the followers of Dominic or to the religious orders that were established in his name.

105. *arbuscelli*: The term is in contrast with "sterpi" (vs. 100) and with the modification "più vivi" suggests plants green and fruitful.

106. *biga*: The two-wheeled chariot of the Church. Cf. *Purg.*
XXIX, 107.

108. *e vinse in campo la sua civil briga*: The reference seems
to apply more precisely to Dominic and his war against
heresy, which in the context is termed a civil war in that
heresy divides the Christian community or the heavenly city
on earth.

109. *assai*: "Enough."

110. *l'altra*: I.e., *rota*. The other wheel is St. Francis.
di cui: "Concerning whom."   *Tomma*: Thomas Aquinas.

112. *Ma l'orbita che fé la parte somma*: Here, matching
what Aquinas the Dominican has done (in the preceding
canto), begins this Franciscan's criticism of his own order,
through a curious series of mixed metaphors.

"The panegyric on Francis is pronounced by a Dominican,
and that on Dominic by a Franciscan (whereas the denuncia-
tion of the unworthy Dominicans and Franciscans is in each
case pronounced by one of themselves). Thus Dante fore-
shadowed what afterwards became a general usage, viz., for
a Dominican to read mass in a Franciscan convent on their
founder's day (Oct. 4), and a Franciscan to do the like for
a Dominican convent on their founder's day (Aug. 4)"
(TC).

112-13. *Ma l'orbita . . . derelitta*: The metaphor obviously
continues the image of the wheel: "But the rut which the
outside of its circumference made is forsaken." The wheel
is St. Francis. His track is deserted by the Franciscans.

112. *orbita*: Cf. *Purg.* XXXII, 30.

114. *sì ch'è la muffa dov' era la gromma*: The change of
metaphor is most abrupt, passing now to wine-making. Good
wine leaves a crust in the barrel, bad wine leaves a mold.
Thus the degeneracy of the Franciscans is scored.

115-17. *La sua famiglia . . . gitta*: In place of the track left
by the wheel the metaphor changes to the footprints of Fran-

cis ("le sue orme") which his first followers held to. Vs. 117 is obscure in its meaning, which is much debated. The phraseology seems, in the context, to imply a backward movement where there should be a forward one, following in the saint's footsteps. (For "backward steps," see *Purg.* X, 123.) It focuses on a single walker who "throws" his forward foot ("quel dinanzi") toward his hind foot ("quel di retro") as he walks, which can only mean that he walks backwards. See M. Barbi (1934), p. 287.

118–20. *e tosto . . . tolta*: "The tare 'shall complain that the bin is taken from it.' Cf. Mat. xiii, 30: 'Gather ye together first the tares, and bind them in bundles to burn them: but gather the wheat into my barn.'—There may be here a reference to the condemnation of a group of the Spirituals by the Pope in 1318" (Gr). See U. Cosmo (1900), pp. 177-82. It is also possible that the bin may be the kingdom of Heaven itself, from which degenerate Franciscans will find themselves excluded.

120. *li = gli*.

121–22. *Ben dico . . . carta*: Again the change in metaphor is abrupt: the volume is the Franciscan order, the leaves are the individual friars of that order.

122. *troveria = troverebbe*.

123. *u' = ubi (ove).* *l' mi son*: The "mi" is the so-called pleonastic reflexive, here in its function of distinguishing and identifying. Cf. *Purg.* XXIV, 52. In metaphor the page (the individual friar) affirms that it is unchanged. Vss. 121-22 suggest that such a page is not easy to find.

124. *fia = sarà*. *Casal*: A town of northern Italy in Piedmont, on the right bank of the Po, about thirty miles east of Turin. The allusion is to Ubertino da Casale, leader of the so-called Spirituals in the Franciscan order, who opposed the relaxations of discipline introduced by Matteo d'Acquasparta as general of the order. Ubertino, who was born in 1259, entered the Franciscan order in 1273; after spending nine

years as lecturer in the University of Paris he returned to Italy, where he became head of the Spirituals. During the pontificate of Clement V his party prevailed, but on the election of John XXII he withdrew from the Franciscan order and entered (in 1317) that of Benedict. His most important work is the *Arbor vitae crucifixae Iesu*, which was begun in March 1305 at La Verna, where he had been ordered to retire, and finished the following September, shortly after the election of Clement V. This work was undoubtedly known to Dante.

Acquasparta: Village in Umbria, about ten miles southwest of Spoleto, at the head of a torrent of the same name. The allusion is to Matteo d'Acquasparta, who was appointed general of the Franciscan order in 1287 and created cardinal by Nicholas IV in the next year. In 1300, and again in 1301, he was sent by Boniface VIII to Florence to act as mediator between the Bianchi and the Neri, but he was unsuccessful in his mission on both occasions (Villani, VIII, 40, 43, 49). He died in 1302. His portrait is preserved in a fresco by Benozzo Gozzoli in the church of San Francesco at Montefalco in Umbria. As general he introduced relaxations in the discipline of the Franciscan order, which allowed abuses to creep in and which were vehemently opposed by the ascetic Ubertino da Casale.

125. *scrittura*: The rule of St. Francis.

126. *ch'uno la fugge*: Matteo d'Acquasparta flees from the rule, which seems to him too strict.   *e altro la coarta*: Ubertino makes it more strict or narrow ("coarta," from the Latin *coarctare*, "to compress").

127-28. *Bonaventura da Bagnoregio*: St. Bonaventura (Giovanni di Fidanza) was born at Bagnoregio, near Orvieto, in 1221, the year of St. Dominic's death. As a child he was attacked by a dangerous disease, which was miraculously cured by St. Francis of Assisi. When the latter heard that the child had recovered, he is said to have exclaimed "buona ventura," whereupon the boy's mother changed his name to Bonaventura. In 1238 or 1243 he entered the Franciscan order. After studying at Paris under Alexander of Hales, he became successively professor of philosophy and theology and in 1257 was made doctor. Having risen to be general of the Franciscan order (in 1257), he was offered the archbishopric of York by Clement IV, which he declined. He was afterwards (1274) created cardinal bishop of Albano by Gregory X, whom he accompanied to the second Council of Lyons, where he died, July 15, 1274. St. Bonaventura was canonized in 1482 by Sixtus IV and placed among the doctors of the Church, with the title of Doctor Seraphicus, by Sixtus V. The authoritative edition of his voluminous works is *S. Bonaventurae opera omnia* (Quaracchi, 1882-1902).

129. *la sinistra cura*: Temporal interests, in which Bonaventura was much involved, as general of the Franciscan order (see preceding note) and cardinal bishop. For the expression and its significance, cf. Thomas Aquinas, *Summa theol.* I-II, q. 102, a. 4, ad 6:

> Sapientia autem pertinet ad dextram, sicut et caetera spiritualia bona; temporale autem nutrimentum ad sinistram, secundum illud Prov. 3, 16: *In sinistra illius divitiae et gloria*. Potestas autem sacerdotalis media est inter temporalia et spiritualem sapientiam; quia per eam et spiritualis sapientia, et temporalia dispensantur.

> And wisdom, like other spiritual goods, belongs to the right hand, while temporal nourishment belongs to the left, according to Prov. iii. 16: *In her left hand [are] riches and glory*. And the priestly power is midway between temporal goods and spiritual wisdom; because thereby both spiritual wisdom and temporal goods are dispensed.

Since *sapientia* is precisely uppermost in the meaning of this sphere and the souls who appear here are *sapienti*, these words are particularly significant. Bonaventura was thus between temporal and spiritual wisdom, and his statement means that he always gave priority to the spiritual side, which signifies contemplation. Bonaventura wrote a well-known treatise entitled *Itinerarium mentis in Deum* (*Itinerary of the*

Mind to God), which might even stand as an appropriate title of the *Paradiso* and of Dante's journey to Paradise.

130. *Illuminato*: Illuminato da Rieti, one of the earliest followers of St. Francis of Assisi. He accompanied St. Francis into Egypt.   *Augustin*: Augustine, another of the earliest followers of St. Francis of Assisi, whom he joined in 1210, was eventually (in 1216) head of the Franciscan order in Terra di Lavoro.

131. *fuor = furono.   scalzi poverelli*: The Franciscans.

132. *nel capestro*: Girt with the rope cord of the order. Cf. *Par.* XI, 87.   *fero = fecero.*

133. *Ugo da San Vittore*: Hugh of St. Victor, celebrated mystic and theologian of the beginning of the twelfth century. He was born near Ypres in Flanders *ca.* 1097 or, as some believe, in Saxony, and he was educated during his early years in the monastery of Hamersleben near Halberstadt in Saxony. In 1115 he removed to the abbey of St. Victor near Paris, which had recently been founded by William of Champeaux, the preceptor of Abelard, and which during the twelfth century was a center of mysticism. He became one of the canons-regular of the abbey and was in 1130 appointed to the chair of theology, which he held until his death in 1141. His reputation was so great that he was known as "alter Augustinus" and "lingua Augustini." He was the intimate friend of Bernard of Clairvaux, and among his pupils were Richard of St. Victor and Peter Lombard.

The writings of Hugh of St. Victor, which are very numerous and are characterized by great learning, are frequently quoted by Thomas Aquinas. The most celebrated are the *Didascalicon,* a sort of encyclopedia of the sciences as then understood, viewed in their relation to theology; the treatises *De arca Noe morali, De arca Noe mystica,* and *De vanitate mundi*; and the *De sacramentis Christianae fidei,* on the mysteries of the faith, comprising a systematic exposition of Catholic theology. He also wrote commentaries on various books of the Old and New Testament (with the latter of which he appears to rank as of equal importance the canons, the decretals, and the writings of the fathers), and upon the *De caelesti ierarchia* of Dionysius.

134. *Pietro Mangiadore*: Petrus Comestor (i.e., Peter the Eater, so called because he was an insatiable devourer of books), priest, and afterwards dean, of the cathedral of Troyes in France, where he was born in the first half of the twelfth century. He became canon of St. Victor in 1164 and chancellor of the University of Paris, and died at St. Victor in 1179, leaving all his possessions to the poor. His chief work was the *Historia scholastica*, which professed to be a history of the Church from the beginning of the world down to the times of the apostles; it consists mainly of a compilation of the historical portions of the Bible, accompanied by a commentary and parallels from profane history. It was the great authority on the subject in the Middle Ages and was translated into several languages.

Pietro Spano: Petrus Hispanus (Petrus Juliani) was born at Lisbon *ca.* 1225, where he at first followed his father's profession of medicine. He studied at Paris, probably under Albertus Magnus; subsequently he was ordained and became (1273) archbishop of Braga. In 1274 he was created cardinal bishop of Tusculum (Frascati) by Gregory X. On September 13, 1276, he was elected pope, under the title of John XXI, at Viterbo, in succession to Adrian V. He died May 20, 1277, after a reign of a little more than eight months, his death being caused by the fall of the ceiling of one of the rooms in his palace at Viterbo.

Besides several medical works of a more or less popular character (one of which, consisting of a collection of prescriptions, is entitled *Thesaurus pauperum*), Petrus Hispanus wrote a manual of logic, which, under the title of *Summulae logicales*, attained a wide popularity in the Middle Ages. In it the logic of the schools was expanded by the incorporation of fresh matter of a semi-grammatical character. In this treatise, which is divided into twelve parts, occurs for the first time the well-known mnemonic formula beginning "Barbara Celarent" for the valid forms of the syllogism.

136. *Natàn*: Nathan, the prophet, who was sent by God to reprove David (II Reg. 12:1-12) for his sin in causing the death of Uriah the Hittite in order that he might marry Bathsheba.

136-37. *'l metropolitano Crisostomo*: *Metropolitan* is the title of a bishop exercising powers over a province consisting of several dioceses. The title first appears in the fourth canon of the Council of Nicaea (325). The reference is to St. John Chrysostom (χρυσόστομος, golden-mouthed), celebrated Greek father of the Church, who was born at Antioch *ca.* 345 and died at Comana in Pontus in 407. He belonged to a noble family and was first a lawyer; he afterward became a monk, in which capacity he so distinguished himself by his preaching that the Emperor Arcadius appointed him (in 398) patriarch of Constantinople. His severity toward the clergy in his desire for reform made him an object of hatred to them and led to his deposition (403) at the instance of Theophilus, patriarch of Alexandria, and the Empress Eudoxia, whose excesses he had publicly rebuked. Sentence of exile was pronounced against him, but the people, to whom he had endeared himself by his preaching, rose in revolt, and he was reinstated in his office. Shortly afterward, he was again banished (404), and he finally died in exile on the shores of the Black Sea. He left nearly one thousand sermons or homilies as evidence of his eloquence.

137. *Anselmo*: Anselm, archbishop of Canterbury from 1093 to 1109, was born at Aosta in Piedmont in 1033, and in 1060, at the age of twenty-seven, he became a monk in the abbey of Bec in Normandy, to which he had been attracted by the fame of Lanfranc, at that time prior. In 1063, on the promotion of Lanfranc to the abbacy of Caen, he succeeded him as prior; fifteen years later, in 1078, on the death of Herluin, the founder of the monastery, he was made abbot, an office he held till 1093. In that year he was appointed archbishop of Canterbury by William Rufus, in succession to Lanfranc, after the see had been vacant for four years; in 1097, in consequence of disputes with William on matters of

ecclesiastical jurisdiction, he left England for Rome to consult the pope and remained on the Continent until William's death in 1100, when he was recalled by Henry I. He died at Canterbury, April 21, 1109 and was canonized, in 1494, by Alexander VI.

Anselm was the author of several theological works, the most important of which are the *Monologion* (to which Anselm gave the sub-title *Exemplum meditandi de ratione fidei*), the *Proslogion* (*Fides quaerens intellectum*), and the *Cur Deus homo* (a treatise on the atonement intended to prove the necessity of the incarnation).

137–38. *Donato . . . mano*: Aelius Donatus, Roman scholar and rhetorician of the fourth century, who is said to have been the tutor of Jerome. He was the author of a commentary on Virgil (now lost, but often alluded to by Servius) and of another on Terence, but his most famous work was an elementary Latin grammar, *Ars grammatica*, in three books, part of which served as a model for subsequent similar treatises. Because of the popularity of this work in the Middle Ages—it was one of the earliest books, being printed even before the invention of movable types—the name of its author became a synonym for grammar, just as Euclid did for geometry. Thus the title of a Provençal grammar of the thirteenth century begins: "Incipit Donatus Provincialis." Rutebeuf says in *L'État du monde* (vs. 158): "Chascuns a son Donet perdu." ("Each one has lost his Donatus.") See also *Piers Plowman* (B text, Passus V, vs. 209): "Thanne drowe I me amonges draperes my donet to lerne."

138. *la prim' arte*: Grammar is the first of the seven liberal arts of the trivium and quadrivium. See Dante, *Conv.* II, xiii, 8-10.

139. *Rabano*: Rabanus (more correctly Hrabanus) Maurus Magnentius, born at Mainz of noble parents *ca.* 776. While still a youth he entered the monastery at Fulda, where he received deacon's orders in 801. Shortly thereafter he proceeded to Tours to study under Alcuin, who in recognition of his piety and diligence gave him the surname of Maurus,

after St. Maurus (who died in 565), the favorite disciple of St. Benedict. He was ordained priest in 814 and after a pilgrimage to the Holy Land returned to Fulda in 817, where he became abbot in 822. He held this office for twenty years until 842, when he retired in order to devote himself more completely to religion and literature. Five years later, however, he was appointed to the archbishopric of Mainz, which he held until his death in 856. Rabanus, who was considered one of the most learned men of his time, wrote a voluminous commentary on the greater portion of the Bible and was the author of numerous theological works, the most important being the *De institutione clericorum*. His treatise *De laudibus sanctae crucis* contains figures in which rows of letters are cut by outlines of stars, crosses, and the like, so as to mark out words and sentences.

140. *Giovacchino*: Joachim of Floris, the Calabrian abbot. He appears to have enjoyed in his own day, and long afterwards, a reputation for prophetic power; hence Bonaventura speaks of him as "di spirito profetico dotato" (vs. 141), words which are taken from the anthem still chanted on the festival of St. Joachim, the father of the Virgin Mary, in the churches of Calabria.

Joachim was born *ca.* 1145 at Celico, about four miles northeast of Cosenza in Calabria. He made a pilgrimage to the Holy Land and on his return to Italy became a monk, entering (*ca.* 1158) the Cistercian monastery of Sambucina. In 1177 he was made abbot of Corazzo in Calabria. In 1185, Pope Urban III appointed a deputy abbot in order that Joachim might have leisure to devote himself to his writings. In 1189 Joachim founded a monastery, San Giovanni in Fiore in the forest of the Sila among the mountains of Calabria, whence he was named "de Floris." From this institution, the rule of which was sanctioned by Celestine III in 1196, ultimately sprang the so-called Ordo Florensis (absorbed by the Cistercians, 1505). Joachim died *ca.* 1202.

The authenticated works of Joachim comprise a commentary upon the Apocalypse (*Expositio in Apocalypsim*), a harmony of the Old and New Testaments (*Concordia novi et veteris Testamenti*), the *Psalterium decem chordarum,* and perhaps the *Adversus Iudeos*. Many works have been attributed to him—among them, the *Liber figurarum*, the authorship of which is much debated. He was credited with the authorship of a book on the popes, in which the persons and names of all the future popes were described.

Joachim "was the reputed author of many prophecies. He was also the first preacher of the doctrine that the dispensation of the Father (Old Testament) and of the Son (New Testament, and the Church as an institution) would be followed by the dispensation of the Holy Spirit, the period of perfection and freedom, without the necessity of disciplinary institutions. This was the 'Everlasting Gospel'—a dispensation, not a book. Joachim was a Cistercian, not a Franciscan; but the Franciscan 'Spirituals' were much influenced by him, and one of them, Gerardus by name, wrote a book entitled *Introduction to the Everlasting Gospel*. 'Joachism' henceforth became a feature of the extreme Spiritual movement among the Franciscans, and as such was opposed by Bonaventura" (TC).

It should be noted that Joachim occupies, in this second circle of *sapienti*, a position corresponding to that of Siger (*Par*. X, 136) in the first: each is the last named, each is to the immediate left of the spokesman. Both were not only controversial figures, but Thomas Aquinas, the spokesman of the first circle, engaged in an attack on Siger's ideas, and Bonaventura attacked the Spirituals of the Joachimite order. The poet's parallelism expresses a spirit of lofty conciliation and heavenly charity.

142. *inveggiar*: The meaning of the verb in this context is much debated. (See Petrocchi's note concerning it.) The most plausible interpretation would seem to be that "inveggiar," deriving from *invidiare*, "to envy," would mean (as does its Provençal equivalent *envejar*) "to envy in a good sense," hence "to praise." Cf. the adjective "invidiosi" as applied to Siger (*Par*. X, 138 and note).   *cotanto paladino*: St. Dominic. The term "paladino" ("warrior") is quite in keeping with "santo atleta" (vs. 56) and the presentation in general of Dominic.

143. *l'infiammata cortesia*: "The ardent [loving] courtesy" of Aquinas refers primarily to the fact that he, as a Dominican, eulogized Francis.

144. *discreto latino*: "Discerning discourse"; but, given the context, the adjective may also bear the suggestion of "reverent." For "latino" in this sense, cf. *Par.* X, 120.

145. *meco = con me.   compagnia*: The eleven companions of Bonaventura just named.

CANTO XIII

1. *cupe*: "Wishes." From the Latin *cupit*.

2. *l'image = l'immagine*.

4–15. *quindici stelle . . . gelo*: On this whole elaborate and complex figure, see Grandgent, who observes: "The better to visualize the scene, the reader is asked to pick out twenty-four of the brightest fixed stars and imagine them arranged in the shape of a double Ariadne's Crown. Fifteen miscellaneous ones are selected first, there being, according to Ptolemaic astronomy, fifteen stars of the first magnitude in the whole sky. Next are added the seven conspicuous members of the Wain (the Great Bear or Dipper), a constellation which in our climate never sinks below the horizon: cf. Dante, *Rime* C, 28-29. The remaining two of the twenty-four are from the hornlike Little Bear (or Little Dipper) whose peak is the North Star; the two chosen—those which, at the other extremity, form the mouth of the horn—are, according to Alfraganus, of the second magnitude."

4. *plage = plaghe*. From the Latin *plagae*.

5. *sereno*: "Brightness."

6. *compage = compagine*,   "composition,"   "condition." From the Latin *compages*.

7. *quel carro*: The Wain (Ursa Major, or the Big Dipper). See n. to vss. 4-15.

7-8. *il seno . . . giorno*: The vault of heaven over the northern hemisphere. Ursa Major cannot literally be seen day and night, but one is asked to imagine it so.

9. *temo = timone*, "pole."   *non vien meno*: "Never disappears," i.e., the pole of the Wain, as it turns about, changing position, never sinks below the horizon, is always visible.

10. *la bocca di quel corno*: The last two stars of the hornlike Little Dipper (Ursa Minor), the mouth ("bocca") of which is formed by the two stars farthest from the polestar.

11. *punta*: The North Star, which forms the pointed end of the horn.   *stelo*: "Axis."

12. *prima rota*: The daily rotation of the heavens.

13. *aver fatto*: Depends on "imagini" in vs. 1.   *di sé*: "Of themselves."   *segni*: "Constellations."

14. *la figliuola di Minoi*: The daughter of King Minos (see *Inf.* V, 4) was Ariadne. In *Metam.* VIII, 174-82 Ovid relates how Ariadne's crown was turned into a constellation. *Minoi*: "The form *Minoi* was taken from the oblique cases of *Minos* (*Minois*, etc.)" (Gr).

16. *ne l'altro*: "Within the other."

18. *che l'uno andasse al primo e l'altro al poi*: "That one should start at the word 'First!' and the other at the word 'Next!' " (Gr).

19. *l'ombra*: "Faint image."

22. *di là da*: "Beyond."

23. *Chiana*: River in east Tuscany and southwest Umbria. It was noted in Dante's time for the sluggishness of its stream. The silting up of its bed turned the whole Val di Chiana into a malarious swamp, which thus became a byword for its unhealthiness.

24. *il ciel*: The Primum Mobile, swiftest of the heavens.

25-27. *Lì si cantò . . . l'umana*: "As celebrants of old sang hymns to heathen deities, so the Heavenly chorus sings of the threefold God and the twofold Christ, perhaps in the words of the Athanasian Creed" (Gr).

25. *Peana*: "*Paean* (accusative *Paeana*) is a name given to Apollo, and also a hymn in his honor" (Gr).

27. *essa*: I.e., "divina natura."

28. *Compié 'l cantare e 'l volger*: "Cantare" and "volger" are subjects of "compié." *sua*: "Their."

29. *attesersi = si attesero.*

30. *felicitando sé di cura in cura*: The spirits rejoice in turning from their dance and song, their first "care," to their next, the satisfying of Dante's other question.

31. *numi*: "Divinities," the blessed spirits. Cf. *Par.* V, 123.

32. *luce*: The "light" of Thomas Aquinas.

32-33. *in che . . . fumi*: Within which the wondrous life of Francis of Assisi was related.

33. *fumi = fummi (mi fu).* For the unusual rhyme, see *Inf.* VIII, 17.

34. *Quando*: "Since." *una paglia*: The question suggested by "u' ben s'impingua" (see *Par.* X, 96; XI, 25). *trita*: "Threshed" (Gr).

35. *riposta*: "Stored away."

36. *l'altra*: I.e., *paglia,* the question raised by "non surse il secondo" (see *Par.* X, 114; XI, 26).

37-39. *petto onde la costa . . . costa*: The "breast" of Adam, whence was taken the "rib" to form Eve.

39. *il cui palato*: Eve's taste for the forbidden fruit.

40. *quel*: That is, *petto*, the breast of Christ.

41. *e prima e poscia*: "Both after [His death on the Cross] and before," i.e., for all generations. Cf. *Par.* VII, 112-20.

43. *quantunque = quanto*.

45. *quel valor*: God, who created Adam and Christ (in his human aspect).

46. *miri*: "You marvel."   *suso = sopra*.

47–48. *quando narrai . . . chiuso*: Cf. *Par.* X, 109-14.

47. *non ebbe*: Thomas once more changes the verb of the affirmation, which first was "surse" (*Par.* X, 114) and then "nacque" (*Par.* XI, 26).

48. *ben*: "Goodness."   *quinta luce*: The light that envelops the soul of Solomon.

51. *nel vero farsi come centro in tondo*: "A circle has but one point as its center. The truth is as a mathematical point, in which the two opinions coincide" (Gr).

52. *Ciò che non more*: Incorruptible things created directly by God: the angels, the heavens, primal matter, and human souls.   *ciò che può morire*: Corruptible things, created by secondary causes (see *Par.* VII, 133-41).

53–54. *non è se non . . . Sire*: Cf. *Par.* X, 1-6. Thus all creation, corruptible and incorruptible, is said to be merely a reflection ("splendor") of God's idea. The idea is the Word, second person of the Trinity, which God the Father ("il nostro Sire") contemplates and through which, in His love, He produces, in His eternity, all things. The Word is the archetype of all things created directly or indirectly. See Thomas Aquinas, *Summa theol.* I, q. 44, a. 3, resp.:

> Deus est prima causa exemplaris omnium rerum. Ad cuius evidentiam considerandum est quod ad productionem alicuius rei ideo necessarium est exemplar, ut effectus determinatam formam consequatur. Artifex enim producit determinatam formam in materia propter exemplar ad quod inspicit, sive illud sit exemplar ad

quod extra intuetur, sive sit exemplar interius mente conceptum. Manifestum est autem quod ea quae naturaliter fiunt, determinatas formas consequuntur. Haec autem formarum determinatio oportet quod reducatur, sicut in primum principium, in divinam sapientiam, quae ordinem universi excogitavit, qui in rerum distinctione consistit. Et ideo oportet dicere quod in divina sapientia sint rationes omnium rerum, quas supra diximus (quaest. 15, art. 1) ideas, id est, formas exemplares in mente divina existentes. Quae quidem, licet multiplicentur secundum respectum ad res, tamen non sunt realiter aliud a divina essentia, prout eius similitudo a diversis participari potest diversimode. Sic igitur ipse Deus est primum exemplar omnium. Possunt etiam in rebus creatis quaedam aliorum exemplaria dici secundum quod quaedam sunt ad similitudinem aliorum vel secundum eamdem speciem, vel secundum analogiam alicuius imitationis.

God is the first exemplar cause of all things. In proof whereof we must consider that if for the production of anything an exemplar is necessary, it is in order that the effect may receive a determinate form. For an artificer produces a determinate form in matter by reason of the exemplar before him, whether it is the exemplar beheld externally, or the exemplar interiorly conceived in the mind. Now it is manifest that things made by nature receive determinate forms. This determination of forms must be reduced to the divine wisdom as its first principle, for divine wisdom devised the order of the universe, which order consists in the variety of things. And therefore we must say that in the divine wisdom are the types of all things, which types we have called ideas—*i.e.*, exemplar forms existing in the divine mind (q. 15, a. 1). And these ideas, though multiplied by their relations to things, in reality are not apart from the divine essence, according as the likeness to that essence can be shared diversely by different things. In this manner therefore God Himself is the first exemplar of all things. Moreover, in things created one may be called the exemplar of another by the reason of its likeness thereto, either in species, or by the analogy of some kind of imitation.

Note that with "amando" the verses bring in the Holy Ghost and thus the Trinity; and this continues by restatement in the next tercet.

55–57. *ché quella . . . s'intrea*: Now the subject of the action becomes the "viva luce," the Word which emanates as light from the Father without ever separating Himself from the Father or from the Love (Holy Ghost), which makes them three (is their third part).

55. *mea*: Literally, "pours."

57. *s'intrea*: The verb is Dante's invention.

58. *per sua bontate il suo raggiare aduna*: "In its goodness, gathers its radiance together."

59. *quasi specchiato, in nove sussistenze*: The "nine sub-sistences" are the nine orders of angels, reflecting God's wisdom, which contains the plan of the universe. The reader will recognize the pattern of the descent of a power from on high through the spheres down to the sublunar world, by way of the nine orders of angels who turn the spheres, which was followed out in *Par.* II. The angels, receiving light from the Word, reflect it in turn and are thus properly termed "mirrors." See *Conv.* III, xiv, 4, where Dante writes:

Lo primo agente, cioè Dio, pinge la sua virtù in cosa per modo di diritto raggio, e in cose per modo di splendore reverberato; onde ne le Intelligenze raggia la divina luce sanza mezzo, ne l'altre si ripercuote da queste Intelligenze prima illuminate.

The prime agent—to wit God—stamps his power upon some things after the manner of a direct ray, and upon others after the manner of a reflected splendour; for upon the intelligences the divine light rays without medium, upon other things it is reflected by those intelligences which are first enlightened.

But, though reflected in so many mirrors, the divine light remains eternally one at its source. Cf. *Par*. XXIX, 142-45.

61-62. *Quindi discende . . . atto*: From the nine orders of angels this creating light descends then to the elements of the sublunar world ("ultime potenze"). Again the verses of *Par*. II (112-41) may be reconsidered as an exposition of this process, but here we are concerned more with what happens to the *virtù* from above when it extends to the sublunar world. Each heaven is a *potenza* insofar as it receives from above and is an *atto* insofar as it transmits to the world beneath it.

63. *contingenze*: Cf. Thomas Aquinas, *Summa theol*. I, q. 86, a. 3, resp.:

> Contingentia dupliciter possunt considerari: uno modo, secundum quod contingentia sunt; alio modo, secundum quod in eis aliquid necessitatis invenitur; nihil enim est adeo contingens, quin in se aliquid necessarium habeat. . . .
>
> Est autem unumquodque contingens ex parte materiae; quia contingens est quod potest esse et non esse. Potentia autem pertinet ad materiam.
>
> Contingent things can be considered in two ways; either as contingent, or as containing some element of necessity, since every contingent thing has in it something necessary. Now contingency arises from matter, for contingency is a potentiality to be or not to be, and potentiality belongs to matter.

Thus "brevi contingenze" signify things of the sublunar world, which are made from the elements, which may be shaped by the descending power but are of brief duration and, viewed from the *material* side, are mere potentialities and have no necessary or enduring existence.

66. *con seme e sanza seme*: Animals and vegetables "with seed," minerals "without seed." *il ciel movendo*: The heavens (singular for plural, as frequently in the poem) in their revolution, which constitutes nature.

67–69. *La cera . . . traluce*: The "wax" of generated things (in the sublunar world) and the heavens (which imprint their form on elemental matter) are not always the same (being variously disposed at different times, the heavens or "stamp" on the one hand, and matter or "wax" on the other). See Virgil, *Aen*. VI, 848: "Vivos ducent de marmore voltus." ("[They] shall from marble draw forth the features of life.") The subject of "traluce" is the wax of the elemental world, and the "segno ideale" is the imprint of the idea which has been transmitted downwards so variously through the heavens (the process followed out in the preceding verses). Generated things shine more or less with the imprint from above, which comes ultimately from the idea or Word, hence "ideale." Cf. *Par.* I, 1-3.

67. *duce*: "Shapes" or stamps (to keep the figure).

68. *però = perciò*.

70. *Ond'*: "Wherefore."   *elli avvien*: "It happens." "Elli" is a pleonastic subject.

70–71. *un medesimo legno, secondo specie*: One tree equal to another as to species.

72. *voi nascete con diverso ingegno*: You human creatures (though all of one species) are born with different dispositions. See *Par.* VIII, 122-48, where this fact is viewed as providential.

73. *Se fosse a punto la cera dedutta*: "If the wax were perfectly disposed." "Dedutta," from the Latin *deducta*, bears the suggestion of "made ready," i.e., to receive.

74. *il cielo*: Again the singular for the plural, "the heavens."

75. *la luce del suggel parrebbe tutta*: The light of the "segno ideale," the stamp, would shine forth, be visible, entirely, perfectly.

76. *la natura*: The whole causal operation of the heavens, which is termed "la circular natura" in *Par.* VIII, 127. In the context here, however, there is something of a personification

of Nature implied, a personification which can lead into the striking figure of the artist which follows.

77–78. *similemente operando . . . trema*: Deficiencies or imperfections in the sublunar world must be explained. They cannot really be assigned to any source above nature, for that would be to derogate from God's idea; they must therefore result from Nature (the revolving heavens) in its downward transmission of the "seal," as if Nature were an artist who has the clear idea (right reason) of that which is to be made, but a hand that trembles. Even so, the image is a daring one, for Nature is, after all, God's agent in this process!

79–81. *Però se 'l caldo amor . . . s'acquista*: The act of creation now is viewed as a disposition whereby the ardent Love (the Holy Ghost) disposes and stamps the clear Vision (the Son, Wisdom, second person of the Trinity) of the first Power (God the Father). When the entire Trinity "stamps" directly, then all perfection is the result; no trembling hand of any intermediary, Nature, and no secondary causes, are involved.

82–84. *Così fu fatta . . . pregna*: Thus without intermediary —but directly—was man created from the dust ("terra") with all possible perfection (see Gen. 2:7); thus, in the womb of Mary, was Christ conceived. Adam and Christ (in his human aspect) were created perfect.

85–87. *sì ch'io commendo . . . persone*: Thus the opinion held by Dante that Adam and Christ in his human aspect represent the summit of perfection in human nature is commended as correct, and that perfection never was nor will be surpassed.

88–90. *Or s'i' non procedesse . . . tue*: Thomas Aquinas now anticipates an objection on Dante's part. If he did not proceed in his discourse, Dante might well put the question as phrased in vs. 89, having understood Aquinas to have affirmed absolutely that Solomon was "without peer" in human nature.

88. *piùe = più.*

91–93. *Ma perché . . . dimandare*: But in order that the con-
cept be made clear (as it is not yet), Dante is urged to think
who Solomon was (a king) and what he (as king) asked of
God. Cf. III Reg. 3:5-12:

Apparuit autem Dominus Salomoni per somnium nocte,
dicens: Postula quod vis ut dem tibi. Et ait Salomon:
Tu fecisti cum servo tuo David patre meo misericordiam
magnam, sicut ambulavit in conspectu tuo in veritate
et iustitia et recto corde tecum; custodisti ei misericordi-
am tuam grandem, et dedisti ei filium sedentem super
thronum eius sicut est hodie. Et nunc, Domine Deus,
tu regnare fecisti servum tuum pro David patre meo.
Ego autem sum puer parvulus, et ignorans egressum et
introitum meum; et servus tuus in medio est populi
quem elegisti, populi infiniti qui numerari et supputari
non potest prae multitudine. Dabis ergo servo tuo cor
docile, ut populum tuum iudicare possit et discernere
inter bonum et malum; quis enim poterit iudicare popu-
lum istum, populum tuum hunc multum?

Placuit ergo sermo coram Domino, quod Salomon
postulasset huiuscemodi rem, et dixit Dominus Sa-
lomoni: Quia postulasti verbum hoc, et non petisti tibi
dies multos, nec divitias aut animas inimicorum tuorum,
sed postulasti tibi sapientiam ad discernendum iudicium,
ecce feci tibi secundum sermones tuos, et dedi tibi cor
sapiens et intelligens, in tantum ut nullus ante te similis
tui fuerit nec post te surrecturus sit.

And the Lord appeared to Solomon in a dream by night,
saying: Ask what thou wilt that I should give thee.

And Solomon said: Thou hast shewn great mercy to
thy servant David my father, even as he walked before
thee in truth, and justice, and an upright heart with thee;
and thou hast kept thy great mercy for him, and hast
given him a son to sit on his throne, as it is this day.

And now, O Lord God, thou hast made thy servant
king instead of David my father. And I am but a child,
and know not how to go out and come in.

And thy servant is in the midst of the people which thou hast chosen, an immense people, which cannot be numbered nor counted for multitude.

Give therefore to thy servant an understanding heart, to judge thy people, and discern between good and evil. For who shall be able to judge this people, thy people which is so numerous?

And the word was pleasing to the Lord that Solomon had asked such a thing.

And the Lord said to Solomon: Because thou hast asked this thing, and hast not asked for thyself long life or riches, nor the lives of thy enemies, but hast asked for thyself wisdom to discern judgment.

Behold I have done for thee according to thy words, and have given thee a wise and understanding heart; insomuch that there hath been no one like thee before thee, nor shall arise after thee.

Cf. Dante, *Conv*. IV, xxvii, 6.

94. *posse = possa*.

97–102. *non per sapere . . . avesse*: The things other than wisdom to govern which Solomon might have asked for are now phrased as specific questions in theology, dialectic, physics, and geometry.

97–98. *il numero in che . . . sù*: The question of the number of the heavenly motors, or angels, was treated by Plato and Aristotle and is discussed by Dante in the *Convivio* (see *Conv*. II, iv and v). The angels are almost countless.

97. *enno = sono*.

98–99. *o se necesse . . . fenno*: "Or whether an absolute premise with a conditional premise has ever produced an absolute conclusion." This is a scholastic problem in logic, also touched upon by Plato and Aristotle. The answer is "no."

100. *non si est dare primum motum esse*: "Not, whether a prime motion is to be admitted," i.e., a motion independent

of any cause. See Aristotle, *Physica* VIII, 1-2, 250^b-253^a. All motion is dependent on God (see Dante, *De mon.* I, ix, 2).

101-2. *o se del mezzo . . . avesse*: See Euclid, *Elements* III, 31. "Note that here again the answer is 'no' " (Gr).

102. *retto*: "Right angle."

103-5. *Onde, se ciò . . . percuote*: "Wherefore—if thou notest what I said, and this—that peerless vision which the arrow of my intention hits is kingly prudence" (Gr).

106. *al "surse"*: To my phrase "non surse il secondo" (*Par.* X, 114).

109. *questa distinzion*: I.e., that Solomon was the wisest of all kings, not of all men.

110-11. *e così puote star . . . Diletto*: My affirmation and distinction are in accord with your belief respecting Adam and Christ.

110. *puote = può*.

114. *e al sì e al no che tu non vedi*: I.e., in affirming or denying in a matter where you cannot see clearly.

115. *bene a basso*: Far down in the scale of foolishness.

117. *ne l'un così come ne l'altro passo*: "In the one case as well as in the other," that is, whether he affirms or denies.

118. *elli 'ncontra*: "It happens." The "elli" is the familiar pleonastic subject.

119. *corrente*: "Hasty." Cf. Dante, *Conv.* IV, xv, 15-16. See Prov. 29:20: "Vidisti hominem velocem ad loquendum? stultitia magis speranda est quam illius correptio." ("Do you see a man hasty in his words? More can be hoped for from a fool!")

120. *affetto*: "Fondness" for one's own opinion. "Affetto" is the subject of "lega," and "intelletto" the object.

121. *Vie più*: "Far worse." *'ndarno = indarno,* "in vain." *da riva si parte*: The metaphor is made clear in vs. 123. The subject of "si parte" is "chi" (vs. 123). *si parte*: "Sails forth."

122. *non torna tal qual e' si move*: "Chi" in vs. 123 is still the subject. Such a person is (out of metaphor) only confirmed in error and false opinions and so is worse off than before.

125. *Parmenide*: Parmenides, an early Greek philosopher, was born at Elea in Italy *ca.* 513 B.C. He is the chief representative of the Eleatic philosophy, in which he was followed by his disciple Zeno; he and Zeno, according to Plato, met Socrates in Athens in *ca.* 448 B.C. Parmenides wrote in verse his philosophical views *On Nature*, of which only fragments are extant. *Melisso*: Melissus, a philosopher of Samos who flourished *ca.* 441 B.C., was a follower of Parmenides. Only fragments of his writings are extant. *Brisso*: Bryson was a Greek philosopher mentioned by Aristotle as having attempted to square the circle, a problem which apparently he tried to solve dishonestly by non-geometrical methods (*Soph. elench.* I, 11, 171[b]; *Anal. post.* I, 9, 75[b]).

127. *Sabellio*: Sabellius, heresiarch of the third century, was born at Pentapolis in North Africa, became presbyter of Ptolemais, and died *ca.* 265. He refused to accept the received doctrine of the Trinity and held that the terms Father, Son, and Holy Ghost were merely different names for the One God. He was excommunicated by Pope Callistus I.
Arrio: Arius, who died in 336, was the originator of the Arian heresy that the Father and the Son are not "one substance," a doctrine which the Athanasian creed was designed to controvert. Arius was presbyter of Alexandria and while holding that position (*ca.* 318) promulgated his heresy, which consisted in the doctrine that Christ was a created being inferior to God the Father in nature and dignity, though the first of all created beings, and that the Holy Ghost is not God, but was created by the power of the Son. This doctrine, which was condemned by the Council of Nicaea in 325,

gained many adherents after the death of Arius, including several emperors, and gave rise to the famous Heterousian and Homoousian controversy, which distracted the Church for three hundred years.

128–29. *come spade . . . volti*: "Instead of reflecting the Scriptures accurately, like a glass, they gave a distorted image of them, similar to faces mirrored in sword blades" (Gr).

130–32. *Non sien le genti . . . mature*: See I Cor. 4:5: "Itaque nolite ante tempus iudicare." ("Therefore, pass no judgment before the time.") See Boethius, *Consol. philos.* IV, vi, ll. 1-210, which deals with God's providence.

130. *ancor*: "Moreover." This serves to turn the admonition from famous men who presumed in their false knowledge, to people generally in their judgments concerning the future, which leads, in the closing verses, to the presumption of knowing the inscrutable ways of God's providence. And in the background of this latter admonition is the case of Solomon, whether he was saved or not (see n. to *Par.* X, 111).

134. *prun*: "Briar."   *rigido*: Dry and hard, as if dead. *feroce*: Covered with thorns.

136. *legno*: "Ship."

139. *donna Berta e ser Martino*: "*Berta* and *Martino* were equivalent to our 'Tom, Dick, and Harry'" (Gr). Cf. Dante, *Conv.* I, viii, 13; *De vulg. eloqu.* II, vi, 5.

140. *per vedere*: "Seeing."   *furare*: "Steal."   *offerere*: "Make pious offerings." Pronounced *offerère*.

142. *quel*: The thief.   *surgere*: "Rise up" (i.e., be saved, by true repentance, before his death).   *e quel*: The devout person.   *cadere*: "Fall" (into sin and damnation).

CANTO XIV

1–3. *Dal centro . . . dentro*: The reader will note that the image of the circle remains uppermost in this heaven of the *sapienti*, the wise, and will remember that the circle is the symbol of intellection. We are to imagine that the water, in this case, is struck in the exact middle of its surface.

1. *cerchio*: "Rim."

2. *movesi* = *si move*.

4. *fé sùbito caso*: "Suddenly fell into" my mind; "suddenly occurred to me." "Caso" here is from the Latin *casus*, "a fall." There are other examples of this usage in early Italian. The subject of "fé" (*fece*) is "questo ch'io dico" in vs. 5.

6. *vita*: "Soul." Cf. *Par.* IX, 7; XII, 127.

7–9. *per la similitudine . . . piacque*: "The sound waves proceeding from St. Thomas, in the ring of bright spirits, and from Beatrice, in the center, remind Dante of the circular ripples in a round vessel, when the water is stirred at the edge or in the middle" (Gr). R. Murari (1905, p. 228) notes a similar comparison that is to be found in Boethius, *De institutione musica* I, 14.

10. *costui*: Dante.

10-11. *e nol vi dice . . . ancora*: Dante has not expressed his question yet, either vocally or—by clear formulation—in his own mind (the spirits in the two circles would of course know his thoughts, which would thus be expressed to them without utterance). Beatrice, however, even before such a formulation in Dante's mind, clearly knows what his question is (cf. *Par.* XV, 61-63) and proceeds to state it. He wishes to "go to the root" of yet another truth (vs. 12).

13. *Diteli = ditegli* (imperative).

13-14. *onde s'infiora vostra sustanza*: "Whereof your souls flower," i.e., are radiant.

15. *ell' = ella*, i.e., *essa*.

16-17. *poi che sarete visibili rifatti*: "Visibili" is here used in the sense of "seeing with one's bodily eyes." After the Last Judgment these souls will be reunited with their glorified bodies, and each will be again the "form" of its body forever.

18. *esser porà ch'al veder non vi nòi*: Since the answer to the first question is affirmative, of course, then the further question is: "How can it be that all this bright radiance in Heaven will not hurt your sight, will not dazzle your bodily eyes?" On this question and the answer that follows, Grandgent observes: "The effulgence that clothes the soul will remain after the restoration of the flesh, but it will not dazzle the bodily eyes; for the glorified body can suffer nothing except through the spirit. This 'claritas' is discussed by St. Thomas in the *Summa Theologiae*, Tertia, Suppl., Qu. lxxxv, Art. 1-3." See *Summa theol.* III, Suppl., q. 85, a. 2, ad 2, where Aquinas says:

> Sicut corpus gloriosum non potest pati aliquid passione naturae, sed solum passione animae, ita ex proprietate gloriae non agit nisi actione animae. Claritas autem intensa non offendit visum, inquantum agit actione animae, sed secundum hoc magis delectat; offendit autem, inquantum agit actione naturae, calefaciendo et dissolvendo organum visus, et disgregando spiritus. Et ideo claritas corporis gloriosi, quamvis excedat claritatem

solis, tamen de sua natura non offendit visum, sed demulcet.

Just as a glorified body is not passible to a passion of nature but only to a passion of the soul, so in virtue of its property of glory it acts only by the action of the soul. Now intense clarity does not disturb the sight, in so far as it acts by the action of the soul, for thus it rather gives delight, but it disturbs it in so far as it acts by the action of nature by heating and destroying the organ of sight, and by scattering the spirits asunder. Hence, though the clarity of a glorified body surpasses the clarity of the sun, it does not by its nature disturb the sight but soothes it.

porà = potrà. *nòi*: "Hurt." "Nòi" is from *noiare*. Cf. *Purg.* IX, 87.

19. *pinti = spinti, sospinti.* *tratti*: "Drawn." For the same notion in metaphor, see *Par.* X, 142.

20. *a la fiata*: "From time to time." See E. G. Parodi (1957), p. 274, n. 121; M. Barbi (1903), p. 6. *vanno a rota*: "Dance a round dance."

22. *orazion*: "Question." *divota*: "Reverent."

23. *mostrar = mostrarono.*

24. *mira nota*: "Wondrous song." For *nota* in this sense, cf. *Purg.* XXXII, 33; *Par.* VI, 124.

25. *Qual*: "Whosoever." *qui*: "Here" on earth.

26. *colà sù*: In Heaven. *quive = quivi*, referring to "colà sù."

27. *lo refrigerio de l'etterna ploia*: Souls in Heaven are constantly "refreshed" by the down-pouring (rain) of God's grace. "Ploia" is from the Provençal *ploia*. For a similar use, see *Par.* XXIV, 91.

28–30. *Quell' uno e due e tre . . . circunscrive*: "Once more the souls celebrate the mystery of the Trinity. Cf. XIII, 26"

(Gr). For parallels to vs. 30 in Gregory, Isidore of Seville, Hugh of St. Victor, and Peter Lombard, among others, see J. S. P. Tatlock (1919), p. 275. Cf. *Purg.* XI, 2. The Empyrean heaven, which does indeed "enclose all," was sometimes identified with the mind of God.

31. *tre volte*: The Trinity is not only celebrated by such a number, but the poet has seen to it that a single tercet expresses what is sung (vss. 28-30).

33. *merto = merito.   muno*: "Reward." "Muno" is from the Latin *munus*.

34. *luce*: The "light" is that of Solomon (see *Par.* X, 109). The Song of Solomon (Canticle of Canticles) celebrates the union of the divine with the human, the resurrection of the body. See *Bullettino della Società Dantesca Italiana* N.S. XX (1913): 236-37.   *dia = diva*, "resplendent."

36. *angelo*: Gabriel. Cf. Luc. 1:28.

37-39. *Quanto fia lunga . . . vesta*: The joy of Paradise will be eternal, and the radiance of the souls eternal, whether in the glorified body or not.

40-42. *La sua chiarezza . . . valore*: "The brightness of the 'garment' of light shall be proportionate to the fervency of love in each soul, the love shall be proportionate to the distinctness of its vision of God, and that vision is a gift of Grace, or predestination, not dependent on merit" (Gr). The point of doctrine here reflected in the sequential order of three (brightness, fervency of love, vision) represents a reversal of the actual order, as vss. 46-51 make clear by a restatement of that order. See Bonaventura, *Soliloquium* IV, v, 27: "Tantum gaudebunt, quantum amabunt; tantum amabunt, quantum cognoscent." ("They shall rejoice in proportion as they shall love; they shall love in proportion as they shall know.")

41. *quella*: Here used for *questa*, i.e., "visione," which is the subject of "séguita," understood as repeated from vs. 40.

42. *sovra suo valore*: "Beyond its desert" (Gr).

43. *Come*: "When."

43–45. *la carne . . . quanta*: The soul is the form of the body, and the human creature is more perfect when it has its body. This point is actually touched on in *Inf.* VI, 103-8 (see n. to *Inf.* VI, 106-7) and derives from Aristotle, even though in his philosophy he never dreamt of a glorified body. The glorified body adds an even greater perfection. Grandgent comments: "Now, inasmuch as man was made to consist of both spirit and matter, it follows that the blessed will be more perfect after the resurrection than before and therefore more like to God, who is absolute perfection. As St. Thomas says (*Summa Theologiae*, Tertia, Suppl., Qu. xciii, Art. 1, ad 1): 'Anima coniuncta corpori glorioso est magis Deo similis quam ab eo separata, inquantum coniuncta habet esse perfectius: quanto enim est aliquid perfectius, tanto est Deo similius.' (The soul united to a glorified body is more like to God than when separated therefrom, insofar as when united it has more perfect being. For the more perfect a thing is the more it is like to God.) The bodiless soul in Heaven has full spiritual happiness; but when clad again in the flesh it will possess bodily happiness as well: its joy will be increased 'extensively.' Therefore the blessed, while feeling no sorrow, look forward with pleasure to the Judgment Day, when, as they know, they will be complete, more akin to their Maker, and endowed with an additional capacity for blessedness. 'Omne autem imperfectum,' says St. Thomas (*loc. cit.* [resp.]), 'appetit suam perfectionem. Et ideo anima separata naturaliter appetit corporis coniunctionem.' (Now every imperfect thing desires its perfection. Hence the separated soul naturally desires reunion with the body.)" See Bernard of Clairvaux, *De diligendo Deo* XI, 30-32; E. G. Gardner (1913), pp. 119-21.

46–48. *per che s'accrescerà . . . condiziona*: The light given to the blessed by God, the supreme good, is the light of glory, by means of which (and *only* by means of which) each can see God. Cf. *Par.* XXX, 100-102.

46. *ne = ci* (indirect object).

48. *ne = ci* (direct object).

49–51. *onde la vision . . . vene*: Now the sequence is stated in its actual order, vision coming first, then love, then radiance. Cf. n. to vss. 40-42.

53. *vivo candor*: This suggests a white-hot glow.   *quella soverchia*: " 'Outshines it' (the flame). The coal glows through the flame that envelops it" (Gr).

54. *sì che la sua parvenza si difende*: "So that its visibility is maintained."

55. *ne = ci*.

56. *apparenza*: "Distinctness."

57. *tutto dì*: "As yet," "still."

58–60. *né potrà . . . dilettarne*: Cf. n. to vs. 18.

60. *dilettarne = dilettarci*. Cf. "affaticarne" (*affaticarci*) in rhyme (vs. 58).

62. *Amme*: "Amen." A clerical Latinism.

63. *mostrar = mostrarono*.

64. *non pur per lor*: "Not for themselves alone."

65. *fuor = furono*.

66. *fosser = fossero*, the subject of which is "l'uno e l'altro coro," vs. 62.

67. *di chiarezza pari*: Of uniform brightness, i.e., in all its parts.

68. *un lustro*: A splendor (cf. *Purg.* XXIX, 16).   *sopra*: "In addition to," i.e., to the splendor of the two circles of lights already there.

69. *orizzonte che rischiari*: The horizon becomes bright, of course, where the sun rises.

70–72. *E sì come . . . vera*: The simile changes abruptly from the moment of sunrise to that of twilight.

71. *nove parvenze*: "New appearances," i.e., of stars, faint in the twilight.

72. *la vista*: The sight of these faint stars.

73. *novelle sussistenze*: "New souls."

74–76. *un giro . . . Spiro*: This third circle of lights (the context and simile clearly suggest that they are a multitude and not merely twelve lights) completes the triad and is obviously yet another way of celebrating the Trinity here. The Holy Ghost, which is Love, illumines all the souls in each of the three circles, but to end the exclamation in the name of the third person of the Trinity points up this very fact, since in the usual order of naming the three persons the Holy Ghost comes last. Moreover, no spirits of this third circle are named, hence their appearance here for the purpose of completing the number three is the more evident.

"Line 76 makes it clear that this third circle specially represents the Holy Spirit, and so completes the symbol of the Trinity. . . .

"In its dimness at first and brightness afterwards, there may be a reference to the difficulty that has always been experienced in finding an adequate *philosophical* basis for the doctrine of the Third Person of the Trinity corresponding to the clearness of the distinction between the conceptions of God in his essence (Father) and God as manifested (Son); whereas to the more strictly *theological* speculation, or rather to the religious experience, the doctrine of the Holy Spirit (God regarded not as the Creator or the Redeemer, but as the Inspirer) has always had a special vividness" (TC).

77. *sùbito e candente*: "Suddenly incandescent." Cf. "candor" in vs. 53.

78. *nol soffriro = soffrirono*, "did not endure it."

81. *si vuol lasciar*: "Must be left." This new sight of Beatrice is such that it surpasses the memory's powers of retention.

Cf. *Par.* I, 7-9. But, as usual, Dante's gazing on Beatrice "empowers" him to rise to the next heaven (cf. *Par.* X, 93), and, looking up now, he is immediately lifted to the fifth sphere.

83. *translato*: "Borne." The word is from the Latin *translatus*.

84. *in più alta salute*: "To a higher degree of blessedness," that of the fifth heaven, the sphere of Mars. The very principle of hierarchy in the order of the heavens requires that this be so. It should be remembered that the sphere of Mars is the midmost of the nine material heavens and so represents a center, even as does the sun in the strictly planetary spheres.

86-87. *l'affocato riso . . . l'usato*: Mars is normally said to be a ruddy planet. Cf. Dante's description of Mars in *Conv.* II, xiii, 21: "Esso Marte dissecca e arde le cose, perchè lo suo calore è simile a quello del fuoco; e questo è quello per che esso pare affocato di colore, quando più e quando meno, secondo la spessezza e raritade de li vapori che 'l seguono." ("This same Mars drieth and burneth things, because his heat is like to the heat of fire; and this is why he appeareth enkindled in colour, sometimes more and sometimes less, according to the thickness and rarity of the vapours which follow him.") Cf. *Purg.* II, 13-15. And now Mars becomes even ruddier in its happiness at receiving Dante and Beatrice within itself (cf. *Par.* V, 94-96).

88-89. *quella favella . . . tutti*: The unspoken language of the heart, in silent thanksgiving.

89. *olocausto*: "Holocaust," offering. Cf. vs. 92: "sacrificio."

90. *conveniesi* = *si conveniva*.

93. *litare*: A Latin infinitive, used here as a noun, "litare" means "offering."   *fausto*: "Propitious."

94. *lucore*: "Brightness."   *robbi*: "Ruddy." "Robbi" is from the Latin *rubeus*.

95. *splendor*: The plural is *splendori*.

96. *Eliòs*: Helios, here used as the name of God, the spiritual sun. The word represents a fusion of the Greek word *helios* (ἥλιος), meaning "sun," and the Hebrew *Ely*, meaning "God." Thus Uguccione da Pisa says in his *Magnae derivationes* (as found in P. Toynbee, 1902, p. 112): "Ab *ely*, quod est deus, dictus est sol *elyos*, quod pro deo olim reputabatur." ("From *Ely*, that is God, the sun is called *elyos*, having been considered a god in former times.") Dante frequently refers to God as *Sole* (see *Par.* IX, 8; X, 53; *Conv.* III, xii, 6).

99. *Galassia*: Pronounced *Galàssia*; the Galaxy or Milky Way. Dante says the Galaxy forms part of the heaven of the fixed stars and discusses (*Conv.* II, xiv, 5-8) the various theories as to its origin. *che fa dubbiar ben saggi*: Aristotle deals with the nature and origin of the Galaxy in his treatise on meteors (*Meteor.* I, 8, 345^{a}-346^{b}). The opinion attributed to him in what Dante calls the Old Translation is probably due to the Arabic translator or editor and was introduced as a correction of his actual opinion (which is recorded in the New Translation). Ptolemy's opinion is given in the *Almagest* (VIII, 2). Dante, however, got his account of the various opinions as to the origin of the Milky Way not from Aristotle, but from Albertus Magnus (*De meteoris* I, ii, 2-5).

100. *costellati*: "Costellati" is in apposition to "quei raggi" of the following verse, the subject of "facean."

100-101. *nel profondo Marte*: "In the depth of Mars." This is a Latin construction.

101. *il venerabil segno*: The cross, meaning in this case the Greek cross, as vs. 102 makes evident.

102. *che fan giunture di quadranti in tondo*: "Which joinings of quadrants make in a circle." Two diameters of a circle, intersecting at right angles, form a cross and divide the circle into four quadrants.

103. *vince la memoria*: "Memoria" is the subject of "vince."

104. *croce lampeggiava*: "Croce" is the subject of "lampeg-giava" ("flashed forth").   *Cristo*: Once more *Cristo* occurs in the rhyme. Cf. *Par.* XII, 71, 73, 75.

105. *essempro = esempio*.

106. *ma chi prende sua croce e segue Cristo*: Cf. Matt. 10:38; 16:24.

107. *lasso = lascio*.

108. *vedendo*: The present participle refers to the first person (Dante the wayfarer): "when I beheld."

109. *corno*: "Horn," arm of the cross. Given the military context, it is important to realize that "corno" also can be used to designate the "flank" of an army.

112–17. *così si veggion . . . acquista*: "The moving lights in the cross are compared to bits of dust dancing in a ray of sunshine in a dark room" (Gr). Cf. Lucretius, *De rerum natura* II, 114-20.

112. *qui*: On earth.   *torte*: "Aslant."

113. *rinovando vista*: "Changing aspect."

114. *minuzie*: "Particles."

115. *onde si lista*: "With which is streaked."

116. *per sua difesa*: "For self-protection" from the sun.

117. *la gente con ingegno e arte acquista*: " 'People obtain,' by building houses. In warm countries the house is regarded primarily as a shelter from the heat" (Gr).

118. *giga*: "Viol."   *tesa*: "Strung."

119. *tintinno*: Cf. *Par.* X, 143.

121. *apparinno = apparirono*.

122. *s'accogliea = s'accoglieva*. Cf. *Purg.* I, 14.

124. *elli = egli*, i.e., the hymn.   *lode*: Plural of *loda*. Cf. *Par.* X, 122.

125. *però = per ciò.* *"Resurgi" e "Vinci":* "The song which Dante cannot entirely catch is evidently a triumphal hymn to Christ, sung by the knights of the Cross" (Gr).

127. *Io:* The word here has two syllables. *quinci:* "With it."

129. *vinci = vincoli,* "ties."

130. *osa:* "Bold." Cf. *Purg.* XI, 126.

131. *posponendo il piacer de li occhi belli:* " 'Subordinating,' giving a secondary place to the eyes of Beatrice. Dante seems to be rating the song above those 'beauteous eyes'; but, as he presently explains, he is not really doing so, since he has not yet looked upon them in this sphere" (Gr). See vs. 135.

133–34. *i vivi suggelli d'ogne bellezza:* " 'The living stamps of all beauty' are Beatrice's eyes, which become more potent from sphere to sphere, as she approaches God" (Gr).

135. *quelli:* The eyes.

136. *escusar = scusare.* *puommi = mi può.*

136–37. *escusar puommi . . . vero:* " 'May excuse me for that (i.e., l. 131) of which I accuse myself in order to excuse myself'—i.e., for the accusation which I bring against myself merely in order to have an opportunity to deny it—'and may see that I am telling the truth' " (Gr).

138. *ché 'l piacer santo non è qui dischiuso:* For that holy delight, the eyes, is not excluded (set aside) as of less account than the song here. *dischiuso:* Cf. *Par.* VII, 102.

139. *più sincero:* "Purer."

CANTO XV

1. *liqua*: "Liqua" (from the Latin *liquet* shifted to the first conjugation in Italian and made reflexive) means "manifests itself."

2. *drittamente*: "Rightly," in the sense of "toward a rightful object." *spira*: For the "spiration" of love, cf. *Par*. X, 2; *Purg*. XXIV, 53.

3. *fa*: Replaces the verb "spira" of vs. 2. *iniqua*: I.e., *volontade*.

4-6. *silenzio puose . . . tira*: The subject is "benigna volontade," benign will on the part of these spirits who, in their configuration of a Greek cross, are metaphorically termed a lyre ("lira"). Similar metaphors, "viol" and "harp," have already been applied to this same figure of the cross (*Par*. XIV, 118), as if the bands of souls might somehow be the strings ("corde") of one such instrument, strings which are now said to be "tuned" ("allenta e tira") by the right hand of Heaven, i.e., by God.

7-12. *Come saranno . . . spoglia*: The two tercets constitute a kind of indirect address to the living, to those who pray righteously, and to those who misdirect their loves on earth.

9. *concorde* = *concordi*.

10. *Bene è che*: "It is right." *sanza termine si doglia*: "Suffer eternal torment" in Hell.

11-12. *per amor di cosa . . . spoglia*: The things that do not last are temporal things, and love of them reflects the notion of "cupidità" in vs. 3, even as "quello amor" refers to "l'amor che drittamente spira," right love in this life and perfect love of God in the next, in Heaven, as "etternalmente" plainly suggests.

13. *li seren*: "Clear skies."

14. *discorre = trascorre*. *sùbito foco*: The light of a shooting star. "Meteors were explained as dry vapors which had risen so high as to take fire and then had plunged back in the direction of the earth" (Gr).

15. *movendo li occhi che stavan sicuri*: Causing the spectator's eyes to move in following the brief sight, eyes that until then had been calmly contemplating the vault of the sky at night.

17. *e' = el*. The shooting star.

18. *nulla sen perde*: No star is missing. *esso*: The "sùbito foco" (vs. 14), referred to by "el" in the preceding verse.

19-21. *tale dal corno . . . resplende*: Again the military overtone (see *Par.* XIV, 109) of the word "corno" may be felt, as this light holds to the figure of the cross in coming toward Dante, who somehow stands at or near the bottom of the great configuration of souls. This soul does not break formation but executes a kind of "soldierly" left-front movement, a fact made further emphatic by vss. 22-23.

22. *né si partì la gemma dal suo nastro*: "The gem did not leave its ribbon." Silk ribbons studded with pearls as ornaments were common in Dante's time.

23. *lista radial*: The band followed by the spirit in its motion is termed radial as if the "tondo" (*Par.* XIV, 102) or circle brought into the picture through simile were actually there.

Here the band followed by this spirit is that which extends from right to center, then from center to the bottom of this circle where Dante stands ("radial," from the Latin *radius*). Some commentators, however, take the adjective to mean "radiant."

24. *che parve foco dietro ad alabastro*: Within the great diffused radiance of the cross made up of many souls in these ribbons, this particular soul now shines the brightest and can be followed in its movement, as it gleams through the general luminosity. "Alabastro" can suggest any translucent screen.

25-27. *Sì pia l'ombra . . . s'accorse*: The reference is to the encounter of Aeneas with his father, Anchises, in the Elysian fields, as related by Virgil in *Aen.* VI, 684-88:

> isque ubi tendentem adversum per gramina vidit
> Aenean, alacris palmas utrasque tetendit,
> effusaeque genis lacrimae et vox excidit ore:
> "venisti tandem, tuaque exspectata parenti
> vicit iter durum pietas? . . ."

And he, as he saw Aeneas coming towards him over the sward, eagerly stretched forth both hands, while tears streamed from his eyes and a cry fell from his lips: "Art thou come at last, and hath the love thy father looked for vanquished the toilsome way?"

26. *se fede merta nostra maggior musa*: "Our greatest muse" (poet) is Virgil, who inspires other poets, as do the Muses. Cf. Dante's wording in *Conv.* IV, xxvi, 8: "Virgilio, lo maggiore nostro poeta" ("Virgil, our greatest poet") and see *Purg.* VII, 16-17. Regarding the implications of the "if" clause as such, cf. *Inf.* II, 13 and the corresponding note.

28-30. *O sanguis meus . . . reclusa*: " 'O blood of mine, O lavish grace of God! To whom was Heaven's gate ever twice opened, as to thee?' Heaven receives Dante now, and will receive him again after his death; such a thing has never happened since the days of St. Paul.—The use of Latin—the language of Church and school—adds dignity to this celestial greeting. It is made more appropriate by the reminiscence of

Anchises, to whom, indeed, the phrase 'sanguis meus' (meaning 'my child') belongs: 'Proice tela manu, sanguis meus' (cast from thy hand the sword, thou blood of mine!) in *Aen.*, VI, 835, where Anchises is addressing Julius Caesar" (Gr). In any case, this is clearly another instance of Dante's prediction of his own ultimate salvation (cf. *Inf.* III, 93; *Par.* X, 87), and behind the exclamation of this soul may perhaps be heard the unexpressed marvel that Dante is visiting Heaven in his body (for the soul is surely not recognizing a disembodied soul—though this is not actually stated). To be sure, Paul did not know whether he had made the heavenly journey in his body or not, but through the words of this soul there is a strong suggestion that Dante actually did. Cf. *Inf.* II, 28-30; *Par.* I, 73-75.

32–36. *poscia rivolsi . . . paradiso*: Until now, Dante has not looked into the eyes of Beatrice in this sphere.

36. *mio paradiso*: "My beatitude."

37. *Indi, a udire e a veder giocondo*: "Then, joyous to hear and see."

38. *giunse = aggiunse*.

40. *né per elezion*: "Not through any choice of his."

42. *al segno d'i mortal si soprapuose*: "Shot above the target of mortals," i.e., above their level of comprehension, as in vs. 45. The poet is using the archery figure continued in the next verse with "arco."

43. *affetto*: Love of God, and gratitude to Him, as expressed in vss. 47-48.

46. *per me s'intese*: For the construction, cf. *Inf.* I, 126.

49. *Grato e lontano digiuno*: The "welcome and long-felt hunger" is the object of "you have relieved" in vs. 52.

50. *tratto*: "Derived."   *del magno volume*: The "book" containing that which God has decreed, the book of the future. Cf. *Inf.* XIX, 54.

51. *du' = dove*, "wherein." *non si muta mai bianco né bruno*: White and black are never altered, i.e., in God's book of the future the text is never changed. This soul, who proves to be Cacciaguida, Dante's great-great-grandfather, knows this, and reading therein of this journey of his great-great-grandson to Heaven, he has felt for all these years the "welcome hunger" of an event destined to come about in the spring of 1300.

52. *solvuto = risolto*, "satisfied" (referring back to "digiuno" of vs. 49). The echo of Virgil's verses continues in Cacciaguida's words (cf. vss. 25-27). *questo lume*: The light from within which Cacciaguida speaks, the radiance that conceals him from view.

53-54. *colei ch' . . . piume*: Beatrice gives Dante wings for his upward flight, the power to rise. Cf. *Par.* X, 74; X, 93; and *passim*.

55. *mei*: "Flows," from the Latin *meare*. Cf. *Par.* XIII, 55.

56-57. *da quel ch'è primo . . . sei*: "Unity is the beginning of number, as God is the beginning of thought; from the conception of unity is derived the conception of all numbers, and in the divine mind all thought is contained" (Gr). "The thought of man rays out, reflected from the mind of God, the prime Unity, as all numbers proceed from the unit; and the thought thus becomes known to the blessed gazing upon God. See Canto ix. 73-75. This is what Donne (Sermon xxiii.) calls 'Gregory's wild speculation,' *Qui videt videntem omnia, omnia videt* ['he who sees Him who sees all, sees all'], because we shall see him that sees all things, we shall see all things in him, for then we should see the thoughts of men" (Norton).

56. *raia*: "Radiates."

58. *però = perciò*. *ch'io mi sia*: The "mi" is the reflexive (sometimes termed pleonastic) that specifies and stresses identity.

60. *che*: "Than," connecting with "più gaudioso" in vs. 59.

62. *questa vita*: That is, in Heaven.   *speglio*: "Mirror," from the Latin *speculum*, i.e., God. Cf. *Par.* XXVI, 106-8.

63. *il pensier pandi*: See n. to vss. 56-57.   *pandi*: "Reveal."

64–65. *ma perché . . . vista*: Cf. *Purg.* XXX, 103-5.

68. *suoni*: Subjunctive used as imperative, "la voce tua" being the subject: "Let your voice sound out."   *suoni la volontà, suoni 'l disio*: "Volontà" here refers to Dante's will or wish taken subjectively, whereas "disio" indicates the object of his wish.

69. *decreta*: A Latinism, meaning "decreed," i.e., "established" (since Cacciaguida, knowing what Dante is about to ask, knows what his own answer is to be).

71. *arrisemi = mi arrise*. Some manuscripts have "arrosemi," but Petrocchi has rightly preferred "arrisemi," according to the manuscript evidence. See his note.

72. *l'ali*: The familiar metaphor reappears. Cf. vss. 53-54.

73–75. *L'affetto e 'l senno . . . si fenno*: " 'As soon as the primal Equality (God, in whom all powers are perfect and therefore equal) revealed himself to you, desire and faculty in each one of you became equal in weight': the blessed have no wish which they have not intelligence to fulfill" (Gr). E. G. Gardner (1913, p. 102) refers to Dionysius, *De divinis nominibus*, in this regard. This is a conception that will re-emerge at the very end of the poem (*Par.* XXXIII, 143-44).

75. *fenno = fecero*.

76. *però = perciò*.   *'l sol*: God.   *v'allumò*: Illumined with His light (the light of glory by which the creature sees God). This light regards the intellect.   *e arse*: That is, caused to glow with His love, which regards the will. Thus the verses continue to keep intellect and will, the two powers of the immortal human soul, central to the conception here expressed. See *Par.* XXX, 100, and the note to *Par.* XXX, 100-102.

77. *col caldo e con la luce*: "Caldo" pertains to the will and to the notion expressed by "arse" in the preceding verse, whereas "luce" pertains to intellect, as is evident in the verb "v'allumò." Now the two faculties are stated or implied in reverse order.   *sì iguali*: "So perfectly balanced." "Iguali" is singular, modifying "sol," vs. 76. It derives from the Latin nominative *aequalis* and is found in early Florentine texts.

78. *simiglianze*: Comparisons.

79-81. *Ma voglia . . . ali*: Whereas the blessed have no wish which they have not the intelligence to fulfill, with mortals it is otherwise, as is to be made plain in this particular case. Dante has the wish ("voglia") to express his gratitude adequately to Cacciaguida, but the expressive means or power to execute that wish is lacking in him, as it so often is in mortals. See "argomenti" in this sense in *Purg*. II, 31. Thus the two essential terms *will* and *intellect* are kept, but now are measured in our mortal condition in contrast with the immortal perfection of these powers in the blessed, "ali" reflecting metaphorically those two powers.

83. *disagguaglianza = disugguaglianza*. The term clearly echoes, by contrast, the statement of vss. 73-78 respecting the condition of the blessed in Heaven as soon as they behold God face to face.   *però = perciò*.

84. *se non col core*: Only with the words of the heart (corresponding to the "voglia" in that this wish belongs to desire, which is in the affective faculty, the will).   *la paterna festa*: The joyous welcome made by a great-great-grandfather to his grandson. The word *festa* in the sense of "welcome" is common, as in the expression *fare festa a qualcuno*, "to welcome someone."

85. *supplico io a te*: The construction with the dative is modeled on the corresponding Latin. Cf. *Par*. XXVI, 94.
    vivo topazio: "Resplendent topaz," which resumes the metaphor of vs. 22. The choice of this particular precious stone meets the requirements of the rhyme, of course; but it is perhaps significant that the most precious of the topazes,

the yellow (also known as the yellow sapphire), is sometimes made red by heating, and red is the color of love and would be most appropriate here, since we are everywhere told that the souls appear as flames.

86. *gioia*: The cross in its total configuration, made up of the many jewels which form it.

88–89. *O fronda mia . . . radice*: The notion of family tree clearly informs the metaphor, Dante being the latest descendant ("leaf") growing on this tree, of which the speaker is the "root." See n. to *Purg.* XX, 43-45.

88. *compiacemmi = mi compiacqui*, in which there may be heard God's words when Jesus was baptized (Matt. 3:17): "Hic est Filius meus dilectus, in quo mihi complacui." ("This is my beloved Son, in whom I am well pleased.") Cf. Mar. 1:11; Luc. 3:22.

90. *femmi = mi feci*.

91. *Poscia mi disse*: In reply to Dante's question concerning the name and identity of this soul, the soul will require many verses to make his answer, and he will not name himself until vs. 135 as Cacciaguida, who, from what he first tells, proves to be the great-great-grandfather of Dante. Of Cacciaguida's life nothing is known beyond what the poet has him tell of himself.

R. Davidsohn (1896, p. 440, including n. 2) cites a document dated April 28, 1131, in which there is mention of one Cacciaguida, son of Adam, whom he identifies with Dante's great-great-grandfather. What Cacciaguida begins to tell of himself in this canto extends into *Par.* XVI as well and may be summarized here. Cacciaguida was born in Florence in the Sesto di Porta San Piero about the year 1091. He belonged, possibly, to the Elisei, one of the old Florentine families which boasted Roman descent. He was baptized in the Baptistery of San Giovanni in Florence and had two brothers, Moronto and Eliseo. Cacciaguida's wife came from the valley of the Po and from her, through his son, Dante got his surname of Alighieri. Cacciaguida followed the Emperor Conrad III on the second Crusade and was knighted by him; finally he fell fighting against the infidel about the year 1147. His existence is attested by the mention of his name in a document (still preserved in Florence), dated December 9, 1189, in which his two sons bind themselves to remove a fig tree which was growing against a wall of the church of San Martino. See R. Piattoli (1950), pp. 3-4.

There is considerable difference of opinion as to the precise date of Cacciaguida's birth, the indications given by Dante (*Par*. XVI, 34-39) being variously interpreted. Cacciaguida says that from the Incarnation of Christ down to the day of his own birth the planet Mars had returned to the sign Leo 580 times (or 553 times, according as "trenta" or "tre" be read in *Par*. XVI, 38), i.e., had made that number of revolutions in its orbit. Two questions are involved. The first involves the reading, "trenta" or "tre." The second concerns whether the period of the revolution of Mars is to be estimated at about two years, as given by Brunetto Latini (*Tresor* I, cx, 5) and implied by Dante in the *Convivio* (II, xiv, 16), or at the correct period, as given by Alfraganus, of approximately 687 days (actually, according to Witte, 686 days, 22 hours, 29 minutes). If we read "trenta" (with the majority) and take the period of Mars at the estimate of Alfraganus, we get (due regard being given to leap years) the year 1091 as the date of Cacciaguida's birth. If, on the other hand, we read "tre," and put the period of Mars at two years, we get the year 1106. In the former case Cacciaguida would have been fifty-six, in the latter forty-one at the time when he joined Conrad III on the second Crusade (1147) and met his death (vss. 139-48). Several of the early commentators (*Anonimo fiorentino,* Buti, and Landino, among others), reading "trenta" and computing the period of Mars at two years, bring the date of Cacciaguida's birth to 1160 (i.e., thirteen years after his death!), while Benvenuto, who avoids this error, brings it to 1054, which on his own showing (since he gives 1154 as the date of the Crusade) would make Cacciaguida a crusader at the age of 100!

Cacciaguida indicates (*Par*. XVI, 40-42) the situation of the house in which he and his ancestors lived in Florence as being "in the place where the last ward is reached by him who runs in your annual game," i.e., on the boundary of the district known later as the Sesto di Porta San Piero. The house of the Elisei (Villani, IV, 11) stood not far from the junction of the Mercato Vecchio and the Corso, apparently just at the angle formed on the north side of the present Via de' Speziali by its intersection with the Via de' Calzaioli. The Sesto di Porta San Piero appears to have been the last of the city divisions to be traversed in the annual *gioco* by the competitors who entered the city probably at the Porta San Pancrazio, close to where the Palazzo Strozzi now stands, crossed the Mercato Vecchio, and finished in the Corso which was thence so called.

92. *cognazione*: " 'Family name': Alighieri. Alighiero (or Allagherius), son of Cacciaguida, was the first male member of the family to bear this name, which, as we learn presently, he derived from his mother. His name occurs in documents of 1189 (where it is joined with that of his brother Preitenitto) and of 1201. The *cent' anni e più* would seem, therefore, to indicate ignorance of the exact date of his death" (Gr).

93. *prima cornice*: The circle of pride, in Purgatory. Dante apparently regarded pride as a family failing. Cf. *Purg.* XIII, 136-38, where he attributes it to himself.

95. *la lunga fatica*: The toil of carrying a huge stone on his back, and this now for more than a century!

96. *li = gli.   opere tue*: "Your prayers."

97. *cerchia antica*: The old city walls. The first medieval walls, probably built in the ninth century, which were virtually identical with the Roman walls. (See Map 3, facing p. 260.)

98. *ond' ella toglie ancora e terza e nona*: Beside these walls stood the ancient abbey, the Badia, whose bell continued, in Dante's day, to mark the hours for the Florentines. Tierce is the third of the canonical hours, or 9 A.M. None, or nones, is the ninth of the canonical hours, or 3 P.M.

3. Florence: the circuits of walls

100. *Non avea = non vi aveva (non c'era).* Cf. the French *il n'y avait.*   *catenella*: "Necklace," or "bracelet."

101. *contigiate*: "Adorned." Cf. the noun *contigia*, meaning "ornament."

102. *la persona*: The wearer.

103–5. *Non faceva . . . misura*: "The marriageable age had not yet become absurdly low, nor the dowry ruinously high" (Gr).

105. *fuggien = fuggivano.*

106. *Non avea case di famiglia vòte*: There were no palaces built on too large a scale for their occupants.

107–8. *non v'era . . . puote*: "Sardanapalus, king of Assyria, was notorious in antiquity for his luxury and effeminacy. He is mentioned by Paulus Orosius and Egidio Colonna" (Gr). Cf. Juvenal, *Satires* X, 362.

109–11. *Non era vinto . . . calo*: "Rome was not yet surpassed in splendor by Florence, which has been swifter in its rise and will be swifter in its fall. Montemalo (or Montemallo), now Montemario, is a hill that affords the approaching traveler a view of Rome; similarly the height called Uccellatoio offers the stranger, as he draws near on the north, an outlook on Florence. In *Uccellatoio* the *-toio* counts as one syllable: cf. *Purg.* XIII, 22; XIV, 66; XX, 52.—*Che* in l. 110 refers to *Montemalo*" (Gr).

111. *calo*: "Decline."

112. *Bellincion Berti*: Florentine of the ancient Ravignani family, father of "la buona Gualdrada" (see *Inf.* XVI, 37), through whose marriage with Guido Guerra IV the Conti Guidi traced their descent from the Ravignani. He lived in the second half of the twelfth century and in 1176 was deputed by the Florentines to take over from the Sienese the castle of Poggibonsi, which had been ceded by the latter. Villani (IV, 1) speaks of him as "il buono messere Bellincione Berti de' Ravignani onorevole cittadino di Firenze" ("the

good Messer Bellincione Berti de' Ravignani, honorable citizen of Florence").

113. *di cuoio e d'osso*: With a plain leather belt fastened with a clasp of bone.

114. *la donna sua*: "His wife."

115. *Nerli*: Ancient noble family of Florence which received knighthood from the Marquis Hugh of Brandenburg, "il gran barone" (*Par.* XVI, 128). *del Vecchio*: Ancient noble family of Florence (otherwise known as the Vecchietti). Villani (IV, 12) couples the Vecchietti with the Pigli and Soldanieri as ancient families residing in the "quartiere della porta di san Brancazio." He says they were Guelphs (V, 39) and as such were expelled from Florence in 1248 (VI, 33) and went into exile in 1260 after the Ghibelline victory at Montaperti (VI, 80). When the Guelph party was split up into Bianchi and Neri they sided, some with one faction, some with the other (VIII, 39).

116. *pelle scoperta*: "Bare leather," i.e., plain dressed skin not covered or lined with cloth.

117. *sue* = *loro*. *al fuso e al pennecchio*: Cf. Prov. 31:19: "Manum suam misit ad fortia, et digiti eius apprehenderunt fusum." ("She puts her hands to the distaff, and her fingers ply the spindle.") *fuso*: "Spindle," as used in spinning. *pennecchio*: The wool or flax that is put upon the distaff. Cf. "conocchia" in *Purg.* XXI, 26.

118-19. *certa de la sua sepultura*: I.e., each knew that she would be buried in her own church or churchyard, and would not die in exile.

119-20. *ancor nulla . . . diserta*: None was abandoned by a husband who journeyed to France as a merchant.

119. *nulla* = *nessuna*.

121. *vegghiava* = *vegliava*. *a studio*: In the sense of the Latin *studium*, "assiduous and affectionate care."

122–23. *l'idioma che prima . . . trastulla*: Baby talk, such as parents use with their children as they play with them.

124. *rocca*: "Distaff."   *chioma*: The wool or flax that is put upon the distaff and drawn off onto the spindle, in spinning. "Chioma" ("hair") is thus figuratively synonymous with "pennecchio" in vs. 117.

125. *famiglia*: "Family" in the sense of "household," i.e., including female servants.

126. *d'i Troiani, di Fiesole e di Roma*: Legends of the founding of Rome by the Trojans, and of the founding of Fiesole and then of Florence by the ancient Romans. Such legends enjoyed a considerable popular diffusion in Dante's day and long before. Cf. Villani, I, 6 and 7. The telling of such "founding" tales attests essentially to the "piety" (in the Latin sense of *pietas*) of the good people of old Florence, as Dante would have it, and this fits into the whole picture as an effective touch.

128. *Cianghella*: Florentine lady of ill repute, contemporary of Dante. She is said to have been the daughter of Arrigo della Tosa and to have died *ca.* 1330. The early commentators say Cianghella was notorious for her arrogance, extravagance, and profligacy. Benvenuto states that she married a certain Lito degli Alidosi of Imola, a native of his own city, after whose death she returned to Florence and led a disreputable life. He says he had heard many stories of her from a neighbor of hers in Imola. One of these he records as a specimen, to the effect that on a certain occasion when she had gone to church to hear a sermon she was so infuriated because none of the ladies present rose to make room for her that she violently assaulted several of them; her blows being returned, a free fight ensued, greatly to the amusement of the male members of the congregation who could not restrain their laughter in which the preacher himself joined and thus the sermon was brought to an end. She appears also to have been in the habit of beating her servants with a stick.

Lapo Salterello: Florentine lawyer and judge, a relative and adherent of the Cerchi, the leaders of the Bianchi faction in Florence. He belonged to the same party as Dante and was included in the same decree of banishment (March 10, 1302), in which his name is second on the list. He was a prominent and active politician, and his name recurs continually in contemporary documents as having been concerned in most of the important public acts in Florence during the twenty years between the institution of the priorate (1282) and the banishment of the Bianchi (1302). In 1294 he went with other Florentines on an embassy to Boniface VIII; and in 1300 he served in the office of prior during the two months (April 15-June 15) preceding Dante's priorate. In this latter year he and two others denounced a conspiracy between certain Florentines and Boniface VIII to incorporate Tuscany with the States of the Church, whereby he incurred the deadly hatred of the pope. After the outbreak in Florence of the Bianchi and Neri feuds, and the triumph of the latter, he attempted to conceal himself in the house of the Pulci, but he was discovered, and proscribed with most of the other members of his party. He appears to have been very corrupt and was specifically accused of having taken bribes to pervert the course of justice. He is said to have died in exile in great poverty. Dante's negative opinion of Lapo Salterello is fully borne out by the early commentators and by Dino Compagni, who frequently mentions him in his chronicle.

129. *Cincinnato*: See n. to *Par.* VI, 43-53. *Corniglia*: Cornelia, daughter of the elder Scipio Africanus, wife of Tiberius Sempronius Gracchus, and mother of the Gracchi, the tribunes Tiberius and Gaius. On being condoled on the death of her sons, who were both slain during her lifetime, she is said to have exclaimed that she who had borne them could never deem herself unhappy. Dante places her, along with Lucretia, Julia, and Marcia, among the noble spirits of antiquity in Limbo (*Inf.* IV, 128).

132. *cittadinanza*: "Citizenry." *ostello*: "Hostelry," "inn."

133. *Maria mi diè, chiamata in alte grida*: For Mary invoked by women in the pains of childbirth, cf. *Purg.* XX, 19-21. *diè = diede.*

134. *Batisteo*: The Baptistery of Florence, in which in early times most children born in Florence received baptism. See n. to *Inf.* XIX, 17.

135. *insieme fui cristiano e Cacciaguida*: I was baptized and at the same time given the name of Cacciaguida.

136. *Moronto fu mio frate ed Eliseo*: Of these two brothers, named (as was Cacciaguida) by their first names only, nothing is known, though it is thought possible that the family of the Elisei, or one branch of it, may have descended from Eliseo. They were Ghibellines and noble, and they were exiled from Florence several times.

137. *mia donna*: "My wife." Cf. vs. 114.   *di val di Pado*: The valley of the Po. It is thought that the lady may have come from Ferrara, where, from the eleventh to the thirteenth centuries, there flourished a family with the name of Aldighieri; but the reference to "the Po valley" has allowed other cities of that valley to lay claim to being the birthplace of Dante's great-great-grandmother.

138. *e quindi il sopranome tuo si feo*: The family name (variously spelled), which the poet thus assigns to himself, might well have been *Alaghieri* in its Italian form (*Alagerius* or *Alagherius* in Latin), whereas *Alighieri* appears later with Boccaccio and is thereby confirmed in the tradition.   *si feo = si fece.*

139. *lo 'mperador Currado*: Conrad III (1093-1152) was the son of Frederick, duke of Swabia. As duke of Franconia, he fought against Lothair II, duke of Saxony, and being elected king by the adversaries of Lothair, in 1127, and being recognized in Italy as well, he was crowned at Milan in the spring of 1128 and recognized as emperor thereafter. As such he undertook the disastrous second Crusade, in company

with Louis VII of France. He returned to Germany in 1149 and died at Bamberg in 1152.

140. *el = egli.* *mi cinse de la sua milizia*: "He made me one of his knights." The ceremony involved the girding on of a sword, hence "cinse." As there is no record of any Florentines having been knighted by Conrad III, some think that Dante may have confused him with Conrad II (1024-39), who according to Villani (IV, 9) undertook an expedition against the Saracens in Calabria, and passed through Florence on his way, knighting several Florentines who accompanied him.

141. *bene ovrar*: For faithful service to him. *li = gli.* *venni in grado*: "I won his favor."

142-44. *Dietro li andai . . . giustizia*: The whole reference is to the second Crusade.

142. *li = gli.*

143. *legge*: "Religion," the Mohammedan, the followers of which are usurping the Holy Land—which rightly belongs to you ("vostra giustizia")—because the popes care nothing about the reconquest of it. Cf. *Inf.* XXVII, 85-90.

145. *Quivi*: In the Holy Land. *turpa = turpe*, "base."

146. *disviluppato*: "Released." *mondo fallace*: Cf. *Purg.* XIX, 108, where the world is so judged by a pope.

147. *deturpa*: "Corrupts."

148. *venni dal martiro a questa pace*: Those who died on a crusade in the Holy Land were considered martyrs of the faith who would therefore go directly to Heaven after suffering their death as crusaders.

CANTO XVI

1-6. *O poca nostra nobiltà . . . gloriai*: " 'Iam vero quam sit inane, quam futtile nobilitatis nomen, quis non videat?' (Likewise, who sees not what a vain and idle thing it is to be called noble?) says Boethius, in *Consolatio Philosophiae*, III [vi, ll. 20-21]. Other authors known to our poet, in Latin, Provençal, and Italian, disparage the glory of birth, and exalt the true nobility of character. Dante himself devotes the 3rd Canzone of the *Convivio* to the development of this theme, and touches upon it in *Monarchia*, II, iii, 4. Yet in the presence of his belted ancestor he cannot check a feeling of family pride, which betrays itself by the use of the respectful 'voi' " (Gr).

3. *qua giù dove l'affetto nostro langue*: On earth the affection of mortals is fainter than in heaven and falls short of its proper goal.

5. *là*: In Heaven.

5-6. *dove appetito . . . gloriai*: Dante is, of course, not yet confirmed in heavenly love, but being a visitor from earth, he succumbs to this kind of pride of family. The whole passage is self-deprecating.

7. *raccorce*: "Shrinks."

8. *se non s'appon*: "Unless we add to you."

9. *lo tempo va dintorno con le force*: Time cuts away at the mantle with its scissors.   *force = forbici*. "Force" is from the Latin *forfices*. The meaning out of metaphor will be evident in the discourse on the decline of families that now follows.

10. *Dal "voi"*: "With the *you*." "Dal 'voi'" depends on "ricominciaron," vs. 12.   *Dal "voi" che prima a Roma s'offerie*: According to tradition, the plural *vos* was first used, in addressing one person, when Julius Caesar made himself emperor. In the entire *Commedia* Dante uses the honorific plural to address only Farinata and Cavalcante (*Inf.* X), Brunetto Latini (*Inf.* XV, 80), Pope Adrian V, when he learns that it is he (*Purg.* XIX, 131), and—always—Beatrice until the very end of the poem, where he very strikingly addresses her with the singular form *tu* (see *Par.* XXXI, 80-90). Thus, his shifting to "voi" here is significant.   *s'offerie*: The reading in some manuscripts is "sofferie" (= *sofferì*), "allowed," but see Petrocchi for his preference of "s'offerie" (= *si offrì*), "offered."

11. *in che la sua famiglia men persevra*: It seems that in the time of Dante the Romans were more inclined to use the familiar *tu*, instead of *voi*; and this remains true of Roman speech in outlying regions in the country around Rome.
la sua famiglia: Her people.

13-15. *onde Beatrice . . . Ginevra*: "Beatrice, 'who stood a little apart,' smiled indulgently at Dante's weakness, just as, in the Old French romance of *Lancelot du Lac* (cf. *Inf.* V, 127-138), the Dame de Malehaut, watching the first clandestine interview of Guinever and Lancelot, coughed on hearing the impassioned speech of the Queen.—*Fallo scritto*, 'recorded fault.'—The Lady of Malehaut, in whose castle Lancelot had for some time secretly lived unrecognized, was hiddenly in love with him.—Guinever, after having drawn from Lancelot the avowal of his love, asks: 'Whence comes this love of yours for me?' Then it is that (in some manuscripts but not in all) the Lady of Malehaut coughs" (Gr).

14. *tossio = tossì.*

16. *il padre mio*: Dante speaks affectionately and reverently in addressing Cacciaguida as his father, meaning the first head of his family.

20. *che di sé fa letizia*: "That it congratulates itself," i.e., at being able to bear so much joy and exultation without "breaking," as the next verse makes clear.

21. *può sostener che non si spezza*: "On being able to endure without bursting."

23. *quai fuor = quali furono.   li vostri antichi*: "Your ancestors."

23–24. *li anni . . . puerizia*: "The recorded years of your youth" in the sense of *anni Domini.*

24. *si segnaro = segnarono.*

25. *ovil di San Giovanni*: John the Baptist is the patron saint of Florence. "Ovil" ("sheepfold") plays into the notion of a small and simple Florence.

26. *quanto era*: How many were its inhabitants.

26–27. *e chi eran le genti . . . scanni*: The reader should remember this particular turn of the question as Cacciaguida replies at length, singling out the families of Florence that were "worthy of the highest offices."

28–29. *Come s'avviva . . . fiamma*: Cf. Ovid, *Metam.* VII, 79-81.

30. *blandimenti*: "Soothing," "reverent" words.

33. *ma non con questa moderna favella*: This "does not imply that Cacciaguida spoke throughout in Latin as he had begun (xv. 28-30), but that he spoke in the ancient Florentine dialect of his day. Dante was well aware of the rapidity with which spoken dialects, not yet fixed by a standard literature, vary. See *De Vulgari Eloquentia*, i. 9 [7-8]" (TC). Cf. also Dante, *Conv.* I, v, 8-9.

34. *Da quel dì che fu detto "Ave"*: From the Annunciation (Luc. 1:28). The Florentine year began with the Conception, March 25.

35. *ch'è or santa*: Who is now among the blessed, in Paradise.'

36. *grave = gravida*.

37–39. *al suo Leon . . . pianta*: " 'This fire (Mars) came 580 times to its Lion, to be rekindled under its paw.' Between the Conception—the beginning of the year 1—and the birth of Cacciaguida, Mars returned 580 times to the constellation of Leo, which, being of like disposition to Mars, reinforces the influence of that planet. As Mars completes its revolution in 687 days, we shall get the year of Cacciaguida's birth by multiplying 687 by 580 and dividing by 365: 1091. He was therefore 56 when he followed the crusade, having lived from 1091 to 1147. Cf. Moore, III, 59-60" (Gr). See n. to *Par.* XV, 91. "Apparently the kinship between Leo and Mars is to be found in the attribute of courage, not in any specific astrological belief of the time" (TC).

41–42. *dove si truova . . . gioco*: "Where the last ward is first reached by the runner in your annual sports." The races were run on June 24 (St. John's day). The horse race (*palio*) began on the west boundary of the city and went along the Corso, thus entering the "last" ward, that of Porta San Piero, at what is still the beginning of Via de' Speziali. In that place were the houses of the Elisei family, whereas those of the Alighieri were later in the so-called *popolo* of San Martino and thus were not near the course of the annual race. (See Map 4, facing p. 270.)

43–45. *Basti d'i miei maggiori . . . onesto*: With this sentence, presumably, Dante veils his lack of further information. Cf. *Inf.* IV, 104.

43. *maggiori*: Cf. *Inf.* X, 42.

44. *si fosser*: This is the familiar so-called pleonastic reflexive *si*, stressing identity.

4. The district around Florence

45. *onesto*: "Modest."

47. *da poter arme*: "Fit for arms," eligible for military service. Cf. the Latin *armipotens*.   *tra Marte e 'l Batista*: Between the old statue of Mars, on the river (cf. vs. 145), and the Baptistery (cf. *Inf*. XIX, 17). The ancient city was measured thus from south to north.

48. *erano il quinto di quei ch'or son vivi*: According to Casini-Barbi, who cites Villani (VIII, 39) as his evidence, in 1300 Florence had a total population of more than 30,000 citizens, perhaps around 40,000, and those subject to military service (all men from the age of eighteen to sixty) must have been approximately 10,000. Therefore, in the time of Cacciaguida, the population would have been between 6,000 and 8,000 citizens, and those subject to military service would have been approximately 2,000.

49-50. *or mista . . . Fegghine*: The citizens of Florence are now mixed with people from the surrounding countryside.

50. *di Campi, di Certaldo e di Fegghine*: These three villages, all in Tuscany, are named as typical of the many small towns situated in the vicinity of Florence. Campi is on the Bisenzio, about nine miles northwest of Florence. Certaldo is in the Val d'Elsa, about seven and a half miles northwest of Poggibonsi, on the road from Poggibonsi to Empoli. Figline (pronounced *Figlíne*) Valdarno is on the Arno, seventeen miles southeast of Florence.

51. *pura*: I.e., pure Florentine.   *vediesi = si vedeva*. *ne l'ultimo artista*: "Even to the lowliest artisan."

52. *fora = sarebbe*.   *vicine*: "Neighboring," hence outside the city of Florence, not inside its limits (cf. vs. 55).

53. *Galluzzo*: Ancient village of Tuscany, to the south of Florence, about two miles from the Porta Romana on the road to Siena, a little to the north of the confluence of the Ema with the Greve.

54. *Trespiano*: Village of Tuscany, to the north of Florence, about three miles from the Porta San Gallo.

56. *Aguglion*: A castle (now destroyed), formerly called Aquilone, in the Florentine territory in the Val di Pesa to the south of the city. The reference "villan d'Aguglion" is to one Baldo d'Aguglione, who is spoken of by Dino Compagni in his *Cronica* (I, 19) as "giudice sagacissimo" and who was one of those who drew up the *ordinamenti di giustizia* in Florence in 1293. His family were Ghibellines, and as such his father Guglielmo and his brother Puccio were exiled from Florence in 1268. Baldo himself, however, took the other side and remained in Florence, where, after playing an important part in the events of 1293, and in the expulsion of Giano della Bella in 1295, he became prior in 1298. In 1299, in consequence of the discovery of his share in the fraud of Niccola Acciaiuoli, he fled from Florence and was condemned in his absence to a fine of 2,000 lire and to a year's banishment. In 1302, when through the intervention of Charles of Valois the Bianchi were expelled, he and Fazio de' Morubaldini da Signa joined the Neri with certain other renegade Bianchi and Ghibellines. From this time forward he occupied a position of great influence in Florence. In 1311, while he was prior for the second time, and the city was anxious to present a united front to Emperor Henry VII, he drew up the decree (dated September 2, 1311) known as the *riforma* of Baldo d'Aguglione, whereby the sentences against a number of the Guelph exiles were revoked and canceled, and a number of others, who are all included under the head of Ghibellines, were expressly excepted, among the latter being Dante Alighieri.

When, in the next year, Emperor Henry VII's army was advancing towards Florence, Baldo d'Aguglione fled from the city and was consequently himself declared an outlaw. He managed, however, to secure a pardon. He returned to Florence, where he died not long after, leaving several sons to succeed him. The family died out before the end of the fourteenth century.

Signa: Village of Tuscany, near the Arno, about ten miles west of Florence. The reference is probably to one Fazio (Bonifazio) from Signa. Fazio or Bonifazio de' Morubaldini da Signa was a lawyer who was *gonfaloniere di giustizia* in

Florence in 1316 and was prior several times. He was sent as ambassador to Clement V in 1310 for the purpose of organizing the opposition to Emperor Henry VII when he came into Italy, and his name figures in consequence on the list of those condemned by the emperor in 1313.

58. *gente*: The clergy.   *traligna*: "Degenerates."

59. *a Cesare noverca*: "Like a stepmother"—that is, hostile —to Caesar, i.e., to the emperor and the Holy Roman Empire.

61. *merca* = *mercanteggia*.

62. *si sarebbe vòlto*: Would have continued to live, more literally, "to go about."

62–63. *Simifonti . . . cerca*: Semifonte was a strong fortress in the Val d'Elsa, southwest of Florence and east of Certaldo, which belonged originally to the Conti Alberti. In 1202, after a four-year siege, it was captured and destroyed by the Florentines, with whom it had long been carrying on hostilities.

The point of Cacciaguida's allusion, which appears to be to some special circumstance, is not now understood. Some think the reference is to an incident in the taking of Semifonte by the Florentines, to whom the fortress was betrayed by one of the defenders, as is recorded by Villani (V, 30). However, Casini-Barbi and Del Lungo think there may possibly be a reference to one of the Velluti family, who were well-known merchants and money-changers in Florence and originally came from Semifonte. The special allusion may be to Lippo Velluti, who is mentioned in Dino Compagni's *Cronica* (I, 18) as belonging to the government which expelled Giano della Bella in 1295. Lippo's father and grandfather were soldiers. If the reference in these lines is not to him, the phrase "andava . . . a la cerca" may have its more common sense of "went begging" or "went about the countryside as peddlers," as Buti understands the phrase.

64. *sariesi* = *si sarebbe*. The reflexive specifies identity and bears also a touch of its distancing function.   *Montemurlo*:

A castle on a hill between Prato and Pistoia which belonged to the Conti Guidi, who were finally (1254) obliged to sell it to the Florentines since they could not hold it against the Pistoians. Its acquisition, therefore, marks a step in the aggressive expansion of Florence.

65. *Cerchi*: Wealthy Florentine family of low origin, who originally came from Acone, a small village in the neighborhood of Florence. In 1215, when Florence was divided into Guelphs and Ghibellines, they espoused the cause of the former and were already at that date rising into prominence. Subsequently, when the Florentine Guelphs split up into Bianchi and Neri, by which time the Cerchi were wealthy merchants and very powerful in the commercial world, they became the leaders of the former, while the Donati, who were of noble origin, headed the Neri.

After their purchase of the palace of the Conti Guidi (Villani, IV, 11) the Cerchi became the near neighbors of the more ancient but less wealthy Donati, and in consequence great jealousy, ending in a deadly feud, arose between the two houses, which led to constant breaches of the peace in Florence. Cacciaguida laments that the feud between the Church and the emperor, among other consequences, brought the Cerchi from their original home at Acone to settle in Florence.

It appears that the people of Acone district were constantly at war with the Florentines on account of the castle of Montecroce, which belonged to the Conti Guidi and was situated in their neighborhood, close to the Florentine territory. After a number of unsuccessful attempts, the Florentines at length, in 1154, captured it by treachery and razed it, on which account the Conti Guidi ever after bore a grudge against Florence, as Villani (IV, 37) relates. It was about this time that the Cerchi came to Florence. *piovier* = *pievania*, a group of parishes under the head (*piovano*) of one of them.

66. *Valdigreve*: The valley of the Greve, a small river of Tuscany, which rises about twenty miles south of Florence

and flows north, joining the Ema close to Galluzzo, about three miles from the Porta Romana of Florence.   *Buondelmonti*: The leaders of the Guelph party in Florence, whose family left the country and took up their residence in Florence in 1135, on account of the destruction of their castle of Montebuono in the Valdigreve close to Florence, in the process of the expansion of the city.

67–68. *Sempre la confusion . . . cittade*: See Aristotle, *Polit.* III, 3, 1277^b-1278^b.

69. *s'appone*: "Is added," i.e., to food still undigested in the stomach, which, it was believed, causes sickness.

70. *più avaccio*: "Faster." For "avaccio," cf. *Inf.* X, 116.

71–72. *e molte volte . . . spade*: "Many times one sword will cut better than five." The article with the number ("le cinque") is common in early Italian.

73. *Luni*: Ancient Luna, a maritime town in Etruria on the left bank of the Magra, not far from Sarzana, on the boundary between Liguria and Etruria. Modern Luni is west of Apuania, Tuscany, near the Carrara marble quarries. The first mention of ancient Luna was in 177 B.C. It fell into decay under the Roman emperors and was sacked by the Lombards in 630, by the Saracens in 849, and again in 1016. The date of its final destruction is uncertain. The site of the ancient town is still marked by the ruins of an amphitheater and circus. The harbor of Luna (the Gulf of La Spezia or the mouth of the Magra) was well known, but the Magra was silted up, and Portovenere took its place. Luni was an episcopal see, which was transferred to Sarzana by Innocent III in 1204. It was from Luni that the district of Lunigiana derived its name.

Orbisaglia: Urbisaglia, the ancient Urbs Salvia, was once an important town, but in Dante's day the ancient city was a collection of ruins. In the region of the Marches, about thirty miles south of Ancona and about six miles southwest of Macerata, the extensive Roman remains consist of an amphitheater, baths, and walls.

75. *Chiusi*: The ancient Clusium, formerly one of the twelve great Etruscan cities. It is situated in the Val di Chiana, close to the lake of the same name, on the borders of Tuscany and Umbria, midway between Florence and Rome on the Via Cassia. The decay of Chiusi was doubtless in great part due to the unhealthiness of its situation in the malarious Val di Chiana, as Benvenuto points out. See Villani, I, 54.

Sinigaglia: Now Senigallia, the ancient Sena Gallica, called Senagallia by Pliny (*Nat. hist.* III, xiv, 113), so named to distinguish it from Sena Julia (Siena). It is situated on the Adriatic at the mouth of the Misa, about seventeen miles northwest of Ancona, in what was formerly the duchy of Urbino, but now forms part of the region of the Marches. The ancient city, which was founded by the Galli Senones, was made a Roman colony in 283 B.C. It was sacked by Pompey in 82 B.C. and ravaged by Alaric, king of the Visigoths, in the fifth century, by the Lombards in the eighth century, and by the Saracens in the ninth century. It was eventually ruined for a time in the thirteenth century by the wars of the Guelphs and Ghibellines and especially by the severities of Guido da Montefeltro. According to Benvenuto the town was practically deserted in his day.

78. *termine*: "An end."

80. *celasi in = si cela in*, "it is not apparent in the case of."

81. *le vite*: Human lives. See Dante, *De vulg. eloqu.* I, ix, 8-9.

82-83. *E come 'l volger . . . posa*: It was the common opinion that tides are due to the influence of the moon (a fact accepted by modern science in the sense that tides are caused by the interaction between the moon and the earth of gravitational forces). Cf. Thomas Aquinas, *Summa theol.* I, q. 110, a. 3, ad 1.

84. *così fa di Fiorenza la Fortuna*: Cf. *Inf.* VII, 67-81. Fortune's realm, the whole sublunar world, is characterized by constant change. "Fortuna" is the subject of "fa."

86. *alti*: "Noble," "distinguished." See Dante's question, vss. 26-27.

88. *Ughi*: Ancient noble family of Florence. Villani (IV, 12) says that in his own day they were extinct.   *Catellini*: Another ancient noble family of Florence mentioned by Villani (IV, 12). They were also extinct in Dante's day.

89. *Filippi*: Of the Filippi, another ancient noble family of Florence, Villani (IV, 13) says: "[I] Filippi, che oggi sono niente, allora erano grandi e possenti, abitavano in Mercato nuovo." ("The Filippi, who are nothing today, were great and powerful then and lived near the Mercato Nuovo.")
Greci: The reference here is to yet another noble family of Florence, extinct in Dante's day. The Borgo de' Greci in Florence (which at the present time leads from the Piazza San Firenze to the Piazza Santa Croce) was named for them. See Villani, IV, 13.

89-93. *Ormanni e Alberichi . . . Bostichi*: All these old families have declined or disappeared. See Villani, IV, 9, 10, 11, 12, 13.

94-95. *Sovra la porta . . . peso*: In 1280 the Cerchi bought the palace of the Conti Guidi, near the Porta San Piero (see Dino Compagni, I, 20). The Cerchi became leaders in party strife. See n. to vs. 65.

96. *jattura*: "Jettison," throwing overboard. Perhaps the reference is to the exile of the Bianchi, including many of the Cerchi, in 1302, the "barca" being the city of Florence itself.

97-99. *i Ravignani . . . preso*: The Ravignani were another of the older families extinct in Dante's day. The head of the family, in Cacciaguida's time, was Bellincione Berti (cf. *Par.* XV, 112), the father of Gualdrada, who was the wife of Guido Guerra IV. The several lines of the Conti Guidi descended from them. The Conte Guido here referred to was doubtless their grandson, that same Guido Guerra of *Inf.* XVI, 38 (see n. to that vs.).

98–99. *e qualunque . . . preso*: The descendants of Ubertino Donati, son-in-law of Bellincione Berti, took the name of Bellincioni, as did some members of the Adimari family.

100. *de la Pressa*: Villani (IV, 10) includes this family among the old families who lived in the neighborhood of the Duomo. They were among the Ghibelline families who were expelled from Florence in 1258 (Villani, VI, 65) and were associated with the Abati in the treachery at Montaperti (VI, 79).

101. *Galigaio*: Galigaio de' Galigai was a member of an ancient noble family of Florence. Villani (IV, 11), who describes the family as "molto antichi," says the Galigai lived in the Porta San Piero. They were Ghibellines (Villani, V, 39) and as such were expelled from Florence in 1258 (VI, 65). In 1293, in consequence of a murderous assault committed in France by one of the family upon a Florentine citizen, their houses in Florence were demolished in obedience to the provisions of the *ordinamenti di giustizia*, under the superintendence of Dino Compagni, who records the fact in his *Cronica* (I, 12).

102. *dorata in casa sua già l'elsa e 'l pome*: A sign of nobility.

103. *la colonna del Vaio*: A representation of a strip of vair (ermine) traversed longitudinally the escutcheon of the Pigli family. Villani (IV, 12) mentions them among the old Florentine families. He says that they became Ghibellines (in 1215), though some of the family afterwards joined the Guelphs (V, 39), and eventually they identified themselves for the most part with the Bianchi (VIII, 39).

104. *Sacchetti*: Villani speaks of this ancient family as Guelph (V, 39) and as having been among those who fled from Florence to Lucca after the great Ghibelline victory of Montaperti (VI, 80).   *Giuochi*: According to Villani (V, 39; VI, 33) this family was Ghibelline and, though originally noble, had suffered a decline by his time.   *Fifanti*: Villani mentions this family as being among the early inhabitants of

Florence. He records that they were Ghibelline (V, 39) and as such were expelled from the city in 1258 (VI, 65).
Barucci: The Barucci family was also Ghibelline and according to Villani (IV, 10) extinct in his time.

105. *Galli*: Villani states that the Galli were Ghibellines (V, 39) who lived in the Mercato Nuovo and in his time had become of no account (IV, 13). Their houses in Florence, like those of the Galigai, were demolished in 1293 in accordance with the provisions of the *ordinamenti di giustizia* (Villani, VIII, 1), on which account, probably, the *Ottimo Commento* speaks of them as being hopelessly ruined.   *quei ch'arrossan per lo staio*: The Chiaramontesi, here spoken of by reference to a fraud of a member of the house who was overseer of the salt customs. This same fraud is also alluded to, together with that of Niccola Acciaiuoli, in connection with the ascent to the church of San Miniato, the steps of which Dante says were made in the days "when the ledger and the stave were safe" in Florence. See nn. to *Purg.* XII, 105 and 104-5.

106. *i Calfucci*: A Guelph family. According to Villani (IV, 11) they were extinct in his time. They descended from the Donati family, their stock ("ceppo").

108. *curule*: Supreme offices of magistrates, high civic offices.   *Sizii e Arrigucci*: Ancient noble families of Florence. The two families are frequently mentioned together by Villani, who says they resided in the "quartiere della porta del Duomo" (IV, 10). They were Guelphs (Villani, V, 39; VI, 33) and were among those who fled from Florence to Lucca after the great Ghibelline victory at Montaperti (VI, 80). They afterwards threw in their lot with the Bianchi (VIII, 39).

109. *quali*: In what glory.

109–10. *quei che son . . . superbia*: The Uberti, who in the latter part of the twelfth century rebelled against the Florentine government and for a while gained control of the city. For Farinata degli Uberti, see *Inf.* X.

110-11. *le palle de l'oro . . . fatti*: The Lamberti family, to which Mosca (*Inf.* XXVIII, 106) belonged, had golden balls on their shield. Both the Lamberti and the Uberti were of German origin.

112-14. *Così facieno . . . consistoro*: The Visdomini and the Tosinghi, patrons of the bishopric of Florence, administered the episcopal revenues whenever the see was vacant, until a successor was chosen, "and thus after the death of a bishop, by securing delay in the appointment of his successor, grew fat on the episcopal revenues" (Norton).

115. *L'oltracotata schiatta*: The reference is to the Adimari family. Villani says that they were Guelphs (V, 39) and as such were expelled from Florence in 1248 (VI, 33). They were among those who took refuge in Lucca after the Ghibelline victory at Montaperti in 1260 (VI, 80); and, when subsequently the Guelph party in Florence split up into Bianchi and Neri, they all joined the former, with the exception of the Cavicciuli branch (VIII, 39). It appears from Villani (VII, 56) that there was a bitter feud between the Adimari and the Donati (who were afterwards leaders of the Neri) long before the division of the Guelph party in Florence, and this feud is doubtless hinted at in Cacciaguida's allusion. *oltracotata* = *oltracotante*, "proud and insolent." *s'indraca*: "Becomes fierce as a dragon." Filippo Argenti (*Inf.* VIII, 61) belonged to this clan.

118. *venìa* = *veniva*.

119-20. *sì che non piacque . . . parente*: Ubertino Donati, who had married one daughter of Bellincione Berti, was displeased when another daughter was given in marriage to one of the humble stock of the Adimari. Cf. n. to vss. 97-99.

120. *il fé* = *lo fece* .

121. *'l Caponsacco*: The singular is used for the plural (the entire family) here as elsewhere (cf. vs. 92). The Caponsacchi, ancient noble family of Florence, originally (in 1125) came from Fiesole. Villani says they were one of the original

Ghibelline families in Florence (V, 39) and records that they took part in the expulsion of the Florentine Guelphs in 1248 (VI, 33) and that they were among the Ghibellines who were themselves expelled in 1258 (VI, 65). After their return from exile in 1280 they appear to have joined the Bianchi and to have been again expelled along with them in 1302.

122. *Fiesole*: See n. to *Inf.* XV, 62.

123. *Giuda*: Again the singular is used for the plural, referring to the Giudi family of Florence. The *Ottimo Commento* says of them: "Questi son gente d'alto animo, Ghibellini, e molto abbassati d'onore e di ricchezze e di persone; e quelli che v'erano al tempo dell'Autore, seguirono coi detti Cerchi la fuga." ("This is a family proud of its lineage, Ghibellines, but it has dwindled in honors, riches and in numbers, and those who were in Florence in the author's time followed the Cerchi in fleeing the city.")   *Infangato*: Name, again in the singular, used to represent the Infangati family. Villani mentions them among the ancient families of note in Florence and says they were Ghibellines (V, 39) and as such were expelled from Florence in 1258 (VI, 65).

125. *picciol cerchio*: The old city walls. Cf. *Par.* XV, 97.

126. *quei de la Pera*: Ancient noble family of Florence. The gate in question is said to have been the Porta Peruzza, one of the minor city gates. The statement that the family gave their name to one of the city gates, which Cacciaguida qualifies as "incredible but true," has been explained in various ways. Some think the incredible point was the smallness of the size of the city of Florence when this was one of the actual city gates. The view taken by the *Ottimo Commento*, however, seems the best: "Dice l'Autore: chi crederebbe, che quelli della Pera fossono antichi? Io dico ch'elli sono sì antichi, che una porta del primo cerchio della cittade fu dinominata da loro; li quali vennero sì meno, che di loro non fu memoria." ("The author says: who would believe that the Pera family was ancient? I tell you, they are so ancient that one of the gates of the first walls of the city was named for

them, but they declined so that the memory of them perished.")

127–29. *Ciascun che . . . riconforta*: The great baron is the Marquis Hugh of Brandenburg. He is said to have come to Florence from Germany with Emperor Otto III, and while there to have conferred knighthood on six Florentine families (the Giandonati, the Pulci, the Nerli, the Gangalandi, the Alepri, and the Della Bella). He died in Florence on the festival of St. Thomas the Apostle and was buried in the Badia of Florence (founded by his mother in 978), where the anniversary of his death was (and is still) solemnly commemorated every year on St. Thomas' day (December 21). The coat of arms referred to as "la bella insegna" consisted of seven red and white staves, which each of the families named above adopted, with variations, in its escutcheon. See M. Barbi (1934), p. 303.

This marquis of Brandenburg appears to be identical with Ugo, marquis of Tuscany from 961 to 1001, who was the son of Uberto, marquis of Tuscany from 936 to 961 (natural son of Ugo, king of Italy and count of Arles from 926 to 945), and of the Countess Willa (foundress of the Badia of Florence in 978).

131–32. *avvegna che . . . fregio*: "One, however, of the knights whose nobility goes back to Hugh, is now 'siding with the people.' This is Giano della Bella, who introduced, in 1293, severe reform measures directed against the nobles, and was banished in 1295. His family has somewhat changed the escutcheon of the 'great baron,' 'bordering' it with a 'fringe' " (Gr). They had a border of gold on their coat of arms.

133. *Gualterotti e Importuni*: These old families had also fallen from high estate by Dante's time. Both were excluded from the magistracy in 1311, and both were Guelphs (Villani, V, 39).

134. *Borgo*: The quarter called Borgo Santi Apostoli, where the Gualterotti and Importuni lived.

135. *se di novi vicin fosser digiuni*: " 'If they had gone on fasting for new neighbors,' i.e., if they had never had any: for this use of *digiuno*, cf. *Inf.* XVIII, 42, and XXVIII, 87. The undesirable new neighbors are the Buondelmonti (cf. l. 66), who, after the destruction of their castle of Montebuono in 1135, returned to take up their abode in Florence" (Gr).

136. *casa*: The Amidei.   *nacque il vostro fleto*: The bloody feud between the Amidei and the Buondelmonti divided all Florence for a long time. See Villani, V, 38. *fleto*: "Weeping," from the Latin *fletus*.

137. *disdegno*:   "Resentment." The indignation of the Amidei against Buondelmonte de' Buondelmonti, who, on his wedding day, in 1215, forsook his betrothed—one of the Amidei—for a daughter of the Donati.   *che v'ha morti*: To avenge this insult, the Amidei murdered him, and this was the beginning of the feud. See *Inf.* XXVIII, 103-11. *v'ha morti*: Here the verb is transitive, "has slain you."

139. *suoi consorti*: "Their associates." "The Uccellini and Gherardini. In the democratic legislation against the Magnates (who systematically defied the civic law and recognised no authority save that of the Family Council), members of a family who had ceased to act with it were regarded as no longer belonging to it, and members of another family who had joined its Tower-club, that is to say, its association for the maintenance of a tower for military purposes, were regarded as its 'consorts,' or associates, forming one *consorteria* with it, and therefore legally identified with it" (TC).

141. *conforti*: "Instigation." Cf. *Inf.* XXVIII, 135. The suggestion came from a certain Gualdrada Donati.

143. *Ema*: Small stream in Tuscany, which rises in the hills south of Florence and falls into the Greve a few miles from the city. It is crossed near Galluzzo by the road from the Val di Greve to Florence, by which the Buondelmonti would have entered Florence in coming from their castle to the city. Though the reference here is, first of all, to the individual named Buondelmonte de' Buondelmonti (vs. 140), also im-

plied of course is the evident involvement of the entire family in the tragic incident and their coming into the city from the country in the first place.

145–47. *Ma conveniesi . . . postrema*: " 'But it was fitting that Florence, in her last peace, should offer a victim to that mutilated stone which guards the bridge'—the old, broken statue supposed to be of Mars (the first patron of Florence) at the end of the Ponte Vecchio. Cf. *Inf.* XIII, 143-150. The victim was Buondelmonte, who was killed on Easter morning at the foot of the statue" (Gr). See also *Inf.* XXVIII, 107-8.

145. *conveniesi* = *si conveniva*.

146. *fesse* = *facesse*.

148. *altre con esse*: As Scartazzini-Vandelli observes, Villani (V, 39) mentions some seventy noble or notable families in 1215, hence Cacciaguida has not even mentioned half of them.

154. *né per division fatto vermiglio*: In 1251, after the expulsion of the Ghibellines, the Guelphs altered the Florentine standard from a white lily in a red field to a red lily in a white field. The Ghibellines kept the old colors. See Villani, VI, 43.

CANTO XVII

1–2. *Qual venne a Climenè . . . udito*: Because Dante has received several dire forecasts of exile and hard years ahead from Farinata, Brunetto Latini, and Vanni Fucci, and has just now heard Cacciaguida mention internal strife in Florence such as often leads to exile, he is naturally anxious to learn something about his own future. Although he had been informed by Virgil (*Inf.* X, 130-32) that Beatrice would tell him about the course of his life, and he remembered this and referred to it later (*Inf.* XV, 89-90), Dante nevertheless now turns to Cacciaguida in his concern. The poet, having doubtless decided while writing the poem to stage an encounter with Cacciaguida, finds it more appropriate to have great-great-grandfather provide this information in Beatrice's place.

Dante compares himself to Phaëthon, who, having been told by a comrade that the god of the Sun was not really his father, went to his mother, Clymene, to find out the truth. Clymene swore to Phaëthon that he was truly the son of the god and urged him to ask his father in person. The result was that Phaëthon induced his father to let him drive his chariot, an enterprise that proved fatal to him. Dante got the story from Ovid; see *Metam.* I, 750-61:

. . . fuit huic animis aequalis et annis
Sole satus Phaethon, quem quondam magna loquentem
nec sibi cedentem Phoeboque parente superbum
non tulit Inachides "matri" que ait "omnia demens
credis et es tumidus genitoris imagine falsi."
erubuit Phaethon iramque pudore repressit
et tulit ad Clymenen Epaphi convicia matrem
"quo" que "magis doleas, genetrix" ait, "ille ego liber,
ille ferox tacui! pudet haec opprobria nobis
et dici potuisse et non potuisse refelli.
at tu, si modo sum caelesti stirpe creatus,
ede notam tanti generis meque adsere caelo!"

He had a companion of like mind and age named
Phaëthon, child of the Sun. When this Phaëthon was
once speaking proudly, and refused to give way to him,
boasting that Phoebus was his father, the grandson of
Inachus rebelled and said: "You are a fool to believe all
your mother tells you, and are swelled up with false no-
tions about your father." Phaëthon grew red with rage,
but repressed his anger through very shame and carried
Epaphus' insulting taunt straight to his mother, Cly-
mene. "And that you may grieve the more, mother," he
said, "I, the high-spirited, the bold of tongue, had no
word to say. Ashamed am I that such an insult could
have been uttered and yet could not be answered. But
do you, if I am indeed sprung from heavenly seed, give
me a proof of my high birth, and justify my claims to di-
vine origin."

See *Inf.* XVII, 106-8.

1. *Climenè*: For the accentuation of Greek proper names,
see the n. to *Inf.* V, 4.

3. *quei ch'ancor fa li padri ai figli scarsi*: The example of
Phaëthon still makes fathers cautious in granting their sons'
requests because of the tragedy that resulted when Phaëthon
was allowed by his father to drive the chariot of the Sun. See
Ovid, *Metam.* II, 31-328.

5-6. *da la santa lampa . . . sito*: The "holy lamp" (light) is the soul of Cacciaguida. For the changing of place, see *Par.* XV, 19-24.

7-9. *Manda fuor . . . stampa*: Dante's desire to know what he now will ask of Cacciaguida is a burning desire (termed a "thirst" in vs. 12) within him to which Beatrice urges him to give adequate expression.

10. *nostra conoscenza*: Beatrice here speaks of herself and all the blessed in Heaven.

11. *ma perché t'ausi*: "But in order that you may accustom yourself."

12. *sì che l'uom ti mesca*: "So that one may pour you [drink]." "Uom" is here used as the equivalent of the French *on*.

13. *piota*: "Sole of the foot," i.e., foundation. (Cf. *Inf.* XIX, 120.) Elsewhere the term "radice" is applied to Cacciaguida (*Par.* XV, 89), and "ceppo" is used in referring to another family (*Par.* XVI, 106).

14-16. *come veggion . . . contingenti*: "The blessed see even 'contingent,' or casual, things—whether they be past, present, or future—as clearly as 'earthly minds' can grasp an eternal, concrete, elementary fact—as for instance the geometrical proposition that 'two obtuse angles cannot be contained in a triangle.' Cf. Aristotle, *Metaphysics*, IX, x" (Gr). Cf. "brevi contingenze" in *Par.* XIII, 63.

16-18. *così vedi . . . presenti*: As has been made clear before, the blessed are able to know many things denied to ordinary mortals, since they see them in God. For God's own knowledge of contingent things specifically, see Thomas Aquinas, *Summa theol.* I, q. 14, a. 13, resp.:

Deus autem cognoscit omnia contingentia, non solum prout sunt in suis causis, sed etiam prout unumquodque eorum est actu in se ipso. Et licet contingentia fiant in actu successive, non tamen Deus successive cognoscit contingentia, prout sunt in suo esse, sicut nos, sed simul;

quia eius cognitio mensuratur aeternitate, sicut etiam suum esse; aeternitas autem tota simul existens ambit totum tempus, ut supra dictum est, quaest. 10, art. 2 et 4. Unde omnia quae sunt in tempore, sunt Deo ab aeterno praesentia, non solum ea ratione qua habet rationes rerum apud se praesentes, ut quidam dicunt, sed quia eius intuitus fertur ab aeterno supra omnia, prout sunt in sua praesentialitate. Unde manifestum est quod contingentia infallibiliter a Deo cognoscuntur, in quantum subduntur divino conspectui secundum suam praesentialitatem, et tamen sunt futura contingentia, suis causis proximis comparata.

Now God knows all contingent things not only as they are in their causes, but also as each one of them is actually in itself. And although contingent things become actual successively, nevertheless God knows contingent things not successively, as they are in their own being, as we do; but simultaneously. The reason is because His knowledge is measured by eternity, as is also His being; and eternity being simultaneously whole comprises all time, as said above (q. 10, [aa. 2, 4]). Hence, all things that are in time are present to God from eternity, not only because He has the types of things present within Him, as some say; but because His glance is carried from eternity over all things as they are in their presentiality. Hence it is manifest that contingent things are infallibly known by God, inasmuch as they are subject to the divine sight in their presentiality; yet they are future contingent things in relation to their own causes.

19–23. *mentre ch'io . . . gravi*: See n. to vss. 1-3. Also see *Purg.* VIII, 133-39; XI, 139-42.

24. *tetragono*: "Foursquare," presenting upon every side a bold front or a show of unyielding resistance. See Aristotle, *Eth. Nicom.* I, 10, 1100^b, "τετράγωνος" ("tetragonus"), and *Rhet.* III, 11, 1411^b. *ventura*: See *Inf.* II, 61 and the corresponding note. Also see *Inf.* XV, 91-93.

27. *ché saetta previsa vien più lenta*: "An arrow foreseen

comes slower," i.e., strikes us with a less violent shock. See Thomas Aquinas, *Summa theol.* II-II, q. 123, a. 9, resp.:

In operatione fortitudinis duo sunt consideranda: unum quidem quantum ad electionem ipsius; et sic fortitudo non est circa repentina; eligit enim fortis praemeditari pericula, quae possunt imminere, ut eis resistere possit, aut facilius ea ferre: quia, ut Gregorius dicit in quadam homil. ([35] in Evang., in princ.), *iacula quae praevidentur, minus feriunt; et nos mala mundi facilius ferimus, si contra ea clypeo praescientiae praemunimur.*

Aliud vero considerandum est in operatione fortitudinis quantum ad manifestationem virtuosi habitus; et sic fortitudo maxime est circa repentina; quia secundum Philosophum in 3 Ethic. (cap. 8, ad fin.), in repentinis periculis maxime manifestatur fortitudinis habitus: habitus enim agit in modum naturae. Unde quod aliquis absque praemeditatione faciat ea quae sunt virtutis, cum necessitas imminet propter repentina pericula, hoc maxime manifestat quod sit fortitudo habitualis in animo confirmata.

Potest autem aliquis, etiam qui habitu fortitudinis caret, ex diuturna praemeditatione animum suum contra pericula praeparare: qua etiam praeparatione fortis utitur, cum tempus adest.

Two things must be considered in the operation of fortitude. One is in regard to its choice: and thus fortitude is not about sudden occurrences: because the brave man chooses to think beforehand of the dangers that may arise, in order to be able to withstand them, or to bear them more easily: since according to Gregory (*Hom.* [xxxv], *in Ev.*), *the blow that is foreseen strikes with less force, and we are able more easily to bear earthly wrongs, if we are forearmed with the shield of foreknowledge.* The other thing to be considered in the operation of fortitude regards the display of the virtuous habit: and in this way fortitude is chiefly about sudden occurrences, because according to the Philosopher (*Ethic.* iii. 8) the habit of fortitude is displayed chiefly in sudden dangers: since a habit works by way of nature. Wherefore if a person without forethought does that which pertains to virtue, when necessity urges on account of some sudden danger, this is a very strong proof that habitual fortitude is firmly seated in his mind.

Yet is it possible for a person even without the habit of fortitude, to prepare his mind against danger by long forethought: in the same way as a brave man prepares himself when necessary.

For the references in this quotation, see Gregory, *Homil.* XXXV, 1 and Aristotle, *Eth. Nicom.* III, 8, 1117ᵃ. See V. Crescini (1918), E. G. Parodi (1918a).

31–33. *Né per ambage . . . tolle*: In no enigmatical or ambiguous terms, such as heathen prophets used in order to ensnare the "foolish folk." In *Aen.* VI, 98-100 Virgil writes:

> Talibus ex adyto dictis Cumaea Sibylla
> horrendas canit ambages antroque remugit,
> obscuris vera involvens . . .

In such words the Cumaean Sibyl chants from the shrine her dread enigmas and echoes from the cavern, wrapping truth in darkness.

On "ambage," see P. Rajna (1920), p. 93. The "gente folle" are the pagans, of course, as the verses make clear. Cf. *Par.* VIII, 1-6.

32. *già s'inviscava*: "Once entangled themselves." The verb is based on *vischio*, "birdlime." Cf. *Inf.* XIII, 57: "m'inveschi." See also *Inf.* XXII, 144.

33. *l'Agnel di Dio che le peccata tolle*: See Ioan. 1:29: "Ecce agnus Dei; ecce qui tollit peccatum mundi." ("Behold, the lamb of God, who takes away the sin of the world!") Cf. *Purg.* XVI, 18.   *tolle = toglie* (cf. *Par.* VI, 57).

35. *latin*: "Discourse." Dante also uses the word in this sense in *Par.* XII, 144.

36. *chiuso e parvente del suo proprio riso*: "Enclosed by his own radiance and manifesting his own joy."

37–39. *La contingenza . . . etterno*: See n. to vss. 16-18 for the quotation from Thomas Aquinas. Here the singular implies the plural, "contingent events." These occur only in the sublunar world, which is also called the elemental world of matter in that the four elements—fire, air, water, and earth—make it up. This notion of the four elements is implied in the term "quaderno" (cf. the English *quaternion*), which in turn also fits the metaphor of book (volume) in the sense of a quire.

40–42. *necessità però . . . discende*: " 'But it [contingency] does not derive inevitability therefrom (from being foreseen by God), any more than a boat going downstream derives inevitability from the eye in which it is mirrored.' Casual things are no more necessary from being anticipated by omniscience than they would be if there were no power to see them coming" (Gr). See n. to vss. 16-18. Here the question concerns the determination of future contingent events in regard to their being foreseen by God, and Aquinas' argument at another point in the *Summa theologica* (I, q. 22, a. 4, resp.) is more pertinent:

> Providentia divina quibusdam rebus necessitatem imponit, non autem omnibus, ut quidam crediderunt.
>
> Ad providentiam enim pertinet ordinare res in finem. Post bonitatem autem divinam, quae est finis a rebus separatus, principale bonum in ipsis rebus existens est perfectio universi; quae quidem non esset, si non omnes gradus essendi invenirentur in rebus. Unde ad divinam providentiam pertinet omnes gradus entium producere. Et ideo quibusdam effectibus praeparavit causas necessarias, ut necessario evenirent; quibusdam vero causas contingentes, ut evenirent contingenter, secundum conditionem proximarum causarum.
>
> Divine providence imposes necessity upon some things; not upon all, as some formerly believed. For to providence it belongs to order things towards an end. Now after the divine goodness, which is an extrinsic end to all things, the principal good in things themselves is the perfection of the universe; which would not be, were not

all grades of being found in things. Whence it pertains to divine providence to produce every grade of being. And thus it has prepared for some things necessary causes, so that they happen of necessity; for others contingent causes, that they may happen by contingency, according to the nature of their proximate causes.

To be sure, the image expressed in vss. 41-42 states the matter in terms of a human eye in which the boat going downstream is mirrored, and this would seem to make a considerable difference. For when the event is mirrored in God, He *could* and (in the sense expressed by Aquinas above) *does* have control over all things, whether contingent or not. Cf. vs. 17.

43. *Da indi*: From the "cospetto etterno," vs. 39. "Da" may be considered redundant here.

43–44. *sì come . . . organo*: Since the prophecies of what is to come are dire indeed for Dante, one may wonder at the comparison with *sweet* music. But Cacciaguida is one of the blessed and in God's will is his peace (*Par.* III, 85), that is, all things willed by God or allowed by God, such as these "contingent things," are "sweet."

46–47. *Qual si partío . . . noverca*: Hippolytus was a son of Theseus by Hippolyte, a queen of the Amazons. Theseus later married Phaedra, who fell in love with her stepson Hippolytus; on his rejecting her shameful proposals, she accused him to his father of having attempted her dishonor. Theseus thereupon cursed his son, who was obliged to flee from Athens. He subsequently met his death in fulfillment of his father's curse. When Theseus afterwards discovered that Phaedra's accusation was false, Phaedra killed herself in despair. Dante got the story of Hippolytus and Phaedra from Ovid (*Metam.* XV, 497-505). See Virgil, *Aen.* VII, 761-82; Cicero, *De officiis* I, x, 32.

47. *noverca* = *matrigna*, "stepmother." Cf. *Par.* XVI, 59.

49–51. *Questo si vuole . . . merca*: Apparently the exile of Dante and other opponents of the papal policy was planned in Rome in April 1300, two months before Dante's priorate. Specifically the reference seems to be to the fact that Boniface VIII and the Roman curia were already plotting to turn the city of Florence over to the faction of the Neri, an event which did indeed lead finally to Dante's exile. At this time the city was in a state of ferment, owing to the feuds between the Neri and the Bianchi. The former were the partisans of Boniface and were clamoring for Charles of Valois as his representative, while the Bianchi, to which faction Dante belonged, were bitterly opposed both to Boniface and to Charles. In October 1301, in order to appeal for a change in the papal policy towards the city and to protest the machinations of the Neri, the Bianchi sent to Rome an embassy of which, according to Dino Compagni's *Cronica* (II, 25), Dante was a member. During Dante's absence, however, Charles of Valois entered Florence (November 1, 1301), and soon afterwards the *podestà*, Cante de' Gabrielli of Gubbio, under the date of January 27, 1302, pronounced a sentence against Dante and other Bianchi, a sentence which in Dante's case was followed by yet others. Dante never returned to Florence.

50. *verrà fatto a chi*: "Will be brought about by him who" —i.e., by Pope Boniface.

51. *là dove Cristo tutto dì si merca*: The place is Rome, where the pope and curia traffic in holy things. Cf. similar judgments in *Inf.* XIX, 52-57, 69-72.

52–53. *La colpa . . . suol*: Compare Boethius, *Consol. philos.* I, 4, ll. 158-59: "Quo fit ut existimatio bona prima omnium deserat infelices." ("By which means it comes to pass that the first loss which miserable men suffer is their esteem and the good opinion which was had of them.")

52. *colpa*: "Blame."   *offensa = offesa*, "wronged."

53–54. *ma la vendetta . . . dispensa*: "Many regarded the disgrace and death of Boniface VIII as a divine punishment for his cruelty and ambition" (Gr). See Dino Compagni, *Cronica* II, 35; Villani, VIII, 64.

58–59. *come sa di sale lo pane altrui*: How bitter is the bread of another, i.e., bread that must be begged of someone else.

58. *sa di sale*: "Tastes salty."

59. *altrui*: The possessive form, as used again in vs. 60. *calle*: "Path."

60. *l'altrui scale*: Literally, the stairs of another, but clearly meaning the begged-for bed and hospitality.

62. *la compagnia malvagia e scempia*: The other Florentine exiles of the party of the Bianchi. Of Dante's movements for some years after his exile, little is known for certain. In 1302 he was at San Godenzo in the Mugello at a meeting of the Bianchi and the next year at Forlì, where he served at one point as an aide to Scarpetta degli Ordelaffi. On July 20, 1304, the exiled Bianchi made an abortive attempt to effect an entry into the city, but from this attempt Dante seems to have held aloof, and about this time he separated himself from the Bianchi, having come to hold them in the bitter disesteem which the adjectives here reflect.

63. *in questa valle*: Vale of tears, of hardship and suffering, which your exile will be for you.

66. *ella*: The company of the exiled Bianchi.   *n'avrà rossa la tempia*: "Shall have its brows red therefrom," i.e., shall blush for shame for its foolishness, stupidity, and wicked deeds.

67–68. *Di sua bestialitate . . . prova*: Their very deeds and ways of proceeding ("processo")—implying the progressive unfolding of their deeds and ways—will be the best proof of their stupidity.

68–69. *sì ch'a te . . . stesso*: It will be more fitting and commendable on your part to have left that wicked company (that party) and to stand aloof and alone, a party by yourself.

69. *averti fatta*: The use of *avere* as auxiliary in reflexive verbs is common in early Italian.

70–72. *Lo primo . . . uccello*: Apparently, after separating himself from the exiled Bianchi, Dante took refuge at Verona, with one of the Scaligers (probably Bartolomeo della Scala). Nearly all the early commentators, including Pietro di Dante, who ought to have known, take the reference to be to Bartolomeo. After the death of Ezzelino III, Mastino della Scala was elected captain of Verona (1262). He was succeeded (in 1277) by his brother Alberto della Scala, who had four sons, Bartolomeo, Alboino, Can Grande, and Giuseppe, the abbot of San Zeno (*Purg.* XVIII, 124-26). Alberto died in 1301 and was succeeded by his eldest son, Bartolomeo, who died in March 1304.

The coat of arms of the Scaliger family was a ladder surmounted by the imperial eagle. For "santo uccello" in this sense, see *Par.* VI, 4. Some commentators have objected to the identification of the "gran Lombardo" as Bartolomeo because in his time the Scaligers did not bear the imperial eagle on their arms. This, however, as Scartazzini-Vandelli points out, is a mistake of Dante himself, and the objection might be urged equally against any of the other members of the family. Dante makes Cacciaguida, speaking in 1300 (the imagined date of the journey), say that the Scaliger in question "bears" ("porta") the imperial eagle on his arms, the fact being that the first of the family to be created imperial vicar was Alboino, who was appointed to the office by Henry VII in 1311. Butler suggests that Bartolomeo adopted the eagle as a sign of devotion to the imperial cause; but even so, since he did not succeed his father, Alberto, until 1301, the description in the text could hardly have applied to him in 1300. For the view that "il gran Lombardo" is Can Grande, see C. Hardie (1963). On this question, see the *Enciclopedia dantesca*, under the entry "Della Scala."

73. *ch'in te = verso di te.*

74. *del fare e del chieder*: "De" (*di*) is here used as in its limiting sense in Latin, "as for."

75. *fia primo quel che tra li altri è più tardo*: The great Lombard will give before you have to ask, which is not usual with benefactors, who wait to be asked before giving.

76-78. *Con lui vedrai . . . sue*: Can Francesco della Scala, called Can Grande, third son of Alberto della Scala (lord of Verona, 1277-1301), was born on March 9, 1291. In 1308 he married Giovanna, daughter of Conrad of Antioch, and died at Treviso on July 22, 1329. In 1308 he was associated with his brother Alboino in the lordship of Verona and was made joint imperial vicar with him by Emperor Henry VII; on the death of Alboino (November 29, 1311) he became sole lord of Verona, a position which he maintained until his death.

To Can Grande Dante dedicated the *Paradiso*, in a lengthy letter addressed (*Epist.* XIII, 1) "magnifico atque victorioso domino domino Cani Grandi de la Scala sacratissimi Cesarei Principatus in urbe Verona et civitate Vicentie Vicario generali" ("to the magnificent and victorious lord, Lord Can Grande della Scala, vicar-general of the most sacred imperial princedom in the city of Verona and in the state of Vicenza"), in which the title and subject of the *Divine Comedy* are discussed. The letter opens with a eulogy of Can Grande's magnificence and bounty, of which Dante says he himself partook, and which he acknowledges to have surpassed even the extravagant reports he had heard of it (*Epist.* XIII, 2-3):

> Inclita vestre Magnificentie laus, quam fama vigil volitando disseminat, sic distrahit in diversa diversos, ut hos in spem sue prosperitatis attollat, hos exterminii deiciat in terrorem. Huius quidem preconium, facta modernorum exsuperans, tanquam veri existentia latius arbitrabar aliquando superfluum. Verum ne diuturna me nimis incertitudo suspenderet, velut Austri regina Ierusalem petiit, velut Pallas petiit Elicona, Veronam petii fidis oculis discursurus audita, ibique magnalia vestra vidi, vidi beneficia simul et tetigi; et quemadmodum prius dictorum ex parte suspicabar excessum, sic posterius ipsa facta excessiva cognovi.

The illustrious praise of your munificence, which wakeful fame scatters abroad as she flies, draws divers in such divers directions as to exalt these in the hope of prosperous success and hurl down those into terror of destruction. Now this report, exceeding all deeds of moderns, I was once wont to think extravagant, as stretching beyond the warrant of truth; but, lest continued doubt should keep me too much in suspense, even as the queen of the south sought Jerusalem or as Pallas sought Helicon, so did I seek Verona, to scrutinise by the faithful testimony of my own eyes the things which I had heard. And there I beheld your splendour, I beheld and at the same time handled your bounty; and even as I had formerly suspected excess on the side of the reports, so did I afterwards recognise that it was the facts themselves that exceeded.

The authenticity of the letter is much disputed. See E. Moore (1903), pp. 284-369; also see F. Mazzoni (1955), who argues for the authenticity of the letter, and B. Nardi (1960) and C. Hardie (1960), who argue against it. The present commentary considers it to be authentic.

77. *forte*: The adjective, used for the adverb, goes with the preceding "sì."

78. *notabili fier l'opere sue*: Can Grande's great deeds were martial, evidence of the fact that he was chiefly influenced, at birth, by the planet Mars. The following is a summary of the most important events in his career:

1308-11. Joint lord of Verona with Alboino.

1311. Imperial vicar in Verona (Villani, IX, 20); November, sole lord of Verona; December, rescued Brescia from the Guelphs (Villani, IX, 32); helped to take Vicenza from the Paduans.

1312. Imperial vicar in Vicenza.

1314. September, repelled Paduan attack on Vicenza (Villani, IX, 63); October, made peace with Padua and was confirmed in lordship of Vicenza.

1315. Attacked Cremona, Parma, and Reggio, in alliance with Passerino Bonaccolsi, lord of Mantua and Modena.

1316. Dante perhaps at Verona.

1317. May, with help of Uguccione della Faggiuola repelled fresh attack of Paduans on Vicenza; December, appointed imperial vicar in Verona and Vicenza by Frederick of Austria; besieged Padua (Villani, IX, 89).

1318. April, took Cremona (Villani, IX, 91); December 16, elected captain general of Ghibelline league in Lombardy at Soncino.

1319. August, besieged Padua (Villani, IX, 100).

1320. August 25, repulsed by Paduans, Uguccione della Faggiuola being killed (Villani, IX, 121).

1322. September, took part with Passerino Bonaccolsi in siege of Reggio (Villani, IX, 167).

1324. June, attacked in Padua by German forces of Otto of Austria, whom he repelled (Villani, IX, 255).

1327. Besieged Padua (Villani, X, 42).

1328. Captured Mantua; September 8, at invitation of Paduan Ghibellines became lord of Padua (Villani, X, 101).

1329. July 18, took Treviso, where he died (July 22); buried at Verona (Villani, X, 137).

fier = *saranno*.

80. *la novella età*: Can Grande was born in March 1291.
pur: I.e., *soltanto*.   *nove anni*: This follows because the imagined date of the "present" in the poem is 1300.

81. *queste rote*: The heavenly spheres.   *torte*: "Revolved."

82. *ma pria che 'l Guasco l'alto Arrigo inganni*: Before 1312, when the Gascon pope, Clement V, after promising to support the emperor, Henry VII, in his expedition to Italy, promoted opposition to it. See *Inf.* XIX, 83; *Par.* XXX, 133-48.

83. *parran* = *appariranno*.

84. *in non curar d'argento né d'affanni*: Indifference to

wealth and to toil is a characteristic of magnanimity. See Thomas Aquinas, *Summa theol.* II-II, q. 129, a. 8.

88. *A lui t'aspetta*: "Look to him," "expect from him," and from his benefactions. The verb is in the imperative. Cf. *Purg.* XVIII, 47.

89. *per lui = da lui.*

89–90. *fia trasmutata . . . mendici*: Cf. Luc. 1:51-53: "Fecit potentiam in brachio suo: dispersit superbos mente cordis sui, deposuit potentes de sede, et exaltavit humiles, esurientes implevit bonis, et divites dimisit inanes." ("He has shown might with his arm, he has scattered the proud in the conceit of their heart. He has put down the mighty from their thrones, and has exalted the lowly. He has filled the hungry with good things, and the rich he has sent away empty.")

91. *portera'ne = ne porterai.*

93. *che fier presente*: "Who shall be witnesses." *presente = presenti.*

94. *giunse = aggiunse.*

94–95. *le chiose . . . fu detto*: Clarifications (glosses) of what had already been predicted.

95. *le 'nsidie*: Cf. vss. 49-51.

96. *pochi giri*: "But a few turns" of the sun, i.e., in the course of but a few years.

97–99. *Non vo' però . . . perfidie*: "Dante's life extended long beyond the miserable end of Boniface and of Corso Donati (*Purg.* XXIV, 82-87). The latter was a 'neighbor' in the strictest sense of the word. It may be, however, that l. 98 refers to Dante's enduring fame, rather than to his bodily existence" (Gr).

97. *invidie = invidii*, "bear hatred toward."

106–7. *sì come sprona . . . darmi*: The metaphor suggests

that time "spurs toward" Dante, like some charging warrior on horseback, with lance lowered to deal him a terrible blow.

108. *ch'è più grave a chi più s'abbandona*: Such a blow is even more terrible to one who is not expecting it, or, out of metaphor, to one who does not know clearly what blows await him, and these Cacciaguida can see and know, since he sees them in the mind of God.

109. *provedenza = previdenza*.

110. *se loco m'è tolto più caro*: Florence. Such is the reading accepted by Petrocchi. Other editors have "se'l loco," which would be normal.

111. *li altri*: Other places, places of refuge in exile. *carmi*: Verses.

112. *lo mondo sanza fine amaro*: Inferno.

113-14. *lo monte . . . levaro*: Purgatory, from the summit of which (beautiful because of the Garden of Eden there) the pilgrim is said to have been lifted by the eyes of Beatrice. Such turns of phrase should not be overlooked, for they are always clear pointers to the allegorical role of Beatrice, as the second of three lights. See C. S. Singleton (1958), pp. 23-31.

114. *levaro = levarono*.

115. *di lume in lume*: From one planet to another.

116-17. *quel che . . . agrume*: Dante has seen things—particularly in Hell, where he has seen the damned and where they are punished there—which, if reported, are going to prove very sour to some of his readers, who might otherwise offer him hospitality in his exile. Shall he make a true report, or shall he withhold certain things?

117. *agrume*: "Sourness."

118-20. *e s'io . . . antico*: To withhold true report of the things seen on this journey, to be a "timid friend of truth," could mean that my fame as poet will endure less with posterity, with those who one day will look upon the year 1300 as ancient.

121–23. *La luce in che rideva . . . d'oro*: Cf. *Par.* XV, 22 and 85. The light which is Cacciaguida, ever resplendent ("rideva"), now becomes more so, at the prospect of counseling his great-great-grandson concerning the question asked.

124. *fusca = offuscata*, "darkened."

126. *pur sentirà la tua parola brusca*: "Will indeed deem your speech harsh," whether on their own account, or for the shameful deeds of their relatives ("altrui vergogna").

128. *vision*: Here, as elsewhere in the poem, the word is used to mean "that which has been seen," and it nowhere implies "vision" in the sense of a dream-experience.

129. *rogna*: " 'Itch.'—Dante chose to write his poem in the 'comic' rather than the 'tragic' style, that he might, when occasion required, sacrifice elegance to vigor" (Gr).

130–32. *Ché se la voce . . . digesta*: See Boethius, *Consol. philos.* III, 1, ll. 13-14: "Talia sunt quippe quae restant, ut degustata quidem mordeant, interius autem recepta dulcescant." ("For the remedies which remain are of that sort that they are bitter to the taste, but being inwardly received wax sweet.")

132. *digesta = digerita*.

133. *Questo tuo grido*: "Grido" is used here in something of the meaning of a "public proclamation," i.e., of all that you have seen.

134. *più alte cime*: The word *cima* can suggest "peak" (as of a mountain) or "treetop," or, out of metaphor, it can mean the mighty of this world.

135. *argomento*: " 'Proof': because it requires exceptional courage to 'strike the highest peaks' " (Gr).

136. *Però = perciò*, which depends on "che" in vs. 139.

138. *pur l'anime che son di fama note*: Cacciaguida's assertion here cannot be taken as literally true, for every reader will recall the many humble, unknown characters encountered in Hell and elsewhere. One has only to think of the riff-raff, generally, of the eighth circle of Inferno.

139–42. *che l'animo . . . paia*: "The listener is never satisfied nor convinced by an unknown example or an obscure argument" (Gr).

140. *aia = abbia*.

CANTO XVIII

1. *verbo*: "Word," i.e., thought. See Thomas Aquinas, *Summa theol.* I, q. 34, a. 1, resp.: "Ex hoc ergo dicitur verbum vox exterior, quia significat interiorem mentis conceptum. Sic igitur primo et principaliter interior mentis conceptus verbum dicitur." ("Wherefore the exterior vocal sound is called a word from the fact that it signifies the interior concept of the mind. Therefore it follows that, first and chiefly, the interior concept of the mind is called a word.")

2. *specchio*: Cacciaguida is called a "mirror" because he reflects God's mind.

3. *lo mio*: My inner thoughts.   *temprando col dolce l'acerbo*: The "sweet" are the consoling parts of the prophecy, the "bitter" are the harsh: exile and the hardships thereof.

6. *colui*: God.   *colui ch'ogne torto disgrava*: Cf. Deut. 32:35: "Mea est ultio, et ego retribuam in tempore." ("To me belongs the vengeance, and I will make recompense in due time.")

8. *mio conforto*: Beatrice. Virgil is so termed in *Inf.* IV, 18; *Purg.* III, 22; and elsewhere.

8–9. *qual io allor . . . l'abbandono*: "At this point I renounce any attempt to express it," i.e., the love I saw in the holy eyes of Beatrice. "Qual" modifies "amor" in this construction, "amor" being the direct object of "vidi."

10. *non perch' io pur del mio parlar diffidi*: "Not only ['pur'] because I have no confidence in my [powers of] expression."

11. *ma per la mente che non può redire*: For the concept, see *Par.* I, 9. *mente*: "Memory." *redire*: "Return." Cf. *Par.* XI, 105.

12. *altri*: God. Cf. *Inf.* V, 81; IX, 9.

13. *Tanto*: "This much only." Cf. *Inf.* XV, 91; *Par.* II, 67.

16. *fin che*: "As long as." *piacere etterno*: Divine beauty.

16–18. *fin che . . . aspetto*: The "secondo aspetto" is the reflected light of beauty. Such expressions continue to underscore the allegory of Beatrice, by and through whose guidance the pilgrim sees by reflected light. Cf. *Par.* I, 49, 64-66.

20. *Volgiti e ascolta*: I.e., turn back to Cacciaguida and listen to him.

21. *non pur ne' miei occhi è paradiso*: "Beatitude consists not only in acceptance of the demonstration of divine truth, but also in the companionship of the blessed and the comprehension of their state as a manifestation of divine grace. This idea is conveyed by Beatrice in a figure as appropriate as it is sweet and modest" (Gr).

22. *qui*: On earth.

23. *vista*: "Eyes."

24. *tolta*: "Rapt."

25. *folgór santo*: Cacciaguida.

28–29. *quinta soglia . . . cima*: "The 'tree' of the heavens, which derives all its sustenance from above, is conceived as a fir, whose branches grow in rings or 'tiers' around the trunk. The fifth ring is the heaven of Mars" (Gr).

28. *soglia*: "Tier." Cf. *Par.* XXX, 113; XXXII, 13.

30. *e frutta sempre e mai non perde foglia*: This "tree" produces beatitude, which never "falls away."

32. *fuor = fuorono*.   *voce*: "Fame."

33. *musa*: "Poet." Cf. *Par.* XV, 26.   *opima*: "Rich."

34. *Però = perciò*.   *corni*: The term doubtless applies now to all the four arms of the cross, lateral and vertical.

35–36. *lì farà l'atto . . . veloce*: We are to conceive that each spirit (light), as it is named, darts through the cross like lightning in a cloud. The ruddy background of the planet itself provides the element that corresponds, in the simile, to the cloud. It should be remembered, throughout this review, that all those named were warriors for the faith.

38. *dal nomar*: "By the mention of."   *Iosuè*: Joshua, successor of Moses and conqueror of the promised land. Cf. *Purg.* XX, 111; *Par.* IX, 124-25.   *com' el si feo*: "When it [the mention] was made."   *feo = fece*.

39. *né mi fu noto il dir prima che 'l fatto*: The response by the light named is instantaneous.

40. *Macabeo*: Judas Maccabaeus, the great Jewish warrior. First under the leadership of his father, Mattathias, and, after his death (*ca.* 166 B.C.), as leader himself, he carried on the war against Antiochus IV Epiphanes, king of Syria, and his successor Demetrius and successfully resisted their attempts to destroy the Jewish religion. After having gained a series of victories over the generals of both kings, and having restored and purified the Temple at Jerusalem (165 or 164 B.C.), Judas was defeated and slain by the Syrians under Bacchides at Elasa (160 B.C.). His valor is glorified in the book of Maccabees (I Mach. 3:3-4).

42. *e letizia era ferza del paleo*: " 'And joy was the whip of the top,' i.e., it was joy that made it (the light) spin. Several times in the *Paradiso* Dante makes a swift rotary motion the symbol of keen delight" (Gr).

43. *per*: "At the naming of."   *Carlo Magno*: Charlemagne (Charles the Great), restorer of the Empire of the West, was born at Salzburg in 742, the eldest son of Pépin le Bref, king of the Franks. On his father's death (in 768) Charlemagne became joint king with his brother Carloman, and on the death of the latter (in 771) he became sole king of the Frankish empire. After his defeat of Desiderius (773-74), he assumed the title of king of Lombardy, and on Christmas Day 800, he was crowned Emperor of the West at Rome by Pope Leo III. He died on January 28, 814 and was buried at Aix-la-Chapelle. He was canonized in 1165.
    Orlando: Roland, the French epic hero who was represented as the nephew of Charlemagne and one of the twelve peers. According to the poetical account, he was slain at Roncesvalles by the Saracens in league with the traitor Ganelon. See n. to *Inf.* XXXI, 18.

44. *due ne*: I.e., *due lumi*. "Due" is the object of "seguì."

46. *Guiglielmo e Rinoardo*: "William, count of Orange, is the hero of a group of Old French epics, of which the best known is the *Aliscans*. He combatted the Saracens in southern France, as Charlemagne and Roland fought against them in Spain. Associated with him is the gigantic Renoart, of Saracen birth but baptized" (Gr). "Guiglielmo" and "Rinoardo" are subjects of "trasse."

47. *'l duca Gottifredi*: Godfrey of Bouillon, leader of the first Crusade (1096), battled with the Saracens in the Holy Land and became first Christian king of Jerusalem.
vista: The object of "trasse."

48. *Ruberto Guiscardo*: Robert Guiscard, a Norman conqueror of the second half of the eleventh century, took a large part of southern Italy and Sicily from the Saracens. If the reader glances back over the list of the warriors thus named,

he will note that a certain chronological order is observed and that some examples are from B.C. and some from A.D. times.

49. *mota e mista*: "Going and mingling."   *mota = mossa*.

50-51. *mostrommi l'alma . . . artista*: Cacciaguida, having returned to his place in this great heavenly "choir," shows his great-great-grandson what an artist (singer) he is there.

55. *luci*: "Eyes."   *mere*: "Pure."

56-57. *la sua sembianza . . . solere*: Beatrice is now seen to be more beautiful than Dante has ever seen her before.

57. *li altri e l'ultimo solere*: The verb "solere" is used as a noun, meaning her wonted appearance ("sembianza"). *Soleri*, in the plural, is understood ("li altri soleri e l'ultimo solere"), thus referring to the many times Dante has looked upon Beatrice, including the very last (vss. 8-18).

58-60. *E come . . . avanza*: See Aristotle, *Eth. Nicom.* II, 3, 1104^{b}.

58. *per sentir*: "Through feeling."

59. *bene operando*: "Through virtuous conduct."

61-63. *sì m'accors' io . . . addorno*: "Thus from an increase of Beatrice's loveliness I inferred that I had risen to a greater and swifter sphere. Since all the heavens revolve together from east to west, the outer must move faster than the inner, just as the tire of a wheel moves quicker than the hub; and as Dante proceeds from the center to one heaven after another, each successive sphere he reaches must, in a given time, cover a greater arc than its predecessor. As long as Dante remains in a sphere, he of course revolves with it" (Gr).

63. *miracol*: Beatrice. See Dante, *Vita nuova* XXI, 4; XXIX, 3.

64-66. *E qual è . . . carco*: The change from the red light of Mars to the whiteness of Jupiter is compared to the change

in a pale lady's face when a blush suddenly passes from it.
For the simile, cf. Ovid, *Metam*. VI, 46-49.

66. *vergogna*: The meaning should be understood as
"modest shame."

68-69. *temprata stella sesta*: The "temperate sixth star,"
Jupiter, is between hot Mars and cold Saturn. See *Conv*. II,
xiii, 25, where Dante writes: "Onde Tolomeo dice . . . che
Giove è stella di temperata complessione, in mezzo de la
freddura di Saturno e de lo calore di Marte. L'altra si è che
intra tutte le stelle bianca si mostra, quasi argentata."
("Wherefore Ptolemy saith . . . that Jove is a star of tem-
perate composition betwixt the cold of Saturn and the heat
of Mars. The other is that he shows white among the stars,
as though of silver.") Cf. *Par*. XXII, 145.

69. *ricolto = raccolto*, "received."

70. *giovial facella*: "Torch of Jove," the planet Jupiter, but
in "giovial" there is doubtless a play on the adjective in its
more common sense of "jovial," since the planet Jove (Jupi-
ter) was thought to make those born under it to be of joyful
and merry disposition.

72. *nostra favella*: "Our human language," here actually let-
ters of the alphabet.

73. *surti*: Past participle of *surgere*.   *surti di rivera*:
"Which have flown up from a riverbank."

74. *congratulando*: "Rejoicing together."   *pasture*: "Food."

76-77. *sì dentro . . . cantavano*: Each soul within its own
light sings as it flies about.

77. *faciensi = si facevano*. The word is pronounced *facìensi*.

79. *a sua nota*: "To their own tune."   *sua = loro*.
moviensi = si movevano. The pronunciation is *movìensi*.

81. *taciensi = si tacevano*. "Taciensi" is pronounced *tacìensi*.

82. *Pegasea*: I.e., Muse. The Muses are associated with the

winged horse, Pegasus. It is not clear whether Dante had in mind any special Muse; nor is it clear, if he was thinking of a particular Muse, whether the one invoked is Calliope (*Purg.* I, 9), Urania (*Purg.* XXIX, 41), or Euterpe (who presided over the sphere of Jupiter). This brief invocation here serves to indicate that some most remarkable thing is about to be recounted. Cf. *Purg.* XXIX, 37-39.

83. *rendili = li rendi.   longevi*: "Long-lived" (through fame).

84. *ed essi teco*: *Rendono longevi* is understood: "renders them long-lived." "Essi" stands for "li 'ngegni."   *teco = con te*, "with your aid."

85. *illustrami = illuminami*, "shed your light [of inspiration] upon me." "Illustrami" is an imperative.   *rilevi*: "Set forth."

86. *concette = concepite* (from the Latin *conceptae*), "beheld."

87. *paia = apparisca.   possa = possanza.*

88. *Mostrarsi = si mostrarono.   in cinque volte sette*: Thirty-five.

90. *le parti*: The single letters.   *come mi parver dette*: In the order in which they were traced out to me, as if spoken.

91–93. *DILIGITE IUSTITIAM . . . sezzai*: "Diligite iustitiam qui iudicatis terram" ("Love justice, you who judge the earth") is from the first verse of the book of Wisdom. Justice is a product of the heaven of Jupiter, and the souls of the just appear in this planet.

91. *primai*: "First." Cf. *Inf.* V, 1.

92. *fur = furono.*

93. *sezzai*: An archaic form meaning "last." Cf. "da sezzo" in *Inf.* VII, 130.

94. *emme*: The Italian name of the letter is *emme*, and the reader is to conceive the "sky-written" letter here to be the type illustrated in Fig. 2a.

2. Figures illustrating the successive changes of the shape assumed by the spirits of the just

96. *d'oro distinto*: "Patterned with gold." The planet looked like a silver background with a golden *M* embroidered on it. For the silvery hue of Jupiter, see n. to vss. 68-69.

97–98. *E vidi scendere . . . quetarsi*: For this second formation, see Fig. 2b. The shape is now not unlike that of a lily. This second moment in the transformation will be referred to later (vss. 112-13).

99. *cantando, credo, il ben ch'a sé le move*: Dante cannot hear clearly the words of their song, hence "credo." *il ben*: God, who moves them "to Himself" in love of Him.

100. *percuoter*: "Stirring."   *ciocchi*: "Logs."

102. *onde li stolti sogliono agurarsi*: The reference is to the superstitious practice of drawing omens from the many sparks that would rise from the log thus struck. Benvenuto observes: "Est enim de more in partibus Italiae, quod pueri stantes in hyeme de sero iuxta ignem percutientes stipitem augurantur sibi, dicentes: tot civitates, tot castella, tot agnelli, tot porcelli; et ita transeunt tempus." ("For it is the custom in some parts of Italy, that on a winter's evening when they are sitting by the fire, children will strike the burning log and draw omens therefrom, saying [according to the quantity of

the sparks]: 'So many cities, so many towns, so many lambs, so many little pigs.' And thus they pass the time.")
agurarsi = augurarsi.

103. *quindi*: From the body or lower parts of the letter *M*.

105. *'l sol*: God.   *sortille = le sortì*, "distributed them," allotting to each its place. Cf. *Par*. IV, 37, and *passim*.

107. *la testa e 'l collo d'un'aguglia*: See Fig. 2c for the third and last stage in the changes of shape assumed by the spirits. The reader must bear in mind that it is an heraldic eagle that is "figured" here by the many lights, and accordingly it is seen only in profile. Thus later only one eye of the bird will be noted, for in profile only one is seen. By this remarkable transformation, the capital *M*, already standing for monarchy, has become the symbol of the Roman Empire, the eagle which every reader of *Par*. VI recalls.

108. *a*: "By."   *distinto*: "Patterned." Cf. vs. 96.

109. *Quei che dipinge lì*: God.

109–11. *non ha chi . . . nidi*: " 'He (God) who paints there has no one to direct him, but he himself directs; and from him we recognize that power which is the essence of nest-building.' The instinct of the little bird, which is able to build its nest without having any need of a pattern, comes from God, and, in its own small way, serves as an image of the creative activity of God, who constructs solely from his inner conception" (Gr). Cf. Thomas Aquinas, *Summa theol*. I, q. 19, a. 4, resp.

112–13. *L'altra beatitudo . . . emme*: The rest of the blessed souls that had seemed content to form a lily in the *M* (see Fig. 2b). Some commentators have thought that these souls might symbolize Guelphs, who, as Grandgent observes, "though seemingly reluctant at first to give up their own standard [the lily], readily conform to the Imperial design [the *imprenta* of the eagle]." Yet others would hold to quite another view, that the group which temporarily, in the second shape, makes the heraldic *M* into a lily thus alludes to the French monarchy, whose heraldic device is the lily. Though momentarily attempting to stand alone, as seemed to happen in 1300, the French monarchy was to yield and merge with the Empire, or in all justice *should* have done so, for the *M* and the eagle are one, and, in Dante's well-known view, as expressed in the *De monarchia*, there is no place for another shape or sign, such as a lily, another separate power.

112. *beatitudo = beatitudine*.

114. *seguitò la 'mprenta*: The group fits itself perfectly into the figure of the eagle which began as an *M*, this *M* being the last letter of the scriptural exhortation to love justice. Thus the symbolic configuration is complete in all its details and transformations, and the poet can end his canto with a prayer for order and justice and with a bitter denunciation of the corrupt papacy.

115. *O dolce stella*: The planet Jupiter.

116. *nostra giustizia*: Human justice on earth.

117. *effetto sia del ciel che tu ingemme*: See n. to vss. 91-93.

118. *la mente*: God.

120. *ond' esce il fummo che 'l tuo raggio vizia*: The smoke that obstructs the downpouring influence of Jupiter for justice is chiefly avarice, as the following verses make clear.

121–23. *sì ch'un'altra fiata . . . martìri*: Cf. Matt. 21:12: "Et intravit Iesus in templum Dei; et eiiciebat omnes vendentes et ementes in templo, et mensas numulariorum et cathedras vendentium columbas evertit." ("And Jesus entered the temple of God, and cast out all those who were selling and buying in the temple, and he overturned the tables of the money-changers and the seats of those who sold the doves.")

123. *che si murò di segni e di martìri*: Cf. Actus 20:28: "ecclesiam Dei, quam acquisivit sanguine suo" ("the Church of God, which he has purchased with his own blood").

124. *milizia del ciel*: See Luc. 2:13: "multitudo militiae caelestis" ("a multitude of the heavenly host").   *cu'* = *cui*, accusative.

125. *adora*: "Pray."

126. *tutti sviati dietro al malo essemplo*: See Rom. 3:12: "Omnes declinaverunt." ("All have gone astray together.") For the notion of misguidance by a corrupt papacy and the "bad example" set by it, cf. *Purg.* XVI, 100-111; *Par.* IX, 127-32.

129. *lo pan*: The sacraments.   *che 'l pio Padre a nessun serra*: Cf. Thomas Aquinas, *Summa theol.* III, q. 80, aa. 3-6. "Nowadays wars are waged by means of excommunications and interdicts" (Gr).   *serra*: "Locks up," "withholds."

130. *Ma tu che sol per cancellare scrivi*: "John XXII, who was Pope when Dante was writing, issued and revoked many excommunications. He amassed a large fortune. In 1317 he excommunicated Can Grande della Scala, who remained under the ban until his death" (Gr).

131. *moriro* = *morirono*.

132. *per la vigna che guasti*: See Isa. 3:14: "Vos enim depasti estis vineam." ("For you have devoured the vineyard.") The "vineyard" is, traditionally, the Church. Cf. *Par.* XII, 86-87.

133–36. *Ben puoi . . . Polo*: "My heart is so set on John the Baptist (i.e., on the gold florin bearing his image) that I have forgotten Peter and Paul" (Gr). Villani (IX, 171) relates how John XXII had a gold coin minted in Avignon that was very similar to the florin of Florence.

134. *volle viver solo*: See Luc. 1:80.

135. *salti*: The dance of Herodias' daughter. See Matt. 14: 1-12.

136. *il pescator*: Peter.   *Polo*: Paul. "Polo" is another form of *Paolo*.

CANTO XIX

1. *Parea = appariva.*

2. *che*: The object of "facevan" in vs. 3.   *frui*: A Latin infinitive used as a noun, meaning "fruition," "enjoyment." For *frui* and its noun *fruitio*, which are used frequently by Augustine, cf. Thomas Aquinas, *Summa theol.* I-II, q. 11, a. 3, ad 3:

> Finis dicitur dupliciter: uno modo ipsa res, alio modo adeptio rei. Quae quidem non sunt duo fines, sed unus finis in se consideratus, et alteri applicatus. Deus igitur est ultimus finis sicut res quae ultimo quaeritur; fruitio autem, sicut adeptio huius ultimi finis. Sicut igitur non est alius finis Deus, et fruitio Dei, ita eadem ratio fruitionis est qua fruimur Deo, et qua fruimur divina fruitione. Et eadem ratio est de beatitudine creata, quae in fruitione consistit.

> We speak of an end in a twofold sense: first, as being the thing itself; secondly, as the attainment thereof. These are not, of course, two ends, but one end, considered in itself, and in its relation to something else. Accordingly God is the last end, as that which is ultimately sought for: while the enjoyment is as the attainment of this last end. And so, just as God is not one end, and the

enjoyment of God, another: so it is the same enjoyment whereby we enjoy God, and whereby we enjoy our enjoyment of God. And the same applies to created happiness which consists in enjoyment.

2–3. *che nel dolce frui . . . conserte*: A more normal prose order would be: "la quale [immagine] le anime conserte formavano, liete nel dolce *frui*."

6. *rifrangesse*: "Reflected." Cf. *Purg.* XV, 22; *Par.* II, 93. *lui*: "It," the sun.

7. *testeso*: "Now." Cf. *Purg.* XXI, 113.

8. *incostro = inchiostro*.

9. *né fu per fantasia già mai compreso*: "Fantasia," here as elsewhere in the *Comedy*, refers specifically to that human faculty of the mind which receives images; hence "compreso" means "grasped," "taken in." Cf. *Purg.* XVII, 25, and see the corresponding note.

11–12. *e sonar . . . "nostro"*: The single voice of the eagle speaks collectively for the just souls comprising it, "an image of the concordant will of the Just, and of the unity of Justice under the Empire" (Norton).

13. *Per esser*: "For being."   *giusto e pio*: The two terms reflect God's two ways (see n. to *Par.* VII, 103), which should also be the ways of the Empire and a good emperor, whose authority derives from God.

15. *che non si lascia vincere a disio*: "Which cannot be surpassed by desire." A higher glory (in Heaven) than that of the eagle (i.e., of the souls that make it up) cannot be desired by us, for it is supreme.

16. *la mia memoria*: "Memory of myself," the record ("la storia," vs. 18) of my deeds (such as are recounted by Justinian in *Par.* VI).

18. *lei*: "La mia memoria," vs. 16.   *la storia*: The record

or history of the Empire, which is in itself exemplary and should be followed.

19–21. *Così un sol calor . . . image*: Once more the unity of Empire, its oneness, is stressed by the imagery, as it is again in vss. 23-24.

24. *tutti vostri odori*: A single perfume comes from the many "flowers" that make up "the one."

25. *spirando*: "By speaking."

27. *trovandoli = trovandogli*, the *gli* meaning "for it," the long hunger.

28–29. *Ben so io . . . specchio*: The angelic order of the Thrones, which reflect God's judgments, presides over the sphere of Saturn. Cf. *Par.* IX, 61-62.

30. *'l vostro*: That is, *cielo*, this heaven of Jupiter.   *non l'apprende con velame*: Whereas souls in other spheres look up to the Thrones for the reflection of God's judgment and justice, it appears that the souls in the heaven of Jupiter (this heaven of justice) see God's justice directly.

31–33. *Sapete come attento . . . vecchio*: The souls that make up the eagle know Dante's past and present thoughts in regard to the question that has troubled him for so long, and they will soon proceed to read those thoughts and formulate his "doubt" (vss. 70-78).

34. *cappello*: "Hood." The falcon was hooded while it was taken to the place of the hunt, but was then unhooded and released when the hunt began.

35. *si plaude*: "Claps." Cf. Ovid, *Metam.* VIII, 238, "plausit pennis" ("clapped her wings"), and XIV, 507, "remos plausis circumvolat alis" ("circled round the rowers with flapping wings").

37. *segno*: From the Latin *signum*, "segno" means the "ensign" of the Roman Empire, its banner. Cf. *Par.* VI, 32. *laude = lodi*. The term is used here to mean those souls who

1. God and compass

declare God's grace and glory by their very actions. See *Inf.*
II, 103 (where this is said of Beatrice) and the note.

39. *quai = quali.   si sa chi là sù gaude*: The "si" here
serves to set off, to mark special distinctness, and has some-
thing of the meaning "he alone knows." Cf. *Par.* III, 108.
gaude = gode.

40–42. *Poi cominciò . . . manifesto*: The eagle's answer to
Dante's "long doubt" begins significantly with words that de-
clare the glory and the might of God the Creator of Heaven
and earth, and the specific answer itself (vss. 86-90, 103-5)
holds to this tone. See Prov. 8:27-29: "Quando praeparabat
caelos, aderam, quando certa lege et gyro vallabat abyssos,
quando aethera firmabat sursum, et librabat fontes aquarum,
quando circumdabat mari terminum suum, et legem ponebat
aquis ne transirent fines suos, quando appendebat funda-
menta terrae." (The following translation is found in the
King James version of the Bible: "When he prepared the
heavens, I was there: when he set a compass upon the face
of the depth: when he established the clouds above: when
he strengthened the fountains of the deep: when he gave to
the sea his decree, that the waters should not pass his com-
mandment: when he appointed the foundations of the
earth.") Cf. Iob 38:5-6.

41. *a lo stremo del mondo*: "Mondo" here, as often in Ital-
ian, has the meaning of "universe," "lo stremo" being the
outer confines and limit, marked off as with a compass.

43–45. *non poté suo valor . . . eccesso*: This should not be
understood as derogating from God's power (as if He could
not do this or that), but rather as being to His greater glory,
since His worth necessarily exceeds all created things (even
though these are created by Him), as does His wisdom
("verbo"). "Cf. XIII, 52-78. God's ideal conception is in-
finite, while the created universe is finite" (Gr).

44. *verbo*: Cf. *Par.* XVIII, 1.

46. *E ciò fa certo che 'l primo superbo*: "And a proof of this

(the inferiority of every created thing to the creative mind) is that the first proud one (Lucifer) . . ." (Gr).

47. *che fu la somma d'ogne creatura*: Lucifer was the most beautiful of all the angels, who are at the very summit of creation. Cf. *Inf.* XXXIV, 34-36.

48. *per non aspettar lume*: Without waiting for God's special grace, the "light of glory," Lucifer sought to attain to it by his own natural means. See Thomas Aquinas, *Summa theol.* I, q. 63, a. 3, resp.: "Sed in hoc appetiit indebite esse similis Deo, quia appetiit ut finem ultimum beatitudinis id ad quod virtute suae naturae poterat pervenire, avertens suum appetitum a beatitudine supernaturali, quae est ex gratia Dei." ("But he desired resemblance with God in this respect,—by desiring, as his last end of beatitude, something which he could attain by the virtue of his own nature, turning his appetite away from supernatural beatitude, which is attained by God's grace.") On the light of glory, which Lucifer did not wait to receive, see C. S. Singleton (1958), pp. 20-23. On the notion that pride (Lucifer's sin par excellence) causes the creature to remain incomplete or "unripe," see n. to *Inf.* XIV, 48; XXV, 18.

50. *è corto recettacolo*: See Thomas Aquinas, *Summa theol.* I, q. 12, a. 4.   *corto*: "Insufficient."

52. *vostra veduta*: Your human sight, the sight of all mortals.

52-53. *convene essere alcun de' raggi*: This statement is best glossed by vss. 64-65.

55. *da*: "By."

56. *che suo principio non discerna*: "As not to discern its origin" (the mind of God).

57. *molto di là da quel che l'è parvente*: Far beyond all that human vision can see. Our intelligence, a product of the intelligence of God, has just power enough to understand how far beyond the range of its comprehension its divine Source lies.
l' = *le*, the "vostra veduta" of vs. 52.

58–60. *Però ne la giustizia . . . s'interna*: The eagle's discourse finally touches on justice and thus approaches Dante's specific question. "Earthly intelligence, then, can no more penetrate eternal justice than a human eye can penetrate the ocean" (Gr). Cf. Ps. 35:7[36:6]: "Iudicia tua abyssus multa." ("Your judgments [are] like the mighty deep.")

61–63. *che, ben che . . . profondo*: The image effectively conveys, with "pelago," what is often referred to as the abyss of God's counsel (*Par.* VII, 94-95).

61. *proda*: "Shore."

62. *pelago*: The deep (cf. *Inf.* I, 23).

63. *èli = vi è* (unaccented *li = vi*).   *lui*: "Il fondo," vs. 61. "It [the bottom] is there, but its depth conceals it."

64. *Lume non è*: "There is no light," i.e., no light for the human intellect.

64–65. *dal sereno . . . mai*: From the eternally serene light of God.

65–66. *anzi è tenèbra . . . veleno*: Without grace (God's light), all that we take to be light is darkness, either the shadow or the poison of the flesh, either ignorance or vice.

67. *Assai*: I.e., *abbastanza*.   *mo*: I.e., *adesso*.   *la latebra*: A Latinism, meaning "hiding-place," referring to the inscrutable depth of God's judgment and justice.

69. *facei = facevi*.   *crebra*: A Latinism, meaning "frequent."

70. *dicevi*: The past descriptive tense conveys the notion that the question is repeatedly put to oneself.

70–71. *a la riva de l'Indo*: The river Indus, in northern India, is used to indicate India itself, as the eastern limit of the habitable world and as a place far removed from the Holy Land and the lands of Christendom generally, where all have heard of Christ.

71–72. *e quivi . . . scriva*: The three verbs here ("ragioni," "legga," "scriva") are all in the hypothetical subjunctive. The hypothetical example of this man so far removed *in space* from knowledge of Christ and belief in Him may be compared to that of those who were far removed from His coming *in time* and so had no knowledge of Him (the most striking examples of which are the virtuous pagans in Limbo).

72. *legga*: "Teaches." Cf. *Par.* X, 137.

73–75. *e tutti suoi voleri . . . sermoni*: "Voleri" looks to the will of the inner man and "atti" to his outward deeds, the key phrase being "quanto ragione umana vede," which clearly implies that our human view and understanding of the case may indeed be a limited one.

75. *in vita o in sermoni*: Cf. Luc. 24:19: "vir propheta potens in opere et sermone" ("a prophet, mighty in work and word").

76. *Muore non battezzato e sanza fede*: Again one thinks of the virtuous pagans in Limbo, who in life were far removed in time from knowledge of Christ and who, according to Virgil (*Inf.* IV, 33-42), did not sin, but who died without being baptized and without having faith in Christ.

77. *ov' è questa giustizia*: As much as to say: "What kind of justice is this?"

79–81. *Or tu chi se' . . . spanna?* The reply of the eagle to the troubling question, in these its opening words, is actually no reply at all, but an outburst against man's very pride and presumption in asking any such question in the first place. There are echoes of passages in the Scriptures here. Note, for example, Sapien. 9:13: "Quis enim hominum poterit scire consilium Dei? aut quis poterit cogitare quid velit Deus?" ("For what man knows God's counsel, or who can conceive what the Lord intends?") See Iob 38 and 39 and Rom. 9:20: "O homo, tu quis es, qui respondeas Deo?" ("O man, who art thou to reply to God?")

79. *sedere a scranna*: "Sit in the judgment seat."
scranna = scranno.

82. *Certo a colui che meco s'assottiglia*: " 'Surely, for him
who sophisticates with me . . .' Dante is putting subtle ques-
tions about justice to the Eagle, who is its embodiment"
(Gr).

83–84. *se la Scrittura . . . maraviglia*: "If you mortals had
not the Bible and its clear utterances to guide you, there
would be no end to your sophistries, since even with the Bible
you enter into such discussions" (Gr).

84. *da dubitar sarebbe a maraviglia*: "There would be a
marvelous chance for questioning."

85. *Oh terreni animali*: Cf. Boethius, *Consol. philos*. III, iii,
l. 1: "Vos quoque, o terrena animalia" ("you also, O earthly
creatures").

87. *da sé, ch'è sommo ben, mai non si mosse*: Cf. Mal. 3:6:
"Ego enim Dominus, et non mutor." ("For I am the Lord
and I change not.")

88. *Cotanto è giusto quanto a lei consuona*: Cf. *De mon*. II,
ii, 5, where Dante says: "Et iterum ex hoc sequitur quod ius
in rebus nichil est aliud quam similitudo divine voluntatis;
unde fit quod quicquid divine voluntati non consonat, ipsum
ius esse non possit, et quicquid divine voluntati est conso-
num, ius ipsum sit." ("And hence it follows again that right
as manifested in things is nought else than the similitude of
the divine will. Whence it comes to pass that whatever is not
consonant with the divine will cannot be right, and whatever
is consonant with the divine will is right.") Also see Rom.
9:14-24:

> Quid ergo dicemus? Numquid iniquitas apud Deum?
> Absit. Moysi enim dicit: Miserebor cuius misereor, et
> misericordiam praestabo cuius miserebor. Igitur non
> volentis neque currentis, sed miserentis est Dei. Dicit
> enim Scriptura Pharaoni: Quia in hoc ipsum excitavi te,
> ut ostendam in te virtutem meam, et ut annuntietur

nomen meum in universa terra. Ergo cuius vult misere-
tur, et quem vult indurat. Dicis itaque mihi: Quid adhuc
queritur? Voluntati enim eius quis resistit? O homo, tu
quis es, qui respondeas Deo? Numquid dicit figmentum
ei qui se finxit: Quid me fecisti sic? An non habet pote-
statem figulus luti ex eadem massa facere aliud quidem
vas in honorem, aliud vero in contumeliam? Quod si
Deus volens ostendere iram et notam facere potentiam
suam, sustinuit in multa patientia vasa irae apta in in-
teritum, ut ostenderet divitias gloriae suae in vasa mise-
ricordiae quae praeparavit in gloriam; quos et vocavit
nos non solum ex Iudaeis sed etiam ex Gentibus.

What then shall we say? Is there injustice with God? By
no means! For he says to Moses, "I will have mercy on
whom I have mercy, and I will show pity to whom I will
show pity." So then there is question not of him who
wills nor of him who runs, but of God showing mercy.
For the Scripture says to Pharaoh, "For this very pur-
pose I have raised thee up that I may show in thee my
power, and that my name may be proclaimed in all the
earth." Therefore he has mercy on whom he will, and
whom he will he hardens.

Thou sayest to me: Why then does he still find fault?
For who resists his will? O man, who art thou to reply
to God? Does the object moulded say to him who
moulded it: Why hast thou made me thus? Or is not the
potter master of his clay, to make from the same mass
one vessel for honorable, another for ignoble use? But
what if God, wishing to show his wrath and to make
known his power, endured with much patience vessels
of wrath, ready for destruction, that he might show the
riches of his glory upon vessels of mercy, which he has
prepared unto glory—even us whom he has called not
only from among the Jews but also from among the
Gentiles?

89. *nullo creato bene a sé la tira*: "No created goodness
draws it [the will of God] to itself."

90. *ma essa, radiando, lui cagiona*: "It [God's will], raying forth, causes it [the 'creato bene']."

91. *sovresso*: "Over."   *si rigira*: The subject of "si rigira" is "la cicogna," to be supplied from vs. 92.

93. *è pasto = è pasciuto*, on the model of the Latin *pastus est*.

94. *cotal*: "Cotal" is the correlative of "quale" in vs. 91. *sì*: "Sì" is the correlative of "come" in vs. 93.

94–95. *cotal si fece . . . imagine*: The image is awesome. The great eagle, made up of so many lights, actually circles about over Dante, even as the stork over its little ones in the nest.

96. *sospinte da tanti consigli*: Again the underscoring of the striking fact, stressed throughout, of the single concerted movement of so many souls together.

98. *le mie note*: "My song."

100. *Poi = poi che.*

101. *nel segno*: See n. to vs. 37.

102. *fé = fece.*

104. *Cristo*: For the third time we have *Cristo* in rhyme with itself: cf. *Par.* XII, 71, 73, 75. See also *Par.* XIV, where the rhyming lines are the same as in this canto: vss. 104, 106, 108.

106. *Ma vedi*: *molti gridan "Cristo, Cristo!"*: See Matt. 7:22-23: "Multi dicent mihi in illa die: Domine, Domine, nonne in nomine tuo prophetavimus, et in nomine tuo daemonia eiecimus, et in nomine tuo virtutes multas fecimus? Et tunc confitebor illis: Quia numquam novi vos; discedite a me, qui operamini iniquitatem." ("Many will say to me in that day, 'Lord, Lord, did we not prophesy in thy name, and cast out devils in thy name, and work many miracles in thy name?' And then I will declare to them, 'I never knew you. Depart from me, you workers of iniquity!' ")

107. *prope*: A Latinism, meaning "near."

109. *e tai Cristian dannerà l'Etiòpe*: See Matt. 12:41-42:

> Viri Ninivitae surgent in iudicio cum generatione ista, et condemnabunt eam; quia paenitentiam egerunt in praedicatione Ionae, et ecce plus quam Ionas hic. Regina austri surget in iudicio cum generatione ista, et condemnabit eam; quia venit a finibus terrae audire sapientiam Salomonis, et ecce plus quam Salomon hic.

> The men of Nineve will rise up in the judgment with this generation and will condemn it; for they repented at the preaching of Jonas, and behold, a greater than Jonas is here. The queen of the South will rise up in the judgment with this generation and will condemn it; for she came from the ends of the earth to hear the wisdom of Solomon, and behold, a greater than Solomon is here.

Etiòpe: Ethiopian, in the sense of "the heathen" generally.

110. *quando si partiranno i due collegi*: Cf. Matt. 25:31-46. *si partiranno = si divideranno.* *collegi*: "Assemblies."

111. *inòpe*: "Poor," from the Latin *inops*, that is, deprived of Heaven, these being the damned.

112. *poran = potranno.* *li Perse = i Persiani.* The word is used here, as "Etiòpe" is in vs. 109, for the heathen in general.

113. *quel volume*: Cf. Apoc. 20:12: "Et vidi mortuos magnos et pusillos stantes in conspectu throni; et libri aperti sunt, et alius liber apertus est, qui est vitae: et iudicati sunt mortui ex his quae scripta erant in libris secundum opera ipsorum." ("And I saw the dead, the great and the small, standing before the throne, and scrolls were opened. And another scroll was opened, which is the book of life; and the dead were judged out of those things that were written in the scrolls, according to their works.")

114. *suoi dispregi*: "Their disgraces."

115. *Lì si vedrà, tra l'opere d'Alberto*: The adverb "lì," used

thrice in this device of anaphora, refers to "the volume" (vs. 113). With this verse begins a series of judgments and condemnations of Christian rulers of Dante's time, their strife held up to scorn by the poet in contrast to the ideal unity and harmony of justice represented by the image of the eagle.

Alberto: Albert of Austria, whom Dante here rebukes for his invasion of Bohemia. See n. to *Purg.* VI, 97.

116. *quella*: That is, *opera*. The devastation of Bohemia in 1304. *penna*: The pen of the recording angel.

117. *Praga*: Prague, on the Moldau (now Vltava), the capital of Bohemia. The allusion is to the invasion of the dominions of Wenceslaus II, king of Bohemia, in 1304 by his brother-in-law, Albert I (Wenceslaus having married, as his first wife, Albert's sister). Albert was jealous of the growing power of Bohemia and wanted to force Wenceslaus to renounce the claim of his son Wenceslaus to the throne of Hungary in favor of Charles Robert, eldest son of Charles Martel. (See Map 1, facing p. 162.)

118. *sovra Senna*: "On the Seine," in France.

119. *falseggiando la moneta*: Philip the Fair, to supply himself with money after the battle of Courtrai in 1302, debased the coinage of the realm, causing great misery.

120. *quel che morrà di colpo di cotenna*: "Philip died in 1314 from a fall occasioned by a wild boar which ran between the horse's legs" (Gr). See Villani, IX, 66. *colpo di cotenna*: " 'Boarskin blow' is an odd phrase: the king's death was due, not to the tusks of the boar, but to its bristly hide brushing against the horse" (Gr).

121–22. *Lì si vedrà . . . folle*: The first part of the fourteenth century saw the wars of Edward I and Edward II against the Scots under Wallace and Bruce.

121. *asseta*: "Quickens thirst."

123. *soffrir*: "Endure," keep.

124. *Vedrassi = si vedrà* (i.e., recorded in God's book).
The anaphora passes now to this verb.

125. *quel di Spagna*: Ferdinand IV of Castile, king of Castile and León from 1295 to 1312. *quel di Boemme*:
Wenceslaus II (*Purg.* VII, 101). *Boemme = Boemia*,
Bohemia. *Boemme* was a common form in Dante's time.

127. *Ciotto di Ierusalemme*: Charles II of Naples, titular
king of Jerusalem, was called "the Cripple" on account of his
lameness. See Villani, VII, 1. Charles derived the title of
Jerusalem from his father, Charles of Anjou, king of Naples
and Sicily, who claimed to have acquired the right to it by
purchase in 1272. He further claimed it in his own right, as
one of the forfeited Hohenstaufen dignities, with which he
had been invested by the pope. The title had come to the
Hohenstaufen through the marriage of Frederick II to Yolande (his second wife), daughter of John of Brienne and
Marie of Montferrat, who was the eldest daughter of Isabella
(daughter of King Amalric I of Jerusalem) and Conrad of
Montferrat. Frederick II became titular king of Jerusalem in
1227 and assumed the crown in 1229.

128-29. *segnata con un i . . . un emme*: "His goodness will
be marked 1, his wickedness 1000." He seems to have had
no virtue except liberality. For Charles' character, see *Purg.*
XX, 79-81.

131. *quei che guarda l'isola del foco*: Frederick II, king of
the volcanic island of Sicily. Cf. *Purg.* VII, 119; *Conv.* IV,
vi, 20; *De vulg. eloqu.* I, xii, 5. After warring for some years
with Charles II of Naples, he made peace with him and married one of his daughters. Upon the death of Emperor Henry
VII, he abandoned the Ghibelline cause.

132. *ove Anchise finì la lunga etate*: See Virgil, *Aen.* III,
707-15.

133-35. *e a dare . . . loco*: "To indicate at the same time his
insignificance and his wickedness, his many misdeeds shall
be recorded in shorthand" (Gr). The anaphora shifts now

to tercets beginning with "e." Thus it is first *l*, then *v* (interchangeable with *u*), then *e*. The term *lue* is thus spelled out, which as a noun (*la lue*) means "pestilence." For a similar device, see *Purg.* XII, 25-63 and the note to *Purg.* XII, 61-63.

137. *barba*: "Beard," but here meaning "uncle," a usage that is still common in Italian dialects. The reference is to James, second son of James I of Aragon and brother of Pedro III. On the death of his father in 1276 he entered into possession of the kingdom of the Balearic Islands, which had been wrested from the Moors by James I in 1232 and of which he had been assigned the sovereignty in 1262. He also claimed Valencia under his father's will, and in order to enforce his claim he joined Philip III of France in his luckless expedition against Pedro III of Aragon in 1284. He supplied the enemy of his house with ships and men, and occupied Perpignan on behalf of the French king. The campaign proved a disastrous failure, and James was deprived of his kingdom. Ten years later, however, in 1295, he was reinstated in accordance with the terms of an agreement between his nephew, James II of Aragon, and Philip IV, the Fair, of France and Charles II of Naples. He died in 1311.
fratel: James II of Aragon. See n. to *Purg.* VII, 119.

138. *nazione*: "Stock," "lineage." *due corone*: Of Majorca and of Aragon. *fatte bozze*: "Dishonored," "betrayed." Literally, *fare bozzo* means "to cuckold."

139. *quel di Portogallo*: Diniz (also known as Dionysius), king of Portugal from 1279 to 1325, was the son of Alfonso III, whom he succeeded, and Beatrice, daughter of Alfonso X of Castile and León. He married Isabel (Saint), daughter of Pedro III of Aragon.

It is not clear on what grounds Dante condemned Diniz, for he has the reputation of being one of the best and ablest rulers of his time, having by his wise government laid the foundations of the future Portugal. Among the benefits he conferred on his country was the foundation (in 1290) of the University of Coimbra, which was at first in Lisbon. As hinted by the *Ottimo Commento*, Dante's censure of him may be explained by the fact that he devoted himself to extending the commerce of Portugal, instead of taking the field against the Moorish infidels, as his predecessors had done. Or possibly Dante misunderstood his action with regard to the Templars in Portugal, who in common with those of Castile and León had in 1310 been declared by the Council of Salamanca innocent of all the charges against them. Nevertheless, when the order was finally suppressed by the Council of Vienne two years later, Diniz, instead of handing their property over to the Knights of St. John, took possession of it and refused to give it up. Dante may have regarded this simply as an act of spoliation, not being aware (at any rate at the time he wrote) that when, in 1319, Diniz founded the Order of Christ he endowed it with the confiscated property of the disbanded Templars, of whom the new order was chiefly composed.

The infidelity of Diniz to his wife, St. Isabel, and the civil wars between him and his heir, Alfonso IV, occasioned by the latter's jealousy of his bastard brother, may also have influenced Dante's judgment against him.

Norvegia: Norway, an independent kingdom until the Union of Kalmar in 1397, when the three kingdoms of Norway, Sweden, and Denmark were united. Since only living sovereigns are in question here, the reference is probably to Haakon V Magnusson, king from 1299 to 1319, who passed his reign in wars with Denmark. But it is quite likely that Dante's knowledge of the Norwegian kings was vague and that the reference is to Haakon's elder brother, Eric II (who ruled from 1280 to 1299), or even to their father, Magnus VI (who ruled from 1263 to 1280).

140. *Rascia*: Name by which the former kingdom of Serbia was known in the Middle Ages, from the name of its capital, Raska or Rashka, the modern Novi Pazar. It comprised parts of the modern Serbia, Bosnia, Croatia, and Dalmatia. (See Map 1, facing p. 162.)

The king in question is Stephen Urosh II (1275-1321), son of Stephen Urosh I (1240-72), and grandson of Stephen, the

first king (1222-28). The reign of Stephen Urosh II, other-
wise known as Milutin, was chiefly occupied with struggles
against the Greeks, in which he was for the most part suc-
cessful. His domestic life was unhappy—he divorced three
wives and caused his only son, Stephen (who was a bastard),
to be blinded on suspicion of treachery. In 1314 he fought
on the side of the Emperor Andronicus against the Turks,
and in the same year forced the republic of Ragusa to pay
him tribute. In 1319 he was deprived of Bosnia by the Hun-
garians, and two years later he died (October 29, 1321, a few
weeks after Dante).

141. *che male ha visto il conio di Vinegia*: Dante's allusion
to Stephen's counterfeiting of the Venetian coinage refers to
the fact that he issued coins of debased metal in imitation of
the Venetian *matapan* or *grosso*. A decree which was issued
March 3, 1282, and repeated May 3, 1306 (both during the
reign of Stephen Urosh II), is preserved in the Venetian
Libro d'oro, whereby it is enacted that all official receivers
of government monies are to make diligent search for the
counterfeit Venetian *grossi* issued by the king of Rascia, and
that all money-changers on the Rialto and their boys from
the age of twelve upwards be bound upon oath to do the
same, the said counterfeits wherever found to be defaced and
destroyed.

It appears from the same source that the Venetians sent
an embassy in 1287 to the king of Rascia about this same
matter of the counterfeit *grossi*. From Venice this debased
coinage found its way to other parts of Italy, among other
places to Bologna, where in 1305 a number of bankers and
money-changers were convicted of purchasing a large quan-
tity of the counterfeit *grossi* for the purpose of exchanging
them (at a profit of 40 per cent) against good Venetian
grossi.

142-43. *O beata Ungheria . . . malmenare*: The throne of
Hungary, which belonged to Charles Martel (*Par.* VIII, 64-
66), was usurped by Andrew III.

143-44. *e beata Navarra . . . fascia*: "Navarre would be

happy if she could protect herself with the mountain chains that enfold her—that is, if she could make the Pyrenees a bulwark against France, which is destined to annex her on the death of her queen, Joanna, married to Philip the Fair" (Gr).

145–48. *E creder . . . si scosta*: "We may regard as a 'fore-taste' and a warning of these great disasters the misfortunes of a couple of towns in Cyprus, which are already bewailing and scolding about their 'beast,' the dissolute King of Cyprus, Henry II of Lusignan" (Gr). Dante here alludes to the sufferings of Cyprus under the unsettled rule of the house of Lusignan. Hugh III of Antioch, king of Cyprus and Jerusalem, who derived the Lusignan title from his mother, died in 1284, leaving several dissolute sons. The eldest of these, John, succeeded, but died within a year, his death being attributed to poison administered by his brother Henry. The latter, second son of Hugh, a prince of feeble character and constitution, assumed the government in 1285, under the title of Henry II. Six years later (1291), Acre, the last possession of the Christians in the Holy Land, having been captured by the Saracens (*Inf.* XXVII, 89), Henry collected a force with the object of attempting its reconquest and gave the command of it to his younger brother Amalric or Amaury, prince of Tyre. The failure of this expedition, and the unpunished depredations of some Genoese galleys on the coast of Cyprus, gave Amalric a pretext for declaring his brother incapable of governing. Having got himself appointed governor of the island by the supreme council (1307), Amalric kept Henry virtually a prisoner and assumed all the power into his own hands. Before, however, he could finally make himself master of the kingdom, he was assassinated by one of his own adherents (1310). On his death, his younger brother attempted to seize the throne; but Henry's following demanded the restoration of the rightful king, who resumed the government and retained it until his death in 1324.

148. *che dal fianco de l'altre non si scosta*: "This little beast trots along beside the big ones on the path of crime" (Gr).

CANTO XX

1. *colui*: The sun.   *alluma = illumina*.

4–6. *lo ciel . . . risplende*: In Dante's time it was generally held that all the stars derived their light from the sun. Hence the many lights that appear in the heavens after sunset are still shining with the light of the sun. Cf. *Conv.* III, xii, 7, as well as II, xiii, 15.

7–11. *e questo atto . . . canti*: The comparison is not intended to be exact, for although the sun disappears in setting, the figure of the eagle does not. However, that figure, which has been speaking as one, now presents the aspect of its many parts, as does the sun after sunset, for the many lights, or souls, that constitute it begin to sing as so many participants in a chorus. Each becomes brighter, which further supports the simile.

8. *come*: "When."   *'l segno del mondo*: The eagle. *suoi duci*: "Its rulers."

9. *rostro*: "Beak." Cf. *Par.* XIX, 10.

10. *però che = perciò che*.

12. *da mia memoria labili e caduci*: These songs are such

331

that the memory of the living man cannot retain them. See *Par.* X, 70-73.   *caduci = caduchi.*

13. *dolce amor*: The love of these spirits for God.   *t'ammanti*: Cf. *Par.* V, 136-37; IX, 70-71.

14. *flailli*: "Pipes." Cf. the OFr *flavel*, "flute."

15. *avieno = avevano.*

16. *lapilli*: "Jewels." Cf. *Par.* XV, 22, 85; XVIII, 115.

17. *il sesto lume*: The planet Jupiter.

18. *squilli*: "Songs," as is clear from the context.

21. *cacume*: "Summit." Cf. *Purg.* IV, 26; *Par.* XVII, 113.

22–24. *E come . . . penètra*: In the cittern, or lute, "the sound is shaped at the neck," where the fingering is done; in the bagpipe, it is at the holes.

24. *sampogna = zampogna.*

25. *rimosso d'aspettare indugio = rimosso ogni indugio d'aspettare*, "removed every delay in waiting," or simply "without delay." The expression in the Italian is somewhat redundant.

26. *salissi = si salì.* The *si* here, as again in "uscissi" (vs. 28), is the so-called pleonastic reflexive which serves to focus attention more emphatically on the subject, in this case on the sound as it is gradually formed and as it then issues as a voice. The poet delights in following such gradual formation, particularly in the matter of a voice. Cf. *Inf.* XIII, 40-44; XXVII, 13-18.

27. *bugio*: "Hollow."

28. *quivi*: In the neck ("collo").   *uscissi = si uscì.* Cf. n. to vs. 26.

30. *quali aspettava il core ov' io le scrissi*: Dante's heart-felt desire is to know the names of the spirits exalted to this heav-

en, and as he now hears some of them, he inscribes them in his heart (memory).

31–32. *La parte in me . . . mortali*: The eagle's eye. The reader should bear in mind that the eagle is seen in profile, hence only one of its eyes is visible. (See Fig. 2, p. 310.)

31. *che vede e pate il sole*: Cf. *Par.* I, 48.

32. *incominciommi = mi incominciò*.

33. *riguardar si vole*: "Must be looked at."

36. *e' = ei (elli)*. The redundant pronoun refers back to "quelli" in vs. 35.   *di tutti lor gradi son li sommi*: The meaning here is not entirely clear, but it probably is that "of the spirits that form my body, these are the highest."

37–39. *Colui che luce . . . villa*: David, as the light which he is here, is the very pupil of the eye, therefore the highest of all that are to be named as forming eye and eyebrow. The psalms written by him were inspired by the Holy Ghost, as were all the canonical books of the Bible. As king of Israel, he had the ark of the covenant moved to Jerusalem (II Reg. 6:2-17).

39. *villa*: "Town."

40–42. *ora conosce . . . altrettanto*: Now (in Paradise) David knows that which he merited by his psalms, written by him insofar as their art, as song, was of his own devising. The whole statement allows for merit deserved by the *human* side of the artistic achievement, distinguishing this from what must be assigned to the dictation of the Holy Ghost. "Consiglio," that is, points to the act of free will and talent on the part of the artist.

It will be noted, in the review of the spirits that make up the eye and brow, that the poet enters into the device of anaphora, with the second tercet of each pair of tercets allotted to each figure beginning with the words "ora conosce." This may be compared with *Purg.* XII, 25-63. The repeated phrase "ora conosce" clearly stresses the distance between the limited human vision of God's justice as had on earth and the revelation thereof which awaits the elect in Paradise.

42. *per lo remunerar ch'è altrettanto*: God's justice rewards according to merit. Cf. *Par.* VI, 118-20.

43. *Dei cinque che mi fan cerchio per ciglio*: See Fig. 2, p. 310.

44-45. *colui che più . . . figlio*: For the story of Trajan's justice to the poor widow for the death of her son, see *Purg.* X, 73-93.

46-48. *ora conosce . . . l'opposta*: The just emperor Trajan lived in Christian times but died a pagan; however, in response to the prayers of Gregory the Great, he was allowed to return from the lower world (probably from Limbo), where conversion is impossible, and to resume his body long enough for him to embrace the true faith and thus win to a place in Heaven. (See n. to vs. 106.) For this legend, see Jacobus de Varagine, *Legenda aurea* XLVI, 10 and n. to *Purg.* X, 75.

48. *opposta*: The life of souls in Limbo.

49-54. *E quel che segue . . . l'odierno*: King Hezekiah, who, when Isaiah told him of his impending death, prayed and had his life prolonged for fifteen years. See IV Reg. 20:1-6. Also see Isa. 38:1-22, where in the words of the prophet, expressing the king's gratitude, there is echoed the latter's sense of his guilt as well as his penitence.

50. *per l'arco superno*: I.e., proceeding now along the rising arch of the Eagle's brow.

53. *preco = preghiera*.

54. *fa crastino là giù de l'odierno*: "Turns today's into tomorrow's down on earth." In such cases the "prayer" and its result are a part of the divine plan.

55-60. *L'altro che segue . . . distrutto*: The Emperor Constantine occupies thus the central and highest part of the arch. The reference is to his ceding Rome to the pope and transferring the capital to Byzantium, thus making himself, the imperial eagle, and the laws Greek. Cf. *Inf.* XIX, 115-17; XXVII, 94-97; *Purg.* XXXII, 124-29; *Par.* VI, 1-3.

58–60. *ora conosce . . . distrutto*: Cf. Thomas Aquinas, *Summa theol.* I-II, q. 20, a. 5, resp.:

> Eventus sequens aut est praecogitatus aut non. Si est praecogitatus, manifestum est quod addit ad bonitatem vel malitiam actus: cum enim aliquis cogitat quod ex opere suo multa mala possunt sequi, nec propter hoc dimittit, ex hoc apparet voluntas eius esse magis inordinata.
>
> Si autem eventus sequens non sit praecogitatus, tunc distinguendum est: quia si per se sequitur ex tali actu, et ut in pluribus, secundum hoc eventus sequens addit ad bonitatem vel malitiam actus. Manifestum est enim meliorem actum esse ex suo genere, ex quo possunt plura bona sequi, et peiorem ex quo nata sunt plura mala sequi.
>
> Si vero per accidens, et ut in paucioribus, tunc eventus sequens non addit ad bonitatem vel ad malitiam actus. Non enim datur iudicium de re aliqua secundum illud quod est per accidens, sed solum secundum illa quod est per se.

> The consequences of an action are either foreseen or not. If they are foreseen, it is evident that they increase the goodness or malice. For when a man foresees that many evils may follow from his action, and yet does not therefore desist therefrom, this shows his will to be all the more inordinate.
>
> But if the consequences are not foreseen, we must make a distinction. Because if they follow from the nature of the action and in the majority of cases, in this respect, the consequences increase the goodness or malice of that action: for it is evident that an action is specifically better, if better results can follow from it; and specifically worse, if it is of a nature to produce worse results.—On the other hand, if the consequences follow

by accident and seldom, then they do not increase the goodness or malice of the action: because we do not judge of a thing according to that which belongs to it by accident, but only according to that which belongs to it of itself.

58. *dedutto*: "Resulting."

59. *li = gli*.

61–66. *E quel . . . ancora*: William II, the Good, king of Naples and Sicily in the Norman line from 1166 to 1189. He was the son (born 1154) of William I, the Bad (who ruled from 1154 to 1166 and was so called on account of his cruelty towards his rebellious barons), and in 1177 married Joan, youngest daughter of Henry II of England, by whom he had no issue. On his death, at the age of thirty-five, the crown passed to his cousin Tancred, whose son and successor was dispossessed by Emperor Henry VI, who had married Constance, the aunt of William II and heiress presumptive to the throne. The kingdom thus passed to the Hohenstaufen line, in the person of Frederick I (afterwards emperor as Frederick II), the son of Henry VI and Constance.

William II's reign was as beneficial to his subjects as that of his father had been the reverse. He was a zealous champion of the Church and spent the large treasures left by William I in founding and endowing pious institutions. His death was sincerely lamented by the Sicilians.

62. *cui*: The direct object of "plora."

63. *Carlo e Federigo*: The kings of Naples and of Sicily who are rebuked in *Par.* XIX, 127-35.

67–72. *Chi crederebbe . . . fondo*: Ripheus was a Trojan hero who was slain during the sack of Troy. "Nowhere, before Dante, do we find any suggestion that this Trojan prince attained Heaven, nor that he was of particular importance. Virgil mentions his name, with those of other Trojans, in *Aen.*, II, 339 and 394. In *Aen.*, II, 426-427, he adds a brief description" (Gr). In this third passage, Virgil writes: "Cadit et Ripheus, iustissimus unus / qui fuit in Teucris et servantis- simus aequi." ("Ripheus, too, falls, foremost in justice among the Trojans, and most zealous for the right.") "Noth- ing more. But these words evidently made a profound im- pression on Dante and led him to conjecture that such devo- tion to justice must have been a result of grace—of that divine plan which no created mind can penetrate. The upright heathen, who has made the most of his natural en- dowments, is met by grace, which moves him to love good above everything else and finally reveals to him the essential truth of salvation through Christ. The choice of such a minor personage as Ripheus emphasizes the mystery of God's pre- destination. On the other hand, Ripheus was a Trojan, a rep- resentative of that noble stock from which the Romans sprang. And among the Trojans he was 'the most righteous of all, and the strictest observer of justice' " (Gr).

Thus, we here "find illustrated the possibility of salvation for a virtuous man living in pagan times. 'Invincible' (that is, insuperable, inevitable) ignorance is not an absolute bar: cf. *Summa Theologiae*, Prima Secundae, Qu. lxxvi, Art. 2. Often, says St. Thomas, has grace been extended to the worthy but otherwise unenlightened" (Gr). In *Summa theol.* II-II, q. 2, a. 7, ad 3 Aquinas notes that "multis gentilium facta fuit revelatio de Christo, ut patet per ea quae prae- dixerunt. . . . Sibylla etiam praenuntiavit quaedam de Christo." ("Many of the gentiles received revelations of Christ, as is clear from their predictions. . . . The Sibyl too foretold certain things about Christ.") He continues:

Si qui tamen salvati fuerunt quibus revelatio non fuit facta, non fuerunt salvati absque fide Mediatoris; quia etsi non habuerunt fidem explicitam, habuerunt tamen fidem implicitam in divina providentia, credentes Deum esse liberatorem hominum secundum modos sibi placi- tos, et secundum quod aliquibus veritatem cognoscenti- bus Spiritus revelasset.

If, however, some were saved without receiving any rev- elation, they were not saved without faith in a Mediator, for, though they did not believe in Him explicitly, they did, nevertheless, have implicit faith through believing in Divine providence, since they believed that God would deliver mankind in whatever way was pleasing to Him, and according to the revelation of the Spirit to those who knew the truth.

"The *Commedia*, however, affords only two individual examples: that of Cato in *Purgatorio* I, and, in the present canto, that of Ripheus" (Gr).

72. *ben che sua vista non discerna il fondo*: Cf. *Par.* XIX, 52-63. With this verse the device of anaphora ends, having served to frame the cases of six just kings, seen in this sixth heaven; it will be recalled that the sixth canto of the *Paradiso* is the canto of the Roman Empire and the imperial eagle, as recounted by Justinian.

73-75. *Quale allodetta . . . sazia*: This figure of the skylark was used before Dante, by the Provençal poets (*la lauzeta* in Provençal) and earlier Italian poets. Cf. Bernard de Ventadour's *canzone* beginning "Can vei la lauzeta mover" (in S. G. Nichols, Jr. and J. A. Galm, 1962, pp. 166-68) and Bondie Dietaiuti's *canzone* beginning "Madonna, me è avenuto similgliante" (in E. Monaci, 1955, pp. 263-64).

73. *allodetta = allodoletta.   si spazia*: "Soars."

76-77. *tal mi sembiò . . . piacere*: "Thus the image appeared to me, [satisfied] with the stamp of God's will," i.e., in the mystery of this salvation of two who were thought to be pagans.

77-78. *al cui disio . . . diventa*: Cf. *Par.* XVIII, 109-11, where this same principle applies to birds' nests.

79-80. *E avvegna . . . veste*: Although my doubt showed through me, as a coat of paint shows through glass. In *Conv.* III, ix, 10 Dante writes: "E però coloro che vogliono far parere le cose ne lo specchio d'alcuno colore, interpongono di quello colore tra 'l vetro e 'l piombo, sì che 'l vetro ne rimane compreso." ("And therefore they who desire to give some particular colour to the things in a mirror, interpose of that colour between the glass and the lead, so that the glass is embraced by it.")

81. *tempo aspettar tacendo non patio*: "It [the doubt] endured not to bide its time in silence." Cf. *Conv.* IV, *canzone* III, 9 and *Conv.* IV, ii, 5-10.   *patio = patì*.

83. *mi pinse = mi spinse*. The subject is "il dubbiar mio" (vs. 79).

84. *per ch'io di coruscar vidi gran feste*: As usual, in the anticipation of being able to satisfy Dante's doubt, the souls rejoice with an increase of brilliance, and with a brighter eye, as the next verse makes clear.

92. *quiditate*: "Quiddity," essence.

93. *prome*: "Discloses," from the Latin *promit*.

94. *Regnum celorum violenza pate*: See Matt. 11:12: "Regnum caelorum vim patitur." ("The kingdom of heaven has been enduring violent assault.") Cf. Luc. 16:16. The eagle's discourse is the more solemn in its beginning for being in Latin, and for being a verse of the Scriptures.

95-96. *da caldo amore . . . volontate*: "Caldo amore" and "viva speranza" constitute a double subject of the verb "vince," in the singular.

97. *a guisa che*: "As."   *a l'om sobranza*: *Sobranza a* is a Provençalism, meaning "overcomes."

98. *vince lei*: "It [love and hope] conquers it [divine will]."

99. *beninanza = benignità*. The word is a Provençalism. Cf. *Par.* VII, 143.

100. *La prima vita del ciglio e la quinta*: The first and fifth are Trajan and Ripheus.   *vita*: Soul. Cf. *Par.* IX, 7.

102. *la region de li angeli*: The heavens which Dante is traversing.   *dipinta*: "Adorned."

103-4. *D'i corpi suoi non uscir . . . Gentili = dai corpi loro non uscirono Gentili*, i.e., they did not die as pagans.

105. *quel d'i passuri e quel d'i passi piedi*: "The one (Ripheus) had faith in the feet (of Christ) that were to suffer (being nailed to the cross), the other (Trajan) had faith in the feet that had suffered. *Passuri* and *passi* are Latin future and perfect participles. Both Ripheus and Trajan had faith in Christ, one before and one after the crucifixion" (Gr). See Dante, *De mon.* III, iii, 10.

106–11. *Ché l'una . . . mossa*: The first of the two cases to be considered is that of Trajan. Cf. n. to vss. 46-48.

106. *'nferno*: This was doubtless Limbo, where there is "good will" among the virtuous pagans. "Good will," however, does not suffice. God's special sanctifying grace is required for salvation, a grace infused from above and given only to the living (with this great exception due to Gregory's prayers, his great hope, "viva spene"). The effectiveness of Gregory's prayers in short is an instance of the doctrine stated in vss. 94-99. It may be noted here that Thomas Aquinas considers the case of Trajan and of Gregory's prayers for him; a passage in his *Summa theologica* may serve here as a gloss on the case (*Summa theol.* III, Suppl., q. 71, a. 5, ad 5):

De facto Traiani hoc modo potest probabiliter aestimari, quod precibus B. Gregorii ad vitam fuerit revocatus, et ita gratiam consecutus sit, per quam remissionem peccatorum habuit, et per consequens immunitatem a poena: sicut etiam apparet in omnibus illis qui fuerunt miraculose a mortuis suscitati, quorum plures constat idololatras et damnatos fuisse. De omnibus talibus enim similiter dici oportet quod non erant in inferno finaliter deputati, sed secundum praesentem propriorum meritorum iustitiam: secundum autem superiores causas, quibus praevidebantur ad vitam revocandi, erat aliter de eis disponendum.

Vel dicendum, secundum quosdam, quod anima Traiani non fuit simpliciter a reatu poenae aeternae absoluta; sed eius poena fuit suspensa ad tempus, scilicet usque ad diem iudicii. Nec tamen oportet quod hoc fiat communiter per suffragia; quia alia sunt quae lege communi accidunt, et alia quae singulariter ex privilegio aliquibus conceduntur.

Concerning the incident of Trajan it may be supposed with probability that he was recalled to life at the prayers of blessed Gregory, and thus obtained the grace whereby he received the pardon of his sins and in consequence was freed from punishment. The same applies to all those who were miraculously raised from the dead, many of whom were evidently idolaters and damned. For we must needs say likewise of all such persons that they were consigned to hell, not finally, but as was actually due to their own merits according to justice: and that according to higher causes, in view of which it was foreseen that they would be recalled to life, they were to be disposed of otherwise.

Or we may say with some that Trajan's soul was not simply freed from the debt of eternal punishment, but that his punishment was suspended for a time, that is, until the judgment day. Nor does it follow that this is the general result of suffrages, because things happen differently in accordance with the general law from that which is permitted in particular cases and by privilege.

110. *per suscitarla*: "To resuscitate" Trajan's soul.

111. *sua voglia*: Trajan's will, now moved by God toward Himself, the supreme good.

112–17. *L'anima gloriosa . . . gioco*: Two more tercets are thus given to the case of Trajan.

114. *credette in lui*: He believed in Christ and thereby was saved. See vss. 104-5.

115–16. *s'accese in tanto foco . . . amor*: The will, the good will of Trajan, is thus stressed, since love pertains to the will.

116. *a la morte seconda*: Trajan's second death.

117. *questo gioco*: The joy of Paradise.

118. *L'altra*: The soul of Ripheus.

118–21. *per grazia . . . drittura*: The inclination of the will to good is a result of grace, and accepted doctrine speaks of two kinds of grace (a point worth considering in the case of Ripheus), namely, of operating grace and of cooperating grace. In *Summa theol.* I-II, q. III, a. 2, resp., Thomas Aquinas defines the two:

> Utroque autem modo gratia dicta convenienter dividitur per operantem et cooperantem. Operatio enim alicuius effectus non attribuitur mobili, sed moventi. In illo ergo effectu in quo mens nostra est mota, et non movens, solus autem Deus movens, operatio Deo attribuitur: et secundum hoc dicitur *gratia operans*. In illo autem effectu in quo mens nostra et movet et movetur, operatio non solum attribuitur Deo, sed etiam animae; et secundum hoc dicitur *gratia cooperans*. Est autem in nobis duplex actus: primus quidem interior voluntatis; et quantum ad istum actum voluntas se habet ut mota, Deus autem ut movens; et praesertim cum voluntas incipit bonum velle, quae prius malum volebat; et ideo, secundum quod Deus movet humanam mentem ad hunc actum, dicitur *gratia operans*. Alius autem actus est exterior, qui cum a voluntate imperetur, ut supra habitum est, quaest. 17, art. 9, consequens est quod ad hunc actum operatio attribuatur voluntati. Et quia etiam ad hunc actum Deus nos adiuvat, et interius confirmando voluntatem, ut ad actum perveniat, et exterius facultatem operandi praebendo; respectu huiusmodi actus dicitur *gratia cooperans*. Unde post praemissa verba subdit Augustinus (ibid., 4): *Ut autem velimus, operatur; cum autem volumus, ut perficiamus, nobis cooperatur*. Sic igitur si gratia accipiatur pro gratuita Dei motione, qua movet nos ad bonum meritorium, convenienter dividitur gratia per *operantem et cooperantem*.

> Now in both these ways grace is fittingly divided into operating and co-operating. For the operation of an effect is not attributed to the thing moved but to the mover. Hence in that effect in which our mind is moved

and does not move, but in which God is the sole mover, the operation is attributed to God, and it is with reference to this that we speak of *operating grace*. But in that effect in which our mind both moves and is moved, the operation is not only attributed to God, but also to the soul; and it is with reference to this that we speak of *co-operating grace*. Now there is a double act in us. First, there is the interior act of the will, and with regard to this act the will is a thing moved, and God is the mover; and especially when the will, which hitherto willed evil, begins to will good. And hence, inasmuch as God moves the human mind to this act, we speak of operating grace. But there is another, exterior act; and since it is commanded by the will, as was shown above (q. 17, a. 9), the operation of this act is attributed to the will. And because God assists us in this act, both by strengthening our will interiorly so as to attain to the act, and by granting outwardly the capability of operating, it is with respect to this that we speak of co-operating grace. Hence after the aforesaid words Augustine subjoins: *He operates that we may will; and when we will, He co-operates that we may perfect.* And thus if grace is taken for God's gratuitous motion whereby He moves us to meritorious good, it is fittingly divided into operating and co-operating grace.

For Aquinas' reference to Augustine, see Augustine, *De gratia et libero arbitrio* XVII.

120. *la prima onda*: The "first wave" of a fountain is the water that is gushing into it from the bottom.

121. *tutto suo amor là giù pose a drittura*: The verse focuses on Ripheus' cooperation with the special grace bestowed on him, and he directs all his love to righteousness or inner justice ("drittura"). It will be noted that the stress here is on love, which pertains to the will, as noted in the case of Trajan.

122-23. *per che, di grazia in grazia . . . futura*: Thus, as with Trajan, the absolute requirement for salvation is met.

Ripheus believes, with an implicit faith comparable to that which God gave to those who were harrowed from Hell and through a special revelation made to him by God ("Dio li aperse l'occhio").

124–29. *ond' ei credette . . . millesmo*: Two more tercets are given to the case of Ripheus, making four in all in this passage: precisely the number of tercets allotted to the case of Trajan (vss. 106-17).

125. *da indi . . . più*: "From that moment on."

126. *riprendiene = ne riprendeva*, "reproved therefor."

127–28. *Quelle tre donne . . . rota*: See *Purg.* XXIX, 121-29. The three theological virtues (whom Dante saw beside the right wheel of the chariot of the Church) were Ripheus' baptism. In this particular reference, which takes the reader back to the advent of Beatrice in the great procession at the summit of Mount Purgatory, it is possible to see that the pilgrim Dante fulfills the same pattern as Ripheus. First he is brought (by Virgil and special grace from Heaven) to "drittura," justice (see *Purg.* XXVII, 139-42), and then he attains to special grace (beyond Virgil's ken) on the other side of the river, the three theological virtues finally presenting him to Beatrice (*Purg.* XXXI, 133-35). On this whole pattern in the journey, see C. S. Singleton (1958), pp. 72-121.

127. *li fur = gli furono.* *per battesmo*: Ripheus thus fulfills an essential requirement for salvation, which is baptism. Cf. *Inf.* IV, 34-36.

129. *dinanzi al battezzar*: It was the baptism of Christ by John the Baptist which instituted the sacrament.

130–32. *O predestinazion . . . tota*: The two exceptional cases of Trajan and Ripheus support the exclamation over God's predestination, hidden from the sight of all creatures.

131. *aspetti*: A Latinism, from *aspicior* ("I see"), here meaning "sight" and used in the plural to include all creatures, even angels and the blessed in Heaven.

132. *tota* (Latin) = *tutta*.

133–35. *E voi, mortali . . . eletti*: The tercet now distinguishes between the vision of God's predestination that mortals have on earth and that which the blessed have in Heaven, which is also limited, even though they see God.

136. *ènne = ci è.   scemo*: "Shortcoming," "want."

137–38. *perché il ben nostro . . . volemo*: " 'For our good is perfected by this good, namely, that we will what God wills.' Our happiness is made perfect by the complete surrender of our will to God" (Gr). Cf. *Par.* III, 85-87.

142–48. *E come a buon cantor . . . fiammette*: "While the Eagle speaks, the lights of Trajan and Ripheus flash together (like the twinkling of a pair of eyes) at the two ends of the semicircle,—just as a lute-player accompanies a singer by touching the strings" (Gr).

143. *seguitar*: "Accompany."

145. *mentre ch'e' = mentre che egli*.

CANTO XXI

3. *intento*: Object of attention.   *s'era tolto = s'era dis-tolto*.

4–6. *non ridea . . . fessi*: Beatrice speaks of her smile, so often bestowed upon Dante in this journey through the heavens, which always implies a radiance. Hence here her radiance in smiling would be such that it would reduce Dante to ashes.

6. *Semelè quando di cener fessi*: Semele, daughter of Cadmus and mother of Bacchus, having insisted on beholding her lover, Jupiter, in all his heavenly majesty, was burned to ashes by his splendor. See Ovid, *Metam*. III, 253-315; cf. *Inf*. XXX, 2.   *fessi = si fece*.

7–8. *le scale de l'etterno palazzo*: The metaphor converts the heavens through which Dante (and contemplation) passes with Beatrice into so many steps which lead finally to the innermost throne-room of God's "palace" (cf. *Par*. XXV, 42). The reader should begin to note a gradual transformation in this journey through the heavens to God; for in the world-picture in which the journey begins, the earth is at the center and the Empyrean heaven is the circumference—sometimes termed the mind of God. But now, through such similes as this of an "eternal palace," the reader is being led to God as to a point and not as to a circumference. The poet will continue this gradual transformation until finally (*Par* . XXVIII, 16) God will be seen symbolically as a *point* of light, and the pilgrim will be puzzled at the way things have turned inside out, so to speak, as he passes from the material world to the purely spiritual.

12. *fronda che trono scoscende*: "Trono" is the subject, "fronda" the object of the verb.   *trono*: "Bolt of lightning." See vs. 108; see also Dante's *Rime* CXVI, 57.
scoscende: Cf. *Purg*. XIV, 135, for the verb used, as here, in the sense of "rend."

13. *sem = siamo*.   *settimo splendore*: The planet Saturn and its heaven.

14–15. *che sotto . . . valore*: Saturn, "the seventh brightness," being in line with the constellation Leo, its cold influence "now radiates downward" mitigated by the heat of the Lion. Dante speaks of the coldness of Saturn in *Conv*. II, xiii, 25: "Giove è stella di temperata complessione, in mezzo de la freddura di Saturno e de lo calore di Marte." ("Jove is a star of temperate composition betwixt the cold of Saturn and the heat of Mars.") See n. to *Purg*. XIX, 3; *Par*. XXII, 145-46. In *Georg*. I, 336, Virgil refers to "frigida Saturni . . . stella" ("Saturn's cold star").

14. *Leone ardente*: The reference is to Leo the Lion, constellation and fifth sign of the zodiac. Cf. *Par*. XVI, 34-39. In the spring of 1300 the planet Saturn was in the constellation of Leo, which, as Lana observes, is of a hot and dry nature, like fire.

18. *questo specchio*: The planet Saturn.   *ti sarà parvente*: It will be remembered that Beatrice and Dante always enter into the planet contained in each heaven. Cf. vs. 25: "dentro al cristallo."

19–20. *Qual savesse . . . beato*: "Anyone who knew how my eyes loved to feed on her blessed countenance" (Gr).

19. *savesse = sapesse.*

21. *quand' io mi trasmutai ad altra cura*: "When I turned my attention to a different object."

24. *contrapesando l'un con l'altro lato*: " 'By balancing the one side with the other': i.e., by weighing in the scales my desire to see Beatrice against my desire to obey her" (Gr).

25. *Dentro al cristallo*: Saturn has been termed a "specchio" (vs. 18). *vocabol*: "Name," in this case, Saturn.

26. *cerchiando il mondo*: "Revolving around the earth," as do all the planets and their spheres.

26–27. *del suo caro duce . . . morta*: The god Saturn, dear to the earth for having ruled there during the Golden Age, when, as vs. 27 reminds the reader, all was perfect. Cf. *Purg.* XXII, 148-50; XXVIII, 139-40. Appropriately, as indicated in the following verses, the ladder seen in this planet is the color of gold.

28. *traluce*: "Shines brightly." For a similar use of this verb, see *Par.* XIII, 69.

29. *uno scaleo = una scala.*

29–30. *uno scaleo eretto . . . luce*: On this ladder, the appropriate symbol of contemplation, Grandgent remarks: "Corresponding to the Cross in Mars and the Eagle in Jupiter, we find in Saturn a Ladder of golden light, the emblem of Contemplation, stretching upward farther than the eye can follow—such a ladder as Jacob once saw. . . . A similar ladder adorns the gown of Lady Philosophy in the *Consolatio Philosophiae* of Boethius (I, Pr. i)." See Gen. 28:12: "Viditque in somnis scalam stantem super terram, et cacumen illius tangens caelum, angelos quoque Dei ascendentes et descendentes per eam." ("He dreamed that a ladder was set up on the ground with its top reaching to heaven; angels of God were ascending and descending on it.")

30. *mia luce*: "My sight."

31. *li gradi*: The rungs of the ladder.

32. *tanti splendor*: "So many lights" (spirits).

32–33. *ogne lume che par nel ciel*: Each and every heavenly body that is visible in the sky.

33. *quindi*: "Thereover."

34. *costume*: "Habit."

35. *pole*: "Daws." See R. T. Holbrook (1903), pp. 44-45.

35–36. *al cominciar . . . piume*: To bring in the coldest time of day and to have these birds flying about to warm their cold feathers, the poet is clearly adding another touch of coldness to that which is already associated with Saturn (cf. n. to vss. 14-15).

37–39. *poi altre . . . soggiorno*: The varied flight of these birds may well be here used to suggest, through metaphor, what properly belongs to contemplation. Grandgent remarks that "in the fragmentary Old Provençal *Boeci*—probably through an error in reading the Latin text—the figures climbing the rungs are called birds; and by an odd coincidence Dante likens to birds the bright spirits that come swarming down the steps to meet him." Richard of St. Victor (*De gratia contemplationis* I, 5) compares the operations of the contemplative mind to the movements of birds.

40–42. *tal modo . . . si percosse*: "When the sparkling host of souls, in its descent, reaches a 'certain round' of the ladder (probably the one nearest Dante), it breaks up into groups that hover and flit like birds" (Gr).

40. *me*: The old language often used the pronouns in *e*, without a preposition, as unstressed dative (as here) or accusative.

42. *si percosse*: The "si" here is the so-called pleonastic reflexive, which actually focuses specifically on the subject, in this case that part of the total "sfavillar" which strikes upon a certain rung of the ladder.

43. *quel*: I.e., "splendor" (vs. 32).

44. *fé = fece.*

45. *accenne = accenni.* Some editors make this the last word of Dante's inner thought and end the quotation here. But Petrocchi has chosen, for quite persuasive reasons, to extend the quotation to the end of vs. 48.

46–48. *Ma quella . . . dimando*: Thus Dante's thought continues.

46–47. *quella ond' . . . si sta*: Beatrice, from whom I take my every cue as to how and when to speak.

47. *si sta*: Freely, "is not doing or saying anything."

48. *contra 'l disio*: "Against my own desire."   *fo = faccio.*

49. *Per ch'ella, che vedea il tacer mio*: Beatrice reads Dante's unexpressed thought.

50. *colui che tutto vede*: God. Cf. *Par.* IX, 73.

51. *Solvi*: "Give vent to." Cf. *Par.* XV, 52; XIX, 25.

55–56. *vita beata . . . letizia*: As so often, the spirit is swathed in the effulgence of its own joy.

56–60. *fammi nota . . . divota*: Dante's two requests, as expressed in these verses, are not answered in the order in which they are asked, but in reverse order. The first (vss. 56-57) seems deliberately introduced by the poet in order to bring in once more the theme of predestination, thus making it the far more important question. The second can be answered in a few words.

59. *sinfonia*: The hymns sung by spirits in the preceding spheres.

60. *l'altre*: The other wheels or heavens.

63. *per quel che*: "For the same reason that." For the phrase, cf. *Purg.* XV, 133; XXXIII, 77-78.

64–66. Giù per li gradi . . . ammanta: The reply to Dante's first question begins.

65. discesi tanto: I.e., descended so far down, even to you. *sol = solo, soltanto*, modifying "per farti festa." *farti festa*: *Fare festa* commonly has the meaning of "welcome."

67. più amor: I.e., greater than that of my companions.

68. quinci sù ferve: "Glows from here up," on the ladder.

69. sì come il fiammeggiar ti manifesta: The measure of love is the brightness of the spirit. Hence above the speaker, at a higher rung of the ladder, there must be spirits brighter and equally bright.

70. l'alta carità: God's love.

71. pronte al consiglio che 'l mondo governa: Quick to obey the counsel or providence (God's) which governs the universe.

72. sorteggia: "Allots."   *osserve = osservi.*

76–78. ma questo . . . consorte: "Why does God choose one soul for a particular office, rather than another? Once more Dante is confronted with the inscrutable mystery of predestination, which perturbs and baffles him. And once more his curiosity is curbed. Cf. XIX, 52-66, 79-90; XX, 130-138" (Gr).

76. cerner: "Make out."   *forte*: "Hard."

78. consorte = consorti.

79–81. Né venni . . . mola: The spirit, in the joy it feels in being able to respond to Dante's question, spins upon itself. See *Par.* XVIII, 41-42.

81. mola: "Millstone." The word suggests a horizontal view of this spinning. Cf. *Par.* XII, 3.

83. s'appunta: "Focuses."

84. questa: I.e., "luce."   *in ch'io m'inventro*: "In which

I am embellied," i.e., contained. The verb was coined by Dante.

85. *cui*: Refers to "luce" in vs. 83.   *col mio veder*: "With my [natural] light."

87. *munta*: "Milked," i.e., drawn. Cf. *Inf.* XII, 135; XXIV, 43.

89. *quant'*: "According as."

90. *la chiarità de la fiamma pareggio*: " 'I match the clearness of my flame.' Again the doctrine that happiness depends on clearness of spiritual vision, which is a gift of grace" (Gr).

91. *alma = anima*.   *più si schiara*: "Is most illumined."

92. *quel serafin che 'n Dio più l'occhio ha fisso*: With this touch the statement comes very close to that of *Par.* IV, 28. The Seraphim are the angels who are closest to God and who represent His love.

93. *satisfara*: "Would satisfy," an old form of the conditional.

94. *però che = perciò che*.

95. *etterno statuto*: That which has been "eternally decreed" by God.   *quel che chiedi*: The subject of "s'innoltra."

96. *creata vista*: The power of vision, both of angels and of men.   *scisso*: "Cut off." Cf. *Purg.* VI, 123.

98. *presumma = presuma*. The double *m* in such forms (like *summa* and *assumma*) is archaic.

99. *segno*: "Goal," i.e., the inscrutable ways of God's providence.

100. *qui*: In Heaven.

101–2. *onde riguarda . . . l'assumma*: Consider, then, how it can do on earth (where it "is smoky") that which it cannot do in Heaven (where it "shines").

102. *perché 'l ciel l'assumma*: "Though heaven receives it into itself."

103. *Sì mi prescrisser*: *Prescrivere* has here the meaning of "set a limit to." Cf. *Par.* XXIV, 6; XXV, 57.

104. *mi ritrassi*: "I limited myself."

105. *umilmente*: In this context the adverb registers resignation respecting the unanswerable and far deeper question of God's providence.

106. *Tra' due liti*: The Adriatic and the Tyrrhenian.
sassi: The Apennines.

107. *e non molto distanti a la tua patria*: The reference proves to be to the mountains of the Apennine chain near Gubbio (cf. vs. 109, "Catria"), which is relatively close to Florence.

108. *tanto*: Modifies "surgon" (vs. 106).   *che ' troni assai suonan più bassi*: The mountains rise so high as to be above the clouds wherein lightning and thunder are formed (cf. "trono," vs. 12). The verb *suonare* points to the meaning "thunder."

109. *gibbo*: "Hump."   *Catria*: Monte Catria, one of the peaks of the Apennines, on the borders of Umbria and the Marches, about ten miles northeast of Gubbio, near the Via Flaminia.

110. *ermo*: "Hermitage" (cf. *Purg.* V, 96), the monastery of Santa Croce di Fonte Avellana.

111. *suole*: "Suole" is evidently equivalent to the imperfect, *soleva*. See, for other persons of the verb, *Inf.* XXVII, 48; *Par.* XII, 123 (cf. *Inf.* XVI, 22).   *latria*: "Worship." Cf. Thomas Aquinas, *Summa theol.* II-II, q. 81, a. 1, ad 3: "Manifestum est autem quod dominium convenit Deo secundum propriam et singularem quamdam rationem, quia scilicet ipse omnia fecit, et quia summum in omnibus rebus obtinet principatum; et ideo specialis ratio servitutis ei debetur; et talis servitus nomine latriae designatur apud Graecos;

et ideo ad religionem proprie pertinet." ("Now it is evident that lordship belongs to God in a special and singular way, because He made all things, and has supreme dominion over all. Consequently a special kind of service is due to Him, which is known as *latria* in Greek; and therefore it belongs to religion.")

112. *ricominciommi = mi ricominciò.   sermo*: "Speech."

114. *mi fe' = mi feci.*

115. *pur con cibi di liquor d'ulivi*: Lenten fare, food seasoned only with olive oil, not animal fat.   *pur*: "Only." *cibi di = cibi da.*

116. *lievemente*: "Easily," i.e., without any sense of privation.   *caldi e geli*: I.e., all seasons of the year.

118-19. *Render solea . . . fertilemente*: "Produce" a great harvest of blessed souls.

119. *vano*: "Void." There seems to be here a reference to some condition or event of which we have no knowledge, but which is so deplorable that it will disclose itself eventually.

121-23. *In quel loco . . . adriano*: There has been much discussion as to the interpretation of vss. 121-23. If "fu'" (i.e., *fui*), "I was," be the reading in vs. 122, "Pietro Damiano" and "Pietro Peccator" must be one and the same person, and the meaning would be: "I was known as Peter Damian in the monastery of Santa Croce di Fonte Avellana, but I was Peter the Sinner in the monastery of Our Lady on the shores of the Adriatic." Or, reading "fu" ("he was"), the meaning would be: "At the monastery of Santa Croce di Fonte Avellana I was Peter Damian, and Peter the Sinner was in the monastery of Our Lady on the Adriatic shore." In the latter case, the remark would be parenthetical, to correct, as it were, a prevailing confusion of the two Peters.

Some early commentators take the latter view, but many modern commentators agree with Benvenuto in the former interpretation and would read "fu'" in vs. 122. In this case, Dante has Peter Damian affirm what was a common confusion of the two Peters in the poet's day. This seems the more plausible interpretation.

121. *Pietro Damiano*: San Pietro Damiani (St. Peter Damian), proclaimed doctor of the Church by Leo XII in 1828, was born of an obscure family at Ravenna *ca.* 1007. In his childhood he was much neglected and after the death of his parents was set by his eldest brother to tend swine. Later on, another brother, named Damiano, who was archdeacon of Ravenna, took compassion on him and had him educated. Peter in gratitude assumed his brother's name and was thenceforth known as Peter Damian (Petrus Damiani).

After studying at Ravenna, Faenza, and Parma, Peter Damian himself became a teacher and soon acquired celebrity. At the age of about twenty-eight, however, he entered the Benedictine monastery of Fonte Avellana on the slopes of Monte Catria, of which in 1043 he became abbot. In this capacity he rendered important services to Popes Gregory VI, Clement II, Leo IX, Victor II, and Stephen IX, by the last of whom he was in 1057, much against his will, created cardinal bishop of Ostia. He appears to have been a zealous supporter of these popes, and of Hildebrand (afterwards Gregory VII), in their efforts to reform Church discipline, and he made journeys into France and Germany with that object. After fulfilling several important missions under Nicholas II and Alexander II, he died at an advanced age at Faenza, February 22, 1072.

122–23. *la casa di Nostra Donna*: The monastery of Santa Maria in Porto, near Ravenna.

123. *lito adriano*: The Adriatic shore.

125. *cappello*: The cardinal's hat. (See n. to vs. 121.) The fact is that the "cardinal's hat" (as still in use today) did not exist at the time of Peter Damian, but was instituted by Innocent IV in 1252.

126. *di male in peggio si travasa*: "Which is shifted only from bad to worse." Each successive cardinal is worse than the one before.   *si travasa*: Literally, "poured."

127. *Cefàs*: St. Peter. See Ioan. 1:42: "Intuitus autem eum Iesus, dixit: Tu es Simon, filius Iona; tu vocaberis Cephas (quod interpretatur Petrus)." ("But Jesus, looking upon him, said, 'Thou art Simon, the son of John; thou shalt be called Cephas, which interpreted is Peter.'") *Petrus* is a translation of the Aramaic *cephas*. Dante also mentions Peter in *Par.* XVIII, 131. *vasello*: St. Paul, the "chosen vessel." Cf. Actus 9:15; *Inf.* II, 28.

128. *magri e scalzi*: Cf. Matt. 10:10.

129. *ostello*: "House." See Luc. 10:5, 7; I Cor. 10:27.

130. *quinci e quindi*: "On either side." *chi rincalzi*: "Someone to prop them up." Some editors prefer the reading "chi i rincalzi," wherein "i" = *li*, "them," redundant for "li moderni pastori" in the following verse. These servants who attended on either side were called *braccieri*.

131. *chi li meni*: This can mean either in sedan chairs, in which case the two who carried the chair were known as *portantini*, or on horseback, flanked by lackeys known as *staffieri*.

132. *e chi di rietro li alzi*: These who held up the prelate's train behind were known as *caudatari*.

134. *due bestie*: The prelate and his palfrey. *pelle*: The prelate's fur-lined mantle.

136. *voce*: "Words."

139. *fermarsi = si fermarono*.

140. *fero = fecero*.

141. *qui*: I.e., on earth.

142. *'ntesi*: "Understood." *il tuono*: "The shout" raised by those who had come on.

CANTO XXII

1. *Oppresso di stupore*: Cf. Boethius, *Consol. philos.* I, ii, ll. 8-9: "Sed te, ut video, stupor oppressit." ("But I perceive thou art become insensible.")

2. *parvol = parvolo*, "child."

3. *colà dove più si confida*: To its mother.

4-6. *e quella . . . disporre*: The simile of child and mother is sustained now in these verses. Beatrice is often seen as "mother" to Dante, in one way or another.

5. *palido = pallido.   anelo*: "Panting."

9. *buon zelo*: Probably, given the context, the expression is here used to denote "righteous indignation," as in *Purg.* XXIX, 23.

10-11. *Come t'avrebbe . . . ridendo*: Cf. *Par.* XXI, 4-6, 58-63.

12. *mosso = commosso.*

13. *se 'nteso avessi i prieghi suoi*: "If you had understood the prayers it contained." Dante, of course, has not understood them.

14-15. *la vendetta . . . muoi*: The prediction is deliberately obscure, and no specific event can be singled out as its fulfillment. It will, in any case, be a "vengeance" wreaked on corrupt prelates and a corrupt Church.

15. *muoi = moia*.

16-18. *La spada . . . l'aspetta*: God's sword ("la spada di qua sù") never cuts either too soon or too late, except as it seems to one who desires it or one who fears it.

17. *ma' ch' = mai che*. Cf. *Inf*. IV, 26; XXI, 20.   *parer*: The infinitive used as a noun, "opinion."

19. *inverso altrui*: "Towards others" (other spirits).

21. *redui = riduci (rivolgi)*. The infinitive is *redurre*, from the Latin *reducere*.

22. *ritornai*: "I turned again." The verb is transitive here and has "li occhi" as its direct object.

23-24. *e vidi . . . rai*: *Sperule* is the diminutive of *spere* and thus could mean "little globes" (of light), but the diminutive here may well be that of enhancement, adding the touch of "precious" to these globes (see vs. 29, where they are termed "pearls"). The same applies to the use of "rubinetto" to designate spirits in *Par*. XIX, 4. "Cento" is here used to mean a multitude.

24. *mutui rai*: The spirits shine to one another in their love. Cf. vs. 32.

25. *represe = reprime*.

26. *punta*: "Prick."   *s'attenta*: "Ventures." Cf. *Purg*. XXV, 11.

27. *del troppo si teme*: "Fears he will go beyond proper bounds." The "si" here is the usual pleonastic reflexive which directs attention back on the subject with the suggestion of "fears, for his own part."

28-29. *la maggiore . . . margherite*: When the reader learns that this is none other than the great St. Benedict, he will understand these superlatives, and just why this flame is so.

29. *innanzi fessi*: *Farsi innanzi* and *farsi avanti* are established expressions in both early and modern Italian. *fessi = si fece*.

30. *di sé*: "Concerning itself."

31. *dentro a lei = dentro ad essa* (the flame or, in metaphor, the "pearl"). The spirit is swathed in its own radiance.

33. *sarebbero espressi = sarebbero già espressi*, i.e., you would not have held back so.

34. *tarde = tardi*, present subjunctive of *tardare*.

35. *a l'alto fine*: The end of the journey and the sight of God face to face.

36. *pur al pensier, da che sì ti riguarde*: "Even to that thought of which you are so chary."   *riguarde = riguardi*.

37–39. *Quel monte . . . disposta*: The mountain referred to is that of Monte Cassino, which is situated on a commanding spur of Monte Cairo, overlooking the valley of the Liri, 1,400 feet below, a few miles from Aquino in the north of Campania, almost halfway between Rome and Naples. The town of Cassino is at the base of Monte Cassino. When St. Benedict first came to the spot, it was still a center of pagan worship, the summit of the hill being crowned by a temple of Apollo and a grove sacred to Venus, both of which he destroyed.

39. *la gente ingannata e mal disposta*: Pagans who worshiped the "false and lying gods" (*Inf.* I, 72), who were "the ancient peoples in their ancient error" (*Par.* VIII, 6). "Ingannata" refers primarily to the intellect, to erroneous beliefs, whereas "disposta" refers to the will, which in them was perverse.

40–42. *e quel son io . . . soblima*: St. Benedict now declares himself. Founder of the Benedictine order, the first religious

359

order of the West, St. Benedict was born of a noble family at Nursia (now Norcia) in the east of Umbria *ca.* 480. In early youth he was sent to school in Rome, but shocked by the wild life of his associates he ran away at about the age of fourteen and hid himself among the mountains near Subiaco on the borders of the Abruzzi. There he lived in solitude for three years in a cave, acquiring a great reputation for sanctity, which led the monks of the neighboring monastery of Vicovaro to choose him as their abbot. Impatient, however, of his severe rule, of which he had warned them before accepting their invitation, they attempted to rid themselves of him by poison. Their attempt being discovered, St. Benedict left them and returned once more to Subiaco, whence he went to Monte Cassino, where *ca.* 529 he founded his famous monastery on the site of an ancient temple of Apollo. He died at Monte Cassino *ca.* 543.

St. Benedict's *Regula monachorum*, which was designed to repress the irregular lives of the wandering monks, was first introduced in this monastery and eventually became the rule of all the western monks. One of the features of his system was that, in addition to their religious exercises, his monks occupied themselves with manual labor and in the instruction of the young.

41. *lo nome di colui*: Christ.

42. *soblima = sublima*, "exalts," "uplifts" (to salvation).

43. *e tanta grazia sopra me relusse*: St. Benedict attributes to God and His grace all he achieved.   *relusse = rilucette*. "Relusse" is from the Latin *reluxit*.

44. *le ville circunstanti*: The neighboring towns.

45. *cólto*: "Cult," i.e., pagan worship.

46–47. *Questi altri . . . fuoro*: This is the explicit declaration that Saturn is the heaven of contemplation, this already having been symbolized by the configuration of a ladder and by what has been said about it.

46. *fuochi*: "Spirits."

47. *accesi di quel caldo*: "Kindled with that fire" of holy love.

48. *che fa nascere i fiori e ' frutti santi*: The "flowers" may be taken to be thoughts and sentiments, which then produce the fruits, i.e., holy works.

49. *Maccario*: St. Macarius. It is uncertain which of the several saints of the name of Macarius is the one intended by Dante. The two best known, between whom perhaps Dante did not very clearly distinguish, are St. Macarius the Elder, called the Egyptian, and St. Macarius the Younger of Alexandria—both disciples of St. Anthony. St. Macarius the Elder (born in 301) retired at the age of thirty into the Libyan desert, where he remained for sixty years, passing his time between prayer and manual labor, until his death, at the age of ninety, in 391. St. Macarius the Younger had nearly 5,000 monks under his charge; he is credited with having established the monastic rule of the East, as St. Benedict did that of the West. He died *ca.* 404.

Romoaldo: St. Romuald, founder of the order of Camaldoli or reformed Benedictines, belonged to the Onesti family of Ravenna, where he was born *ca.* 950. He entered the Benedictine order *ca.* 970 and lived a hermit's life. In 998 he was named abbot of Sant'Apollinare in Classe, but soon renounced the office. He then began to establish the hermitages of his order, one of which was the famous monastery of Camaldoli in the Casentino about thirty miles from Florence. He died *ca.* 1027. A purely contemplative life was enjoined on the members of his order, which received the papal sanction from Alexander II in 1072.

51. *fermar = fermarono*.

52-54. *E io a lui . . . vostri*: The reader should note that Dante, who has been speaking only to St. Benedict, now refers to all the spirits in this heaven.

56-57. *come 'l sol fa la rosa . . . possanza*: Cf. *Inf.* II, 127-29.

58. *Però = perciò.*   *m'accerta*: I.e., *fammi certo* (imperative).

60. *con imagine scoverta*: I.e., in your true human semblance, and not concealed by the radiation that hides you. The reader will recall, with this request by Dante, how long it has been since any semblance whatsoever of a human countenance or figure has been seen. By such a question, and considering how great the saint is to whom he is speaking, the poet causes the wayfaring Dante to express a wish that may well be that of the reader by now. The answer, moreover, points to the end, and such signals are beginning to come (see vs. 124). By the answer we are also given the first hint of the special grace that awaits the pilgrim at the end (*Par.* XXX, 43-45), to which end the ladder of contemplation rises (vs. 68).

61. *Frate*: Again this form of address introducing a corrective or admonitory tone. Cf. *Purg.* IV, 127; XI, 82; XVI, 65; *Par.* III, 70, and *passim.*   *alto disio*: "Alto" anticipates the reply, for it is a desire (for vision, let it be remembered) that will be satisfied only at the summit of the ladder of contemplation.

62. *l'ultima spera*: The Empyrean.

64. *Ivi*: In the Empyrean.   *perfetta, matura e intera*: These adjectives, implying perfection, maturation, and fulfillment, will be better understood when the journey to God reaches the experience that awaits the pilgrim at the final summit. *Perfetto* would seem to take its meaning from the Latin *perficio*, "to complete."

65-66. *in quella sola . . . sempr' era*: In the Empyrean, a spiritual heaven, all is as it ever was, and all is at rest, whereas the other nine heavens revolve, their parts changing place.

67. *loco*: "Space."   *non s'impola*: "It has no pole," it does not revolve, like the material heavens.

68. *e nostra scala infino ad essa varca*: The ladder of contemplation reaches all the way to the Empyrean. "Varca"

brings in the notion of fording, from one shore to another, i.e., from time to eternity.

69. *dal viso ti s'invola*: Cf. *Par.* XXI, 30.   *viso*: "Sight."

70–72. *Infin là sù . . . carca*: Cf. Gen. 28:12: "Viditque in somnis scalam stantem super terram, et cacumen illius tangens caelum, angelos quoque Dei ascendentes et descendentes per eam." ("He dreamed that a ladder was set up on the ground with its top reaching to heaven; angels of God were ascending and descending on it.")

73. *Ma*: With this "ma" begins St. Benedict's denunciation of corruption in monastic orders and in the Church, which extends through vs. 96 and is strong indeed. Since he speaks in terms, first, of the ladder of contemplation which reaches all the way to the Empyrean, his words are important for the basic allegory of the *Paradiso*, which is that of a journey of contemplation. And Contemplation, let it be remembered, is one of Beatrice's names, so that the very journey with her is seen through St. Benedict's words, even though they apply more to monastic orders and their neglect of the ladder.

73–75. *per salirla . . . carte*: To climb this ladder no one leaves the earth, all are so attached to worldly things.

75. *per danno de le carte*: "As so much waste paper," i.e., not worth the paper on which the "regola" is written, since no one follows it any longer.

76–77. *Le mura . . . spelonche*: What were abbeys have become caves—here with the overtone, perhaps, of such passages from the Bible as Ier. 7:11: "Numquid ergo spelunca latronum facta est domus ista, in qua invocatum est nomen meum, in oculis vestris?" ("Is this house then, in which my name hath been called upon, in your eyes become a den of robbers?") See also Matt. 21:13: "Scriptum est: Domus mea domus orationis vocabitur; vos autem fecistis illam speluncam latronum." ("It is written, 'My house shall be called a house of prayer'; but you have made it a den of thieves.")

77. *cocolle*: "Cowls." Cf. *Par.* IX, 78, "coculla."

78. *sacca*: Feminine plural of *sacco*, "sack."

79–81. *Ma grave usura . . . folle*: But exorbitant usury (interest paid by the borrower) when exacted ("si tolle") is not so much against God's will as the taking of that fruit (Church moneys) which makes the hearts of monks so wild, i.e., avid for more (see "folle" in this sense in *Par.* XIX, 122).

82–84. *ché quantunque . . . brutto*: For all the material goods which the Church has in its keeping belong to the people who ask in God's name (that is, the worthy poor) and is not for family or worse (i.e., concubines and bastards). Cf. Dante, *De mon.* III, x, 17.

85–87. *La carne . . . la ghianda*: Human nature is so weak ("blanda," "soft") that down in the world a good beginning does not last ("basta") as long as it takes the oak to sprout and form its fruit, the acorn. Early commentators assure us that this is a period of some twenty years, but less time is implied by the figure, indeed a very short time. For a similar judgment, see *Par.* XXVII, 136-38.

88. *Pier cominciò sanz' oro e sanz' argento*: Cf. Actus 3:6: "Petrus autem dixit: Argentum et aurum non est mihi." ("But Peter said, 'Silver and gold I have none.' ")

90. *Francesco*: St. Francis of Assisi. See *Par.* XI, 43-117.

93. *tu vederai del bianco fatto bruno*: "You will see the white turned dark," as in a withered flower. Again the imagery is close to that of *Par.* XXVII, 136-38.

94. *Veramente*: "Nevertheless." *Iordan vòlto retrorso*: "Jordan turned back." See Iosue 3:14-17; Ps. 113[114]:3.

95. *più*: "Più" is to be connected with "mirabile," vs. 96. *e 'l mar fuggir*: Cf. Exod. 14:21-29. *volse = volle*.

96. *mirabile a veder che qui 'l soccorso*: "The turning back of the Jordan and the parting of the Red Sea were examples of divine intervention 'more wonderful to behold than succor here.' Therefore we must not despair" (Gr).

97. *indi*: From where he was, near me.

97–98. *si raccolse . . . collegio*: "He withdrew to his company."

98. *e 'l collegio si strinse*: "And the company drew together into a single group."

99. *turbo*: "Whirlwind."   *s'avvolse*: "Whirled away."

100. *La dolce donna*: Beatrice.

100–102. *dietro a lor mi pinse . . . vinse*: Here one may hear, in allegory, an echo of the words by which Virgil first recognized Beatrice (see *Inf.* II, 76-78).

103. *qua giù*: Down here on earth.

105. *la mia ala*: "My flight."

106. *S'io torni mai*: "As I hope ever to return."   *lettore*: Scartazzini-Vandelli notes that this is the last of Dante's sixteen apostrophes to the reader.

109–11. *tu non avresti . . . esso*: This main clause swears by the asseveration of the author's true hope to return to the immortal world above. Again one notes the figure of *hysteron proteron* or the "last first" ("tratto e messo / nel foco il dito"). See n. to *Par.* II, 23-24. Rapidity of motion is certainly expressed here by the reversal, but there is more to it than just that.

112–23. *O gloriose stelle . . . tira*: God's providence has seen to it that the pilgrim Dante "lands" precisely in the constellation under which he was born, Gemini, or the Twins, and his apostrophe to these stars constitutes the most eloquent witness to the belief in the influence of the heavenly bodies on human character that is found anywhere in the poem. That these bodies do have such influence is granted in *Purg.* XVI, 73-81; but that the poet would grant, in his prayer here, that these glorious stars gave him "tutto, qual che si sia" (*all,* whatever it may be) of his genius was perhaps hardly expected by the reader.

This tribute is then turned into a devout invocation, that *virtù*, power, may come to him, as poet, from these stars, that he, the poet, may be equal to the hard pass that "draws his soul to it." Thus, as a little invocation, the verses signal the end, the final challenge to the poet, and beseech the power, from his own stars, to achieve it. Whereupon Beatrice's first words (vs. 124) join in this signal of the final course to be run: "Tu se' sì presso a l'ultima salute."

115–17. *con voi nasceva . . . tosco*: The sun, "padre d'ogne mortal vita," was rising and setting with Gemini when Dante first breathed "the Tuscan air." He was born, then, between May 21 and June 21.

115. *vosco*: "With you."

127–54. *e però . . . belli*: On these verses, which close this canto, and on the theme they present, Grandgent observes: "Between Saturn and the fixed stars is a distance greater than any hitherto traversed by Dante. The long, swift ascent symbolizes the uplifting of the soul by contemplation. In the 8th sphere, which contains countless heavenly bodies, the poet enters the constellation of Gemini, under whose influence he was born. Thus, in a spiritual sense, he returns, like Plato's departed, to his native star: cf. *Par.* IV, 52-57. At this point of his journey, he is told to look back (*Purg.* IV, 54): 'che suole a riguardar giovare altrui.' Beneath him are the sun, the moon, and all the planets, and, lowest, our little earth, so tiny that its pettiness makes him smile. Once St. Benedict, standing at a window, had a similar vision, suddenly beholding the whole world collected, as it were, under one sunbeam (Gregory the Great, *Dialogi*, II, xxxv)."

Grandgent notes that "a closer parallel to Dante's experience, however, is to be found in Cicero's *De Re Publica*, VI, where Scipio [Africanus the Younger], in a dream, is lifted to the skies." See *De re publica* VI, xvi, 16:

Erant autem eae stellae, quas numquam ex hoc loco vidimus, et eae magnitudines omnium, quas esse numquam suspicati sumus, ex quibus erat ea minima, quae ultima a caelo, citima terris luce lucebat aliena. stella-

rum autem globi terrae magnitudinem facile vincebant.
iam ipsa terra ita mihi parva visa est, ut me imperii
nostri, quo quasi punctum eius attingimus, paeniteret.

There were stars which we never see from the earth, and
they were all larger than we have ever imagined. The
smallest of them was that farthest from heaven and
nearest the earth which shone with a borrowed light.
The starry spheres were much larger than the earth; in-
deed the earth itself seemed to me so small that I was
scornful of our empire, which covers only a single point,
as it were, upon its surface.

Grandgent, noting that Scipio "sees the starry sphere, the
seven planets (including sun and moon), and the earth,"
cites *De re publica* VI, xx, 21-22:

Omnis enim terra, quae colitur a vobis, angustata verti-
cibus, lateribus latior, parva quaedam insula est circum-
fusa illo mari, quod Atlanticum, quod magnum, quem
Oceanum appellatis in terris, qui tamen tanto nomine
quam sit parvus, vides. ex his ipsis cultis notisque terris
num aut tuum aut cuiusquam nostrum nomen vel Cau-
casum hunc, quem cernis, transcendere potuit vel illum
Gangen tranatare?

For that whole territory which you hold, being narrow
from North to South, and broader from East to West,
is really only a small island surrounded by that sea
which you on the earth call the Atlantic, the Great Sea,
or the Ocean. Now you see how small it is in spite of its
proud name! Do you suppose that your fame or that of
any of us could ever go beyond those settled and ex-
plored regions by climbing the Caucasus, which you see
there, or by swimming the Ganges?

Comments Grandgent: "So Dante sees the whole inhabited
continent—short from north to south, but broad from east
to west—exposed 'from hills to river mouths,' from Caucasus
to Ganges and Ebro. This, then, is 'the little threshing floor
that makes us so ferocious'! Like a threshing floor our earth
appeared to Alexander the Great, when, according to an
ancient legend, he had himself carried up to the sky by eagles

or griffins. Equally insignificant it seemed to Boethius." See
Consol. philos. II, vii, vss. 1-6:

> Quicumque solam mente praecipiti petit
> Summumque credit gloriam,
> Late patentes aetheris cernat plagas
> Artumque terrarum situm.
> Brevem replere non valentis ambitum
> Pudebit aucti nominis.

> He that to honour only seeks to mount
> And that his chiefest end doth count,
> Let him behold the largeness of the skies
> And on the strait earth cast his eyes;
> He will despise the glory of his name,
> Which cannot fill so small a frame.

Grandgent continues: "In Canto XXVII, ll. 76-87, Dante de-
scribes a second downward look from the same constellation,
with which he has been revolving. It would appear from this
passage that during his first observation he reached the
meridian of Jerusalem, the center of the inhabited earth. The
phrase 'while I was circling with the eternal Twins' [vs. 152]
indicates that this first gaze lasts a considerable length of
time. When it began, he was presumably in line with central
Asia, and saw the whole of that region, as far east as the
mouth of the Ganges; when it ended, he was on the meridian
of the Holy City, and could see the entire westerly stretch of
land to the Atlantic. If the sun, too, had been in Gemini, he
could have taken in the whole continent (which is 180°
broad) at one sweep, from a position on the line of Jeru-
salem; but inasmuch as the sun was in Aries, some 40° west
of the observer, the part of the earth illumined by its light did
not coincide with Dante's field of vision."

127. *t'inlei*: A verb coined by Dante on the same model as
others (e.g., "s'inluia," *Par.* IX, 73).

129. *ti fei = ti feci.*

131-32. *s'appresenti a la turba . . . tondo*: Thus the an-
nouncement is made of what is now to be expected in the
action.

132. *etera tondo*: "This round heaven." *Etera* is from the Latin accusative *aethera*, which is generally used to refer to the matter of which the heavens are made.

133–34. *Col viso ritornai . . . spere*: The seven planetary heavens that have now been traversed. This backward glance sums them up, and their number, which is seven, is not insignificant.

134–35. *vidi questo globo . . . sembiante*: Then, after and below the glorious seven, he sees the earth with its "vil sembiante," so much so that anyone who sets his thoughts elsewhere is truly to be praised.

139–41. *Vidi la figlia di Latona . . . densa*: The moon shows her spots only on the side toward the earth (see n. to *Par.* II, 52-148).

142–50. *L'aspetto del tuo nato . . . riparo*: The planets are then variously distinguished, by names and in ways the reader will at once recognize.

142. *Iperione*: Hyperion is often called by ancient poets the father of the Sun. See Ovid, *Metam.* IV, 192, "Hyperione nate" ("son of Hyperion"), and IV, 241.

144. *lui*: The sun.   *Maia e Dione*: "Maia" and "Dione" are probably to be taken as vocatives like "Iperione" in vs. 142. These persons are invoked because, like Hyperion, they are parents of gods whose names are borne by heavenly bodies. Maia is the mother of Mercury; Dione, the mother of Venus. Cf. Statius, *Theb.* II, 1, "Maia satus" ("son of Maia") and Virgil, *Aen.* I, 297, "Maia genitum" ("son of Maia"). See *Par.* VIII, 7.

146. *padre*: Saturn.   *figlio*: Mars.

150. *riparo*: "Abode."

151–53. *L'aiuola che . . . foci*: See n. to vss. 127-54. The "threshing-floor" (the inhabited part of the earth) makes us ferocious not only in our striving to possess as much of it as we may, but because of the grain that is on it at harvest time, which can only diminish by division or partnership, as this poem's central thesis makes clear (*Purg.* XV, 49-75). For the Latin *area* (the word from which *aiuola* derives) in the sense of "threshing-floor," see Virgil, *Georg.* I, 178-81.

154. *poscia rivolsi li occhi a li occhi belli*: Dante's turning away from the whole visible universe to Beatrice's eyes implies an upward gaze now that rejects and negates all the rest. The beautiful eyes reflect a spiritual universe that is immeasurably more important.

CANTO XXIII

1-9. *Come l'augello . . . nasca*: These three opening tercets, presenting the first term of a simile, are laden with sentiment, as every reader will feel: "augello," "amate fronde," "dolci nati," "aspetti disiati," "ardente affetto."

2-3. *posato al nido . . . la notte*: "Having sat on the nest throughout the night." It is important that the reader should get his bearings with the first term of the simile: the present action of the mother bird, after having sat on the nest through the night, is given in vss. 7-9.

2. *dolci nati*: Her beloved nestlings.

4-9. *che, per veder . . . nasca*: The mother bird has longed all night for the sight of the faces of her nestlings and for the light of day, so that she may find food for them, and such labor is sweet to her.

6. *labor = lavori*. "Labor" is a Latinism.   *li = gli.* There is no feminine form for *uccello*, hence the construction is in the masculine, though the bird in question is certainly the mother bird.   *aggrati*: Adjective probably formed on the adverbial phrase *a grato* and meaning "pleasant," "to one's liking."

7. *previene il tempo*: Anticipates daybreak, as vs. 9 makes clear. *in su aperta frasca*: The mother bird thus leaves the nest for the open bough that she may see her "dolci nati" and the coming of the dawn.

9. *pur che l'alba nasca*: "Pur" stresses the mother bird's persistent waiting for the dawn. Through all the sentiment-laden first term of the simile, the awaiting of sunrise is the guiding central motif, and it should be remembered that the rising sun is the image of the coming of Christ (cf. *Purg.* XXX, 22-27, and see C. S. Singleton, 1958, p. 73). That His Advent is to be realized now symbolically in the action of the poem the reader does not yet know, but will soon realize as the canto develops.

10-12. *così la donna mia . . . fretta*: Thus, in the second term of the simile, Beatrice replaces the mother bird, and Dante must somehow replace her nestlings (but in the singular). Spiritual is the food that now comes for him, food that comes by way of Beatrice, in the allegory. But the most curious feature of the simile is that *this* "dawn," this advent, is expected, not on the horizon, but at the zenith: "la plaga sotto la quale il sol mostra men fretta." Christ and the hosts of the blessed appear there, descending from on high. (Actually, Beatrice and Dante are above the sun, hence the indication is metaphorical and not literal at this point.)

11-12. *la plaga . . . fretta*: In the middle of the sky the sun seems to move more slowly than it does near the horizon. *plaga*: "Quarter." Cf. *Par.* XIII, 4.

13. *vaga*: "Eager."

14. *fecimi = mi feci.*   *quei = quegli* (singular).

15. *vorria = vorrebbe.*   *sperando s'appaga*: "Contents himself with hope."

16. *quando*: Here used as a noun, "moment."

18. *lo ciel venir più e più rischiarando*: This keeps this advent as a dawn, even though it is at the meridian.

19–21. *e Beatrice . . . spere*: Finally we are told what comes, though the whole scene is entirely symbolical, as the reader must realize. Christ will now appear as a sun illuminating many stars, and the action of the canto will develop from and through such symbolism. Here is the host of the blessed who were, so to speak, "harvested" out of time, the fruit gathered in from the turning of the spheres, a turning which is the very image of time, for it determines time for mortals on earth. This notion of "harvest out of time" also appears at the end of the canto, vss. 130-32. "Triunfo," as distinguished from *militia* (Christ's army still on earth and in time), bears in itself this latent metaphor. Such, then, is the wayfarer's experience in the heaven of the fixed stars, where, unlike the planetary heavens, there is no single body, no planet, but a multitude of bodies, *all* the stars.

22. *Pariemi = mi pareva.*

24. *che passarmen convien sanza costrutto*: "That it behooves me to leave it without phrasing." For *costrutto* in this sense, cf. *Par.* XII, 67.   *passarmen = passarmene.*

26. *Trivia*: "The goddess at the three ways," a term applied by Virgil (e.g., *Aen.* VI, 13, 35; VII, 516, 774) and other Latin poets to Diana (whose temple was frequently placed where three roads met), and hence by Dante to the moon, Diana being goddess of the Moon.   *ride*: "Shines."
ninfe: "Stars." Thus even as nymphs made up the following of the goddess, so here the stars make up the following of the moon. Cf. Horace, *Epodes* XV, 1-2: "Nox erat et caelo fulgebat Luna sereno / inter minora sidera." ("Twas night, and in a cloudless sky the moon was shining amid the lesser lights.") The poet has been obliged to shift, through simile, to a night scene as we now see, in order to have the major body (which at first was the sun but now is the moon) shining amidst many lesser lights. And yet, in the second term of the simile, that body is still the sun, and since the stars derive their light from the sun, it is proper that this symbolic sun should illumine all the lights, "lucerne" (vs. 28) here.

373

27. *seni*: "Parts." Cf. *Par.* XIII, 7.

28. *sopra migliaia di lucerne*: Some commentators attempt to determine just which particular group of the blessed is here intended by these "thousands of lights," but surely the symbolism is calculated to convey the meaning that there is represented here the entire host of the blessed, *all* of Christ's "triumph" in that sense—*represented*, not all necessarily *present* in the many lights.

29–30. *che tutte quante . . . superne*: "Christ illumines all the blessed, just as our material sun illumines all the stars—'the phenomena on high' (cf. II, 115). See *Conv.*, II, xiii, 15: 'del suo lume tutte le altre stelle s'informano' ['all the other stars are informed by his light']. Cf. *Par.* XX, 6.—A. Santi, *Giorn. dant.*, XXII, 229, attempts to show that in Dante's belief the light of the stars does not come entirely from the sun. We find that both opinions were current in the Middle Ages" (Gr).

30. *viste*: Cf. "vedute" in *Par.* II, 115; also see *Par.* XXX, 9.

31–32. *e per la viva luce . . . chiara*: Through the effulgence of this sun, the person of Christ, the source of this light, which is itself a shining substance, can be seen. "Sustanza" is used in the scholastic sense (*substantia*), denoting that which has separate existence, as contrasted with "accident," which is a quality existing in a substance. See Dante's use of these terms in *Vita nuova* XXV, 1-2. With this term the stress is rather on the human Christ. The whole vision is symbolic, however—a point not to be forgotten.

35. *sobranza*: "Overcomes." Cf. *Par.* XX, 97.

36. *virtù*: "Power." Cf. vs. 37, "possanza."   *nulla*: That is, *virtù*.

37. *Quivi è la sapienza e la possanza*: See I Cor. 1:24: "Christum Dei virtutem et Dei sapientiam." ("Christ, the power of God and the wisdom of God.") Usually Christ is identified with wisdom.

38. *ch'aprì le strade tra 'l cielo e la terra*: From Adam's sin to the Advent of Christ, the way to Heaven was closed. Even the virtuous who believed in Him went to Limbo to await His "opening of the way." And there in Limbo the long desire for His coming was felt, as it was on earth among those who believed in Him as the Redeemer. Adam, as he tells us later (*Par.* XXVI, 118-20), waited in Limbo 4,302 years for Christ's harrowing, which took him forth.

40. *foco*: "Lightning."   *di nube = dalla nube.*

41. *per dilatarsi*: "Expanding."   *non vi cape*: "Is no longer contained therein."   *cape*: From *capere*.

42. *e fuor di sua natura in giù s'atterra*: It is the nature of fire to rise. Cf. *Par.* I, 115; *Conv.* III, iii, 2.   *fuor di*: "Contrary to."

43. *dape*: Meaning "viands," from the Latin *dapes,* but with a plural ending in *e* instead of *i*.

44. *di sé stessa uscìo*: This is the *excessus mentis* of the mystics, wrought by the power of Christ, here present symbolically.   *uscìo = uscì.*

45. *che si fesse*: "What it became." The pleonastic reflexive (here "si") is very commonly used, in older Italian, after *non sapere.*   *fesse = facesse.*   *sape = sa.*

46–48. *Apri li occhi . . . mio*: Dante has not seen Beatrice's smile since entering the heaven of Saturn, because he could not have endured it (*Par.* XXI, 4-12), but now that he has seen the "triunfo di Cristo" (vs. 20) and Christ in His effulgence, his eyes can endure the sight of her radiant smile.

49. *come quei che si risente*: "As one who comes to himself."

50. *di visione oblita*: "From a vision that has faded away." "Oblita" is a Latinism, "obliterated."

51. *ridurlasi = ridursela.*

53. *grato*: "Gratitude."   *stingue = estingue.*

54. *del = dal.*   *libro che 'l preterito rassegna*: The book
of memory. For the book of memory, cf. Dante, *Rime* LXVII,
59; *Vita nuova* I; C. S. Singleton (1949).   *preterito*: A
Latinism.   *rassegna*: "Records."

55. *quelle lingue*: The tongues of poets.

56. *Polimnia*: Here pronounced *Polimnìa*. Polyhymnia, the
Muse of the Sublime Hymn.   *con le suore*: "With her sis-
ters," the other Muses. The Muses nourish (or "fatten") the
tongues of poets.   *fero = fecero*.

59. *verria = verrebbe*.

60. *e quanto il santo aspetto facea mero*: It (the smile)
"lighted up" the face of Beatrice.

61. *figurando*: "Depicting."

62. *poema*: The subject of "saltar."

63. *riciso*: "Cut off," "barred."

67. *pareggio*: There has been much discussion concerning
the correct reading here, whether "pileggio" or "pereggio"
or "poleggio." There is also a Low Latin *parigium* to be reck-
oned with. Petrocchi's acceptance of "pareggio" seems justi-
fiable. See his vol. I, *Introduzione*, pp. 240-41, where he ad-
mits that other forms are possible, but that in any case the
poet means by the term "a long and difficult stretch of sea."
In fact, the metaphor here returns the reader to the opening
of *Par*. II, particularly with the touch "che fendendo va
l'ardita prora" (vs. 68).

69. *a sé medesmo parca*: "Who would [seek to] spare him-
self"; from the Latin *sibi parcat*.

70-72. *Perché la faccia mia . . . s'infiora?* Cf. *Par*. XVIII,
20-21.

71. *bel giardino*: Now all the lights of the blessed, irradi-
ated by the sun, who is Christ, become a beautiful garden.
The flower metaphor continues in the following verses.

73. *la rosa*: Mary, the "Mystic Rose" of the liturgy. Cf. *rosario*, rosary, a series of prayers to the Virgin.   *verbo divino*: Christ. See Ioan. 1:14: "Et Verbum caro factum est." ("And the Word was made flesh.")

74. *gigli*: The apostles. "In his unfinished commentary on Isaiah, St. Thomas discusses the resemblance of saints to lilies" (Gr). See G. Busnelli (1911a), pp. 128-29, n. 3.

75. *a*: "By."   *al cui odor si prese il buon cammino*: See II Cor. 2:14: "Deo autem gratias, qui semper triumphat nos in Christo Iesu, et odorem notitiae suae manifestat per nos in omni loco." ("But thanks be to God who always leads us in triumph in Christ Jesus, manifesting through us the odor of his knowledge in every place.")

78. *cigli*: "Brows," for "eyes."

79–87. *Come a raggio . . . possenti*: In three tercets the poet suggests, by such a transition from the preceding image, the Ascension of Christ: the sun withdrawn—having risen, as it were, above the clouds—but still shining through upon the company of the elect. Grandgent comments: " 'As ere now my eyes, covered by a shadow, have seen a flowery meadow under a sunbeam that streams clear through a rifted cloud': an exceedingly beautiful simile used to describe the vast throngs of flowerlike souls illumined from above by the dazzling light of Christ, who has risen once again to the Empyrean, in order that Dante's own eyes may not be entirely blinded by his brightness."

79. *mei*: "Pours down." Cf. *Par.* XIII, 55. "Mei" is subjunctive to suggest the hypothetical though common scene.

80. *fratta*: "Broken," here "rifted." Cf. *Purg.* XVII, 42.

83. *folgorate*: "Illuminated."

84. *principio di folgóri*: In this instance, Christ, the sun, withdrawn, "arisen," as the following tercet makes clear.

85. *li 'mprenti*: "Do stamp them."

87. *non t'eran possenti*: "Were not able to endure Thee" (your light).

88. *nome*: The mention of Mary by Beatrice in vs. 73. Among the bright lights, hers is now the greatest (vs. 90).

89. *mane = mattina*.

89–90. *tutto mi ristrinse l'animo*: Made me concentrate all my attention on.

90. *avvisar*: "Make out," "distinguish."

91. *come*: "When."   *luci*: "Eyes."   *dipinse*: The subject of "dipinse" is the phrase in vs. 92.

92. *il quale e il quanto*: "The quality and bigness." Cf. *Par.* II, 65.   *la viva stella*: "Stella" is another of the names of Mary in the liturgy: "stella mattutina," "maris stella."

93. *che là sù vince come qua giù vinse*: Mary outshines all the other stars up there, even as on earth she outshone all other creatures.

94–96. *una facella . . . ella*: The "torch" seems certainly to be the Archangel Gabriel, the messenger of the Annunciation. He now forms a circling halo around the head of the Virgin, re-enacting, as it were, the great moment. But this is only a ritualistic celebration of the Annunciation and does not take its place *chronologically* in the events symbolized, for Christ has already "ascended."

96. *cinsela = la cinse.   girossi = si girò.   ella = lei*.

99. *parrebbe nube che squarciata tona*: See Ovid, *Metam.* XII, 51-52: "qualemve sonum, cum Iuppiter atras / increpuit nubes, extrema tonitrua reddunt" ("or like the last rumblings of thunder when Jove has made the dark clouds crash together").

100. *quella lira*: The singing Gabriel who circles and thus "crowns" Mary, the most beautiful sapphire in Heaven. Cf. a similar crowning of Dante, described in *Par.* XXIV, 152-54.

102. *il ciel più chiaro*: The Empyrean.

103. *giro*: "Encircle."

104. *ventre*: "Womb."

105. *nostro disiro*: Christ, the object of desire. Cf. vss. 37-39.

106. *girerommi* = *mi girerò*.

106-8. *mentre che . . . entre*: I.e., until Mary shall rise to the highest heaven, following Christ, which she does (vs. 120).

107. *dia*: "Divine." Cf. *Par.* XIV, 34.

108. *perché li entre*: "By entering it."   *li*: The unaccented "li" here is the unemphatic adverb, corresponding to *vi.   entre = entri.*

110. *si sigillava*: "Sealed itself," i.e., ended.

112-13. *Lo real manto . . . mondo*: "The royal cloak of all the revolutions of the world" is the ninth sphere, the Primum Mobile, which encircles the eight revolving heavens, the seven planetary spheres plus the sphere of the fixed stars where the wayfarer now is.

112. *volumi*: For the word in this sense, cf. *Par.* XXVI, 119; XXVIII, 14. Also see Ovid, *Metam.* II, 71.

113-14. *che più ferve . . . costumi*: The Primum Mobile, or ninth sphere, is said to "burn" most (with desire) and be most "living" through the spirit ("alito") of God and His operations or ways ("costumi"). Cf. Dante, *Conv.* II, iii, 8-9:

> Veramente, fuori di tutti questi, li cattolici pongono lo cielo Empireo, che è a dire cielo di fiamma o vero luminoso; e pongono esso essere immobile per avere in sè, secondo ciascuna parte, ciò che la sua materia vuole. E questo è cagione al Primo Mobile per avere velocissimo movimento; chè per lo ferventissimo appetito ch'è'n ciascuna parte di quello nono cielo, che è im-

mediato a quello, d'essere congiunta con ciascuna parte
di quello divinissimo ciel quieto, in quello si rivolve con
tanto desiderio, che la sua velocitade è quasi incom-
prensibile.

But beyond all these the Catholics assert the empyrean
heaven, which is as much as to say the heaven of flame,
or the luminous heaven; and they assert it to be immov-
able, because it hath in itself with respect to every part
that which its matter demandeth. And this is the cause
of the *primum mobile* having the swiftest motion, be-
cause by reason of the most fervid appetite wherewith
every part of this ninth heaven, which is next below it,
longeth to be conjoined with every part of this divinest,
and tranquil heaven, it revolves therein with so great
yearning that its swiftness is scarce to be compre-
hended.

It should be remembered that the desire which the spheres
have for the unmoved Mover is basically Aristotelian in con-
ception. The very last verse of the whole poem will echo this
doctrine. Moreover, in imagery that is to come (*Par.* XXX,
106-8) the reader will see how this ninth heaven receives
God's light and power.

115-17. *avea sopra . . . appariva*: The concave inner surface
("bank") of the ninth heaven is said to be so far beyond the
reach of Dante's eyes that, as he looks up, he cannot see it.
The reader should recall that, in this cosmology, each of the
nine spheres is conceived as having material existence.

117. *ancor non appariva*: "Ancor" has reference to the up-
ward journey, of course, and clearly implies that the "bank"
will be visible later.

118. *però = per ciò*.

119. *la coronata fiamma*: Mary.

120. *sua semenza*: Christ, the "seed" or child of Mary.

121-26. *E come fantolin . . . palese*: The simile clearly casts
the Virgin Mary in the role of mother (*mater gratiae, mater*

misericordiae) and is an excellent example of the vivid earth-ly and everyday imagery which the poet introduces, in the first terms of his similes, throughout this rarified realm of Paradise. All readers will remember having seen the flush on a baby's face after it has suckled and the way it may reach out its little arms towards its mother. Literally, flames are conceived of as "reaching upward," through their desire to reach home (the sphere of fire), and this conception forms the background of the second term of the simile, these "flames" being souls.

123. *per l'animo che 'nfin di fuor s'infiamma*: " 'Because of the spirit (of grateful love) which breaks even into external flame'—which, in default of words, finds expression in a gesture" (Gr).

124. *ciascun di quei candori in sù si stese*: All the bright souls extend their flames upward after Mary.   *candori*: "Glowing lights" (cf. *Par.* XIV, 77).   *si stese = si protese.*

126. *avieno = avevano.*

128. *Regina celi*: "Regina coeli," antiphon in praise of the Virgin Mary, Queen of Heaven, which is sung in the Office at Easter. See P. Guéranger (1888), p. 39:

> Regina coeli, laetare, alleluia,
> Quia quem meruisti portare, alleluia,
> Resurrexit sicut dixit, alleluia.
> Ora pro nobis Deum, alleluia.
> Gaude et laetare, Virgo Maria, alleluia.
> Quia surrexit Dominus vere, alleluia.
>
> Rejoice, O Queen of heaven, alleluia,
> For he whom thou deservedst to bear, alleluia,
> Hath risen, as he said, alleluia.
> Pray to God for us, alleluia.
> Rejoice and be glad, O Virgin Mary, alleluia.
> For the Lord hath truly risen, alleluia.

130. *ubertà*: "Abundance."   *si soffolce*: "Is stored," from the Latin *suffulcire*.

131. *arche*: "Bins" or "coffers," the blessed souls.

132. *bobolce*: Feminine plural of *bobolco*, from the Latin *bubulcus*, "a ploughman." The plural reflects *anime*. The meaning is "husbandmen," "tillers and sowers." The souls are now filled with the good which they sowed on earth. Cf. Gal. 6:8[7]: "Quae enim seminaverit homo, haec et metet." ("For what a man sows, that he will also reap.") Other commentators take "bobolce" to mean "fields," but this seems less fitting in the context.

134–35. *lo essilio di Babillòn*: The "exile of Babylon" is the earthly life. Cf. Ps. 136[137]:1: "Super flumina Babylonis illic sedimus et flevimus, cum recordaremur Sion." ("By the streams of Babylon we sat and wept when we remembered Sion.")

135. *Babillòn = Babilonia.   ove si lasciò l'oro*: "On earth 'they forsook gold,' following the precept of Jesus" (Gr). See Matt. 19:21: "Ait illi Iesus: si vis perfectus .esse, vade, vende quae habes, et da pauperibus, et habebis thesaurum in caelo." ("Jesus said to him, 'If thou wilt be perfect, go, sell what thou hast, and give to the poor, and thou shalt have treasure in heaven.'")

137. *di sua vittoria*: "By his victory." The canto ends on the note of "triumph" and "victory" with which it began.

138. *e con l'antico e col novo concilio*: "In company with the souls of the Old and the New Covenant. Prophets and Apostles preached the same faith" (Gr).

139. *colui*: "Colui," St. Peter, is the subject of "triunfa" in vs. 136.   *tien le chiavi di tal gloria*: Cf. Matt. 16:19: "Et tibi dabo claves regni caelorum." ("And I will give thee the keys of the kingdom of heaven.") The final verse thus presents Peter—who, as the reader will soon see, is the most prominent of these figures—with keys and an examination suggesting that the journey has now reached an "entrance-way" into Heaven.

CANTO XXIV

1–3. *O sodalizio . . . piena*: There are clear scriptural echoes in Beatrice's opening words, which are addressed to the whole company of the blessed that is before her and Dante, like so many flames.

1. *sodalizio*: The word means "company," but Pietro di Dante and other early commentators sense that the term already tends to single out the apostles in particular. Commenting on this point, Pietro speaks of the apostles as those "qui fuerunt sodales, quasi simul sedentes ad mensam cum Christo" ("who were intimate companions, as those who sat together at table with Christ"). *eletto*: Cf. Matt. 22:14: "Multi enim sunt vocati, pauci vero electi." ("For many are called, but few are chosen.")

1–2. *cena del benedetto Agnello*: Cf. Apoc. 19:9: "Beati qui ad cenam nuptiarum Agni vocati sunt." ("Blessed are they who are called to the marriage supper of the Lamb.") For "Agnello," see Ioan. 1:29: "Ecce agnus Dei; ecce qui tollit peccatum mundi." ("Behold, the lamb of God, who takes away the sin of the world.")

2–3. *vi ciba sì . . . piena*: Cf. Ioan. 6:35: "Dixit autem eis Iesus: Ego sum panis vitae; qui venit ad me non esuriet."

("But Jesus said to them, 'I am the bread of life. He who comes to me shall not hunger.'") The desire of the blessed in Paradise is always satisfied, but there *is* desire and not cessation of desire, a fact which will be reflected in the experience of Dante the pilgrim at the end of his journey (*Par.* XXXIII, 143-44).

4. *questi preliba*: "This man [Dante] foretastes."

5. *di quel che cade de la vostra mensa*: Cf. Matt. 15:27: "Nam et catelli edunt de micis quae cadunt de mensa dominorum suorum." ("For even the dogs eat of the crumbs that fall from their masters' table.") Dante develops this image and idea in *Conv.* I, i, 10, and it is reflected in the very title of that work.

6. *prima che morte tempo li prescriba*: "Before death cuts off his time" (i.e., his lifetime on earth).   *li = gli.*
prescriba = prescriva. For the word in this sense, cf. *Par.* XXI, 103; XXV, 57.

7. *affezione immensa*: "Great desire," i.e., Dante's desire to know the truth, or (to continue the opening metaphor) to participate in the "feast" of the blessed, who are feasting on the truth.

8. *roratelo*: "Bedew him," give him a few drops from the fount of truth, on which his desire is set. "Rorate, coeli" belongs to liturgical language, and dew is the well-established symbol of grace given from Heaven. This shifts the metaphor, of course, to the notion of drinking, rather than eating bread, to thirst instead of hunger, as is at once evident.

8-9. *voi bevete . . . pensa*: You, the elect, drink eternally at the fountain of God's wisdom, i.e., you gaze upon God and thus see the very origin of this man's thoughts. Cf. *Purg.* XXI, 1-3.

11. *si fero spere sopra fissi poli*: It is evident from vs. 30 and from *Par.* XXV, 14, that "spere" means "circles," rings of spirits dancing in a round, or carol. It is also clear, from vss. 16-17, that the flames (souls) form different groups, or

carols, this being implied also by the clock image which now comes.

12. *fiammando, volte*: Some editors have adopted "forte" here, in place of "volte," but Petrocchi's choice seems the better.   *a guisa di comete*: The image implies that each of these flames, thus spinning, leaves a certain trail of light behind it.

13. *cerchi*: The *cerchi* or wheels of a clock's works.
tempra: The total mechanism of the clock, including the escapement as well as the wheels.

14–15. *'l primo . . . pare*: The first wheel that one observes is the largest and in the clock's mechanism the slowest to turn, so slow that it seems to stand still.

15. *e l'ultimo che voli*: The smallest wheel of the mechanism turns so fast that it seems to "fly" around.

16–18. *così quelle carole . . . lente*: The second term of the simile confirms what is already evident: that the flames form different rounds, or carols, and now are seen to spin at different velocities, like the wheels of a single mechanism. This latter metaphor of the *whole* clock stresses one total harmony in these different round dances.

16–17. *differentemente*: "An adverb like *differentemente* was originally a phrase made up of an adjective and the ablative *mente*; its composite nature long continued to be felt" (Gr).

17. *de la sua ricchezza*: The pace of the circling rings of dancers is a measure of their "wealth" of gladness.   *sua*: I.e., *loro*.

18. *facieno = facevano*.

19. *quella*: That is, *carola*.   *carezza*: "Wealth," connecting with "ricchezza," vs. 17. Some editors have preferred the reading "bellezza" here; but see Petrocchi, whose choice of "carezza" is persuasive. Thus the flame that comes forth from

the dance now belongs to the "richest" of the rounds, that of greatest worth.

20–21. *sì felice . . . chiarezza*: Joy is the cause of brightness. The flame that comes now is not only from the richest "round," but is the brightest flame in that dance.

22–24. *e tre fiate . . . ridice*: This same flame will circle Dante's head an equal number of times (see vs. 152) and thus seems to have a predilection for the number three.

23. *divo = divino*.

24. *la mia fantasia*: Here, as usual, the term "fantasia" is used in the sense of that faculty which receives images (cf. *Purg.* XVII, 25; *Par.* X, 46; and *passim*); but that faculty in Dante, in this case, does not *hold* the image so that memory can deliver it up (*ridire*).   *nol mi = non me lo*.

25. *Però = per ciò.   salta la penna*: "La penna" is the subject of "salta," literally, "jumps," "passes over."

26–27. *ché l'imagine . . . vivo*: " 'For our imagination—not to say our speech—is too bright a color for such folds.' Human speech and even human memory are not profound enough to describe or retain an impression of such depth of holiness. The metaphor is taken from the technique of painting (in V.N., [XXXIV], Dante appears as an artist): pictures, in our poet's day, consisted mainly of faces and garments, the latter falling in folds, and these folds presented the deepest shades; skill was required to find a color dark enough to portray them, while preserving the purity of tone the Tuscans loved" (Gr).

28. *suora = sorella*, one who is herself of the company of the elect.   *ne prieghe = ci prieghi*.

29. *per*: "By" or "through."   *affetto*: Charity, love.

30. *da quella bella spera*: From the carol that was in fact the most beautiful (see vs. 19).   *mi disleghe = mi disleghi*, "you unloose me."

31. *Poscia*: First (vss. 22-23) the shining spirit circles about Beatrice and sings, "then" ("poscia") it stops and speaks the words just cited. For this use of *poscia*, cf. *Inf.* XXIV, 118.

32. *spiro*: "Voice." Cf. *Par.* XXVI, 3.

33. *favellò*: "Spoke."

34-36. *O luce etterna . . . miro*: When we learn that this is none other than St. Peter, the overtones of "gran" become clear.

34. *viro*: "Man," from the Latin *vir*. The Latinism confers solemnity.

35. *le chiavi*: Cf. *Par.* XXIII, 139.

36. *di questo gaudio miro*: "Of this wondrous delight" in Heaven. The phrase depends on "le chiavi."

37. *tenta*: "Probe," "examine."   *punti lievi e gravi*: Points both minor and major.

38. *intorno de la fede*: Faith is thus the first point on which Dante is to be examined. The other two will be hope and charity. Thus, the total examination will prove to be one on the three theological virtues and will constitute, as it were, an entrance examination to Heaven (which is above, and towards which the pilgrim moves). See Bonaventura, *Itinerarium mentis in Deum* IV, 2; Dante, *Conv.* III, xiv, 15. Grandgent comments: "Dante's examiners are St. Peter, St. James, and St. John, the disciples most closely associated with Jesus, and the traditional representatives of the virtues he preached. The fitness of Peter and John to stand for Faith and Love is obvious; less clear is the special appropriateness of the assignment of Hope to James." Grandgent notes that "after his colloquy, in this sphere, with the Apostles and Adam, Dante converses only with those who serve as his guides, Beatrice and St. Bernard."

39. *per la qual tu su per lo mare andavi*: See Matt. 14:28-29: "Respondens autem Petrus dixit: Domine, si tu

es, iube me ad te venire super aquas. At ipse ait: Veni. Et descendens Petrus de navicula ambulabat super aquam, ut veniret ad Iesum." ("But Peter answered him and said, 'Lord, if it is thou, bid me come to thee over the water.' And he said, 'Come.' Then Peter got out of the boat and walked on the water to come to Jesus.")

40. *S'elli ama bene e bene spera e crede*: The verse reverses the usual order of statement (faith, hope, and charity), but also signals what the total examination will involve.

41. *viso*: "Sight."

41-42. *quivi dov' ogne . . . vede*: "Quivi" is "in God"; the fact that the elect can read all things in Him has been frequently stated in a variety of images.

43-45. *ma perché questo regno . . . arrivi*: This realm of Paradise has formed its citizenry through the true faith, and therefore, in order to glorify faith, "it is well that he [Dante] be called upon to speak of it."

43. *civi*: "Citizens."

45. *arrivi*: Equivalent to *tocchi*, "befall."

46-48. *Sì come . . . terminarla*: To understand the simile the modern reader needs to know that in the medieval examination, or *disputatio*, leading to the degree of doctor of theology, a time was appointed for the discussion of a given question. On this occasion the master or doctor examining the candidate would state the question, whereupon the "bachelor" was expected to adduce proofs (*approvare*), that is, bring arguments to bear on it (both *pro* and *con*), but he did not presume to settle or decide the question (*terminare*), since this privilege belonged only to the examining doctor and was called the *determinatio*. See M. Barbi (1927). The bachelor had a brief time (as Dante has here with St. Peter) in which to collect himself and muster his arguments ("s'arma").

46. *baccialier*: Petrocchi prefers the form *baccialier* to the more common *baccellier*.

49–51. *così m'armava . . . professione*: Dante "arms himself" even before hearing the question, especially since, this being St. Peter, that question is bound to concern faith.

51. *tal querente*: "Such a questioner." *professione*: This anticipates "profession of faith," which Dante already surmises his examination will be on.

52–53. *Dì, buon Cristiano . . . è?* St. Peter's manner is most direct and his words are simple. Moreover he knows already that the "candidate" is a good Christian. The first question, then, is simply: what is faith?

54. *in*: "Toward." *spirava*: Cf. "spiro," vs. 32. *questo*: These words.

56. *sembianze femmi*: "Signed to me" ("with her eyes and look" being implied). *femmi = mi fece*.

56–57. *perch' io . . . fonte*: Cf. Ioan. 7:37-38: "Si quis sitit, veniat ad me et bibat. Qui credit in me, sicut dicit Scriptura, flumina de ventre eius fluent aquae vivae." ("If anyone thirst, let him come to me and drink. He who believes in me, as the Scripture says, 'From within him there shall flow rivers of living water.'")

59. *da l'alto primipilo*: "By the high commander," Peter, the first commander of the Church. Note that *primopilus* is the title of a Roman military officer, strictly the *centurio primi pili*, centurion of the front rank of the *triarii* (the veteran Roman soldiers who formed the third rank from the front when the legion was drawn up in order of battle), hence the chief centurion of the legion. Dante probably got the term from the *Epitoma rei militaris* (II, 8) of Vegetius, whom he mentions in *De mon.* II, ix, 3.

61. *'l verace stilo*: "The veracious pen."

62. *ne = ci.* *tuo caro frate*: St. Paul. Cf. II Pet. 3:15: "sicut et carissimus frater noster Paulus secundum datam sibi

sapientiam scripsit vobis" ("just as our most dear brother Paul also, according to the wisdom given him, has written to you").

63. *che mise teco Roma nel buon filo*: "Who, with you, brought Rome into the right line," i.e., the path of Christianity.

64–65. *fede è sustanza . . . parventi*: The definition of faith is, as stated, St. Paul's. See Heb. 11:1: "Est autem fides sperandarum substantia rerum, argumentum non apparentium." ("Now faith is the substance of things to be hoped for, the evidence of things that are not seen.") "This formula, says St. Thomas, although some say that it is not a definition, contains all the elements of one" (Gr). See Aquinas, *Summa theol.* II-II, q. 4, a. 1, resp.: "Licet quidam dicant praedicta Apostoli verba non esse fidei definitionem . . . tamen si quis recte consideret, omnia ex quibus fides potest definiri, in praedicta descriptione tanguntur." ("Though some say that the above words of the Apostle are not a definition of faith, yet if we consider the matter aright, this definition overlooks none of the points in reference to which faith can be defined.") Aquinas adds: "Si quis ergo in formam definitionis huiusmodi verba reducere velit, potest dicere quod *fides est habitus mentis, quo inchoatur vita aeterna in nobis, faciens intellectum assentire non apparentibus.*" ("Accordingly if anyone would reduce the foregoing words to the form of a definition, he may say that *faith is a habit of the mind, whereby eternal life is begun in us, making the intellect assent to what is non-apparent.*")

66. *quiditate*: "Essence."

67. *senti*: "Think," "conceive."

68. *la ripuose*: "He [Paul] placed it [faith]."

69. *tra le sustanze, e poi tra li argomenti*: On this and Dante's comments, which follow, Grandgent observes: "But why, demands St. Peter, did St. Paul call Faith first a 'substance' (*sustanza*) and then an 'evidence' (*argomento*)? The

eternal Heavenly life, replies Dante, is beyond the perception
of mortals and, for them, exists only in their belief; hence
Faith, from the human point of view, is the material, or sub-
stance, of which the hoped-for joys consist. Moreover, while
in ordinary matters we argue from proved facts, in religion
we use as our basis for further reasoning a belief; and so
Faith, in theological questions, takes the place which in
worldly syllogisms is taken by evidence."

71. *che mi largiscon qui la lor parvenza*: "Which here [in
Heaven] allow themselves to be seen by me." *Largire* implies
"bounty," "grace."

72. *a li occhi di là giù*: To the eyes of mortals on earth.
ascose = nascoste.

73. *che l'esser loro v'è in sola credenza*: That their existence
is there founded only on belief.

74. *spene = speme, speranza.* This is the hope of eternal
beatitude.

75. *però = perciò.   sustanza*: "Substance" or "material,"
with the verb "si fonda," in the preceding verse, suggesting
the meaning "foundation." Cf. vs. 69.   *prende intenza*:
" 'It assumes the concept': it falls into the category. *Intenza*
is the scholastic Latin *intentio*, 'notion' or 'concept'; English
intention has often been used in this sense" (Gr).

77. *silogizzar*: "Argue."   *vista*: "Proof," "visible evi-
dence."

78. *però = perciò.   tene = tiene.*

81. *non li avria loco ingegno di sofista*: "The sophist's wit
would have no place there."   *li*: Here the unaccented "li"
= *vi*.

83. *trascorsa*: "Inspected," "examined."

84. *lega*: "Composition," "alloy."   *peso*: "Weight," these
being the two essential "tests" of a coin.

86. *Sì ho*: The repetition of the verb adds emphasis to the

affirmation, and in such cases the omission of the object pronoun (*lo, la,* etc.) was common in early Italian. See M. Barbi (1934), p. 291. *sì lucida e sì tonda*: The verbs reflect the tests of a coin (see vs. 84), the *lucidezza* attesting a good composition (with high gold content) and the *tondezza* referring to its weight, for coins could be shaved down around the outer edge (a not uncommon practice), thus reducing the weight.

87. *conio*: "Stamp." *s'inforsa*: "Is questionable." The verb is coined by Dante.

89. *Questa cara gioia*: Faith.

90. *sopra la quale ogne virtù si fonda*: See Thomas Aquinas, *Summa theol.* II-II, q. 4, a. 7, resp.:

Aliquid potest esse prius altero dupliciter; uno modo per se; alio modo per accidens. Per se quidem inter omnes virtutes prima est fides. Cum enim in agibilibus finis sit principium, ut supra dictum est, 1-2, quaest. 13, art. 3, et quaest. 34, art. 4, ad 1, necesse est virtutes theologicas, quarum obiectum est ultimus finis, esse priores caeteris virtutibus. Ipse autem ultimus finis oportet quod prius sit in intellectu quam in voluntate; quia voluntas non fertur in aliquid, nisi prout est in intellectu apprehensum. Unde cum ultimus finis sit quidem in voluntate per spem et charitatem, in intellectu autem per fidem; necesse est quod fides sit prima inter omnes virtutes; quia naturalis cognitio non potest attingere ad Deum, secundum quod est obiectum beatitudinis, prout tendit in ipsum spes et charitas.

One thing can precede another in two ways: first, by its very nature; secondly, by accident. Faith, by its very nature, precedes all other virtues. For since the end is the principle in matters of action, as stated above (I-II, q. 13, a. 3: q. 34, a. 4, *ad* 1), the theological virtues, the object of which is the last end, must needs precede all the others. Again, the last end must of necessity be present to the intellect before it is present to the will, since the will has no inclination for anything except in so far as it is apprehended by the intellect. Hence, as the last end is present in the will by hope and charity, and in the intellect, by faith, the first of all the virtues must, of necessity, be faith, because natural knowledge cannot reach God as the object of heavenly bliss, which is the aspect under which hope and charity tend towards Him.

91. *ploia = pioggia* (cf. *Par.* XIV, 27), "rain," inspiration.

93. *cuoia*: "Parchments," Testaments. Cf. vss. 97-98.

94. *silogismo = sillogismo*, "argument."   *la m'ha conchiusa = me l'ha conchiusa*. "Conchiusa" ("demonstrated") extends the metaphor of "silogismo."

95. *che 'nverso d'ella = che inverso di essa*, "compared to it."

96. *ottusa*: "Unconvincing," opposed to "acutamente," vs. 95.

98. *proposizion*: "Premise." The Old Testament and the New Testament are the premises from which the conclusion is deduced.

101. *opere seguite*: "Works that followed," the miracles.

102. *non scalda ferro mai né batte incude*: Many editors have accepted the reading of some MSS that have these verbs in the preterite (*scaldò, battè*), but Petrocchi argues well for the present tense here. The figure obviously involves the metaphor of the smith, which Nature, as artist, was often said to be. The "works that followed," therefore, are divinely wrought miracles, not natural occurrences.   *incude = incudine*, "anvil."

104. *che quell' opere fosser*: "That those works [miracles] took place, existed."

104-5. *Quel medesmo . . . giura*: " 'The very thing that is to be proved (the revealed Truth), and naught else, is thy voucher for it.' St. Peter, wishing, as examiner, to draw out Dante more fully, tells him that he is arguing in a circle" (Gr).

106–8. *Se 'l mondo . . . centesmo*: "If the world was con-
verted to Christianity without the miracles related in the
Bible, this conversion was itself a far greater miracle, and
quite sufficient proof of divine intervention. The argument
is taken from St. Augustine, *De Civitate Dei*, XXII, v: 'hoc
nobis unum grande miraculum sufficit, quod . . . terrarum
orbis sine ullis miraculis credidit.' ('This one grand miracle
suffices for us, that the whole world has believed without any
miracles.') St. Thomas also, *De Veritate Catholicae Fidei*,
I, vi, discourses on the miracle of the conversion of the world
to Christianity" (Gr).

108. *non sono il centesmo*: All the other miracles are not
worth the hundredth part of this one.

109–10. *ché tu . . . campo*: "For you [and the other apostles]
entered the field poor and fasting." "Field" introduces the
familiar metaphor of cultivation, good or bad, and—with
"vite" (vs. 111)—of the "vineyard of the Lord."

111. *fu già vite*: The verb has its full force of the past abso-
lute here.   *pruno*: The vine is said to have become wild
like a thorn bush (cf. *Inf.* XIII, 32).

113. *spere*: The rounds or carols (cf. vs. 11).   *Dio
laudamo*: The "Te Deum." Cf. *Purg.* IX, 140.

115. *baron*: "Lord," i.e., Peter. Cf. *Par.* XXV, 17, where
the term is applied to James as well.

115–17. *sì di ramo . . . appressavamo*: The examination
becomes, in metaphor, a tree, and the end thereof the "last
boughs."

118. *donnea*: "Holds amorous discourse"; from the Pro-
vençal *domnejar*.

119–20. *la bocca . . . si dovea*: With these words Peter as-
signs all the merit of the answers to grace, and not to Dante.

121. *emerse*: "Has issued."

122. *quel che credi*: The specific truths you hold in your belief.

123. *e onde a la credenza tua s'offerse*: "And whence these truths came to you for your belief."

124-26. *O santo padre . . . piedi*: "St. Peter now sees in God that which on earth he accepted through faith. This faith was so strong that it impelled him to enter the Sepulchre before John, although the younger disciple reached it first: John xx, 3-8. Cf. *Mon.*, III, ix, 16" (Gr).

128. *forma*: "Essence," "substance."   *pronto*: "Unhesitating" and without need of proofs.

129. *la cagion di lui*: "Its cause."

130-32. *E io rispondo . . . disio*: Dante's Credo follows the accepted one in its essentials, but contains Aristotelian touches as well.

131-32. *che tutto 'l ciel move . . . disio*: Here *il ciel* has its usual plural meaning (*i cieli*, all the heavens or spheres) and, like the unmoved mover who moves those heavens with desire on their part, is from Aristotle. (Cf. *Par.* I, 76-77.) Only the love—if this means, as it seems to, love on the part of God for His creation, so that He moves the heavens with *His* love—is specifically Christian.

133. *pur*: "Only."

133-34. *prove fisice e metafisice*: "St. Thomas, *Summa Theologiae*, Prima, Qu. ii, Art. 3, gives five physical and metaphysical proofs of the existence of God: the impossibility of explaining the world without the assumption of a first motor, of a first efficient cause, of a first necessity, of a first goodness, of a first governing intelligence. In Prima, Qu. 1, Art. 5, he tells us that theology makes use of philosophy" (Gr).

134. *dalmi = me lo dà*. The subject is "verità" in vs. 135.

135. *piove*: See n. to *Par.* XIV, 27.

136. *per Moisè, per profeti e per salmi*: See Luc. 24:44: "Haec sunt verba quae locutus sum ad vos, cum adhuc essem vobiscum, quoniam necesse est impleri omnia quae scripta sunt in lege Moysi et prophetis et psalmis de me." ("These are the words which I spoke to you while I was yet with you, that all things must be fulfilled that are written in the Law of Moses and the Prophets and the Psalms concerning me.")

137. *l'Evangelio*: The narrative parts of the New Testament.

137–38. *e per voi . . . almi*: The Acts, Epistles, and Apocalypse—thus, the whole of the Bible is implied in vss. 136-38.

138. *poi che l'ardente Spirto vi fé almi*: The reference is to Actus 2:1-4, which describes the time of Pentecost, when the Holy Ghost, as tongues of fire, descended upon the apostles. *almi*: "Reverend" (cf. *Inf.* II, 20).

141. *soffera*: The word is pronounced *sòffera* and means "it admits." When speaking of the Trinity, it is possible to use either a singular or a plural verb. *este*: *Este* (from the Latin *est*) for *è* is not uncommon in early Italian.

143. *mente*: The object of "sigilla" ("stamps").

144. *l'evangelica dottrina*: Various passages in the Bible are cited in support of the doctrine of the Trinity. See Matt. 28:19; II Cor. 13:13[14]; I Pet. 1:2; and I Ioan. Apos. 5:7: "Quoniam tres sunt qui testimonium dant in caelo: Pater, Verbum, et Spiritus Sanctus; et hi tres unum sunt." ("For there are three that bear witness in heaven: the Father, the Word, and the Holy Spirit; and these three are one.") This truth, therefore, is entirely based on revelation.

145–47. *Quest' è . . . scintilla*: The existence of God, One and Three, a principle given by revelation through the Holy Scriptures, is the source, therefore, of all articles of faith, is the "spark" which becomes a great flame (and flame or fire can always suggest love).

147. *come stella in cielo*: My "guiding star," as it were, my "north star."

148. *i* = *gli*. Cf. *Inf.* XXII, 73.

149. *da indi*: From the Latin *de inde*, "then."   *gratu-lando*: "Rejoicing with him."

150. *novella*: "News."   *el* = *egli*.

152. *tre volte cinse me*: St. Peter "crowns" Dante thrice, even as he crowned Beatrice (vss. 22-24).   *cinse*: "En-circled." The subject is "lume" in vs. 153.

154. *sì nel dir li piacqui*: Thus Dante has "passed" the first part of what proves to be an "entrance" examination, with the highest mark possible, considering the examiner: nothing less than a *summa cum laude*!   *li* = *gli*.

CANTO XXV

1–12. *Se mai continga . . . fronte*: "Until the very end of his life Dante cherished, at the bottom of his heart, a hope that he might be called back to his city, to that Florence which he so loved and so reviled. Pathetic indeed is the yearning expressed in the opening lines of this canto. Some day, he thinks, his great poem may win such fame as to 'overcome the cruelty that locks him out'—'la crudeltà che fuor mi serra.' In earlier years, addressing one of his lyrics as he sent it forth, he had said (*Rime*, CXVI, 77-79):

> Forse vedrai Fiorenza, la mia terra,
> Che fuor di sè mi serra,
> Vota d'amore e nuda di pietate.

[. . . mayhap to see my city Florence, who bars me out from her, void of love and stripped of pity.]

The longing to return is voiced in the *Convivio*, I, iii, 4; and the same sentiment is treated half playfully, half sadly, in the first Eclogue, 39-50" (Gr).

1. *continga*: Subjunctive form of *contingere*; cf. the Latin *contingat*. In the present context the meaning is: "should it happen." *poema sacro*: Cf. *Par*. XXIII, 62: "sacrato poema."

2. *ha posto mano e cielo e terra*: The verb in the singular serves a plural subject, as so often in the poem, and is effective here in binding together, as it were, the whole universe, declaring that nothing less than the whole is the subject of this poem.

3. *molti anni*: The received opinion is that Dante composed his poem between 1310 and 1320, a period of only ten years —and what years for the exile! Now he is within nine cantos of the end, as he opens with one of the most poignant and personal passages in the entire work. Can the number nine be accidental in this case?   *macro*: Cf. *Purg.* IX, 138.

4. *la crudeltà che fuor mi serra*: The Neri, or Blacks, exiled Dante from Florence in 1302, and the poet was never allowed to return to the city.

5. *ovile*: Cf. "l'ovil di San Giovanni" in *Par.* XVI, 25. *agnello*: Cf. Ier. 11:19; Ecclus. 13:21; Isa. 11:6, 65:25. See P. Villari (1905), p. 293, for the opening passage of a law proposed in Florence in 1291, in which the metaphor of lambs, wolves, and fold occurs.

6. *nimico*: Following upon the figure of Dante as the lamb, "nimico" is the object of the "wolves" who devised against him as he grew up in the city and took finally an active role in its political life. For *nemico* as object in such a construction, see n. to *Inf.* II, 61.

7. *vello*: "Fleece," obviously continuing the metaphor of the lamb and the sheepfold.

8. *fonte*: In the Baptistery, where he was baptized. Cf. *Inf.* XIX, 17.

9. *cappello*: "Wreath." Cf. the OFr and Provençal *chapel*, and see Boccaccio, *Decam.* I, 1 (vol. I, p. 29, ll. 4-7).

10. *però = perciò.   conte = cognite*, "known." Cf. Gregory, *In Ezech.* I, iii, 1: "Per fidem namque ab omnipotenti Deo cognoscimur." ("Now we are known to almighty God through faith.")

12. *lei*: I.e., *essa*, meaning "la fede." *girò*: See *Par.* XXIV, 151-52.

14–15. *la primizia . . . suoi*: "The first fruit which Christ left of his vicars" is Peter, first of the popes. Cf. *Inf.* II, 24.

17–18. *ecco il barone . . . Galizia*: This is James the Apostle, also known as St. James the Great and St. James of Compostela. Son of the fisherman Zebedee and of Salome, and brother of John the Apostle and Evangelist, he was put to death by Herod Agrippa I shortly before the day of the Passover in 44 (Actus 12:2). According to tradition, James preached the Gospel in Spain. He later returned to Jerusalem, and after his death his body was miraculously transferred to Santiago de Compostela, then the capital of Galicia. The relics of the saint were said to have been discovered in 835 by Theodomir, bishop of Iria, who was guided to the spot by a star, whence the name (*Campus Stellae*).

Pilgrimages to the tomb of St. James at Santiago de Compostela were so frequent in the Middle Ages as to be second only to those to Rome itself, and in fact, as Dante explains in the *Vita nuova* (XL, 6-7), those who made the pilgrimage to St. James' tomb are properly and specifically known as *peregrini*, as distinguished from *palmieri* and *romei*:

> Peregrini si possono intendere in due modi, in uno largo e in uno stretto: in largo, in quanto è peregrino chiunque è fuori de la sua patria; in modo stretto non s'intende peregrino se non chi va verso la casa di sa' Iacopo o riede. E però è da sapere che in tre modi si chiamano propriamente le genti che vanno al servigio de l'Altissimo: chiamansi palmieri in quanto vanno oltremare, là onde molte volte recano la palma; chiamansi peregrini in quanto vanno a la casa di Galizia, però che la sepultura di sa' Iacopo fue più lontana de la sua patria che d'alcuno altro apostolo; chiamansi romei in quanto vanno a Roma, là ove questi cu' io chiamo peregrini andavano.

> *Pilgrims* may be understood in two ways, one wide and another narrow. In the wide sense, in so far as whoever

is outside his fatherland is a pilgrim; in the narrow sense, none is called a pilgrim save him who is journeying towards the sanctuary of St. James, or is returning: and therefore it should be known that there are three ways of properly naming folk who journey for the worship of the Most High. They are called *palmers*, in so far as they journey over the sea, there, whence many times they bring back palm branches; they are called *pilgrims* in so far as they journey to the sanctuary of Galicia, because the tomb of St. James was farther from his own country than that of any other apostle; they are called *romers*, in so far as they journey to Rome, where these which I call *pilgrims*, were going.

17. *barone*: Cf. *Par.* XXIV, 115, where Peter is so termed.

18. *vicita = visita.* There are other examples of the form *vicitare* in early Italian. On Petrocchi's preference for this form, see his vol. I, *Introduzione*, p. 443.   *Galizia*: Galicia (ancient Gallaecia), region and ancient kingdom in northwest Spain; in Dante's day it was a province of León and Castile.

19. *il colombo*: Both the masculine and the feminine form could be used generically. Thus in the famous simile which introduces Francesca and Paolo the poet uses the feminine form (*Inf.* V, 82), since a woman dominates in that scene, whereas here, for the two apostles, he chooses the masculine form, even though the act of pouting and circling commonly seen among pigeons or doves normally involves male and female as an act of love.

20. *pande*: "Extends," "unfolds," "manifests," from the Latin *pandit*. "Affezione," vs. 21, is the object of the verb.

23. *principe*: Now the apostles are termed "princes," as St. James was called a "baron" before (vs. 17).

24. *il cibo*: Cf. *Par.* XXIV, 1-3.   *prande*: "Feeds," from the Latin *prandet*.

25. *'l gratular*: The reciprocal manifestation of joy and affection. *assolto*: From the Latin *absolutum*, "ended."

26. *coram me*: Latin, meaning "before me." Cf. *Par.* XI, 62. It should be noted that here, as so often in the *Paradiso*, the use of Latin and of Latinisms in Italian lends solemnity and elevation to the style. One remembers Cacciaguida, who spoke in Latin first (*Par.* XV, 28-30) and then "descended" to Italian (*Par.* XV, 44-45).

27. *ignito*: Another Latinism, from *ignitus*, "fiery," "glowing." *volto*: "Face" for "eyes."

29. *Inclita*: Pronounced *ìnclita*, this is yet another Latinism, from *inclitus*, meaning "illustrious." *vita*: "Soul." *larghezza*: "Bounty."

29-30. *la larghezza . . . scrisse*: "In the Epistle of James there are some references to divine liberality" (Gr). See Iac. 1:5: "Deo qui dat omnibus affluenter et non improperat" ("God, who gives abundantly to all men, and does not reproach"), and 1:17: "Omne datum optimum et omne donum perfectum desursum est, descendens a Patre luminum." ("Every good gift and every perfect gift is from above, coming down from the Father of Lights.") Also see Iac. 2:5: "Nonne Deus elegit pauperes in hoc mundo divites in fide et heredes regni, quod repromisit Deus diligentibus se?" ("Has not God chosen the poor of this world to be rich in faith and heirs of the kingdom which God has promised to those who love him?")

30. *basilica*: The "court" of Heaven.

31-33. *fa risonar . . . carezza*: "Three of the disciples (Peter, James, John) were chosen by Jesus to be present, and to receive the clearest revelation of his character, on three different occasions: at the Transfiguration (Mat. xvii, 1-8), in the Garden of Gethsemane (Mat. xxvi, 36-38), and at the raising of the daughter of Jairus (Luke viii, 50-56). On these three occasions Peter, James, and John stand respectively for Faith, Hope, and Love" (Gr). See G. Busnelli (1911a), pp. 151-58.

32–33. *tu sai . . . carezza*: "You know that you personified it [hope] as many times as Jesus bestowed more honor on the three."

33. *fé = fece.   fé più carezza*: Some editors follow the reading "chiarezza" of certain MSS, but the expression *fare carezza* in the meaning "to honor" is well documented in early Italian and fits better here.

38. *ond' io levai li occhi a' monti*: See Ps. 120[121]:1: "Levavi oculos meos in montes, unde veniet auxilium mihi." ("I lift up my eyes toward the mountains, from whence comes my help.")

40. *vuol*: The subject of "vuol" is "Imperadore" in vs. 41.
    t'affronti: "T'affronti" is to be connected with "co' suoi conti" in vs. 42.

42. *conti*: The counts in the imperial court of Heaven are the saints. The feudal terminology, following "barone" in vs. 17 and "Imperadore" in vs. 41, continues now with "conti." With such a figure as is suggested by "aula più secreta," the reader should realize that such metaphors, in their cumulative effect, will finally make it credible to come to God and the vision of Him, not as to a circumference (the Empyrean heaven, synonymous with the mind of God) but as to a center, to God as *the* center.

44. *spene*: "Spene" is the object of "conforte" in vs. 45.
là giù bene innamora: Begets righteous love on earth.

45. *di ciò conforte*: " 'Thou mayest strengthen therewith'— with the recital of what thou hast seen" (Gr).   *conforte = conforti*.

46–47. *dì quel . . . venne*: "Three questions are asked: what is Hope, to what degree dost thou possess it ('how does thy mind blossom with it'), and from what source dost thou derive it? Beatrice (l. 51) forestalls Dante's response to the second question, since his affirmative answer would imply that he thought himself worthy of salvation, and hence might smack of vainglory; to the other two he replies" (Gr). It will be noted that St. James' three questions correspond very closely in nature to those of St. Peter in *Par.* XXIV (53, 85, 91) respecting faith.

49-50. *E quella pia . . . volo*: Over and over again Dante employs figures such as this, which stress Beatrice's allegorical role in the journey. Cf. the first of these, which appears as early in the poem as *Inf.* II, 76-78 (and see the corresponding note).

52-54. *La Chiesa militante . . . stuolo*: "Our band" ("nostro stuolo") is the symbolical representation of the Church Triumphant. This pair of terms (Church Militant and Church Triumphant), firmly established in its Christian concept, will come into play very often as the journey of this living man, still engaged in the warfare of life, approaches the end and the "harvest out of time" which is the Church Triumphant. Cf. *Par.* XXIII, 19-21. Thus "Egypt" and "Jerusalem" in the verses immediately following are established terms for the two conditions, the living on the one hand and the blessed on the other.

55. *Egitto*: By "Egypt" is meant life on earth. See Ps. 113[114]:1; cf. Dante's *Letter to Can Grande* (*Epist.* XIII, 21).

56. *Ierusalemme*: Jerusalem was commonly used to indicate the city of God on high. Cf. Heb. 12:22: "Sed accessistis ad Sion montem et civitatem Dei viventis, Ierusalem caelestem et multorum millium angelorum frequentiam." ("But you have come to Mount Sion, and to the city of the living God, the heavenly Jerusalem, and to the company of many thousands of angels.")

57. *militar*: "Service." Cf. Iob 7:1: "Militia est vita hominis super terram." ("Man's life on earth is a warfare.") *prescritto*: "Closed."

59. *perch' ei rapporti*: "That he may relate" on earth.

60. *quanto questa virtù t'è in piacere*: "Souls in Heaven have no further use for Hope, but St. James loves it still" (Gr).

61. *li = gli.   forti*: "Hard" to reply to.

62. *né di iattanza*: Nor cause for vainglory.

63. *ciò li comporti*: "Help him therein."

64–65. *Come discente . . . esperto*: The simile may be compared with that of the *baccialiere* in *Par.* XXIV, 46-48, and continues to stress the fact of formal examination.

64. *discente*: "Pupil."   *seconda*: "Replies."

65. *libente*: "Willing."   *ch' = che*, i.e., *in cui*.

66. *si disasconda*: "May be disclosed."

67–69. *Spene . . . merto*: The definition of hope given by Dante here is that of Peter Lombard in *Sent.* III, xxvi, 1: "Est enim spes certa expectatio futurae beatitudinis, veniens ex Dei gratia et meritis praecedentibus." ("Now hope is a certain expectation of future beatitude proceeding from God's grace and antecedent merits.") He adds: "Sine meritis aliquid sperare non spes sed praesumptio dici potest." ("Without merits, to hope for something is not hope but presumption.") "When we say that Hope comes from Grace and from antecedent merits, we must remember that these two sources are not of the same kind: the impulse to hope springs from Grace alone, while our merits are, as we know, a necessary condition of the fulfillment of our assurance of salvation. This is explained by St. Thomas in the *Summa Theologiae*, Secunda Secundae, Qu. xvii, Art. 1" (Gr).

67. *uno attender certo*: "A sure expectation."

68. *il qual*: The object of "produce," of which "grazia" and "merto" (vs. 69) are subjects.

70. *Da molte stelle mi vien questa luce*: Cf. Dan. 12:3: "Qui autem docti fuerint fulgebunt quasi splendor firmamenti, et qui ad iustitiam erudiunt multos quasi stellae in perpetuas aeternitates." ("But they that are learned shall shine as the brightness of the firmament: and they that instruct many to justice, as stars for all eternity.")

71. *quei*: David.   *distillò*: "Instilled."

73–74. *Sperino in te . . . tuo*: See Ps. 9:11[10]: "Et sperent in te qui noverunt nomen tuum." ("They trust in you who cherish your name.")

73. *teodia*: "Theody," sacred song.

76. *Tu mi stillasti, con lo stillar suo*: "You did instill it into me with his instilling."

78. *vostra pioggia repluo*: Grace and revelation are commonly symbolized by rain or dew, as that "refreshment" which descends from on high. The reader will note the shift to the plural "vostra," the second person plural which includes both David and St. James.   *repluo*: The Latin *repluo*, "rain down again." The poet has shifted the accent from the first syllable to the penultimate for the sake of the rhyme.

80–81. *un lampo . . . baleno*: James and John, the sons of Zebedee, were surnamed by Jesus (Mar. 3:17) "Boanerges, quod est filii tonitrui" ("Boanerges, that is, Sons of Thunder").

83. *virtù*: Hope.   *seguette = seguì*.

84. *palma*: The victory of martyrdom. He was put to death by Herod Agrippa. See Actus 12:2.   *campo*: "The 'battlefield' of life. James was a strenuous and rigid ascetic" (Gr).

85. *respiri*: "Breathe [i.e., speak] once more."   *ti dilette*: "Are gladdened."

86. *emmi = mi è*.   *diche = dica*.

88–90. *E io . . . amiche*: " 'The token' set up by the Old and the New Testament is indicated in ll. 91-96.—*Ed esso* etc., 'and it (the token) points it out to me,' i.e., points out what blessedness in Heaven means—perfect joy of the body and the spirit" (Gr).

91–92. *Dice Isaia . . . vesta*: See Isa. 61:7: "Propter hoc in

terra sua duplicia possidebunt, laetitia sempiterna erit eis."
("Therefore shall they receive double in their land. Everlast-
ing joy shall be unto them.") Also see Isa. 61:10: "Quia
induit me vestimentis salutis." ("He hath clothed me with
the garments of salvation.") The "double garment" is the
effulgence of the soul and the glorified body.

94. *fratello*: John.   *assai vie più digesta*: "Far more
explicitly."

95. *là dove tratta de le bianche stole*: "St. John 'treats of the
white robes' of the elect in Rev. iii, 5, and vii, 9-17. The
'white robes' symbolize the brightness or glory of 'the souls
that God has made his friends.' The body, after the Resur-
rection, will become bright and pure like the spirit, and will
share in its happiness. According to St. Bonaventure, *Brevi-
loquium*, VII, vii, the body is called the 'second robe' " (Gr).

98. *Sperent in te*: Cf. vs. 73.

99. *tutte le carole*: All the "dances" or circles of the blessed.
Cf. *Par.* XXIV, 16.

100. *lume*: The "light" of St. John.   *si schiarì*: "Bright-
ened."

101-2. *se 'l Cancro . . . dì*: "In mid-winter the constellation
of Cancer, for a month, shines all night long. If it contained
a star as bright as this newly appeared 'crystal,' night, during
that month, would be as light as day. In other words, the ef-
fulgence of St. John is as bright as the sun" (Gr).

103-11. *E come surge . . . immota*: The three representa-
tives of the Christian virtues dance before Beatrice, as the
virtues themselves did (in allegorical form) in *Purg.* XXIX,
121-29.

105. *novizia*: "Bride."   *fallo*: "Failing," i.e., vanity or
love of display.

108. *conveniesi = si conveniva*.

112-13. *Questi è . . . pellicano*: See Ioan. 13:23: "Erat ergo

recumbens unus ex discipulis eius in sinu Iesu, quem dilige-
bat Iesus." ("Now one of his disciples, he whom Jesus loved,
was reclining at Jesus' bosom.")

113. *pellicano*: See Ps. 101:7[102:6]: "Similis factus sum
pellicano solitudinis." ("I am like a pelican of the wilder-
ness.") "It was generally believed that the pelican brings its
young back to life with its own blood; hence this bird was
taken as the symbol of Christ" (Gr).

113-14. *questi fue . . . eletto*: John was entrusted with the
care of Mary. See Ioan. 19:27: "Deinde dicit discipulo: Ecce
mater tua. Et ex illa hora accepit eam discipulus in sua."
("Then he said to the disciple, 'Behold, thy mother.' And
from that hour the disciple took her into his home.")

115-17. *né però . . . sue*: The construction is somewhat in-
volved. "La vista sua" ("her eyes") is the object of
"mosser," of which the subject is "le parole sue" ("her
words"). That is, her speaking did not cause her to turn her
eyes away from the three apostles, neither as she made ready
to speak ("prima"), nor after she had spoken ("poscia").

115. *però = per ciò*.

118. *adocchia*: Cf. *Inf.* XV, 22, and *passim*.   *s'argo-
menta*: "Strives." Cf. *Inf.* XXII, 21.

119. *di vedere eclissar lo sole un poco*: "Dante had an op-
portunity to see seven eclipses of the sun, two of them total
in Italy" (Gr).

123. *per veder cosa che qui non ha loco*: "Dante is trying
to see, through the effulgence, the body of St. John, believ-
ing, according to an old legend, that John was taken up to
Heaven in the flesh" (Gr). See Ioan. 21:22-23: "Dicit ei
Iesus: Sic eum volo manere donec veniam, quid ad te? Tu
me sequere. Exiit ergo sermo iste inter fratres quia discipulus
ille non moritur; et non dixit ei Iesus: Non moritur; sed: Sic
eum volo manere donec veniam, quid ad te?" ("Jesus said
to him [Peter], 'If I wish him [John] to remain until I come,
what is it to thee? Do thou follow me.' This saying therefore

went abroad among the brethren, that that disciple was not to die. But Jesus had not said to him, 'He is not to die'; but rather, 'If I wish him to remain until I come, what is it to thee?'") "In a fresco, attributed to Giotto, in Santa Croce, John is rising in body, obliquely, from the grave to God" (Gr).

124. *saragli = vi sarà.*

125. *tanto . . . che*: "Until."

126. *con l'etterno proposito s'agguagli*: "Shall be equal to the eternal purpose." See Eph. 1:4: "sicut elegit nos in ipso ante mundi constitutionem" ("even as he chose us in him before the foundation of the world"). In *Conv.* II, v, 12, Dante tells us that the elect are to fill the places of the fallen angels, who were "forse in numero de la decima parte" ("[perhaps in] the number of a tenth part") of all the angelic orders.

127. *le due stole*: The "two robes" are the effulgence of the spirit and the glorified body.

128. *son le due luci sole che saliro*: On Christ's rising from death in His body, see Thomas Aquinas, *Summa theol.* III, q. 53, a. 3.

130–32. *A questa voce . . . spiro*: I.e., at the *beginning* of the words spoken by St. John, not at the end, both the dance ("giro") of the three apostles and their song (see vss. 106-8) cease.

131. *con esso*: "Together with."   *mischio*: The apostles' song is now called a "mischio" because the voices are three and a "triune breathing" ("trino spiro").

133. *cessar*: "Avoid."

134–35. *li remi . . . fischio*: The vigorous simile is taken from Statius, *Theb.* VI, 799-801.

134. *ripercossi*: "Driven."

138. *per non poter*: "At being unable."

CANTO XXVI

1–79. *Mentr' io . . . poi*: The reader will note that during the entire examination on *caritas*, or love, the third theological virtue, Dante is blinded, a fact which can hardly fail to bring to mind Cupid blindfolded and many another such traditional association of blindness with love. In this striking context it should also be noted that no definition of love is given in the examination, as it is with faith and hope. This serves to stress the fact that love is primarily a matter of the will, not of the intellect. Dante is simply asked *what* he loves, and *why*. The examination concludes what amounts to a kind of "entrance examination," the "entrance" being into the region of eternal blessedness above. Cf. *Conv.* III, xiv, 14, where Dante writes: "onde la nostra buona fede ha sua origine; da la quale viene la speranza, [che è] lo proveduto desiderare; e per quella nasce l'operazione de la caritate. Per le quali tre virtudi si sale a filosofare a quelle Atene celestiali" ("whence our excellent faith hath its origin, from which cometh the hope of that for which we long and which we foresee, and from this is born the activity of charity; by which three virtues we rise to philosophise in that celestial Athens").

The fact that this examination on the three virtues is indeed an entrance examination is precisely what is underscored, for the attentive reader, by the closing words of *Par.* XXIII, that is, just before the examination is to begin, with *Par.* XXIV and with St. Peter as first examiner. Now it will be remembered that the two keys that were left to Peter by Christ are (as the poet has chosen to conceive the matter) in the hands of the guardian angel at the gate of Purgatory proper, the *entrance* to Purgatory (*Purg.* IX, 117-29). But Peter's presence here in Paradise, framing the examination cantos XXIV-XXVI (for Peter appears centrally on the scene in *Par.* XXVII), and the reference in *Par.* XXIII, 139, to him as "the one who holds the keys to such glory" (the glory above this heaven, in the Empyrean) clearly signal the fact that the wayfarer here passes through a kind of "gateway" (symbolically conveyed), if not a material gate such as that of Purgatory, where the keys actually are.

1. *dubbiava*: The verb conveys the sense of hesitation and of fear. Cf. *Inf.* IV, 18; *Purg.* III, 72; XX, 135.

2. *de = da.*   *fiamma*: That of St. John.

3. *spiro*: "Voice" (a breathing forth); cf. *Par.* XXIV, 32.

4–5. *risense de la vista*: "Regain your sight."

5. *in me consunta*: "Lost by looking upon me."

6. *la compense*: "You make up for it," i.e., by speaking with me and using the light of the mind in place of actual sight.

7–8. *ove s'appunta l'anima tua*: That is, whither, at what principal "target" (vs. 24), does your soul aim? "Aiming," it should be noted, is a matter of the will primarily (see n. to vss. 1-79), and love is primarily of the will. And, as noted, no definition of love is required here.

8. *e fa ragion che*: "And know that," "and realize that." Cf. *Inf.* XXX, 145.

9. *non defunta*: "Not lost forever," but only temporarily "confounded."

10. *dia*: I.e., *divina*. Cf. *Par*. XIV, 34; XXIII, 107. This is the "region de li angeli" (*Par*. XX, 102).

11. *lo sguardo*: It should be recalled that Beatrice has kept her eyes on the three apostles and has not yet turned from them to look at Dante. Cf. *Par*. XXV, 110-11; 115-17.

12. *Anania*: Ananias, the disciple at Damascus, cured St. Paul of his blindness by "laying his hands upon him." See Actus 9:17-18:

> Et abiit Ananias, et introivit in domum; et imponens ei manus dixit: Saule frater, Dominus misit me Iesus, qui apparuit tibi in via qua veniebas, ut videas et implearis Spiritu Sancto. Et confestim ceciderunt ab oculis eius tamquam squamae, et visum recepit; et surgens baptizatus est.

> So Ananias departed and entered the house, and laying his hands upon him, he said, "Brother Saul, the Lord has sent me—Jesus, who appeared to thee on thy journey—that thou mayest recover thy sight and be filled with the Holy Spirit." And straightway there fell from his eyes something like scales, and he recovered his sight, and arose, and was baptized.

13. *Al suo piacere*: "At her pleasure," "whenever it may please her."

14-15. *che fuor porte . . . ardo*: Cf. *Purg*. XXX, 41-42.

16. *Lo ben che fa contenta questa corte*: This is divine love and the gift of eternal beatitude to human souls.

16-18. *Lo ben . . . forte*: Thus Dante answers St. John's query (vss. 7-8) concerning the object of his love. The subject of the sentence is "Amore," the object is "lo ben," at the beginning, and the verb "legge" clearly bears the meaning of "read" in the sense of "teach."

17. *Alfa e O*: Alpha and omega are the first and the last letters of the Greek alphabet. In the Apocalypse (1:8)—which, it should be remembered, was in Dante's time attributed to

the same apostle John who wrote the fourth Gospel—we find: "Ego sum A et Ω, principium et finis, dicit Dominus Deus." (" 'I am the Alpha and the Omega, the beginning and the end,' says the Lord God.") "The Vulgate in the 13th century read 'alpha et ω' or 'α et ω' " (Gr).   *scrittura*: Out of metaphor this means "all possible objects of love."

18. *o lievemente o forte*: "With lesser or greater emphasis."

19. *voce*: The voice of St. John.

20. *abbarbaglio = barbaglio*.

22. *Certo*: "However," "but."   *a più angusto vaglio*: "With the finer sieve" (one that separates the bran from the flour), that is, "you must make your declaration more precise, you must 'refine' it."

23. *schiarar = chiarire*.

25. *Per filosofici argomenti*: The nature of these is made explicit in vss. 38-39. This amounts to a statement of what human reason can see, what an Aristotle could teach in this regard, as distinguished from divine revelation.

26. *per autorità che quinci scende*: Divine revelation, revealed truth, as conveyed in the Holy Scriptures.

27. *convien che in me si 'mprenti*: "Must needs stamp on me," so that I will be "imprinted by it." For the figure of the stamp on wax, so common in the poem, but more specifically in a context of love, see *Purg.* XVIII, 38-39. Cf. "imprenta" in *Par.* X, 29.

28–30. *ché 'l bene . . . sé comprende*: "For good, as such, kindles love in proportion as it is understood, and kindles the greater love, the more goodness it contains within it" (Gr). This is the philosophical argument, common to Aristotle and other pagan thinkers; it thus corresponds to the "filosofici argomenti" and represents them, continuing through vs. 36. Although love is primarily of the will, Dante's position is repeatedly and consistently on the side of those philosophers and theologians who hold that perception and understanding (acts of the intellect) precede love (an act of the will). Cf. *Purg.* XVIII, 22-27; *Par.* XXVIII, 109-11; and *passim*.

29. *maggio* = *maggiore*. Cf. *Inf.* VI, 48.

31-36. *Dunque a l'essenza . . . prova*: "Since love is attracted by goodness, and all goodness is in God, he must be the primal object of love" (Gr).

31. *a l'essenza*: "A l'essenza" is to be connected with "si mova" in vs. 34.

33. *altro non è ch'un lume di suo raggio*: Cf. *Par.* XXXI, 22-24.

34. *più che in altra convien che si mova*: "Must turn more than to any other [essence]." The subject of "si mova" is "la mente . . . di ciascun che cerne / il vero in che si fonda questa prova" of the next two verses.

35. *cerne*: "Discerns," from the Latin *cernit*.

36. *in che*: "Upon which."   *prova*: "Argument."

37-39. *Tal vero . . . sempiterne*: "This is clearly Aristotle, who teaches that God is the supreme object towards whom the heavens yearn. . . . The extension of this idea from the heavens to the Angels or Deities is not remote from Aristotle's spirit, and is entirely germane to Dante's conception of it. (Compare *Conv.* ii. [4]; and also *Parad.* ii. 139-144. . . .) The principle of lines 28-30 underlies all Aristotle's philosophy; but perhaps Dante had specially in mind the passage in the *Metaphysics* where Aristotle says that what moves other things, though itself unmoved, is 'the object of longing' or 'the object of intellectual apprehension'; and adds that 'the principles of these two are identical.' Albertus (with whom Thomas substantially agrees) interprets them as meaning *appetibile bonum* and *intelligibile bonum*, 'that which asserts itself as good to our desire' and 'that which asserts itself as good to our intellect.' He goes on to explain that the former may be delusive and may be resisted, but the latter 'provoketh our longing without let and without intermediary; because there is no need that it should first announce itself as good through the sense in order to stir the appetite; nor is there any clog to it on the part of the receiving intellect, since the thing loved is good in itself and . . . winneth the undivided longing of him upon whom it is poured' " (TC). See *Inf.* VII, 74, and *Par.* XXVIII and XXIX.

37. *sterne*: "Unfolds," from the Latin *sternit*.

40. *Sternel* = *lo sterne*.   *autore*: God.

42. *Io ti farò vedere ogne valore*: See Exod. 33:19: "Ego ostendam omne bonum tibi." ("I will make all my beauty pass before you.")

43. *Sternilmi tu* = *tu me lo sterni*.

44. *preconio*: "Preconio" is a Latinism. The reference is most probably to the Gospel of John (and this most appropriately, since Dante is speaking with him), for his is the most "theological" of the four Gospels, opening solemnly and mysteriously (see "arcano" in this verse) with the announcement of the Incarnation, God's great sacrifice to man: "In principio erat Verbum." ("In the beginning was the Word.") See also Ioan. 3:16. Some interpreters, however, have held that the reference is to Apoc. 1:8 (see n. to vs. 17). Those who adopt such a view should bear in mind that, for Dante, the author of the fourth Gospel and the author of the Apocalypse are the same author.   *grida*: "Proclaims."

45. *bando*: "Heralding."

46. *Per intelletto umano*: That is, the philosophical arguments which a pagan such as Aristotle was able to formulate by purely human reason.

47. *e per autoritadi*: Cf. vs. 26. These are scriptural authorities. The method of basing a demonstration in theology on both Aristotle and the Scriptures is, of course, constant with Thomas Aquinas and Albertus Magnus, to name but

two theologians.　　*concorde* (from the Latin *concordes*) = *concordi*.

48. *d'i tuoi amori a Dio guarda il sovrano*: "The highest of your loves looks to God." In the examination of a Christian's love, this is the supreme test. Cf. *Purg.* XVII, 97.

49–51. *Ma dì ancor . . . morde*: This is an odd combination of metaphors, but such mixing is common in Dante, as every reader knows by now.

50. *suone* = *suoni* (subjunctive), "you may declare." Cf. *Par.* XV, 68.

53. *l'aguglia di Cristo*: John. The four beasts of Apoc. 4:7 are traditionally identified with the four Evangelists. St. John is the "flying eagle."

54. *professione*: "Declaration," in this examination on love.

55. *Però* = *perciò*.　　*morsi*: The metaphor continues from vs. 51.

56. *lo cor volgere a Dio*: Again, the supreme test. Cf. n. to vs. 48.

57. *caritate*: Love of God is more specifically signified by *caritas* than by *amor*.

58. *l'essere*: "Existence."

59. *la morte ch'el sostenne perch' io viva*: Cf. I Ioan. Apos. 4:7-9: "Carissimi, diligamus nos invicem, quia caritas ex Deo est, et omnis qui diligit ex Deo natus est et cognoscit Deum. Qui non diligit non novit Deum, quoniam Deus caritas est. In hoc apparuit caritas Dei in nobis, quoniam Filium suum unigenitum misit Deus in mundum ut vivamus per eum." ("Beloved, let us love one another, for love is from God. And everyone who loves is born of God, and knows God. He who does not love does not know God; for God is love. In this has the love of God been shown in our case, that God has sent his only-begotten Son into the world that we may live through him.") The reader should not forget that

in Dante's time the apostle John was commonly regarded as the author of the three epistles as well as of the Gospel and of the Apocalypse.   *el = egli* (Christ, both God and man).

60. *quel che spera ogne fedel com' io*: Salvation, eternal beatitude, and the vision of God.

61. *la predetta conoscenza*: See vss. 25-45.

62–63. *tratto m'hanno . . . riva*: The metaphor takes the reader back as far as *Inf*. I, 22-27, the first simile of the poem (see the note corresponding to those verses). See also *Purg*. XVII, 91-139; *Purg*. XVIII; and the opening of *Purg*. XIX.

64–66. *Le fronde . . . porto*: Dante is saying that he loves the various creatures of God's creation (the leaves of His garden) that make up the world, in proportion to the goodness which their Maker (the eternal Gardener) in His predestination has bestowed upon them. The good Christian should love God alone for Himself and love creatures only insofar as they participate in the goodness of God. Cf. Ioan. 15:1: "Ego sum vitis vera, et Pater meus agricola est." ("I am the true vine, and my Father is the vine-dresser.") Again Dante chooses a metaphor from John. The examination on love ends at this point, and therewith the entire "entrance examination" on the three virtues, conducted by the three apostles who represent those virtues.

68–69. *e la mia donna . . . "Santo, santo, santo!"* These words of praise (and now Beatrice joins all the host in chanting them) constitute a "passing mark" for the whole examination that could hardly be higher, for these are words which the Seraphim chant around the throne of God, according to Isa. 6:2-3, and which the four animals chant around the throne in Apoc. 4:8.

70–71. *E come a lume . . . ricorre*: "And as one is awakened by a keen light, because of the spirit of sight running to meet. . . ." Cf. *Conv*. III, ix, 7-10, where the act of sight is described scientifically. Also see *Conv*. II, ix, 5, where Dante speaks of the "nervo per lo quale corre lo spirito visivo" ("nerve along which the visual spirit runs").

70. *si disonna*: Impersonal and passive.

72. *gonna*: "Coat" or membrane of the eye. In *Conv*. III, ix, 13, it is termed a tunic ("tunica").

73. *aborre*: "Shrinks" (from looking too intently). The infinitive is *aborrire*.

74. *nescia*: "Unknowing," "senseless."   *vigilia*: "Awakening."

75. *la stimativa*: The faculty which discerns (the form *estimativa* is also common). This faculty is referred to by circumlocution in *Purg*. XXIX, 49 (see n. to that verse). See B. Nardi (1949), pp. 172-73.

76. *quisquilia*: "Mote."

78. *rifulgea da più di mille milia*: The radiance of Beatrice's eyes would have been visible a thousand miles away.

79. *mei = meglio*. Cf. *Inf*. I, 112, and *passim*.

81. *un quarto lume*: A fourth light has now joined the other three—presumably it did this while Dante was blinded. This proves to be Adam, hidden by his own radiance like all other souls here.

83. *vagheggia*: "Lovingly contemplates." Cf. *Purg*. XVI, 85; *Par*. X, 92; and *passim*. The subject is "l'anima prima," Adam.

84. *la prima virtù*: The power of the "fattor" (vs. 83), God. Cf. *Par*. X, 3; *Conv*. III, vii, 5.

85–87. *Come la fronda . . . soblima*: Cf. Statius, *Theb*. VI, 854-57.

85. *fronda*: "Bough."   *flette*: "Bends."

87. *soblima*: "Uplifts."

88. *fec' io*: "So I stood" (i.e., with bowed head).   *in tanto in quant'*: "While."

89. *stupendo*: "Amazed."   *mi rifece sicuro*: Dante raises his head again.

91–93. *O pomo . . . nuro*: Dante as poet delights in circum-locutions that distinguish Father Adam from the rest of the human race, who descended from him. Cf. *Par.* VII, 26: "quell' uom che non nacque." Now he addresses him as "pomo" (one would think that since Adam's great sin was by way of a *pomo* the term might be avoided in his pres-ence!) and as "padre antico," each circumlocution serving to identify him among all men. "Pomo" is clear enough in its meaning, as is "padre antico" when one realizes that the meaning of "nuro" (from the Latin *nurus*) is "daughter-in-law" in the sense of "wife of any descendant."

94. *a te supplìco*: For the dative construction, cf. the Latin *tibi supplico*. The requirements of the rhyme cause a shift of accent from *sùpplico* to *supplìco*. Cf. *Par.* VI, 91, "re-plìco," and *passim* for other instances of such a shift.

95. *tu vedi*: That is, you see in God my wish to know from you.

97. *Talvolta un animal coverto broglia*: It is not clear, in vss. 97-99, just what kind of creature the poet has in mind—a falcon, or cat, or little pig in a sack, or a horse covered with its trappings?   *broglia*: Cf. the Provençal *brolhar*, "to move," as well as the French *brouiller*.

98–99. *sì che l'affetto . . . 'nvoglia*: "So that its desire [or feeling] is perforce revealed by the response that its wrapper makes to it."

99. *la 'nvoglia*: The modern Italian is *involucro*. Cf. "co-verta," vs. 101. For a like notion respecting these spirits, cov-ered as they are by their radiance, see *Par.* VIII, 54, the image of a silkworm: "quasi animal di sua seta fasciato."

100. *primaia = prima.*

101. *la coverta*: The soul's covering is, of course, pure radiance, spiritual and not material.

102. *quant' ella a compiacermi venìa gaia*: "How joyously it came to do me pleasure."

103. *spirò*: "Breathed forth," i.e., "spoke." Cf. *Par*. XXV, 82.   *proferta = proferita*, "uttered."

106. *speglio = specchio* (i.e., as *passim*, the mind of God).

107-8. *che fa di sé . . . pareglio*: "Which makes itself a [complete or perfect] image of other things, while nothing makes of itself a [perfect] image of it [the mirror]." God reflects everything, but nothing can wholly reflect God. See Thomas Aquinas, *Summa theol*. I, q. 57, a. 2, resp.: "Deus per essentiam suam, per quam omnia causat, est similitudo omnium." ("By His essence, by which He causes all things, God is the likeness of all things.")

108. *lui = a lui,* corresponding to "a l'altre cose."
pareglio: Cf. the French *pareil*. Here the adjective is used as a noun.

109-42. *Tu vuogli udir . . . sesta*: Dante addresses four questions to Adam, who first formulates and then answers them. The questions are answered, however, not in the order in which they are put, but in the order of their importance. First comes the reply to question number three: What was the real nature of Adam's sin? Then follows the answer to question number one: How long ago was he created? Next comes the reply to question number four, which concerns the language that the first man invented and spoke. And last is offered the answer to question number two: How long did Adam stay in the Garden of Eden?

109. *quant' è che*: "How long it is since."

110-11. *costei a così . . . dispuose*: Beatrice, who is beside Dante, and who, in the Garden of Eden, disposed Dante to the ascent: "puro e disposto" (*Purg*. XXXIII, 145).

111. *così lunga scala*: The ladder of contemplation which

reaches from the summit of the mountain all the way to God. The reader will recall the image of the ladder in connection with the heaven of Saturn, heaven of the contemplatives (*Par.* XXII, 68-75).

112. *quanto fu diletto*: In this construction "diletto" is probably a noun.

113. *la propria cagion*: "The true reason." *disdegno*: The wrath of God, resulting from the sin of Adam and Eve in the Garden of Eden.

114. *e che fei*: This anticipates Adam's answer (vss. 124-38) in which he makes it clear that he *did* create or "make" the language he spoke.

115. *Or*: The word clearly signals the beginning of the answers, which now follow. *non il gustar del legno*: For the notion as applied to the tree of the Garden of Eden, cf. *Purg.* XXXII, 43-44.

117. *il trapassar del segno*: "Transgressing the bound." Adam's sin was disobedience, caused by pride (see Thomas Aquinas, *Summa theol.* II-II, q. 163, a. 1) not gluttony, though gluttony resulted from that sin (cf. *Purg.* XXIV, 116-17). See also Augustine, *De civ. Dei* XIV, xii-xiv.

118. *Quindi onde mosse tua donna Virgilio*: "Therefore, in the place whence your lady drew Virgil," i.e., in Limbo. See *Inf.* II, 52-69.

119. *volumi*: "Revolutions," i.e., solar years in the sense expressed in the following tercet with the phrase "tutt' i lumi de la sua strada," that is, all the signs of the zodiac.

120. *questo concilio*: The "assembly" of the blessed (cf. *Purg.* XXI, 16) for which Adam longed for centuries before he was taken from Limbo by Christ (*Inf.* IV, 55).

121. *lui*: The sun. *lumi*: The signs of the zodiac (cf. vss. 119-20).

122–23. *novecento trenta fiate . . . fu'mi*: Cf. Gen. 5:5: "Et

factum est omne tempus quod vixit Adam anni nongenti tri-
ginta, et mortuus est." ("The whole lifetime of Adam was
nine hundred and thirty years; then he died.")

Adding the number of years that Adam lived on earth
(930) to the number of years he spent in Limbo (4,302)
gives a total of 5,232 years between the creation of Adam
and the Crucifixion (cf. *Purg.* XXXIII, 62), hence 6,498
years between the Creation and the date of the journey (i.e.,
5,232 years before the Crucifixion + 1,266 years after the
Crucifixion (cf. *Inf.* XXI, 112-14).

123. *in terra fu'mi*: "Mi" here is the familiar so-called pleo-
nastic reflexive in its distancing function, the distance in this
case, concerning Adam's life on earth, being one both of time
and of space: "down on earth and so long ago," as it were.
For a similar example of the pronoun in this function, cf.
Purg. XXII, 90.

124-26. *La lingua . . . attenta*: "The 'unaccomplishable
task' which Nimrod's people attempted was the building of
the Tower of Babel: Gen. xi, 4-9. Cf. *Inf.* XXXI, 77-78;
Purg. XII, 34.—Dante evidently changed his opinion on this
subject, for in *Vulg. El.*, I, vi, 5-7, he had said that Adam's
language was spoken by all men until the confusion of
tongues, and by the Hebrews after that event. His study of
human speech doubtless led him to the conclusion that an un-
written language could not last without change through
many generations" (Gr). See B. Nardi (1949), pp. 217-47,
and the *Enciclopedia dantesca* under the first "Adamo"
entry.

126. *Nembròt*: Cf. *Inf.* XXXI, 77; *Purg.* XII, 34-36.

127-29. *ché nullo effetto . . . durabile*: "For no product of
reason was ever permanent for all time, because of human
inclination, which varies with the sky" (Gr). "Il cielo" in the
singular refers to the heavenly spheres, the turning of which
constitutes the operation of Nature, as every reader of the
poem knows by now; and reason, in its purely human aspect,
within the realm of Nature, is a human construction. As for

man's variability (as of all other things within the realm of Nature and beneath the sphere of the moon), cf. *Par.* V, 98-99, where, of Dante himself, it is said: "io che pur da mia natura / trasmutabile son per tutte guise!" See also *De vulg. eloqu.* I, ix, 6: "cum . . . homo sit instabilissimum atque variabilissimum animal" ("since . . . man is a most unstable and changeable animal").

130. *Opera naturale è ch'uom favella*: " 'It is a natural operation for man to speak': hence he always does speak, in some fashion" (Gr).

131-32. *ma così o così . . . v'abbella*: Nature here appears as the subject of this statement and is almost personified in the usual sense of "the operation of the heavenly spheres on the sublunar world." Nature leaves it to man to speak as he pleases, literally "as it suits him" ("secondo che v'abbella"). For the notion in the scholastic view of language in this regard, cf. Thomas Aquinas, *Summa theol.* II-II, q. 85, a. 1, ad 3: "Significare conceptus suos est homini naturale; sed determinatio signorum est secundum humanum placitum." ("It is natural to man to express his ideas by signs, but the determination of those signs depends on man's pleasure.") The idea is common to scholastic thought. See P. Rotta (1909), pp. 186-87.

132. *abbella*: A common Provençalism. Cf. *Purg.* XXVI, 140.

134. *I s'appellava*: "We do not know where Dante got the idea that the first name of God was *I*. This letter is the initial of *Jehovah*, and also of *Jah*: cf. Ps. lxviii (Vulg. lxvii), 4 ('extol him . . . by his name Jah'). Moreover, standing for the number 1, it is the symbol of unity. See D. Guerri, 'Il nome adamitico di Dio' in *Di alcuni versi dotti della 'Divina Commedia*,' 1908" (Gr).

136. *El*: "*El* is the Hebrew name. St. Isidore, *Etymologiae*, VII, i: 'Primum apud Hebraeos Dei nomen *El* dicitur.' ('The first name of God with the Hebrews was El.')" (Gr). The names Jehovah and Elohim are the two chief names used for the Deity throughout the Hebrew Scriptures.

137–38. *ché l'uso . . . vene*: Cf. Horace, *Ars poetica*, vss. 60-63:

> ut silvae foliis pronos mutantur in annos,
> prima cadunt; ita verborum vetus interit aetas,
> et iuvenum ritu florent modo nata vigentque.
> debemur morti nos nostraque. . . .

As forests change their leaves with each year's decline, and the earliest drop off: so with words, the old race dies, and, like the young of human kind, the new-born bloom and thrive. We are doomed to death—we and all things ours.

139–42. *Nel monte . . . sesta*: Adam now replies to the second question (see vs. 112), and many readers (especially readers of Milton) will be surprised to learn how brief a time our first parents sojourned in the Garden of Eden: only a little more than six hours! Among the various estimates (Genesis has nothing precise to say on the matter), Dante chose one of the shortest, that of Petrus Comestor (whom the poet mentions in *Par.* XII, 134), *Hist. schol., Liber Genesis* XXIV: "Quidam tradunt eos fuisse in paradiso septem horas." ("Some hold that they were in the garden for seven hours.") This brief time is said by Dante to have been "from the first hour to the one that follows the sixth, when the sun changes quadrant" (that is, passes from the first quadrant, or 90°, to the second), i.e., from sunrise (6:00 A.M., apparently, at the time of the Creation, when the sun was in Aries —see *Inf.* I, 37-40) to the hour that follows noon.

139. *Nel monte che si leva più da l'onda*: Cf. *Purg.* III, 14-15; XXVIII, 97-102.

140. *con vita pura e disonesta*: I.e., "before my sin and after."

142. *l'ora sesta*: Students of the numerical architecture in the *Commedia* may find it significant that, by answering this question last, the poet is able to present, as the last word, the number *six* explicitly expressed ("sesta"), but the number seven in actual meaning (the seventh hour). Since there are

thirty-three cantos in the *Paradiso*, this last word of the present canto may be seen to mark off the remaining area of the poem, made up of seven cantos. This is the more remarkable, architecturally, since the first seven cantos of the *Inferno* were marked off as such by the special beginning of *Inf.* VIII (see n. to *Inf.* VIII, 1-2). Thus a seven-canto area at the beginning and the same at the end underscore a "framing" number seven. On this number as the central number of the whole structure, see C. S. Singleton (1965).

CANTO XXVII

1–5. *Al Padre . . . l'universo*: The host of souls seen in the eighth heaven now sing the Gloria Patri of the liturgy of the Church: "Gloria Patri et Filio et Spiritui Sancto, sicut erat in principio et nunc et semper et in saecula saeculorum." ("Glory to the Father, to the Son, and to the Holy Ghost, even as in the beginning so now and ever throughout all time.") In this particular context, following Dante's brilliant passing of his entrance examination, this represents the highest mark conceivable! A soul out of time, a living man in this case, now crosses over to the "celestial Athens" (see n. to *Par.* XXVI, 1-79) that lies ahead and above. The reader will not forget, in such a context, the "Gloria in excelsis" (*Purg.* XX, 136) that was sung by *all* Purgatory when Statius was liberated therefrom, and as it was sung for him, so is it sung for each soul when it has finished its period of purgation. Thus here all Paradise joins in the singing (though this is a little hard to conceive, and many commentators insist that it is only the souls of the eighth circle who sing). The poet's language is hyperbolic in the visual field as well, for what the pilgrim sees now seems to him "un riso de l'universo," no less, the radiance of all the triumphant souls in their joy over this wayfarer's successful progress toward God.

8. *intègra*: Pronounced *ìntegra* in modern Italian; here the word means "perfect."

9. *sanza brama sicura ricchezza*: The souls of the elect enjoy full beatitude, as the reader was told by Piccarda as the journey entered into the first of the heavens (see *Par*. III, 64-85). Nor do they fear ever to lose this condition. It is truly a "secure wealth," as is here declared.

10. *face* (from the Latin *faces*) = *faci* (cf. "concorde" in *Par*. XXVI, 47). The four "torches" are the lights of Peter, James, John, and Adam.

11. *quella*: The flame of St. Peter.

13–15. *e tal ne . . . penne*: If the planets Jupiter and Mars were birds and should molt and exchange feathers with each other, Jupiter would turn red and Mars white. Cf. *Purg*. II, 14, and *Par*. XIV, 87, for the red color of Mars; for Jupiter's whiteness, see Dante's comment in *Conv*. II, xiii, 25: "Giove è stella di temperata complessione, in mezzo de la freddura di Saturno e de lo calore di Marte." ("Jove is a star of temperate composition betwixt the cold of Saturn and the heat of Mars.") Dante notes that Jupiter "intra tutte le stelle bianca si mostra, quasi argentata" ("shows white among the stars, as though of silver"). Cf. *Par*. XVIII, 96. Thus Peter's effulgence reddens for indignation, as will now be clear. Grandgent judges the figure "whimsical." It *is* curious, at least. However, the early commentator Buti does not find it too far-fetched to compare planets to birds, observing: "Le penne dei pianeti s'intendono li colori de' raggi dei quali risplendono, come le penne de li uccelli appaiano diverse, per diversi colori che dimostrano." ("By feathers of the planets we are to understand the colors of the rays wherewith they are resplendent, just as the feathers of birds appear diverse because of the different colors which these display.")

15. *cambiassersi* = *si cambiassero*.

16. *comparte*: "Distributes" (cf. *Inf*. XIX, 12). Perhaps the most striking example of the direction of providence in

the configuration of the souls in a given sphere is the great eagle formed by the lights (souls) in the heaven of Jupiter (note there too an association with birds). See *Par.* XIX.

17. *vice*: "Vice" (from the Latin *vices*) is actually a plural here (cf. "face," vs. 10), meaning "turns" in speaking, singing, silence, movement, rest.   *officio*: The specific function each soul must serve.

19–21. *Se io mi trascoloro . . . costoro*: St. Peter has blushed red with shame, and as he explains the cause of his indignation all the souls of this heaven will also blush. Hence the change from white to red comes to affect the whole heaven in this sense.

22–24. *Quelli ch'usurpa . . . Dio*: The reference is to Boniface VIII, and Peter's denunciation of him, with the phrase "il luogo mio" used three times, could not be couched in stronger language.

22–23. *il luogo mio . . . mio*: For the repetition of "il luogo mio," cf. Ier. 7:4, where "the temple of the Lord" occurs three times.

23. *vaca*: "Is vacant." Some commentators would take this to mean that Boniface's very election to the supreme office was invalid, but it is necessary to consider the perspective of this judgment from Heaven, looking down to earth, and the very important qualifying phrase "ne la presenza del Figliuol di Dio" (vs. 24). It is not the validity of Boniface's election to the office that is pointed to, but the corruption which he brought to the office, he and his curia.

It seems well not to forget other verses concerning Boniface (among them, *Purg.* XX, 85-90), where he is recognized as the true vicar of Christ on earth. Those verses express indignation from quite another—a human and earthly —perspective. As the reader will soon see, there is yet to come a still more terrible thrust at him (*Par.* XXX, 148).

24. *ne la presenza*: "In the sight of."

25. *cimitero mio*: St. Peter's "burial place" is Rome, where

he suffered martyrdom (see *Par*. IX, 139-41).   *cloaca*:
"Sewer," one which carries all the blood that is being shed
in Rome, and near Rome, among Christians (see *Inf*.
XXVII, 85-90) as well as all the corruption of the papal
court.

26-27. *'l perverso . . . sù*: This is Satan, of course. Cf. *Inf*.
XXXIV, 121-26.

27. *si placa*: "Is well pleased," "is content."

28-29. *Di quel color . . . mane*: Cf. Ovid, *Metam*. III,
183-85:

> qui color infectis adversi solis ab ictu
> nubibus esse solet aut purpureae Aurorae,
> is fuit in vultu visae sine veste Dianae.

And red as the clouds which flush beneath the sun's
slant rays, red as the rosy dawn, were the cheeks of
Diana as she stood there in view without her robes.

28. *che*: The subject of "dipigne" in vs. 29.   *per lo sole
avverso*: "The sun being opposite."

32. *di sé sicura*: Certain of her own blamelessness.   *fal-
lanza*: An archaic form of *fallo*, some blameworthy act.

33. *pur*: "Merely."   *fane = fa*. Cf. "pòne" in *Inf*. XI,
31; "vane" (= *va*) in *Purg*. XXV, 42; and *passim*.

34. *così Beatrice trasmutò sembianza*: Commentators debate
the exact meaning here. Does Beatrice blush as do Peter and
all the other souls, even the whole heaven? Or does she grow
pale? Certainly, as many have pointed out, a passage in the
Convivio (IV, xxv, 7) can appropriately be brought to bear
here, as a gloss:

> Lo pudore è uno ritraimento d'animo da laide cose, con
> paura di cadere in quelle; sì come vedemo ne le vergini
> e ne le donne buone e ne li adolescenti, che tanto sono
> pudici, che non solamente là dove richesti o tentati sono
> di fallare, ma dove pure alcuna imaginazione di venereo
> compimento avere si puote, tutti si dipingono ne la fac-
> cia di palido o di rosso colore.

Pudicity is a shrinking of the mind from foul things, with the fear of falling into them; as we see in virgins and in good women and in the adolescent, who are so modest that not only where they are urged or tempted to err, but where only a bare imagination of venereal pleasure can find place, are all painted in the face with pale or with red colour.

But, as is clear, this gloss would allow for either blush or pallor. And the implied simile of vss. 35-36 adds the implication that her countenance grows "dark" in some way comparable to the darkness that came over the earth at the Crucifixion. In any case, this must carry out the first part of the true simile (vss. 31-33), but the answer is left unclear.

35-36. *e tale eclissi . . . possanza*: Cf. Matt. 27:45: "A sexta autem hora tenebrae factae sunt super universam terram usque ad horam nonam." ("Now from the sixth hour there was darkness over the whole land until the ninth hour.") Also see Luc. 23:44-45; Mar. 15:33.

36. *la supprema possanza*: Jesus Christ, the Word made flesh—God and man.

37. *procedetter = proseguirono*.   *sue*: St. Peter's.

39. *piùe*: "More," that is, than his voice had changed.

40. *Non fu la sposa di Cristo allevata*: St. Peter's terrible denunciation of the corrupt papacy and Rome begins here and extends through vs. 66. It is the most impressive of all the denunciations of its kind in the poem, because it is pronounced by St. Peter himself, the first and greatest of popes (cf. *Inf.* II, 24), but the reader will recall many another in the course of the poem, such as that pronounced by Dante as he stood over the simoniac pope Nicholas III (*Inf.* XIX, 90-117).   *allevata*: "Established and nurtured."

41. *Lin*: St. Linus, generally considered the immediate successor to Peter as pope. Jerome gives the year A.D. 67 as the date of his accession; others place it in the year A.D. 64. He is said to have been beheaded by one Saturninus in 76 or 79.

Cleto: St. Cletus (or Anacletus), pope from *ca.* A.D. 79 to *ca.* A.D. 90, was the successor of St. Linus. He was martyred under Domitian.

42–43. *per essere . . . lieto*: Cf. I Pet. 5:1-4:

Seniores ergo qui in vobis sunt, obsecro consenior et testis Christi passionum, qui et eius quae in futuro revelanda est gloriae communicator: pascite qui in vobis est gregem Dei, providentes non coacte sed spontanee secundum Deum, neque turpis lucri gratia sed voluntarie, neque ut dominantes in cleris sed forma facti gregis ex animo; et cum apparuerit princeps pastorum, percipietis immarcescibilem gloriae coronam.

Now I exhort the presbyters among you—I, your fellow-presbyter and witness of the sufferings of Christ, the partaker also of the glory that is to be revealed in time to come—tend the flock of God which is among you, governing not under constraint, but willingly, according to God; nor yet for the sake of base gain, but eagerly; nor yet as lording it over your charges, but becoming from the heart a pattern of the flock. And when the Prince of the shepherds appears, you will receive the unfading crown of glory.

Compare the denunciation in *Inf.* XIX, 90-117.

44. *Sisto e Pio e Calisto e Urbano*: Sixtus I was pope (*ca.* 115-125) during the reign of the Emperor Hadrian. Pius I, pope from *ca.* 140 to *ca.* 155 or 157, was contemporary with the Emperor Antoninus Pius. Callistus I, pope from 217 to 222, was succeeded by Urban I as pope from 222 to 230. All four were known as early martyrs.

45. *fleto*: "Weeping," from the Latin *fletus*. The tears were shed for the persecutions and martyrdoms of the early Church.

46–48. *Non fu . . . cristiano*: Peter is saying that the first popes never intended that their successors should treat the Guelphs (papal supporters) as sheep and the Ghibellines as goats. Cf. Matt. 25:31-33.

49–51. *né che le chiavi . . . combattesse*: Nor, Peter continues, was it intended that the keys that were consigned to him should become an emblem on a standard. For the keys, cf. *Purg.* IX, 117-19; *Par.* XXIV, 35; and Matt. 16:19. Members of the papal troop sent against Frederick II in 1229 wore this token on their shoulders and were called *chiavi-segnati* ("those marked by the keys"). In Dante's own time the pope was warring against Christians (see *Inf.* XXVII, 85-90).

50. *signaculo = segnacolo*, "ensign," "emblem," from the Latin *signaculum*.

52. *figura di sigillo*: The papal seal bears the image of St. Peter.

55–56. *In vesta . . . paschi*: Cf. Matt. 7:15: "Attendite a falsis prophetis, qui veniunt ad vos in vestimentis ovium, intrinsecus autem sunt lupi rapaces." ("Beware of false prophets, who come to you in sheep's clothing, but inwardly are ravenous wolves.")

55. *vesta = veste*.

57. *difesa di Dio*: God's providential prevention of these terrible things.   *perché pur giaci?* "Pur" here has a function similar to that in *Inf.* V, 21, denoting continuation. Freely, this means: "Why do you continue to refrain from intervention?" For this kind of question addressed to the Lord, cf. Ps. 43[44]:23-24: "Exurge, quare obdormis, Domine? exurge, et ne repellas in finem. Quare faciem tuam avertis?" ("Awake! Why are you asleep, O Lord? Arise! Cast us not off forever! Why do you hide your face?") The reader will recall other passages where the poet addresses the Deity in similar anguish. Cf. *Purg.* VI, 118-20, for example. But Dante never lost faith in the ultimate intervention of God's providence, a faith which is expressed here (vss. 61-63) by St. Peter.

58. *Caorsini*: Cahors, capital of the ancient province of Quercy in southern France, was a nest of usury (see *Inf.* XI,

50). John XXII, pope from 1316 to 1334, came from that town. He is referred to by Dante in *Par.* XVIII, 130-36.

Guaschi: The predecessor of John XXII, Clement V, was a Gascon; he is mentioned in *Inf.* XIX, 82-87; *Purg.* XXXII, 148-60; *Par.* XVII, 82. The Gascons had generally the reputation of being avaricious and grasping (see Villani, VIII, 80).

59. *principio:* "Beginning."

61-63. *Ma l'alta provedenza . . . concipio:* Dante's optimism and abiding faith in God's providence, so often expressed throughout the poem, return, after the dismay expressed. The reference to Scipio Africanus obviously looks to a temporal power, as directed by God, to restore order and justice to the world; many similar passages in the poem, beginning with the very first canto, express the confidence that such will be the way God will choose (cf. *Inf.* I, 101-11, and the n. to *Inf.* I, 101-2). See also the *De monarchia* in its total thesis in this regard.

61. *Scipio:* Scipio Africanus the Elder, who conquered Hannibal and thus saved Rome. See *Conv.* IV, v, 19.

62. *difese a Roma:* "Defended *for* Rome."   *la gloria del mondo:* It was the "glory" of the Romans that they conquered and governed the whole world.

63. *soccorrà = soccorrerà.   io concipio:* St. Peter is reading in the "book" or seeing in the "mirror" that is the mind of God, hence this is no personal revelation, but vouchsafed by God's providence.

64-66. *e tu, figliuol . . . ascondo:* The living man on this exceptional journey is solemnly charged by St. Peter himself to disclose to the living that which he, Peter, has not concealed from him. The poet's mission is a lofty one indeed, in this respect.

64. *per lo mortal pondo:* The phrase clearly stresses the fact that the pilgrim is a living man, here in the flesh, and thus one who bears a "weight" which will cause his sojourn in

these lofty regions to be brief. This point is brought out more emphatically toward the very end of the poem (*Par.* XXXII, 139). Cf. also *Par.* I, 73-75.

65. *ancor giù*: "Back down to earth."

67-72. *Sì come di vapor . . . soggiorno*: These lines present the strange and lovely picture of an inverted snowstorm. Dante sees "the ether grow beautiful, flaked with triumphant vapors"—the swarm of bright spirits returning to the Empyrean—"just as our air flakes downward with frozen vapors" in midwinter when the sun is in Capricorn: "when the horn of the Sky Goat and the Sun touch each other." It must be remembered that "wet vapors" produce rain, snow, and hail, while wind, lightning, and meteors are caused by "dry vapors." The reader may recall an inverted rain referred to by Dante in *Vita nuova* XXIII, 25. These inversions (such as that of the inverted "plant" of time itself in vss. 118-19 of the present canto) are contributing to an experience which the reader will undergo as he passes, with the pilgrim Dante, from time to eternity, from the universe with earth at the center to a universe that has God as its center: a complete change in gravitation, from the material to the spiritual.

70. *etera*: Cf. *Par.* XXII, 132.

71. *fioccar*: The verb is intransitive here.   *vapor triunfanti*: The flames of those who are already part of the Church Triumphant.

72. *avien = avevano*.

73. *viso*: "Sight."   *suoi = loro*, "their."

74. *'l mezzo*: "The intervening space." Cf. *Purg.* I, 15; XXIX, 44-45.   *lo molto*: "Its great extent."

75. *li = gli* (my sight).   *li tolse il trapassar del più avanti*: "Prevented it from passing beyond." "Mezzo" is the subject of "tolse." "Il più avanti" is used substantively.

76. *assolto*: "Freed." Cf. *Par.* XXV, 25.

77. *Adima*: A verb created by Dante, based on the Latin adjective *imus*, "lower." Cf. *Purg.* XIX, 100.

78. *se' vòlto*: "How you have revolved."

79. *Da l'ora ch'io avea guardato prima*: See *Par.* XXII, 127-54. Repeating explicitly a previous downward look at the material universe, this amounts to a kind of "farewell" gaze earthwards, from this point so near the confine of that universe (for the tenth heaven, the Empyrean, is a purely spiritual heaven, and only one material heaven, the ninth, remains). It will be recalled that this eighth heaven is also the one from which Scipio Africanus the Younger, uplifted thereto, according to Cicero's *De re publica*, saw the universe beneath him (see n. to *Par.* XXII, 127-54).

80–81. *i' vidi mosso . . . clima*: "Compare xxii. 124-154. The 'climata' are latitudinal divisions which may be applied equally to the heavens and the earth. There is some difference of usage amongst the mediaeval geographers, but it seems probable that Dante regarded the Twins, in which he was situated, as lying on the upper confines of the first clima. The passage, therefore, seems to mean simply, 'I had revolved, with the first clima, through a whole quadrant'" (TC). See E. Moore (1903), pp. 101-5.

But perhaps the entire passage, vss. 80-87, presents serious difficulties generally for the modern reader, who would profit from the clear explanation and illustration which Grandgent gives it: "When Dante once more gazes down at the earth, he finds that during the interval since the end of his previous observation (XXII, 133-153) he has traversed 90°, or a quarter of the whole circumference. Six hours, then, have elapsed. At the close of the first look, he was on the meridian of Jerusalem; he is now in line with the Strait of Gibraltar, having covered the whole length of the Mediterranean, whose extent was curiously exaggerated by the ancients (cf. IX, 82-87). Had the sun been under Gemini (but so placed as not to obstruct his sight), he could have beheld, from his present viewpoint, the whole western hemisphere, from Jerusalem to the Island of Purgatory; but, as he tells us (ll. 86-87), 'the sun was ahead of me, distant a sign and more beneath my feet.' The signs of the zodiac are, of course, all in the eighth heaven. Dante is in Gemini; and the sun is 'in,' or under, Aries. Between Gemini and Aries is Taurus. We may suppose that the poet is at or near the western extremity of Gemini, and we know that the sun is in line with a point something less than a third of the way from the eastern end of Aries. Each of the twelve signs is 30° long. A line drawn from Dante to the center of the earth, and a line drawn from the sun to the same point, would then be separated by an arc of not more than 40°. It follows that some 40° of Dante's field of vision, on the eastern side, is in the dark, or at least in the twilight. Instead, therefore, of seeing clearly to the Phoenician coast, at the eastern end of the Mediterranean, he sees 'almost the shore' (l. 83)—perhaps as far as Greece. It should be remembered that all this Mediterranean region was observed by him at the time of his first inspection." See Fig. 3.

3. Dante's view of the earth from the heaven of the fixed stars

82–83. *sì ch'io vedea . . . Ulisse*: Thus, beyond Cadiz, Dante from this lofty point is able to see the "mad track," or, more exactly, the "mad fording" of Ulysses. This is the second time since it was first recounted (in *Inf.* XXVI) that Ulysses' journey has been remembered. The first was, most significantly, at the moment when Dante, issuing from Hell, came to stand on the shore of the mountain of Purgatory to look out over the waters offshore where Ulysses and his crew had perished (see *Purg.* I, 131-32, and nn. to *Purg.* I, 132 and 133). Ulysses' journey may be called a "varco," for he sailed from one shore, that of the Strait of Gibraltar, almost to another, that of the mountain-island of Purgatory. When (in *Purg.* I) this "varco" was first recalled, Dante had just come from Hell to stand on the shore of this mountain-island, had accomplished, that is, a kind of fording himself. This was followed by the arrival of the boatload of souls on a journey which had followed the attempted course of Ulysses' fording, and again the notion of "fording" is brought out, by the phrase "tra liti sì lontani" (*Purg.* II, 33). In short, the wayfaring Dante and the souls of those who pass to Purgatory both complete successfully a fording which is denied Ulysses.

And now, as the pilgrim is about to cross over from "the human to the divine, from time to eternity" (*Par.* XXXI, 37-38), his last glance earthwards takes in the "mad crossing" of Ulysses: again he stands on a "shore" that will forever be denied to the ancient hero.

83–84. *di qua presso il lito . . . carco*: "Nearly the shore" (see n. to vss. 80-81), the Phoenician shore, where Europa mounted the back of Jupiter disguised as a bull (see Ovid, *Metam.* II, 833-75, especially vss. 868-69).

85. *fora = sarebbe* in the sense of *sarebbe stato*.

86. *aiuola*: The word marks a definite recall to the previous time when Dante looked down (*Par.* XXII, 151).

87. *sotto i mie' piedi un segno e più partito*: See the quotation from Grandgent in n. to vss. 80-81.   *partito*: "Separated," "distant."

88. *donnea*: From an original Provençal word, *domnejar*, which had much the same sense as here. The verb is used three times in Dante's works: *Rime* LXXXIII, 52; *Par.* XXIV, 118; and the present verse. Essentially amorous in significance, the word means "to court," or (like *vagheggiare*, which is often used in the poem) it may mean "to gaze amorously upon."

89. *ridure* (from the Latin *reducere*) = *ridurre*. Such northern Italian forms were occasionally used by Tuscan poets (e.g., *condure*, *redure*, *trare*). See E. G. Parodi (1957), p. 237. Cf. *Par.* XXII, 21: "redui."

91–93. *e se natura . . . pitture*: "And if nature or art ever made bait of human flesh or paintings of it, to catch the eyes in order to possess the mind" (Gr). For some reflections on this basic aesthetic principle of art as Dante saw it and practiced it in the *Divine Comedy* and other works, see C. S. Singleton (1969).

91. *fé* = *fece*, in the sense which Grandgent has seen: "*ever* made."

94. *tutte*: *Tutte le pasture.* *adunate*: I.e., *raccolte*, "gathered together."

95. *refulse*: Cf. *Par.* IX, 32, 62; XXVI, 78.

96. *viso*: "Face," but especially the eyes.

97. *virtù*: "Power." *indulse*: "Granted," a Latinism. Cf. *Par.* IX, 34.

98. *del bel nido di Leda*: "Leda's nest" is the constellation of Gemini, in which Dante has been while in the sphere of the stars (see *Par.* XXII, 110-20); it is so called because the twins Castor and Pollux were the children of Leda. According to late versions of the story, Jupiter visited Leda in the form of a swan, and she brought forth two eggs, from one of which issued Helen, and from the other the twin brothers Castor and Pollux. (Cf. Ovid, *Heroides* XVII, 55-56.) At their death Jupiter placed the twins among the stars as the

constellation of Gemini. Cf. *Inf.* I, 105, and the correspond-
ing note.

99. *ciel velocissimo*: The ninth heaven, or Primum Mobile,
which contains no bodies, neither stars nor planets, but is the
outermost of the moving spheres, imparting its motion to the
rest. It is bounded by the Empyrean. For its rapidity, see
Conv. II, iii, 8-9, where Dante writes:

> Veramente, fuori di tutti questi, li cattolici pongono lo
> cielo Empireo, che è a dire cielo di fiamma o vero lumi-
> noso; e pongono esso essere immobile per avere in sè,
> secondo ciascuna parte, ciò che la sua materia vuole.
> E questo è cagione al Primo Mobile per avere velocis-
> simo movimento; chè per lo ferventissimo appetito ch'è
> 'n ciascuna parte di quello nono cielo, che è immediato
> a quello, d'essere congiunta con ciascuna parte di quello
> divinissimo ciel quieto, in quello si rivolve con tanto
> desiderio, che la sua velocitade è quasi incompre-
> hensibile.

> But beyond all these the Catholics assert the empyrean
> heaven, which is as much as to say the heaven of flame,
> or the luminous heaven; and they assert it to be immova-
> ble, because it hath in itself with respect to every part
> that which its matter demandeth. And this is the cause
> of the *primum mobile* having the swiftest motion, be-
> cause by reason of the most fervid appetite wherewith
> every part of this ninth heaven, which is next below it,
> longeth to be conjoined with every part of this divinest,
> and tranquil heaven, it revolves therein with so great
> yearning that its swiftness is scarce to be comprehended.

impulse: "Thrust," from the Latin *impellere*.

100. *vivissime*: "Quickest," as compared with the eight
heavens revolving within it (see n. to vs. 99). This reading
has been much debated, some texts having "vicissime" or
"vicinissime." Petrocchi, however, for reasons completely
cogent (see his long note on this, in vol. I, *Introduzione*,
pp. 245-47) has accepted "vivissime," which stresses the ex-

treme rapidity of this heaven.　　*eccelse*: This is the highest
of the moving heavens.

101. *uniforme = uniformi*. All the parts of this ninth heaven
are said to be uniform, in contrast with the other heavens,
since unlike the others it contains no planet or star.

101–2. *ch'i' non so dire . . . mi scelse*: In the other heavens
the place chosen for Dante has been either the planet con-
tained by each or the constellation. But in this ninth heaven,
where there are no such bodies, Dante cannot say just where
he was received into it, what place Beatrice chose for him
therein.

103. *'l mio disire*: The desire to know just where he is, in
this last of the material heavens.

106–8. *La natura . . . meta*: "Natura" here means specifi-
cally "the natural property or principle in virtue of which";
cf. a similar use in *Par*. IV, 131. But a more general sense of
the word is also part of the meaning, since the whole opera-
tion of Nature in this Aristotelian-Ptolemaic universe is
synonymous with the turning of the spheres, which begins
with the Primum Mobile.

106–7. *che quieta il mezzo*: The natural principle holds the
earth motionless at the center of this universe.

107. *tutto l'altro*: All the nine revolving heavens or spheres.

108. *meta*: A primary meaning of *meta* in Latin is "bound-
ary" or "limit." Thus, according to the way in which a *meta*
may be regarded, it may signify either "beginning" or "end."
In this case it is being viewed as "beginning," for here, in the
Primum Mobile, is initiated the whole movement of all the
spheres.

109–11. *e questo cielo . . . piove*: "La mente divina" is
synonymous with the tenth, or Empyrean, heaven. See *Conv*.
II, iii, 8-9, quoted in n. to vs. 99. The passage continues
(*Conv*. II, iii, 10-11):

E quieto e pacifico è lo luogo di quella somma Deitade
che sola [sè] compiutamente vede. Questo loco è di spi-

riti beati, secondo che la Santa Chiesa vuole, che non
può dire menzogna; e Aristotile pare ciò sentire, a chi
bene lo 'ntende, nel primo De Celo et Mundo. Questo
è lo soprano edificio del mondo, nel quale tutto lo mon-
do s'inchiude, e di fuori dal quale nulla è; ed esso non
è in luogo ma formato fu solo ne la prima Mente, la
quale li Greci dicono Protonoè. Questa è quella magni-
ficenza, de la quale parlò il Salmista, quando dice a Dio:
"Levata è la magnificenza tua sopra li cieli."

But still and tranquil is the place of that supreme deity
which alone completely perceiveth itself. This is the
place of the blessed spirits, according as holy Church,
which may not lie, will have it; and Aristotle likewise
seemeth to agree hereto (to whoso rightly under-
standeth) in the first *Of Heaven and the World*. This
is the sovran edifice of the world, wherein all the world
is included, and outside of which there is nought; and
it is not itself in space, but was formed only in the
primal mind, which the Greeks call *protonoë*. This is
that "magnificence" whereof the Psalmist spoke when
he saith to God: "Thy magnificence is exalted above the
heavens."

The reader will note that as the journey approaches this end
(the mind of God and the vision of God) the question of
where something is arises frequently ("dove" is here used as
a noun, as in *Par.* III, 88; XII, 30; XXII, 147). The general
principle affirmed in these verses will be repeated in the
cantos ahead: namely, that the location of things (each of the
revolving heavens, for instance) can only be determined by
reference to that which contains it, or finally by reference to
the one Absolute, whether this be the all-containing Em-
pyrean heaven (the mind of God, as above) or God as a
fixed point (*Par.* XXVIII, 95).

111. *l'amor che 'l volge*: See the quotation from the *Con-
vivio* in n. to vs. 99, where Dante terms this *amore* an "ap-
petito" and "desiderio."   *la virtù ch'ei piove*: The power
which it (the ninth heaven) transmits to the rest of the
world. See *Par.* II, 112-32.

112–14. *Luce e amor . . . intende*: On the "light" and "love" of the Empyrean heaven, see the quotations from the *Convivio* in nn. to vss. 99 and 109-11. Grandgent sums up the matter as follows: " 'Light and love envelop it round about, as it envelops the other heavens; and that belt (the Empyrean, or Heaven of light and love) is governed only by him (God) who girds it.' Every sphere except the ninth is surrounded by another sphere; but the ninth, the outermost sphere of the material universe, is surrounded only by the world of spirit, the Heaven of light and love, the Empyrean, which is the Mind of God. Moreover, every material heaven is directed by an order of angelic Intelligences; but in the Empyrean the only governing Intelligence is the Lord, in whom it exists." The nine spheres are turned by intellection: cf. *Par.* VIII, 37, where the poet cites that *canzone* of the *Convivio* (*canzone* I, 1, *Conv.* II) which, in its first verse, with " 'ntendendo," brings out this principle, a principle which derives ultimately from Aristotle's conception. "Intende" here (vs. 114) concerns this principle, as applied to God and His tenth heaven.

113. *precinto*: Cf. *Inf.* XXIV, 34.

115–16. *Non è suo moto . . . questo*: This statement relates to the principle of the *dove*, as glossed in n. to vss. 109-11. The outermost, or tenth, heaven, which is motionless, "measures" the ninth, or Primum Mobile, because it contains it; this ninth heaven "measures" the other eight, on the same principle. The essentially hierarchical nature of the principle is clear.

116. *mensurati = misurati*, "measured," but also "regulated."

117. *come diece da mezzo e da quinto*: Just as ten is determined by five (its "half") and two (its "fifth").

118–19. *e come il tempo . . . fronde*: The unit of time is the day, which is determined by the revolution of the Primum Mobile, which transmits that motion to the other spheres; the other spheres are included in the total revolution which

makes time. Some readers have judged this metaphor gro-
tesque, mainly because of the inversion involved: time grows
downward, having its roots in the Primum Mobile, where it
originates, and since the movement of this ninth heaven is in-
visible to mortals (no heavenly body being contained in it),
the "roots" of this potted plant are hidden. The reader should
see the inversion in the context of others: the upside-down
trees of Purgatory (*Purg.* XXII, 133-34; XXXII, 40-41),
the inverted snowstorm of the present canto (vss. 70-71),
and yet other inversions to come. Benvenuto aptly terms the
ninth sphere the "radix temporis" ("root of time").

121–23. *Oh cupidigia . . . onde*: The whole metaphor may
remind the reader of other metaphorical waters in the poem,
including the first simile (*Inf.* I, 22-27). See also *Inf.* II,
107-8, and *Inf.* VI, 7-21, which describes the constant down-
pour on the gluttons who were never satisfied and who lay
face down and hence did not raise their eyes. Cf. the figure
of "amor torto" as a stream (*Par.* XXVI, 62-63). A flood
of water and incessant rain becomes the dominant feature of
the figure here and leads at once into what is another principal
theme of this poem at so many points, degeneration in the
human race (see, e.g., *Purg.* XIV, near the center of the
poem, where in vss. 86-87 human degeneration is seen to
have its cause in cupidity of earthly things, as here now in
Paradise). And this will now lead into that other familiar
theme, of humanity without proper guidance, either spiritual
or temporal, which is even closer to the exact center of the
whole poem (*Purg.* XVI, 94-129).

126. *bozzacchioni*: "Abortions." The word is still used in
Tuscany to designate plums that are spoiled on the tree by
too much rain.

127. *son reperte*: From the Latin *repertae sunt*.

129. *pria fugge che le guance sian coperte*: Before the child
becomes a man, with a beard (cf. *Purg.* XXIII, 110), faith
and innocence are fled.

132. *per qualunque luna*: At no matter what time or season.

443

"Luna," however, suggests a period of fasting such as is prescribed by the Church according to a lunar calendar (Lent).

134. *loquela intera*: This matches "lingua sciolta" in vs. 131.

136-38. *Così si fa . . . sera*: This is a much-debated tercet, but the most plausible view of its meaning is the following. "He who brings morning and leaves evening" is obviously the sun. Now Circe was the daughter of the Sun and, according to the familiar story, had the power to change men into beasts. It is also possible that the "old witch" seen in the second dream of Purgatory (*Purg.* XIX, 7-24) represents Circe, since she declares that she turned Ulysses from his way, and she certainly symbolizes the sins of upper Purgatory, among which is avarice, or cupidity, the keynote of Beatrice's present discourse. Thus Circe, daughter of the Sun, would represent worldly goods generally, viewed as tempting man and turning him from heavenly things. "Aspetto" can here bear the meaning of "sight." On the basis of these several possible meanings in the detail, Beatrice is saying that the white skin of human nature (the innocent child) turns "black" (i.e., is corrupted by sinful desire) as soon as it looks upon worldly goods, that is, at the first sight of them ("primo aspetto"), in their power to tempt. Thus Circe is called "bella" in precisely the sense of having this power as temptress. Such an interpretation of this notoriously difficult tercet has the merit of fitting perfectly into the line of Beatrice's discourse, from vs. 121 to the end of the canto. For the many other interpretations, see the *Enciclopedia dantesca* under the entry "Circe." For Circe as the daughter of the Sun, cf. Virgil, *Aen.* VII, 11; Ovid, *Metam.* XIV, 346.

139. *facci = faccia*.

140-41. *pensa che . . . famiglia*: See the end of n. to vss. 121-23.

142. *gennaio*: "Gennaio" is to be counted as two syllables. Cf. "migliaio" in *Purg.* XIII, 22; "primaio" in *Purg.* XIV, 66; and "beccaio" in *Purg.* XX, 52. *si sverni*: "Be unwintered," become a spring instead of a winter month.

143. *per la centesma ch'è là giù negletta*: "Through an inac-
curacy in the Julian calendar, which made the year of 365
days and 6 hours, the solar year gained over the standard
year about one day in a century; in the course of something
less than 90 centuries, then, January would have been pushed
into the spring, if the error had not been corrected (as it was
in 1582 under Gregory XIII, when the present calendar was
adopted). The line means: 'But before 9000 years have gone
by,' i.e., 'within a little while'" (Gr). The statement thus
represents a familiar form of irony, through overstatement.

144. *raggeran*: Other editors have followed the reading
"ruggiran." See Petrocchi, vol. I, *Introduzione*, pp. 247-48.
The verb "raggeran" obviously brings in the heavenly bodies,
with the influence which they "ray down" upon earth, and
the stars can bring the needed temporal leader, through God's
providence. See *Purg.* XXXIII, 40-45; *Inf.* I, 101-5, and the
corresponding notes.

145. *fortuna*: "Storm."

146–48. *le poppe . . . fiore*: In this figure the "umana fami-
glia" (vs. 141) which is *sviata* for lack of leadership of the
temporal monarch so long awaited, becomes a fleet of many,
many ships ("classe," from the Latin *classis*), which, as a
result of the storm, will turn to sail in the opposite (and cor-
rect) direction. Then, with a shift of metaphor of the sort
which the poet delights in, the final verse returns to the meta-
phor of vs. 126.

1. *'ncontro a*: Beatrice's judgment on the present deplorable condition of the human family is adverse, hence "against."

2. *miseri mortali*: Cf. Virgil, *Georg.* III, 66: "miseris mortalibus" ("hapless mortals"). *aperse*: The subject of "aperse" is "quella" (Beatrice), in vs. 3. See "apersi" in this sense in *Inf.* X, 44.

3. *quella che 'mparadisa la mia mente*: The whole verse reflects perfectly the role which Beatrice has had as guide, all the way through Paradise, and "la mia mente" keeps to the proper focus on the allegory. *'mparadisa*: The verb was created by Dante; cf. "inciela," *Par.* III, 97.

4. *doppiero*: A large torch (termed *duplerius* in medieval Latin) consisting of two candles.

5. *che se n'alluma retro*: "Who is illuminated by it from behind himself." The reflexive construction is thus passive in meaning.

6. *o in pensiero*: Or even before he is expecting it.

8. *li = gli*.   *el*: "It," the truth.

9. *con esso*: "With it," the glass or mirror.   *come nota*

con suo metro: "Nota" is the singing, "metro" the rhythm of the musical accompaniment. Cf. "nota" in *Purg.* XXXII, 33.

11. *ch'io feci*: "I became."

12. *onde a pigliarmi fece Amor la corda*: "Corda" is used here in the sense of "noose" or "snare," formed by a cord or small rope. (Cf. *Inf.* XVI, 106-8.) "Amor" represents the typical personification of the god of love, as common in the early love lyric and in Dante's *Vita nuova*; and in this sense the reference goes back to the time when Dante first became enamored of Beatrice, as recounted in the *Vita nuova*. Here, of course, Beatrice's eyes, as mirrors revealing something sacred and mysterious, have the function they have had since she became the guide in this journey. Cf., for example, *Purg.* XXXI, 118-23, where they are said to mirror the griffin in his dual nature. Vision with Beatrice is always fundamentally by reflection, in the allegory of the three lights. See C. S. Singleton (1958), p. 18 and *passim*.

13-39. *E com' io . . . s'invera*: Dante now turns from gazing on the image reflected in Beatrice's eyes to behold directly a symbolic vision that represents the relation of God to His first creatures, the angels.

13. *tocchi = toccati*.

14. *volume*: "Revolution," i.e., heaven. Cf. *Par.* XXIII, 112; XXVI, 119. "Quel volume" is this very ninth heaven, the Primum Mobile.

15. *quandunque nel suo giro ben s'adocchi*: Apparently whenever someone gazes intently upon this heaven one sees the astounding vision which is now presented (vss. 16-39). This can only mean a gazing in absorbed contemplation, of course, and points to the basic allegory through the *Paradiso*, which is that of a rising in contemplation, by the "ladder" which reaches all the way to the Empyrean (*Par.* XXI, 29; XXII, 68). In climbing this ladder, the verse is implying, one would always come upon such a vision in the ninth heaven, acknowledged heaven of the angels.

16. *un punto*: The point represents God symbolically and most appropriately. "In Dante's new vision God appears as a microscopic point of exceeding brightness. The center of a circle is like the Almighty in its immobility and its lack of extension. Minuteness is a token of indivisible unity; and the one Indivisible Unit is the center and source of all light" (Gr). Cf. Thomas Aquinas, *Summa theol.* I, q. 3, a. 7; q. 11, aa. 2-4.

19. *quinci*: "From here below," from the earth.   *poca =* *piccola*. Cf. *Inf.* XX, 115.

20. *locata con esso*: "Placed near it" or "placed beside it," as the next verse makes clear.

21. *come stella con stella*: The comparisons continue to be with heavenly bodies and phenomena, all suggesting that Dante is here looking upwards to the symbolic vision disclosed to him.

22-23. *Forse cotanto . . . dipigne*: "*Cotanto* is to be connected with *distante* in l. 25, and *cotanto distante* is correlative with *quanto appresso*: 'as near as' . . . 'so far away' . . ." (Gr). The distance suggested is "quite near," as compared with other distances in the heavens, among stars and planets. Cf. *Par.* X, 67-69.

23. *alo*: "Halo," from the Latin *halos*.   *luce*: "Light," the moon or a star. "Luce" is the object of the verb "cigner."   *'l = lo*, as also in vs. 24: "che 'l porta."

25. *igne*: From the Latin *ignis*, "fire."

26-27. *si girava . . . cigne*: The "motion that circles the world with the greatest velocity" is the Primum Mobile or ninth heaven, where Dante now finds himself. See also *Purg.* XXXIII, 90; *Par.* I, 123; XIII, 24; XXVII, 106-8.

This reference, comparing the innermost circle in the vision with the ninth heaven of the material universe, is a signal of a correspondence that will be developed now.

27. *mondo*: The universe.

28. *circumcinto*: "Girt round."

31–33. *Sopra seguiva . . . arto*: The reader may note that only the seventh sphere in Dante's vision receives as much as a whole tercet in this enumeration. For other pointers to the number seven as a special number, see *Par.* XXVI, 141-42, and the n. to *Par.* XXVI, 142.

31. *sparto*: "Widespread."

32. *'l messo di Iuno*: Juno's messenger is Iris, the rainbow. Cf. *Purg.* XXI, 50-51; *Par.* XII, 12.

33. *intero*: That is, if the rainbow were a complete circle and not an arc.   *arto*: "Narrow." Cf. *Inf.* XIX, 42; *Purg.* XXVII, 132.

34–36. *Così l'ottavo . . . l'uno*: In the spiritual world of Dante's vision each successive circle of fire, counting out from the innermost to the outermost, moves more slowly in proportion to its distance from the point of light.

37–38. *e quello . . . pura*: And the innermost of the wheels of fire, closest to the point of light, is the brightest and purest ("sincera").

38. *cui*: "Cui" is the dative here, depending on "distava." "La favilla" is the subject.

39. *credo*: The verb represents Dante's continuing attempt to understand the symbolic vision before him. What he believes is, of course, the truth in this regard.   *però che* = *perciò che*.   *di lei s'invera*: "Partakes of its truth." Vss. 107-8 of this canto can serve as a further gloss.

40. *cura*: Dante's doubt and desire to know and understand.

41–42. *Da quel punto . . . la natura*: This clearly reflects Aristotle's statement in the *Metaphysics* summarizing his speculations on the unmoved mover as final cause and supreme good. In the Latin translation of Aristotle known to Thomas Aquinas this reads (*Metaphys.* XII, 7, 1072[b]): "Ex tali igitur principio dependet caelum et natura." ("It is on such a principle, then, that the heavens and the natural world depend.") Aquinas, in his commentary on this point in the *Metaphysics,* states (*Exp. Metaphys.* XII, lect. 7, n. 2534):

> Ex hoc igitur principio, quod est primum movens sicut finis, dependet caelum, et quantum ad perpetuitatem substantiae suae, et quantum ad perpetuitatem sui motus; et per consequens dependet a tali principio tota natura, eo quod omnia naturalia dependent a caelo, et a tali motu eius.

> Hence it is on this principle, i.e., the first mover viewed as an end, that the heavens depend both for the eternality of their substance and the eternality of their motion. Consequently the whole of nature depends on such a · principle, because all natural things depend on the heavens and on such motion as they possess.

Typically, Aristotle speaks of "the heaven" in the singular (as does Dante frequently, here and elsewhere), but the meaning is plural, meaning all the revolving heavens. Nature is synonymous with those revolving heavens. But "il cielo e tutta la natura" is not tautological, for "tutta la natura" points to the operation of the heavens and their influence on the earth at the center and on all things on earth.

It may be noted that here begins, for the reader, the sure experience of a "turning inside-out" which is the culmination, in a sense, of the other experience of "turning upside-down" (see n. to *Par.* XXVII, 67-72). The reader is led into this through Dante's puzzlement and Beatrice's explanation, and the whole matter can be most simply stated in terms of circumference and center. Up to now we have been moving with the wayfarer within a universe that has the motionless earth as the center, and the "mind of God," the Empyrean, as the circumference. But now, in this symbolic vision, the center is shown to be a point, which is God, the circumference is the order of angels which preside over the sphere of the moon—and the earth is nowhere! This experience, as it is prepared for and then finally achieved, is one of the most impressive of the whole poem.

43. *li = gli.*   *congiunto*: "Near."

44–45. *e sappi che . . . punto*: In the vision before the way-
farer the innermost wheel of fire is made up of the highest
order of angels, the Seraphim, as we are soon to realize from
Beatrice's explanation. But the correspondence between the
Seraphim and the Primum Mobile over which they preside
is already emerging, for the knowledgeable reader, from the
touches concerning the rapid movement and the "fiery love,"
for in Aristotle's conception, which Dante follows, the heav-
ens move through desire for the unmoved mover.

45. *ond'*: I.e., *da cui*, "by which."   *punto*: "Pricked,"
i.e., impelled.

46. *mondo*: "Universe."

48. *sazio*: "Satisfied."   *che m'è proposto*: Cf. *Par.* X, 25.
"Proposto" means "set before," as food upon a table.

49. *mondo sensibile*: The physical (material) universe, the
nine spheres with the earth at the center.

50. *volte*: "Revolutions," the revolving heavens or spheres.
Cf. *Purg.* XXVIII, 104.

50–51. *tanto più divine . . . remote*: In the material universe
each heaven, counting out from earth, is more "divine" than
that immediately beneath it, a principle of hierarchy which,
in the medieval conception of the universe, is always
remembered.

51. *centro*: The earth.

52. *disir*: The desire to understand what is stated in
vss. 55-56.

53. *miro*: From the Latin *mirus*, "marvelous."   *angelico
templo*: "Angelic temple" signals the fact that this ninth
heaven is indeed the "heaven of the angels" and that this,
consequently, was (for the poet) the appropriate place for
them to be seen as they are and for them to become the cen-
tral concern and theme.

54. *che solo amore e luce ha per confine*: The wayfarer still has the material universe surrounded by the Empyrean as his "world picture," which explains his puzzlement. Cf. *Par.* II, 112.

55–56. *udir convienmi . . . modo*: It seems best to understand "essemplo" as "model," or "original," and "essemplare" as the "copy." Thus "essemplo" is the symbolic vision before Dante's eyes, with God as a point at the center (a purely spiritual "model," in which the wheels of fire *seem* spheres, but are orders of angels), and "essemplare" is the physical universe bounded by the Empyrean, with the earth at its center surrounded by nine material spheres. Cf. the verb "assemplare" as used in *Vita nuova* I.

55. *convienmi = mi conviene*.

60. *tanto, per non tentare, è fatto sodo*: Few, if any, philosophers have attempted to solve the problem of the relation of the spiritual to the material world, and this "knot," for not being tried ("per non tentare"), has become hard ("sodo").

63. *intorno da esso t'assottiglia*: "Sharpen your wits on it."

64. *Li cerchi corporai*: "The material heavens." The modern reader should bear in mind that in Dante's conception, as in that of Thomas Aquinas and many another philosopher following Aristotle, these heavens are both form and matter conjoined.   *arti*: Cf. vs. 33.

65–66. *secondo il più . . . parti*: The "material heavens" contain, each in itself, a *virtù*. For this virtue and the way in which it is shed upon the earth, see *Par.* II, 112-38.

67. *Maggior bontà vuol far maggior salute*: What has just been termed a *virtù* is now called a "bontà," or goodness, viewed as a beneficent influence shed downwards.   *vuol far*: "Needs must" (no act of volition is implied).

68. *maggior salute maggior corpo cape*: "Corpo" is the subject here, "salute" the object. "Cape" (present indicative of *capere*, "to contain") implies "capability" to contain. Hence

"the greater the material heaven or sphere, the greater its capacity to contain *virtù* or goodness," with the proviso that follows.

69. *s'elli ha le parti igualmente compiute*: "If all its parts are complete," i.e., if it is perfect in all its parts. The qualification is already pointing to the ninth heaven, the Primum Mobile, which is indeed "complete" in all its parts, being entirely "uniform" therein (see *Par.* XXVII, 100-101 and n. to *Par.* XXVII, 101).

70–71. *costui che tutto quanto . . . seco*: The Primum Mobile where Dante and Beatrice now find themselves. The demonstrative denotes proximity.

70. *rape*: "Drags," "pulls," from the Latin *rapit*.

71. *l'altro universo*: All the other spheres contained by the Primum Mobile.   *seco = con sé*, i.e., by its motion.
corrisponde: This is the cardinal point awaited in Beatrice's discourse, of course.

72. *cerchio che più ama e che più sape*: The "circle that loves most and knows most" is the innermost circle of fire, made up of myriads of sparks which represent the Seraphim, the highest order of angels, distinguished always for their most ardent love of God, but here also for their knowledge or vision of God. Cf. *Conv.* II, v, 9, where Dante notes that the Seraphim "veggiono più de la Prima Cagione che nulla angelica natura" ("see more of the first cause than any other angelic nature").

73–75. *per che, se tu . . . tonde*: Dante is invited to take the measure of the problem of correspondence in terms of *virtù*, applied now to the wheels of fire or orders of angels ("le sustanze che t'appaion tonde"), which means of course that the order of the Seraphim, which *seems* ("parvenza") smallest in its circling, is actually the greatest.

76–78. *tu vederai . . . intelligenza*: The correspondence between the "essemplo" (the wheels of fire in the present vision) and the "essemplare" (the wheels or material spheres of the physical universe)—the point that has so puzzled Dante, vss. 46-56—is now evident: it is a correspondence of greater size of the material heavens to the greater love and knowledge of each of the orders of angels that presides over a given heaven.

78. *a sua intelligenza*: With respect to the order of angels from which the *virtù* comes to a given heaven. The singular is used for the plural.

80. *l'emisperio de l'aere*: The air that envelops the earth, our atmosphere.

80-81. *quando soffia . . . leno*: The wind-gods were often represented as heads blowing a threefold blast from the middle and the two corners of their mouths. See the description of Ristoro d'Arezzo, *Della comp.* VII, 3 (pp. 232-33). According to Brunetto Latini (*Tresor* I, cvi, 14) the direct north wind brings clouds and cold, the northwest wind brings snow and hail, while the northeast wind keeps off rain and clouds. It appears evident that Dante is here speaking of the northeast wind.

81. *leno = lene*, "mild."

82. *per che = per cui*.   *roffia*: The word in Tuscan usage, in Dante's time, apparently meant the refuse of tanned hides (see E. G. Parodi, 1957, p. 283), hence the meaning here is "impurity," mists, and the like.

83. *ne*: "In consequence."

84. *paroffia*: "Parish," quarter. *Paroffia* is an old form for *parrocchia*. See E. G. Parodi (1957), p. 282; A. Schiaffini (1922).

85. *così fec'io = così rimasi io*.   *provide*: "Bestowed upon me."

88. *restaro = restarono*, "had ceased."

89-90. *ferro disfavilla che bolle*: Cf. *Par.* I, 60.

90. *come i cerchi sfavillaro*: "The sparks into which the fiery

rings resolve themselves represent the individual angels that compose the orders. Every angel constitutes a species by itself, but nevertheless it belongs to one of the nine orders, and never leaves it (cf. l. 91)" (Gr).

91. *incendio*: "Incendio" is the object of "seguiva."
suo: I.e., *loro*.

92. *'l numero loro*: In *Conv.* II, v, 5, Dante states that the angels are "quasi innumerabili" ("as it were, innumerable"). Thomas Aquinas declares as much in *Summa theol.* I, q. cxii, a. 4, ad 2, quoting Dan. 7:10: "Millia millium ministrabant ei et decies millies centena millia assistebant ei." ("Thousands of thousands ministered to him, and ten thousand times a hundred thousand stood before him.") Aquinas is making the point that "sic ministrantium numerus ponitur indefinitus, ad significandum excessum" ("thus the number of those who minister is indefinite, and signifies excess").

93. *più che 'l doppiar de li scacchi s'inmilla*: "S'inmilla" is a verb invented by Dante; cf. "s'incinqua," *Par.* IX, 40; "s'intrea," *Par.* XIII, 57. Its meaning here is "reaches into the thousands." The "doppiar de li scacchi" refers to an old story according to which the inventor of the game of chess asked of the king of Persia, as a reward, one grain of corn for the first square, two for the second, four for the third, eight for the fourth, and so on, with successive doubling through the sixty-four squares of the chessboard. The total is about eighteen and one half million, million, million. The Provençal poets Peire Vidal and Folquet de Marseille both refer to this tale.

94. *osannar*: "Hosanna sung."

95–96. *che li tiene . . . fuoro*: That is, the fixed point holds each and every angel to its appointed place in the order of the circlings.

95. *ubi*: Latin adverb meaning "where." For "ubi" again, see *Par.* XXIX, 12; and cf. "dove," its Italian equivalent, which is used as a noun in *Par.* XXVII, 109 and elsewhere

in the poem. It may be noted that *ubi* as a substantive is commonly used in scholastic Latin.

97. *dubi = dubbi*. Dante is wondering about the orders of the angels.

99. *Serafi = serafini.   Cherubi = cherubini.*

100. *i suoi vimi = i loro vimi*. "Vimi" (from the Latin *vimen*) are the "bonds" or respective rings to which they are bound, elsewhere termed "incendio" (vs. 91) or "cerchio d'igne" (vs. 25).

101–2. *per somigliarsi . . . soblimi*: Some commentators would interpret "per somigliarsi" as meaning "because they resemble," others take the phrase to mean "in order to resemble." The latter meaning is certainly more in keeping with the following verse and is the correct one. The reader is to see that the Trinity itself is made up of three "circlings," and the meaning of the "point" will open up to that meaning. Cf. *Par*. XXXIII, 116, "tre giri," and 127, "circulazion."

101. *ponno = possono*.

102. *e posson quanto a veder son soblimi*: Cf. I Ioan. Apos. 3:2: "Similes ei erimus, quoniam videbimus eum sicuti est." ("We shall be like to him, for we shall see him just as he is.")
    soblimi = sublimi, "exalted." Their possibility of resembling God is proportionate to the loftiness of the vision which they have of him. Circling is a sign of "intellection," which is "vision," in one of its common meanings.

103. *amori*: For the word as applied to the angels, cf. *Par*. XXIX, 18.   *li = gli*, standing for the dative *loro*, as it often does in spoken Italian. It here refers to the two orders of the Seraphim and the Cherubim.   *vonno = vanno*. The form was used in southern Tuscany and in Umbria. See E. G. Parodi (1957), p. 254.

105. *per che 'l primo ternaro terminonno*: " 'Therefore,' when God created the world 'they closed the first triad.' The

Thrones, like the Cherubim and the Seraphim, receive God within them. . . . The line is very obscure; but the idea seems to be that the designation 'Thrones' is appropriate because these angels form the bottom of the highest set, the sovereign angels being (so to speak) seated upon them. According to Dionysius (*De Caelesti Hierarchia*, VII), the Thrones are so called because they are remote from everything earthly, are close to the highest, receive the divine advent without matter and without motion, carry God, and are fit for divine offices" (Gr). See *Par.* IX, 61-63; Thomas Aquinas, *Summa theol.* I, q. 108, a. 5. It will be noted, here and in the following verses, that the nine orders of angels are carefully divided into three triads.   *terminonno = terminarono.* The tense is narrative, as Grandgent indicates above with the phrase "when God created the world." The ending *-onno* is characteristic of Lucca and Pisa and is here adapted to the rhyme, even though, in *De vulg. eloqu.* I, xiii, 2, Dante actually condemns this as of the Pisans.

106–14. *e dei saper . . . procede*: As vs. 114 suggests, that which is observed in these verses interrupts the exposition of the angelic orders as such to state the nature of the blessedness of them all. Here, as elsewhere, Dante takes his stand with those philosophers and theologians (Thomas Aquinas, Albertus Magnus, and the Dominicans generally) who assigned primacy to the intellect rather than to the will (this latter position being more commonly held by the Augustinian-Franciscan school). Vss. 109-11 take a very clear and explicit stand in the matter. Cf. *Par.* XIV, 40-42, and *passim.*

107. *sua veduta = loro veduta.*

107-8. *si profonda . . . intelletto*: Cf. vs. 39.

110. *atto che vede*: "The act of sight."

111. *quel ch'ama*: The act of loving, which belongs to the will, not to the intellect or to sight, as such.   *poscia seconda*: "Follows after."

113. *che grazia partorisce e buona voglia*: "Che" (i.e., *mer-*

457

cede) is the object of "partorisce," of which "grazia" and "buona voglia" constitute the dual subject. On the point of doctrine, cf. *Par.* XXIX, 61-66. "These are the 'steps': Grace begets good will, Grace and good will constitute desert, desert determines the degree of sight, and sight is the source of love" (Gr). Cf. Thomas Aquinas, *Summa theol.* I, q. 62, a. 4.

115. *L'altro ternaro*: The second ternary. Cf. vs. 105, and the corresponding note.

117. *che notturno Ariete non dispoglia*: "Nocturnal Aries" indicates autumn, because in that season (September 21-October 21) Aries is the constellation opposite the sun.

118. *sberna*: From the Latin *exhibernare*, "sings," as the song of birds in the spring. Cf. *svernare*. See "verna," *Inf.* XXXIII, 135. The cognate expression in this sense is found in early Provençal poetry: the birds celebrate the spring with their song. "Osanna" is the object of the verb.

119. *melode = melodi*. Or quite possibly "melode" is the plural of *meloda*.   *tree = tre*. See "èe" (vs. 123), which is used in rhyme here, as it frequently is in the poem (see, for example, *Inf.* XXIV, 90, and *Purg.* XXXII, 10).

120. *s'interna*: "Threefolds itself." The verb is created by Dante. Cf. "s'intrea," *Par.* XIII, 57.

121. *gerarcia = gerarchia*.   *dee*: "Divinities," orders of angels. The term has been applied to angels before (*Purg.* XXXII, 8). Here it should be noted that the three names of the *orders* are feminine.

124. *tripudi*: "Dances," i.e., orders of angels in their round dance. "Ludi," in rhyme (vs. 126), bears a similar suggestion of sport, diversion, play.

126. *l'ultimo è tutto d'Angelici ludi*: Since this verse concludes the exposition of the angelic orders, the reader might review the whole through the following note by Grandgent: "The nine rings represent the heavenly Intelligences, which

fall into three hierarchies, each composed of three orders: Seraphim, Cherubim, Thrones; Dominations, Virtues, Powers; Principalities, Archangels, Angels. They preside respectively over: the Primum Mobile, the Starry Heaven, the sphere of Saturn; the spheres of Jupiter, Mars, the sun; the spheres of Venus, Mercury, the moon. All these names of angels occur in one place or another in the Bible, but with no suggestion of system; five of them are mentioned by St. Paul (Ephesians i, 21, and Colossians i, 16), who had visited Paradise. St. Ambrose, *Apologia Prophetae David*, V, 20, enumerates nine angelic choirs; but for an exact designation and classification of the orders—with a lengthy but confused account of their functions—we must look to a fifth or sixth century Neoplatonic Greek treatise, *De Caelesti Hierarchia*, sometimes called the Pseudo-Dionysius. . . . The matter is discussed by St. Thomas in the *Summa Theologiae*, Prima, Qu. cviii, and by Dante in the *Convivio, II*, [v]. The present canto corrects an error of arrangement made by the author (and others) in his previous description—a shifting of Thrones, Dominations, Powers, and Principalities. In this chapter of the *Convivio*, 7-11, Dante informs us that the three hierarchies contemplate respectively the three persons of the Trinity—Power, Wisdom, and Love, embodied in the Father, the Son, and the Holy Ghost. And inasmuch as each person can be regarded in three ways—in itself, and in its relation to each of the other two—every hierarchy is divided into three orders. St. Thomas ascribes to the nine orders the following functions: Seraphim, love; Cherubim, sight; Thrones, taking and holding; Dominations, command; Virtues, execution; Powers, judgment; Principalities, direction of nations; Archangels, direction of leaders; Angels, direction of individuals." See the *Enciclopedia dantesca*, under the entry "angelo."

127–29. *Questi ordini . . . tirano*: The principle of hierarchy is now reaffirmed in terms of operation, here the attraction upwards toward God.

127. *di sù tutti s'ammirano*: All the angels of a given order gaze upon God, of course, both in the symbolic representa-

tion of the wheels of fire and in actuality, but the suggestion here is that each order looks with ecstasy or wonder ("s'ammirano") on the next *higher* order and each in turn sheds its knowledge and influence on the next *lower* order, so that the whole hierarchical chain, so to speak, pulls toward God, higher pulling lower (exceptions must be granted in the case of the highest order, the Seraphim, who gaze directly on God, and in that of the lowest, the Angels, who have no order below them which they "pull" upwards).

128. *vincon*: "Prevail."

130. *Dionisio*: Dionysius the Areopagite, an eminent Athenian, whose conversion to Christianity by the preaching of Paul is mentioned in Actus 17:34. He is said to have been the first bishop of Athens and to have been martyred in that city about A.D. 95. There is a tradition that he visited Paris, and an attempt has been made to identify him with St. Denis (third century), the patron saint of France. In the Middle Ages he was universally credited with the authorship of works on divine names, on mystic theology, on ecclesiastical hierarchy, and on celestial hierarchy, all of which now bear the name Pseudo-Dionysius and are admitted to be the productions of a Neoplatonist or of Platonists of the fifth or sixth century. The work on celestial hierarchy, *De caelesti ierarchia*, was translated into Latin in the ninth century by Johannes Scotus Erigena and became the medieval textbook of angelic lore. Dante mentions Dionysius in *Par.* X, 116-17.

133. *Ma Gregorio da lui poi si divise*: Gregory, in *Moral.* XXXII, xxiii, 48, arranges the angelic orders thus: Seraphim, Cherubim, Powers; Principalities, Virtues, Dominations; Thrones, Archangels, Angels. This sequence is followed by Brunetto Latini in the *Tresor* (I, xii, 5) and by Dante in *Conv.* II, v, 6. Elsewhere Gregory has a still different arrangement. See G. Busnelli (1911b); P. Toynbee (1911).

134-35. *sì tosto . . . rise*: The suggestion is that Gregory, in passing through the heavens to his eternal reward in the Empyrean, was shown the present symbolic truth concerning the hierarchical ordering of the angels. Seeing the truth, he laughed at himself and his mistake, then and there!

137. *mortale*: Dionysius.

138. *chi 'l vide qua sù*: St. Paul, who was "caught up to the third heaven" (II Cor. 12:2-4). Cf. *Inf.* II, 28.   *gliel discoperse*: In fact, in *De caelesti ierarchia* (VI) Dionysius affirms that he learned this truth directly from Paul.

CANTO XXIX

1-6. *Quando ambedue . . . dilibra*: At the vernal equinox, when, at dawn and at sunset, the sun and the moon are opposite each other on the horizon, one rising and the other setting.

1. *ambedue li figli di Latona*: "Latona's children" are Apollo and Diana, the Sun and the Moon.

2. *coperti del Montone e de la Libra*: The sun is in Aries (the Ram, "Montone"), the moon is in Libra (the Scales).

3. *fanno de l'orizzonte insieme zona*: "The two luminaries 'belt themselves with the horizon': the horizon line bisects them both" (Gr).

4-6. *quant' è dal punto . . . dilibra*: "As long as is the time between the moment when the horizon runs through the middle of the moon and the sun and the moment when the horizon no longer touches either body, i.e., about a minute." See M. Porena (1930), pp. 201-6. "The sun and the moon, exactly balanced for an instant on opposite sides of the horizon, suggest to the poet the figure of a gigantic pair of scales, suspended from the zenith. And just as, in a balance, one scale immediately goes down, and the other up, so one of the two luminaries rises above the horizon and the other sinks below it" (Gr).

4. *cenìt = zenìt.*

5. *infin che*: "Until."   *cinto*: "Girdle," the horizon.

6. *si dilibra*: "Is unbalanced."

7. *tanto*: " 'So long': correlative with the *quanto* of l. 4. The simile of the sun and moon in balance is used to convey the idea of one instant of intermediate stillness and suspense— the silence that intervenes between Beatrice's speech at the end of the last canto and her discourse that begins in l. 10" (Gr). The simile also serves to open this canto with a sweeping universal kind of view, which "uplifts" and introduces the amplitude of the act of creation itself, which Beatrice is now to present.

8–9. *Beatrice, riguardando . . . vinto*: Thus the stage is set for Beatrice's exalted discourse on the act of creation, as she gazes intently on the point which, symbolically, is God. This is the second of two cantos dealing essentially with angelology. For a reader unfamiliar with the standard procedure of a *summa* of theology, it should perhaps be pointed out that the poem is proceeding thematically in the opposite direction to that of a *summa*: the journey moves ever upwards, toward God, and here comes to a treatise on angels, in these two cantos so near the end, whereas a *summa* begins with God, in its first section of questions, and then passes to the creation or procession of creatures from God (cf. *Summa theol.* I of Thomas Aquinas as it passes from question 43 to question 44), beginning with the highest creatures, which are the angels.

10. *dico*: "Declare."

12. *là 've s'appunta ogne ubi e ogne quando*: Beatrice is looking fixedly at the point which is God, in the symbolic vision, but her declaration means that she is actually seeing reflected in the mind of God (not in this heaven but in the Em-

pyrean) Dante's thought and wish, as so often she and the other blessed have done.   *s'appunta*: "Are centered." The phrase "ogne *ubi* e ogne *quando*" is the dual subject of the verb. Here the vision which has God as center rather than circumference is fully affirmed. All space and all time depend on the one Absolute.   *ogne ubi e ogne quando*: "Ubi" (the Latin adverb) is here used as a noun. (On the similar use of the Italian adverb *dove*, see n. to *Par*. XXVIII, 95.) For *ubi*, cf. *Par*. XXVIII, 95, and for *quando* (also Latin here), see *Par*. XXI, 46, where it is the identical, but Italian, form.

13–18. *Non per aver . . . amore*: These two tercets present the act of creation (a creation *ex nihilo*, be it remembered) as motivated in God not by any desire to add to His own goodness (which is inconceivable, since He is *all* goodness), but by a desire to have other beings, creatures, who might share in that goodness—consequently God's creation is essentially an overflowing or opening-up of His love. This is the doctrine of Thomas Aquinas in *Summa contra Gentiles* II, 46, which extends to the creation of intelligent creatures: "Ad productionem creaturarum nihil aliud movet Deum nisi sua bonitas, quam rebus aliis communicare voluit secundum modum assimilationis ad ipsum." ("The only thing that moves God to produce creatures is His own goodness, which He wished to communicate to other things by likening them to Himself.") Aquinas continues:

> Similitudo autem unius invenitur in altero dupliciter: uno modo quantum ad esse naturae, sicut similitudo caloris ignis est in re calefacta per ignem; alio modo secundum cognitionem, sicut similitudo ignis est in visu vel tactu. Ad hoc igitur quod similitudo Dei perfecte esset in rebus modis possibilibus, oportuit quod divina bonitas rebus per similitudinem communicaretur, non solum in essendo, sed etiam in cognoscendo. Cognoscere autem divinam bonitatem solus intellectus potest. Oportuit igitur esse creaturas intellectuales.

> Now, the likeness of one thing is found in another thing in two ways: first, as regards natural being—the likeness

of heat produced by fire is in the thing heated by fire;
second, cognitively, as the likeness of fire is in sight or
touch. Hence, that the likeness of God might exist in
things perfectly, in the ways possible, it was necessary
that the divine goodness be communicated to things by
likeness not only in existing, but also in knowing. But
only an intellect is capable of knowing the divine good-
ness. Accordingly, it was necessary that there should be
intellectual creatures.

Cf. *Par.* VII, 64-66.

14. *splendore*: "Dante is careful in the use of *splendor* for
reflected, not direct light. (*Epist. ad Can Grand.*, [XIII, 53-
65] and *Conv.* iii. 14 [3-6]). Therefore we must not under-
stand this passage as declaring the manifestation of his own
glory to be God's motive in creation, but rather the confer-
ring of conscious being, the sense of existence, upon his crea-
tures. 'In order that his creatures (*i.e.* his reflected glory, his
splendor) might be able to say: *I am*' " (TC).

15. *Subsisto*: Latin, meaning "I am."

16. *di tempo fore*: "Outside of time," i.e., before time
existed. See vss. 20-21.

17. *comprender*: The infinitive is used as a noun and signi-
fies both spatial and intellectual comprehension.   *i = gli.*

18. *s'aperse*: The verb suggests the opening of a flower. Cf.
Par. XXII, 56, and *Conv.* IV, xxvii, 4: "E conviensi aprire
l'uomo quasi com'una rosa che più chiusa stare non puote."
("And man should open out like a rose that can no longer
keep closed.")

19-21. *Né prima . . . acque*: Time has reference only to cre-
ated things; for God, all time is present, and "before" and
"after" have no significance. Therefore we may not say that
God was inactive "before" the act of creation. See Augustine,
Conf. XI, 13:

At si cuiusquam volatilis sensus vagatur per imagines
retro temporum, et te, deum omnipotentem et omni-

creantem et omnitenentem, caeli et terrae artificem, ab
opere tanto, antequam id faceres, per innumerabilia
saecula cessasse miratur, evigilet atque adtendat, quia
falsa miratur. nam unde poterant innumerabilia saecula
praeterire, quae ipse non feceras, cum sis omnium sae-
culorum auctor et conditor? . . . Cum ergo sis operator
omnium temporum, si fuit aliquod tempus, antequam
faceres caelum et terram, cur dicitur, quod ab opere
cessabas? id ipsum enim tempus tu feceras, nec prae-
terire potuerunt tempora, antequam faceres tempora.
si autem ante caelum et terram nullum erat tempus, cur
quaeritur, quid tunc faciebas? non enim erat tunc, ubi
non erat tempus.

    . . . Tu autem idem ipse es, et anni tui non deficient.
anni tui nec eunt nec veniunt: isti autem nostri eunt et
veniunt, ut omnes veniant. anni tui omnes simul stant,
quoniam stant, nec euntes a venientibus excluduntur,
quia non transeunt: isti autem nostri omnes erunt, cum
omnes non erunt. anni tui dies unus, et dies tuus non
cotidie, sed hodie, quia hodiernus tuus non cedit cras-
tino; neque enim succedit hesterno. hodiernus tuus
aeternitas: ideo coaeternum genuisti, cui dixisti: ego
hodie genui te. omnia tempora tu fecisti et ante omnia
tempora tu es, nec aliquo tempore non erat tempus.

IF any giddy brain now wildly roves over the images of
fore-past times, and wonders with himself, that thou the
God Omnipotent, All-creator and All-supporting, Mak-
er of heaven and earth, didst for innumerable ages for-
bear to set upon such a work, before thou wouldst make
it: let him wake himself and consider well; since he
wonders at mere false conceits. For how could innu-
merable ages pass over, which thyself hadst not made;
thou being the author and creator of all ages? . . . Seeing
therefore thou art the Creator of all times; if any time
had passed before thou madest heaven and earth, why
then is it said, that thou didst forbear to work? For that
very time hadst thou made: nor could there any times
pass over, before thou hadst made times. But if

before heaven and earth there were no time, why is it then demanded, what thou didst? For there was no THEN, whenas there was no time.

. . . Whereas thou art still the same, and thy years shall not fail. Thy years neither go nor come; whereas these years of ours do both go and come, that in their order they may all come. Thy years stand all at once, because they stand: nor are those that go thrust out by those that come, for they pass not away; but these years of thine shall all be ours, when all time shall cease to be. Thy years are one day; and thy day is not every day, but to-day: seeing, thy to-day gives not place unto to-morrow, for neither comes it in place of yesterday. Thy to-day is eternity: therefore didst thou beget him co-eternal to thyself, unto whom thou saidst: This day have I begotten thee. Thou hast made all times; and before all times thou art: nor in any time was time not.

See also *Conf.* VII, 15.

21. *lo discorrer di Dio sovra quest' acque*: "The moving of God upon these waters" means the act of creation. See Gen. 1:2: "Et Spiritus Dei ferebatur super aquas." ("And the spirit of God was stirring above the waters.") The figure is particularly appropriate here, because the ninth sphere was often called the "aqueous heaven." See B. Nardi (1944), pp. 307-13.

22. *Forma e materia, congiunte e purette*: The poet is speaking of pure form (i.e., spirit without matter: the angels), pure matter (i.e., matter without spirit: the stuff of which the earth was made), and form and matter conjoined (i.e., the heavens). Aristotle, in *De anima* II, 2, 414[a], distinguishes between form, matter, and a compound of the two. See E. G. Parodi (1918b), p. 131. Cf. *Par.* VII, 64-72; 130-38. *purette*: "Unmixed," "absolutely pure."

23. *usciro ad esser che non avia fallo*: This threefold creation "issued forth" into an existence that was faultless, perfect.   *avia = aveva*.

24. *come d'arco tricordo tre saette*: Not only is the creation by a triune God threefold, bearing the imprint of its own number upon itself, but the figure of the three-stringed bow and three arrows expresses aim, intention in itself. Cf. *Par.* I, 119; IV, 60; VIII, 103.

25-27. *E come in vetro . . . intervallo*: "It was a received point in the Aristotelian physics that light occupies no time in diffusing itself through a translucent medium or substance. Beatrice, then, declares that the creation of the Angels, of the *Prima Materia*, of the physical heavens (and also time and space) was instantaneous. The successional creation recorded in *Genesis* was a subsequent process of evolution which took place in time, and through the instrumentality of the Angels" (TC).

28. *effetto*: "Work" (vss. 22-24). *del suo sire*: "From its lord."

29. *raggiò*: "Shot forth."

31-32. *Concreato fu ordine . . . sustanze*: "Concreato" may well bear a technical philosophical meaning in this context, as may be seen from the following passage in *Summa theol.* I, q. 45, a. 4, resp., which begins: "Creari est quoddam fieri." ("To be created is, in a manner, to be made.") Aquinas continues:

Fieri autem ordinatur ad esse rei. Unde illis proprie convenit fieri et creari quibus convenit esse; quod quidem convenit proprie subsistentibus, sive sint simplicia, sicut substantiae separatae, sive sint composita, sicut substantiae materiales. Illi enim proprie convenit esse quod habet esse, et est subsistens in suo esse. Formae autem, et accidentia et alia huiusmodi non dicuntur entia quasi ipsa sint, sed quia eis aliquid est; ut albedo ea ratione dicitur ens, quia ea (1) subiectum est album. Unde, secundum Philosophum (7 Metaphys., text. 2), accidens magis proprie dicitur entis quam ens. Sicut igitur accidentia et formae, et huiusmodi quae non subsistunt, magis sunt coexistentia quam entia; ita magis debent dici concreata quam creata; proprie vero creata sunt subsistentia.

Now, to be made is directed to the being of a thing. Hence to be made and to be created properly belong to whatever being belongs to; which, indeed, belongs properly to subsisting things, whether they are simple things, as in the case of separate substances, or composite, as in the case of material substances. For being belongs to that which has being—that is, to what subsists in its own being. But forms and accidents and the like are called beings, not as if they themselves were, but because something is by them; as whiteness is called a being, forasmuch as its subject is white by it. Hence, according to the Philosopher (*Metaph.* vii, text. 2) accident is more properly said to be *of a being* than *a being*. Therefore, as accidents and forms and the like non-subsisting things are to be said to co-exist rather than to exist, so they ought to be called rather *concreated* than *created* things; whereas, properly speaking, created things are subsisting beings.

Regarding Aquinas' reference to Aristotle, see *Metaphys.* VII, 1, 1028ᵃ.

Seen in this light, "ordine" and "costrutto" do not belong to being, the existence of the angels, but co-exist with those creatures.

31. *costrutto*: There is some doubt among commentators as to the syntax of "costrutto," but the above view would strongly suggest that it is a noun along with the noun "ordine."

32. *e quelle furon cima*: The verb "furon" is narrative in meaning here: the substances, i.e., the angels, "became" the summit.

33. *puro atto*: "The three kinds of beings above named were arranged in due order. At the top (*cima*) were 'those in which pure activity was produced,' i.e., the angels, which, having no body, are pure intelligence, or 'form'; and form,

or character, begins to operate as soon as it exists, and continues to operate completely and incessantly. The angels have no powers that are not in constant and full activity" (Gr). See Thomas Aquinas, *Summa theol.* I, q. 50, a. 2. "*Act* or *actuality* is opposed to *potentiality.* Man's intellect is 'possible' or 'potential,' that is to say, we know potentially much that we do not know actually, and (in another but allied sense) are potentially thinking and feeling many things that we are not actually thinking and feeling; whereas the whole potentialities of an angel's existence are continuously actualised" (TC).

34. *pura potenza tenne la parte ima*: "Pure potentiality" is characteristic of brute matter (or *materia prima*), which is capable of no independent activity.   *ima*: From the Latin *imus*, "lowest."

35. *mezzo*: The material heavens.   *strinse*: "Bound"; the subject is "vime" in the following verse.

36. *vime*: "Tie." Cf. *Par.* XXVIII, 100.   *che già mai non si divima*: Spirit and matter are always united in the spheres.
   divima: "It is untied." The verb is probably Dante's invention.

37–39. *Ieronimo vi scrisse . . . fatto*: A curious Latinizing construction: "Jerome wrote you down a long lapse of ages from the creation of the angels." Jerome's opinion—that the angels existed countless ages before the creation of the world —is recorded by Thomas Aquinas in *Summa theol.* I, q. 61, a. 3, together with the contrary view, which was generally held by the Greek fathers, as Aquinas' reference to Gregory of Nazianzus suggests. Article 3 opens with the following "objection":

Videtur quod Angeli fuerint creati ante mundum corporeum. Dicit enim Hieronymus (super epistolam ad Titum, cap. 1 . . . *Sex millia nondum nostri temporis complentur annorum; et quanta tempora, quantasque saeculorum origines fuisse arbitrandum est, in quibus Angeli, Throni, Dominationes, ceterique ordines Deo*

470

servierunt! Damascenus etiam dicit (in 2 lib. orthod. Fidei, cap. 3, circa fin.): *Quidam dicunt quod ante omnem creationem geniti sunt Angeli, ut theologus dicit Gregorius. Et primum quidem Deus excogitavit angelicas virtutes et coelestes; et excogitatio opus eius fuit.*

It would seem that the angels were created before the corporeal world. For Jerome says (*In Ep. ad Tit.* i. 2): *Six thousand years of our time have not yet elapsed; yet how shall we measure the time, how shall we count the ages, in which the Angels, Thrones, Dominations, and the other orders served God?* Damascene also says (*De Fid. Orth.* ii): *Some say that the angels were begotten before all creation; as Gregory the Theologian declares, He first of all devised the angelic and heavenly powers, and the devising was the making thereof.*

But in the response Aquinas allows the view expressed by Jerome:

Circa hoc invenitur duplex sanctorum doctorum sententia. Illà tamen probabilior videtur, quod Angeli simul cum creatura corporea sunt creati.

Angeli enim sunt quaedam pars universi; non enim constituunt per se unum universum; sed tam ipsi quam creatura corporea, in constitutionem unius universi conveniunt. Quod apparet ex ordine unius creaturae ad aliam. Ordo enim rerum ad invicem est bonum universi. Nulla autem pars perfecta est a suo toto separata. Non est igitur probabile quod Deus, *cuius perfecta sunt opera*, ut dicitur Deut. 32, 4, creaturam angelicam seorsum ante alias creaturas creaverit.

Quamvis contrarium non sit reputandum erroneum, praecipue propter sententiam Gregorii Nazianzeni, cuius *tanta est in doctrina christiana auctoritas, ut nullus unquam eius dictis calumniam inferre praesumpserit, sicut nec Athanasii documentis, ut Hieronymus dicit.*

There is a twofold opinion on this point to be found in the writings of the Fathers. The more probable one holds that the angels were created at the same time as corporeal creatures. For the angels are part of the uni-

471

verse: they do not constitute a universe of themselves; but both they and corporeal natures unite in constituting one universe. This stands in evidence from the relationship of creature to creature; because the mutual relationship of creatures makes up the good of the universe. But no part is perfect if separate from the whole. Consequently it is improbable that God, Whose *works are perfect*, as it is said Deut. xxxii. 4, should have created the angelic creature before other creatures. At the same time the contrary is not to be deemed erroneous; especially on account of the opinion of Gregory Nazianzen, *whose authority in Christian doctrine is of such weight that no one has ever raised objection to his teaching, as is also the case with the doctrine of Athanasius,* as Jerome says.

Clearly, Dante is not so tolerant of Jerome's view.

39. *l'altro mondo*: "The rest of the universe."

40–41. *ma questo vero . . . Spirito Santo*: "This truth" refers to what is stated in vss. 22-24 and 28-30. Thus Dante finds firm scriptural support for the one view he so positively affirms. Cf. Ecclus. 18:1: "Qui vivit in aeternum creavit omnia simul." ("He who lives throughout eternity created all things at the same time.") It was also argued from Gen. 1:1 that there had been no long previous creation: "In principio creavit Deus caelum et terram." ("In the beginning God created the heavens and the earth.") Thomas Aquinas, in *Summa theol.* I, q. 61, a. 3, ad 3, does make reference indeed to the opening words of Genesis as the text which supports the one view of simultaneous creation.

41. *li scrittor de lo Spirito Santo*: In *De mon.* III, iv, 11, Dante writes: "Nam quanquam scribe divini eloquii multi sint, unicus tamen dictator est Deus, qui beneplacitum suum nobis per multorum calamos explicare dignatus est." ("For though the scribes of the divine utterance be many, one is he who dictates to them, even God, who has deigned to set forth his will to us by the pens of many writers.")

42. *agguati*: "Agguati" is formed on the verb *guatare* and means "watch," "consider."

43–45. *e anche la ragione . . . cotanto*: Beatrice here passes from revelation to reason, as scholastic theology so often does. One might say that, typically, she passes to the authority of Aristotle. See the Busnelli-Vandelli edition of the *Convivio*, vol. I, p. 124, col. 1, where the quotation "si aliquae substantiae essent non moventes, essent otiosae" ("if certain substances were not movers, they would be idle") from Aristotle is given with reference to Averroës' commentary on the *Metaphysics*, but where it is pointed out that Albertus Magnus attributes these words to Plato.

To be sure, Aristotle and the Arab commentators on him conceive of all the Intelligences as being "movers," whereas Christian thought came to conceive of the angels as of two kinds, the "contemplatives" and the "movers." Dante's own opinion as expressed in the *Convivio* (II, iv, 9-13), where the poet argues precisely this point, may be cited here:

Nessuno dubita, nè filosofo nè gentile nè giudeo nè cristiano nè alcuna setta, ch'elle non siano piene di tutta beatitudine, o tutte o la maggior parte, e che quelle beate non siano in perfettissimo stato. Onde, con ciò sia cosa che quella che è qui l'umana natura non pur una beatitudine abbia, ma due, sì com'è quella de la vita civile, e quella de la contemplativa, inrazionale sarebbe se noi vedemo quelle avere la beatitudine de la vita attiva, cioè civile, nel governare del mondo, e non avessero quella de la contemplativa, la quale è più eccellente e più divina. E con ciò sia cosa che quella che ha la beatitudine del governare non possa l'altra avere, perchè lo 'ntelletto loro è uno e perpetuo, conviene essere altre fuori di questo ministerio che solamente vivano speculando. E perchè questa vita è più divina, e quanto la cosa è più divina è più di Dio simigliante, manifesto è che questa vita è da Dio più amata: e se ella è più amata, più le è la sua beatanza stata larga: e se più l'è stata larga, più viventi le ha dato che a l'altrui. Per che si conchiude che troppo maggior numero sia quello di quelle creature che li effetti non dimostrano. E non è contra quello che par dire Aristotile nel decimo de l'Etica, che a le sustanze separate convegna pure la speculativa vita. Come pure la speculativa convegna loro, pure a la speculazione di certe segue la circulazione del cielo, che è del mondo governo; lo quale è quasi una ordinata civilitade, intesa ne la speculazione de li motori.

No one—neither philosopher, nor Gentile, nor Jew, nor Christian, nor any sect—doubts that either all of them, or the greater part, are full of all blessedness, or doubts that these blessed ones are in the most perfect state. And inasmuch as human nature, as it here exists, hath not only one blessedness but two, to wit that of the civil life and that of the contemplative life, it were irrational did we perceive those others to have the blessedness of the active that is the civil life, in guiding the world, and not that of the contemplative life, which is more excellent and more divine. And inasmuch as the one that hath the blessedness of guiding may not have the other, because their intellect is one and continuous, there must needs be others exempt from this ministry whose life consists only in speculation. And because this life is the more divine, and because in proportion as a thing is more divine it is more like to God, it is manifest that this life is more loved by God; and if it be more loved, its share of blessedness hath been more ample; and if it be more ample, he hath assigned more living beings to it than to the other. Wherefore we conclude that the number of these creatures is very far in excess of what the effects reveal. And this is not counter to what Aristotle seems to say in the tenth of the *Ethics*, to wit that the speculative life alone fits with the sejunct substances, for if we allow that the speculative life alone fits with them, yet upon the speculation of certain of these followeth the circulation of the heavens, which is the guiding of the world; which world is a kind of ordered civility perceived in the speculation of its movers.

The whole argument rests on the basic principle that every-
thing is created for a purpose (the movers for moving) and
that the fulfillment of that purpose is the perfection of the
thing.

46. *questi amori*: Cf. vs. 18.

49–51. *Né giugneriesi . . . alimenti*: On this question (stand-
ard in a *summa* of theology), see Thomas Aquinas, *Summa
theol.* I, q. 63, a. 6, which bears the heading: "Utrum aliqua
mora fuerit inter creationem, et lapsum Angeli" ("Whether
there was any interval between the creation and the fall of the
angel"). The response is:

Circa hoc est duplex opinio.

Sed probabilior et sanctorum dictis magis consonans
est quod statim post primum instans suae creationis
diabolus peccaverit. Et hoc necesse est dicere, si pona-
tur quod in primo instanti suae creationis in actum liberi
arbitrii proruperit, et cum gratia fuerit creatus, ut supra
diximus, quaest. 62, art. 3. Cum enim Angeli per unum
actum meritorium ad beatitudinem perveniant, ut supra
dictum est, quaest. 62, art. 5, si diabolus in primo in-
stanti, in gratia creatus, meruit, statim post primum
instans beatitudinem accepisset, nisi statim impedimen-
tum praestitisset peccando.

Si vero ponatur quod Angelus in gratia creatus non
fuerit, vel quod in primo instanti actum liberi arbitrii
non potuerit habere, nihil prohibet aliquam moram
fuisse inter creationem et lapsum.

There is a twofold opinion on this point. But the more
probable one, which is also more in harmony with the
teachings of the Saints, is that the devil sinned at once
after the first instant of his creation. This must be main-
tained if it be held that he elicited an act of free-will in
the first instant of his creation, and that he was created
in grace; as we have said (q. 62, a. 3). For since the
angels attain beatitude by one meritorious act, as was
said above (q. 62, a. 5), if the devil, created in grace,
merited in the first instant, he would at once have re-

ceived beatitude after that first instant, if he had not placed an impediment by sinning.

If, however, it be contended that the angel was not created in grace, or that he could not elicit an act of free-will in the first instant, then there is nothing to prevent some interval being interposed between his creation and fall.

Dante expresses his opinion in the *Convivio* (II, v, 12), where what becomes in the present passage "the count to less than twenty" is expressed simply by "tosto": "Dico che di tutti questi ordini si perderono alquanti tosto che furono creati, forse in numero de la decima parte." ("I say that out of all these orders some certain were lost as soon as they were created, I take it to the number of a tenth part.")

49. *giugneriesi = si giungerebbe.*

51. *turbò il suggetto d'i vostri alimenti*: "Alimenti" is used for *elementi* (see Petrocchi, vol. I, *Introduzione*, p. 231). The entire meaning of the phrase has been the subject of much discussion, with the specific meaning of "suggetto" as the main problem. It is possible to understand that "suggetto" means the *substrate* of the elements, the *prima materia,* at first formless, "the elaboration of the elements being the subsequent work of the Angels and the heavens" (TC). (Cf. *Par.* VII, 130-38.) However, it is not possible to overlook the account of Satan's fall to earth and his place at the center of the earth as clearly set forth in *Inf.* XXXIV, especially vss. 118-26, and (though there is evidently an inconsistency here between two views as expressed in the poem) to understand "il suggetto d'i vostri alimenti" to mean "that one of your elements that underlies the rest," i.e., earth. The verb "turbò" seems to point back to the account of Satan's fall, since the earth actually shrank away from him (*Inf.* XXXIV, 122-26).

52. *L'altra*: I.e., *parte*, meaning the good angels of vss. 58-60. *quest' arte*: "This art" is the angels' circling of the point, a circling which here symbolically represents intellection that is both contemplation and action, since by intel-

lection the angels turn the heavens. See Dante's *canzone* as cited by Charles Martel in *Par.* VIII, 37, and the corresponding note. "Arte," in itself, seems to stress the turning of the heavens more than it does contemplation, but "circuir" (vs. 54) must include both contemplation and moving.

55–57. *Principio del cader . . . costretto*: *Inf.* XXXIV provides the best gloss on these verses, but *Par.* XIX, 46-48, should also be remembered: Satan was the "first proud creature," "the highest of all creatures," but "for not waiting on the light he fell unripe" (see n. to *Par.* XIX, 48). "Principio" here may well have not only a temporal sense ("beginning"), but also a causal sense, for Satan induced the other bad angels to become bad. See Thomas Aquinas, *Summa theol.* I, q. 63, a. 8, resp.:

> Peccatum primi Angeli fuit aliis causa peccandi, non quidem cogens, sed quadam quasi exhortatione inducens.
>
> Cuius signum ex hoc apparet quod omnes daemones illi supremo subduntur, ut manifeste apparet per illud quod dicit Dominus Matth. 25, 41: *Ite, maledicti, in ignem aeternum, qui paratus est diabolo et angelis eius.* Habet enim hoc ordo divinae iustitiae, ut cuius suggestioni aliquis consentit in culpa, eius potestati subdatur in poena, secundum illud 2 Pet. 2, 19: *A quo quis superatus est, huic servus addictus est.*

> The sin of the highest angel was the cause of the others sinning; not as compelling them, but as inducing them by a kind of exhortation. A token thereof appears in this, that all the demons are subjects of that highest one; as is evident from our Lord's words: *Go* (Vulg., *Depart from Me*), *you cursed, into everlasting fire, which was prepared for the devil and his angels* (Matth. xxv. 41). For the order of Divine justice exacts that whosoever consents to another's evil suggestion, shall be subjected to him in his punishment; according to (2 Pet. ii. 19): *By whom a man is overcome, of the same also he is the slave.*

The essence of Satan's pride ("not waiting for the light") in-

volves a basic tenet in the matter which, on its simplest state-
ment, is as follows: all the angels were first given a "natural"
light, consistent with their nature, but God was to give them,
in a second instant, that light by which He sees Himself and
that light by which—and *only* by which—a creature may see
God in direct vision (cf. *Par*. XXX, 100-101 and n. to *Par*.
XXX, 100-102) which is known in theology as the light of
glory. Satan and the others who followed his example did not
wait for God's bestowal of this light, but presumed to attain
to it by their own natural powers. In this way, Satan aspired
to be "similis altissimo," as it is stated in Isa. 14:14: "Similis
ero Altissimo." ("I will be like the most High.") He did not
recognize his creaturely dependence on God, as did the good
angels (vss. 58-60). On the light of glory, see C. S. Singleton
(1958), pp. 20-23.

58-60. *Quelli che vedi . . . presti*: "Modesti" stresses the
opposite of pride, namely humility, the recognition of the
creature's dependence on the Creator and His goodness, i.e.,
His great gift of intellection ("tanto intender"), while
"presti" points to their natural endowment for intellection,
which they had in their first moment of creation (see preced-
ing note).

59. *riconoscer*: For this use of the verb, cf. *Par*. XXII, 113;
XXXI, 84.

61-63. *per che le viste . . . volontate*: The angels who waited
for the bestowal of the higher light, the light of glory, re-
ceived that light (here termed "grazia illuminante"). Their
merit ("merto") was precisely that humility and their wait-
ing upon the Lord to bestow that higher light. With that be-
stowal they were forever confirmed in this highest grace, and
accordingly they are now bound thereby to the good and to
do the good. They have fullness of vision and of will, and
they cannot sin. See Thomas Aquinas, *Summa theol*. I, q.
62, a. 8, resp.:

Angeli beati peccare non possunt.
Cuius ratio est quia eorum beatitudo in hoc consistit
quod per essentiam Deum vident. Essentia autem Dei

est ipsa essentia bonitatis. Unde hoc modo se habet Angelus videns Deum ad ipsum, sicut se habet quicumque non videns Deum ad communem rationem boni. Impossibile est autem quod aliquis quidquam velit vel operetur, nisi attendens ad bonum, vel quod velit divertere a bono, inquantum huiusmodi. Angelus igitur beatus non potest velle vel agere, nisi attendens ad Deum; sic autem volens vel agens non potest peccare. Unde Angelus beatus nullo modo peccare potest.

The beatified angels cannot sin. The reason for this is, because their beatitude consists in seeing God through His essence. Now, God's essence is the very essence of goodness. Consequently the angel beholding God is disposed towards God in the same way as anyone else not seeing God is to the common form of goodness. Now it is impossible for any man either to will or to do anything except aiming at what is good; or for him to wish to turn away from good precisely as such. Therefore the beatified angel can neither will nor act, except as aiming towards God. Now whoever wills or acts in this manner cannot sin. Consequently the beatified angel cannot sin.

65–66. *che ricever . . . aperto*: The degree of openness depends on love (*caritas*) which is a result of foreordained disposition. See Thomas Aquinas, *Summa theol.* I, q. 62, a. 5, resp.:

Angelus post primum actum charitatis, quo beatitudinem meruit, statim beatus fuit.

Cuius ratio est quia gratia perficit naturam secundum modum naturae, sicut et omnis perfectio recipitur in perfectibili secundum modum eius. Est autem hoc proprium naturae angelicae quod naturalem perfectionem non per discursum acquirat, sed statim per naturam habeat, sicut supra ostensum est, art. 1 huius qu., et qu. 58, art. 3 et 4. Sicut autem ex sua natura Angelus habet ordinem ad perfectionem naturalem, ita ex merito habet ordinem ad gloriam; et ita statim post meritum in Angelo fuit beatitudo consecuta. Meritum autem beatitudinis non solum in Angelo, sed etiam in homine esse potest per unicum actum: quia quolibet actu charitate informato homo beatitudinem meretur. Unde relinquitur quod statim post unum actum charitate informatum Angelus beatus fuit.

The angel was beatified instantly after the first act of charity, whereby he merited beatitude. The reason whereof is because grace perfects nature according to the manner of the nature; as every perfection is received in the subject capable of perfection, according to its mode. Now it is proper to the angelic nature to receive its natural perfection not by passing from one stage to another; but to have it at once naturally, as was shown above (a. 1; q. 58, aa. 3, 4). But as the angel is of his nature inclined to natural perfection, so is he by merit inclined to glory. Hence instantly after merit the angel secured beatitude. Now the merit of beatitude in angel and man alike can be from merely one act; because man merits beatitude by every act informed by charity. Hence it remains that an angel was beatified straightway after one act of charity.

67. *consistorio*: Cf. "consistoro," *Purg.* IX, 24.

69. *aiutorio*: From the Latin *adiutorium*, a word that is used frequently in the Bible. Dante uses the form more than once in the *Convivio* (e.g., III, x, 8).

70–72. *Ma perché . . . vole*: With these verses begins what Beatrice eventually will term a digression (vs. 127): a denunciation of erroneous and deceitful practices on earth in willfully teaching false doctrine.

70. *vostre scole*: Cf. *Purg.* XXXIII, 85.

71. *si legge*: It is taught in the lectures of doctors of theology. For this use of *leggere*, cf. *Par.* X, 137; XXVI, 18.

72. *'ntende e si ricorda e vole*: "These are the precise powers which Dante believed the disembodied human soul actually to possess before assuming its provisional aerial body. (See *Purg.* XXV. 83.) As far as *intelligence* and *will* are con-

cerned, the assertion is equally true of the Angels, but not so
as to *memory*" (TC).

73. *dirò*: "I shall explain."   *veggi = vegga*.

75. *lettura*: The noun corresponds in meaning to the verb
leggere as it is used in vs. 71.

76. *Queste sustanze*: The angels.   *fur = furono*.

76–77. *poi che fur gioconde . . . Dio*: I.e., from the mo-
ment when the good angels were granted the light of glory,
which made it possible for them to have direct vision of God
("*faccia*" suggests the conception of vision face to face).

77–78. *non volser viso da essa*: In their direct vision of God
the angels are fully satisfied, for therein they see all things as
well ("*da cui nulla si nasconde*"). They have therefore no
reason to turn away from gazing on Him, and they do not do
so.

79. *però = per ciò.   non hanno vedere interciso*: Noth-
ing ever intervenes between their mind and the image of all
things in God.   *interciso*: "Intercepted."

80–81. *non bisogna . . . diviso*: " 'They have no need of re-
membering by reason of interrupted concept.' Forgetfulness
is the intervention of a new concept between the former one
and the consciousness. With the angels, no concept, or per-
ception, is ever interrupted by another.—St. Thomas inclines
to the opinion that angels do not need—and therefore do not
possess—memory, but he admits the possibility of their pos-
sessing it in a certain sense, if memory be considered as a fac-
ulty of the mind: *Summa Theologiae*, Prima, Qu. liv, Art. 5.
Cf. St. Augustine, *De Trinitate* [X, 11]. Dante is more posi-
tive than his masters. Angels have only intelligence and will"
(Gr). See E. Moore (1917), pp. 154-56. E. G. Parodi
(1918b, p. 132, n. 1) notes that Thomas Aquinas uses the
term *dividendo* in describing forgetfulness in *Summa theol.*
I, q. 58, a. 4, which is entitled: "Utrum Angeli intelligant
componendo et dividendo" ("whether the angels understand
by composing and dividing"). Cf. *De mon.* I, iii, 7, where

Dante, in speaking of intellection in the angels, refers to it as "sine interpolatione" ("continuous").

82. *sì che là giù, non dormendo, si sogna*: "So that on earth men dream waking dreams" (Gr).

84. *ma ne l'uno è più colpa e più vergogna*: In those who preach what they do not believe there is malice involved; they are the worse set.

85–86. *Voi non andate . . . filosofando*: "Voi" refers to "you mortals," and "giù" to the earthly life. Cf. *Purg.* XXXIII, 82-90.

85. *un sentiero*: The way of the truth is *one*.

87. *l'amor de l'apparenza e 'l suo pensiero*: "The love and thought of mere show."

88. *si comporta*: "Is suffered."

89. *posposta*: "Put aside" (preferring to deal in false reasonings).

90. *quando è torta*: Cf. *Par.* XIII, 127-29.

91. *vi*: On earth.   *costa = è costato*, in blood shed by martyrs to the faith.

93. *con essa*: "Con" here, rather than the usual *a*, expresses greater adherence.

94. *Per apparer*: In order to cut an impressive figure, for mere show. Cf. "apparenza" in vs. 87.   *face = fa*.

95. *trascorse*: "Amply developed," "expatiated on."

96. *Vangelio = Vangelo*.

97–102. *Un dice . . . rispuose*: See Matt. 27:45: "A sexta autem hora tenebrae factae sunt super universam terram usque ad horam nonam." ("Now from the sixth hour there was darkness over the whole land until the ninth hour.") "To explain this darkness at the Crucifixion, some said that the moon left its course to make an eclipse, others that the sun

hid its own rays. Dionysius ([*Par.*] XXVIII, 130) favored
the first explanation, St. Jerome the second. Both are re-
corded by St. Thomas in *Summa Theologiae*, Tertia, Qu. xliv,
Art. 2. The second theory has the advantage of accounting
for an obscuration 'over all the land' ['super universam ter-
ram'], whereas an ordinary eclipse would darken only a part
of it. The miraculous eclipse recorded in the Bible 'answered
for the Spaniards and the Indians'—at the two extremes of
the habitable world—'as well as for the Hebrews' " (Gr). Cf.
Mar. 15:33; Luc. 23:44.

100. *mente* = *mentisce* (from the infinitive *mentire*), though
the form *mente* is still found in literary use. The word is pro-
nounced *mènte*.

102. *rispuose* = *corrispuose*.

103. *Lapi e Bindi*: Lapo and Bindo seem to have been very
common names in Florence. They were originally nicknames
for Jacopo and Ildebrando, respectively.

104. *per anno* = *ogni anno*.

105. *quinci e quindi*: "Here and there," i.e., on every hand.

106. *le pecorelle*: The flock, in the familiar sense of faithful
Christians that is used in the Bible. Cf. *Par.* XI, 124-29.

108. *non le scusa non veder lo danno*: Cf. *Purg.* XXII, 47,
"per ignoranza," and what Statius affirms in that canto. Igno-
rance is no excuse when it is a matter of certain fundamental
notions and articles of faith which every good Christian is
bound to hold.

109. *convento*: "Congregation," i.e., the apostles. Cf. Mar.
16:15: "Et dixit eis: Euntes in mundum universum, praedi-
cate evangelium omni creaturae." ("And he said to them,
'Go into the whole world and preach the gospel to every
creature.' ")

111. *ma diede lor verace fondamento*: See I Cor. 3:10-11:
"Secundum gratiam Dei quae data est mihi, ut sapiens archi-
tectus fundamentum posui. . . . Fundamentum enim aliud

nemo potest ponere praeter id quod positum est, quod est
Christus Iesus." ("According to the grace of God which has
been given to me, as a wise builder, I laid the foundation. . . .
For other foundation no one can lay, but that which has been
laid, which is Christ Jesus.")

112. *quel tanto*: "That alone," i.e., the true foundation. For
this use of *tanto* cf. *Par.* II, 67; XVIII, 13.   *sue = loro*,
the apostles'.

114. *fero = fecero*.   *scudo e lance*: The "shield" is clear-
ly for defense, and the "lance" for their attack on false beliefs.

115. *motti*: "Jests," "witticisms."   *iscede = scede*, "buf-
fooneries."

117. *gonfia il cappuccio*: "The cowl [of the preacher] puffs
up" with self-satisfaction.   *e più non si richiede*: And the
congregation hearing the sermon asks for nothing else but
this sort of "wind" (vs. 107).

118. *Ma tale uccel nel becchetto s'annida*: Devils are termed
uccelli in *Inf.* XXII, 96, and XXXIV, 47, as well as here.
Thus a devil is nestling in the "hoodtail" as in a pocket, wait-
ing to snatch the preacher's soul. For a similar notion, cf.
Inf. XXVII, 117.

120. *la perdonanza di ch'el si confida*: "What kind of indul-
gence it places its trust in."

121. *per cui*: Through such trust placed in promises of in-
dulgence ("promession," vs. 123).

123. *ad ogne promession*: "To any promise."   *si cor-
rerebbe = si accorrerebbe*, they "would flock."

124. *Di questo*: On this credulity of the people.   *sant' An-
tonio*: The order of St. Anthony, here the subject of "in-
grassa," with "porco" as the object. This is St. Anthony the
Great, the Egyptian hermit (not to be confounded with his
namesake of Padua), who was born in Upper Egypt (*ca.*
250) and died at the age of 105. He is regarded as the found-

er of monastic institutions, the disciples who followed him in his retirement to the desert having formed, as it were, the first community of monks. His symbol is a hog (perhaps as a type of the temptations of the devil, or possibly as a token of the power ascribed to him of warding off disease from cattle), which is generally represented lying at his feet. His remains were miraculously discovered long after his death and transported to Constantinople, whence *ca.* 960 a portion of them was transferred to Vienne in Provence. The monks of the order of St. Anthony kept herds of swine, which they fattened with the proceeds of their alms, and which were allowed to roam the streets of towns and feed at public charge. They were regarded by the common folk with superstitious reverence, a fact which the monks turned to account when collecting alms. For a famous story concerning one of the order, see Boccaccio, *Decam.* VI, 10. A story of the evil fate which befell a Florentine who tried to kill one of these hogs of St. Anthony forms the subject of one of Sacchetti's stories (*Novelle* CX).

125. *e altri assai che sono ancor più porci*: These others, even more "swinish," are concubines, natural sons, and the like, the object of "ingrassa" along with "il porco" of the preceding verse.

126. *moneta sanza conio*: False money, i.e., false indulgences.

127. *siam digressi*: From the Latin *digressi sumus*. By such a touch, all that Beatrice has said in vss. 70-126 is viewed as a "digression."

127-28. *ritorci li occhi . . . strada*: Turn back your eyes, i.e., your mind, toward the true path, that is, the "way" of vs. 129. Such a turn of phrase, with the stress on eyes, points to the journey to God as the true concern and to that journey as an intellectual ascent from truth to truth, especially in the *Paradiso* (cf. *Par.* IV, 124-32).

129. *sì che la via col tempo si raccorci*: The time allotted to their stay in this heaven is growing short, as is their time for

the intellectual journey as such, i.e., what remains to be said here in the ninth heaven.

130. *Questa natura*: Angel kind. *sì oltre s'ingrada*: "Rises by degrees so high in numbers." Hierarchy is stressed by the verb invented by Dante.

133-35. *e se tu guardi . . . cela*: Cf. Dan. 7:10: "Millia millium ministrabant ei et decies millies centena millia assistebant ei." ("Thousands of thousands ministered to him, and ten thousand times a hundred thousand stood before him.") See n. to *Par.* XXVIII, 92.

135. *determinato numero si cela*: This ambiguous verse must mean: "No definite number is discernible." For this use of "cela," cf. *Par.* XVI, 80. Thus Daniel's thousands indicate that the number of the angels is greater than man can conceive.

136. *La prima luce, che tutta la raia*: The light of God shines upon all the angelic kind ("la" refers to "questa natura," vs. 130).

137. *per tanti modi in essa si recepe*: Every angel constitutes a species by itself, hence no two perceive God alike, i.e., no two receive of His light alike. *per tanti modi*: "In as many ways." *recepe = riceve*.

138. *a chi s'appaia*: "With whom it [the light] unites." Some editors have "che" instead of "chi"; but see Petrocchi's note explaining his preference for the more personal form *chi*. There is the suggestion of "matching," that is, to each angel is given all of the light that it is able to receive.

139. *però che = per ciò che*.

139-40. *a l'atto che concepe segue l'affetto*: Again the poet takes his stand on this issue (see *Par.* XXVIII, 109-11, and the note to *Par.* XXVIII, 106-14). The "act that conceives" is the act of intellect, whereas "affetto" refers to the will, where love is seated.

140-41. *d'amar la dolcezza . . . tepe*: Hence, even as the reception of the light varies with each angel, so also its love varies in measure depending on the light received, i.e., on its vision of God.

141. *tepe*: A Latinism, meaning "is tepid," i.e., less fervent than in other angels.

142. *l'eccelso*: The sublime height of the whole angelic hierarchy.   *la larghezza*: "The breadth," with special reference to the immense number of the angels; cf. *Par.* XXV, 29-30.

143. *etterno valor*: God; cf. *Par.* I, 107; X, 3.

143–44. *tanti speculi*: The angels who reflect God's light, which shines in each one of them (the figure should be connected with vss. 14-18 of the present canto).

144. *si spezza*: Literally, "divides" or "breaks" Itself, that is, "gives of Itself" to each. Cf. *Par.* XIII, 55-60.

145. *uno manendo in sé come davanti*: Vs. 60 of *Par.* XIII expresses almost exactly this idea of God's "self-contained-ness."   *manendo = rimanendo*.

CANTO XXX

1-3. *Forse semilia . . . piano*: "Dante is about to describe
the aspect of the sky, with the stars gradually fading, a
little before dawn. 'The sixth hour (i.e., noon) is glowing'
some '6,000 miles away from us.' Noon is separated from
sunrise by a quarter of the earth's circumference—that is,
according to our author's geography (*Conv.*, III, v, 11), by
5,100, a quarter of 20,400. If noon, then, is 6,000 miles off,
sunrise must still be 900 miles (or about an hour) away. The
sun is below our horizon on one side, and the earth's conical
shadow, projected into space, is correspondingly above our
horizon on the other. As the sun rises, the shadow sinks; and
when the middle of the sun shall be on the horizon line, the
apex of the shadow will be on the same plane in the opposite
quarter. An hour before dawn, therefore, 'this earth is al-
ready bowing its shadow down almost to the level bed' of the
horizon" (Gr). See also *Conv.* IV, viii, 7; E. Moore (1903),
pp. 58-59.

2. *ci*: This is the adverb of place, conjoined in meaning with
"lontano."

4. *'l mezzo del cielo*: This is not the meridian, but the whole
atmosphere visible above and reaching all the way to the
heaven of the stars. "Mezzo" is thus used here in the meaning

4. Dante's view of the sky a little before dawn

of a medium through which we see any object (cf. *Purg.* I, 15; XXIX, 45; *Par.* XXVII, 74). *a noi profondo*: "Deep above us."

5. *comincia a farsi tal*: The "mezzo" begins to be brightened by the dawn so much that . . .

5–6. *ch'alcuna stella . . . fondo*: The first stars to disappear would be those in the east, near the oncoming dawn.

6. *parere = apparire.* The infinitive is used as a noun.
questo fondo: "This bottom" of the universe, the earth's surface.

7. *ancella*: Aurora, the dawn. Cf. *Purg.* XII, 81; XXII, 118.

8–9. *'l ciel si chiude di vista in vista*: Concerning the term *vista* as applied to stars, see *Par.* II, 115, and XXIII, 30. Cf. also the use of *parvenza* in *Par.* XIV, 71.

9. *la più bella*: This is possibly Venus, which is the brightest star (planet) towards dawn. Cf. *Purg.* I, 19-21.

10–11. *il triunfo . . . punto*: Cf. *Par.* XXVIII, 22-39.

10. *il triunfo*: The circling orders of angels.   *lude*: From the Latin *ludit*, "sports."

11. *vinse*: See *Par.* XXVIII, 16-18.

12. *parendo inchiuso da quel ch'elli 'nchiude*: See n. to *Par.* XXVIII, 41-42. This verse is the final seal on the mystery: the point which is God in the symbolic vision that has been before Dante's eyes in this ninth heaven is also the circum-

ference of the whole universe in the sense that the tenth and last heaven is the Empyrean, which is the mind of God. For the "fade-out" of this symbolic vision, see *Summa theol.* II-II, q. 180, a. 5, ad 2, where Thomas Aquinas quotes from the *De caelesti ierarchia* of Dionysius:

> Dicit enim Dionysius . . . quod *angelorum hierarchias manifestat nobis divina claritas in quibusdam symbolis figuratis, ex cuius virtute restituimur in simplum radium,* idest, in simplicem cognitionem intelligibilis veritatis. Et sic intelligendum est quod Gregorius dicit, quod *contemplantes corporalium rerum umbras non secum trahunt,* quia videlicet in eis non sistit eorum contemplatio, sed potius in consideratione intelligibilis veritatis.

> For Dionysius says . . . that *the Divine glory shows us the angelic hierarchies under certain symbolic figures, and by its power we are brought back to the single ray of light,* i.e., to the simple knowledge of the intelligible truth. It is in this sense that we must understand the statement of Gregory that *contemplatives do not carry along with them the shadows of things corporeal,* since their contemplation is not fixed on them, but on the consideration of the intelligible truth.

13. *stinse* = *estinse* (*estinguere*).

14. *per che* = *per la qual cosa,* "wherefore."   *tornar*: "Tornar" depends on "costrinse" in vs. 15.

15. *nulla vedere e amor mi costrinse*: "Nulla vedere" ("seeing nothing") and "amor" are the subjects of "costrinse."

16. *Se quanto infino a qui di lei si dice*: The poet's affirmation here includes all the early praise of Beatrice, to be found in the *Rime,* in the *Convivio,* and, above all, in the *Vita nuova.*

17. *conchiuso*: "Gathered together."   *una loda*: "In one single praising" (a praising that will be attempted here, at this point in the poem).

18. *vice*: A Latinism, meaning "turn," "moment," i.e., right

here, at this point in the narrative. Some commentators take the term to mean "office," but see *Par.* XXVII, 17, where it is paired with "officio."

19. *si trasmoda*: "Transcends measure." The verb is formed on the Latin *modus* in this sense, with *trans-* added.

20. *pur*: I.e., *soltanto*, or "solo," as in vs. 21.

21. *solo il suo fattor*: These are strong words, for they exclude *all* creatures, even the angels.

22. *mi concedo*: "I declare myself," "I confess myself."

23. *punto di suo tema*: Some especially difficult passage to be rendered in the matter undertaken.

24. *soprato = superato*, "surpassed." *comico o tragedo*: The modern reader needs to remember that a "comic poet" is one who writes in familiar style, whereas a "tragic poet" is one whose style is exalted. See Dante's *Letter to Can Grande* (*Epist.* XIII, 30). Thus the *Comedy* (cf. *Inf.* XVI, 128) is written by a *comico*, whereas the Dante of the *canzoni* (in the *Rime*, the *Vita nuova*, and the *Convivio*) is a *tragedo*, as was Virgil in writing the *Aeneid* (cf. *Inf.* XX, 113).

25. *come sole in viso che più trema*: "Viso" is to be understood here as "eyes" (as also in vs. 28), which, with the modifying phrase, means: "the weakest eyes." Cf. *Conv.* III, *canzone* II, 59-60: "Elle soverchian lo nostro intelletto, / come raggio di sole un frale viso." ("They transcend our intellect, as the sun's ray a feeble vision.")

27. *scema*: Literally, "reduces," here in the sense of "takes from."

28. *il suo viso*: The reference is primarily to Beatrice's eyes, but it is also to the beauty of her countenance. This verse takes us back, in its affirmation, to Dante's first sight of Beatrice when he was nine years old (as related in the *Vita nuova*). The total statement here, as the verses continue, amounts to the highest praise yet bestowed on Beatrice and

the beginning of a kind of "goodbye" to her in the poem, which will terminate in the paean addressed to her in *Par.* XXXI, 79-90.

30. *preciso*: "Cut off," from the Latin *praecisum*.

31. *desista*: The subject of the verb is *io* (understood), the object is "mio seguir."

33. *come a l'ultimo suo ciascuno artista*: "'As every artist (must stop) at his utmost.'—Now that Beatrice has reached her own home, the Empyrean, she is seen in her full beauty, which defies description" (Gr). For analogous points, see *Par.* XIV, 79-81; XVIII, 8-12; XXIII, 22-24, 55-63.

34. *Cotal*: "Such," that is, in all her indescribable beauty.
bando: "Heralding." Cf. *Purg.* XXX, 13; *Par.* XXVI, 45.

35. *tuba*: I.e., *tromba*. "Tuba" is a Latinism. Cf. *Par.* VI, 72, and *passim*.   *deduce*: A Latinism, meaning "to draw out" (a term in spinning). The word is used in connection with wax in *Par.* XIII, 73.

36. *sua matera terminando*: The signal of the approaching end of the poem is clear and emphatic here.

37. *spedito duce*: A leader whose duty has been discharged. For *spedito* in this special sense, cf. *Par.* XVII, 100.

38–39. *Noi siamo . . . luce*: It has been Beatrice's role as guide to lead Dante to the last heaven. She has fulfilled that role now, and her words explain even more clearly the sense of "spedito" above.

39. *maggior corpo*: The Primum Mobile, or ninth heaven, which is indeed the "biggest body" since it is the largest in circumference of all the material heavens and surrounds them.   *ciel ch'è pura luce*: The Empyrean, a purely spiritual heaven, as the following tercet makes clear. See n. to *Par.* I, 4.

40–42. *luce intellettual . . . dolzore*: The tercet, as it further defines the nature of the Empyrean, presents the pattern of a "trinity," light to love to joy. The order is significant, for light, intellectual light, coming first, stresses seeing (intellection), which pertains to intellect; love, which is of the will, follows on seeing (see *Par.* XXVIII, 109-11, and the n. to *Par.* XXVIII, 113). Joy, which is fulfillment of intellectual desire to see and of love resulting from the seeing, is that which completes the triad. On joy as the culminating experience of love fulfilled, see *Purg.* XVIII, 33, and n. to *Purg.* XVIII, 32-33.

42. *dolzore = dolcezza.* The word is a Provençalism, common in the early Provençal poets.

43-45. *Qui vederai . . . giustizia:* "In the Empyrean are two victorious armies, the 'soldiery' of blessed souls that resisted temptation, and the host of good angels that triumphed over the bad" (Gr). Cf. *Purg.* XXXII, 22; *Par.* XVIII, 124; XXXI, 2.

44-45. *e l'una in quelli aspetti . . . giustizia:* By a very special privilege the wayfarer, a living man who has attained to this ultimate goal, is to be shown the human souls of the elect as they will be seen after the Last Judgment, when they will have their bodies (glorified bodies) again. Here the poet is quite on his own, for no accepted doctrine concerning the attainment of this pinnacle of contemplation on the part of a living man allows any such privilege. But now the poet allows it and crowns his poem with such embodied vision (by special privilege), thus climaxing the whole structure with the kind of vision which is the very substance of his poetry (see C. S. Singleton, 1969, pp. 25-29). Human souls that have been flames, without human countenance or bodily semblance throughout most of the *Paradiso*, are now to be seen in their glorified bodies. The reader will recall that the wayfarer had had the desire to see souls in this embodied way during the upward journey (*Par.* XXII, 58-60). This was denied him then, but the promise was made that is here fulfilled (*Par.* XXII, 61-63), and he was told that the ladder of contemplation is capable of attaining to such vision (*Par.* XXII, 68).

It may also be recalled at this point that the wayfarer was clearly told that only two have risen to Heaven in their bodies —the resurrected Christ and His mother, Mary (*Par.* XXV, 128)—at a point where Dante tried to see if St. John was in Paradise with his body, which John denied.

45. *che tu vedrai*: This is one among many assurances of his own personal salvation that Dante receives in the course of his journey. The first of these was expressed by Charon (*Inf.* III, 91-93).

46. *discetti*: "Scatters," from the Latin *disceptare*.

47. *spiriti visivi*: The spirits (or sense) of sight. Cf. *Par.* XXVI, 71, and n. to *Par.* XXVI, 70-71.

47-48. *sì che . . . obietti*: "So that it [the flash] deprives the eye of the effect of stronger objects," i.e., of sight of *any* objects, said to be "stronger" because of the dazed eyes. This understanding of the verse is confirmed in the second term of the simile, vs. 51. "Forti," that is, is to be referred to the eyes, in this sense, not to actual objects as "stronger" in themselves.

49-51. *così mi circunfulse . . . m'appariva*: Cf. Actus 22:6, St. Paul's words concerning his own experience of the blinding light that came to him on the road to Damascus: "Factum est autem eunte me et appropinquante Damasco, media die, subito de caelo circumfulsit me lux copiosa." ("And it came to pass that, as I was on my way and approaching Damascus, suddenly about noon there shone round about me a great light from heaven.") Also see Actus 22:11: "et cum non viderem prae claritate luminis illius" ("and as I could not see because of the dazzling light"). The poet's phrasing here seems to echo deliberately Paul's words, a fact which is highly significant, for St. Paul was the prime example of one who was "caught up to Heaven" in the experience of rapture and is cited as such in most discussions of the experience of rapture, an experience which Dante is now beginning to have. See C. S. Singleton (1958), pp. 15-23. Paul's experience has been recalled more than once in the poem up to this point: cf. *Inf.* II, 28, and *Par.* XXVIII, 138-39, and see the echo of Paul's own words respecting his rapture in *Par.* I, 5-6. Also see n. to *Par.* I, 5-9, and *Epist.* XIII, 79.

52. *l'amor che queta questo cielo*: God's love and the love of God make the Empyrean the "heaven of divine peace" (*Par.* I, 122; II, 112; and *passim*).

53. *accoglie*: "Receives," "welcomes." The understood object of the verb is "every soul as it joins the company of the elect," having risen from Purgatory to this place.   *salute*: The term is used in the equivocal sense it has in the *Vita nuova* (XI, 3), for example, where of Beatrice it is said: "e quando questa gentilissima salute salutava" ("and when this most gentle lady gave salutation"). That is, "salute" has its normal meaning of "health," "weal," "salvation" (see, for example, *Inf.* I, 106) and also bears the suggestion of *saluto*, meaning "salutation," "welcome," as if the light were a welcoming light.

54. *per far disposto a sua fiamma il candelo*: The reader will do well to bear this metaphor in mind as the pilgrim advances now through higher and higher vision to the ultimate. He is the "candle" that must be gradually rendered able to bear the "flame," that is, this vision which so exceeds normal human capacity (vs. 57). Thus he undergoes a transformation and an enabling process, from here on to the end. *candelo = candela* (*Par.* XI, 15).

57. *me sormontar di sopr' a mia virtute*: The experience which Dante begins to have now is that of rapture, which all theologians agree is one that is far, far above natural human power, a fact declared in the opening verses of the *Paradiso* (I, 4-9) and in *Epist.* XIII, 78-82.

58. *mi raccesi*: The verb continues the metaphor of the "candelo," vs. 54.

59. *mera*: "Bright." Cf. *Par.* XI, 18; XVIII, 55.

60. *non si fosser difesi*: "Would not have withstood it."

61–63. *e vidi lume . . . primavera*: Compare Dan. 7:10: "Fluvius igneus rapidusque egrediebatur a facie eius." ("A swift stream of fire issued forth from before him.") Also see Apoc. 22:1: "Et ostendit mihi fluvium aquae vitae, splendidum tamquam crystallum, procedentem de sede Dei et Agni." ("And he showed me a river of the water of life, clear as crystal, coming forth from the throne of God and of the Lamb.") Cf. Isa. 66:12. Bernard of Clairvaux, *Sermones de diversis* XLII, 7, says: "Torrente voluptatis potantur iusti." ("The just shall drink of the torrent of delight.") Dante makes of this traditional river a symbol of grace, or, more specifically, of the light of glory. See C. S. Singleton (1958), pp. 15-23.

61. *rivera*: "River." Cf. *Inf.* XII, 47; *Purg.* XXVIII, 47. Because of subsequent transformations, the reader should note that he quite naturally imagines this "river" to be flowing more or less horizontally between its two banks, like any river.

63. *primavera*: For *primavera* in this sense of "spring flowers" or "spring flowering," cf. *Purg.* XXVIII, 51. As will now be disclosed, these flowers which cover the banks are (in prefatory vision, that is, for the moment incomplete) the souls of the elect, even as the "sparks" (vs. 64) will prove to be the other *milizia* of Heaven, the angels, who nestle in the flowers. Angels are compared to bees by St. Anselm (see G. Busnelli, 1911a, p. 232).

65. *d'ogne parte*: On either bank of the stream.

66. *quasi rubin che oro circunscrive*: "Like rubies set in gold." *rubin = rubini*. When it is understood that these are angels who assist in the transmission of love, their red color will seem most appropriate since red is the color of love. In this first incomplete vision, the "gold" obviously suggests that the "flowers" that grow on the banks are of golden color, even as the "river" itself.

68. *miro*: "Marvelous," from the Latin *mirus*. *gurge*:

From the Latin *gurges*. Cf. Virgil, *Aen.* I, 118; VI, 296. The word means "torrent."

70. *L'alto disio*: Cf. *Par.* XXII, 61.   *urge*: Cf. *Par.* X, 142.

71. *vei = vedi*. The form was used in prose in early Italian. See E. G. Parodi (1957), p. 258.

72. *turge*: "Swells." Cf. *Par.* X, 144.

73. *bei = beva*. The reader is soon to see what an extraordinary "drinking" this proves to be.

75. *il sol de li occhi miei*: Cf. *Par.* III, 1. Such an epithet for Beatrice is common enough, by implication, but to use it here is to stress the action as being primarily in terms of vision.

76. *li topazi*: The metaphor changes for the angels, from ruby to topaz, which may seem somewhat curious since the topaz is characteristically yellow. However, yellow topaz is sometimes made red by heating, and perhaps the poet is suggesting just this, since these precious stones, first called rubies, are aflame with love and are the bearers of love.

77. *'l rider de l'erbe*: The "mirabil primavera" of vs. 63.

78. *son di lor vero umbriferi prefazi*: "Prefazi" (from the Latin *praefatio*, literally, a saying beforehand) can be understood metaphorically as "preface," of course, and with its adjective "umbriferi" as a veiled preface of what is to be disclosed, that truth or real nature of these "flowers" and "bees" and this marvelous "river."

79. *da sé = per sé*, "in themselves."   *acerbe*: "Unripe," i.e., not fully matured. Cf. *Inf.* XXV, 18; *Purg.* XXVI, 55; *Par.* XIX, 48, and the corresponding note.

80–81. *difetto da la parte . . . superbe*: This affirmation continues the metaphor of the candle that must be disposed to receive the flame. Cf. vs. 54.

81. *viste*: "Eyes."   *superbe*: Here, in the good sense of "exalted," "strong."

82. *fantin* = *fantino*, i.e., *bambino*. *rua*: Literally, "plunges," from the Latin *ruat*. Cf. *Inf.* XX, 33.

84. *l'usanza sua*: His usual nursing time. The implied simile presents an innocent and humble Dante hungry now for the higher and truer vision promised him.

85–86. *per far . . . occhi*: "To make better mirrors of my eyes" continues the stress on seeing by reflection which has prevailed throughout the journey with Beatrice and was there at the beginning: cf. *Purg.* XXXI, 109-23. On this kind of vision as belonging to the second kind of light which Beatrice represents, see C. S. Singleton (1958), pp. 23-31. Here, at the point of transition from guidance by her kind of light to guidance by another, the light of glory, Dante's eyes rather than Beatrice's become the mirrors. This touch, clearly stressing vision by contemplation, may recall Rachel (*Purg.* XXVII, 104-8), who sat before her mirror all day to look upon her own eyes. And in the heaven of the contemplatives (Saturn) the word *specchi* is used in exactly the sense it has here (*Par.* XXI, 17).

87. *che si deriva perché vi s'immegli*: "Which pours forth that we may better ourselves there," i.e., improve our vision on the upward way. The implication is that any pilgrim who attains to this high place in the journey "where the candle must be made able to bear the flame" (vs. 54) would undergo this experience—and perhaps that any soul on its upward way to the beatific vision would also be made ready in this way, though this is not clearly stated. *s'immegli*: This could be the impersonal construction, but it might also imply that "one," "we," is the subject of the reflexive verb.

88–90. *e sì come di lei . . . tonda*: This moment of "drinking" in this striking way (which so stresses vision as the medium of the journey) is one of the most impressive in the long line of events which gradually transform the wayfarer. There was another such transforming moment signaled at the beginning of the upward journey with Beatrice, where the verb *trasumanar* was used and Glaucus' metamorphosis was recalled (*Par.* I, 67-71). And since the wayfarer now drinks of a river, his drinking of Lethe may also be remembered (*Purg.* XXVIII, 130-33; XXXI, 100-102), which was also a necessary preparation for higher vision at that point, through reflection in Beatrice's eyes as mirrors (*Purg.* XXXI, 121-23).

88. *lei*: The "onda" (vs. 86).

88–89. *la gronda de le palpebre*: "The eaves of my eyelids" are the lashes.

90. *di sua lunghezza divenuta tonda*: The light from God, first seen as a river and therefore as a horizontal flowing (this being a "veiled preface" of the reality there), now becomes a downstreaming light, vertical from horizontal. Since the wayfarer is passing now, in vision, from time to eternity, the reader should be aware of the full burden of symbolic suggestion involved in this transformation, since the downpouring light becomes, by reflection, a great circle: a river is a familiar symbol of time, whereas the circle is the symbol of eternity. In a single verse, with the terms "lunghezza" and "tonda," the poet has conveyed such a "crossing over."

91. *larve*: "Masks," from the Latin *larva*. See the word already used in this sense, *Purg.* XV, 127. The simile operates, of course, within the frame-notion of "umbriferi prefazi," vs. 78.

93. *la sembianza non sua*: The semblance of flowers adorning the banks of the river, in the first "unripe" vision (vss. 62-63), for the human souls, and the sparks for the angels.
  disparve = era sparita.

94. *maggior feste*: Figures more joyous or "festive."

95. *vidi*: "Note the insistence on the reality of the vision of Heaven, implied in the repetition of *vidi* in rhyme with itself in ll. 95, 97, 99" (Gr).

96. *ambo le corti del ciel*: The two militias (vs. 43), angels and human souls, are now termed "courts."

97–99. *O isplendor . . . vidi*: The tercet constitutes an invocation on the part of the poet, not to the Muses now, but to the very light of God.

100–102. *Lume è là sù . . . pace*: The tercet presents the downstreaming light of God in terms that define it specifically as the light of glory, and it is no accident that this occurs with a verse numbered 100, in a canto numbered 30! See Thomas Aquinas, *In Isaiam prophetam expositio* I, 1:

> Est enim quaedam visio ad quam sufficit lumen naturale intellectus, sicut est contemplatio invisibilium per principia rationis: et in hac contemplatione ponebant philosophi summam felicitatem hominis. Est iterum quaedam contemplatio ad quam elevatur homo per lumen fidei sufficiens, sicut sanctorum in via. Est etiam quaedam beatorum in patria ad quam elevatur intellectus per lumen gloriae, videns Deum per essentiam, inquantum est obiectum beatitudinis; et hoc plene et perfecte non est nisi in patria: sed quandoque ad ipsam raptim elevatur aliquis etiam existens in hac mortali vita, sicut fuit in raptu Pauli.

> There is [1] a kind of vision for which the natural light of intellect suffices, such as the contemplation of invisible things according to the principles of reason; and the philosophers placed the highest happiness of man in this contemplation; [2] there is yet another kind of contemplation to which man is raised by the light of faith, as are the saints in this life [*in via*]; and [3] there is that contemplation of the blessed in Heaven [*in patria*] to which the intellect is uplifted by the light of glory, seeing God in His essence, as the object of beatitude—and this contemplation is not full and perfect except in Heaven; yet sometimes one is uplifted to this contemplation by rapture even while still in this mortal life, as was Paul when in rapture.

See C. S. Singleton (1958), pp. 20-23.

100. *che visibile face*: "Che" is the subject, "creatore" (vs. 101) the object of the verb.   *face = fa*.

101. *a quella creatura*: This means, in the context, both angels and human creatures, for they, and they alone, are capable of the beatific vision, through the light of glory.

102. *ha la sua pace*: Cf. *Par.* III, 85, and see Augustine, *Conf.* I, 1: "Fecisti nos ad te et inquietum est cor nostrum, donec requiescat in te." ("Thou hast created us for thyself, and our heart cannot be quieted till it may find repose in thee.")

103. *E'* = *egli* (the "lume" of vs. 100).   *si distende* = *si estende*.

103-5. *E' si distende . . . cintura*: It should be remarked that, as the following verses then explain, the downstreaming light of glory is first seen primarily as reflected light and will continue, by implication, to be seen primarily thus. The journey still moves with Beatrice, and reflected light is the kind of light by which she guides in the journey. Of course she and Dante will look up directly to see the human souls and angels, but they will see them by a light that is thrown back from the convex surface of the Primum Mobile (surely one of the most astounding conceptions and images known to poetry!). Thus we now learn how it is that the light became round (vs. 90). It does so in a pool of reflected light or, given its dimensions—larger than the disk of the sun itself (vs. 105)—it were better called an "ocean."

106-8. *Fassi di raggio . . . potenza*: The whole material universe forms a globe, whose exterior is that of the Primum Mobile. The downpouring light of glory descends upon the convex outer surface of the Primum Mobile and, reflected upon its surface, becomes the circular ocean of light that appears as the "floor" of Paradise.

106. *Fassi* = *si fa*.

108. *che prende quindi vivere e potenza*: From this ray of God's light striking upon it, the Primum Mobile takes its motion ("vivere," motion being its very life) and the power ("potenza") which it transmits to the other heavens in a hier-

archical descent to the earth at the center. Cf. *Par.* II, 112-23; XXVII, 106-14.

109-11. *E come clivo . . . opimo*: This remarkable simile presents, in its first term, the image of a hillside with a pool or lake at its base which reflects that base in its greenery and its flowers. The important symbolic point is that such an image is deliberately calculated to continue the stress on seeing by *reflected* light (see notes above), the verb *specchiarsi* appearing in both terms of the simile (vss. 110 and 113): that is, the whole amphitheater or rose of the blessed in their seats is first seen by reflection.

109. *clivo*: "Hillside."   *di suo imo*: "At its base."

110. *si specchia, quasi per vedersi addorno*: The hillside is, as it were, personified, gazing at its own beauty in the mirroring water. But see n. to vss. 112-14, on the corresponding "specchiarsi" of vs. 113.

111. *opimo*: "Rich." Cf. *Par.* XVIII, 33.

112-14. *sì, soprastando . . . ritorno*: Thus, "all of us who have returned on high," that is, all the elect (human souls), are seen by Dante reflected in the ocean of light at the center of what will be called a rose and is actually an amphitheater. Some commentators are inclined to misunderstand the verb "specchiarsi" here. Strictly speaking, to match the same notion in the first term of the simile, this would mean that the blessed "look *down*" into the ocean of light which is the "lake" at the center in order to see themselves therein, as in a mirror. But this cannot be the meaning intended by the poet, since all souls seated in the amphitheater look upwards, to enjoy their vision of God face to face, not downwards, to see themselves (an absurdity from the doctrinal point of view). Thus it is the wayfarer who sees the reflection, not the blessed, and the verb *specchiarsi* can bear such a meaning here perfectly well: "vidi specchiarsi" ("I saw reflected"). The repetition "intorno intorno" clearly implies that Dante sees the amphitheater in its whole extent and circumference, which would not follow from the image of the hillside reflecting itself at its base.

113. *soglie*: "Tiers." Cf. *Par.* III, 82; XVIII, 28.

115–17. *E se l'infimo . . . foglie*: These verses, exclaiming over the almost inconceivable size of this amphitheater, refer back to the statement of vss. 103-5, where we were told that the reflected ocean of light is bigger than the sun in its circumference. Now we are reminded that this means, of course, that the lowest tier of the amphitheater encloses that ocean of light; therefore, how vast in circumference must be the uppermost tiers! But the image shifts from that of an amphitheater to that of a single rose with its sections termed petals, and this striking image, rich in connotation, will remain dominant now in this and the next two cantos.

118–20. *La vista mia . . . allegrezza*: We no longer see with Dante by reflected light, but the wayfarer now surveys ("prendeva," "took in") the entire amphitheater directly.

120. *il quanto e 'l quale*: "The extension and the nature" of the whole scene of the blessed in their seats, termed an "allegrezza" with reference to their festivity there (cf. vs. 94, "feste"), in their enjoyment of the ultimate beatitude: the direct vision of God.

121. *Presso e lontano, lì, né pon né leva*: "There, nearness and distance neither add nor subtract," i.e., make no difference. *pon = pone (porre)*.

122. *sanza mezzo*: "Directly," without mediation of the secondary powers of the world of nature (the "legge natural" of the following verse).

123. *nulla rileva*: "Does not apply," "is inoperative."

124. *Nel giallo*: "Into the yellow" is to be connected with "mi trasse Beatrice" in vs. 128. The "yellow of the rose" is its center, the sea of light which has already been termed "fulvido" (in vs. 62) when it first appeared as a "river." Here, in his astounding imagery, the poet draws upon the

imagery of John in Apoc. 4:6: "Et in conspectu sedis tam-
quam mare vitreum simile crystallo." ("And before the
throne there is, as it were, a sea of glass like to crystal.")

125. *si digrada e dilata e redole*: "Which expands, and rises
in steps, and gives off fragrance."   *redole*: From the Latin
redolet. This verb, rare even in Latin, is used transitively
here, "odor di lode" (vs. 126) being its object.

126. *al sol che sempre verna*: The one flower, so vast in size,
this rose, blossoms and is fragrant through all eternity under
the light of God, its "sun," declaring His glory through its
beauty and especially its fragrance, which, out of metaphor,
is the love and praise that rise from its petals (the souls of the
elect) to the Creator above, whom they now see face to face.
    sempre verna: "Makes eternal spring." The verb is not to
be confused with *vernare* (from *hibernare*), meaning "to
pass the winter" (*Inf.* XXXIII, 135; *Purg.* XXIV, 64). Here
the form derives from the Latin *vernare*, meaning "to
bloom," "to renew itself," "to make spring."
    It should be noted that the sun above, which is God, is not
seen directly by the wayfarer (nor by the reader, in conse-
quence) until the very end of the poem. Our view of the rose
is by reflected light. This, as noted above, is a very important
fact, symbolically and in terms of the three lights of the
journey.

127–29. *qual è colui . . . stole*: "Colui" refers to Dante, of
course, i.e., to "mi," the object of "trasse."

129. *convento*: "Assembly." Cf. *Purg.* XXI, 62; *Par.* XXII,
90.   *bianche stole*: See Apoc. 3:5: "Qui vicerit sic vestie-
tur vestimentis albis." ("He who overcomes shall be arrayed
thus in white garments.") Also see Apoc. 7:13: "Hi qui
amicti sunt stolis albis, qui sunt et unde venerunt?" ("These
who are clothed in white robes, who are they? and whence
have they come?") Cf. *Par.* XXV, 88-96.

130–32. *Vedi nostra città . . . disira*: The image of a city
could scarcely fail to appear in this context and these verses,

for it is so central to the Christian concept of Heaven: the city of God, the heavenly Jerusalem, the "true city" (*Purg.* XIII, 95), and "Rome" (*Purg.* XXXII, 102: "quella Roma onde Cristo è romano").

131. *scanni*: The term appears early in the poem (*Inf.* II, 112) when Beatrice in Limbo refers to her seat in Heaven as a "beato scanno," and it has been used throughout the *Paradiso*.

132. *poca gente più ci si disira*: "Men are so wicked, and the end of the world is so near, that only a few more souls are expected in Paradise" (Gr). Cf. *Conv.* II, xiv, 13: "Noi siamo già ne l'ultima etade del secolo." ("We are already in the final age of the world.")

As for the few empty seats still available in the amphitheater, the reader will learn soon (*Par.* XXXII) that the assembly is divided down the middle into two sections wherein are seated those of the elect who lived in B.C. time and those who lived in A.D. time. Obviously, the empty seats are all in the A.D. section, for the B.C. section became full following the harrowing of Hell. (See Fig. 5, p. 534.)

It should also be remembered that, according to accepted doctrine, humankind was created by God to replace the fallen angels. See *Conv.* II, v, 12, where Dante refers to this.

133–38. *E 'n quel gran seggio . . . disposta*: "The impressive episode of a vacant chair in Heaven is found in several medieval legends: in the Syriac version of the *Visio S. Pauli*, in the vision of Tundal, and in the *Dialogus Miraculorum* of Caesarius of Heisterbàch. The homage which Dante, in these lines, pays to his worshipped Henry acquires tremendous force from the unfitness of a symbol of mundane sovereignty in Paradise. Cf. *Purg.* XIX, 133-138" (Gr).

It should be remembered, however, that in Dante's view (as made clear in his treatise *De monarchia* and throughout the *Divine Comedy*) the temporal power of the emperor, whoever he may be, is directly ordained by God, from Heaven, so that a special seat for an emperor there is not a total or entirely shocking incongruity. And an empty chair, in the fictional date of 1300, registers the fact that in that year, in Dante's view, the seat of Empire is indeed empty.

135. *nozze*: For the "wedding" in Heaven, cf. *Purg.* XXXII, 75, and *Par.* XXIV, 1-3. See Apoc. 19:9. This is clearly yet another prediction of Dante's salvation. (See n. to vs. 45.) As for the prediction of the death of Henry VII, that was easily made at the time the poet was writing this canto, for Henry died in 1313.

136. *fia = sarà*.   *agosta = augusta*,   imperial,   invested with imperial authority.

137. *l'alto Arrigo*: Dante is speaking here of the Emperor Henry VII. Henry, count of Luxemburg (born *ca.* 1275), was at the instance of Clement V unanimously elected emperor on November 27, 1308, in opposition to Charles of Valois, the candidate of the French king, Philip the Fair. Henry, who had been recommended to Clement by the Cardinal da Prato as "il migliore uomo della Magna, e il più leale e il più franco e più cattolico" ("the best man of Germany, the most loyal, the most honest, and the most catholic") according to Villani, VIII, 101, was crowned at Aix-la-Chapelle on January 6, 1309. In the following June he sent ambassadors to Florence to announce that he was coming into Italy to receive the imperial crown, a ceremony which had been neglected by his predecessors for many years.

To this advent of Henry Dante looked anxiously for a settlement of the affairs of Italy and for a means to secure his own return to Florence. But his hopes were doomed to bitter disappointment. The emperor crossed the Alps in late October 1310, with a force of about 5,000 men, with less than 500 cavalry, and at first was well received. The cities of Lombardy opened their gates; Milan (where he assumed the iron crown, January 6, 1311) decreed a vast subsidy; Guelph and Ghibelline exiles alike were restored, and imperial vicars appointed everywhere. Supported by the Avignonese pontiff, who dreaded the restless ambition of his French neighbor, Philip the Fair, Henry had the interdict of the Church as well as the ban of the Empire at his command.

But this success did not last long. Tumults and revolts broke out in Lombardy; and at Rome, whither he went (early May 1312) to be crowned, Henry found St. Peter's in the hands of King Robert of Naples and the Tuscan Guelphs, so that the coronation had to take place, shorn of its ceremony, in St. John Lateran, on the southern bank of the Tiber (June 29, 1312). The hostility of the Guelphic league, headed by the Florentines, with King Robert as their acknowledged leader, compelled the emperor to hasten back to Tuscany, for the purpose of laying siege to Florence, which had persistently defied him. To counterbalance the opposition of the Guelphs, he was obliged to abandon his policy of impartiality and to identify himself with the Ghibellines, whose aid he secured by granting to their chiefs the government of cities. Meanwhile Clement V, yielding to the menaces of the French king, had secretly withdrawn his support from the emperor (*Par.* XVII, 82). Henry arrived before Florence in September (1312); but in October he was obliged to raise the siege and retire to Pisa, whence on August 8 of the next year he set out with the intention of reducing Naples. On his way south he was seized with illness, and on August 24, 1313, he died at Buonconvento near Siena. His somewhat sudden death, which was probably due to a malarial fever contracted at Rome, was currently ascribed to poison administered by a Dominican friar in the consecrated wafer. The emperor's body was taken to Pisa and interred in the cathedral, where a monument (removed in 1830 to the Campo Santo), ascribed to Giovanni Pisano, was erected to him.

138. *prima ch'ella sia disposta*: Dante wrote three letters with especial reference to the Emperor Henry VII—one addressed to the princes and peoples of Italy, exhorting them to receive him (*Epist.* V), the second to the rebellious Florentines who opposed his coming (*Epist.* VI), the third addressed to the emperor himself, beseeching him to come into Tuscany and chastise Florence without delay (*Epist.* VII). These letters make clear, as does the preceding note, in what sense Dante in retrospect had reason to view the advent of Henry into Italy as having taken place before she was ready to allow him to "set her straight."

139–41. *La cieca . . . balia*: The words "la cieca cupidigia" have occurred before in the poem (*Inf.* XII, 49), as have similar denunciations of this besetting vice (see, for instance, *Par.* XXVII, 121-23). See also Dante's words addressed to the Florentines in *Epist.* VI, 12, "o male concordes! o mira cupidine obcecati!" ("oh, harmonious in ill, oh, blinded by wondrous greed") and VI, 22: "Nec advertitis dominantem cupidinem, quia ceci estis, venenoso susurrio blandientem." ("Nor in your blindness do ye perceive the lust that hath sway over you, lulling you with poisonous whisper.")

139. *ammalia*: "Bewitches." This is the only instance of the use of this verb in the poem. It is formed on the noun *malia* (cf. *Inf.* XX, 123). For the conception of such bewitching, cf. *Purg.* XIX, 25-33. The overtones of meaning suggest that the bewitching blinds humankind and, in this case, the Italians who oppose the lofty Henry, as Dante's letter, just cited, clearly states.

140. *fantolino*: "Babe." Cf. *Purg.* XXX, 44, and *passim*. Also see "fantin" in vs. 82 of this canto.

142–44. *E fia prefetto . . . cammino*: The pope, or "prefect in the sacred court," is Clement V. The poet has already denounced Clement and assigned him to the circle of the simonists in Inferno (*Inf.* XIX, 82-87). For particulars, see n. to *Inf.* XIX, 83. His treachery toward the Emperor Henry has also been referred to, prophetically (*Par.* XVII, 82). When in 1308, on the assassination of the Emperor Albert of Austria, the imperial crown became vacant, Clement was pressed by Philip to support (as some suppose, in fulfillment of the secret sixth condition of his election) the candidacy of his brother, Clement's old enemy, Charles of Valois. Ostensibly the pope complied, but, dreading any further extension of the formidable power of France, he secretly exerted all his influence against Charles, and favored the claims of his rival, Henry of Luxemburg, who was elected as Henry VII. When the new emperor descended into Italy to assert his imperial rights, Clement for a time loyally cooperated with him; but, yielding to the menaces of the French king, he gradually withdrew his support, leaving Henry to carry out his task alone, unaided, if not actually opposed, by the papal influence. Clement survived the emperor he had betrayed less than a year.

142. *fia = sarà.*

145. *sofferto = tollerato.*

146–48. *ch'el sarà . . . giuso*: Clement shall fall into the third pouch of the eighth circle of Hell, where simonists are planted upside down with burning soles. In the hole reserved for simoniacal popes, each new arrival pushes his predecessors farther down and takes his turn on top (*Inf.* XIX, 73-75), being thus "thrust down" into this hole.

146. *detruso*: "Thrust down," from the Latin *detrusus.*

147. *Simon mago*: For Simon Magus, see *Inf.* XIX, 1.

148. *farà quel d'Alagna intrar più giuso*: "Clement's predecessor in simony is Boniface VIII: *Inf.* XIX, 51-57. He is called 'the man of Anagni' because he was born in that town, and in 1303 was assaulted and taken prisoner there: *Purg.* XX, 85-90. Anagni was known also as *Alagna* and *Anagna.* —These fearful words are the last spoken by Beatrice" (Gr). As such words, it may be added, they amount to a kind of last look earthwards and a last denunciation of cupidity on earth as the sin that most besets mankind there, a fact that was conveyed in the action of the poem at its very beginning, when the she-wolf proved to be the most troublesome of the three beasts blocking the wayfarer's progress up the mountainside. The poem, on this point, comes full circle.

   The poet's indignation is righteous indignation, from his point of view, and this last denunciation of Boniface is just. Some readers of the poem may pause to wonder, however, over the fact that (since the poet Dante and the wayfarer Dante are one person, and since the poet writing his poem is the wayfarer returned to earth from this long journey) Dante shows no more charity toward Boniface than he did at the beginning (*Inf.* VI, 69) and in the many references thereafter, culminating in this one. Has the wayfarer learned no lesson of Christian charity in the long journey to God, and does he, being now so near to God, not love his fellow man, not forgive? But one has only to entertain such reflections for a mere instant to realize that no such transformation of the Christian pilgrim is shown in this journey to God. Dante the character who returns to be Dante the poet is finally quite unchanged by his experience.

With such thoughts the reader should not forget, however, that these words are, after all, Beatrice's and not, in the fiction of the poem, spoken by the poet, but only recorded by him.

CANTO XXXI

1. *candida*: See *Par*. XXX, 129, the "convento de le bian-che stole." The adjective can also suggest the noun *can-dore*, which in itself connotes a "glowing." Cf. *Par*. XIV, 37-39, and "candente" in *Par*. XIV, 77.   *candida rosa*: "The figure of the rose seems to be Dante's own, although Paradise is sometimes represented in roselike form in early Italian art. The rose, too, was sometimes used as a symbol of the Passion. On the fourth Sunday of Lent, the Pope blesses a gold rose ('rosa aurea mixta cum balsamo et musco'), with a ceremonial that indicates an association of this flower with Christ and Heaven: see G. Busnelli, *Il con-cetto e l'ordine del 'Paradiso' dantesco*, I, 1911, 233-238. The Old French *Roman de la Rose*, the great literary success of the 13th century, made all western Europe familiar with the rose as a symbol of earthly love; Dante's white flower is the rose of Heavenly love. It may be that a sight of the Ro-man Coliseum influenced his conception of the great amphi-theater of Paradise (cf. Busnelli, I, 239-242). The figure of the rose is also an homage to Mary, who presides in the as-sembly. See Albertus Magnus, *De laud. b. Mariae Virginis*, XII, iv, 33: 'Et nota, quod Christus rosa, Maria rosa, Ec-clesia rosa, fidelis anima rosa.' ['And note that Christ is a rose, Mary is a rose, the Church is a rose, the faithful soul is a rose.']" (Gr).

2. *la milizia santa*: Cf. *Par.* XXX, 43.

3. *nel suo sangue Cristo fece sposa*: Cf. Actus 20:28: "Attendite vobis et universo gregi in quo vos Spiritus Sanctus posuit episcopos regere ecclesiam Dei, quam acquisivit sanguine suo." ("Take heed to yourselves and to the whole flock in which the Holy Spirit has placed you as bishops, to rule the Church of God, which he has purchased with his own blood.")

4. *l'altra*: I.e., the "milizia," the angels.

5. *la gloria di colui che la 'nnamora*: Love is stressed here, as it is in the verses that recount the creation of the angels (see *Par.* XXIX, 18). But the *seeing* which precedes love is indicated by the "vede" of the preceding verse. See *Par.* XXVIII, 109-11.

6. *la fece cotanta*: See *Par.* XXIX, 59-60.

7. *ape = api*. "Ape" is from the Latin *apes*. *s'infiora*: "Enflowers itself," dips into flowers. The simile of bees and flowers is first suggested as part of the "umbriferi prefazi" (*Par.* XXX, 78) seen by Dante in this last heaven (see *Par.* XXX, 64-65).

8. *e una*: I.e., e un'altra volta. *si ritorna*: Chimenz notes that this is the pleonastic reflexive, as indeed it is, in its distancing function.

9. *là*: To the hive. *s'insapora*: "Turns savory," the nectar being changed to honey.

11. *foglie*: "Petals," i.e., the blessed in their thrones in the great amphitheater. *quindi*: "From there," i.e., from the rose.

11-12. *quindi risaliva . . . soggiorna*: The angels' love is God, who so far in all this scene of the heavenly Paradise remains above and beyond any direct vision of Him on the part of Dante or the reader. Direct vision of Him will only be given at the end; here we still see by reflected light.

13. *Le facce tutte avean di fiamma viva*: Cf. Ezech. 1:13: "Aspectus eorum quasi carbonum ignis ardentium." ("Their appearance was like that of burning coals of fire.")

14. *e l'ali d'oro*: Ruby red and gold were colors in the first "prefatory" vision (cf. *Par.* XXX, 66).

14–15. *e l'altro tanto bianco . . . arriva*: Cf. Dan. 7:9: "Vestimentum eius candidum quasi nix." ("His garment was white as snow.") See also Matt. 28:3; Apoc. 10:1. This is the robe which angels wear, apparently, corresponding to the white "stole" (*Par.* XXX, 129) of human souls. The reader will recall a scene in Purgatory where angels descended wearing robes of a tender green color (*Purg.* VIII, 28-30), but there that color was a symbol of hope, whereas the angel that piloted the boat bringing souls to Purgatory had a white robe, but also white wings (*Purg.* II, 22-26). The angels who stand at the exits of the terraces in that second realm are robed in white (see, for example, *Purg.* XII, 89).

16–18. *Quando scendean . . . fianco*: It now appears that this simile of bees bearing nectar is actually the reverse of the normal activity of bees in nature, which is to bear from the flower to the hive. Here the "bees" bear their "nectar" from the hive (God) to the flower. For other inverted similes, see *Par.* XXVII, 71 and 118-19, and see nn. to *Par.* XXVII, 67-72 and 118-19.

16. *di banco in banco*: "From tier to tier." Cf. "soglie," *Par.* XXX, 113.

17. *porgevan de la pace e de l'ardore*: Peace and ardor (love) are the "honey" which the angels bear to the petals of the great flower. This is in addition to the "honey" (to keep the metaphor) which each human soul receives by gazing directly upon God, through the light of glory. In connection with such a multiplication of love in Heaven the reader may recall a lesson on this subject in *Purg.* XV, 55-57.

18. *ventilando il fianco*: "By fanning their sides," i.e., by the action of their wings as they fly upward. One should also

visualize the fluttering robes of the angels as well, even as in *Purg.* VIII, 29-30.

19-21. *Né l'interporsi . . . splendore*: These verses are clearly concerned to remove a doubt in the reader's mind: Would not the host of angels in their fluttering robes obstruct the vision of God which the human souls enjoy in their eternal beatitude? The "splendore" is the descending light of glory which makes such vision possible.

19. *'l disopra*: God, who is gazed upon in direct vision, face to face, by the souls, but not yet by Dante the pilgrim.

22-24. *ché la luce . . . ostante*: The opening verses of the *Paradiso* are an excellent gloss to these verses, as are those of *Par.* II, 112-48.

24. *essere ostante*: "Be an obstacle." See *Conv.* III, vii, 5, where Dante tells us that angels are diaphanous.

26. *frequente*: "Abounding." "Frequente" is a Latinism, from *frequens*.   *in gente antica e in novella*: Members of the old (Hebrew) and the new (Christian) church. We are to see the distinction strikingly observed in the seating arrangement in the amphitheater.

27. *viso e amore*: The two terms correspond respectively to the activity of the intellect and that of the will.   *tutto*: The adjective is here used adverbially: "entirely."   *ad un segno*: God, who is the goal of all. By now, it will be noted, the Deity is definitely located as a point above (still not seen by reader or wayfarer), as is further brought out by the words "unica stella" in the following verse. It will be remembered that there was a time, in the total picture of all existence, when God was a circumference, not a center or a point. See n. to *Par.* XXVIII, 41-42.

28. *Oh trina luce che 'n unica stella*: The verse clearly indicates God in His tri-unity.

29. *scintillando a lor vista, sì li appaga*: By giving of His light, the light of glory (see *Par.* XXX, 100), which makes

it possible for the creature to gaze upon Him, God gives that creature the only peace that can ever completely satisfy (*appagare*).   *appaga*: It seems best to understand this as the third-person form of the verb. See E. G. Parodi (1957), p. 398.

30. *guarda qua giuso a la nostra procella*: The "storm" referred to is that which is agitating all mankind in life on earth —and the reader knows well from the poem by now how great it is, in the poet's view. The exhortation, turned earthwards in its focus, anticipates that of vss. 37-39.

31–36. *Se i barbari . . . sopra*: Perhaps the "barbarians" who served in the Roman army, or came for whatever reason to the city before it was destroyed by them, are meant, for then the Lateran and many another building in Rome ("l'ardua sua opra") were truly splendid and amazing to behold.

31–33. *tal plaga . . . figlio*: "The 'zone' that is always 'covered by Helice' is the North. The nymph Helice or Callisto was transformed into the constellation of the Great Bear, and her son Arcas or Boötes into the Little Bear: *Met.*, II, 496-530, especially 515-17; cf. *Purg.* XXV, 131. The Bears, or Dippers, are close to the North Star" (Gr).

33. *ond' ella è vaga*: "Whom she loves" (Gr).

34. *l'ardua sua opra*: "Her lofty buildings."

35. *stupefaciensi = si stupefacevano.   Laterano*: Cf. *Inf.* XXVII, 86. The Lateran was the old papal palace in Rome, first the residence of emperors, then of popes down into Dante's time. According to tradition it was given to Pope Sylvester by the Emperor Constantine and thus became the seat of Christian dominion. The present palace, dating from *ca.* 1586, was built on the ruins of the original structure, which was destroyed by fire in 1308 and was said to have belonged originally to the Laterani family.

36. *a le cose mortali andò di sopra*: "Surpassed all other mortal things," i.e., man-made edifices.

37. *io, che al divino da l'umano*: On this verse and others in the present canto, Grandgent observes: "The verses of the present canto offer an unusual abundance of examples of hiatus and diaeresis, which would seem to indicate a slow, thoughtful, impressive delivery. In such cases as *cominciò / elli* and *farà / ogni* (where a final vowel is stressed) hiatus is the rule in our poet. Also, in words like *ardüa, fïata, gaudïoso* (contrasted with *gaudio*), *glorïose, orïental, regïon, rïaccesa, süadi*—mostly Latinisms—diaeresis is rather to be expected in the *Commedia*; although the number of such forms is uncommonly large in this canto. Very rare indeed, on the other hand, are lines comparable to 37, 47, and 53:

> ï/o, che / al divino da l'umano,
>
> menava / ï/o li occhi per li gradi,
>
> già tutta mï/o sguardo avea compresa."

On vs. 39 Grandgent also notes: "This phrase, the climax of the tiercet, is Dante's last and bitterest fling at Florence."

40. *compiuto*: "Filled."

41. *tra esso e 'l gaudio*: "It [my amazement] and my joy together" (dual subject of the verb "facea").

42. *libito*: "Pleasing." Cf. *Inf.* V, 56.   *non udire*: This refers to Beatrice's silence.

43–45. *E quasi . . . stea*: It will be recalled that the journey was termed a pilgrimage (that is, the wayfarers were termed pilgrims) only after Dante's arrival in Purgatory (see *Purg.* II, 63), where positive ascent began. The reader will remark how frequently, now at the end of the long upward way, the pilgrim simile and metaphor come into the poem, and often, as here, in a notably strategic way, for the very notion of pilgrimage raises the question of "whereto" and of "return home." (See, for example, the opening verses of *Purg.* VIII.) A pilgrim may finally, in his outward journey away from home, reach "the temple of his vow," as here implied, and then make his way back home, where he hopes to tell of all the wonderful things he saw. This, applied to Dante the wayfarer at this high terminal point, projects, by clear implica-

tion, his "return home"—and his poem is the telling of it all
to those "back home." In short, the poem here, at the end,
is using the pilgrim image so as to point to a return to earth
which must necessarily be that of the living man who then
writes the poem.

43. *si ricrea*: "Refreshes himself," "restores himself" after
the hardships of the way.

44. *tempio del suo voto*: The shrine which he has vowed to
visit.

45. *ridir*: To tell the people at home.   *ello*: The *tempio*.
stea = stia.

46–48. *su per la viva luce . . . recirculando*: The pilgrim
scans the whole amphitheater from where he stands, "walk-
ing" with his eyes over the whole, an "eye tour," as it were.
The "viva luce," it should be remembered, is still *reflected*
light (*Par.* XXX, 106-8).

49. *Vedea = vedevo*.   *süadi*: From the Latin *suadus*,
meaning "conducive to" or "persuasive" in its commonest
usage. In the present context, however, it seems best to take
the meaning to be passive rather than active, thus "per-
suaded" to charity, i.e., "centered on" love, "all given to"
love.

50. *d'altrui lume*: God's light.   *fregiati e di suo riso*:
"Radiant with their own smiles." This is *riso* expressed as a
radiance. Cf. *Par.* IX, 70-71.

51. *atti*: "Demeanor."   *onestadi*: "Decorum."

52–59. *La forma general . . . Beatrice*: It will be noted that
the verbs in these verses are all in the past descriptive, thus
building up to the dramatic shift to the narrative past abso-
lute at the surprise moment, "vidi" (vs. 59). And it is a mo-
ment when the reader is bound to recall another, when Dante
had taken in, as it were, the whole procession at the top of
Purgatory, including finally Beatrice at her appearance on the
chariot, and turned, as he thought, to confide in Virgil, only

to find that Virgil was no longer with him (*Purg.* XXX, 40-54).

58. *Uno intendea, e altro mi rispuose*: "I expected one thing, but another presented itself to me." *rispuose*: I.e., *corrispose*.

59. *sene*: "Elder," from the Latin *senex*. The Latinism confers greater dignity on the figure and suggests much reverence toward him on the part of the poet. The term is repeated in vs. 94, modified with "santo." This proves to be Bernard of Clairvaux, but identification is withheld until vs. 102, and full attention now centers on Beatrice and the "goodbye" to her. For particulars regarding Bernard, see n. to vs. 102.

60. *vestito con*: "Clad like," i.e., dressed in the white "stole," as are all the other blessed (*Par.* XXX, 129). *gloriose*: The adjective conveys the notion of *gloria* in its full theological sense: those who now enjoy eternal beatitude, with a vision of God made possible through the light of glory. For an earlier use of the word in this sense, see *Vita nuova*, II, 1, where Dante refers to Beatrice (dead and already in Paradise) as "la gloriosa donna de la mia mente" ("the glorious lady of my mind").

61. *gene*: "Cheeks," from the Latin *genae*. Again a Latinism contributes to the dignity and reverence of the figure.

62. *pio*: Given the context, the primary meaning of the word is "loving."

64. *Ov' è ella?* With this the poet has impressively dramatized the immediate and most anxious concern of the pilgrim for his Beatrice, no longer by his side, an over-riding anxiety which admits of no curiosity in regard to the identity of the "elder" who has replaced her.

65. *A terminar lo tuo disiro*: The desire is, of course, the innate desire of natural love, common to every human creature, to attain to God and to the vision of Him face to face. Cf. *Purg.* XVII, 127-29. The fact that this "sene," who

518

proves to be St. Bernard, has been sent by Beatrice to bring about this *terminus* of all "unquiet hearts" says much about Beatrice's limits as guide in the journey. On this point, see C. S. Singleton (1958), pp. 23-31, and on Bernard's specific role as Beatrice's replacement, see pp. 20-23.

66. *mosse*: Cf. *Par.* XXVI, 118.

67-68. *e se riguardi . . . rivedrai*: "Beatrice's own seat is 'in the third row from the top tier.' The 1st row is that of Mary, the 2nd that of Eve, the 3rd that of Rachel, beside whom Beatrice sits: see *Inf.* II, 102; *Par.* XXXII, 8-9. Contemplation and Revelation sit side by side. The number 3 (as well as the number 9) has always been mysteriously associated with Beatrice: see *V.N.*, XXIX" (Gr). See Fig. 5, p. 534.

69. *che suoi merti le sortiro*: Despite the symbolism of the number three (see preceding note), this phrase concerning Beatrice's merits focuses on her primarily as the particular human individual and soul that she was, for she now, like all the other particular souls in the great amphitheater, has her seat according to the original endowment of grace given to her by God when He "breathed" her immortal soul into existence. See *Purg.* XXV, 67-75; *Par.* XXXII, 61-66. Such a focus upon Beatrice leads to the striking change of address to her, a change from *voi* to *tu* (see n. to vs. 80).   *sortiro* = *sortirono*. For this use of *sortire*, see *Par.* XVIII, 105.

72. *reflettendo da sé li etterni rai*: Beatrice, who had guided by reflected light, is now seen (as is the whole rose) by that same kind of light. The wayfarer does not attempt, as yet, to see God directly, by the light of glory, this experience being reserved for the last canto and the very end.

73-76. *Da quella region . . . vista*: An "eye" at the very bottom of the sea "is not so far away" from the top of the earth's atmosphere—the "region that thunders highest up" (cf. *Purg.* XXI, 43-57; XXXII, 111).

75. *qualunque*: I.e., *qualunque occhio mortale*.

76. *vista*: Eyes, or post of observation.

77. *effige*: "Image."

78. *per mezzo mista*: I.e., "blurred by anything between." Here, in this spiritual heaven, there is no air or atmosphere to impede vision. Cf. *Par.* XXX, 122-23.

79–87. *O donna . . . potestate*: The verses which now follow, in this final address to Beatrice, constitute not only a prayer, but a kind of paean in an original sense of the word: a hymn of praise, which serves, from this terminal point, to look back over the whole journey, from the first two cantos of the *Inferno*. The reader will note that the poem begins to come full circle, so to speak, at several such points here near the end. Cf. *Par.* XXXII, 133-38.

79. *vige*: "Is strong."

80. *soffristi*: Dante has addressed Beatrice, without exception up to now, with the respectful second person plural (*voi*); but now with this verb in the second person singular (and then the confirming adjectives and subject pronoun *tu*), it is clear that in these final words to her he shifts to the more familiar second person singular. The reader who may be following the translation, which does not use *thou* or *thee*, will do well to take note of this shift, which should strike every reader with surprise and leave him wondering as to the reason for it. Would Dante the pilgrim become less respectful to Beatrice at such a point and in such a context? This is hardly conceivable. The shift clearly signals something else, namely the fact that Beatrice is no longer *the guide* (with a burden of allegorical meaning) but that, as she has taken her seat among the blessed, she is now seen as the individual historical personage, or the immortal individual soul, as she sits in eternal beatitude.

It will be noted, in the next canto, that Dante addresses St. Bernard with the familiar form and for the same reason (*Par.* XXXII, 100-102) even when he begins to speak with the words "O santo padre." This is in sharp contrast with, for example, Dante's shift from *tu* to *voi* in Purgatory (*Purg.* XIX, 95 and 131) when he realizes that he is speaking to the soul of Pope Adrian V. Surely Dante would not show *less* respect to St. Bernard! But he addresses him immediately with the familiar form. Thus, insofar as Bernard can be viewed as the third guide in the journey, the reader may see, as he remembers the forms of address to the three guides as such, the pattern of *tu* with Virgil, *voi* with Beatrice (as long as she guides), and *tu* with Bernard.

It should be noted that Bernard cannot be a "light" in the sense that Virgil and Beatrice are such, as guides, for the third light is the light of glory, which is God's very own light. See C. S. Singleton (1958), pp. 20-23.

81. *in inferno lasciar le tue vestige*: That is, in Limbo (*Inf.* II, 52-108). With this turn of phrase the reader gets a glimpse of the analogy Beatrice-Christ, for it was to Limbo only that Christ descended in the harrowing of Hell (*Inf.* IV, 52-63). For a strong reinforcement of this analogy, see *Purg.* XXIX-XXXI and the pertinent notes, on the advent of Beatrice in the procession at the top of Mt. Purgatory. See especially *Purg.* XXX, 139-41. *vestige*: Cf. the form "vestigge" in *Purg.* XXXIII, 108.

82. *di tante cose quant' i' ho vedute*: The whole phrase depends on "grazia" and "virtute" in vs. 84.

83-84. *dal tuo podere . . . virtute*: "I owe the grace and efficacy . . . to thy power and goodness" (Gr). For the meaning of *virtù* here in the sense of "power," and of a power which Beatrice specifically has, see Virgil's words of recognition of her in Limbo, *Inf.* II, 76-78. Also see C. S. Singleton (1956).

84. *riconosco*: Cf. *Par.* XXII, 113; XXIX, 59.

85. *Tu*: The expressed subject pronoun is emphatic. *m'hai di servo tratto a libertate*: Cf. Rom. 6:22. In *Summa theol.* II-II, q. 183, a. 4, resp., Thomas Aquinas writes:

> Invenitur autem in rebus spiritualibus duplex servitus et duplex libertas: una quidem est servitus peccati; altera vero est servitus iustitiae. Similiter etiam est duplex libertas; una quidem a peccato; alia vero a iustitia,

ut patet per Apostolum; qui dicit ad Rom. 6, 20: *Cum servi essetis peccati, liberi fuistis iustitiae; nunc vero liberati a peccato, servi estis facti Deo.*

Est autem servitus peccati vel iustitiae, cum aliquis vel ex habitu peccati ad malum inclinatur, vel ex habitu iustitiae inclinatur ad bonum; similiter etiam libertas a peccato est, dum aliquis ab inclinatione peccati non superatur: libertas autem a iustitia est, cum aliquis propter amorem iustitiae non retardatur a malo. Verumtamen quia homo secundum naturalem rationem ad iustitiam inclinatur, peccatum autem est contra naturalem rationem, consequens est quod libertas a peccato sit vera libertas quae coniungitur servituti iustitiae; quia per utrumque tendit homo in id quod est conveniens sibi: et similiter vera servitus est servitus peccati; cui coniungitur libertas a iustitia, quia scilicet per hoc homo impeditur ab eo quod est proprium sibi.

Hoc autem quod homo efficiatur servus iustitiae vel peccati, contingit per humanum studium, sicut Apostolus dicit ibidem: *Cui exhibetis vos servos ad obediendum, servi eius estis, cui obedistis, sive peccati ad mortem, sive obeditionis ad iustitiam.*

Now in spiritual things there is a twofold servitude and a twofold freedom: for there is the servitude of sin and the servitude of justice; and there is likewise a twofold freedom, from sin, and from justice, as appears from the words of the Apostle (Rom. vi. 20, 22), *When you were the servants of sin, you were free men to justice; . . . but now being made free from sin,* you are . . . *become servants to God.*

Now the servitude of sin or justice consists in being inclined to evil by a habit of sin, or inclined to good by a habit of justice: and in like manner freedom from sin is not to be overcome by the inclination to sin, and freedom from justice is not to be held back from evil for the love of justice. Nevertheless, since man, by his natural reason, is inclined to justice, while sin is contrary to natural reason, it follows that freedom from sin is true

freedom which is united to the servitude of justice, since
they both incline man to that which is becoming to him.
In like manner true servitude is the servitude of sin,
which is connected with freedom from justice, because
man is thereby hindered from attaining that which is
proper to him. That a man become the servant of justice
or sin results from his efforts, as the Apostle declares
(*ibid.*, *verse* 16): *To whom you yield yourselves serv-
ants to obey, his servants you are whom you obey,
whether it be of sin unto death, or of obedience unto
justice.*

In this light the whole *Divine Comedy* might be said to have
as its central theme the attainment of liberty, which is com-
plete subjection to God's will. Cf. *Purg.* XVI, 80, and the
corresponding note.

87. *che = per cui.   avei = avevi.*

88. *magnificenza*: "*Magnificence* in mediaeval writings is
often to be interpreted by the use of *magnificentia* in the
Latin Aristotle. It is the translation of μεγαλοπρέπεια which
means *munificence*, i.e. liberality or generosity, but on a
grand scale" (TC). Cf. Ps. 70[71]:21: "Multiplicasti mag-
nificentiam tuam." ("Renew your benefits toward me.")
custodi: "Preserve intact."

89-90. *sì che . . . disnodi*: Dante's last words to Beatrice
touch on the state of his soul at death, the overriding consid-
eration in the matter of salvation, as all readers know by now.
Virgil, in his dismissal of Dante, declared his will to be
"sano" (*Purg.* XXVII, 140). Now the "prayer" concerns the
entire soul, and the same adjective is used. The reader is
surely expected to think that Dante's prayer is to be
answered. Beatrice's smile down at him would seem to be the
full assurance that it will be so.

91. *Così orai*: Thus the paean is explicitly termed a prayer,
as it clearly is.   *sì lontana*: Cf. vss. 73-76.

92. *parea = appariva.   sorrise e riguardommi*: Beatrice's

smile, as she looks down reassuringly to the man whom she has brought to spiritual freedom, provides an unforgettable last glimpse of her, the bearer of beatitude who first appeared to the poet when he was but nine years old (as recounted in the *Vita nuova*).

93. *poi si tornò a l'etterna fontana*: No reader can fail to feel the import of Beatrice's last gesture, which serves to pass on to God above the full praise which belongs to Him and not to her or any other creature. In fact, Dante's paean to her was under some sense of tension for the Christian reader in this regard, for his praise seemed to end with her and not to refer beyond her and above, to the true and only Power (and eternal source of power) capable of leading Dante to this high destination.

94. *assommi*: "Complete."

96. *a che priego e amor santo mandommi*: Bernard now resumes his role as guide, sent by Beatrice. (Cf. vss. 65-66.) The perfect completion is, of course, the vision of God face to face at the end. But that time has not yet come, and Bernard's words, as they continue, speak in terms of a further preparation of the pilgrim for that culminating experience, a "preparation" which has already begun (see *Par.* XXX, 52-54). See vss. 98-99.

99. *montar per lo raggio divino*: These words anticipate the terminal event in *Par.* XXXIII. But the reader will note that the pilgrim has not yet entered into any such event and that he continues to see by reflected light of the divine radiance, or the light of glory, as he enters upon the "eye tour" of the rose, which now begins with Mary, who is a rose herself (see n. to vs. 1).

100–102. *E la regina del cielo . . . Bernardo*: "Bernard's devotion to the Virgin Mary is expressed in his four homilies, '*De laudibus Virginis matris,*' and his nine sermons for the feasts of her *Purification, Assumption, Nativity,* etc., as well as incidentally in other works. It is noteworthy that he opposed the celebration of her Immaculate Conception. His contemporary, Peter Cellensis, says of him: 'He was the most intimate fosterling of Our Lady, to whom he dedicated not only one monastery, but the monasteries of the whole Cistercian order' " (TC).

101. *ne farà = ci farà.*

102. *però = perciò.   Bernardo:* Only now is the replacement for Beatrice named. There has been some suspense in this regard, which now is resolved. St. Bernard, the great abbot of Clairvaux and preacher of the disastrous second Crusade, was born of noble parents in the village of Fontaines, near Dijon in Burgundy, in 1091. After studying in Paris, in 1113, at the age of twenty-two, he joined the newly founded Benedictine monastery of Cîteaux, at the head of which was Stephen Harding, an Englishman. Two years later, in 1115, Bernard was selected by Harding to be the head of one of the branches that the increasing fame of Cîteaux made it necessary to establish. He set out with a small band of devoted followers, journeying north until he came to a spot in the diocese of Langres in Champagne, where he made a clearing and founded his famous abbey of Clairvaux.

Bernard's influence soon spread beyond the limits of his monastery, and from this time until his death he was one of the most prominent figures in the history of his time. After the death of Honorius II in 1130 his championship secured the triumph of Innocent II over his rival Anacletus; and in 1140 at the Council of Sens he secured the condemnation of Peter Abelard. The news of the capture of Edessa by the infidels in 1144 led Bernard, with the approval of the pope, to preach a new Crusade, which resulted in the disastrous expedition of Louis VII and Conrad III (1147-49). The failure of the Crusade was a crushing blow to Bernard, from which he never recovered, and though he continued to take an active part in public affairs, he gradually failed and died on August 20, 1153. He was canonized by Pope Alexander III in 1173.

Bernard's numerous writings consist of epistles, sermons, and theological treatises, which are conspicuous for his devotion to the Virgin Mary, whence on his canonization he was described as "alumnus familiarissimus Dominae Nostrae." One of his most important works is the *De consideratione* (referred to by Dante in *Epist.* XIII, 80), written in the last year of his life and addressed to his disciple, Pope Eugenius III. It is precisely a work on contemplation which is the allegorical basis for the whole upward ascent to the culminating experience that Dante the wayfarer is now to have, with Bernard praying for it and then standing by.

103. *Qual è colui che forse di Croazia*: Readers of Petrarch might well remember here his famous sonnet (*Rime* XVI) beginning: "Movesi il vecchierel canuto e bianco." ("The old man, white and pallid, sets out.") Thus here yet another simile of pilgrimage, with continuing stress on this fact (see n. to vss. 43-45).　*forse*: This touch allows that the pilgrim might come from any distant land, but "let it be Croatia."

104. *Veronica*: The Veronica is the true image (*vera icona*) of the Saviour, left on a kerchief which a holy woman had handed him, on his way to Calvary, to wipe the sweat from his face. It was shown at St. Peter's in Rome on certain days. Hosts of pilgrims went from afar to see it, as Dante tells us in *Vita nuova* XL, 1-7.

105. *che per l'antica fame non sen sazia*: " 'Who, having craved it for so long, cannot look enough.'—Some would read *fama* for *fame*" (Gr). See M. Barbi (1934), pp. 253-54.

106. *fin che si mostra*: "As long as it is exhibited."

108. *or fu sì fatta la sembianza vostra?* "Was your semblance really so!" "Or" is an exclamatory "now" with the overtone of "really." It should be noted that the second person plural is used in this case, whereas the Deity is addressed with the second person singular (cf. the Lord's Prayer of *Purg.* XI, 1-24).

109-10. *la vivace carità*: Love is stressed, with Bernard, who has already spoken in terms of love and lover (vss. 100-101).

110-11. *che 'n questo mondo . . . pace*: Bernard's two prin-
cipal qualifications to serve as final guide in the journey stem
from his special devotion to the Virgin Mary and from his
fame as one dedicated to mystical contemplation with special
emphasis on the affective movement of the mind as it rises
to God, an emphasis which later Franciscan thought and de-
votion adopted and stressed. It was believed that Bernard,
in such meditation, had a foretaste of the peace of Heaven.
In the *Meditationes piissimae* (XIV, 36-37), ascribed to
Bernard, there is a rhapsody on the joys of contemplation.
See also Bernard, *Sermones in Cantica Canticorum* XXIII,
15-16. As noted above, Dante in his *Letter to Can Grande*
(*Epist.* XIII, 80) refers the reader of his *Paradiso* to Ber-
nard's work *De contemplatione*.

111. *contemplando, gustò di quella pace*: "Gustò" and
"pace" stress precisely the affective aspect of the experience,
the peace attained by the will, rather than the vision attained
by the intellect. See preceding note.

112. *quest' esser giocondo*: This happy existence, the condi-
tion of the blessed, which, for the human creature, is of
course the happiest that can be conceived. Bernard's words
thus initiate the invitation to begin the "eye tour" of the great
amphitheater where the blessed sit, a tour that will occupy
most of the next canto and is a preparation of the wayfarer
for the supreme experience described in the final canto, as
is stated in vss. 97-99.

114. *tenendo li occhi pur qua giù al fondo*: Dante has al-
ready looked up almost to the rim of the amphitheater, to see
Beatrice. Bernard now refers to the fact that Dante is looking
at him and not upwards.

115-17. *ma guarda . . . devoto*: Bernard's first exhortation
to the wayfarer, as the "eye tour" begins, is that he should
look first at Mary, truly the queen of heaven as he states it.
Any other beginning for the tour would have been most
unseemly on the part of Bernard, Mary's great lover. But
Bernard's exhortation also follows a hierarchical prin-
ciple requiring that one begin at the summit, which a

medieval poet would hardly fail to observe in any case. And the reader may pause to consider that with this focus on the Virgin Mary, here so near the end, the action of the poem is, in a sense, coming full circle, for it was due to Mary's direct intervention in Heaven that the wayfarer was rescued from the dark slope at the beginning through that relay of grace that ended with Virgil's coming to the man who was being pushed back into the darkness (*Inf.* I-II). Of course, ineffably higher than Mary but not directly seen as yet is the triune God whose "duro giudicio" was swayed by Mary (*Inf.* II, 96) and with whom the descent of grace originates. Mary was serving her familiar role as our advocate in heaven. The reader is soon to see that the focus returns to Mary with the prayer that opens the last canto of the poem, a prayer for another descent of grace here at the end, a prayer that the wayfarer may truly complete his journey. For the seating arrangement of Mary and many others to be named in the next canto, see Fig. 5, p. 534.

116. *veggi* = *veda* or *vegga*.

118-26. *Io levai li occhi . . . scemo*: Two similes now make it clear that Mary's seat is on the highest rim of the amphitheater and in the best place on that rim, that being the eastern point (as if there were *directions* here in this spiritual heaven!). But the reader knows that the emphatic suggestion (through simile) that her place is indeed in the east puts Mary's throne at the point where, on earth, we see the sun rise, and on the horizon of that east whither we turn to pray and according to which all medieval cathedrals were oriented. Cf. *Purg.* IV, 53-54; XXIX, 12; and the notes to these verses. On medieval world maps east, rather than north, is "up." It will be remembered that Beatrice appeared finally in her procession at the top of Purgatory in the figure of a rising sun (*Purg.* XXX, 22-27).

120. *soverchia*: "Surpasses" in brightness.

121-22. *quasi di valle . . . occhi*: The phrase "di valle . . . a monte," obvious in its meaning, is an established one, yet to use it here, thus bringing in "monte" in the context of looking up to Mary there, would seem clearly to call to mind Ps. 120[121]:1: "Levavi oculos meos in montes, unde veniet auxilium mihi." ("I lift up my eyes toward the mountains, whence help shall come to me.") And this too suggests the completion of a circle in the action of the poem, for this is what the pilgrim Dante did at the very outset of the journey (*Inf.* I, 16-18).

122. *parte ne lo stremo*: "A part of the highest edge" or "rim."

123. *l'altra fronte*: "The rest of the rim."

124-25. *E come quivi . . . s'infiamma*: The adverb "quivi" functions here, with its modifying phrase, as a noun, subject of "s'infiamma": "And as on earth the point of the horizon where the chariot pole of the sun is expected."

125. *Fetonte*: For Phaëthon and his unhappy attempt to drive the chariot of the Sun, see *Inf.* XVII, 106-8; *Purg.* XXIX, 118-20; *Par.* XVII, 3.

126. *e quinci e quindi*: "On either side."

127. *quella pacifica oriafiamma*: "The Oriflamme (*aurea flamma*) was the standard given by the Angel Gabriel to the ancient kings of France, representing a flame on a golden ground. No one who fought under it could be conquered" (TC). *oriafiamma* = *orifiamma* (French *oriflamme*).

128. *nel mezzo*: There where Mary will be seen with the thousand and more angels paying homage to her. Thus, through the total figure, Mary is seen to be throughout eternity as a rising sun on the horizon of this amphitheater.

130. *con le penne sparte*: This is clearly a posture of devotion and of angelic obeisance to the mother of the Son of Man. And it will be remembered that Mary is a human creature, and that man was created lesser than the angels. See *Par.* IX, 137-38.

132. *ciascun distinto di fulgore e d'arte*: According to established angelology, each angel constitutes in itself a distinct species. Cf. *Par.* XXIX, 136-38 and n. to *Par.* XXIX, 137.

arte: "Ministry," in this instance the "giochi" and "canti" of the following verse. For "arte" in this sense, as applied to the angels, cf. *Par.* XXIX, 52.

135. *li altri santi*: The rest of the blessed (human souls). The phrase focuses on Mary as a human creature, like the rest. It should be remembered that she, like her Son, is here in her glorified body already and is the only purely human soul to have that radiant body before the Last Judgment (cf. *Par.* XXV, 127-28).

136. *divizia*: "Wealth." This is the modern Italian *dovizia*.

137. *imaginar*: It should be remembered that the faculty known as the *imaginativa* is primarily an image-receiving faculty (see *Purg.* XVII, 13, and n. to *Purg.* XVII, 13-18), and the verb in its meaning corresponds to that of the noun. However, in this context, since this is the voice of the poet speaking, it has the added meaning of "recovery in memory" of that which had been experienced in the receptive *imaginativa*. In this sense the verb takes on a less passive meaning.

140. *nel caldo suo caler*: Warmth or heat expresses love, *affetto*, and "caldo" with "caler" stresses this, with "affetto" following in the next verse. Bernard is the great lover of Mary, as noted above. Petrocchi has preferred the variant "caler" to "calor," which other editors have, for persuasive reasons, terming it a Latinism, the verb *calere* in Latin meaning either "to grow warm" or "to feel warm." Here it is the infinitive used as a noun, in the objective focus, much as *disio* can refer to the object of desire (cf. *Purg.* XXXI, 54, and see "disiri," *Purg.* XXXI, 22). In objective reference, accordingly, "caler" is Mary, the object of Bernard's "calore." See the use of *piacere* which immediately follows in the opening of the next canto (*Par.* XXXII, 1).

142. *rimirar*: Dante had turned to Bernard and now turns again to gaze on Mary.

CANTO XXXII

1. *Affetto al suo piacer*: "Lovingly intent on his delight."
The whole phrase is a kind of ablative modifier. "Piacer" is
here the *object* of delight. Cf. *Inf.* V, 104; *Purg.* XXXI, 52;
and *passim*. Compare "disio" in a similar objective focus in
Purg. XXIV, 111. Thus "piacer" here signifies the Blessed
Virgin, whose great lover Bernard was. *contemplante*:
Again there is stress on Bernard's qualification for his role
here. See *Par.* XXXI, 111, and n. to *Par.* XXXI, 110-11.

2. *libero*: Spontaneous and generous. Cf. "liberamente" in
Inf. XIII, 86, and *Purg.* XXVI, 139.

3. *parole sante*: The use of the adjective may be compared
with the use of the adjectives in "morta poesì," *Purg.* I, 7,
and "alta fantasia," *Par.* XXXIII, 142. Bernard's words are
sante because they focus on and expound "holy" things.

4-6. *La piaga . . . punse*: The wound (*vulnus* or *vulneratio*)
of original sin. See Thomas Aquinas, *Summa theol.* I-II, q.
85, a. 3, resp.:

> Per iustitiam originalem perfecte ratio continebat in-
> feriores animae vires; et ipsa ratio a Deo perficiebatur
> ei subiecta. Haec autem originalis iustitia subtracta est
> per peccatum primi parentis, sicut iam dictum est, qu.

81, art. 2. Et ideo omnes vires animae remanent quodammodo destitutae proprio ordine, quo naturaliter ordinantur ad virtutem; et ipsa destitutio *vulneratio naturae* dicitur.

As a result of original justice, the reason had perfect hold over the lower parts of the soul, while reason itself was perfected by God and was subject to Him. Now this same original justice was forfeited through the sin of our first parent, as already stated (q. 81, a. 2); so that all the powers of the soul are left, as it were, destitute of their proper order, whereby they are naturally directed to virtue; which destitution is called a wounding of nature.

The reader may recall that the figure of Dante the wayfarer, as seen at the outset of the journey, exemplified the wound, in that he was "limping man." See *Inf.* I, 30, and the note to that verse. On the loss of original justice, see C. S. Singleton (1958), pp. 230-45.

"Mary is often represented as the counterpart of Eve. The word *Ave*, with which she is greeted, is the reverse of *Eva*; so says, among others, Dante's son Pietro. St. Bernard, *Sermo de Beata Maria Virgine,* compares Mary to a rose, Eve to a thorn: G. Busnelli, *Il concetto e l'ordine del 'Paradiso' dantesco,* I, 1911, 227-228" (Gr).

It is interesting to note that the early commentary of Buti finds in the "richiuse e unse" of vs. 4 and in the "aperse" and "punse" of vs. 6 an instance of the rhetorical figure of *hysteron proteron,* which the poet uses elsewhere (*Par.* II, 23-24; XXII, 109-10): "Usa qui l'autore una figura di Grammatica; *hysteronproteron,* imperò che prima è pungere che aprire." ("Here the author uses a grammatical figure: hysteron proteron, since 'pricking' precedes 'opening.'") Buti continues: "E così ne la sentenzia di sopra, prima è ungere la piaga che richiudere, et elli mette innanti *chiuse,* e poi *unse*; ecco che la sentenzia muta lo diritto ordine." ("And thus in the preceding sentence salve is applied to the wound before it is closed, but he puts 'closed' first and then 'applied the salve'; therefore, the sentence changes the normal order.") See nn. to *Par.* II, 23-24 and XXII, 109-11. Sapegno observes that the whole sentence is constructed in such a way as to place the memory of redemption before that of sin. Indeed this serves to commemorate the plan of providential history in terms of final cause, and to begin our "eye tour" of the rose with the note that Eve is seated at Mary's feet is to begin to delight in that providential order which is thus manifest.

4-11. *Maria . . . cantor*: In the descending order of this seating arrangement one notes a chronological principle which allows the higher seat to the elder. It should also be noted that since seven, and seven only, are named in this line beginning with Mary, the number can scarcely be accidental. It was underscored before, in the count of the angelic orders first seen as wheels of fire. Cf. *Par.* XXVIII, 31-33, and the corresponding note; and see, on the number seven, C. S. Singleton (1965).

4. *unse*: "Dressed with ointment," as a wound.

7. *ordine*: The "order" is the entire third tier of seats.
sedi: Plural of *sedio* (archaic for *seggio*).

8-9. *siede Rachel . . . Beatrice*: The seating arrangement here noted is true to Beatrice's report to Virgil in Limbo. That Rachel stands for contemplation all readers know, from a certain dream—the *third* dream—in Purgatory (*Purg.* XXVII, 100-108; see nn. to *Purg.* XXVII, 100-108, 106). The number is significant here, and it was brought out in the first transmission of grace, as recounted by Beatrice to Virgil in Limbo (see *Inf.* II, 94-114), grace passing as it did from the Virgin Mary to Lucy (note, in Fig. 5, Lucy's position directly opposite Adam in the rose), and then from Lucy to Beatrice. The reader will note from Fig. 5 that Lucy had to move through a whole semicircle of seats in order to go, as was said, to where Beatrice was sitting with ancient Rachel (*Inf.* II, 102).

It should be observed that to have Beatrice sit on Rachel's right is to accord her an honored position, directly under

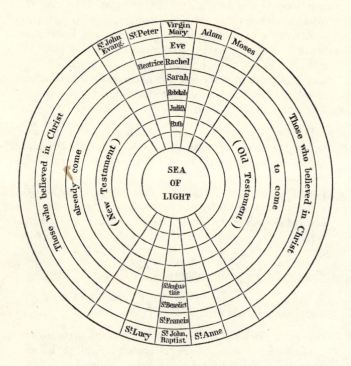

5. The celestial rose

none other than St. Peter, who sits to the right of the Virgin Mary.

8. *di sotto da = di sotto di.*   *costei*: Mary.

10. *Sarra = Sara* (see Petrocchi's justification of this older form). Sarah was the wife of Abraham and mother of Isaac.

  Rebecca: Rebecca, daughter of Bethuel and sister of Laban. Rebecca married Isaac, her father's cousin, by whom she became the mother of Esau and Jacob (see vss. 67-69).

  Iudìt: Judith is the heroine of the book of Judith, in which she is represented as the ideal type of piety (Iudith 8:6), of beauty (11:19), and of courage and chastity (16:26). When Holofernes, general of the armies of Nebuchadnezzar, was besieging Bethulia, Judith entered his camp, and, having by her beauty gained free access to his tent, she one night took advantage of his being in a drunken sleep to cut off his head with his own sword. She then returned to Bethulia with it and had it displayed upon the walls of the city. The Assyrians, struck with panic at the death of their leader, took to flight and were pursued with great slaughter by the Jews, who hailed Judith as their deliverer (Iudith 10-15).

10-11. *e colei . . . cantor*: Ruth, the Moabitish wife of Boaz, by whom she became the great-grandmother of David (Matt. 1:5-6), the "cantor" here referred to.

11-12. *al cantor . . . mei*: David, who is thus named by circumlocution, even if his place in the amphitheater is not specified. Cf. *Inf.* IV, 58; *Purg.* X, 65 (where he is referred to as the "umile salmista"); and *Par.* XX, 37, where he is allowed the most honored place in the eagle, the pupil of its eye. "Fallo" here alludes to David's adultery with Bathsheba (II Reg. 11-12) and his compassing the death of Uriah (II Reg. 11).

12. *Miserere mei*: "Have mercy upon me" (Ps. 50:3[51:1]). Cf. *Purg.* V, 24, and Dante's cry to Virgil, *Inf.* I, 65.

13. *soglia*: Tier of seats, as before.

14. *giù digradar*: "In graded descent."

14-15. *proprio nome . . . foglia*: Actually Bernard will not rebegin the specific naming until vs. 118.

15. *foglia*: "Foglia" here means "petal" of the rose, i.e., each of the blessed in his or her assigned seat, as is even clearer from vss. 22-24, where the metaphor is used again.

16. *settimo grado*: See n. to vss. 4-11 on this singling-out of the number seven.

17. *succedono Ebree*: Thus a most remarkable feature of

the seating arrangement and total order of the rose is made manifest: the seats in the direct line below Mary are all occupied by Hebrew women of the Old Testament who, by such a line, together with one directly across from them (see vss. 31-36), divide vertically the entire amphitheater into two equal parts, from top to bottom.

18. *dirimendo*: "Parting."   *chiome*: The "locks" of the flower are the tiers of seats, which are then termed "le sacre scalee" (vs. 21).

19–20. *secondo lo sguardo . . . Cristo*: "According to the look which faith turned on Christ," i.e., according as the faith of the Hebrews and of certain pagans looked forward to Christ to come, whereas the faith of Christians looks back to Christ crucified (see the principle in miniature in *Par.* XX, 105). Cato (*Purg.* I), Ripheus (*Par.* XX, 68), and presumably many another pagan must not be forgotten here.

20–21. *queste sono . . . scalee*: On the line of women as one great dividing line, Tommaseo observes that this wall both separates and unites: between the Old and New Testament these women are a bond, a bond of maternity, of expectation, of love.

It should be noted that since B.C. time and A.D. time become the basis for this great dividing line, the Virgin Mary, in the topmost position of the line, figures as one who lived in both spans of time, even as did John the Baptist, who will occupy the top position in the line of men opposite.

21. *scalee*: The tiers of the amphitheater.

22. *Da questa parte*: This phrase suggests a gesture or pointing by Bernard as he utters the words. The reader knows that he and Dante are standing in the yellow center of the rose, on the floor of the amphitheater. They are presumably facing the line of Hebrew women that begins with the Virgin Mary, and so, significantly enough, they face towards her for this exposition, and Bernard must be pointing to the left of Mary (see Fig. 5, p. 534), which means to his right.

22–24. *onde 'l fiore . . . venturo*: *Foglie* in the sense of "petals" is again used. Thus Bernard is saying, in metaphor, that all the B.C. half of the amphitheater is completely filled, no seats remain, and he is soon to say that the other half is almost full (in A.D. 1300, at least, the fictional year of the journey). This is according to God's providential plan, *as conceived by the poet*. To take a view of the matter from out side the fiction of the poem (which is not presented as a fiction, of course) the reader should realize that the poet has given us a view of God's providence in this respect that is, in a certain sense, astounding, even "absurd" according to some commentators (see Chimenz' n. on *Par.* XXXII, 37-39). One has only to think how many souls of those who lived in B.C. time would have had to be taken forth from Limbo in the harrowing of Hell, for one thing! But also one might well ask: Did the actual Advent of Christ, opening the door to salvation, not count for more than this, i.e., for more than the salvation apparently effectuated in God's plan for B.C. time?

The fact is that we glimpse here, in the poet's conception, a completely overriding desire to witness, in God's providential plan and His foreordained seating arrangement of His amphitheater, the principle of symmetry and balance, a principle everywhere apparent in His creation of the universe itself, which Dante's great poem everywhere mirrors in itself. But that principle, carried out so exactly in the rose and its petals, puts something of a strain on Christian doctrine and a cardinal tenet of the faith, namely, that Christ's coming *did* count for more than this balance with salvation out of B.C. time. The balance, this symmetry, we are asked in vss. 37-39 to wonder over, as we contemplate it.

25-27. *da l'altra parte . . . visi*: Bernard now points to his left and thus to the Virgin Mary's right—the more honored sector because right is simply better than left, and Mary is the fixed point of reference (cf. *Par.* XXXIII, 3, "termine fisso") —where sit those souls who lived in New Testament times.

25. *intercisi*: A Latinism, meaning "interspersed." The semi-circles in this sector are interspersed or "broken" by empty space, that is, some seats here and there are still vacant in the A.D. half of the rose.

26. *vòti = vuoti.   semicirculi*: Actually this conception of
two semicircular divisions is not made clear until we read
of the other great dividing line that establishes this fact (vss.
31-36).   *si stanno*: The reflexive here is the so-called
pleonastic reflexive, serving its usual function of setting apart,
of distinguishing.

In conceiving that, as of A.D. 1300, there are but few seats
left in the A.D. sector, the poet is introducing an abiding con-
ception in Christian doctrine, namely, that the end of the
world and of time may be at hand. If the salvation of souls,
the "harvest out of time" (cf. *Par*. XXIII, 20-21, and n. to
Par. XXIII, 19-21), continues at a normal rate (whatever
that might mean!), all seats are soon to be filled, and the cur-
tain must then fall on the drama of salvation. The fact that
only a few seats remain in the one sector has been noted by
Beatrice already (see *Par*. XXX, 131-32). And Dante, in the
Convivio (II, xiv, 13), echoes the familiar notion, which is
out of the Gospel truth, moreover, for more than once Christ
himself spoke of the imminent end of the world. See n. to
Par. XXX, 132.

30. *cerna = cernita*, "division," from the Latin *cernere*.

31-33. *quel del gran Giovanni . . . anni*: Here again, in his
choice of the top figure in the great dividing line opposite
Mary, the poet has chosen one who lived in both B.C. time
and A.D. time, thus matching her. The poet's choice of John
the Baptist finds ample support in the Gospels. See Matt.
11:11: "Non surrexit inter natos mulierum maior Ioanne
Baptista." ("Among those born of women there has not risen
a greater than John the Baptist.") Also see Luc. 7:28.

32. *sempre santo*: See Luc. 1:15: "Spiritu Sancto replebitur
adhuc ex utero matris suae." ("He shall be filled with the
Holy Spirit even from his mother's womb.")   *'l diserto*:
Cf. *Purg*. XXII, 151-52.   *'l martiro*: Cf. *Par*. XVIII, 135.

33. *l'inferno*: In Limbo, where John, after his death, had to
wait some two years for the descent of Christ to the harrow-
ing of Hell.   *da*: The preposition has the value here of

circa. John died in August and Jesus in April, two years later; thus John was in Limbo for some twenty months.

34. *cerner sortiro*: It "fell to their lot [in God's ordinance] to divide." Cf. the noun "cerna" in vs. 30.

35–36. *Francesco . . . giro*: Thus the poet has chosen for the highest seats, after that of the great John, only three names of saints (in contrast with the six of Hebrew women under Mary directly opposite), all of whom lived, it is clear, in A.D. time. Hence we are to admit another feature of God's symmetry and balance here: both Mary and John span B.C. and A.D. time. But the figures under Mary all belong to the Old Testament sector, whereas the three saints mentioned here (and presumably those unnamed who continue the line) belong to the A.D. half.

It will also be noted that St. Francis is given the highest place after John the Baptist and that this is not on any chronological principle, as in the Hebrew women, but solely, it would seem, on the principle of excellence. This being the case, it is interesting to note that St. Benedict rates a higher seat than St. Augustine. On St. Francis, see *Par.* XI, 43-117; on Benedict, see *Par.* XXII, 28-98. Augustine is barely named in the *Paradiso* (*Par.* X, 120).

40–42. *E sappi . . . si siede*: The dividing line running horizontally around the amphitheater half way down is now pointed to as one evidenced by all the children who are assigned to this lower half. Though the poem does not again make the point, the reader should remember that the adults who fill the two vertical dividing lines that begin with Mary and with John the Baptist must extend from the top to the very bottom. Therefore all in the lower half are children except these adults who extend the two lines beyond the halfway point.

Since the amphitheater slopes inward from its upper rim to its floor (the yellow center of the rose where Dante and Bernard are standing), it follows that, in actual number, there are fewer seats in the lower half than in the upper half. Still, even as before, the reader may be surprised at the poet's conception (see n. to vss. 22-24), surprised in this case that so many children are saved, one half of all the elect (with the reservation just noted)! And there is another surprise here for any reader familiar with established opinion in medieval theology, for according to that opinion the bodies of all the elect will rise, at the Resurrection, in the aspect of the prime of life, no matter at what age they die. But we already know, since Bernard has been seen as an old man, that the poet does not intend to follow any such opinion. And now all the babes! The opinion of Thomas Aquinas is stated in *Summa theol.* III, Suppl., q. 81, a. 1, resp.:

> Homo resurget absque omni defectu humanae naturae; quia sicut Deus humanam naturam absque defectu instituit, ita sine defectu reparabit. Deficit autem humana natura dupliciter: uno modo quia nondum perfectionem ultimam est consecuta; alio modo quia jam ab ultima perfectione recessit; et primo modo deficit in pueris, secundo modo deficit in senibus. Et ideo in utrisque reducetur humana natura per resurrectionem ad statum ultimae perfectionis, qui est in juvenili aetate, ad quam terminatur motus augmenti, et a qua incipit motus decrementi.

> Man will rise again without any defect of human nature, because as God founded human nature without a defect, even so will He restore it without defect. Now human nature has a twofold defect. First, because it has not yet attained to its ultimate perfection. Secondly, because it has already gone back from its ultimate perfection. The first defect is found in children, the second in the aged: and consequently in each of these human nature will be brought by the resurrection to the state of its ultimate perfection which is in the youthful age, at which the movement of growth terminates, and from which the movement of decrease begins.

On the poet's differing from this ruling in established doctrine, Grandgent remarks: "In his striking departure from current belief, Dante was influenced certainly by a desire for significant visible contrast and also, we may conjecture, by

that love of little children which he has more than once re-
vealed. The sweet conception of an encircling sea of baby
faces, all twittering with baby voices, must have charmed him
as it charms us."

43. *per l'altrui*: "Altrui" is here possessive, thus "per l'altrui"
("through [the merit] of others," i.e., of the parents, as will
be made clearer as certain conditions are set forth).

44. *asciolti*: "Released" from the burden of original sin. See
Inf. IV, 30 ("infanti") and 33-39.

45. *prima ch'avesser vere elezioni*: These children died be-
fore reaching the age of free will or free choice.

46–48. *Ben te ne puoi . . . ascolti*: See n. to vss. 40-42.

49–51. *Or dubbi . . . sottili*: "Dante is silently wondering
why, if these children never won merit by the exercise of their
free will, some have higher seats than others. He learns pres-
ently that the degree of beatitude (symbolized by the height
of the seat) is determined by predestination, not by one's
own acts" (Gr).

49. *dubbi = dubiti.   sili*: "You are silent," from the
Latin *siles*.

50. *discioglierò = scioglierò*.

51. *li pensier sottili*: The subtle thoughts with which in vain
you try to resolve a question of faith.

52–54. *Dentro a l'ampiezza . . . fame*: Not a particle of
chance can find a place here in the rose. Everything has a
definite cause. "Punto" contrasts with "ampiezza" (and how
vast the rose is we have been told).

54. *se non come*: "Any more than." The three conditions
here named are obviously inconceivable in the state of eternal
beatitude. See Apoc. 7:13-17:

> Et respondit unus de senioribus et dixit mihi: Hi qui
> amicti sunt stolis albis, qui sunt et unde venerunt? Et
> dixi illi: Domine mi, tu scis. Et dixit mihi: Hi sunt qui

venerunt de tribulatione magna, et laverunt stolas suas
et dealbaverunt eas in sanguine agni; ideo sunt ante
thronum Dei, et serviunt ei die ac nocte in templo eius,
et qui sedet in throno habitabit super illos: non esurient
neque sitient amplius, nec cadet super illos sol, neque
ullus aestus, quoniam agnus qui in medio throni est
reget illos, et deducet eos ad vitae fontes aquarum; et
absterget Deus omnem lacrimam ab oculis eorum.

And one of the elders spoke and said to me, "These who
are clothed in white robes, who are they? and whence
have they come?" And I said to him, "My lord, thou
knowest." And he said to me, "These are they who have
come out of the great tribulation, and have washed their
robes and made them white in the blood of the Lamb.
Therefore they are before the throne of God, and serve
him day and night in his temple, and he who sits upon
the throne will dwell with them. They shall neither hun-
ger nor thirst any more, neither shall the sun strike them
nor any heat. For the Lamb who is in the midst of the
throne will shepherd them, and will guide them to the
fountains of the waters of life, and God will wipe away
every tear from their eyes."

55. *etterna legge*: God's "eternal law" is His predestination,
which is here witnessed, respecting the degree of beatitude
in the seating of these babes, explicitly stated in vss. 58-60.

56–57. *giustamente ci si risponde . . . dito*: There is exact
correspondence, even as there should be between the size of
a ring and the finger it is to fit.

57. *ci si risponde*: I.e., *si corrispondono fra loro. Rispondere*
is used impersonally.

58. *però = perciò.* *festinata*: "Hurried," as it were,
coming as babes to eternal beatitude, "a vera vita" (vs. 59).
For *festinare* in this sense, cf. *Purg.* XXXIII, 90.

60. *intra sé qui più e meno eccellente*: The often-quoted
scriptural verse from Ioan. 14:2, "in domo Patris mei man-
siones multae sunt" ("in my Father's house there are many

mansions"), is brought out by the assignment of higher and lower seats even to babes, for the reason now to be stated.

61. *Lo rege = il re*, i.e., God.   *pausa = posa*, i.e., *riposa*, "is at rest." "Pausa" is a Latinism.

62. *in tanto amore e in tanto diletto*: It will be recalled from the lesson in love at the center of the poem that love does not rest until it attains its object (in this case the vision of God face to face), and with the attainment comes joy ("diletto"). See *Purg*. XVIII, 28-33, and n. to *Purg*. XVIII, 32-33.

63. *è di più ausa*: "Ventures to aspire to more."   *ausa = oso* (cf. *Purg*. XI, 126; XX, 149; *Par*. XIV, 130). "Ausa" is a Latinism comparable to "pausa."

64–65. *nel suo lieto aspetto creando*: Cf. *Purg*. XVI, 85-90. The reader already knows of the "happy Creator" and His joyous act of creating the individual human soul. See also *Purg*. XXV, 70-75.

65–66. *a suo piacer . . . diversamente*: See Peter Lombard, *Sent*. III, xxxii, 2: "Electorum ergo alios magis, alios minus dilexit." ("Of the elect therefore He loved some more and some less.") See also Thomas Aquinas, *Summa theol*. I-II, q. 112, a. 4.

66. *e qui basti l'effetto*: "And let the fact itself suffice" (that is, ask no further). Cf. *Purg*. III, 37, Virgil's "quia"; also see *Par*. XX, 130-35; XXI, 91-99.

67–69. *E ciò espresso . . . commota*: Grandgent notes that "Jacob and Esau 'struggled together' in their mother's womb" (Gen. 25:22-25[22-26]), and he calls attention to the following passages from the Bible. See Mal. 1:2-3: "Dilexi vos, dicit Dominus, et dixistis: In quo dilexisti nos? Nonne frater erat Esau Iacob? dicit Dominus; et dilexi Iacob, Esau autem odio habui." ("I have loved you, saith the Lord. And you have said: Wherein hast thou loved us? Was not Esau brother to Jacob, saith the Lord, and I have loved Jacob, but have hated Esau?") Also see Rom. 9:10-15:

Non solum autem illa, sed et Rebecca ex uno concubitu

habens Isaac patris nostri: cum enim nondum nati fuissent aut aliquid boni egissent aut mali, ut secundum electionem propositum Dei maneret, non ex operibus sed ex vocante, dictum est ei: Quia maior serviet minori; sicut scriptum est: Iacob dilexi, Esau autem odio habui.

Quid ergo dicemus? Numquid iniquitas apud Deum? Absit. Moysi enim dicit: Miserebor cuius misereor.

And not she only; but also Rebecca, who conceived by one man, Isaac our father; for before the children had yet been born, or had done aught of good or evil, in order that the selective purpose of God might stand, depending not on deeds, but on him who calls, it was said to her, "The elder shall serve the younger"; as it is written, "Jacob I have loved, but Esau I have hated."

What then shall we say? Is there injustice with God? By no means! For he says to Moses, "I will have mercy on whom I have mercy."

See Thomas Aquinas, *Summa theol.* I, q. 23, a. 3.

67. *vi*: "To you" mortals.

70. *Però* = *perciò*.

70–72. *Però, secondo . . . s'incappelli*: " 'Therefore the heavenly light must crown us fitly, according to the complexion of that grace.' Our halo, or reward, in Heaven is proportionate to the grace bestowed on us at birth. For *s'incappelli*, cf. XXV, 9. The odd expression, 'the color of the hair of that grace,' was evidently suggested by Esau's red hair: Gen. xxv, 25. Esau, without apparent reason, differed in looks from Jacob, just as he differed from him in character and in divine favor" (Gr).

73. *mercé*: "Merit." *costume*: "Conduct," "actions," as is made clear in vss. 76-84.

75. *primiero acume*: The original endowment of spiritual sight and capacity for it, which is bestowed by God when He creates the soul.

76. *Bastavasi = bastava. Bastarsi* is an archaic reflexive form.   *secoli recenti*: These first centuries are "new" in the sense of being fresh from creation. "New" is the original meaning of the Latin *recens*. The period referred to is the time from Adam to Abraham. See Thomas Aquinas, *Summa theol.* III, q. 70, a. 2, ad 1:

> Immediate post peccatum primi parentis, propter doctrinam ipsius Adae, qui plene instructus fuerat de divinis, adhuc fides et ratio naturalis intantum vigebat in homine, quod non oportebat determinari hominibus aliqua signa fidei et salutis: sed unusquisque pro suo libito fidem suam aliquibus signis protestabatur. Sed circa tempus Abrahae diminuta erat fides, plurimis ad idololatriam declinantibus: obscurata etiam erat ratio naturalis per augmentum carnalis concupiscentiae usque ad peccatum contra naturam. Et ideo convenienter tunc et non ante fuit instituta circumcisio ad profitendum fidem, et ad minuendum carnalem concupiscentiam.

> Immediately after the sin of our first parent, on account of the knowledge possessed by Adam, who was fully instructed about Divine things, both faith and natural reason flourished in man to such an extent, that there was no need for any signs of faith and salvation to be prescribed to him, but each one was wont to make protestation of his faith, by outward signs of his profession, according as he thought best. But about the time of Abraham faith was on the wane, many being given over to idolatry. Moreover, by the growth of carnal concupiscence natural reason was clouded even in regard to sins against nature. And therefore it was fitting that then, and not before, circumcision should be instituted, as a profession of faith and a remedy against carnal concupiscence.

78. *la fede d'i parenti*: This faith in adults, in the first period, sufficed to render meritorious of salvation such of their children who died in their innocence.

79. *le prime etadi*: The division into "ages" here may reflect

the customary distinction of two ages from Adam to Abraham: the age from Adam to Noah, and that from Noah to Abraham.

80–81. *convenne ai maschi . . . virtute*: Thomas Aquinas (*Summa theol.* III, q. 70, a. 1, resp.) writes:

Baptismus dicitur sacramentum fidei, inquantum scilicet in baptismo fit quaedam fidei professio; et per baptismum aggregatur homo congregationi fidelium. Eadem autem est fides nostra, et antiquorum patrum, secundum illud Apostoli 2 Cor. 4, [13]: *Habentes eumdem spiritum fidei credimus*. Circumcisio autem erat quaedam protestatio fidei . . . unde et per circumcisionem antiqui aggregabantur collegio fidelium. Unde manifestum est quod circumcisio fuit praeparatoria ad baptismum et praefigurativa ipsius secundum quod antiquis Patribus omnia in figuram futuri contingebant, ut dicitur 1 Corinth. 10, sicut et fides eorum erat de futuro.

Baptism is called the Sacrament of Faith; in so far, to wit, as in Baptism man makes a profession of faith, and by Baptism is aggregated to the congregation of the faithful. Now our faith is the same as that of the Fathers of old, according to the Apostle (2 Cor. iv. 13): *Having the same spirit of faith . . . we . . . believe*. But circumcision was a protestation of faith; wherefore by circumcision also men of old were aggregated to the body of the faithful. Consequently, it is manifest that circumcision was a preparation for Baptism and a figure thereof, forasmuch as *all things happened* to the Fathers of old *in figure* (1 Cor. x. 11); just as their faith regarded things to come.

In *Summa theol.* III, q. 70, a. 2, resp., Aquinas continues:

Sicut dictum est art. praec., circumcisio erat praeparatoria ad baptismum, inquantum erat quaedam professio fidei Christi, quam etiam in baptismo nos profitemur. Inter antiquos autem patres primus Abraham promissionem accepit de Christo nascituro, cum dictum est ei Gen. 22, 18: *In semine tuo benedicentur omnes gentes*

terrae. Ipse etiam primus se a societate infidelium segre-
gavit, secundum mandatum Dei dicentis sibi, Gen. 12,
1: *Egredere de terra tua et de cognatione tua.* Et ideo
convenienter circumcisio fuit instituta in Abraham.

As stated above (a. 1) circumcision was a preparation
for Baptism, inasmuch as it was a profession of faith in
Christ, which we also profess in Baptism. Now among
the Fathers of old, Abraham was the first to receive the
promise of the future birth of Christ, when it was said
to him: *In thy seed shall all the nations of the earth be
blessed* (Gen. xxii. 18). Moreover, he was the first to
cut himself off from the society of unbelievers, in ac-
cordance with the commandment of the Lord, Who said
to him (Gen. xii. 1): *Go forth out of thy country and
from thy kindred.* Therefore circumcision was fittingly
instituted in the person of Abraham.

For the metaphor of "wings" and "strength" ("virtute"), cf.
Purg. XII, 95. In circumcision the male is singled out, in the
belief that the guilt of original sin is transmitted through the
male, beginning with Adam. Aquinas notes (*Summa theol.*
I-II, q. 81, a. 5, resp.):

Manifestum est autem secundum doctrinam Philosopho-
rum, quod principium activum in generatione est a
patre, materiam autem mater ministrat. Unde peccatum
originale non contrahitur a matre, sed a patre. Et secun-
dum hoc, si Adam non peccante, Eva peccasset, filii
originale peccatum non contraherent; e converso autem
esset, si Adam peccasset, et Eva non.

Now it is evident that in the opinion of philosophers, the
active principle of generation is from the father, while
the mother provides the matter. Therefore original sin
is contracted, not from the mother, but from the father:
so that, accordingly, if Eve, and not Adam, had sinned,
their children would not contract original sin: where-
as, if Adam, and not Eve, had sinned, they would con-
tract it.

82-84. *ma poi che 'l tempo . . . si ritenne*: "After the Cruci-

fixion, the unbaptized innocent children were 'confined be-
low' in the Limbus: cf. *Inf*. IV, 30, 34-36. Since the Redemp-
tion, there has been no salvation without baptism in Christ"
(Gr). See *Summa theol*. III, q. 70, a. 2, ad 3, where Aquinas
writes: "Baptismus in se continet perfectionem salutis, ad
quam Deus omnes homines vocat." ("Baptism contains in
itself the perfection of salvation, to which God calls all
men.") Aquinas then states: "Circumcisio autem non con-
tinebat perfectionem salutis, sed figurabat ipsam ut fiendam
per Christum." ("On the other hand, circumcision did not
contain the perfection of salvation, but signified it as to be
achieved by Christ.") See *Summa theol*. III, q. 62.

83. *Cristo*: Readers interested in numerology and the bal-
ance of symmetries expressed in numbers in this great struc-
ture may be interested to note that *Cristo* in rhyme with itself
occurs four times in the poem, the present instance being the
last. But this four were perhaps best construed as three plus
one. See C. S. Singleton (1965). The other three instances
also occur in the *Paradiso*: *Par*. XII, 71-75; XIV, 104-8; XIX,
104-8.

84. *tale innocenza là giù si ritenne*: "It is noteworthy that
Bernard himself, in a treatise addressed to Hugo of St. Vic-
tor, shrinks from the appalling conclusion that unbaptized
children are doomed to Limbo. See *Inf*. iv. 'We must suppose
that the ancient sacraments were efficacious as long as it can
be shown that they were not notoriously prohibited. And
after that? It is in God's hands. Not mine be it to set the
limit!' " (TC).

85–87. *Riguarda omai . . . Cristo*: The prompting of Ber-
nard, urging Dante to look upon Mary's face, brings the "eye
tour" of the rose to a return upon itself and thus completes
a circle, for Bernard began the tour with Mary. Her bright-
ness alone can further dispose the pilgrim to greater vision,
the vision of Christ which will be granted him at the end of
the journey that is now so near. And it is with the vision of
Christ, second person of the Trinity, that the whole experi-
ence will be concluded.

The reader will recall that the disposing of the pilgrim to this higher vision begins in *Par.* XXX, 52. But the pilgrim has yet to realize that Christ will not be seen at the end in any human form that resembles, in countenance, the features of his mother, as these verses seem to suggest.

88. *sopra lei*: In Mary's face, the "allegrezza" being expressed in a radiance of beatitude.

89–90. *portata ne le menti . . . altezza*: The "holy minds" are the angels, also called Intelligences. They are pure spirit, pure mind, of course, even though they have, in the poet's conception, the semblance of a body, as witnessed so often throughout the poem. They were created for Heaven, of course, and have wings to fly there. They were first glimpsed, as the final vision began to open up to the eyes of the pilgrim, as sparks that flew in and out of flowers (*Par.* XXX, 64-69) and then became bees in metaphor. In *Par.* XXXI, 7-9, and the verses following there, it is made clear that their chief occupation is to carry the blessings of beatitude to the petals of the rose.

91. *quantunque*: Cf. vs. 56, where the word bears the same meaning: "everything." *davante*: I.e., *prima*.

93. *di Dio tanto sembiante*: "Such resemblance to God." But see n. to vss. 85-87.

94. *amor*: The angel Gabriel. *che primo lì discese*: The exact meaning of "lì," the emphatic adverb, is somewhat obscure. Most commentators take it to refer to the symbolic vision of the Annunciation which the pilgrim beheld in the eighth heaven (*Par.* XXIII, 94-96), and accordingly "primo" would refer to that preceding moment in the poem. But, though the angel Gabriel was there seen symbolically to descend as a light which circled Mary, declaring that he would continue to do so (*Par.* XXIII, 106-8) as Mary symbolically rose in what represented her Assumption, it was not said that he "sang" then the words he spoke to Mary at the Annunciation: "Ave, Maria, gratia plena." It seems best, therefore, to take the "primo" and the "lì" of this verse to

refer to the actual Annunciation to Mary, of which this now is the re-enactment and celebration in eternity of that great moment in time (Luc. 1:28). Note also how that moment in history is then explicitly celebrated in the poet's verses (vss. 112-14) while Gabriel remains at the center of attention.

97. *cantilena*: The term implies a solemn chant.

98. *la beata corte*: Both "courts" of Heaven, angels and human souls, are here seen as one, even though they were named as two courts in *Par.* XXX, 96.

99. *vista*: "Face."   *serena*: "Luminous," with joy. For this meaning of the adjective, cf. *Par.* XIII, 5.

100. *comporte*: "Deign." Dante's words express humble gratitude.

102. *sorte*: Cf. the corresponding verb *sortire* as repeatedly used in such a context, e.g., in vs. 34 of the present canto.

103-5. *qual è . . . foco?* The narrator Dante has already answered the question, of course, but the pilgrim Dante is now represented as one who asks it; and his question is phrased so as to celebrate again the great moment of the Annunciation and Gabriel's enamorment of Mary, which continues throughout eternity.

103. *gioco*: I.e., *festa*, implying joyous celebration. Cf. *Par.* XX, 117.

105. *par di foco*: Cf. *Par.* XXIII, 94, where Gabriel is symbolically represented as a "torch" ("facella").

106-7. *la dottrina . . . Maria*: Cf. "dottore," as Bernard is termed in vs. 2.

107. *ch'abbelliva = che si abbelliva* (cf. *Par.* XXII, 24).

108. *stella mattutina*: Venus. The reference adds further meaning to the context of love here.

109-11. *Ed elli a me . . . sia*: This and the following tercet, in this final celebration of the angel Gabriel's great role, serve to single him out among all the angels as the greatest, for the poem nears its end and no other angel will be brought into such central focus.

109. *Baldezza = baldanza.* The term bears a connotation of pride, which can only be good pride here, pride in the great role assigned to him.   *leggiadria*: Joy of spirit and beauty in bearing.

110-11. *quant' esser puote . . . lui*: The statement is clear in its uplifting of Gabriel to the highest position among all creatures (excepting Mary) be they angels or human souls.

111. *e sì volem che sia*: "And we are in accord," we (all creatures, angels and men) are willing that Gabriel should be so exalted—even as it is God's will that it should be so. Cf. *Par.* III, 70-78; XX, 138.

112-13. *portò la palma giuso a Maria*: "Giuso" in this phrase would seem to support the meaning of "lì" as construed in vs. 94. See n. to vs. 94. Gabriel is commonly represented in painting as bearing a palm frond in one hand, this being the symbol of victory which declared Mary to be above all other women.

114. *carcar si volse de la nostra salma*: When Christ, the second person of the Trinity, chose to become flesh and take on our burden of sin. Cf. *Par.* VII, 30-33.   *carcar = caricar.*   *volse = volle.*

115-16. *Ma vieni omai . . . parlando*: "Omai" implies that it is now time to get on with the "eye tour" of the rose, which has paused for so long with Mary and Gabriel in the central focus.

116. *i gran patrici*: The term, along with "Agusta" as applied to Mary (vs. 119), bears the explicit suggestion of empire. These now are to be the greatest of those who sit in this great colosseum.   *patrici = patrizi*, the patricians of this court of which Mary is the empress.

118. *Quei due*: These, as we are to be told, are St. Peter and Adam, to whom are assigned the highest seats of all (after Mary) on this (Mary's) side of the rose, for they are nearest to "the Empress."

119. *Agusta = Augusta. Augusta* was an established title for the wife of the emperor. Mary is, of course, the mother. Cf. "agosta," the corresponding adjective, in *Par*. XXX, 136; see also *Inf*. XIII, 68. The term "imperio" (vs. 117) has prepared the way for this.

120. *son d'esta rosa quasi due radici*: This use of "roots" as it comes in the context of the rose exalts these two to a place of the highest importance, after Mary's. Both are then termed "fathers," as the verses continue to focus on them.

121-23. *colui che . . . gusta*: It will be noted that Adam sits on the left of "the Empress," a place of less honor, obviously, than St. Peter's, on her right. In this we are to admire, as everywhere in the seating arrangement, the marvelous balance and symmetry in God's providential ordering, borne out on the grandest scale in having the whole rose divided into halves, with a B.C. half and an A.D. half. Adam is thus properly seated in the former. See Fig. 5, p. 534.

121. *le s'aggiusta*: "Is next to her." Cf. the Latin *iuxta*.

122. *ardito gusto*: Adam's tasting of the fruit was an act of pride, hence "ardito" as none other.

123. *tanto amaro*: All the bitter consequences of original sin are implied. Cf. *Purg*. I, 26-27, the lament that points to this, and Adam's own words in *Par*. XXVI, 115-17.

124-26. *dal destro . . . venusto*: St. Peter sits in the seat of highest honor—after Mary—on Mary's right.

124. *vetusto*: "Ancient."

125-26. *le chiavi . . . venusto*: See Matt. 16:19. Cf. *Inf*. XIX, 91-92; XXVII, 104; *Purg*. IX, 117-20. The angel at the gate of Purgatory proper holds the keys to that realm. And now, by the turn of phrase here, the keys are said to be "keys to this lovely flower," the Rose. St. Peter's keys were also remembered when Dante was passing his "entrance examination" with Peter himself (*Par.* XXIV, 35-36).

127-29. *E quei . . . clavi*: This is St. John, the author of the Apocalypse, who prophesied the difficult times and the calamities of the Church. Cf. *Purg.* XXIX, 143-44, and such prophecies as set forth in the dumb show of *Purg.* XXXII, 109-60, on the model of St. John's prophecy.

128. *sposa*: The Church, as so often in the poem (*Par.* X, 140; XI, 32-33; XXVII, 40).

129. *con la lancia*: Cf. Ioan. 19:34: "Sed unus militum lancea latus eius aperuit." ("But one of the soldiers opened his side with a lance.")   *clavi*: I.e., *chiodi*, referring to the nails that nailed Christ to the Cross. For the form, which is latinizing (*clavi* for *chiavi*), cf. the verb *chiavare* as it is used in *Inf.* XXXIII, 46; *Purg.* VIII, 137; *Par.* XIX, 105.

130. *esso*: Peter. St. John the Evangelist sits on Peter's right, always the "better" side.   *lungo l'altro*: Beside Adam.

131-32. *quel duca . . . retrosa*: Moses. See Exod. 16:14-35; for the manna given to the Israelites in the desert, see Exod. 16:14-16. As every reader of the account of the Exodus knows, the people led by Moses did indeed prove to be "fickle and backward-looking," many times over.

133-35. *Di contr' . . . osanna*: St. Anna, the mother of Mary, sits directly opposite St. Peter (see Fig. 5, p. 534). This gives her the position of honor, since it places her to the right of John the Baptist, so that in this respect her seat corresponds to that of Peter, to the right of Mary. To conceive that Anna keeps her gaze constantly on her daughter, on the opposite rim of the great amphitheater, even as all the while she continues to join in the chorus that sings the praises of the Lord, is a strikingly human touch introduced by the poet at this point. Mother gazes constantly at daughter, instead of gazing upwards to enjoy the direct vision of God!

135. *per cantare*: "While singing" or perhaps "despite her singing," that is, she does not allow her singing to interfere with her gazing constantly upon her beloved daughter Mary.

136–38. *e contro . . . ciglia*: St. Lucy, who twice came to Dante's aid, first in the relay of grace that took place in Heaven, as recounted by Beatrice in Limbo (see *Inf*. II, 97-108), then in carrying Dante up the steep mountain to the gate of Purgatory proper (*Purg*. IX, 52-63).

137–38. *che mosse . . . ciglia*: The reference is to the moment (*Inf*. I, 55-60) when the she-wolf was driving Dante back into the darkness ("where the sun is silent") and to the moment then reported by Beatrice to Virgil, in *Inf*. II, when Lucy, having come to where Beatrice sat beside ancient Rachel, exhorted Beatrice to proceed to the rescue of her "faithful" one with words that refer to his being thrust back "on that flood over which the sea has no vaunt" (see *Inf*. II, 103-8). Thus, at the end of the poem the action is again coming full circle, in coming back to Lucy now, as to Mary (with whom it began) and to Beatrice, whose role was remembered in the paean addressed to her (*Par*. XXXI, 79-90).

138. *quando chinavi, a rovinar, le ciglia*: The words give to Dante's falling back into the darkness (as told in *Inf*. I, 55-63) the connotation of falling asleep, that is, a falling back into the sleep of sin. See C. S. Singleton (1948), p. 274.

139. *Ma perché 'l tempo fugge che t'assonna*: Since, within the poem, this journey to the afterlife has never been termed a *dream*, but has always been presented as *real*, it is not possible to understand this verse, with the verb *assonnare*, to contradict this fundamental postulate of the experience. Many differing views have been held of the meaning (see *Enciclopedia Dantesca*, s.v. *assonnare*). The view that seems most persuasive in the total context would see in the phrase *che t'assonna*, modifying *tempo*, a clear reference to the accepted fact that the experience of rising so high, all the way to God, on the part of a man who is still mortal, must of necessity be of the briefest duration. (Cf. "mortal weight," *Par*.

XXVII, 64.) The blessed and the angels are privileged to gaze upon God through all eternity, but a mortal man can have the experience through the *light of glory* only momentarily. Thus Thomas Aquinas, under the standard heading "Of Rapture" (*Summa theol.* II-II, q. 175, a. 3, ad 2), states: "Divina essentia videri ab intellectu creato non potest nisi per lumen gloriae, de quo dicitur in psal. 35, 10: *In lumine tuo videbimus lumen.* Quod tamen dupliciter participari potest. Uno modo per modum formae immanentis: et sic beatos facit sanctos in patria. Alio modo per modum cuiusdam passionis transeuntis." ("The Divine Essence cannot be seen by a created intellect save through the light of glory, of which it is written [Ps. XXXV. 10 (36:9)]: *In Thy light we shall see light.* But this light can be shared in two ways. First by way of an abiding form, and thus it beatifies the saints in heaven. Secondly, by way of a *transitory passion* [italics added].") The "transitory passion" was the experience of St. Paul when rapt to the third heaven.

Thus St. Bernard, with his phrase *il tempo che t'assonna*, is (given the moment and the context) referring to the fundamental difference between the pilgrim's mortal condition (his mortal weight that will pull him down) and the condition of the blessed, which is his own. "Your experience here," he means, "is necessarily *transitory* and can last only for the briefest time." Accordingly, the following simile of the tailor suggests, "Let us make the most of the time that is left to you." *Assonnare* is thus not literal in its meaning but bears an allusion that makes it metaphorical. "Sleep" is a falling away from the final experience, which must happen soon, for the mortal man's experience of the light of glory is most transitory. (On the *light of glory* see Singleton, 1958, pp. 15-23.)

The "falling away" from the vision will be insistently represented in the final experience as given in the last canto, but there as a "fading away" in the poet's memory as he strives to regain a true recollection of the experience had.

The reader will note how the reference to sleep and a falling-back into sleep serves to clinch the coming "round to full circle" of the action, here so near the end. Dante was about to "fall asleep" at the beginning, i.e., fall back into the "sleep of sin," because of his burden of original sin (hence he was limping; see *Inf.* I, 30, with the corresponding note, as well as the note to vss. 4-6 of this canto). Now he is about to "fall asleep," not in the sense of "sleep" at the beginning, but to "fall away" from the high experience of rapture here at the end, due to his "mortal pondo" (*Par.* XXVII, 64), because no living man can endure, except ever so briefly, any such experience.

140–41. *come buon sartore . . . gonna:* The reader will not fail to remark the very humble simile which this medieval poet uses here at the height of his great argument and so near to God. One imagines an everyday scene in a tailor shop in the Florence of Dante's day, the tailor sitting cross-legged over his work and carefully measuring the amount of cloth he has left for making the skirt (*gonna* should be conceived as the typical garment of a man; see n. to *Inf.* XV, 24). How far we are from Milton and a Renaissance conception of the sublime! One does well to recall, in this connection, that Dante termed his style humble and low-pitched (*Epist.* XIII, 30: "comedia vero remisse et humiliter") in justifying his title *Comedia*. And how constant the poet has been in maintaining this level of style from beginning to the very end, even now before God!

142–44. *e drizzeremo . . . fulgore:* The tercet states completely the final "act" of the *Comedy* in precise terms, and the reader should reflect (through such terms) on the cardinal fact that Dante the pilgrim, though in this Empyrean heaven he has been made ready for the final vision of God by all he has seen (cf. *Par.* XXX, 54), has been seeing by reflected light all the while and has never actually ventured to look directly upwards into the descending light of glory through which alone the vision of God face to face can be had (cf. *Par.* XXX, 100-103, where this is clearly stated).

It should be noted that God is specifically termed *amore*, "primo amore." Thus God as the God of love is stressed by Bernard (whose accent on the affective nature of the final experience has been witnessed) here, as it is by the poet at the very end and in the very last verse of the whole poem: "l'amor che move il sole e l'altre stelle."

144. *quant' è possibil per lo suo fulgore*: It is important to note the qualification made by the phrase "as far as possible" and to bear it in mind in reading of Dante's final experience as reported in the last canto, for that touch brings out an accepted point of doctrine regarding the beatific vision on the part of human soul or angel, on the part of any and all creatures, namely, that each sees according to the measure of the divine endowment of capacity made by the Creator when He creates the soul (cf. vs. 75, "primiero acume," and the note to that verse). Hence what the poet reports as his own limit in the attainment of the beatific vision (*Par.* XXXIII, 139-41) should be viewed within the context of this qualification as expressed here by Bernard. And the final experience will indeed be represented as a penetration ("penètri" here). "Fulgore" signifies, of course, the light of glory.

145. *Veramente*: "Veramente," from the Latin *verum*, here means "but," as it so often does in the poem (cf. *Par.* I, 10, and *passim*).   *ne*: Latin, meaning "lest."

146. *movendo l'ali tue*: Thus, the final upward penetration into the light of glory is presented as an upward flight in which the wayfarer strives to move his own "wings." This *cooperation* on the part of the living man in the final gradual attainment of the supreme vision will be insistently brought out in the next canto. But it is God's grace that makes the cooperation effective.   *credendo oltrarti*: The phrase may recall *Purg.* XI, 14-15, in the paraphrase of the Lord's Prayer.

147. *orando grazia conven che s'impetri*: Other editors have adopted the punctuation: "orando, grazia . . ." But it seems better to understand "grazia" as the object of "orando."

148. *grazia da quella che puote aiutarti*: Grace, through Mary, must now be sought, in Bernard's prayer opening the last canto. No reader forgets, of course, that it was grace ob-

tained through Mary's intervention that made the journey of
this living man possible, a journey recounted in no fewer than
ninety-nine cantos. And now the last lap of this journey,
above and beyond Mary and all human creatures, is to be
made possible by another intercession on her part. The way
in which the action of the poem thus comes full circle and
then extends beyond that circle in a final upward line may
easily be represented by the simple diagram seen in Fig. 6,

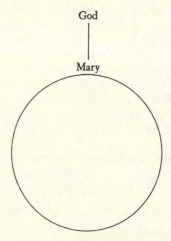

6. Diagram suggesting the return full circle of the action from
the Virgin Mary to Mary and then the ultimate rise to the
Transcendental One

which graphically brings out the presence, symbolically, of
a Transcendental One, throughout the poem. Ninety-nine
cantos have that one canto added to them in which the vision
of God face to face is had and by which the perfect number
one hundred is attained. This "plus one" feature is brought
out in the number of verses allotted to each of the cantos
(which vary in length, as the reader knows), in that in no
canto is the total number of verses exactly divisible by three.
The division by three always leaves a "plus one" verse.

149–51. *e tu mi seguirai . . . orazione*: Bernard continues, with "affezione" and with "cor," to stress the affective aspect of the final experience. It is *love* that finally attains the Object, or so he seems to imply. We know however that *vision* (which is intellective) must precede the love that attains (which is of the will). See *Par.* XXVIII, 109-11. Bernard's injunction also emphasizes the necessity of Dante's cooperation ("tu mi seguirai . . . sì che . . . lo cor non parti").

150. *parti = parta*, "separate."

151. *orazione*: Thus the ninety-ninth canto is so designed that its last word is "orazione" and the number of its verses is 151, which (by the established practice in medieval numerology of adding the digits) presents the number seven, which is also found at the exact center of the whole structure. See C. S. Singleton (1965).

CANTO XXXIII

1–3. *Vergine Madre . . . consiglio*: Bernard's prayer to the Blessed Virgin makes use of a phraseology that belongs to liturgical style, particularly in characteristic antitheses. As Sapegno observes, the opening of the prayer, in this first tercet, offers antithetical and contradictory attributes, if considered according to a *natural* criterion, whereas all are true on the *supernatural* plane: virgin and mother, daughter and mother of God, the most humble of creatures and the most exalted. He also notes in the liturgy such phrases as *Dei genitrix Virgo* ("Virgin mother of God") and *genuisti qui te fecit* ("Thou didst give birth to Him who made thee"). All point, of course, to the inconceivable miracle of the Word made flesh, to incarnation of Deity. As readers of Chaucer well know, the English poet adapted a great part of this prayer in his *Second Nun's Tale*, vss. 29-84.

2. *umile*: For Mary's humility in particular, cf. *Purg.* X, 34-45, and Luc. 1:46-49.

3. *termine fisso*: This refers to God's providential plan wherein Mary *ab aeterno* (from eternity) was chosen for her humble-exalted role. Her very seat in this heavenly rose underscores the fact, since, with her, B.C. time ends, so to speak, and A.D. time begins.

4–6. *tu se' colei . . . fattura*: In *Conv.* IV, v, 5, Dante writes:

> E però [che] anche l'albergo, dove il celestiale rege in-
> trare dovea, convenia essere mondissimo e purissimo,
> ordinata fu una progenie santissima, de la quale dopo
> molti meriti nascesse una femmina ottima di tutte l'altre,
> la quale fosse camera del Figliuolo di Dio: e questa pro-
> genie fu quella di David, del qual [di]scese la baldezza
> e l'onore de l'umana generazione, cioè Maria.

And because the abode wherein the celestial king must
enter ought to be most clean and pure there was likewise
ordained a most holy family from the which after many
merits should be born a woman supremely good
amongst all the rest, who should be the treasure house
of the Son of God. And this family is that of David. And
the triumph and honour of the human race, Mary to wit,
was born from it.

5–6. *che 'l suo fattore . . . fattura*: The Creator of human na-
ture did not deem it unbecoming that He should make Him-
self a human creature (called, in the Holy Scriptures, the Son
of Man).

7–9. *Nel ventre tuo . . . fiore*: The flower, this rose, was part
of God's providential plan, as we know, and it is very strik-
ingly said to have germinated and blossomed in Mary's
womb, in the conception of Jesus. The statement is made
essentially in terms of love, and the verb *raccese* (*re*kindled)
is used to underscore the fact that God, following Adam's sin
in the Garden of Eden, withdrew his special love from the
mass of mankind. Cf., for the same great event, again in
terms of love, the metaphor of *Purg.* X, 41-42.

10. *Qui*: The three opening tercets of the prayer (nor is the
number accidental!) regard Mary and the Incarnation in the
focus of time, of providential history. The "qui" turns
the focus to Mary's *place* here in the rose.   *a noi*: Ber-
nard's words refer not only to the human souls that make
up the rose, but to the angels who fly about it as well.
meridiana face: Literally, "noonday torch," i.e., a "sun"

when it is brightest and warmest, both radiance and heat symbolizing love ("face di caritate"). It will be recalled that Mary was first seen as a sun dawning on the horizon (*Par.* XXXI, 118-29). She now becomes a "noonday sun."

11. *e giuso, intra ' mortali*: This turn of phrase, balancing the "qui" of Heaven, returns us to earth and history, to a focus that will end on the figure of Dante, the mortal man who has been uplifted to this highest of places from that lowly world.

12. *speranza*: "Hope" is very much of the mortal world and has no *active* place in the immortal world of the angels and the elect, despite the fact that St. James could represent that virtue and love it still (*Par.* XXV, 82-84). *vivace*: "Inexhaustible."

13. *Donna*: "Donna" is here used with its full etymological force of *Domina*, as applied to the "Queen of Heaven." It will be noted that, beginning with this term of address, three tercets now follow which exalt Mary to the highest, from the point of view of mortal hope, and which precede the specific grace implored in vss. 22-39, which terminate the prayer.

tanto vali: "Thou dost so avail," i.e., in interceding with God on the part of mortal sinners.

14–15. *che qual vuol grazia . . . ali*: What Dante claims here is not, of course, literally so, or all prayers directed "directly" to God would be misdirected! But it is a becoming part of this highest of praise for Mary as uttered by Bernard, her great lover. In fact, St. Bernard had expressed it so in his *Sermones de tempore* (*In vigilia nativitatis Domini* III, 10): "Nihil nos Deus habere voluit, quod per Mariae manus non transiret." ("God wills that we should have nothing that does not pass through Mary's hands.")

14. *qual*: "Whosoever."

15. *disianza*: This is an archaic form for *desiderio*. *vuol volar sanz' ali*: This seems to have been a standing phrase. See M. Barbi (1934), p. 254.

16–18. *La tua benignità . . . precorre*: Mary intervenes on behalf of the sinner, seeing his plight and need down in the world of mortals, and obtains grace for him without his asking for it. All readers will recall a cardinal instance of this very fact at the outset of this poem, for in the first canto of the *Inferno* we watched the wayfarer struggle alone and lose ground before the three beasts (and he was not seen to pray to Mary), only to learn later through Virgil's account of Beatrice's report to him that Mary had interceded on Dante's behalf, so that "stern judgment" was "broken thereabove" (*Inf.* II, 96).

18. *liberamente*: "Freely." Cf. *Inf.* XIII, 86; *Purg.* XI, 134; XXVI, 139.

19–21. *In te misericordia . . . bontate*: This third of the three tercets specifically dedicated to the praise of Mary is the culminating one. Note especially vss. 20-21, where it is said that *all* goodness to be found in any and all creatures is to be found in her.

20. *magnificenza*: The word may be understood as "munificence" as well as "magnificence" in the sense of "power to achieve lofty things."

22. *Or*: "Or" signals the beginning of the specific request that Bernard would make of Mary.   *questi*: "This man."

22–24. *che da l'infima . . . una*: Many commentators have taken "lacuna" (which does indeed have "pool" as one of its meanings) to mean Cocytus, the lake of ice at the center of the earth. But this, in the context of what is then said concerning seeing the "spiritual lives" one after another, can scarcely be the meaning here, for Bernard would not omit reference to the journey down through Hell, nor exclude the souls of Hell from the experience of that "descent before ascent" which comprised one third of the whole. "Lacuna" should be taken to refer to the whole pit of Hell at the center of the earth. Cf. Dan. 6:7, 12, 17, where the "lion's den" is termed *lacus leonum*. Thus *lacuna* here should be construed as referring to the entire *den* of the cavity of Hell, and it should thus include the many souls seen in Hell.

Although the specific meaning of "lacuna" here would seem to be the cavity of Hell, we might well consider that, in a certain medieval view, the earth itself is *infimo* and that this may be a part of the meaning here. See A. O. Lovejoy (1936), pp. 101-2:

> It has often been said that the older picture of the world in space was peculiarly fitted to give man a high sense of his own importance and dignity; and some modern writers have made much of this supposed implication of the pre-Copernican astronomy. Man occupied, we are told, the central place in the universe, and round the planet of his habitation all the vast, unpeopled spheres obsequiously revolved. But the actual tendency of the geocentric system was, for the medieval mind, precisely the opposite. For the centre of the world was not a position of honor; it was rather the place farthest removed from the Empyrean, the bottom of the creation, to which its dregs and baser elements sank. The actual centre, indeed, was Hell; in the spatial sense the medieval world was literally diabolocentric. And the whole sublunary region was, of course, incomparably inferior to the resplendent and incorruptible heavens above the moon. Thus Montaigne, still adhering to the older astronomy, could consistently describe man's dwelling-place as "the filth and mire of the world, the worst, lowest, most lifeless part of the universe, the bottom story of the house."

See n. to *Par.* XXII, 134-35.

In Dante's phraseology the reference to "le vite spiritali *ad una ad una*" suggests a great chain of beings, reaching down, then up, leading (as an experience of the wayfarer) all the way to God.

25. *supplica*: "Supplica" with the dative is a latinizing construction. Cf. *Par.* XV, 85.

25-26. *di virtute tanto*: "For so much power." *Virtù* has

been used frequently in the poem in this sense, and for the present context a first notable example might be recalled in Virgil's address to Beatrice at the beginning (*Inf.* II, 76): "O donna di virtù."

26–27. *con li occhi levarsi più alto*: The phrase should remind the reader that Bernard and Dante stand on the floor of the amphitheater, in the yellow center of the rose, and that the whole "eye tour" of that amphitheater has so far been by reflected light. That is, though Dante has perforce been standing at the center of the area where the descending light of glory strikes upon the convex surface of the Primum Mobile, hence has been standing in the direct downward line of that light, he has thus far not ventured to look *directly* up into that light nor to seek to see God through it, something he will now do, on Bernard's urging, and through the grace that comes from Mary's granting and God's granting of the saint's prayer. The remainder of this journey is up through the downpouring light of glory, up along its beam. Dante's position, standing beside Bernard at the center of the rose, corresponds to that of the blessed where they sit gazing up into the light. It should be remembered that the light of glory was defined in verses numbered 100-102 (a tercet), in a canto numbered 30 or XXX. See n. to *Par.* XXX, 100-102.

27. *più alto verso*: The phrase is important in this context, for it introduces a modification that bears a touch of relativity. Is the wayfarer merely to *approach* God ("l'ultima salute")? Is he not actually to *attain to* God, move upwards *all the way to Him*? The answer is yes, of course—otherwise this journey could not be said to reach its goal. Yet it should be recalled that each of the blessed—each of the human souls, that is, as well as each of the angels—attains to that *measure* of the beatific vision which an original endowment of grace (see "primiero acume," *Par.* XXXII, 75, and the corresponding note) makes it possible for him to receive. So is it with this living man, who is now to be permitted to attain to *his own particular limit* of vision. And as the action of the poem narrows to this single and simple focus of attainment in these terms, the reader should remember that what this

mortal wayfarer reports of his *limited* experience is to be taken as just that: one living man's final experience in what theological doctrine knows as "rapture." St. Paul's uplifting is always cited as the exemplary instance of rapture, the only difference being that Paul confessed that he could not give a report of what he saw, whereas this poet is now to strive (with all the labor and difficulty which he declares) to convey to the reader, in rhymed words, his own final experience: his vision of God, face to face, *in raptu.*   *l'ultima salute*: "The beatific vision" termed "fine di tutt' i disii" in vs. 46 and "sommo piacer" in vs. 33.

28-30. *E io . . . scarsi*: Bernard's phrasing "che mai per mio veder non arsi," with "arsi" in the preterite, points back to his own ardor, as a "contemplante," when on earth he "burned" with the desire to have the experience in rapture which he now implores for this living man. See *Par.* XXXI, 111, and n. to *Par.* XXXI, 110-11.

29. *prieghi*: The use of "prieghi" here, then "priego" in the next verse, followed by "prieghi" (vs. 32) and "priego" again (vs. 34) clearly builds up a sense of ardor and urgency which Bernard puts into this his prayer to the Queen of Heaven.

30. *scarsi*: "Insufficient." Cf. *Par.* VII, 118.

31. *perché*: "That," as the following subjunctive ("disleghi") makes clear.   *disleghi*: "Dispel."

31-32. *perché tu . . . tuoi*: Cf. Boethius, *Consol. philos.* III, ix, 25-28:

Dissice terrenae nebulas et pondera molis
Atque tuo splendore mica! Tu namque serenum,
Tu requies tranquilla piis, te cernere finis,
Principium, vector, dux, semita, terminus idem.

Cast off the earthly weight wherewith I am opprest,
Shine as Thou art most bright, Thou only calm and rest
To pious men whose end is to behold Thy ray,
Who their beginning art, their guide, their bound,
    and way.

The reader should look closely at the original Latin of Boethius here, rather than at the English translation, for "terrenae nebulas" corresponds exactly to Bernard's "nube," and "pondera molis" points to what has already been termed the "mortal pondo" of the wayfarer (*Par.* XXVII, 64); see n. to *Par.* XXXII, 139. The living man brings clouds inherent in his mortal condition to this loftiest of all experiences, to the sight of God face to face; and these mists must be dispelled, a matter quite in line with the whole preparation for final vision which is stated in *Par.* XXX, 54, in terms of "making the candle able to bear the flame."

32. *co' prieghi tuoi*: It is Bernard's prayer that Mary, in her turn, should pray for this.

33. *sì che 'l sommo piacer*: "Piacer" is here in the objective focus, as frequently in the poem, beginning with *Inf.* V, 104. It is now used in referring to God as the final goal (cf. n. to vs. 27). Other such phrasings may be recalled, for example, *Par.* VIII, 87: "là 've ogne ben si termina e s'inizia."   *li* = *gli*.   *si dispieghi*: "Be manifested to him." The manifesting will indeed prove to be a gradual unfolding, which is the literal meaning of the verb *dispiegare*.

35-36. *che conservi sani . . . suoi*: Bernard's particular request looks back to earth, to the return of this living man to the mortal world, where he will need Mary's continuing guardianship, especially to keep him from the sin of pride, the pride he might feel in having been granted, while still among the living, this most extraordinary experience of the beatific vision ("tanto veder"). The phrases "vinca tua guardia" and "i movimenti umani" of vs. 37 make this meaning clear. That the wayfaring Dante while on earth prayed to Mary every morning and every evening we have been assured by the poet (*Par.* XXIII, 88-89), who has repeatedly caused his own ultimate salvation to be predicted in his poem, beginning with Charon's words to him in *Inf.* III, 91-93.

38-39. *vedi Beatrice . . . le mani*: This is our last glimpse of Beatrice, the last mention of her name in the poem; and the singling out of her in the impressive scene in which so many other blessed souls clasp their hands, as they join Bernard in his prayer, is the culminating tribute to Beatrice by this poet who first began to write of her in youthful verses, and then in the *Vita nuova* (XXVI, 6) as that "miracle on earth" which was leading him to God.

39. *per*: "Per" is the equivalent of the Latin *pro*.

40. *Li occhi*: Mary's eyes, which of course can be clearly discerned by the wayfarer, even though he stands so far below her, since such is the nature of vision here (cf. *Par.* XXX, 121-23).

41. *orator = orante* (Bernard).   *ne = ci*, "us."

42. *son grati*: The verb in the present tense bears a touch of exhortation to mortals to direct their prayers to her.

43. *indi a l'etterno lume s'addrizzaro*: Mary's looking down to Bernard, then turning her eyes to the eternal light, may be compared to Beatrice's similar posture and act, after Dante addresses his paean to her (cf. *Par.* XXXI, 91-93).

44-45. *nel qual . . . chiaro*: It will be seen that the phrase "nel qual" brings out the point in the note to vss. 26-27, namely, that vision through the descending light of glory is an upward ascent reaching, for each creature, the limit of the individual capacity given at birth by God. Mary's limit in this regard is thus the highest of any creature, including even that of the highest angel. For this concept, see Richard of St. Victor, *In Cantica Canticorum explicatio* XXXIX: "[Maria] supra angelos quoque est, quia eos puritate supergreditur, dum divinitatem clarius illis contemplatur." ("Moreover, Mary is above the angels, because she surpasses them in purity, while she contemplates more clearly the divinity than they do.") This is implied in earlier verses (*Par.* IV, 28-30). The verb "s'invii" here further brings out this most essential point, with its clear suggestion of penetration and of reaching, on the part of the creature, the limit of its powers.

As this kind of penetration up through the light to his own limit is now to begin on the part of the wayfaring Dante, it may be well to recall the "coming full circle" again in the statement of such a truth, for it is emphatically affirmed in the opening verses of the *Paradiso* (*Par.* I, 7-9) in the phrase "appressando sé al suo disire" and in the verb "si profonda."

And, as the final lap of the wayfarer's journey begins, the poem itself may be said to complete a circle, in its action, for it opened by focusing on a man struggling to attain to a light which was illuminating a summit, the summit of a mountain (*Inf.* I, 13-30). The scene there and the action was as simple as could be: a man, a light, and struggle to reach the light. The poem has returned, here at its end, to this simplest kind of "stage set" and to this line of action.

46–48. *E io ch'al fine . . . finii*: The first words of this tercet turn the focus of the action into the simplest possible terms, as noted: only an "io" now and a light to be penetrated, upwards to the "goal of all desires" (cf. *Par.* XXII, 61-65). Virgil's promise to the wayfarer, as the journey reached a first but (as is now clear) subordinate goal, may be remembered (see *Purg.* XXVII, 115-17).

47. *appropinquava*: I.e., *mi avvicinavo.   sì com' io dovea*: Cf. *Purg.* XII, 7: "sì come andar vuolsi rife'mi."

48. *l'ardor del desiderio in me finii*: The meaning of the verb in this verse is much debated, but one aspect of that meaning seems beyond discussion: "finii" cannot here be in a normal signification of "bring to an end." Indeed, the context requires that the meaning be the exact opposite, i.e., "I brought the ardor of my desire to its highest intensity." Bernard is urging the wayfarer on in precisely this sense, and the importance of the wayfarer's co-operation in the final act is thus stressed—and continues to be stressed. The "desiderio" (here, and as it continues) is the desire to attain to the highest possible vision of the Godhead. This implies a maximum effort on the part of the wayfarer which can only succeed if grace from above uplifts at every step. It should be noted, in any case, that the poet's conception of the final act is not that of the mystic passive surrender, or the ideal of nirvana. Grace from above descends to help the struggling soul, but

it is a soul that itself *struggles* toward the final attainment. Some commentators (with a certain measure of justness) have viewed this final act of the poem as epic in its nature.

49–51. *Bernardo m'accennava . . . volea*: Strictly speaking, the poet is once more guilty of a momentary slip in maintaining the point of view, a slip that may be compared with that of *Purg.* XXI, 10-12 (which is perhaps the only other instance of this), for if, as is affirmed, he was "already such as Bernard desired," he was indeed already completely intent on gazing into the light, and therefore could not have seen that Bernard was gesturing and smiling to urge that he do so. Bernard, in any case, disappears from the reader's attention at this point, and the poem enters into the simplest of focuses: one actor (one who would *see*) and one goal, God.

52–54. *ché la mia vista . . . vera*: The action of the poem is now entirely a matter of vision ("vista"), of ever increasing vision, and of vision that is given from above, through grace, a fact which "venendo" stresses, for vision *comes* in this sense, and *be*comes ever clearer.

52. *sincera*: "Pure."

53. *e più e più intrava per lo raggio*: The essential nature of this last stretch of the journey is thus declared, from the wayfarer's point of view. He (i.e., his gaze) penetrates (cf. *Par.* XXXII, 143) farther and farther upwards through the descending light of glory, which sheds greater and greater grace upon him (i.e., greater and greater revelation). It is essential to follow this double movement: upwards on the part of the mortal man's seeing (penetration to the highest mystery) and downwards on the part of the divine revelation ("venendo," vs. 52).

54. *che da sé è vera*: Cf. Thomas Aquinas, *Summa theol.* I, q. 16, a. 5, resp.:

> Veritas invenitur in intellectu, secundum quod apprehendit rem ut est; et in re, secundum quod habet esse conformabile intellectui. Hoc autem maxime invenitur in Deo. Nam esse eius non solum est conforme suo in-

tellectui, sed etiam est ipsum suum intelligere; et suum intelligere est mensura et causa omnis alterius esse, et omnis alterius intellectus; et ipse est suum esse et intelligere. Unde sequitur quod non solum in ipso sit veritas, sed quod ipse sit ipsa summa et prima veritas.

Truth is found in the intellect according as it apprehends a thing as it is; and in things according as they have being conformable to an intellect. This is to the greatest degree found in God. For His being is not only conformed to His intellect, but it is the very act of His intellect; and His act of understanding is the measure and cause of every other being and of every other intellect, and He Himself is His own existence and act of understanding. Whence it follows not only that truth is in Him, but that He is truth itself, and the sovereign and first truth.

But "vera" here stresses not only intellect in God and understanding, but Being as well. The verse looks to the origin of the high light, the light of glory (which is soon to be disclosed to the wayfarer), looks to God as the supreme Existence.

55-57. *Da quinci innanzi . . . oltraggio*: It is the *poet's* voice that now breaks in upon the action, speaking in the present tense and reaffirming what is declared at the beginning of the *Paradiso* (a fact that should be clearly recalled by the reader, for through it he sees again how, thematically, this third *cantica* of the poem comes full circle, how it describes a circle, as the *Inferno* and the *Purgatorio* do not). By now no reader of the *Paradiso* can fail to be aware that "circle" (and "circling") *is* the dominant pattern of this last lofty realm, in so many ways; and he is soon to see that the very last image of the *Paradiso* is precisely circle and circling. The verses at the beginning should be remembered in this regard. See *Par.* I, 4-9:

> Nel ciel che più de la sua luce prende
> fu' io, e vidi cose che ridire
> né sa né può chi di là sù discende;

perché appressando sé al suo disire,
nostro intelletto si profonda tanto,
che dietro la memoria non può ire.

The poet now, returned to earth and struggling to go back
over the way of the journey in memory, in order to report
this final experience, step by step (as St. Paul had *not* done
of his), becomes an active figure (as a voice) in the remain-
ing narrative. The voice speaks, of course, in the present
tense, for the poet's struggle is *now*. This *now* alternates
from here on with the *then* of the narrative, and when the
then and the *now*, as two lines of this final action, merge, the
poem ends, in a focus of eternity.

55. *maggio = maggiore*.

56. *che 'l parlar mostra*: Some editors have accepted the
reading "che 'l parlar nostro," but Petrocchi's acceptance of
"mostra" seems justifiable (see his note on this). The theme
is not only that of memory's shortcoming, but of the inability
even to convey that which is remembered. Thus the poet's
struggle is a double one, to remember and to express, each
of these efforts falling short of full attainment, as subsequent
verses now repeatedly affirm.

57. *oltraggio*: The best gloss to the meaning here is to be
found in *Par.* I, 8: "nostro intelletto si profonda tanto." In
older Italian, as Sapegno points out, *oltraggio* did not have
the pejorative connotation that it has in modern usage. (Cf.
the English cognate *outrage* and the French *outrance*, all
forms being based on the Latin *ultra*, "beyond.") The mean-
ing here is "excess," but only in the sense of *profondarsi
tanto*, as above, and since this penetration was made possi-
ble by God, it is not possible that the term should be pejora-
tive: here there can be no *hubris*!

58–63. *Qual è colui . . . essa*: This simile of the dreamer
trying to recall his dream should not suggest in any way that
the actual experience reported *is* that of a dream. (See n. to
Par. XXXII, 139.) This is a simile, after all!

59. *la passione impressa*: The "emotion" or "feeling" left by the dream.

60. *l'altro*: What was actually seen in the dream.

61. *cotal son io*: "Such am I." The verb in the present tense emphatically declares that this is indeed the poet speaking, voicing his struggle *now*. It may be further observed that this voice which breaks into the narrative (in the past tense) affirms not only time, but place as well. Dante's achievement in terminating his great structure should not be overlooked in this regard, nor taken for granted, for it should be noted that in its stress on place (down here on earth, where the wayfarer, now returned from his journey, speaks out as the poet) the poem bears explicitly and emphatically in its end the *return to earth* (see the note on the closing verse of the *Comedy*).   *cessa*: "Falls away," "fades out."

62. *mia visione*: "Visione" is not to be understood as "dream vision," of course (cf. *Par.* XXXII, 139), but simply as "that which I saw, and now see in memory." Cf. *Par.* XVII, 128, where Cacciaguida uses *visione* in this sense as he enjoins Dante to "make manifest all his vision," i.e., "everything you have seen."   *distilla*: "Drips," drop by drop, as it were. Grandgent observes: "Both the sweetness and the thinness of the recollection are reflected by the tinkling rhyme in *-illa*."

63. *il dolce = la dolcezza.*   *che nacque*: The verb in the preterite moves the narrative back into the past again.

64–66. *Così la neve . . . Sibilla*: The theme of "fade-out of vision" is conveyed by some of the most beautiful verses in this ending of a great structure.

64. *si disigilla*: "Unseals itself," "melts away," "loses its shape." Cf. *sigillare* in the opposite sense of "giving form," *Par.* VII, 69.

65–66. *così al vento . . . Sibilla*: The reference is to the Cumaean Sibyl or prophetess of Cumae in Campania, who was consulted by Aeneas before he descended to the infernal regions and accompanied him on his journey, as is related in *Aen*. VI. The description here is borrowed from Virgil; see *Aen*. III, 441-52, where Helenus, son of Priam, king of Chaonia, describes to Aeneas how he is to consult the Cumaean Sibyl on his arrival in Italy:

> huc ubi delatus Cumaeam accesseris urbem
> divinosque lacus et Averna sonantia silvis,
> insanam vatem aspicies, quae rupe sub ima
> fata canit foliisque notas et nomina mandat.
> quaecumque in foliis descripsit carmina virgo,
> digerit in numerum atque antro seclusa relinquit.
> illa manent immota locis neque ab ordine cedunt;
> verum eadem, verso tenuis cum cardine ventus
> impulit et teneras turbavit ianua frondes,
> numquam deinde cavo volitantia prendere saxo
> nec revocare situs aut iungere carmina curat;
> inconsulti abeunt sedemque odere Sibyllae.

And when, thither borne, thou drawest near to the town of Cumae, the haunted lakes, and Avernus with its rustling woods, thou shalt look on an inspired prophetess, who deep in a rocky cave sings the Fates and entrusts to leaves signs and symbols. Whatever verses the maid has traced on leaves she arranges in order and stores away in the cave. These remain unmoved in their places and quit not their rank; but when at the turn of the hinge a light breeze has stirred them, and the open door scattered the tender foliage, never does she thereafter care to catch them, as they flutter in the rocky cave, nor to recover their places, nor to unite the verses; uncounselled, men depart, and loathe the Sibyl's seat.

67-75. *O somma luce . . . vittoria*: These three tercets constitute a final invocation by the poet, who no longer appeals to the Muses (*Inf*. II, 7; *Purg*. I, 8) or to Apollo (*Par*. I, 13), but to God himself and to that light "which in itself is true" (vs. 54). This is the last invocation in the poem and is followed by the closing verses which recount that which (invoked by grace) "returned *somewhat* to memory" (vs.

73), that which is the merest particle or glimpse of the supreme vision of God face to face. What grace grants to the poet's memory now will be passed on to future generations of readers and will, though the tiniest spark, be *ad maiorem Dei gloriam* (for a similar use of "favilla," cf. the invocation addressed to Apollo, *Par.* I, 34, and for a similar entreaty in that invocation, see *Par.* I, 22-24).

68. *da'*: "Above."   *mente*: "Memory."

69. *parevi = apparivi.*

73. *per tornare*: "By returning."

75. *tua vittoria*: Thy power and excellence whereby Thou dost surpass all things.

76–78. *Io credo . . . aversi*: For a similar statement, cf. *Par.* XXV, 118. Dante is able to "endure" the brightness of God's light of glory, a brightness increasing, as through it he draws ever nearer to the vision face to face. In vss. 100-102 we are to be told that it is not possible to turn away from this light.

78. *aversi*: "Averted."

79. *E' mi ricorda*: The impersonal use of the verb, now with the impersonal subject expressed, "e'" ("it")—literally, "it remembers me."   *ardito*: "Bold" (but in a good sense). The adjective serves to keep to the fore the wayfarer's active participation in the final movement toward final vision, which is now declared.

80–81. *tanto ch'i' giunsi . . . infinito*: The upward movement through the ray of light has finally reached its goal, as a verse numbered eighty-one declares! (In medieval numerology it is expected that the digits be added together, and nine is the number of miracle, as every reader of the *Vita nuova* knows.)

81. *aspetto*: "Gaze."   *valore infinito*: God is thus named "the Infinite Worth" as the journey in gazing attains to Him through the light of glory by which He sees Himself. See C. S. Singleton (1958), pp. 20-23.

82–84. *Oh abbondante grazia . . . consunsi*: The exclamatory tercet looks ahead to the end of the action, i.e., the increase of vision, as expressed finally in vs. 142.

82. *presunsi*: "Presumed," but in the same good sense that was connoted by "ardito" before (vs. 79), for now it is emphatically affirmed that this "presumption" was through abounding grace from above.

84. *la veduta vi consunsi*: The wayfaring Dante will reach the limit of vision that was accorded him potentially at birth, by an original act of grace on the part of the Creator. See n. to *Par.* XXXII, 75.

85–87. *Nel suo profondo . . . si squaderna*: The gradual advance in vision continues. It has been termed a penetration, and now "profondo" suggests "deep" mystery and further penetration thereunto. Thus, up through the light of glory, the wayfarer begins to see more particularly the Infinite Worth which has become visible, finally, through the light. This first sight of that Worth presents the aspect of the "all-containing" Godhead of established doctrine. (See *Par.* XIII, 53-54.) This, in one conception of the universe, was expressed in terms of the Empyrean heaven being the mind of God, thus obviously containing all. But now we come into ever clearer vision of God, not as a circumference, but as an all-containing center. See n. to *Par.* XXVIII, 41-42.

85. *s'interna*: "Is contained within itself" (it is possible that the poet intended the choice of verb in this case to reflect the Trinity or triune Godhead, a *terno*).

86. *legato con amore in un volume*: For the familiar metaphor of the book of the created universe, see C. S. Singleton (1949), pp. 37-41. This book is now seen to be contained in the Godhead and there bound by love.

87. *ciò che per l'universo si squaderna*: The book of the universe is contained in God and is bound there, whereas, as it exists outside of the Godhead, in the physical universe, it is "unbound" ("si squaderna"), it is so many separate quires

(Italian *quaderni*, from the Latin *quaterni*, "four each," by fours, from *quattuor*, "four"). Thus a quire (*quaderno*), in the making of a medieval manuscript book, consisted of four sheets of paper or parchment, folded together to make eight leaves or sixteen pages, these quires being then bound together to make the book.

Now, even as "s'interna" in vs. 85 bears within itself the number three (*ter*), so *quaderno* (the noun from which the poet has formed the verb *squadernarsi*) exhibits the number four. This symbolism of a number three and a number four will again appear in the closing verses of the canto and concerns the established symbolism of *three* for spirit and of *four* for matter, the elemental world (the elements being four: fire, air, water, earth). Thus the book which is bound with love in God is, in the material universe created by God, "unquired" or reduced to so many "fours," and their relations to each other. See n. to *Par.* XVII, 37-39.

88–90. *sustanze e accidenti . . . lume*: That which is here seen "bound" in God are the substances and accidents and their relationships which are scattered throughout the universe. A "substance" is that which subsists in itself (a creature, a person, or an angel, for example), whereas an "accident" is that which subsists, not in itself, but as a quality in some substance. For an extended discussion of the terms *sustanzia* and *accidente* in such meanings, see *Vita nuova* XXV (see C. S. Singleton, 1949, pp. 75-77), and see the frequent use of *sustanza* in this sense throughout the *Comedy*. Neither substances nor accidents exist in God, but may be seen reflected in Him as in that mirror that reflects all things (*Par.* XXVI, 107), and *as* reflected in Him they are seen to be "conflati insieme" ("fused together"), along with their relationships ("costume"), all this in such a miraculous way that the poet's expression of it gives but the vaguest glimpse ("semplice lume") or slightest notion of what he thus sees.

What the poet here observes is treated in a *summa* of theology in terms of the perfection of God. Thus Thomas Aquinas, *Summa theol.* I, q. 4, a. 2, resp., writes:

Cum ergo Deus sit prima causa effectiva rerum, oportet

omnium rerum perfectiones praeexistere in Deo secun-
dum eminentiorem modum. Et hanc rationem tangit
Dionysius cap. 5 de divin. Nomin. (a med. lect. 1),
dicens de Deo, quod *non quidem hoc est, hoc autem non
est; sed omnia est, ut omnium causa.*

Secundo vero ex hoc quod supra ostensum est, quaest.
3, art. 4, quod Deus. est ipsum esse per se subsistens;
ex quo oportet quod totam perfectionem essendi in se
contineat. Manifestum est enim quod si aliquod calidum
non habeat totam perfectionem calidi, hoc ideo est, quia
calor non participatur secundum perfectam rationem;
sed, si calor esset per se subsistens, non posset ei aliquid
deesse de virtute caloris. Unde cum Deus sit ipsum esse
subsistens, nihil de perfectione essendi potest ei deesse.
Omnium autem perfectiones pertinent ad perfectionem
essendi: secundum hoc enim aliqua perfecta sunt, quod
aliquo modo esse habent; unde sequitur quod nullius rei
perfectio Deo desit. Et hanc etiam rationem tangit
Dionysius, 5 cap. de div. Nom. (a med. lect. 1), dicens,
quod *Deus non quodam modo est existens; sed simplici-
ter, et incircumscripte totum in se ipso uniformiter esse
praeaccipit*: et postea subdit, quod *ipse est esse
subsistentibus.*

Since therefore God is the first effective cause of things,
the perfections of all things must pre-exist in God in a
more eminent way. Dionysius implies the same line of
argument by saying of God (*Div. Nom.* v): *It is not that
He is this and not that, but that He is all, as the cause
of all.* Secondly, from what has been already proved,
God is existence itself, of itself subsistent (q. 3, a. 4).
Consequently, He must contain within Himself the
whole perfection of being. For it is clear that if some hot
thing has not the whole perfection of heat, this is be-
cause heat is not participated in its full perfection; but
if this heat were self-subsisting, nothing of the virtue of
heat would be wanting to it. Since therefore God is sub-
sisting being itself, nothing of the perfection of being
can be wanting to Him. Now all created perfections are

included in the perfection of being; for things are per-
fect, precisely so far as they have being after some fash-
ion. It follows therefore that the perfection of no one
thing is wanting to God. This line of argument, too, is
implied by Dionysius (*loc cit.*), when he says that,
*God exists not in any single mode, but embraces all be-
ing within Himself, absolutely, without limitation, uni-
formly*; and afterwards he adds that, *He is the very
existence to subsisting things.*

91–93. *La forma . . . godo*: By "the universal form of this
knot" is meant the absolute principle of this union, this "con-
flation" or fusion of all things temporal and eternal in the
Creator (see the quotation from Thomas Aquinas in the pre-
ceding note). And this is such a supreme revelation to any
mortal eye that the poet, in the very affirmation of his glimpse
of it, feels a glow of contentment which seems to confirm that
his report is correct.

94–96. *Un punto solo . . . d'Argo*: Vs. 93 brings in the voice
of the poet again, in the present tense ("mi sento ch'i'
godo"). Now that voice continues in a most remarkable ref-
erence to the falling-away of memory of this his high experi-
ence. Thus one single moment of that experience, his "oltrag-
gio" (vs. 57) as now recovered in memory, comports more
forgetfulness (oblivion, loss of memory) "than twenty-five
centuries have been for the adventure which made Neptune
marvel at the shadow of Argo." The expedition of the Argo-
nauts, under Jason, in search of the golden fleece (*Inf.*
XVIII, 86-87; *Par.* II, 16-18) was thought to have occurred
in the thirteenth century B.C. Philalethes computes the
twenty-five centuries which Dante supposes to have elapsed
between the date of his journey and that of the expedition of
the Argonauts as follows: to the birth of Christ, 1,300 years;
to the founding of Rome, 750 + 1,300 = 2,050 years; to
the fall of Troy, 431 + 2,050 = 2,481 years; to the sailing
of the *Argo*, 42 + 2,481 = 2,523 years, or rather more than
twenty-five centuries. The *Argo*, a fifty-oared ship built by
Argus, son of Phrixus (or of Danaus), was the first ship ever

built: hence Neptune's surprise at seeing it cast a shadow upon the sea.

97–99. *Così la mente mia . . . accesa*: The voice of the narrator returns, in the past tense, as always, and the "così" returns the reader to the line of the narrative. The verb *mirare*, here stressed by repetition, can always connote "marvel," as it does in this case, and for a moment now the wayfarer remains "fixed" and "motionless" in his contemplation of the marvel that is disclosed to him: God in His perfection, as containing all things within Himself.

99. *faceasi = si faceva.   accesa*: "Kindled," with burning desire to see more and more.

100–102. *A quella luce . . . consenta*: "In that Light one becomes such that it is impossible ever to consent to turn from it to see aught else" (Gr). In *Summa theol.* I-II, q. 5, a. 4, resp., Thomas Aquinas notes that "perfecta beatitudo hominis in visione divinae essentiae consistit. Est autem impossibile quod aliquis videns divinam essentiam velit eam non videre." ("Man's perfect Happiness consists in the vision of the Divine Essence. Now it is impossible for anyone seeing the Divine Essence, to wish not to see It.") Aquinas continues: "Visio autem divinae essentiae replet animam omnibus bonis, cum coniungat fonti totius bonitatis. . . . Sic ergo patet, quod propria voluntate beatus non potest beatitudinem deserere." ("But the vision of the Divine Essence fills the soul with all good things, since it unites it to the source of all goodness. . . . It is thus evident that the happy man cannot forsake Happiness of his own accord.")

103. *però = perciò.   'l ben, ch'è del volere obietto*: Good is the object of the will, of volition, even as knowledge or seeing is the object of the intellect. Will and intellect, and their respective objects, must be kept in mind for a proper understanding of the end of the poem. We are now told that *all* good is contained in the Godhead, therefore it is impossible for the will to turn away from such an object. It is the end or goal of all desires (vs. 46).

104. *tutto s'accoglie in lei*: Cf. vss. 85-87.

104–5. *e fuor di quella . . . perfetto*: See n. to vss. 88-90 on the perfection of God.

106–14. *Omai sarà . . . si travagliava*: Three tercets stress again the inability of the poet to express what he saw. "Henceforth, even in the things I remember, my speech will fall shorter than that of a babe" (Gr).

107. *fante*: Cf. *Par.* XXX, 82: "fantin."

109. *sembiante*: "Appearance," but with the suggestion of "face," and therefore already the suggestion of person, of a personal God. This is merely a suggestion, of course, for a face as such is not actually beheld here (unless in our human image within the Second Person), but such is not the meaning.

111. *che tal è sempre qual s'era davante*: Here the poet shows his responsibility to the dogmatic truth that God is unchanging in Himself, therefore the gradual revelation and increase of vision which he reports must be assigned to the mortal beholder, whose powers of vision are growing by the moment: "la vista che s'avvalorava in me guardando" (vss. 112-13).   *s'era davante*: Si ("s'") here is the pleonastic reflexive, distancing and identifying.

112–14. *ma per la vista . . . si travagliava*: The wayfarer's powers of vision increase momentarily, as *he* changes (it being unthinkable that the object of his vision should change). The verb *travagliare* suggests, however, the *struggle* on the part of the wayfarer toward clearer and clearer vision (cf. the English *travail*).

115–17. *Ne la profonda . . . contenenza*: The object of vision, the triune Godhead, now becomes visible in Its triunity.

115. *sussistenza*: Cf. "sustanze" in vs. 88 and see n. to vss. 88-90.

116. *parvermi = mi parvero, mi apparvero*.

116–17. *tre giri . . . contenenza*: The reader will come to see that *giro* here means "circling" as well as "circle," since it can also be termed a "circulazion" (vs. 127). It is important to conceive the concrete image so: the three "giri" are not motionless, but are spinning and are thus completely active, not stationary; and spinning in this instance (as everywhere in the *Paradiso*) symbolizes intellection and perfection in complete actualization. All is active in God, nothing is passive.

117. *di tre colori e d'una contenenza*: The poet's phrase does complete justice to the theological truth: three persons in one nature, three colors in one and the same dimension.

118–19. *e l'un . . . reflesso*: One, the second *giro*, seems reflected from the first (cf. *Par*. XIII, 55-57), just as one arch of a double rainbow is reflected from the other (cf. *Par*. XII, 10-13). This is the second person of the Trinity, the Son begotten by the Father, the first *giro*.

119–20. *e 'l terzo . . . si spiri*: This is the third person of the Trinity, the Holy Ghost, who is, by definition, the love of the Father for the Son, and of the Son for the Father. Cf. *Par*. X, 2, where the verb *spirare* is used to connote love. (Cf. also *Purg*. XXIV, 53, in this regard.) "Si" here is the pleonastic reflexive stressing identification. Fire symbolizes love, of course, for the third person *is* Love.

120. *quinci e quindi*: From the Father to the Son, and from the Son to the Father.

121–23. *Oh quanto . . . "poco"*: Again the poet's voice conveying the familiar theme of the inexpressibility of this final experience.

122. *al mio concetto*: "Compared to what I remember now," conceive now in memory.

122–23. *e questo . . . "poco"*: And what I now remember is such (i.e., so little) that it is not enough to say "little." One should rather say "almost nothing."

124–26. *O luce . . . arridi*: This remarkable tercet, turning—

indeed, *circling*—upon itself, expresses in its very movement the self-containedness of the Trinity, One and Three. The Light is addressed as one self-contained supreme Being.

124. *sidi*: "Abidest," from the Latin *sidio*.

125. *sola t'intendi*: The movement, the circling upon itself, begins.   *e da te intelletta*: The understanding person is here the Son.

126. *e intendente te*: Now it is the Father who understands the Son.   *ami e arridi*: This is the third person, the Holy Ghost, who is Love and the joy that comes from love. Cf. Matt. 11:27: "Nemo novit Filium nisi Pater, neque Patrem quis novit nisi Filius." ("No one knows the Son except the Father; nor does anyone know the Father except the Son.") Thomas Aquinas (*Summa theol.* I, q. 34, a. 1, ad 3) writes: "Pater enim intelligendo se, et Filium, et Spiritum sanctum . . . concipit Verbum." ("For the Father, by understanding Himself, the Son, and the Holy Ghost . . . conceives the Word.")

127-32. *Quella circulazion . . . messo*: The reader is now brought into the final focus of the poem, which is on Christ, second person of the Trinity, as the phrases "sì concetta" and "lume reflesso" make clear. On the symbolical implications of such a final focus, see C. S. Singleton (1969), pp. 22-25.

129. *alquanto circunspetta*: How intently, how closely this wayfarer studies what is revealed to him!   *circunspetta*: A Latinism, from *circumspicere*, meaning "scrutinized."

130. *dentro da sé, del suo colore stesso*: "Our image," Christ incarnate, the Word made flesh, second person of the Trinity, God who became man, is now exclusively focused upon and will be all the way to the end—the mystery of the Incarnation. How can our mortal flesh be any part of the Godhead, second person of the Trinity? And yet Christ has risen in the flesh (even as Mary, His mother is there, in her body) and flesh in "our image" *must* be here (for our faith *must* have it so)! Cf. *Par.* II, 37-42; XXV, 127-28; also Phil. 2:7.

Dante's phrases are emphatic as they insist on the mystery of the Word-made-flesh.

131. *pinta*: This does not suggest an addition of color, but simply affirms appearance, that which the wayfarer beheld.

   nostra effige: "Our human image," Christ in the flesh, the Son of Man.

132. *per che 'l mio viso in lei tutto era messo*: The final focus of attention on the part of the wayfarer absolutely excludes all else: "tutto era messo."

133–35. *Qual è 'l geomètra . . . indige*: No poet was ever more daring in his final simile, in so long a poem, daring to bring into this very end the notion and image ("cold," as in geometry or mathematics!) of the geometer who studies the circle in the vain attempt to square it. "First readers" of the poem, students generally, are of course amazed at the simile, in its strong suggestion of calm, cool study of the greatest mystery of the Christian faith, the Incarnation. But so it is! And the amazement of the modern reader must arise from the abstractness, the geometrical nature, of the vision of God that terminates so long a journey. The poet's conception is Byzantine in nature and as far from the anthropomorphic as can be—except for the final scrutiny of "our effigy" in the second person, which is perhaps a corrective of the geometrical and abstract. But the reader who feels amazement at the geometrical abstractness of the final vision, face to face, should ask himself how *he* would present God to the reader, were he the poet. Would God the Father be an elder with a long gray beard, would the Son appear anthropomorphically as such (as in so many Italian paintings), and would the Holy Ghost be a dove? Would he have his poem end in such a vision of the Deity?

133. *geomètra*: "Geometer."   *s'affige*: "Applies himself."

134. *per misurar lo cerchio*: In *De mon.* III, iii, 2, Dante notes: "Geometra circuli quadraturam ignorat." ("The geometrician knows not how to square the circle.") See *Conv.* II, xiii, 27: "Lo cerchio per lo suo arco è impossibile

a quadrare perfettamente." ("The circle, because of its curve, is impossible to square perfectly.")

135. *indige*: "Is in need."

136–38. *tal era io . . . s'indova*: The posture of cool scrutiny continues, scrutiny of the deepest mystery of the faith, the Incarnation. This geometer (in metaphor) really desires to square the circle, meaning to make out how the flesh, our human flesh and image, can be fitted, *is* fitted, into the circle of divinity.

137. *si convenne*: The verb expresses commensurability, which is precisely the principle that makes the squaring of the circle impossible, even for modern geometry. And incommensurability is at the heart of the mystery of the Incarnation: how can the Word have become flesh, when Word (divinity) and flesh are so incommensurate?

138. *e come vi s'indova*: "How it finds a place there." "Indova" is a verb invented by Dante, based on the adverb *dove*.

139. *ma non eran da ciò le proprie penne*: Again the metaphor of "wings," i.e., power for the upward flight to complete vision of the where and the wherefore. "Proprie penne" underscores the aspect of the wayfarer's struggle in the attainment of vision, which the poet continues to keep to the fore, to the very end.

140–41. *se non che . . . venne*: The wayfarer's wings were themselves not powerful enough to uplift him to the vision of the deepest mystery, but divine grace now intervenes to raise his sight and comprehension to that transcendental point. His mind, his power of vision, is uplifted by a flash, a lightning bolt from above, and the desired vision and comprehension is given to him, through highest grace. Established theology speaks of "man on the way to God" as a *viator* and of "man who attains to the beatific vision" as a *comprehensor*. The wayfarer, in his long journey, attains to the latter condition in these final verses. In a flash his desire to see, to *comprehend*, is granted him.

141. *voglia*: The term "voglia" should be carried forward by the reader to that of "disio" in vs. 143; they are synonymous. The desire (be it *voglia* or *disio*) is the desire of intellect, for comprehending vision.

142. *A l'alta fantasia qui mancò possa*: The modern reader must take care to understand the term *fantasia* in its exact meaning. *Fantasia*, as noted before (see *Purg.* XVII, 25, where it is termed "alta"), is an image-receiving faculty, not image-making. Hence, to affirm that the high (high because of its object—cf. the analogous "morta poesì" of *Purg.* I, 7, and see the corresponding note) "fantasia" failed in its power at this point is equivalent to saying that the wayfarer reaches the limit of his capacity for vision, for the reception of images; that is, he cannot see (receptively) that which he desires to see (and seeing, it must be remembered, is a function of intellect and is, in the wayfarer, a desire of the intellect which is, at the moment, unfulfilled). See Dante's comment in *Conv.* III, iv, 9:

> Nostro intelletto, per difetto de la virtù da la quale trae quello ch'el vede, che è virtù organica, cioè la fantasia, non puote a certe cose salire (però che la fantasia nol puote aiutare, ché non ha lo di che), sì come sono le sustanze partite da materia; de le quali se alcuna considerazione [sanza] di quella avere potemo, intendere non le potemo né comprendere perfettamente.

> Our intellect, by defect of that power whence it draws whatsoever it contemplates (which is an organic power, to wit the fantasy), may not rise to certain things, because the fantasy may not aid it, for it hath not wherewithal. Such are the substances sejunct from matter, which, even though a certain consideration of them be possible, we may not understand nor comprehend perfectly.

Cf. also *Par.* XXIV, 24.

143–45. *ma già . . . stelle*: "Ma" has been preceded by another "ma" (vs. 139) and a "se non che." The reader will do well to keep his bearings with these qualifications and correctives. This "ma," however, is the final one.

143. *già volgeva*: The reader will note that the subject of "volgeva" is effectively withheld until the final verse, when it emerges as "l'amor," as love. And let it be noted at this point that all English translations of these last three verses of the poem are obliged (if they wish to keep "stars" as the very last word, which seems essential) to reduce the final sentence to a passive construction, which is symbolically incongruent with Dante's positive active construction, with "l'amor" as the subject and first word of the final verse.   *il mio disio*: In the context there can be no mistake about the meaning: the desire is the "voglia" of the wayfarer (*viator*) who suddenly, through an act of grace, becomes *comprehensor*, whose condition as such is analogous to that of the blessed, who enjoy through eternity the vision of God face to face. Why should this mortal man ever return to earth? How can he fall away from such a vision (cf. vss. 100-102)? The answer is evident: his is the experience of a *living* man, and he must fall from such high vision (which is like a flash of lightning) because of his "mortal pondo" (see *Par*. XXXII, 139). But for ever so brief a moment he has become, from *viator* in contemplation (and what a long *via* he has come!), a *comprehensor*, and he now has a *foretaste* of the beatitude that awaits him at the end of life.   *e 'l velle*: Coupled with "disio" (which is of the intellect, desire for vision), "velle" refers to the will specifically, which, of the two faculties of the immortal soul, is that which attains to *the object* which (in this case) is intellectually desired. *Velle* is Latin and as such expresses the fact that the attainment of the will (thus matching the desire of the intellect) is made possible from above, by grace descending. Thus desire (of intellect) and will to attain (of "velle," a will that is both human and divine) emerge, at the end of this poem, as equally balanced as a wheel that evenly turns. See the verses which are the best gloss on this, at *Par*. XV, 73-81. Cf. also *Par*. XXVIII, 109-11 (intellect comes first, will follows, as here). See Thomas Aquinas, *Summa theol*. I-II, q. 3, a. 4, resp.:

Ad beatitudinem, sicut supra dictum est, quaest. 2, art. 6, duo requiruntur: unum, quod est esse beatitudinis; aliud, quod est quasi per se accidens eius, scilicet delectatio ei adiuncta.

Dico ergo, quod quantum ad id quod est essentialiter ipsa beatitudo, impossibile est quod consistat in actu voluntatis. Manifestum est enim ex praemissis, art. 1 huius quaest., quod beatitudo est consecutio finis ultimi. Consecutio autem finis non consistit in ipso actu voluntatis; voluntas autem fertur in finem et absentem, cum ipsum desiderat, et praesentem, cum in ipso requiescens delectatur. Manifestum est autem, quod ipsum desiderium finis non est consecutio finis, sed est motus ad finem. Delectatio autem advenit voluntati ex hoc quod finis est praesens; non autem e converso ex hoc aliquid fit praesens, quia voluntas delectatur in ipso. Oportet igitur aliquid aliud esse quam actum voluntatis, per quod fit finis ipse praesens voluntati. Et hoc manifeste apparet circa fines sensibiles. Si enim consequi pecuniam esset per actum voluntatis, statim, a principio cupidus consecutus esset pecuniam, quando vult eam habere; sed a principio quidem est absens ei, consequitur autem ipsam per hoc quod manu ipsam apprehendit, vel aliquo huiusmodo; et tunc iam delectatur in pecunia habita. Sic igitur et circa intelligibilem finem contingit. Nam a principio volumus consequi finem intelligibilem; consequimur autem ipsum per hoc quod fit praesens nobis per actum intellectus; et tunc voluntas delectata conquiescit in fine iam adepto. Sic igitur essentia beatitudinis in actu intellectus consistit.

Sed ad voluntatem pertinet delectatio beatitudinem consequens, secundum quod Augustinus dicit 10 Confess. (cap. 23, ante med.), quod *beatitudo est gaudium de veritate*, quia scilicet ipsum gaudium est consummatio beatitudinis.

As stated above (q. 2, a. 6) two things are needed for happiness: one, which is the essence of happiness: the other, that is, as it were, its proper accident, *i.e.*, the de-

light connected with it. I say, then, that as to the very
essence of happiness, it is impossible for it to consist in
an act of the will. For it is evident from what has been
said (aa. 1, 2; q. 2, a. 7) that happiness is the attain-
ment of the last end. But the attainment of the end does
not consist in the very act of the will. For the will is di-
rected to the end, both absent, when it desires it; and
present, when it is delighted by resting therein. Now it
is evident that the desire itself of the end is not the at-
tainment of the end, but is a movement towards the
end: while delight comes to the will from the end being
present; and not conversely, is a thing made present, by
the fact that the will delights in it. Therefore, that the
end be present to him who desires it, must be due to
something else than an act of the will.

This is evidently the case in regard to sensible ends.
For if the acquisition of money were through an act of
the will, the covetous man would have it from the very
moment that he wished for it. But at that moment it is
far from him; and he attains it, by grasping it in his
hand, or in some like manner; and then he delights in
the money got. And so it is with an intelligible end. For
at first we desire to attain an intelligible end; we attain
it, through its being made present to us by an act of the
intellect; and then the delighted will rests in the end
when attained.

So, therefore, the essence of happiness consists in an
act of the intellect: but the delight that results from hap-
piness pertains to the will. In this sense Augustine says
(*Conf.* x. 23) that happiness is *joy in truth*, because, to
wit, joy itself is the consummation of happiness.

144. *sì come rota ch'igualmente è mossa*: "The circle, being
the perfect figure, is an emblem of perfection; and circular
motion symbolizes full and faultless activity. St. Thomas, *In
Librum B. Dionysii De Divinis Nominibus*, Caput iv, Lectio
7: 'Et ideo circularitas motus animae completur in hoc quod
ad Deum manuducit.' ['And therefore circularity completes
the movement of the soul in that it leads to God.']" (Gr).

145. *l'amor che move il sole e l'altre stelle*: The last verse of the poem bears the image of Aristotle's unmoved mover, the spheres turning in desire of him, being moved by desire of him. As such, this vision of universal movement is from the earth, looking up. Thus the final verse of the poem returns the point of view to earth, with the *upward* gaze at stars here as at the end of the *Inferno* and the *Purgatorio*. The final injunction in each case is "look upwards," *up* being the right direction for our mind and heart. It is an injunction that was carefully built into the center of the poem as well (see C. S. Singleton, 1965). And was it not there at the beginning, too, in the figure of a wayfarer gazing toward the summit of a height illumined by the sun ("the planet that leads men aright by every path") and longing to attain to it?

List of Works Cited
and of Abbreviations

ABBREVIATIONS

a.   articulus

Aen.   Aeneid (Virgil)

Anal. post.   Posteriora analytica (Aristotle)

Anonimo fiorentino   Commento alla Divina Commedia d'anonimo fiorentino del secolo XIV

Conf.   Confessiones (Augustine)

Consol. philos.   Consolatio philosophiae (Boethius)

Conv.   Convivio (Dante Alighieri)

Decam.   Il Decameron (Giovanni Boccaccio)

De civ. Dei   Ad Marcellinum De civitate Dei contra paganos (Augustine)

Della comp.   Della composizione del mondo (Ristoro d'Arezzo)

De mon.   De monarchia (Dante Alighieri)

De vulg. eloqu.   De vulgari eloquentia (Dante Alighieri)

Epist.   Epistolae (Dante Alighieri)

Eth. Nicom.   Ethica Nicomachea (Aristotle)

Exp. Eth. Nicom.   In decem libros Ethicorum ad Nicomachum expositio (Thomas Aquinas)

Exp. Metaphys.   In duodecim libros Metaphysicorum expositio (Thomas Aquinas)

Georg.   Georgics (Virgil)

Gr   Grandgent

Hist.   Historiarum adversum paganos libri septem (Orosius)

Hist. schol.   Historia scholastica (Petrus Comestor)

Homil.   Quadraginta homiliarum in Evangelia libri duo (Gregory I)

In Ezech.   Homiliarum in Ezechielem prophetam libri duo (Gregory I)

Inf.   Inferno (Dante Alighieri)

LCL   Loeb Classical Library

lect.   lectio

Metam.   Metamorphoses (Ovid)

Metaphys.   Metaphysica (Aristotle)

Meteor.   Meteorologica (Aristotle)

MLN   Modern Language Notes

Moral.   Moralium libri, sive Expositio in librum b. Iob (Gregory I)

Nat. hist.   Naturalis historia (Pliny)

obj.   objectio

OFr   Old French

Par.   Paradiso (Dante Alighieri)

Phars.   Pharsalia (Lucan)

P.L.   Patrologiae cursus completus: Series Latina, ed. J.-P. Migne. Paris, 1844-64 (with later printings).

Polit.   Politica (Aristotle)

Purg.   Purgatorio (Dante Alighieri)

q.   quaestio

resp.   respondeo

Rhet.   Rhetorica (Aristotle)

RIS   Rerum Italicarum scriptores ab anno aerae Christianae quingentesimo ad millesimum quingentesimum, ed. L. A. Muratori. Milan, 1723-51. New edn.: *Rerum Italicarum scriptores; Raccolta degli storici italiani dal cinquecento ad millecinquecento,* rev. under the direction of G. Carducci, V. Fiorini, P. Fedele. Città di Castello, Bologna, 1900— (in progress).

Sent.   Sententiarum libri quatuor (Peter Lombard)

Soph. elench.   *De sophisticis elenchis* (Aristotle)
Summa theol.   *Summa theologica* (Thomas Aquinas)
Suppl.   Supplementum
TC   Temple Classics
Theb.   *Thebaid* (Statius)

LIST OF WORKS CITED

Unless specifically and otherwise stated, all classical Greek and Latin texts cited in the *Commentary* of the *Paradiso* are those of the Loeb Classical Library, to which the reader should refer.

Albertus Magnus. *Opera omnia*, ed. Auguste and Émile Borgnet. Paris, 1890-99: *De meteoris*, vol. IV.

Alighieri, Dante. *La Commedia secondo l'antica vulgata*, ed. Giorgio Petrocchi. Vol. I: *Introduzione*; vol. IV: *Paradiso*. Milan, 1966, 1967.

—————. *Il Convivio*, ed. G. Busnelli and G. Vandelli. Vol. I. Florence, 1953.

—————. *Le opere di Dante: Testo critico della Società Dantesca Italiana*. 2d edn. Florence, 1960:

> *Convivio*, ed. Ernesto Giacomo Parodi and Flaminio Pellegrini, pp. 143-293.
>
> *De vulgari eloquentia*, ed. Pio Rajna, pp. 295-327.
>
> *Epistole*, ed. Ermenegildo Pistelli, pp. 383-415.
>
> *Monarchia*, ed. Enrico Rostagno, pp. 329-81.
>
> *Questio de aqua et terra*, ed. Ermenegildo Pistelli, pp. 429-42.
>
> *Rime; Rime dubbie*, ed. Michele Barbi, pp. 51-142.
>
> *Vita nuova*, ed. Michele Barbi, pp. 1-49.

————. TRANSLATIONS

The Convivio of Dante Alighieri, trans. Philip H. Wicksteed. The Temple Classics. London, 1903.

A Translation of the Latin Works of Dante Alighieri. The Temple Classics. London, 1940:

> *The De monarchia,* trans. Philip H. Wicksteed, pp. 125-280.
>
> *The De vulgari eloquentia,* trans. A. G. Ferrers Howell, pp. 1-115.
>
> *Epistolae,* trans. Philip H. Wicksteed, pp. 293-368.
>
> *The Quaestio de aqua et terra,* trans. Philip H. Wicksteed, pp. 387-423.

The Vita Nuova. In *The Vita Nuova and Canzoniere of Dante Alighieri,* ed. and trans. Thomas Okey and Philip H. Wicksteed, pp. 2-153. The Temple Classics. London, 1906.

Antonelli, Mercurio. "La 'Malta' dantesca e l'isola Bisentina." *Giornale storico della letteratura italiana* LXXVII (1921): 150-52.

Aquinas, Thomas. *Opera omnia.* Parma, 1852-73. Photolithographic reimpression, with Introduction by Vernon J. Bourke, New York, 1948-50:

> *De veritate Catholicae fidei contra Gentiles seu Summa philosophica,* vol. v
>
> *In X libros Ethicorum ad Nicomachum expositio,* vol. XXI
>
> *In XII libros Metaphysicorum expositio,* vol. XX
>
> *In Isaiam prophetam expositio,* vol. XIV
>
> *Summa theologica,* vols. I-IV.

————. MARIETTI PUBLICATIONS

In decem libros Ethicorum Aristotelis ad Nicomachum expositio, ed. Raimondo M. Spiazzi, O.P. 3rd edn. Turin, 1964.

In duodecim libros Metaphysicorum Aristotelis expositio, ed. Raimondo M. Spiazzi, O.P. Turin, 1964.

————. TRANSLATIONS

Commentary on the Metaphysics of Aristotle, trans. John P. Rowan. Vol. II. Chicago, 1961.

Commentary on the Nicomachean Ethics, trans. C. I. Litzinger, O.P. Vol. I. Chicago, 1964.

On the Truth of the Catholic Faith, Summa contra Gentiles. Book II: Creation, trans. James F. Anderson. Garden City, N.Y., 1962. *Book IV: Salvation,* trans. Charles J. O'Neil. 1957.

Summa theologica, trans. Fathers of the English Dominican Province. 3 vols., the edition used throughout being that of Benziger Brothers, New York, 1947-48.

Aristotle. "Antiqua Translatio" in Thomas Aquinas, *Opera omnia,* Parma, 1852-73. Photolithographic reimpression, with Introduction by Vernon J. Bourke, New York, 1948-50:

> *De anima,* vol. xx
>
> *De caelo,* vol. xix
>
> *Ethica Nicomachea,* vol. xxi
>
> *Metaphysica,* vol. xx
>
> *Meteorologica,* vol. xix
>
> *Physica,* vol. xviiii
>
> *Politica,* vol. xxi
>
> *Posteriora analytica,* vol. xviii

————. MARIETTI PUBLICATIONS

De anima. In Thomas Aquinas, *In Aristotelis librum De anima commentarium,* ed. Angelo M. Pirotta, O.P. 2d edn. Turin, 1936.

De caelo. In Thomas Aquinas, *In Aristotelis libros De caelo et mundo, De generatione et corruptione, Meteorologicorum expositio,* ed. Raimondo M. Spiazzi, O.P. Turin, 1952.

Ethica Nicomachea. In Thomas Aquinas, *In decem libros Ethicorum Aristotelis ad Nicomachum expositio,* ed. Raimondo M. Spiazzi, O.P. 3rd edn. Turin, 1964.

Metaphysica. In Thomas Aquinas, *In duodecim libros Metaphysicorum Aristotelis expositio,* Ed. Raimondo M. Spiazzi, O.P. Turin, 1964.

Meteorologica. In Thomas Aquinas, *In Aristotelis libros De caelo et mundo, De generatione et corruptione, Meteorologicorum expositio,* ed. Raimondo M. Spiazzi, O.P. Turin, 1952.

Politica. In Thomas Aquinas, *In libros Politicorum Aristotelis expositio*, ed. Raimondo M. Spiazzi, O.P. Turin, 1951.

――――. TRANSLATIONS

Metaphysics. In Thomas Aquinas, *Commentary on the Metaphysics of Aristotle*, trans. John P. Rowan. Vol. II. Chicago, 1961.

Nicomachean Ethics. In Thomas Aquinas, *Commentary on the Nicomachean Ethics*, trans. C. I. Litzinger, O.P. Vol. I. Chicago, 1964.

Augustine. *Ad Marcellinum De civitate Dei contra paganos.* In Migne, *P.L.* XLI.

――――. *Gratia et libero arbitrio.* In Migne, *P.L.* XLIV.

――――. *St. Augustine's Confessions*, trans. William Watts (1631), preface by W.H.D. Rouse. 2 vols. LCL, 1912.

Barbi, Michele. Review of Dante Alighieri, *La Divina Commedia riveduta nel testo e commentata da G. A. Scartazzini*, 4th edn., revised by G. Vandelli, 1903. In *Bullettino della Società Dantesca Italiana* N.S. x (1903): 1-8.

――――. "La similitudine del baccelliere (*Par.* XXIV, 46-48)." *Studi danteschi* XII (1927): 79-82.

――――. *Problemi di critica dantesca: Prima serie (1893-1918).* Florence, 1934.

Bernard de Ventadour. *See* Nichols, Stephen G., Jr., and Galm, John A. (1962).

Bernard of Clairvaux. *De diligendo Deo.* In Migne, *P.L.* CLXXXII.

――――. *Meditationes piissimae de cognitione humanae conditionis.* In Migne, *P.L.* CLXXXIV.

――――. *Sermones de diversis.* In Migne, *P.L.* CLXXXIII.

――――. *Sermones de tempore.* In Migne, *P.L.* CLXXXIII.

――――. *Sermones in Cantica Canticorum.* In Migne, *P.L.* CLXXXIII.

Boccaccio, Giovanni. *Il Decameron*, ed. Charles S. Singleton. 2 vols. Bari, 1955.

Boethius. *The Consolation of Philosophy.* In *The Theological Tractates*, ed. and trans. H. F. Stewart and E. K. Rand; *The Consolation of Philosophy*, trans. "I.T."

(1609). Revised by H. F. Stewart, pp. 128-411. LCL, 1962.

———. *De institutione musica*. In *De institutione arithmetica; De institutione musica*, ed. Gottfried Friedlein, pp. 175-371. Leipzig, 1867.

Bonaventura. *Opera omnia*, ed. PP. Collegii a S. Bonaventura. Quaracchi, 1882-1902:

    Itinerarium mentis in Deum, vol. v

    Legenda sancti Francisci, vol. viii

    Soliloquium de quatuor mentalibus exercitiis, vol. viii

Bullettino della Società Dantesca Italiana N.S. iv (1897): 180-81.

Bullettino della Società Dantesca Italiana N.S. xx (1913): 236-37. Review of Carlo Steiner, La *"luce più dia" del canto XIV del Paradiso e l'episodio del cielo del Sole*, 1913.

Busnelli, Giovanni. *Il concetto e l'ordine del 'Paradiso' dantesco. Parte I: Il concetto*. Città di Castello, 1911a.

———. "L'ordine dei cori angelici nel *Convivio* e nel *Paradiso. Bullettino della Società Dantesca Italiana* N.S. xviii (1911b): 127-28.

Chaucer, Geoffrey. *The Works of Geoffrey Chaucer*, ed. F. N. Robinson. 2d edn. London, 1957.

Compagni, Dino. *La cronica di Dino Compagni delle cose occorrenti ne' tempi suoi*, ed. Isidoro Del Lungo. In *RIS* ix, pt. 2. New edn.

Cosmo, Umberto. "Noterelle francescane." *Giornale dantesco* viii (1900): 163-82.

Crescini, Vincenzo. "L'origine d'un pentametro attribuito a Ovidio." *Giornale storico della letteratura italiana* lxxii (1918): 192-93.

Curtius, Ernst Robert. *European Literature and the Latin Middle Ages*, trans. from the German by Willard R. Trask. New York, 1953.

Davidsohn, Robert. *Geschichte von Florenz*. Vol. i: *Aeltere Geschichte*. Berlin, 1896.

Dietaiuti, Bondie. *See* Monaci, Ernesto (1955).

Dionysius. *De caelesti ierarchia.* In Migne, *P.L.* cxxii.

Enciclopedia dantesca, ed. Umberto Bosco. 5 vols. Rome, 1970—(in progress).

Euclid. *The Thirteen Books of Euclid's Elements,* ed. and trans. Sir Thomas L. Heath. In *The Thirteen Books of Euclid's Elements; The Works of Archimedes, including the Method; On Conic Sections; Introduction to Arithmetic,* pp. 1-396. Chicago, 1952.

Gardner, Edmund G. *Dante and the Mystics.* London and New York, 1913.

Gibbon, Edward. *The History of the Decline and Fall of the Roman Empire,* ed. J. B. Bury. Vol. iv. 3rd edn. London, 1908.

Gregory I. *Homiliarum in Ezechielem prophetam libri duo.* In Migne, *P.L.* lxxvi.

———. *Moralium libri, sive Expositio in librum b. Iob.* In Migne, *P.L.* lxxvi.

———. *XL Homiliarum in Evangelia libri duo.* In Migne, *P.L.* lxxvi.

Guéranger, R. R. Dom Prosper. *The Liturgical Year. Paschal Time,* trans. from the French by the Rev. Dom Laurence Shepherd. 2d edn. Vol. i. London, 1888.

Hardie, Colin. "The Epistle to Cangrande Again." *Deutsches Dante-Jahrbuch* xxxviii (1960): 51-74.

———. "Cacciaguida's Prophecy in *Paradiso* 17." *Traditio* xix (1963): 267-94.

Holbrook, Richard T. "Romanic Lexicographical Miscellanies." *MLN* xviii (1903): 42-45.

Jacobus de Varagine. *Legenda aurea vulgo historia lombardica dicta,* ed. T. Grässe. Photographic reproduction of the 3rd edn., 1890. Osnabrück, 1969.

Latini, Brunetto. *Li livres dou tresor de Brunetto Latini,* ed. Francis J. Carmody. Berkeley, 1948.

Levi, Ezio. *Piccarda e Gentucca: Studi e ricerche dantesche*. Bologna, 1921.

Le Liber pontificalis, ed L. Duchesne. 2d edn. Vol. 1. Paris, 1955.

Lovejoy, Arthur O. *The Great Chain of Being. A Study of the History of an Idea*. Harper Torchbooks. New York, 1960.

Mazzoni, Francesco. "L'epistola a Cangrande." *Atti della Accademia Nazionale dei Lincei, Rendiconti, Classe di scienze morali, storiche e filologiche* ser. 8, x (1955): 157-98.

Monaci, Ernesto (ed.). "Canzone di Bondie Dietaiuti." In *Crestomazia italiana dei primi secoli*, pp. 263-64. New edn., revised by Felice Arese. Rome, 1955.

Moore, Edward. *Studies in Dante. First Series: Scripture and Classical Authors in Dante*. Oxford, 1896 (reprinted 1969). *Third Series: Miscellaneous Essays*, 1903 (reprinted 1968). *Fourth Series: Textual Criticism of the Convivio and Miscellaneous Essays*, 1917 (reprinted 1968).

Murari, Rocco. *Dante e Boezio*. Bologna, 1905.

Nardi, Bruno. *Saggi di filosofia dantesca*. Milan, 1930.

——. *Nel mondo di Dante*. Rome, 1944.

——. *Dante e la cultura medievale: Nuovi saggi di filosofia dantesca*. 2d edn. Bari, 1949.

——. *Lectura Dantis Scaligera: Il punto sull'epistola a Cangrande*. Florence, 1960.

Nichols, Stephen G., Jr. and Galm, John A. (eds.). *The Songs of Bernart de Ventadorn*. Chapel Hill, N.C., 1962.

Orosius. *Historiarum adversum paganos libri VII*, ed. Karl Zangemeister. Leipzig, 1889.

——. *Seven Books of History against the Pagans: The Apology of Paulus Orosius*, trans. Irving Woodworth Raymond. New York, 1936.

Parodi, E. G.   Review of Paget Toynbee, "Dante's Obliga-
tions to the *Magnae derivationes* of Uguccione da Pisa,"
Romania XXVI (1897): 537-54. In *Bullettino della So-
cietà Dantesca Italiana* N.S. V (1898): 199.

————. Review of V. Crescini, "L'origine d'un pentametro
attribuito a Ovidio," *Giornale storico della letteratura
italiana* LXXII (1918): 192-93. In *Bullettino della Società
Dantesca Italiana* N.S. XXV (1918a): 108-9.

————. Review of Edward Moore, *Studies in Dante, Fourth
Series: Textual Criticism of the Convivio and Miscellane-
ous Essays*, 1917. In *Bullettino della Società Dantesca
Italiana* N.S. XXV (1918b): 121-36.

————. Lectura Dantis: *Il canto II del Paradiso letto da
Ernesto Giacomo Parodi nella Sala di Dante in Orsan-
michele.* Florence, 1922.

————. *Lingua e letteratura: Studi di teoria linguistica e di
storia dell'italiano antico*, ed. Gianfranco Folena, pt. 2.
Venice, 1957.

Peter Lombard.   *Sententiarum libri quatuor.* In Migne, *P.L.*
CXCII.

Petrarca, Francesco.   *Rime, trionfi e poesie latine*, ed. F.
Neri, G. Martellotti, E. Bianchi, N. Sapegno. Milan, 1951.

Petrus Comestor.   *Historia scholastica.* In Migne, *P.L.*
CXCVIII.

Piattoli, Renato (ed.).   *Codice diplomatico dantesco.* New
edn. Florence, 1950.

*Piers Plowman. The Vision of William Concerning Piers
the Plowman*, ed. Walter W. Skeat. Vol. I. Oxford, 1886.

Porena, Manfredi.   "Note dantesche." *La Rassegna* ser. 4,
XXXII (1924): 147-58.

————. "Noterelle dantesche." *Studj romanzi* XX (1930):
201-15.

Proto, Enrico.   "La dottrina dantesca delle macchie lunari."
In *Scritti varii di erudizione e di critica in onore di Rodolfo
Renier*, pp. 197-213. Turin, 1912.

Ptolemy.   *The Almagest*, ed. and trans. R. Catesby Talia-
ferro. In *The Almagest, by Ptolemy; On the Revolutions
of the Heavenly Spheres, by Nicolaus Copernicus; Epit-*

ome of Copernican Astronomy: IV and V; The Harmonies of the World: V, by Johannes Kepler, pp. xi-464. Chicago, 1952.

Rajna, Pio. "Arturi regis ambages pulcerrime." *Studi danteschi* I (1920): 91-99.

Richard of St. Victor. *De gratia contemplationis, seu Beniamin maior.* In Migne, *P.L.* cxcvi.

———. *In Cantica Canticorum explicatio.* In Migne, *P.L.* cxcvi.

Ristoro d'Arezzo. *Della composizione del mondo di Ristoro d'Arezzo*, ed. Enrico Narducci. Milan, 1864.

Rolandino. *Cronica in factis et circa facta Marchie Trivixane*, ed. Antonio Bonardi. In *RIS* viii, pt. i, pp. 1-174. New edn.

Rotta, Paolo. *La filosofia del linguaggio nella Patristica e nella Scolastica.* Turin, 1909.

Rutebeuf. *L'État du monde.* In *Œuvres complètes de Rutebeuf*, ed. Edmond Faral and Julia Bastin. Vol. 1, pp. 382-88. Paris, 1959.

Sacchetti, Franco. *Delle novelle di Franco Sacchetti cittadino fiorentino.* Florence, 1724.

Schiaffini, Alfredo. "Del tipo 'parofia' parochia (Dante, *Par.*, XXVIII, 84." *Studi danteschi* v (1922): 99-131.

Singleton, Charles S. "'Sulla fiumana ove 'l mar non ha vanto' (*Inferno*, II, 108)." *The Romanic Review* xxxix (1948): 269-77.

———. *An Essay on the Vita Nuova.* Cambridge, Mass., 1949; Baltimore, Md., 1977.

———. "Virgil Recognizes Beatrice." *Annual Report of the Dante Society* lxxiv (1956): 29-38.

———. *Dante Studies 2: Journey to Beatrice.* Cambridge, Mass., 1958; Baltimore, Md., 1977.

———. "The Poet's Number at the Center." *MLN* lxxx (1965): 1-10.

———. "The Vistas in Retrospect." *MLN* LXXXI (1966): 55-80.

———. "The Irreducible Vision." In *Illuminated Manuscripts of the Divine Comedy*, by Peter Brieger, Millard Meiss, and Charles S. Singleton. Vol. I, pp. 1-29. Princeton, N.J., 1969.

Spiazzi, Raimondo M. (ed.). *See* Aquinas, Thomas (Marietti publications); Aristotle (Marietti publications)

Tatlock, John S. P. "*Purgatorio* XI.2-3 and *Paradiso* XIV.30." *The Romanic Review* X (1919): 274-76.

Toynbee, Paget. *Dante Studies and Researches.* London, 1902.

———. "Dante's Arrangement of the Celestial Hierarchies in the *Convivio.*" *Bullettino della Società Dantesca Italiana* N.S. XVIII (1911): 205.

———. *A Dictionary of Proper Names and Notable Matters in the Works of Dante*, revised by Charles S. Singleton. Oxford, 1968.

Vegetius. *Epitoma rei militaris*, ed. Carl Lang. Editio altera. Leipzig, 1885.

Villani, Giovanni. *Cronica di Giovanni Villani*, ed. F. Gherardi Dragomanni. 4 vols. Florence, 1844-45.

Villari, Pasquale. *I primi due secoli della storia di Firenze.* New edn. Florence, 1905.

EARLY COMMENTATORS

Anonimo fiorentino. Commento alla Divina Commedia d'anonimo fiorentino del secolo XIV, ed. Pietro Fanfani. Vol. III. Bologna, 1874.

Benvenuto da Imola. *Comentum super Dantis Aldigherij Comoediam*, ed. Giacomo Filippo Lacaita. Vols. IV, V. Florence, 1887.

Buti, Francesco da. *Commento di Francesco da Buti sopra la Divina Comedia di Dante Allighieri*, ed. Crescentino Giannini. Vol. III. Pisa, 1862.

Lana, Jacopo della. *Comedia di Dante degli Allagherii col commento di Jacopo della Lana bolognese*, ed. Luciano Scarabelli. Vol. III. Bologna, 1866.

Landino, Cristoforo. *Dante con l'espositioni di Christoforo Landino et d'Alessandro Vellutello. Sopra la sua Comedia dell'Inferno, del Purgatorio, e del Paradiso*. Venice, 1596.

L'Ottimo Commento della Divina Commedia, ed. Alessandro Torri. Vol. III. Pisa, 1829.

Pietro di Dante. *Super Dantis ipsius genitoris Comoediam commentarium*, ed. Vincenzio Nannucci. Florence, 1845.

MODERN COMMENTATORS

Butler, Arthur John. *The Paradise of Dante Alighieri*. 2d edn. London, 1891.

Casini, Tommaso and Barbi, S. A. *La Divina Commedia di Dante Alighieri*, comm. Tommaso Casini. 6th edn. revised by S. A. Barbi. Florence, 1926.

Chimenz, Siro A. *La Divina Commedia di Dante Alighieri*. Turin, 1962.

Del Lungo, Isidoro. *La Divina Commedia*. Florence, 1944.

Grandgent, C. H. *La Divina Commedia*, ed. C. H. Grandgent, rev. Charles S. Singleton. Cambridge, Mass., 1972.

Norton, Charles Eliot. *The Divine Comedy of Dante Alighieri*. Rev. edn. Vol. III: *Paradise*. Boston, 1902.

Petrocchi, Giorgio. *La Commedia secondo l'antica vulgata*. Vol. I: *Introduzione*. Vol. IV: *Paradiso*. Milan, 1966, 1967.

Philalethes, *pseud.* [Johann, king of Saxony]. *Dante Alighieri's Göttliche Comödie*. Vol. III: *Das Paradies*. Leipzig, 1891.

Sapegno, Natalino. *La Divina Commedia*. Milan, 1957.

Scartazzini, G. A. and Vandelli, Giuseppe. *La Divina Commedia: Testo critico della Società Dantesca Italiana*, comm. G. A. Scartazzini. 17th edn. revised by Giuseppe Vandelli. Milan, 1958.

The Temple Classics. *The Paradiso of Dante Alighieri*, ed. H. Oelsner, with translation and arguments by P. H. Wicksteed. London, 1965.

Tommaseo, Niccolò. *Commedia di Dante Allighieri*. Vol. III: *Il Paradiso*. Milan, 1869.

Witte, Karl. *Die Göttliche Komödie des Dante Alighieri*, ed. Karl Ludwig Kannegiesser, 5th revised edn. ed. Karl Witte. Leipzig, 1873.

NOTE

"L'Amor che move il sole e l'altre stelle": if one might only know what the poet's feelings were when he conceived and finally wrote down that last of the 14,233 verses! A great vision of this life and of the next, a wondrous structure, "monument of unaging intellect" if ever human mind produced one, had been brought to completion, in all the symmetry, the balance, the harmony among the parts, that makes it the imitation of God's created universe and of His providential plan for man and all creatures that it is and that it must have been conceived to be from a verse which reads: "Nel mezzo del cammin di nostra vita."

One readily imagines that no poet could have endured a greater tragedy than Dante, had exile and then death at the age of 56 forced him to leave his *Comedia* unfinished—which would have meant that a structure (in 100 Cantos and in *terza rima*), designed to reflect God's work in *its* completeness and perfection, would have failed of its goal. But at some time before that fatal date of mid-September, 1321, that last verse, speaking of Love to the very end, had been conceived and penned, and that *Comedy* to which Heaven and earth had set hand and which had made its author lean through many years, *was done*, an "imitation" finished in its perfection.

The dividing line which, after such reflections on a poet's finished work, must be drawn by a commentator before speaking of the unfinished nature of his own work must be firm indeed, for reasons obvious to each and all who have followed him through to this last verse. *His* labors have not been poetic in the least, even his translation is in prose. In short, somewhat like M. Jourdain, he has been speaking prose throughout.

In some essential sense he now finds that the nature of his efforts were best set forth in a first *Note* to the reader, at the outset: so much so that one cannot do better than to quote that paragraph here:

"Many a problem in understanding awaits reader and commentator down the long unfolding line of this poem, hard problems indeed, in allegory, in symbolism, in patterns of meaning broad in nature and visible only from great pivotal points in this journey to God. Solutions to such problems will be attempted only in a supplementary volume which may well bear the title *Essays and Excursuses*. Meanwhile, the reader will have to bear with patience an ever-growing burden of unresolved meanings until he himself has won to the vantage ground of a fuller experience of the whole and to those vistas in retrospect through which a full, or a fuller, understanding of the total meaning may be had."

Thus, even with the completion of this sixth volume, an explicator's work remains unfinished. Perhaps, by its very nature, it will ever be so. But, at least, in this promised *seventh* volume, his work will be more nearly finished: se piacere sarà di colui a cui tutte le cose vivono, che la mia vita duri per alquanti anni. . . .

C.S.S.

Sept. 14, 1973.